Coinage in the Roman Economy, 300 B.C. to A.D. 700

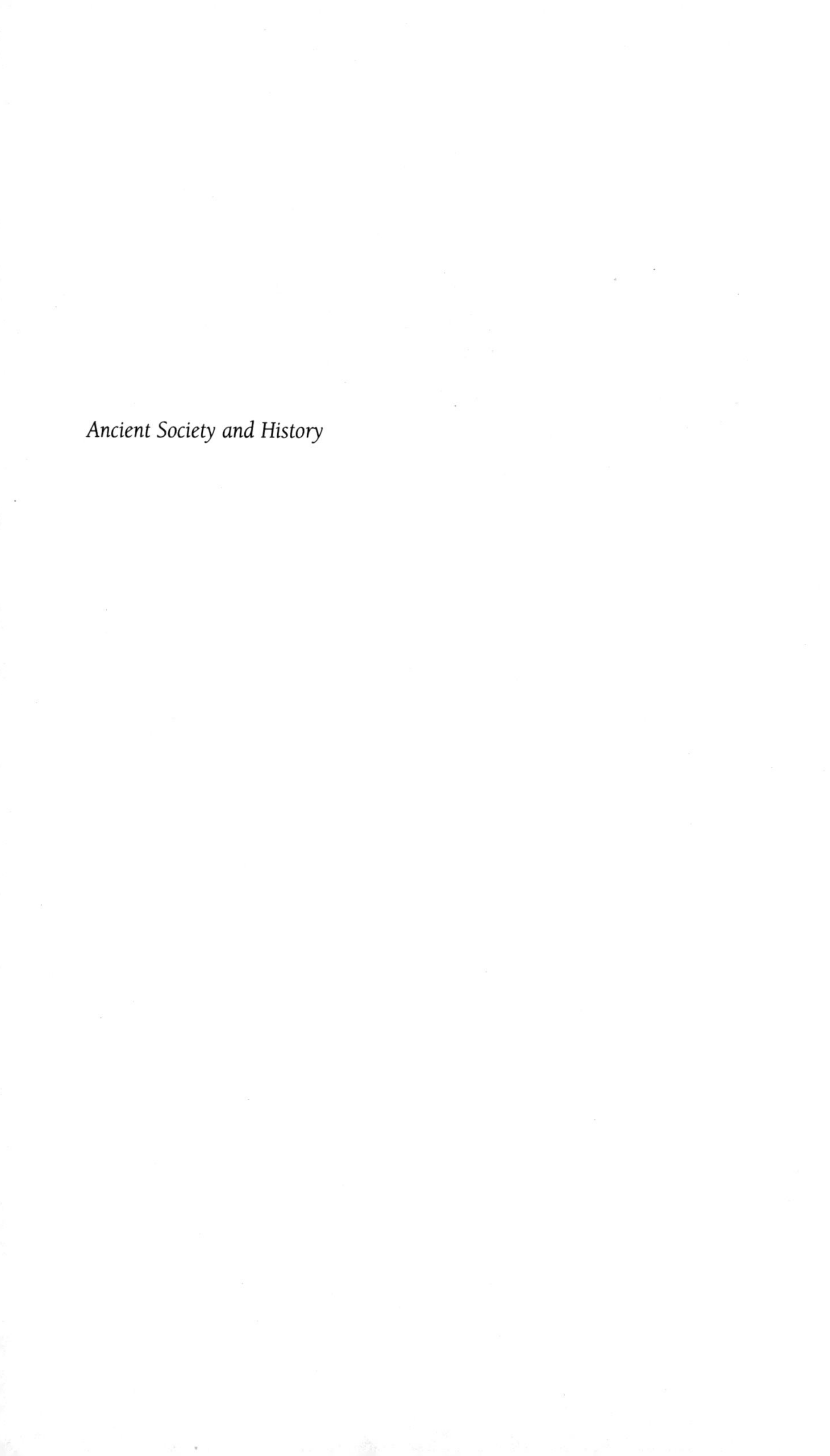

*Ancient Society and History*

# *Coinage in the*

KENNETH W. HARL

# *Roman Economy, 300 B.C. to A.D. 700*

The Johns Hopkins University Press
Baltimore and London

 Published 1996
Printed in the United States of America on acid-free paper
05 04 03 02 01 00 99 98 97 96 5 4 3 2 1

The Johns Hopkins University Press
2715 North Charles Street
Baltimore, Maryland 21218-4319
The Johns Hopkins Press Ltd., London

A catalog record for this book is available from the British Library.

Library of Congress Cataloging-in-Publication Data

Harl, Kenneth W.
Coinage in the Roman economy, 300 B.C. to A.D. 700 / Kenneth W. Harl.
p. cm.
Includes bibliographical references (p.) and index.
ISBN 0-8018-5291-9 (alk. paper)
1. Coins, Roman. 2. Coinage—Rome—History. 3. Rome—Economic conditions. I. Title.
CJ843.H35 1996
737.4937—dc20 95-50043

# Contents

# Acknowledgments

In writing this book, I have enjoyed encouragement and assistance of many friends and scholars. I foremost thank Eric Halpern for approaching me with the idea of writing this work. I must single out the friendship and sage advice of Keith Hopkins, J. Edward Lendon, Ramsay MacMullen, Thomas Martin, Elizabeth Meyer, Jonathan Roth, and William E. Metcalf. I thank especially Roger S. Bagnall for his indispensible assistance on Roman Egypt and papyri and Bruce Frier for his expertise on Roman law and his kindness in sharing his unpublished work on prices in legal documents. My dear friends Frank Campbell and Carla Lukas are deserving of far more than this brief special thanks for their toils on my behalf.

I am, as ever, in debt to the staff of the American Numismatic Society as well as curators of coin cabinets and scholars working on both sides of the Atlantic. Space permits me only brief thanks for their many varied services: Michel Amandry, Melih Aslan, Michael Bates, Andrew Burnett, Eugene Borza, Kevin Butcher, Miribelle Corbier, Günther Dembski, Georges Depeyrot, Peter R. Franke, Christopher Howgego, Ursula Kampmann, Wolfgang Leschhorn, Johannes Nollé, Bernhard Overbeck, Joseph Scholten, Alan Stahl,

John Vanderspoel, Colin Wells, Peter Weiss, Richard Weigal, and Ruprecht Ziegler.

My home university, Tulane, has provided me with invaluable support throughout this project, and it is a privilege to acknowledge my debt of gratitude to my colleagues in the Department of History, and to my students Vasilios Manthos and Jaclyn Maxwell for their editorial comments and David Endler for his expert aid in computer programing. Finally, I must thank my parents for their constant support and faith in me, inasmuch as they were the inspiration in seeing this project to completion, and it is to my nieces, Melissa and Jessica, I dedicate this book.

# One

# Coins, the Money of the Roman Economy

The objective of this book is an examination of how the Romans used coined money—its role in payrolls, tax collection, trade, and daily transactions—over the course of a millennium, 300 B.C. to A.D. 700. Although there are many books about Roman coins, they are, for the most part, numismatic works devoted to the study of the coins as objects rather than as evidence for the economic and social life of the Roman world. This is an attempt to redress the imbalance by dealing with coins both as fiscal instruments of the Roman state and as the medium of exchange employed by the Roman public. This focus, however, requires generalization: coins by their very nature offer terse evidence subject to several plausible interpretations. Whenever my interpretations have departed from those of leading numismatic authorities, alternate opinions can be found in the notes.

Since this is a history of the currency of the Roman world, its geographic expanse widens with the growth of Roman power, and it includes the civic and provincial coinages that formed a large part of the money used for the five centuries from 200 B.C. to A.D. 300. Although this vast local coinage cries out for further study, enough is known to write not only of the roles such coins played in provincial taxation and local markets but also of the lessons Romans gained from these coinages and applied to their own. This is nowhere more true than for the coinage of Roman Egypt, which has been viewed, and neglected, as an unusual currency in a closed economy. Yet, in Egypt the Romans created the world's first successful fiduciary currency. Minted from billon, an alloy of less than 25 percent silver, it earned the trust of the Egyptians, who constituted 10 to 15 percent of the empire's population, for more than two centuries. The Egyptian experience gave the imperial government a model for its own billon currencies in the third and fourth centuries. Private accounts and tax registers reveal that, when it came to paying taxes and using coins, Egyptians had far more in common with inhabitants of the rest of the Roman world than has heretofore been recognized.

Several issues and questions must be faced in any study of Roman currency, among them, the extent to which Romans used and were accustomed to coins; what forces drove debasements and reforms that affected currency, state revenues, and prices; and what inferences may be drawn from that evidence underlying current opinions about the size and composition of the Roman currency. Precisely how Romans employed coins is a question central to any assessment of the success of the Roman economy, indeed of imperial civilization itself. Classical numismatists and historians, with the notable exception of Sture Bolin, have seldom ventured to explain the precise role of coins. Bolin's work, *State and Currency in the Roman Empire,* has drawn sharp criticism because of its reliance on theoretical mathematics and the premise, demonstrably false, that gold and silver coins of the Roman Empire were tariffed far in excess of their intrinsic or metallic value.[1] An understanding of the place of coins in the Roman economy can be enhanced by comparison to the role of coins in medieval and early modern European economies. The more numerous documents and coins available for these periods have enabled historians to examine in detail the commercial and fiscal roles of coins. Since these later coinages were rooted in a Roman past, they reflect many of the features that existed in the Roman age.

The use and importance of Roman coins are often discounted on the grounds of their limited numbers, but this view springs from the assumption that because mints in the ancient world seldom struck on an annual basis coins were in short supply. On the other hand, down to the nineteenth century most states struck coinage intermittently, so the fact that Rome produced coins on an intermittent basis hardly supports Finley's sweeping assertion for the whole of ancient history that "shortage of coins was chronic, both in total numbers and in the availability of preferred types or denominations."[2] References cited in support of this claim date from 66 B.C. to A.D. 33, when Roman aristocrats ran short of hard cash in their eagerness to acquire the vast amounts of Italian land available in the wake of civil war. Notices of brief shortages are matched by those of abundance, and neither set of circumstances can be pressed as evidence to what was the "typical" volume of money in circulation.[3] The important point so often missed is that coins could remain in use for over a century. Finley penned his words just as numismatists were beginning to apply statistical methods to the study of hoards and dies to estimate output. While they are far from agreement on the methods and the meaning of their analyses, numismatists agree that ancient mints could strike on short notice coinages as great as the largest coinages on record for medieval European mints from the thirteenth century on.[4] The combined coinages of imperial Rome constitute perhaps the largest in history; Diocletian (A.D. 284–305) alone directed a recoinage on a scale that dwarfed all coinages until this century.

Roman coins, even when their great numbers and diversity are acknowledged, are minimized on two other grounds. First, since the Roman world was tied to the soil, coins, it is argued, played a limited role in what is dubbed an "underdeveloped" economy. A second criticism often advanced is that coins were invented for fiscal purposes alone and their use in commerce was only incidental because throughout Roman history state demands took precedence over public needs and economic growth. Most scholars who minimize the role of coins—and some have gone so far as to deny the existence of market forces in most Roman commerce—write primarily on agriculture and the peasantry. The comparatively few coins recovered from rural sites have fostered a perception that coins were not widely used, but the record is defective, reflecting accidents of survival rather than the absence of markets and a negligible use of coins. The extent of circulation of coins in the countryside is best understood by an analogy to medieval Europe, which was at least as rural as much of the Roman Empire. Documents from A.D. 1000–1350 reveal that great numbers of "black money," low-grade silver *deniers,* circulated between countryside and city every year in a seasonal cycle; so too *denarii* and bronze coins of the Principate or billon *nummi* of the Dominate must have traveled for centuries.[5] There was nothing inherently backward in the structure of the Roman economy that limited such a pattern of circulation. The Roman world, like other civilized societies prior to the industrial age, drew its wealth from the land, but seaborne trade stimulated growth so that Rome approached the economic diversity of late medieval and early modern Europe. The classical city was not just a political center that drained wealth from the countryside in taxes and rents. As a settlement boasting only a few thousand souls it was intimately tied to the villages of a spreading countryside. Such small cities had the same commercial, religious, and social bonds that drew together late medieval towns and their hinterlands.

The second criticism, if valid, is more potent. If coins are classified solely as fiscal instruments, then they may be removed from serious discussion of economic life. Scholars such as Crawford and Hendy have advocated this view primarily as a reaction to suggestions that the Roman state issued coins to meet the needs of the marketplace.[6] These criticisms have some validity, for coins usually entered circulation in government payrolls or payments to contractors. But the distinction is more apparent than real, because fiscal and commercial activities have been and still are two sides of a single economy. While fiscal in origin, coins had long proved their convenience in commerce and this role continued even in the world that followed the collapse of the Roman Empire. The success of token bronze coins and the creation of fiduciary billon coins in the third century A.D. were possible only because a Roman public dealt and reckoned in coined money. The total coins recovered from scores of sites in Western Europe and Italy, when plotted on a graph, document vividly how demand for Roman coins rose steadily from

50 B.C. to A.D. 400. Romans employed coins in great numbers, whether or not the imperial government pursued a formal monetary policy. This fact alone vitiates claims that the minting of coins was little more than an act of political sovereignty that impeded rather than promoted trade.[7] It is thus proper to speak of Roman monetary habits, because for nearly a thousand years Romans reckoned and settled private and public obligations in coin. Although commodities such as grain and oil were never displaced as staples in Mediterranean trade, Roman coins became the preferred medium of exchange and the preferred store of value, because they were portable, nonperishable, and easily negotiated into any other commodity.

Finally, while it is necessary to guard against investing modern notions of money in coins of the ancient world, coins are often emptied of their economic significance by comparisons to the use of money in what Polanyi and his disciples have termed an "embedded society." Coins, in anthropological schemes, are interpreted as gifts exchanged to cement social bonds or common kinship rather than to facilitate commerce. The evidence, however, does not warrant any such conclusion: Strabo and Posidonius, reporting what is interpreted as a "gift exchange," note only that the Gallic chieftan Lurius scattered from his chariot gold and silver coins among his countrymen. The scene is more aptly viewed as a Celtic version of a later, more elaborate Roman ceremony when emperors of the fourth century scattered gold *solidi* to buy the loyalty of their subjects.[8] Large numbers of denarii survive in Scandinavia not because the northernmost Teutonic peoples prized them for "gift exchanges," but because Roman merchants carried them directly by sea to pay for amber and other commodities.[9]

The pre-Roman coinages of Western and Central Europe were derived from those of the Mediterranean world, and they are best understood by reference to roles coins performed in the Roman economy. Celtiberians and Gauls minted silver denarii or *obols* to hire mercenaries, to pay wages of their men serving under Roman eagles, or to render tribute to Rome. They also quickly learned the value of silver and base metal fractions in markets where traders of the Mediterranean world offered many fine wares or in the collection of lucrative tolls on transit trade. Coinage in these lands reflected a high level of economic development and prepared the way for rapid monetization under Roman rule. In northern and western Europe, the Romans conquered and assimilated provinces where native peoples dwelled in towns and handled coins. Likewise, in the sixth century A.D., Justinian's armies recovered provinces where town life and coinage had survived the collapse of the Western Empire. The Romans owed coinage to the Greeks and found native currencies in their provinces, but they carried the use of coins to unparalleled heights. They spread their coins across Europe, North Africa, and the Near East and transmitted their notions of money as one of many legacies to the peoples of medieval Europe, Byzantium, and Islam.

The success of Roman currency rested upon its silver coins, which over the centuries often suffered recoinage, debasement, and revaluation that directly affected the supply and use of coins, and thus state expenses, taxes, and prices in the marketplace. Romans employed as their principal coin a modest-sized silver denomination, the *denarius* (measuring 22–20 mm in diameter), for nearly five centuries (264 B.C.–A.D. 238); bronze and gold coins served as its subsidiary fractions and multiples. Various billon coins, reckoned in notational denarii (*denarii communes* or d.c.), followed for a century (A.D. 251–367), but they yielded primacy again to fine silver coins that recalled the denarius and inspired the pennies and deniers of medieval Europe and the *dirhems* of the Caliphate.

The Roman state often manipulated the silver currency to keep pace with inflation or to expand the supply of money in an emergency, but even during periods of prosperity and stable prices, currency had to be replenished periodically because of its deterioration in circulation. Duncan-Jones estimates the loss from wear suffered by the principal denominations of the High Roman Empire was as follows: the gold *aureus* lost 1/4330 or 0.0225 percent of its weight each year; the silver denarius, 1/1673 or 0.0598 percent; and the brass *sestertius,* 1/583 or 0.1715 percent. The loss of the sestertius was 7.6 times, and that of the denarius 2.65 times, the loss suffered by the aureus reflecting the higher velocity of the less valuable coins.[10] Annual rates of wear, however, usually were the least important loss suffered by Roman currency. Silver and gold coins fell prey to abuses such as clipping and "sweating," and many coins left the mint below full standard. Wear reduced the stock of coined silver by 2 to 2.5 percent each decade or about 10 to 12 percent every half-century, but stocks often dwindled much more rapidly due to export of silver in trade, war, and diplomacy.[11]

Coins retained their exchange value as long as they were of proper weight, but heavy, purer pieces ordinarily disappeared into savings or melting pots, while baser, lighter specimens were discounted at the tables of moneychangers. Even under the best of circumstances there was a deterioration of the currency that in time affected values assigned to denominations, often driving up prices. The state could react in one of three ways.[12] First, it could demonetize, melt down, and restrike old coins, but the task required additional moneyers or mints, and the state lost money whenever a significant proportion of recalled coins were base, underweight, or counterfeit. During the two centuries when the Romans established the denarius as the currency of the Mediterranean world (187 B.C.–A.D. 64), they enjoyed an ample supply of silver from overseas revenues and mines. Since imported silver far exceeded losses due to wear and export, Rome never resorted to comprehensive recoinage to maintain the standard of the denarius. The Roman denarius stands in sharp contrast to its closest counterpart from medieval Europe, the English penny; English monarchs in 1100–1300 had to conduct seven recoinages to maintain the penny at the sterling standard (92.5 percent). As a second option, the state could revalue the circulating coin, most often by lowering its official tariffing against new coins. This move, called in the parlance of medieval England "crying down" the money, outraged saving classes and risked triggering panicked hoarding. Finally, the state could issue new coins with the same silver content as the worn pieces in circulation so that new and old circulated at par. The standard was adjusted either by lowering the weight of new coins or by alloying new coins so that they were of traditional weight but contained less silver. As an example of the first method, the Roman Republic, to account for wear sustained by its earliest coins, lowered slightly the weight of subsequent issues (ca. 310–268 B.C.). An example of the second may have occurred when Antoninus Pius alloyed the denarius slightly in A.D. 148.

The Roman state seldom implemented recoinage or revaluation just to replenish the worn stock of coins in circulation. Instead, it employed one or both measures in tandem with a debasement or reform. In crisis Rome invariably debased the silver currency to cover costs, and then, once the emergency passed, often reformed the currency to its previous level. The Republic in 213–212 B.C. thus revalued its heavy denarius, or *quadrigatus,* and began recoining quadrigati into lighter denarii at two-thirds the old weight. Nero revived the device of recoinage on a grand scale, and emperors in the next three centuries were driven to pay off bills by reminting silver or billon coins into more numerous, baser ones. Sometimes improvement of standards followed debasements—Domitian (A.D. 81–96), Pertinax (A.D. 193), and Macrinus (A.D. 217–18) each restored the fineness of the denarius.

The Roman state sometimes revalued older coins to save the costs of a recoinage. In 141 B.C. the Republic retariffed the denarius from ten to sixteen *asses,* probably because aged bronze coins were so worn that sixteen passed as the equivalent of ten minted to the uncial standard under which one as weighed a full ounce. More often revaluation accompanied at least a partial recoinage in a major reform or debasement. Spiraling inflation in the late third and fourth centuries A.D. made such recoinages and revaluations commonplace. In A.D. 293 Diocletian cut by 60 percent the tariffing of radiate billon coins in circulation when he introduced a silver-washed nummus as their replacement. His "crying down" the money sparked speculation, hoarding, and price increases so that twice within eight years he had to revalue upward the nummus to five times its original notational value.

The forces driving debasement and reform affected the numbers and kinds of coins in circulation, but conversely the size and structure of the currency dictated to large extent decisions the Roman state took to secure revenues, meet payrolls, or stabilize prices. Literary and documentary sources offer brief glimpses of coins in use at different periods, giving a series of disjointed scenes rather than a panoramic view of the history of Roman currency. In the absence of better records, it is necessary to allow the coins themselves to reveal how many and what kinds of coins the Roman government and public employed. Current scholarship in numismatics bristles with detailed analyses of hoards, reports of stray finds from archaeological sites, catalogues of major collections, and die studies. Specialists have devised a battery of tests to deduce the size and composition of the Roman currency, tests that contribute to our understanding of the metrology, output, and circulation of Roman coins.

Modern spectral analysis can give us accurate information about the source of the metal in Roman coins. These metrological analyses reveal that much of the coinage of the ancient world was reminted from older coins. For example, Shah Shapur of Persia (A.D. 240–70) struck base dirhems from captured Roman *antoniniani* and the Dacians manufactured silver coins and jewelry from Republican denarii. On the other hand, we know that Axumite emperors of Ethiopia minted their fractional gold pieces from East African gold rather than late Roman solidi. Metrological analyses of gold and silver coins of the Roman Empire provide virtually the only information concerning their rates of debasement. Estimates of output, composition, and circulation offer more controversial results. The objective of analyses of hoards and stray coins lost casually is to determine the place of origin, region of circulation, and use of coins in trade as well as the size and structure of the overall currency. The analyses are statistical, and so accuracy hinges upon large samples of representative coins. Given this critical limitation, it is best to review what these methods can offer on output, composition, and circulation.

Romans struck their coins from engraved dies, except in the early Republic when they cast bronze ingots and coins from molds. Since each die was cut separately, even dies of the most routine design betray peculiarities so that a trained eye can detect the different dies used to mint a surviving population of coins. The method used to manufacture ancient and medieval coins facilitates a calculation of the minimum number of coins that might have been struck from a die.[13] Simply stated, a prepared coin blank, or "flan," was positioned by a man using tongs (called a *suppostor* at the imperial mint) between two engraved dies and a second man (the *malleator* at Rome) delivered a blow with a mallet to stamp the designs on the coin blank. Since more pressure was placed on the moveable or punch die on which the reverse was engraved, it wore out more quickly than the obverse die, which was firmly set in an anvil. Dies had relatively short life spans, and whenever an obverse die was matched with three or four reverse dies, it was likely that mint workers used that die to full capacity. A count of obverse dies that were worked to capacity permits an estimate of the minimum size of a coinage.

The crux of the problem is twofold. How many coins were produced from an obverse die, and how representative of the total are the dies detected from the existing specimens? As to the first question, Greeks and Romans have been credited with minting between ten and twenty thousand coins per obverse die, but the estimate is based on experiments conducted by Sellwood in the early 1960s with modern tools that only approximated ancient conditions. In a recent restudy of the Amphictyonic financial accounts and coins of Delphi, Kinns argues for a range of thirty to forty thousand coins. This figure is of the same order as hammered silver coinages of England and Venice in the thirteenth and fourteenth centuries that can be verified by surviving mint records.[14] Although medieval coins were engraved in lower relief which might have facilitated striking, the hand technology in manufacturing coins had not improved significantly by the fourteenth century. Thus, throughout this book the figure of forty thousand coins per obverse die has been employed, with the warning that this is only an estimate.

Calculation of the number of dies originally employed to mint any ancient coinage is even less certain, because survival of large numbers of coins depends upon their recovery from hoards. Since the largest coinages that have survived from the ancient world defy cataloguing every die, the total dies are often estimated by one of several probability formulas applied to a sample of dies counted in a large hoard.[15] The approach is based upon the premise that every coin in a hoard had an equal chance of survival and that the hoard preserves a representative sample of a coinage. Neither assumption is well founded. Figures of output calculated from estimates of total obverse dies can only suggest a minimum for the order of magnitude of a series or the relative size of different coinages, and, consequently, they are to be treated with extreme caution. The limits of these statistics lead us to consider the characteristics of their basis, hoards.

Hoards of coins underpin much of what is written about the size and use of ancient and medieval coinages, but hoards distort rather than mirror the image of the money in circulation at the time of their concealment. Owners invariably preferred higher value and more portable denominations in gold or silver over fractional coins, and they also chose heavier or purer coins over lighter, more circulated specimens. As a consequence, most hoards preserve only the most valuable coins on hand. This is true whether a hoard represents a gradual accumulation of savings or a cache of coins suddenly drawn out of circulation during troubled times. Those who could afford to put aside large caches of coins in emergencies could also convert many low-value or base metal denominations into portable high-value gold or silver pieces on short notice. Samuel Pepys, when he fled seventeenth-century London on rumor of an approaching Dutch fleet, converted his savings into portable gold guineas and silver crowns for transport and concealment at his country estate.[16] In a similar vein, Josephus reports that during the siege of Jerusalem (A.D. 66–70), Jews planning to escape the doomed city or at least to conceal their wealth had sought out gold aurei and scorned silver denarii.[17]

Hoards from the Roman world usually do not reflect the relative numbers of the various denominations in circulation. Since ratios of the relative numbers of denominations deduced from Roman hoards cannot be checked against mint records, comparison to Swedish hoards deposited in 1700–1721 can serve as a warning of the distorting mirror of hoards.[18] The thirty-one published Swedish hoards from this period are composed overwhelmingly of silver *carolin* denominations, the purest coins available for hoarding (the limited issues of gold *ducat* and silver *riksdaler* and *christen* were for export). Yet, mint records of 1664–1721 record that carolin coins totaled in face value less than one-half the value of the heavy bronze plate money and only 25 percent more than the total value of the billon and bronze fractional coins that are scarcely represented in hoards.

Hoards have just as many pitfalls as evidence for the size of different coinages in the Roman world. For example, Crawford based his estimates of obverse dies, and hence output, of denarii of ca. 160–30 B.C. on hoards that totaled nearly 27,000 denarii, but this is less than 10 percent of the 275,000 coins found in Swedish hoards for 1664–1721 that provide the statistical basis for devising probability formulas.[19] Hoards of the Roman Republic preserve a paltry fraction of the original coinage and the surviving denarii will never be sufficiently representative for meaningful estimates of the relative size of most series. In interpreting hoards, then, it is just as important to determine not only when they were deposited but also why owners failed to retrieve them. Hoards survive in clusters from periods of natural calamity or war when death or enslavement prevented many owners from recovering their savings. The record of coin hoards in Italy from 218 B.C. to A.D. 1 peaks during the Second Punic War and the Civil Wars in 90–71 and 49–31 B.C., while it shows more modest rises that might represent the failure of soldiers to return from the Celtiberian Wars in the 150s B.C. and the Jugurthine and Cimbric Wars in 116–100 B.C. (Figure 1.1).

What is noteworthy is that even a cluster of hoards gives us only a fraction of the total coins issued during any particular period. Hoarding in both tranquil and troubled times was and still is a common practice in societies without deposit banking, but the vast majority of coins secreted in antiquity were recovered and returned to circulation. Classical authors casually refer to what must have been a continual cycle of concealing and finding treasures, and they saw discovery of a pot of coins as the best way to reverse a man's fortune. Artemidorus of Daldis, the dream analyst of the second century A.D., considered dreams of recovering buried treasures so common as to warrant several different interpretations.[20] Pompey had to indulge his soldiers for two weeks in 81 B.C. as they wandered the ruins of Carthage (sacked in 146 B.C.) looking for treasures.[21] When Roman soldiers burst into Rhodes and Lycian cities in 43 B.C., they forced residents to give up treasures in wells, under entry ways, and in dozens of other well-known places of conceal-

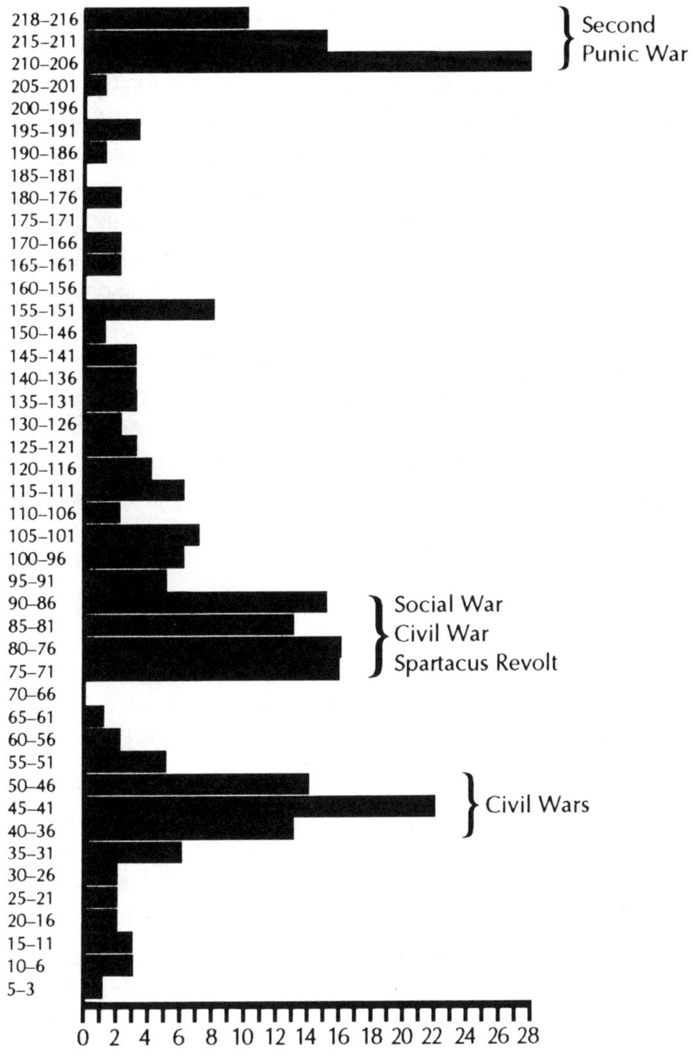


*Figure 1.1* Roman Republican Coin Hoards, 218 to 3 B.C.

*Source*: M. H. Crawford, "Coin Hoards and the Pattern of Violence in the Late Republic," *PBSR* 37 (1969), 79. Reprinted by permission of the University of Oklahoma Press from P. J. Casey, *Understanding Coins: An Introduction for Archaeologists and Historians* (Norman, 1986), p. 64.

ment.[22] On a far more humble note, a certain Orseniouphis in A.D. 28/9 filed a police report at Hermopolis charging a mason with absconding with the family fortune of four pieces of jewelry and twenty *tetradrachmae*.[23]

Since most coin hoards were recovered and returned to circulation, they reentered the cycle of being melted down and reminted. Coins surviving in hoards thus beat the odds of reminting. What the record of hoards presents is a set of snapshots of the coins that were set aside and not recovered rather than a coherent picture of the money in circulation. This fact must temper any conclusions drawn from the failure of certain coins to surface in hoards. It is inevitable that the denarii of 200–160 B.C. are poorly represented because most hoards were recovered and dispersed during the comparative tranquility of this period. It is, therefore, unwarranted to postulate a "gap" in the production and infer that the Roman state suffered chronic shortages of hard cash during the years 200–157 B.C. when literary sources report the opposite.[24]

Carradice has calculated the output of denarii under Domitian (A.D. 81–96) by reference to the number of obverse dies as estimated from hoards (Figure 1.2).[25] The low mintage shown for 82–87 most likely is not a true reflection of the relative size of the output for these years. In 82–85 Domitian improved the silver standard, and older coins, averaging 88 to 92 percent silver, were reminted into purer denarii (98 percent fine). These purer coins had scarcely entered the marketplace when Domitian in mid-85, pressed for money to pay off war bills, again changed the standard, reducing it to 93 percent fine. Much of the silver for these new coins undoubtedly was obtained by melting down their purer predecessors, so the majority of the fine denarii of 82–85 ended up in the melting pot rather than in hoards. What the graph shows as peak years reflects not so much an increase in relative output as the thoroughness of recalling and reminting of the purer coins minted in 82–85. The graph, thus, distorts rather than mirrors the coinage and finances of Domitian.

The lack of minting records and budgets for the Roman state are irretrievable losses, while coins surviving in hoards are too few to offset the impact of the innumerable remintings coins underwent

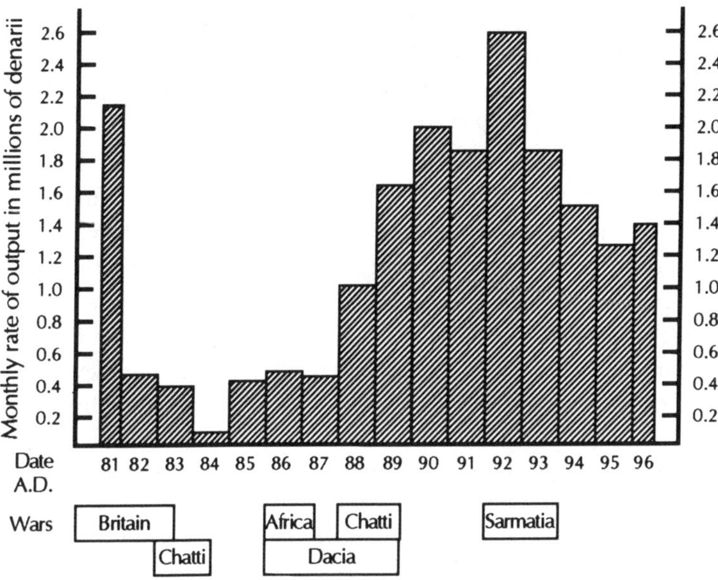


*Figure 1.2* Volume of Denarii under Domitian (A.D. 81–96), Reconstructed from Surviving Hoards.

*Source*: From A. M. Burnett, *Coinage in the Roman World* (London, 1987), p. 93. Reprinted by permission of Seaby, imprint of B. T. Batsford.

over the centuries. Even if large numbers of hoards are consulted, surviving coins and statistical methods cannot produce a reasonable guess as to the numbers of coins in circulation at any time in Roman history.[26] The best that studies of dies and output can achieve are figures that convey an order of magnitude of coinages that are now well represented due to their survival in hoards. Nor can these methods tell us how much coined money the Roman state accumulated or spent each year. Instead, literary and documentary sources, when they preserve plausible figures such as in triumphal inventories reported by Livy or state reserves cited by Pliny the Elder, remain the foundation to understanding state revenues and expenditures. Therefore, the figures on production employed in this book are limited to coinages whose original or surviving number of dies are reasonably well known, but even these figures cannot yield much more than a minimum of an order of magnitude.

Given the selective composition of hoards, archaeologists have pioneered statistical analysis of stray coins found in excavations of military sites, towns, and villas. Stray finds are coins that owners casually lost rather than a cache of coins deliberately secreted for later recovery. Coins found under such conditions distort the record just as much as those in hoards, because owners lost those coins they could most afford, namely small change of low purchasing power. Given their occupation, place of residence, and personal attitudes, owners had varying opinions about what was an acceptable loss. Peasants took care to guard hard-earned money, and, not surprisingly, few coins of any type have been found in villages or at roadside marts. Legionaries, on the other hand, had frequent nights out on the town, and they could always borrow or take advances on salary to recoup losses, so they were prone to lose many more coins. Roman military sites across the empire show a remarkable uniformity in the types of coins lost over the centuries. In Julio-Claudian army camps in the Rhineland, soldiers seldom lost denarii, but they cared far less when they lost worn base metal fractions. Excavations yield mostly Republican asses, the middle and lower imperial fractions of asses, *semisses,* and *quadrantes* (which are often countermarked), halved coins, forgeries (so-called plated coins), and a sprinkling of Celtic coins that were curiosities of little monetary value. Excavation reports from the Roman world confirm what is inferred from economic activity, namely that coins were more numerous in cities, military centers, and villas than in the countryside. The reports, however, are far less helpful for determining the types or numbers of coins in use, and it is dangerous to conclude from casual finds alone that peasants lived in a world of barter and seldom used any coins or that Roman soldiers received the bulk of their wages in bronze coins.[27]

Coins recovered at Pompeii, which was suddenly buried by the eruption of Mt. Vesuvius in A.D. 79, point to a very different structure of Roman currency than that reflected by stray coins or hoards. Nearly one-half the coins found were silver denarii (48 percent) while base metal fractions (48 percent), and a handful of gold aurei (4 percent) make up the rest. The structure of Pompeii's currency diverges from the typical pattern suggested by other excavated sites.

*Table 1.1*
Structure of Currency in Finds, ca. 30 B.C.–A.D. 80: Select Italian Sites and Western Military Camps

| Denomination* | | Pompeii | Minturnae | Military Sites | | |
|---|---|---|---|---|---|---|
| | | | | Camulodunum | Moguntiacum | Haltern |
| AU | Aureus | 4% | —— | —— | <1% | <1% |
| AR | Denarius | 48% | 1% | 3% | 4% | 5% |
| AE | Sestertius | 9% | 8% | 10% | 10% | 3% |
| AE | Dupondius | —— | 5% | 20% | 5% | 6% |
| AE | As | 27%** | 67% | 65% | 80% | 85% |
| AE | Semis | —— | —— | —— | <1% | —— |
| AE | Quadrans | 11% | 18% | 1% | <1% | <1% |
| Non-Roman | | 1% | 1% | 1% | <1% | <1% |

*AU = gold; AR = silver; and AE = copper, bronze, or orichalum.

**Dupondii and asses reckoned together.

*Source:* The table is based on L. Breglia, "Circolazione monetale ed aspetti di vita economica in Pompei," in *Raccolta di studi per il secondo centenario degli scavi di Pompei* (1950), pp. 41–59; W. E. Metcalf, "Roman Coins from the River Liri II," *NC* 7, 14 (1974), 42–53; L. Houghtalin, "Roman Coins from the River Liri, III," *NC* 145 (1984), 67–81 (Minturnae); C. F. C. Hawkes and M. R. Hall, "The Coins," in *Camulodunum: First Report on the Excavations at Colchester 1930–1939* (London, 1940), pp. 129–67; P. R. Franke, *Die Fundmünzen der römischen Zeit in Deutschland* IV. *Rheinland-Plfaz* 1. *Rheinhessen* (Berlin, 1960), pp. 198–410 (Moguntiacum); B. Korzus, *Die Fundmünzen der römischen Zeit in Deutschland* VI. *Nordrhein-Westfalen* 4. *Münster* (Berlin, 1971), pp. 57–115 (finds at Haltern).

Four other such sites are offered for comparison; they are the finds of discarded votive offerings near Minturnae at the crossing of the Liri River, coins found in the debris of Camulodunum (Colchester) when British rebels sacked the colony in A.D. 61, and stray finds from two typical Julio-Claudian military sites in the Rhineland, the legionary camp at Moguntiacum (Mainz), and the auxiliary camp at Haltern (Table 1.1). Finds at Pompeii illustrate best the pitfalls in drawing conclusions about structure and circulation from the casual loss of coins at sites. In short, coins lost casually on sites are equivalent to small change lost today in the parking lot of a shopping center, where many more cupronickel dimes and quarters dated from 1964 on are likely to be recovered than early silver ones. A collation of finds from fifty such parking lots and calculation of "annual loss" for the period 1945–90 would give little sense of the size or structure of the coinage of the United States in the twentieth century.

Furthermore, Roman coins could remain in circulation for a long time, especially when monetary standards and prices were stable, so that it is impossible to know, except within broad limits, when coins were lost. Catalogues and graphs of coins found at sites cannot yield an annual rate of loss of small change, and thus they fail to reflect velocity of circulation. Coins from Pompeii, which still await final publication, confirm that many Republican denarii struck in the late second century B.C. were still circulating in A.D. 79 so that perhaps one-half to one-third of the denarii in Italy were Republican as late as the reign of Trajan (98–117). This fact must temper any conclusions regarding the supply of money in circulation based on statistical estimates of output or the rates of annual loss on sites. The speed whereby coins circulated is simply unknown. A single issue of 10 million denarii could, in a year, have sufficed for five, ten, or twenty times their worth in transactions.

The casual finds of coins at a site, when properly catalogued and compared to other sites, may illuminate other aspects of monetary structure and circulation. Casey has devised a histogram to compare casual losses of coins found at Romano-British sites (see Figure 1.3).[28] Total coins found on each site are divided according to reign and then standardized as a function of the number of coins lost in each reign per 1,000 coins. Standard histograms illustrate the scourge of inflation. More coins were lost as their numbers mounted and their purchasing value plunged due to debasements in the third and fourth centuries A.D. More long-term changes can also be detected. The "open" deposit at the crossings of the Liri River in southern Italy yields coins extending over the whole course of the time covered in this book, for travelers discarded their humblest coins as offerings to the river god. The Liri finds, in tandem with those at other sites such as the colony of Cosa, show that Roman coins displaced earlier currencies of Italy soon after 200 B.C.[29] Such reports also document how inflation over the centuries slowly reduced the value of denominations. In Italy, over the course of 450 years (200 B.C.– A.D. 250), the bronze *sextans, quadrans, as,* and finally sestertius each in its turn declined to the lowest

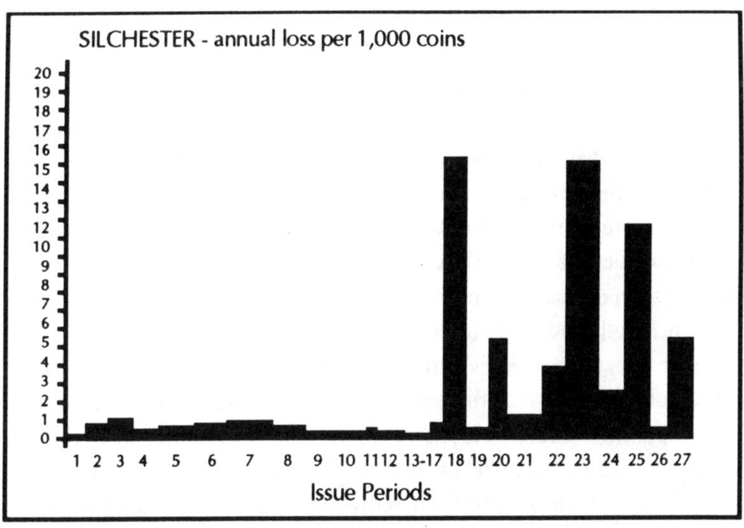


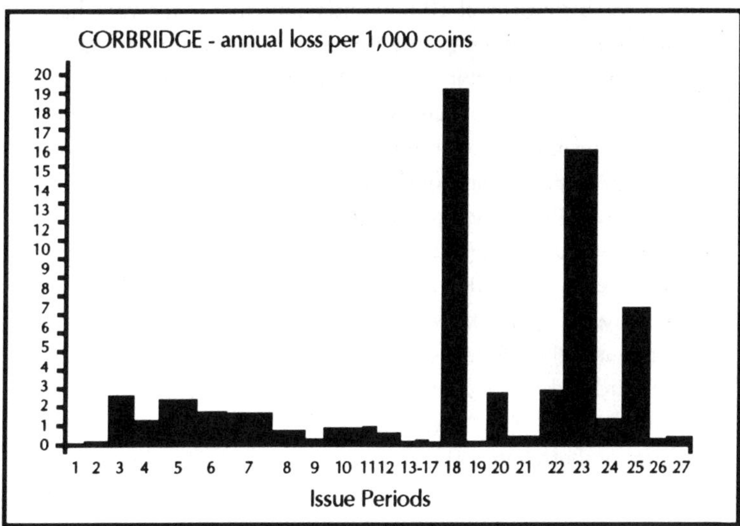


*Figure 1.3* Standardized Histograms of Casual Loss at the Romano-British Sites of Silchester and Corbridge.

*Source*: J. Casey, *Roman Coinage in Britain* (Aylesbury, 1980), p. 31, Figs. 5–6. Reprinted by permission of the University of California Press from K. Greene, *The Archaeology of the Roman Economy* (Berkeley, 1986).

fraction in the currency and became, before it dropped out of circulation, the most frequently lost coin. After A.D. 250 these bronze denominations were replaced by billon antoniniani and, in the fourth century, by silver-clad nummi.

Casual losses and hoards, taken together, can document shifts in patterns of circulation both within and beyond imperial frontiers. Since late Roman and early Byzantine coins carry mintmarks, they give direct evidence for sources of money for regions of the Roman world. For Britain in the period of A.D. 300–400, Fulford has collated finds of Roman coins to illustrate how the island province first drew its currency primarily from mints in Londinium (London) and Treveri (Trier), and then from more distant mints in southern Gaul and Italy after Londinium was closed in 325 and production at Treveri was disrupted by civil wars and barbarian assaults after mid-century.[30] In the late sixth and seventh centuries, coins from excavated sites and hoards show that the North African provinces were thrown on their own resources for coined money while Syria was cut off from fresh supplies of coin by Persian and Arabic attacks.[31]

Although advances in numismatic and archaeological methods cannot offer definitive answers as to the role of coins in Roman economic life, they have provided many crucial details missing in the literary and documentary sources. The aim of this book is to combine the most significant results of these studies, long the preserve of the specialist, with the other sources to write an account of the salient features in the evolution and use of Roman currency.

Two

# Monetization of Roman Italy, 500–200 B.C.

Italic peoples of the early Iron Age (ca. 900–500 B.C.) employed as their media of exchange iron spits or cast bars of bronze. Pliny the Elder in the first century A.D., recalling a popular etymology, relates that the clumsy first forms of money (*pecunia*) substituted for cattle (*pecus*), and he cited a much later cast oblong ingot of bronze bearing a bull as testimony to this association. Later Romans credited to their fifth king, Servius Tullius, the innovation of casting ingots of *aes*, the Latin for copper or any of its alloys. Instead, Servius Tullius probably merely decreed that the unit of the *as* (plural *asses*) was equal to one pound of bronze.[1] In the world of the Twelve Tables (451–450 B.C.) Italians, long after Greeks had arrived carrying the first true silver coins, conducted exchanges by weighing out bars or lumps of bronze (*aes rude*) and converting the weight into local units of asses or nummi. Etruscan towns, the most sophisticated centers in Italy during the sixth and fifth century B.C., never struck gold or silver coins even though they had extensive trade with the Greeks and Carthaginians. Etruscans reserved gold and silver, which were costly metals imported from Central Europe or the East, for plate and jewelry. The nearest they came to issuing coin was the casting of unrefined copper into bars of variable weight (*ramo secco*), apparently for ease in storage and shipment.[2]

Western Greeks introduced the notion of coinage into the Italian peninsula as they adapted the monetary systems of their homeland to local needs. Greek settlers on the Bay of Naples and along the shores of the toe and heel of Italy (Italiots), and in Sicily (Siceliots) as early as the sixth century B.C. struck silver coins from engraved dies, the first such coins in the western Mediterranean. Their monetary units were the *drachma* and its sixth, the obol, but the principal trade coin was a multiple known as a *stater,* which varied in weight and denomination from city to city. Dorian Siceliots, who enjoyed a brisk trade with their mother city Corinth, imported engravers who designed beautiful staters of *decadrachmae* and *tetradrachmae* (pieces of ten and four drachmae) on the commonly used Attic weight standard. Taras (Tarentum) and Heraclea headed the towns of Magna Graecia in striking a more modest *tridrachma* (8 g) and sundry fractions on a regional Achaean standard, while the Campanian cities on the fringes of Greek Italy adopted an even lighter stater, a didrachma (7.5 g; pl. 1.1).[3]

Italiot and Siceliot cities received silver in exchange for grain, timber, slaves, and other exports to the Aegean world. By the end of the sixth century B.C. they were drawing silver in coin and bullion from the three main silver-producing regions of the Greek world: Thrace, Macedon, and the Athenian mines at Laurium. Greeks might have exploited silver deposits in the Liri Valley, but they apparently did not tap other Italian sources or import Sardinian or Spanish silver.[4] Cities of Magna Graecia and Campania were the last consumers in a chain of exchanges that moved silver from the North Aegean and Attica to Sicily, and thence to Italy. Italiots either overstruck Sicilian coins or melted and reminted them into lighter staters and fractions for home consumption, opting for coins on the lighter Achaean or Campanian weight standards to discourage export of their silver money. They were, for the most part, successful. Few of their coins penetrated beyond the Greek cities of the southern shores into the Italic hinterlands prior to the fourth century B.C. when Apulian communities began minting silver obols and *diobols* in tandem with cast bronze denominations on a local Italic standard.[5] When Oscan-speaking highlanders overran the Greek colonies Cumae and Poseidonia (Paestum) in 423–420 B.C., they adopted the practice of minting Greek-style silver coins, while Oscan towns in the Campanian interior commenced coining their own versions of didrachmae and obols.

In the fifth century B.C., none of the Italiot cities had access to mines, and, of greater importance, the need to mint huge silver coinages on the scale of Periclean Athens. The Athenians, as a consequence of their imperial experience, were the first to forge fiscal institutions that pumped coins throughout an economy. Each year the Athenian mint poured out huge quantities of tetradrachmae and varied fractions to meet growing payrolls of magistrates, citizen soldiers and rowers, jurors, and laborers on the great building projects.[6] This monetization of Athenian economic life was repeated in cities of Greek Italy and Sicily at the opening of the next century, and eventually offered a model for Rome.

The shift from citizen to mercenary armies promoted the use of coins throughout the Greek world in the fourth century B.C. In Sicily the tyrants of Syracuse, Dionysius (406–367 B.C.) and Agathocles (317–289 B.C.), and their Carthaginian foes struck vast numbers of tetradrachmae and even gold staters to buy great mercenary armies.[7] In Italy, Taras emerged as the leading mint as it increased production to fulfill contracts offered to Spartan and Epirote kings summoned to repel Italic foes, and lesser cities suspended production as Taras furnished much of the gold and silver money of Magna Graecia (pl. 1.2).[8] Equipping and supplying mercenary armies expanded the numbers and types of transactions in coin, and the many Italians serving in the armies of Taras, Syracuse, and Carthage acquired the habit of dealing in coin. For example, Mamertines, once in the employ of Syracuse, started issuing their own bronze coins soon after seizing Messana in 288 B.C.

Demand for coins for small-scale daily purchases forced Greeks to turn to bronze as a metal of coinage. As early as the mid-fifth century B.C. some Siceliots had already found large bronze fractional coins more practical than tiny divisions of the silver obol, and during the fourth century B.C. Italic peoples from the borders of Etruria to the Ionian shores were casting refined bronze into regularly shaped oblong or rectanglar ingots of fixed weight and carrying simple designs (*aes signatum* or "stamped bronze money"). By the end of the century Romans, too, were casting such bars in units of five Roman pounds, and they then took the simple step of casting fractions of the bars as discs (*aes grave* or "heavy bronze money") made in the fashion of Greek coins.[9] Although Siceliots used engraved dies to manufacture bronze coins, Etruscans, Romans, and Samnites resorted to casting as an economical means of producing round local bronze denominations. By 300 B.C. the Romans' primary unit of value was the as (pl. 3.23), a coin weighing a full Roman pound (*libra*), and they manufactured fractions in increments of an ounce (*uncia*), twelve of which went to the as.

The diffusion of cast bronze currency vastly extended the range of daily transactions conducted in coin and marked a major step in the monetization of Italy. Molds for casting coins were cheap to manufacture, easily repaired, and capable of producing far more coins than engraved dies.[10] On the other hand, *aes grave* were easily counterfeited, singularly ugly, and the clumsiest coins ever handled until Swedish plate money of the seventeenth century. Such ungainly coins circulated within a restricted area, and Latin authors delighted in reporting how notoriously difficult the coins were to transport. Production was by necessity local, and so inevitably regional weight standards and denominations proliferated. Despite their drawbacks, *aes grave* provided the currency of most of Italy down to the opening of the third century B.C. They were accepted in commercial transactions and set aside in savings.[11] The Republic reckoned fiscal needs and legal penalties in asses, and Roman soldiers drew their salaries (*stipendium*) in asses at least until the end of the First Punic War (264–241 B.C.). The Italic peoples by transmuting their traditional bronze money into true coins compensated for a dearth of gold and silver specie, and their descendants eventually turned bronze coins into subsidiary denominations of a Greek-style silver stater.

By the second half of the fourth century B.C., Rome had emerged as the paramount power in peninsular Italy once she had defeated the Samnites and had incorporated the Campanian cities. In Campania, the Romans encountered fine silver coins, which Hellenic

*Table 2.1*
Roman Denarii (Didrachmae), 310–241 B.C.

| Date and Type | Ethnic | Weight: Grams | Weight: Fineness | Silver Content: Grams |
|---|---|---|---|---|
| 310–300 B.C. | | | | |
| Mars/Horsehead | ROMANO | 7.3 | 93.5 | 6.8 |
| 269–264 B.C. | | | | |
| Apollo/Horse | ROMANO | 7.2 | 93.5 | 6.7 |
| Hercules/Wolf and twins | ROMANO | 7.1 | 92.0 | 6.5 |
| 264–241 B.C. | | | | |
| Roma/Victory | ROMANO | 6.6 | 95.0 | 6.3 |
| Mars/Horsehead | ROMA | 6.6 | 97.0 | 6.4 |
| Apollo/Horse | ROMA | 6.6 | 97.0 | 6.4 |
| Mars/Horse | ROMA | 6.6 | 97.0 | 6.4 |

*Source:* Table based on the sequence and weight standards in Thomsen, *ERC* III, pp. 78–81, and Crawford, *RRC* I, pp. 44–45 and nos. 13/1, 15/1b, 20, 22, and 25–27. Fineness is based on Walker, *Metallurgy in Numismatics*, I, pp. 55–56.

and Oscan cities had issued for over two centuries, and discovered the convenience of meeting large-scale payments in purses of silver coins rather than carts of bronze asses. In about 310–300 B.C. the Romans minted their own version of the Campanian stater, a *didrachma* (7.3 g; pl. 1.3), bearing on the obverse a heroic head of Mars, progenitor of the Romans, and on the reverse a horsehead sacred to Mars together with the Latin inscription ROMANO(rum) adapted from Greek genitive ethnics to designate "coin of the Romans" (Table 2.1).[12] They might have obtained much of the metal from northern Etruscan towns looted by Q. Fabius Maximus Rullianus in 310 B.C. From the start Romans probably called their silver coins "denarii" (or "pieces of ten"), because the Roman didrachma was tariffed at ten asses, the reckoning for Roman denominations down to 141 B.C.[13]

Rome minted fine Hellenic-style didrachmae in part to announce her entrance into the concert of civilized powers, but she also acquired with her hegemony of Italy commitments requiring a silver coinage. In 312–308 B.C. censors sold contracts to publicans for the construction of the Via Appia and for ships ordered by a new naval board (*duo viri*) charged with patroling Italian waters. Since the *lex Iulia Papiria* (430 B.C.) fixed the price of one ox or ten sheep at 100 libral asses (equal to 100 pounds of bronze), at such prices in 300 B.C. publicans would have faced major shipping charges for conveying payments of bronze currency whenever purchasing livestock to provision shipwrights or laborers. The equivalent price of ten silver denarii weighed less than one-quarter of a Roman pound.[14] Rome, however, had neither the mines nor the commerce to furnish a steady flow of silver, and, if Livy is to be trusted, *aes grave* and ingots were still the principal money of Italian towns at the opening of the third century. Designs for the early bronzes, headed by an as bearing the portrait of Janus (pl. 3.23), were kept simple for ease of mass production, and consequently specific types became associated with certain denominations. Since the coins were cast, the size of the early issues can not be accurately estimated. Furthermore, when the Romans abandoned full-weight bronze coins, the valuable heavy coins were melted down in droves either to be reminted into token coins or turned into other objects. Bronze coins, however numerous, were so cumbersome that they must have impeded rather than facilitated transactions beyond the most elementary, and their great bulk discouraged transport over any great distance.

In the opening decade of the third century B.C., Rome's main source of precious metals was plunder, but Roman armies seized only modest amounts of gold and silver when they pacified Etruria and Samnium. In 293 B.C. the consuls L. Papirius Cursor and Sp. Carvilius Maximus deposited in the state vaults almost 3 million *aes grave* (or 3 million pounds of bronze), but silver bullion equivalent to only 82,350 denarii (or about 1,830 Roman pounds of silver with the denarius at 1/45 pound).[15] It was the conquest of the proud cities of Magna Graecia, the main source for silver currency in Italy, that netted Rome sufficient stocks of silver from plunder and the sale of captives to recommence minting denarii. In 269/68 B.C., according to Livy, "then for the first time the Roman people began to use silver coins."[16] Two series of denarii were struck on the standard of 45 to the Roman pound in the period 269–264 B.C. One bore the head of Apollo on the obverse and a prancing horse on the reverse (pl. 1.4); on the other Hercules is depicted on the obverse and the reverse carries the wolf and twins (pl. 1.5). On each the ethnic is rendered as ROMANO, as it was on the earlier issue. Yet, the conquest of Magna Graecia did not assure Rome of long-term supplies of specie. Early denarii were high-value coins struck in limited numbers that passed at par with Italiot didrachmae. Rome cast far more bronze coins to serve as fractions of the five-pound bronze ingots.[17]

In the second quarter of the third century B.C., Roman Italy had not yet passed the threshold into a monetized economy, and the Roman Republic entered the First Punic War with a rudimentary currency, few fiscal institutions, and no significant reserves of precious metal. Although victory over Carthage would eventually furnish the specie that enabled Rome to mint her first great silver coinage and monetize her finances, at the beginning of the war the Republic faced financial crisis. Rome minted a mere 6.5 million denarii, whereas Carthage paid for her mercenary armies in Sicily and great fleets by striking over thirty-seven times this amount in gold, electrum, and silver coins valued at 245 million denarii.[18] Rome, therefore, was forced to finance by means other than silver or gold coins most of the enormous costs of the expeditionary forces that served in Sicily and the 700 quinqueremes commissioned for service in 260–249 B.C. Roman soldiers presumably drew their pay in asses, but even at a subsistence wage of perhaps 4 to 8 asses per month, 300,000 to 600,000 Roman pounds of coined bronze money would have been shipped to legionaries in Sicily each campaigning season.[19] The Roman state—like its allies, who compensated their soldiers with rations of grain and oil—might have reduced money payments by furnishing provisions directly to legionaries. The naval allies Taras, Locri, Velia, and Neapolis furnished ships and paid their crews in their own civic didrachmae, relieving Rome of the burden of another monetary obligation (pl. 1.2).[20] In addition Rome demanded extraordinary sacrifices by her citizens. The fleet that won the decisive victory off the Aegetes Islands was financed by a group of senators, just one example of the contributions of materiel and services that saved the state direct expense.

In 263 B.C. the Romans sacked Agrigentum (Acragas) and extorted from King Hiero II of Syracuse an indemnity of 100 *talents,* the equivalent of 384,000 denarii.[21] C. Duilius boasts in his memorial that in 260 B.C. he captured from the Carthaginian fleet off Mylae 3,600 gold staters and silver shekels with a total value between 200,000 and 300,000 denarii.[22] This windfall and prizes taken at sea in 257–255 B.C. might well have been the source of the metal used to strike the last four issues of Roman didrachmae (pl. 1.6–10). These later issues were struck on the lighter standard (48 to the Roman pound) current in Magna Graecia, and bore traditional types (see Table 2.1). Great profits probably were reaped from the sale of captives, but those sold in Italian markets brought no new specie into Italy since many Romans might well have made purchases in bronze asses. The proceeds of sales in Sicily seldom left the isle, for Syracuse, it seems, was unaffected by any specie drain as Hiero II continued striking gold and silver coins. Desultory fighting after 249 B.C. brought Rome no new plunder and so depleted the treasury that it is doubtful the mint coined new money in the final years of the war.

The scarcity of silver and gold during the First Punic War caused the production of bronze currency throughout Italy to climb to new levels, as Rome and her allies had to meet the wages of their citizens serving in armies overseas and in the fleets. Latin and Roman communities in central Italy—notably Tarquinii, Reate, Praeneste, Carseoli, and Firmum—sprang into operation casting local versions of the Roman libral as and its fractions. Elsewhere communities revived ancestral denominations. Umbrian and Etruscan towns based their bronze currency on an as two-thirds the weight of its Roman counterpart (200 g), while the Latin colonies Ariminum and Hadria on the Adriatic shores adopted a pre-Roman heavy as (350–400 g) subdivided into 10 rather than the customary 12 unciae. Greek and Oscan cities of Campania poured out their traditional *aes,* upon which the Latin colony of Beneventum based its first coinage. Arpi led the Apulian towns in resuming large-scale production of local bronze money. Rome soon adopted a practice that would be repeated for centuries: the weight of the principal circulating coin, the as, was reduced, but its monetary value remained unchanged. The reduction was by 2 full ounces or one-sixth below the libral weight of 12 ounces (268 g).[23] The introduction of this "light libral" as reduced the cost of transport and expanded the stock of circulating coins. Rome thereby took the first step in transforming Italic bronze money into a token coinage. The 5-pound ingots still being manufactured in the opening years of the First Punic War and the "heavy money" coins issued on the libral standard disappeared into the melting pot.

Rome had, by 238 B.C., become an imperial power after annexing first Sicily and then Sardinia and Corsica and was committed to a navy to protect her expanded interests. This new role was to transform the Italian economy and society just as similar forces had transformed the Athenian economy in the fifth century B.C. Her financial institutions, however, were not yet adequate for the task. The Roman state solved its immediate monetary deficiencies by imposing unprecedentedly high indemnities upon Carthage. By the treaty in 241 B.C. Carthage was assessed 3,200 talents of silver, payable in ten annual installments, or the equivalent of 1,228,800 denarii per year. In 238 B.C. a second indemnity of 1,200 talents was exacted from Carthage. The Roman people thus netted the equivalent of nearly 17 million denarii in the indemnity payments of 241–231 B.C.[24] With this vast supply of silver, the Roman mint commenced large-scale production of a new denarius of the same weight and fineness as the issues of 264–241 B.C. The new denarius was nicknamed "quadrigatus" (four-horsed) for the design on its reverse.[25] The quadrigatus, its silver fractions, and contemporary bronze asses all carry the head of a youthful Janus on their obverses, a celebration of the closing of the doors of the god's temple to mark the return of peace in 241 B.C. On the reverses of the silver coins, Jupiter hurls a thunderbolt from his *quadriga* as he races across the field and below is a tablet inscribed ROMA (pl. 2.11). On the reverse of asses the prow of a ship denoted naval victories and it became the standard design for the next 150 years so that asses were still dubbed "ships" in the Augustan age (pl. 4.24).[26]

Quadrigati were struck in vast numbers during the next three decades, but Rome did not recall earlier silver coins in circulation, for quadrigati were of the same fineness and weight as denarii of the

ROMANO and ROMA series minted during the First Punic War. Quadrigati circulated alongside earlier Roman denarii, silver coins of Neapolis, Taras, Cales, and even drachmae of Massilia (Marseilles) at the mouth of the Rhone. Although many heavier pieces of the early third century B.C. survived only in savings, Italy's silver money was still a mixed brew at the outbreak of the Second Punic War. Hoards from Italy, Spain, and Sicily dating from the early years of the Second Punic War indicate that the Roman state began paying military payrolls in portable silver coins, perhaps soon after 241 B.C. as Rome waged tough frontier wars in North Italy, Sardinia, and Corsica.[27]

The Second Punic War (218–201 B.C.) put Roman finances to an even greater test. The outbreak of war cut off sources of fresh specie. Rome had, since the 230s B.C., indirectly exploited Spanish mines since Carthage had met its indemnity payments by exacting tribute, in silver, from the Iberian tribes. After 230 B.C., New Carthage, the seat of Punic power, turned Spanish gold and silver to its own uses by striking the staters and shekels that bought the great mercenary armies commanded by Hannibal, Hasdrubal, and Mago. Rome mobilized fleets and armies in many theaters on a scale far exceeding those in the First Punic War, and from the start Rome's extraordinary war effort fueled tremendous demands for coined money that far outstripped the Republic's ability to supply. Rome already faced severe shortages of silver in the first year of the war and debased the quadrigatus by reducing its silver content from 97 to 91 percent.[28] Gold bullion in the treasury, sacred objects, and Syracusan staters loaned by Hiero II were converted into aurei and *quinarii,* Rome's first gold coins. Aurei, struck at the weight standard of a quadrigatus (1/48 pound) and tariffed by the bullion ratio between gold and silver, were high-value coins used in bulk payments as an emergency proxy for quadrigati (pl. 2.12). The head of Janus graces the obverse of aurei, and on the reverse two warriors exchange oaths as a call to arms. Aurei, however, proved too few to meet the demand for more coinage; known dies suggest a mintage of 1,280,000 aurei, equivalent, perhaps, to eight to ten times their number in silver quadrigati.[29]

Roman armies suffered colossal defeats on the battlefields of Italy in 218–216 B.C., and, along with the losses of men and equipment, huge numbers of quadrigati and *aes* fell into the hands of Hannibal. Rebellions in Cisalpine Gaul, Sicily, and southern Italy strained Roman financial resources to the breaking point by 212 B.C. Capua, second city of Italy, defected and minted gold staters, quadrigati, and bronze fractions based on a *quincunx* in 216–211 B.C., while the city of Taras (Tarentum), the Bretti and the Lucanians each struck coins for a veritable Carthaginian military government in southern Italy.[30]

Rome was confronted by shortages of bronze currency after defeats at Trebbia and Lake Trasimene and thereupon slashed the weight of asses by one-half. Successive reductions followed until 212 B.C. when "the Roman people, oppressed by debts during the Punic War, divided the one pound as into six, each of which was to have the value of the one pound as."[31] In desperation the Roman state created a fiduciary bronze currency based on an as (40.5 g) minted on a sextanal standard (pl. 5.25–29). These bronze coins, however, were not temporary substitutes for silver coins as they were in Classical Greece, but rather they were tokens taking the place of full-weight bronze coins. Romans expected even token coins to be of substantial size and weight to guarantee their official exchange value. Scarcity of bronze afflicted both sides of the war since the Campanian towns Capua, Atella, and Calatia, which obtained most of their metal by overstriking Roman pieces, also adopted the lighter standards. With so many cuts in standard, and demonetization of coins of rebels, "heavy bronze coins" (*aes grave*) of all types were reminted so that by 200 B.C. only token coins on the sextanal standard circulated throughout Italy.

Rome also faced critical shortages of silver immediately after the crushing defeat at Cannae in 216 B.C. The Senate defrayed six months of wages for legions in Sicily by borrowing money and grain from Hiero II, while Sardinian communities made voluntary contributions in kind. In the next year, the Republic doubled the land tax (*tributum duplex*), but the measure netted insufficient sums of silver for coinage, for Rome could not repay Hiero II and postponed payment of contractors victualing forces in Spain. More short-term loans followed in 214 B.C. Surcharges on the propertied classes paid salaries of crews in the fleet dispatched to Sicily, while officers and centurions served without pay, saving the state perhaps 20 percent of a legion's payroll. At the same time, the mint issued on a quadranal standard bronze multiples of the as to substitute for quadrigati, including a *decussis* (10 asses), *quincussis* (5 asses), *tressis* (3 asses), and *dupondius* (2 asses).[32] Such heavy, cumbersome emergency pieces aggravated rather than solved shortages of metal because bronze was needed for arms and armor.

The Roman state solved its financial dilemma by its first devaluation and recoinage of silver currency in 213 or 212 B.C.[33] The denarius was devalued by 50 percent. It was minted on a standard of 72 to the Roman pound (4.5 g), but its fineness was improved (96 percent). The Republic thus paid off its debts in denarii devalued by one-half. The new denarius carried stirring appeals. Its obverse bears the head of a helmeted Roma; across its reverse field charge the mounted twins the Dioscuri, Castor and Pollux, who had turned the tide of battle at Lake Regillius when the Romans had defeated their Latin foes and forged their confederacy (pl. 2.16). The first new denarii, along with silver fractions of the half (quinarius) and quarter (sestertius), were marked with values in asses (pl. 2.17–18). Roman soldiers nicknamed the lighter denarii "bigati" (two horsed) to distinguish them from earlier quadrigati.[34]

Rome and auxiliary mints in Southern Italy and Sicily melted and reminted earlier silver coins into the new denarii, although quadrigati struck from alloyed silver since 218 B.C. briefly circulated at a new tariffing of 15 asses or 1.5 denarii. The Roman mint struck in tandem with its new denarius large numbers of *victoriati* which were halves of a quadrigatus and carried types inspired from the iconography found on the reverse of the quadriagtus—an obverse portrait of Jupiter and a Victoria crowning a trophy on the reverse (pl. 2.19). There were thus five silver denominations of varying fineness circulating at the end of the third century B.C. Victoriati were used to pay forces serving in Sicily and Southern Italy, for they have survived in hoards mainly from these theaters of the war, and few quadrigati or denarii were set aside in the same hoards.[35] Meanwhile, denarii, along with quinarii and sestertii, were shipped in lieu of quadrigati to all forces, even those serving in

North Italy and Spain, immediately after the reform. Whereas quadrigati dropped out of use soon after the reform, victoriati circulated to the end of the second century B.C. long after Rome ceased to mint them. They were popular in Cisalpine Gaul, passing as equivalents of Massiliot drachmae and Celtic imitative pieces of the Po Valley. Victoriati that sustained heavy wear during the Second Punic War were later revalued downward at 5 asses or one-half of the denarius, the reckoning Cato the Elder employed in 180 B.C.[36] Since victoriati were of a base alloy, their greater weight and size made them much more handy fractions than the tiny, easily lost quinarii and sestertii.

The new silver coinage was accompanied by a full range of bronze fractions on the sextanal standard from a dupondius (2 asses) to a semuncia (1/24 as) as well as multiples of the denarius in gold bearing the obverse portrait of Mars and an eagle standing on a thunderbolt on the reverse. The aureus of this second gold issue weighed one-half of the first (1/96 pound), and denominations of six, four, and two denarii were coined to provide wages to soldiers and rowers in 212–209 B.C. (pl. 2.13–15).[37] The gold coins were deliberately undervalued at a bullion ratio of 1:8 due to wartime demands for silver money. When great hauls of booty poured into Rome from Africa and Spain in 205–200 B.C., bullion ratios shifted back to a more typical 1:10 or 1:12, thereby condemning the emergency aurei to the melting pot. Based on surviving obverse dies, Rome in 212–207 B.C., despite the best efforts of her financial commissioners, could only mint perhaps 65 to 70 percent of the gold she struck in 218–214 B.C. Earlier aurei as well as stocks of plate and ornaments collected from state, sacred, and private reserves were recoined, but the bulk of the metal came later from foreign coin captured at Capua, Syracuse, New Carthage, Taras, and Hasdrubal's camp at the Metaurus.[38]

In the Second Punic War, the Republic reforged its silver and bronze currency into a system of denominations that endured for the next 450 years. Rome also learned how to avoid massive default in a crisis by devaluing the silver coinage, adopting a fiduciary bronze currency and minting emergency gold coins. The Romans added these measures, well known to Greek states since the fifth century B.C., to their arsenal of financial expedients. They drew the even more important conclusion that control of overseas sources of specie and revenues alone could solve their financial weaknesses. The brilliant victories of P. Cornelius Scipio Africanus in 206–201 B.C. gained Rome control over the rich Spanish mines and an annual indemnity from Carthage equivalent to 1,152,000 denarii (201–151 B.C.).[39] Thereafter, Rome was committed to the imperial axiom, best expressed by Polybius, that "the Romans amass their financial resources in order to wage war."[40] Roman triumph on the battlefield also ensured the triumph of the new Roman currency throughout Italy and the provinces of Sicily, Sardinia, Corsica, and Cisalpine Gaul. Revolts gave Rome an excuse to sack her rivals Capua, Syracuse, and Taras. Hundreds of thousands of gold and silver *litrae* of Syracuse, Corinthian-style *pegasi*, Campanian and Italiot didrachmae, and shekels of Carthage and her Italian allies were melted down and struck into denarii in massive recoinages in 211–200 B.C. that changed the face of currency in the western Mediterranean.

The Republic decentralized minting denarii, victoriati, and bronze coins in Italy and Sicily in 213–204 B.C. to expedite recoining old money and meeting payrolls promptly, and the denarius quickly ousted all earlier silver coins. The Etruscan ports Populonia and Vetulonia, alone of Rome's allies, issued silver currency—didrachmae tariffed at ten local asses and initially struck on the standard similar to the heavy Italiot one of the early third century B.C. (8 g). During 216–207 B.C. each city twice reduced the weight of her stater by 25 percent, and each introduced gold and silver multiples as well as base metal fractions, but these coins seldom traveled beyond Etruria (pl. 2.20–22).[41] In Southern Italy, Latin colonies, which served as bases for Roman legions operating against Hannibal, expanded production of their own bronze currency in 215–205 B.C. to provide change for denarii and victoriati spent in their marts by Roman and allied soldiers. The Latin colonies Luceria and Venusia, bases to a consular army each year for a decade, manufactured great numbers of Apulian asses, each of which was divided into ten unciae. Brundisium, a Latin colony founded at the terminus of the Via Appia in 244 B.C. and serving as a station for the

Roman fleet in the Ionian Sea, likewise minted Roman-style bronze denominations. Other ports such as Paestum, Rhegium, Messana, and Catana similarly minted their own fractional token coins. Decentralized minting furthered the use of Roman coins and systems of reckoning. Although cities often premised their bronze currency on earlier systems of reckoning, they pegged their principal denomination to the Roman denarius. Consequently, native bronze coins of Southern Italy or Greek Sicily were assimilated as local variants of the Roman denominational system by the early second century B.C.

The legacy of the Second Punic War was the Romanization of Italy's currency and the monetization of her economy. Stray coins recovered at sites such as Cosa, or from the open deposit that was an accumulation of coins discarded for good luck by travelers crossing the Liri River, reveal that non-Roman coins disappeared from general circulation after 200 B.C. The finds also suggest that Italians had many coins on hand for daily transactions. The Second Punic War greatly expanded the supply of hard cash—the hard-pressed Roman Republic, as well as Hannibal's Italian allies, reminted vast reserves of gold and silver long immobilized in private plate and sacred objects. The plunder of Spain, Greece, and Africa dumped even larger windfalls of specie on Italian markets. Since over half of the draftable Italians of a generation served either in Roman or Carthaginian forces, they had grown accustomed to receiving wages and conducting daily transactions in coin.

In all theaters of the Second Punic War, Roman and Carthaginian commanders habitually ran short of funds and thus recycled older coins. Roman and Syracusan-Carthaginian forces traded Sicilian towns and districts several times during the fighting in 215–210 B.C. Hoards of this chaotic period contain mixes of silver coins from all sides. Carthaginian mercenaries at Agrigentum in 212–210 B.C. overstruck captured Roman denarii as half-shekels, while the Romans halved bronze coins of Hiero II to serve as semunciae.[42] Very often, commanders on both sides must have just reissued coins of the opponents as booty and saved the cost of reminting. In Spain, P. Cornelius Scipio and later his son the great Africanus acted on their own authority to raise cash and supplies, which might explain the poor record of hoards of Roman coins that have survived from this war.[43] Arrival of large Roman forces also stimulated allied communities in Spain, Gaul, and Sicily to increase production of their own coins because under the terms of their treaties with Rome they were obliged to pay local contractors for supplies or the wages of their own forces. Massilia and her dependencies of Rhode and Emporiae (Ampurias) stepped up production of drachmae and Roman friends in Sicily, notably Tauromenium and Messana, resumed striking coins. Iberian and Massiliot drachmae and old Italiot didrachmae were regularly included with Roman quadrigati and denarii in caches secreted by Carthaginian mercenaries who served in Spain, Sicily, and Italy.[44]

The evolution of the Roman coinage in the third century B.C. hinged on victories in the First and Second Punic Wars that delivered Rome the silver to sustain a major coinage. Imperialism, not commerce, propelled the monetization of Roman Italy. In contrast to her Hellenistic rivals, Rome did not engage mercenary armies but rather drafted citizens and allies who received minimal wages, and, as a consequence, the Republic had little need for the gold staters and silver tetradrachmae minted by her opponents Taras, Syracuse, and Carthage. Romans also engaged in little commerce calling for heavy, wide-flan silver denominations, like the Athenian tetradrachma, which were the trade coins of history. Instead, Rome created a smaller silver denomination, the denarius, and a chain of token bronze denominations suited for the many small-scale payments of her peculiar military budget. Once in circulation, the denarius and its token bronze fractions proved ideal for daily exchanges and so they penetrated the markets of Italian towns and the countryside. Monetization of Roman fiscal institutions and Italian economic life henceforth proceeded as a single process.

Finally, the Roman state could not help but conclude from its experience in the third century B.C. that the profits of overseas imperialism ultimately balanced the books and netted a profit. The Romans learned to use debasement of the currency as a sophisticated expedient, along with short-term loans, to bridge the gap between high costs in the early stages of a war and the spoils of victory. Once the dark days of the Second Punic War passed, the Roman state never again had cause to develop long-term, self-liquidating debt and bills of exchange like those that revolutionized international finances and the Western European economy in the seventeenth and eighteenth centuries. Despite brief shortages during the Civil Wars of the 80s and 40s B.C., Rome by conquest redirected the flow of specie in the Mediterranean world into Italy and thereby assured herself of ample reserves of coined money.

In 200 B.C. Rome scarcely possessed either the major fiscal commitments to overseas provinces or a volume of overseas trade that required placing her currency on the international Attic standard. The Romans, however, were fast assimilating the currencies of the western Greeks and incorporating Sicily, Sardinia, Corsica, and Cisalpine Gaul into the monetary system of a greater Italy. With control of the Spanish mines and a prostrate Carthage, the Roman Republic commanded the financial resources to dominate the Mediterranean world. By dint of sacrifices in war Roman Italy passed the threshold into an increasingly monetized world by 200 B.C. The imperial experience of the next two hundred years accelerated the pace of change many times as the Roman state acquired ever more obligations in coin in the form of military payrolls, building contracts, and distributions to the Roman people. For the next two centuries the Romans embarked on spectacular transmarine conquests that gained an empire and transformed their coins into a Mediterranean currency.

# Three

# The Denarius and Overseas Expansion, 200–30 B.C.

The Roman Republic emerged from the Second Punic War with a new silver denarius and a token bronze currency that met the challenge of financing the great imperial conquests of the next century (200–91 B.C.), but the Republic then faced an even more severe test in the Civil Wars of the first century (90–31 B.C.). The first era of overseas conquest spread Roman coins and monetary habits throughout greater Italy. In the second period, *imperatores* from Sulla to Augustus, who waged their own great wars of conquest or civil wars, extended the use of Roman money to the provinces. From the opening of the second century B.C. the Republic, even though the Senate often strove to cut such commitments, steadily assumed more military and administrative obligations that required payrolls in coin. Starting in the late 140s B.C. the Republic faced not only rising military costs, but also greater expenditures to implement demands of reformers agitating to alleviate the conditions of poorer citizens and allies who had suffered from the social dislocation arising from the monetization of the Italian economy and the great migrations from the countryside to Rome and the Campanian cities.

Roman generals and legionaries who conquered and plundered

the overseas provinces, and Italian contractors, publicans, and traders who followed to exploit them, transformed the currencies of the Classical world. Roman victories from 200 to 90 B.C. altered the flow of specie so that Italy became the prime silver-consuming region. Silver drained out of Spain and the Greek world, and although coin and bullion often flowed back in trade, Roman armies repeatedly returned to plunder the provinces. Most Greek trade coins disappeared: regal Macedonian gold staters shortly before the mid-second century B.C., and the last great civic tetradrachmae, the "New Style" Athenian coins, soon after the mid-first century B.C. The influx of silver wrought economic changes at home, encouraging the use of coins in daily transactions, but it also fueled inflation. The Roman mint became capable of turning out on short notice hundreds of millions of denarii of virtually pure silver on a consistent standard (84 to the pound) for the next two centuries.[1] Change also was wrought in the provinces. In some cases, for example in Asia and Syria, the Romans turned regal silver currencies into provincial ones. More often the denarius supplanted local coinages, although cities or friendly dynasts minted silver fractions or turned to bronze currency for home consumption. It remained for Augustus to integrate the surviving regional and civic coinages into a Roman imperial currency.

When Hannibal withdrew from Italy, the production of coins, which had been dispersed during the wars of the late third century, was returned to Rome. For over sixty years after 200 B.C. Rome struck coins of unchanging design—denarii bearing the types of Roma and the Dioscuri, asses bearing the head of Janus and the prow, and assorted bronze fractions. In the final years of the Second Punic War, standards had deteriorated as many denarii were deliberately minted below their legal weight of 72 to the pound on standards ranging from 76 to 80 to the pound. By 187 B.C. Rome fixed the standard at 84 denarii to the pound, in part to put newly minted denarii at par with the heavily worn or often underweight denarii struck during the Second Punic and Second Macedonian wars.[2] This standard persisted down to the Neronian recoinage in A.D. 64, and its long period of stability led Pliny the Elder to believe that denarii had always been minted at 84 to the pound.[3] The as and its fractions were minted on an array of weight standards. Some wartime mints, such as Luceria, even at the start of the reform of 213–212 B.C., struck bronze coins well below the 2 ounces required by the sextanal standard. Pliny credits the dictator Q. Fabius Maximus (216 B.C.) with the introduction of the uncial standard of 1 full ounce for the as, but in truth the weight was progressively lowered to the uncial standard over the period 210 to 201 B.C.[4] In the early years of the second century B.C., many asses, henceforth struck from engraved dies rather than cast, left the mint one-third to one-quarter below the legal ounce since bronze coins were often manufactured *al marco,* a practice stipulating a fixed number of coins per pound without close regulation of the weight of individual coins (pl. 5.30). The uncial standard became accepted as the appropriate fiduciary ratio between token bronze coins and a "full-bodied" or fine silver denarius, and, as a consequence, uncial asses of the Republic circulated down to the Augustan age.

The profits from eastern wars and from the Spanish mines in 200–187 B.C. brought unprecedented quantities of specie into state vaults which the Roman mint either coined into denarii or cast into certified ingots of gold or silver.[5] Soon after 200 B.C. Rome discontinued the pure silver fractions, quinarius and sestertius, in favor of the victoriatus whose fineness (80 percent) and weight (3.75 g) were set so it passed as the half of the denarius.[6] Despite the steady flow of bullion from indemnities, booty, and the Spanish mines, Rome did not mint silver coins on a regular basis, but rather struck denarii as the need for new money arose. The relative size of these coinages is difficult to estimate, because the hoards do not preserve a representative sample of total coinage throughout the period.[7] Livy and Polybius, however, furnish details about the indemnities, booty, and profits of Spanish mines netted by the Republic in 201–151 B.C. (Table 3.1); Livy also preserves the rates of donatives paid out in triumphs, from which estimates of the total amounts paid can be derived (Table 3.2). These figures, although they cannot replace budget or mint records, still give some sense of the scale of change affecting Roman coinage in the first half of the second century B.C. The treasury is reported to have acquired silver plate and foreign coin equivalent to nearly 620 million denarii, and another 50 mil-

*Table 3.1*
Silver Bullion and Coin Available to Roman Mint, 201–151 B.C.

| Amounts of Silver (Stated in Attic Talents) | | | | | | |
|---|---|---|---|---|---|---|
| Date | Indemnities | Booty in Triumphs | Spanish Mines | Macedon Tribute | Total | Denarii (at 84 to the Pound) |
| 201 B.C. | 200 | 1,462.5 | 500 | | 2,162.5 | 14,532,000 |
| 200 B.C. | 200 | 555.1 | 500 | | 1,255.1 | 8,434,272 |
| 199 B.C. | 200 | 15.0 | 500 | | 715.0 | 4,804,800 |
| 198 B.C. | 200 | | 500 | | 700.0 | 4,704,000 |
| 197 B.C. | 200 | 22.9 | 500 | | 722.9 | 4,857,888 |
| 196 B.C. | 700 | 921.5 | 500 | | 2,121.5 | 14,256,480 |
| 195 B.C. | 350 | 703.9 | 500 | | 1,553.9 | 10,442,208 |
| 194 B.C. | 300 | 410.6 | 500 | | 1,210.6 | 8,135,232 |
| 193 B.C. | 300 | | 500 | | 800.0 | 5,376,000 |
| 192 B.C. | 300 | | 500 | | 800.0 | 5,376,000 |
| 191 B.C. | 200 | 242.5 | 500 | | 942.5 | 6,333,600 |
| 190 B.C. | 200 | 237.3 | 500 | | 937.3 | 6,298,656 |
| 189 B.C. | 900 | 1,616.6 | 500 | | 3,016.6 | 20,271,552 |
| 188 B.C. | 2,750 | | 500 | | 3,250.0 | 21,840,000 |
| 187 B.C. | 1,550 | | 500 | | 2,050.0 | 13,776,000 |
| 186 B.C. | 1,250 | | 500 | | 1,750.0 | 11,760,000 |
| 185 B.C. | 1,250 | 328.8 | 500 | | 2,078.8 | 13,969,536 |
| 184 B.C. | 1,250 | 300.0 | 500 | | 2,050.0 | 13,776,000 |
| 183 B.C. | 1,250 | 116.3 | 500 | | 1,866.3 | 12,541,536 |
| 182 B.C. | 1,200 | | 500 | | 1,700.0 | 11,424,000 |
| 181 B.C. | 1,200 | | 500 | | 1,700.0 | 11,424,000 |
| 180 B.C. | 1,200 | 25.8 | 500 | | 1,725.8 | 11,597,376 |
| 179 B.C. | 1,200 | | 500 | | 1,700.0 | 11,424,000 |
| 178 B.C. | 1,200 | 750.0 | 500 | | 2,450.0 | 16,464,000 |
| 177 B.C. | 1,200 | 52.1 | 1,500 | | 2,752.1 | 18,494,112 |
| 176 B.C. | 1,200 | | 1,500 | | 2,700.0 | 18,144,000 |
| 175 B.C. | 200 | | 1,500 | | 1,700.0 | 11,424,000 |
| 174 B.C. | 200 | 125.0 | 1,500 | | 1,825.0 | 12,264,000 |
| 173 B.C. | 200 | | 1,500 | | 1,700.0 | 11,424,000 |
| 172 B.C. | 200 | | 1,500 | | 1,700.0 | 11,424,000 |
| 171 B.C. | 200 | | 1,500 | | 1,700.0 | 11,424,000 |
| 170 B.C. | 200 | | 1,500 | | 1,700.0 | 11,424,000 |
| 169 B.C. | 200 | | 1,500 | | 1,700.0 | 11,424,000 |
| 168 B.C. | 200 | | 1,500 | | 1,700.0 | 11,424,000 |

(*continued*)

*Table 3.1* (*Continued*)

| | Amounts of Silver (Stated in Attic Talents) | | | | | |
|---|---|---|---|---|---|---|
| Date | Indemnities | Booty in Triumphs | Spanish Mines | Macedon Tribute | Total | Denarii (at 84 to the Pound) |
| 167 B.C. | 200 | 2,987.3 | 1,500 | | 4,687.3 | 31,498,656 |
| 166 B.C. | 200 | | 1,500 | 100 | 1,800.0 | 12,096,000 |
| 165 B.C. | 200 | | 1,500 | 100 | 1,800.0 | 12,096,000 |
| 164 B.C. | 200 | | 1,500 | 100 | 1,800.0 | 12,096,000 |
| 163 B.C. | 200 | | 1,500 | 100 | 1,800.0 | 12,096,000 |
| 162 B.C. | 200 | | 1,500 | 100 | 1,800.0 | 12,096,000 |
| 161 B.C. | 200 | | 1,500 | 100 | 1,800.0 | 12,096,000 |
| 160 B.C. | 200 | | 1,500 | 100 | 1,800.0 | 12,096,000 |
| 159 B.C. | 200 | | 1,500 | 100 | 1,800.0 | 12,096,000 |
| 158 B.C. | 200 | | 1,500 | 100 | 1,800.0 | 12,096,000 |
| 157 B.C. | 200 | | 1,500 | 100 | 1,800.0 | 12,096,000 |
| 156 B.C. | 200 | | 1,500 | 100 | 1,800.0 | 12,096,000 |
| 155 B.C. | 200 | | 1,500 | 100 | 1,800.0 | 12,096,000 |
| 154 B.C. | 200 | | 1,500 | 100 | 1,800.0 | 12,096,000 |
| 153 B.C. | 200 | | 1,500 | 100 | 1,800.0 | 12,096,000 |
| 152 B.C. | 200 | | 1,500 | 100 | 1,800.0 | 12,096,000 |
| 151 B.C. | 200 | | 1,500 | 100 | 1,800.0 | 12,096,000 |
| Totals | 26,950 | 10,873.2 | 52,500 | 1,600 | 91,923.2 | 617,723,904 |

*Source:* Table based on sources collected by Frank, *ESAR* I, pp. 126–41.

lion denarii worth of gold, including several hundred thousand regal Macedonian staters that passed at rates between 22 to 26.5 denarii.[8] Even with the profits of the Spanish mines, the treasury often ran short of hard cash in the opening stages of wars. Expeditionary forces in 200–168 B.C. required enormous cash expenditures for mobilizing fleets and consular armies at a time when Rome was also locked in desultory fighting against Cisalpine Gauls and Ligurians. Annual wages of a legion totaled between 550,000 and 600,000 denarii down to the age of Julius Caesar, but costs of equipping, clothing, and victualing at least doubled the price of mobilizing a citizen legion to well over 1 million denarii per year even when provisions were acquired from allies or by foraging.[9]

Although by 200 B.C. the wealth of Rome had increased suffi-

*Table 3.2*
Estimated Donatives, 201–167 B.C.

| Date | Action | Triumphator | Recipients | Donatives (Denarii) |
|---|---|---|---|---|
| 201 B.C | Carthage | P. Cornelius Scipio | 23,000 | 920,000 |
| 200 B.C. | Spain | L. Cornelius Lentulus | 8,000 | 96,000 |
| 200 B.C. | Cis. Gaul | L. Furius Purpurio | 9,500 | 75,000 |
| 197 B.C. | Cis. Gaul | C. Cornelius Cethegus | 20,000 | 200,000 |
| 197 B.C. | Cis. Gaul | Q. Minucius Rufus | 21,500 | 210,000 |
| 196 B.C. | Cis. Gaul | M. Claudius Marcellus | 14,000 | 140,000 |
| 194 B.C. | Spain | M. Porcius Cato | 21,000 | 650,000 |
| 194 B.C. | Macedon | T. Quinctius Flamininus | 17,500 | 530,000 |
| 191 B.C. | Cis. Gaul | P. Cornelius Scipio Nasica | 21,200 | 290,000 |
| 189 B.C. | Asia | L. Cornelius Scipio | 17,250 | 500,000 |
| 187 B.C. | Asia | Cn. Manlius Vulso | 17,500 | 850,000 |
| 187 B.C. | Aetolia | M. Fulvius Nobilior | 22,600 | 625,000 |
| 181 B.C. | Liguria | L. Aemilius Paullus | 18,100 | 635,000 |
| 180 B.C. | Spain | Q. Fulvius Flaccus | 10,700 | 600,000 |
| 179 B.C. | Liguria | Q. Fulvius Flaccus | 20,200 | 735,000 |
| 178 B.C. | Spain | T. Sempronius Gracchus | 11,200 | 335,000 |
| 178 B.C. | Spain | A. Postumius Albinus | 11,200 | 335,000 |
| 177 B.C. | Liguria | C. Claudius Pulcher | 20,100 | 255,000 |
| 167 B.C. | Macedon | L. Aemilius Paullus | 27,000 | 3,100,000 |
| 167 B.C. | Naval | Cn. Octavius | 13,000 | 1,265,000 |
| 167 B.C. | Illyria | L. Anicius Gallus | 18,350 | 925,000 |
| Totals | | | 362,900 | 13,271,000 |

*Source:* Table 3.2 is based on sources collected by Brunt, *Italian Manpower,* pp. 393–94 and 694–97.

ciently so that debasement was not necessary to finance overseas wars, payments on contracts were postponed, sometimes by offering public land at a nominal rent as collateral.[10] The propertied classes in the Centuriate Assembly defrayed many costs by imposing on themselves a *tributum,* a war-tax levied at 1 to 2 percent on property assessed above 1,500 asses, although they expected repayment in the wake of victory. Such taxes were levied to finance the wars against Philip V, Antiochus III, and Perseus.[11] Each triumph glutted the treasury with silver, and the mint swung into large-scale production, turning out denarii in brief bursts of activity in the 190s, 180s, and 160s B.C. to pay off contracts and war debts. In 187 B.C., Cn. Manlius Vulso carried off so much plate and coin from Asia that the Senate ordered state ledgers cleared of debt—including the refund in a single payment of an onerous *tributum* at 2.55 percent, most likely levied during the Asian War—in what must have been a massive recoinage of captured Greek staters.[12] In 167 B.C., the Roman mint turned Macedonian tetradrachmae, taken as spoils, into denarii, many bearing a new reverse design of Victoria driving a *biga* (two-horsed chariot) in honor of the great Roman triumph (pl. 6.36).[13] The Macedonian treasures, whose value totaled 30 million denarii, filled state coffers to the brim, providing the basis of a reserve that swelled to over 18 million denarii by 157 B.C. With this reserve plus the annual Macedonian tribute of 672,000 denarii and the income from Spanish mines, the Republic never again had to tax Roman soil.[14] This pattern of production was repeated during the next half-century as it peaked again after the sacks of Corinth and Carthage in 146 B.C., and in the wake of later victories in Asia, Africa, and North Italy.

Triumphs, which brought specie to Rome, also became a means of putting coins into circulation as generals rewarded their soldiers with donatives.[15] Although soldiers received Roman coins recaptured from defeated foes in the triumphs celebrating Spanish and Ligurian victories, the lavish donatives distributed by triumphators rewarding eastern victories must have been paid in newly minted denarii. Donatives reported for 201–167 B.C. put at least 13 million denarii into circulation; the great triumphs of four years—194, 189, 187, and 167 B.C.—account for over 60 percent of this total. Generals returning from the East kept breaking records in generosity. A donative of 100 denarii in 167 B.C., equal to one year's pay for a legionary, rose to fifteen times this sum in 61 B.C. Donatives also suggest the scale of specie that entered Italy in the hands of returning soldiers. While still in Epirus in 167 B.C., L. Aemilius Paullus rewarded his army with donatives totaling some 6.4 million denarii realized from the sale of 150,000 prisoners.[16] A century later a Sullan veteran of eastern wars concealed near Poggio Picenze his savings of denarii and Greek coins with a value of over 800 denarii (almost eight times a legionary's annual pay).[17] Much gold and silver taken in private plunder was spent overseas or immobilized in plate, but considerable sums eventually found their way into the markets of Italy.

Coins also were put into circulation as payments for the spate of public building that invariably followed a major victory. The censors of 184 B.C., M. Porcius Cato and M. Valerius Flaccus, employed the Asian spoils to let a number of contracts, notably renovation of the drainage system for Rome at a cost of 6 million denarii.[18] An even more ambitious building program followed in 179 B.C. paid from the booty of Spanish wars. As profits from imperial expansion mounted, so did the scale and cost of projects at Rome; the Marcian aqueduct was built in 144–143 B.C. at a cost of 4.5 million denarii.[19] The construction of military highways in North Italy in 150–100 B.C., and then of extensions into Narbonese Gaul and Spain, spread Roman coins to provincial markets in the West. The influx of silver from Spanish mines and the conquests in the East enabled the Roman mint to improve the fineness of the denarius to virtually pure silver (from 96.5 to 98 percent) after the Third Macedonian War (172–168 B.C.). Old denarii, provided they were of acceptable weight, passed at the same rate as freshly minted ones, and consequently the supply of silver money in Italy constantly expanded during the second century B.C. Expansion of the money supply is reflected by Pliny the Elder's reports of reserves in the treasury (*aerarium*) on three occasions (only two of which survive intact) after a decade of prosperity and relative peace. In 157 B.C. the Republic accumulated from booty and a rudimentary system of provincial taxation over 18 million denarii, as well as a comparable sum in 91 B.C., although the numbers are lost. In 49 B.C., despite greater annual expenditures, the treasury held over 22.6 million denarii.[20] It is noteworthy that most of these reserves—over 80 percent in 157 B.C. and 55 percent in 49 B.C.—was in gold bullion, which, presumably, was readily convertible into silver coin or negotiable in major transactions.

By the mid-second century B.C., denarii were produced on a more regular basis. Systematic exploitation of the Spanish mines and the collection of annual tribute from Macedon gave Rome a predictable income, but, perhaps of more importance, she was accumulating annual commitments for the administration and defense of her overseas provinces. By 150 B.C. production from the silver mines near New Carthage, the most famous of the Iberian mines feeding the Roman mint with metal for two centuries, soared to peak levels of 1,500 talents (or some 10 million denarii) per year.[21] The Republic was awash in so much silver from Spain that for ten years (167–158 B.C.) the Senate could afford to close the Macedonian gold and silver mines. The great size of state reserves and coinages suggests that optimate senators in 133–91 B.C. were obstructionists when they cried impoverishment should the state fund popular reforms advocated by the Gracchi, L. Appuleius Saturninus, or M. Livius Drusus. The tribune M. Livius Drusus probably offered his proposal to debase the denarius by 12.5 percent to counter well-worn conservative claims that lack of funds precluded reform.[22]

Proliferation of control marks, names of issuing moneyers, and types on denarii coincided with the growth of the money supply. As early as the 180s B.C. moneyers designated coins issued under their authority by adding personal symbols or abbreviations of their names that evolved into the full fledged names and control marks found on most denarii after the 160s B.C. Moneyers also began to favor designs honoring the Republic or ancestors of the moneyers, but denarii for the most part remained free of partisan political iconography until the time of the Civil Wars.[23] Engravers also favored more compact flans and tighter execution of figures, freely experimenting in techniques that culminated in the superbly designed denarii of the late first century B.C. Many denarii were struck on flans notched by the chisel before striking. Denarii struck from such decorated flans, serrate denarii (*serrati*), were long preferred in commerce because of their high purity and ease of recognition (pl. 6.40).

The pace of inflation from 200 to 30 B.C. is virtually undocumented, but the coinage itself reflects inflation since the silver fractions, the quinarius and sestertius, were discontinued as unnecessary or unprofitable to mint. Striking of victoriati was suspended early in the second century B.C. so that as stocks of silver fractions wore out, denarii were frequently cut in half or quarters. As economic activity increased during the first half of the second century B.C. so did production of bronze fractions of the denarius. At the same time, loyal communities in Italy recoined many sextanal *aes* as semisses, quadrantes, sextantes, and unciae premised on a local as which ranged from 18 to 32 to the Roman pound. Former Greek cities such as Paestum and Velia, the Latin colony Brundisium, and even the new maritime colonies of Copia (Thurii) and Vibo Valentia issued bronze coins, often distributed as *sportula* during holidays, to function as small change to Roman denarii. Initially Rome, along with Velia, Paestum, and Brundisium, concentrated on striking bronze coins on the old heavy standard, but excavated sites reveal a high incidence of casual loss of all denominations between the as and sextans, indicating that a widespread use of bronze money accompanied the vast increase of denarii in circulation. Although they amounted to no more than 10 to 15 percent of the total value of money in circulation, their numbers must have equaled or exceeded the number of circulating denarii.[24]

Production of bronze coins peaked by 150 B.C. and then fell sharply. Rome could not maintain an uncial standard in the face of growing demand for bronze money. Many asses worn from heavy use weighed no more than two-thirds of an ounce, so that official tariffing fell short of the 10 ounces of bronze (or fourth-fifths of a Roman pound) to a denarius. Moneychangers thus discounted light asses and rates of exchange fluctuated. In 141 B.C. the denarius was retariffed at 16 asses, and for a brief time denarii carried the new value on their obverses, but the standard and types of the denarius were otherwise unchanged (pl. 6.37).[25] By retariffing at 16 asses to the denarius, the Republic saved the cost of reminting a vast body of underweight bronze coins, since 16 worn asses, at two-thirds of an ounce, equaled in weight just over 10 uncial asses of full weight. Revaluation alleviated the problem for a generation, and Rome minted mostly divisions of the as, notably semis, triens, and quadrans, and suspended minting *aes* for lengthy periods down to the outbreak of the Social War (90–88 B.C.). Furthermore, in ca. 101 B.C. a *lex Clodia* revived production of the silver quinarius to ease the demand for fractional currency. Given their purity (94 percent fine) and light weight (2 g), quinarii passed as equivalents of worn victoriati and they even carried the types of the popular victoriatus (pl. 6.38).[26]

Between 225 B.C. and A.D. 1, the number of consumers of coins at least doubled as the population of peninsular Italy climbed to 6 million. Migration from the countryside and import of slaves concentrated in Rome and the cities of Campania nearly 2 million plebeians who required token bronze coins for their innumerable small purchases for daily wants in urban markets. The vast output of bronze currency in the first half of the second century B.C. was sufficient for the populace of Rome as it doubled to some 325,000 by 130 B.C., but the mint thereafter failed to keep pace with public need when the city's population nearly doubled again to 600,000 by 60 B.C. Although costs of living rose, prices of the last century of the Republic indicate that the Roman public still needed large numbers of low-denomination bronze coins for daily purchases. Official prices of a *modius* of wheat, which was 25 percent of the monthly intake of grain for an adult male, remained stable for much of the second century B.C. and it was probably one-half denarius (8 asses) in 100 B.C. In the next century, it rose to 12 asses by Cicero's day and then to 16 asses or a full denarius by the Augustan age. Official prices at Rome give but an impression of the rate of inflation, for most commodities and luxuries underwent far greater increases in price. By the end of the second century B.C., inflation made the striking of bronze denominations below the quadrans (one-quarter as) unprofitable, and the silver divisions of the denarius were revived. Romans were perhaps facing shortages of adequate fractions even before the Social War. The vast majority of fractional coins consisted of aged asses between 50 and 100 years old. In ca. 91 B.C. a *lex Papiria* authorized minting silver sestertii (quarters of a denarius) and bronze asses on a semuncial standard (one-half ounce to the coin). The initial series of bronze denominations, marked as products of "the Papirian law concerning the weight of the as," were rejected as overvalued as vendors and customers haggled over the value of new and old asses (pl. 5.31).[27] The outbreak of the Social

War quickly ruined this reform as Rome faced her first serious challenge at home since the days of Hannibal.

Denarii and asses formed just one element of the money of the imperial Roman Republic, for the same bullion flows carrying silver specie into Italy also drained the provinces of their gold. Triumphators paraded tens of thousands of captured gold staters of Macedonian monarchs, while for half a century Carthaginian envoys rendered part of their annual indemnity in staters minted from African gold. The Senate chose not to mint a gold currency, since Romans preferred silver for their coins and viewed gold as a regal metal better dedicated to the gods. The minting of gold also would give magistrates the chance to exalt their largess above the rest of the aristocracy by distributing gold coins at triumphs or public games. The sole gold coins struck during the second century B.C. justified such fears. T. Quinctius Flamininus, victor over King Philip V of Macedon, received extravagant honors from Greeks including an issue of gold staters in 196–94 B.C., probably distributed at festivals celebrating his restoration of "Freedom of the Greeks." In weight and iconography they were identical to Macedonian regal staters except they carried the portrait of a Roman consul and Latin inscriptions.[28] Coins so defying Republican conventions reenforced the policy of denying aristocrats the chance for regal fame by minting staters. The Republic, with no need to hire mercenaries and with limited long distance trade, could afford to dispense with an international gold currency. The Senate instead banned export of specie when a crisis, such as those in 67 or 63 B.C., depleted the treasury of hard cash, or when it wished to deny gold to foes.[29]

If payments were made in gold they were made either in Macedonian staters ("philippics") captured in the eastern wars of 200–167 B.C. or in certified ingots. Philippics passed in international commerce long after Macedonian monarchs ceased to mint them, and demand prompted peoples from Britain to the Indus to strike imitative versions of the coins. The Roman Republic probably adopted a common practice of employing philippics in sealed bags of fixed value whenever gold payments were required, in a fashion similar to that of Venetians and Crusaders in the thirteenth century who used bags of *besants,* the pure Byzantine *hyperpyra* (20.5 carats) struck more than a century earlier during the Comnenian age.[30] More often the Republic settled large purchases in ingots of gold or silver, cast in convenient multiples of the pound and certified by official stamps. Such bars (*lateres*) composed most of the Republic's cash reserve seized by Julius Caesar in 49 B.C.

The Social War marked the failure of political reform and plunged Rome into civil wars that transformed the Republic into the Principate, the monarchy that Augustus cloaked in constitutional symbols and religious sanctions. In 91–90 B.C. Rome and her Italian opponents mobilized a quarter of a million men. Later rounds of this civil war, which raged over Italy down to 81 B.C. and in the western provinces until 71 B.C., also called to arms a number of legions unequaled since the Second Punic War. Rome met the financial challenge by an increase in the production of denarii and minting semuncial asses, which at times were overstruck on heavier older coins.[31] Denarii struck by the moneyers D. Silanus and L. Calpurnius Piso Frugi (91–90 B.C.) numbered in the tens of millions. Italian insurgents, accustomed to denarii from military service overseas, struck comparable quantities at their capital Corfinium, renamed Italia, or at mobile mints accompanying commanders who were named on denarii in Oscan or Latin (pl. 6.39).[32] Both sides were driven to debase the denarius from 97.5 to about 95 percent fine as stocks of metal ran low.[33] Rome, however, entered the Social War with the considerable advantage of control over the Spanish silver mines and a reserve of gold and silver on the order of 20 million denarii. Rome, by adroit political concessions, surmounted the crisis at home just when King Mithridates VI of Pontus overran the East and cut off the revenues from Asia. The Social War so exhausted the Roman treasury that the Senate in 88 B.C. turned to sacred treasures to finance the reconquest of the East by L. Cornelius Sulla, raising 9,000 pounds of gold to meet payrolls and contracts of the first campaigning season.[34] Sulla's rivals, C. Marius and L. Cornelius Cinna who occupied Rome in the next year, faced the daunting task of restoring the currency, clearing state debts, and amassing a reserve so vital for pulling Rome through crisis.

Widespread forgery and abuses such as sweating and clipping of denarii undermined public confidence in denarii and semuncial bronze coins issued during the Social War. Cicero recalled considerable confusion over exchange rates, "for in that time the nummus [i.e., denarius] was so tossed about that no one was able to know what it held in value."[35] In 86 B.C. the praetor M. Marius Gratidianus reimposed by edict the exchange rate of 16 uncial asses to the denarius, and he devised a test for detecting counterfeit "plated" denarii manufactured as a bronze core with a silvered surface.[36] Appropriate measures followed to stabilize currency and prices. Bronze coins of uncial weight were returned to their original value, and unpopular semuncial ones were demonetized (hoards reveal thereafter that only uncial pieces circulated until the Augustan reform of 23 B.C.). Uncial asses of 84 B.C. carry declarations of being produced "by consent of the Senate" (denoted by the letters "S.C.") as a guarantee of their value.[37] At the same time, the consuls L. Cornelius Cinna and L. Valerius Flaccus repudiated three-quarters of all debts, both public and private, thereby absolving the treasury of many wartime loans. Fresh stocks of silver were acquired from the legacy that King Ptolemy Alexander willed to the Roman people, and the fineness of the denarius was improved to 96 percent. Many of the new coins declare themselves as made "from public silver."[38]

Since so many Cinnan soldiers fell in battle and thus failed to retrieve their savings, Italian hoards concealed in 83–81 B.C. preserve the most representative sample of any coinage of the Republic. The estimated number of dies employed in 86–82 B.C. suggests that the Cinnan goverment coined at least 116 million denarii, our best sense of the scale of great coinages during this civil war.[39] In the East, L. Cornelius Sulla, declared a public enemy by the Marian Senate, laid the foundations for the future currency of imperial Rome when he minted his own coinage as he prosecuted the war against King Mithridates VI and then a civil war in Italy. His spectacular victories gained from Mithridates an indemnity of 2,000 or 3,000 talents, and he fined the cities of Asia for five years of back taxes amounting to a staggering 20,000 talents. Although many cities fell desperately into arrears, Sulla raised gold and silver specie with a value of at least 100 million denarii in 85–83 B.C.[40] From this windfall, Sulla minted not only denarii but the first Roman gold coins in over a century. His aurei and denarii—with the head of Roma on the obverse and Sulla himself, named *imperator,* standing in a triumphal *quadriga* on the reverse—exalted his regal pretensions in defiance of Republican custom. Sullan aurei, minted at 30 to the Roman pound (10.75 g) were ideal for the donatives that bought the loyalty of soldiers in civil war and for advertising the achievements of the *imperator*. While on the march Sulla and his allies seized and turned into aurei and denarii metal long immobilized in private and temple treasuries of Italy. After the Battle of the Colline Gate in late 82 B.C., Sulla occupied Rome and issued aurei hailing him as *imperator* a second time for his triumph over the Samnites. Even more regal-looking aurei followed in 81 B.C. carrying on the reverse the equestrian statue of Sulla voted by the Senate as well as his honorific "fortunate" (*felix*) and extraordinary office of dictator (pl. 6.32). Of all Sulla's lieutenants only Pompey dared to mint aurei, a series of light-weight coins celebrating his victory over Cinnan forces in Africa.[41]

After Sulla retired from public life, his restored Senate suspended the minting of aurei, regarding gold coins as the money of kings. Sulla and his Senate, however, could not abolish his example. When the civil wars that destroyed the Republic erupted in 49 B.C., Caesarians and Republicans alike coined hundreds of thousands, if not millions, of aurei as donatives to their legions. Cicero in 43 B.C. condemned L. Antonius for bribing soldiers with "golden coins" (*aurei nummi*) rather than denarii.[42] The convenience of aurei can be readily grasped by comparing the weight of the silver denarii that Pompey paid to each soldier at his triple triumph in 61 B.C. to that of the donatives Julius Caesar and Augustus paid in gold.[43] Pompey distributed 1,500 denarii per man, a total of nearly 18 pounds of silver; Julius Caesar, in 46 B.C., quadrupled the payment to 240 aurei (equal to 6,000 denarii) weighing 6 pounds; and Augustus, in 29 B.C., paid 120 aurei or 3 pounds of gold. The payments by Julius Caesar and Augustus, if made in silver, would have weighed nearly 71.5 and 35.75 Roman pounds, respectively.

Sullan aurei probably passed at a rate between 28 to 34 denarii (suggesting a price of 840 to 1,020 denarii per pound of gold), but

Suetonius reports that in the 50s B.C. Julius Caesar glutted the Italian money market with so much Gallic gold that the price of bullion sank to 750 denarii per pound.[44] In 46 B.C. the mint of Rome settled on a standard of 40 aurei to the pound and fixed the rate of exchange of 25 denarii to each aureus, which gave rise to the reckoning of 1,000 silver coins to a pound of gold that persisted into the Byzantine age. Caesarian aurei (8 g) succeeded in part because they resembled in weight and fabric regal Macedonian staters that had circulated as the international trade coin. For the next century, Caesar's heirs Octavian and Mark Antony, his assassins the Liberators, and Julio-Roman emperors minted aurei on the standard of Julius Caesar. The Sullans also created the mobile military mint, distinct from the mint of Rome directed by the Senate, which struck the bulk of their coinage in 85–82 B.C. Q. Caecilius Metellus Pius, to pay his forces in North Italy, struck in his camp denarii honoring his virtues and his father's victories in Africa. The Sullan proconsuls C. Valerius Flaccus and C. Annius likewise minted denarii as *imperatores* "with the consent of the Senate" as they pursued the Cinnan forces that Q. Sertorius rallied in Spain. In later civil wars, each side appealed to constitutional legitimacy on coins and employed mobile mints.

The Civil Wars far more than the Social War released into circulation aurei and denarii struck from reserves of gold and silver accumulated in private hands and temples for over a century. The Cinnans obtained silver for their huge coinages of denarii in 84–82 B.C. by seizing temple treasuries throughout Italy. The younger Marius held Praeneste with treasures of 14,000 pounds of gold and 6,000 pounds of silver, representing over 12 million denarii in uncoined money.[45] This reserve fell into the hands of Sulla who paraded it at his triumph along with other spoils taken in the East and Italy. Pliny the Elder reports that the money amounted to 15,000 pounds of gold and 115,000 pounds of silver, which could have been recoined into 450,000 aurei and 9,660,000 denarii.[46] Partisan politics during the Civil Wars added Roman coins to the list of captured coins triumphators reminted. Sulla, notorious for his hatred of the Samnites, restruck the gold staters and denarii the insurgents had issued during the Social War, and so he was the first to pursue *damnatio memoriae* ("condemnation of memory"), the later imperial policy of consigning to the melting pot coins of disgraced predecessors.

Sulla's war had replenished the treasury, and he restored the denarius to its purity (98 percent fine) when moneyers resumed production of denarii in 81 B.C.[47] Fractional currency, so important in daily transactions, suffered the most as the mints during the Civil Wars concentrated on aurei and denarii and suspended the striking of bronze coinage. For nearly sixty years Romans made do with uncial pieces of the second and early first century B.C. Failure to replenish the bronze currency resulted in hardship, for as they deteriorated coins were discounted below official tariffing. Cities of Italy and Sicily, except for Paestum and Velia, did not relieve local shortages, because they had, in adopting Roman coins, weights, and measures, ceased striking their own municipal bronze coins.

The post-Sullan Senate, facing challenges at home and abroad, mobilized as many as forty legions and fleets numbering several hundred vessels against Q. Sertorius in Spain, a slave uprising in Italy (73–71 B.C.), and another Asian war against Mithridates VI (74–63 B.C.). Sertorius threatened to disrupt the flow of Spanish silver until Pompey secured the province. In the East, L. Licinius Lucullus smashed Mithridates at Cyzicus and carried the war eastward, so that Roman legions looted new royal treasuries in Pontus and Armenia and Lucullus reformed the taxation of Asia. The denarius suffered a slight lowering to 96 to 97 percent fine only during the heaviest fighting in Spain. The volume of denarii minted in 81–49 B.C. cannot be estimated with any degree of certainty, but the Senate met payrolls and contracts without resorting to further debasements or striking aurei, voting Lucullus 18 million denarii for the Asian War, and, in 67 B.C., 36 million denarii to Pompey for the Pirate War.[48]

Pompey reorganized Spain and the eastern provinces so that taxation in coin replaced predatory plundering; in 62 B.C. he is reported to have raised annual revenues from 50 million to 85 million denarii, and then Julius Caesar with the tribute of Gaul raised them to 95 million.[49] Military expenditures had mounted substantially since the second century B.C. Each year in the era between the Civil Wars (78–50 B.C.) the Republic fielded an army—averaging twenty to twenty-five legions—that approached the size of the later imperial army. Enfranchisement of Italy more than doubled payrolls because all Italians in the legions became citizens eligible for *stipendium*. Costs of mobilizing legions rose at greater rates because the state defrayed most costs for equipping recruits drawn from landless citizens so that by 70 B.C. the price of mobilizing a legion had risen to 1.5 million denarii.

In 73 B.C. the Roman state acquired the second-largest item in its annual budget, when it assumed the obligation to supply grain to the urban plebs. Despite grain tributes from Sicily, Sardinia, and Africa, the treasury still purchased additional stores, and the disparity between purchase and sale prices was considerable. The Republic in 73 B.C., at the Gracchan retail price, would have recovered only 40 percent of the 2,950,000 denarii that C. Verres expended on Sicilian grain. In 58 B.C., P. Clodius Pulcher legislated distributions free of charge and to these higher annual costs were added the cost of purchasing grain on the spot market during emergencies such as in 56 B.C. when the state had to lay out 10 million denarii.[50] The Republic, despite these increased costs and the peculations rampant in the age of Cicero, amassed its greatest reserve by 49 B.C., which, ironically, Julius Caesar seized to finance his destruction of the Republic. When Caesar seized the state reserves, he immediately struck denarii bearing his name and an elephant trampling a dragon to symbolize the justice of his cause. Within a year he was forced to lower the standard of his denarii to 95 to 96 percent fine. Pompey in the East followed suit, but Republican commanders in Spain, who controlled rich silver mines, continued to strike pure denarii. Q. Caecilius Metellus Pius Scipio and M. Porcius Cato, who regrouped defeated Republican forces in Africa in 47–46 B.C., and their ally King Juba of Numidia minted alloyed denarii from metal obtained by melting down old coin.[51]

Most moneyers continued to strike coins conforming to Republican canons of iconography. Although Pompey's coins proclaim his office (proconsul) and his *cognomen* (Magnus, "the great"), Pompey (as did most Republican commanders) shared credit for his coins with proquaestors, thereby asserting his legitimacy by issuing money under collective authority as mandated by Republican traditions.[52] Caesar, however, broke with custom as his titles and symbols of office, his ancestors and patroness Venus, and finally his own portrait displaced all other symbols on the money of the Roman state (pl. 6.41). Transformation of Republican symbols on coins into those of a Julian monarch was so complete that after the Ides of March in 44 B.C. moneyers produced denarii in the name of the deified Julius Caesar. The Caesarian prefects, A. Hirtius and L. Mutatius Plancus, coined commemorative aurei at Rome in 46 and 45 B.C. for distributions on a scale far grander than any Sulla had offered (pl. 6.33). Caesar paraded at his triumph in 46 B.C. silver booty reckoned at 436,800,000 denarii and gold equivalent to 800,000 aurei (or 20 million denarii). Lavish donatives to legionaries alone would have consumed two-thirds of this windfall, as Julius Caesar put more coined money into circulation than any previous *imperator*.[53] The celebrations of 46 B.C. marked the birth of the Roman imperial currency, as Rome emerged as the capital of a monarchy committed to military, administrative, building, and ceremonial expenses that required tens of millions of aurei and denarii each year. Along with this imperial budget, Julius Caesar transmitted a reserve of 175 million denarii and a private estate of 25 million denarii.[54] Unfortunately, this reserve and the revenues of the reorganized empire were squandered on yet another series of civil wars.

Moneyers at Rome under the Caesarian dictatorship addressed the shortage of "small change" by resuming production of quinarii and sestertii, but the production of adequate numbers of base metal fractions was a more pressing need for the markets of Italy and soldiers serving overseas. Soldiers always needed change for dice and drink, as shown by the scattering of asses and semisses recovered from Roman siegeworks at Numantia (153–133 B.C.) or hoards of *aes* concealed in Greece on the eve of Pharsalus in 48 B.C.[55] Caesar drew on experience gained in the provinces to reform the bronze coinage in 45 B.C. His prefect C. Clovius supervised minting dupondii (double asses or one-eighth of a denarius) intended to head a new fractional currency. In design the coins broke with conventions since the third century B.C., for the head of Victoria and name of Caesar grace the obverse. Dupondii were minted from orichalcum, a shiny brass alloy of copper and zinc tariffed at twice the value of bronze in the Augustan age (pl. 6.43). Although the Caesarian dupondius (15.25 g) weighed less than the most worn of uncial asses (16 to 18 g), the public welcomed the pieces because of their more esteemed metal and attractive color.[56] His heir Octavian followed with his own orichalcum dupondii in the early 30s B.C. with matching obverse and reverse portraits of Octavian and the deified Julius Caesar (pl. 6.44).[57] The dupondius provided a precedent for subsidiary coinages of the Principate whereby each denomination was coined from a specific base metal. At the same time, the legates of Mark Antony devised the base metal denominational system of the imperial age based upon the sestertius rather than the as. Each denomination of this "Fleet Coinage," minted in bronze, carries an appropriate value mark as well as portraits and titles of Mark Antony and Octavia that anticipate imperial nomenclature. The first series was struck at Corinth on a semuncial standard so that the bronze sestertius equaled the weight of its predecessor, the uncial as of the second century B.C. The weight of later series at Corinth and Cyprus was halved due to financial difficulties ensuing from Antony's eastern wars (37–35 B.C.), and the semisses and quadrantes were discontinued (pl. 7.45).[58] Sestertii, dupondii, and asses thus circulated among Mark Antony's soldiers as the principal fractions of the aureus and denarius.

The renewal of civil war with the assassination of Julius Caesar ended the coinage of the Republic. The competing dynasts Octavian and Mark Antony reminted many of the aurei and denarii of their fallen foes in 42–31 B.C. In the opening months of 44 B.C. Mark Antony quickly spent the state reserves and private wealth of Caesar as legacies to soldiers and urban plebeians or bribes to politicians. When Octavian returned to Italy to claim his political heritage, he had to draw on the resources of Caesarian lieutenants and his own equestrian associates C. Maecenas and Q. Salvidienus Rufus. Mark Antony and Octavian put so many coins into circulation so rapidly that the mint was starved of metal, because the treasury could not recover the money by direct taxation. Only limited issues were minted in the name of divus Julius in 44–43 B.C.

As the Liberators cut off the revenues of the East and Sex. Pompeius, prefect of the Republic's fleet, threatened silver shipments from Spain, Octavian and Mark Antony were reduced to depending upon booty to strike their own coins. In 43 B.C., each issued coins more to declare his claim as Caesar's heir than to pay donatives. Octavian minted aurei and denarii after he marched on Rome and seized the consulship. Mark Antony on his retreat from Italy minted his own denarii that countered Octavian's claims as consul, and then he sealed his alliance with M. Aemilius Lepidus in Gaul by a joint issue of denarii and quinarii. When the three dynasts—Octavian, Mark Antony, and Lepidus—settled their differences and formed the Triumvirate in November 43 B.C., their mobile mints celebrated the settlement with another wave of aurei bearing their portraits and Julian slogans. With state and sacred reserves exhausted, the triumvirs extorted the wealth of Italy's landed classes by a welter of capital taxes and outright confiscation. In 42 B.C. the state's mint at Rome converted this income into tens of millions of aurei and denarii bearing the names and portraits of the triumvirs, who thereupon raised forty-three legions to avenge Caesar, crushing the Republican cause at Philippi (pl. 6.34).[59]

The aureus proved its worth as the coin that won civil wars. In 44 B.C. Octavian and Mark Antony countered each other by offering a donative of 500 denarii per man, neatly paid as 20 aurei or one-half pound of gold.[60] During the fighting and countermarching in Italy, Antony and Octavian concentrated on minting aurei, and the lesson was not lost on Republicans, who swallowed their scruples and minted their own aurei. In Greece and Asia Minor, C. Cassius Longinus and M. Junius Brutus taxed and looted at Sullan proportions; Brutus was credited with levying 16,000 talents (or 96 million denarii).[61] Cassius held firm to Republican principles, decorating his aurei and denarii with the optimate slogans of Libertas, but Brutus appealed to soldiers as an *imperator* and the living embodiment of Republican liberties. He struck aurei bearing his own portrait, while on the reverse they commemorated his victories, the founding of the Republic, or the assassination of Caesar (pl. 6.35). Other Republican commanders issued coins extolling their personal valor to appeal to soldiers, but most were more circumspect about stamping their portrait on coins. Only the renegade Q. Labienus, who joined forces with Parthian invaders in 39 B.C., placed his portrait on his coins. The sea adventurer Sex. Pompeius, who styled himself as prefect of the fleet, depicted Neptune and the portrait of his father Pompey the Great on aurei and denarii that he minted in 44–36 B.C.[62]

By the victory at Philippi, Mark Antony and Octavian shared mastery of the Roman world; Antony raised revenues in the East while Octavian settled the West. During 44–42 B.C. the triumvirs had debased the denarius to 95 to 96 percent fine, but, as he secured the East in 41–38 B.C., Mark Antony struck purer denarii (98.5 percent fine), obtaining metal from Greek staters, Republican denarii, and bullion stocks collected by the Liberators. He also concentrated on aurei needed for donatives. A major proportion of his coins traveled west in the hands of veterans returning to Italy or as subsidies to Octavian. Antony's coinage down to 38 B.C. tactfully honored his wife Octavia and his colleague and brother-in-law Octavian. Octavian coined fewer and baser denarii (95 percent fine) so long as the fleet of Sex. Pompeius threatened shipments of Spanish silver to Italy. Pressed for hard cash to provide donatives and land for the 120,000 legionaries discharged after Philippi, Octavian probably met most expenditures in old coin or money dispatched from the East by Antony. The mint at Rome seems to have suspended operations by 40 B.C., probably due to a dearth of bullion. The chronology and relative size of Octavian's later coinages is unclear, but he resumed striking substantial issues from mobile mints during his wars against Sex. Pompeius in Sicily (38–36 B.C.) and the Illyrians (34–33 B.C.).[63] Quite possibly Octavian financed the Actian War (32–31 B.C.) by short-term loans so that his greatest coinages paid off debts in the wake of victory.

Mark Antony cast away his initial financial advantage by waging abortive campaigns against Parthia (37–36 B.C.) and Armenia (34 B.C.). The decline of his fortunes after 38 B.C. is reflected in the progressive deterioration of the purity of his denarii from 98.5 to 92 percent fine within a decade (41–31 B.C.), whereas Octavian, once he secured the sea lanes and the Spanish mines, improved the fineness of his later denarii to 97 percent. In 32–31 B.C. Mark

Antony prepared for civil war by undertaking the greatest recoinage since the Second Punic War, restriking tens of millions of Roman and Greek silver coins into base denarii commemorating his legions (pl. 6.36). Legionary denarii, given their numbers and low-grade silver, escaped later recoinages so that a century later Pliny the Elder could still find large quantities of them in every corner of the Roman world. The scale of the recoinages during the Civil Wars of 49–31 B.C. is suggested by the output estimated from surviving dies of Antony's legionary coinage: 1 million aurei and 35 million denarii. Each of twenty-three legions was individually honored on aurei and denarii so that coins were presumably struck in sufficient numbers to be distributed as donatives and pay.[64]

Mark Antony and Octavian completed the transformation of the Republican coinage into an imperial one. Each paved the way for a reform of the subsidiary bronze currency, and each turned Caesarian appeals into an imperial iconography. Above all, Mark Antony and Octavian together had recoined much of the gold and silver money of the Mediterranean world by 31 B.C., and in so doing they ensured the triumph of aureus and denarius as the prime coins of the new imperial order born at Actium, the Principate.

Although Rome never intended to create a Mediterranean empire or currency, her conquests transformed the monetary systems throughout the Mediterranean world. Since Roman coins and systems of reckoning arrived in the wake of piecemeal conquest, the impact on indigenous coinages varied from province to province, ranging from the elimination of the native money, as in the case of the Celtic world, to its conversion into a provincial currency, as in the case of the Hellenistic East. As long as Roman armies plundered rather than annexed territories, the Republic did not incur the costs of overseas administration and defense, and had no need for a currency acceptable in overseas markets.

The impact of specie entering the Italian economy from 200 to 30 B.C. can be discerned, but virtually nothing is known of the outflow of denarii to the provinces. Few Roman coins of the second century B.C. have surfaced outside of Italy. In Spain, the scene of so many of Rome's bloodiest overseas wars, Roman coins are seldom found in hoards from the period between the Second Punic War and the last quarter of the second century B.C. In Greece and Macedon, denarii are found in hoards from the eve of the first century B.C., but they appear in sizeable numbers only after 81 B.C. In Asia Minor, they appear even later so that the denarius was not the main coin east of the Aegean until the Flavian age. In North Africa, Roman silver and bronze coins appear, and then in small numbers, only during the Jugurthine (116–105 B.C.) and Civil wars (49–46 B.C.). To a great extent the absence of Roman coins reflects the nature of the Republic's military operations, since, in the second century B.C., legions seldom remained in one area long enough to spend sufficient numbers of denarii to alter the region's currency. Republican forces on the move did not set up base camps comparable to those of the Principate where soldiers could spend their pay in markets offering the necessities, luxuries, and vices demanded by every army. In the Principate, Roman coins traveled from such marts into provincial markets, but this flow of Roman coins in the Republic was irregular, diffuse, and haphazard. Major finds of Roman coins in Spain during the second century B.C. come only from siegeworks around Numantia where successive Roman armies from 153 to 133 B.C. beleaguered the defiant Celtiberian capital.[65] Roman soldiers who came to loot and leave seldom concealed their savings and booty in an unfamiliar locale to which they might not return. Even if legionaries gambled away or spent most of their pay, coins more often than not ended up in the hands of Italian contractors rather than native vendors. If an army is aptly described as a traveling city, then much of its currency never left the city limits into an ever changing countryside through which it traversed. As Rome organized more permanent provincial administration in the late second century B.C., denarii, arriving to pay officials and contractors, stayed in circulation, and local money either disappeared or was modified into a provincial currency.

On the other hand, commerce carried many Roman coins to the provinces. Much of the initial seaborne traffic supplied Roman armies, but by 150 B.C. there was a rising volume of trade between Italian and foreign markets. Delos, declared a free port under Athenian control in 167 B.C., emerged as the money market and clearing house of the transit trade in the eastern Mediterranean. Campanians, Italiots, and Syracusans flocked to Delos as bankers, publicans, and traders carrying denarii eastward to buy foodstuffs, textiles, luxuries, and slaves. Delian inventories as early as 153 B.C. include denarii, although Athenian tetradrachmae, Rhodian drachmae, and Attalid cistophori were the principal trade coins down to the First Mithridatic War (89–86 B.C.).[66] By the 80s B.C. Greek merchants of the North Aegean substituted denarii for tetradrachmae among the exports exchanged for gold, grain, and slaves in Moesia and Dacia.[67] Italian traders, financiers, and moneylenders also followed publicans into the Asian and Spanish provinces. They advanced hard cash to cities to pay tribute to Rome, and to provincials to finance trade or the acquisition of property and municipal licenses. Commerce and banking steadily wove the provinces and Italy into a complicated single financial web, thereby popularizing Roman coins and systems of reckonings. To varying degrees, such outflows of cash from Italy redressed the wholesale plundering and tribute that removed so much specie from the provinces to Rome.

By 30 B.C. Republican imperialism had resulted in Romanizing the money of the western Mediterranean and northwestern Europe. The Punic Wars drew the islands of Sardinia, Corsica, and Sicily as well as the thinly populated northern regions of Italy known as Cisalpine Gaul into the Roman monetary orbit. In Sicily the Romans encountered prolific gold and silver coinages minted by Greek cities and Carthaginian military authorities. Trade and warfare since the sixth century B.C. had monetized the commercial life of Sicily, but the seesaw fighting raging across Sicily from 215 to 210 B.C. had ruined the native currency, and Carthaginian and Greek gold and silver coins had disappeared from circulation.[68] Thereafter, Sicilians employed denarii as their silver money, but favored cities—such as Catana, Leontini, and Syracuse—struck their own bronze currency bearing Greek inscriptions and value marks. The Sicilian bronze litra, subdivided into 12 unciae, was the equivalent of the Roman uncial as, and the Sicilian denominations circulated side by side with Roman bronze coins down to the Augustan age when Panormus issued the last native bronze coins.[69]

Rome emptied Punic Africa of its specie by collecting enormous indemnities from Carthage and then by sacking the city in 146 B.C. To facilitate indemnity payments, Carthage turned imported West African gold into staters and minted tetradrachmae from silver acquired in seaborne commerce. Most Carthaginian gold staters and tetradrachmae passed through the Roman mint, reemerging as certified ingots or denarii, and even large stocks of Punic bronze coins taken in 146 B.C. were melted down or overstruck.[70] Lesser Punic cities of the African province employed a mix of imported silver coin—Roman, Massiliot, Iberian, and Athenian—for the next century (146–46 B.C.) and issued their own bronze coins. The Roman civil war injected aurei and denarii into the African economy. In 47–46 B.C. the Republican commanders, Metellus Pius Scipio and M. Porcius Cato, and Julius Caesar issued aurei and denarii from mobile mints in Africa. The client kings, Juba I of Numidia and Bogud of Mauretania, followed with their own base denarii.[71] Some Punic towns issued local Roman-style bronze denominations, but their coins quickly gave way, as African towns drew their currency from the imperial mints of Augustus.

Rome faced a far more daunting task in imposing monetary order upon the Iberian peninsula. In 200 B.C. few Spaniards, other than Celtiberian mercenaries once in the pay of Carthage or the residents of Hellenized and Punic towns on the Levantine shores, dealt in coins on a daily basis. When Scipio Africanus stormed New Carthage in 209 B.C., he signaled the end of the trimetallic currency the Barcids had coined from Spanish bullion to buy Carthage's great mercenary armies, and Punic coins were exported wholesale to Rome for reminting. Mounting Roman military commitments in Spain between the arrival of Scipio Africanus in 210 B.C. and the settlements of Tib. Sempronius Gracchus in 179–178 B.C. steadily transformed Spain's currency. While the native peoples originally viewed silver coins as gifts to seal alliances or symbols of social rank, they acquired monetary habits from the Romans in the course of the second century B.C. Rome levied tribute in coin, drafted Spanish warriors who received wages in coin, and founded cities to whose markets coins arrived with many other wares of the imperial civilization of Rome. The influx of denarii into the northeastern corner of the peninsula popularized the smaller sized denomination over Carthaginian shekels and heavy Greek staters. From 200 B.C. on, Iberian towns such as Bolskan (Osca), Iltirta (Ilerda), and Kelsa (Celsa) minted denarii bearing native inscriptions and types inspired from Sicilian, Punic, Tarentine, and Roman prototypes which Celtiberians had seen in mercenary service. Iberian towns must have minted millions of civic denarii to hire Celtiberian mercenaries in their struggle against Rome and later to pay wages of auxiliary forces demanded by Rome under treaty.[72] Legionaries, who carted off Iberian denarii as spoils reported in triumphs of the 190s and 180s B.C., nicknamed the coins *argentum oscense* (Oscan-looking silver pieces) because the native script resembled Oscan-Umbrian scripts back home. Since Iberian denarii in weight and purity stood at parity to Roman denarii, governors also found them a convenient medium for collection of tribute. Iberian denarii circulated as the prime silver coins in Spain well into the first century B.C. and long after cities had ceased to mint them. Large numbers of worn Iberian pieces appear with Roman denarii in hoards deposited in 125–90 B.C., and thereafter they are an important, if diminishing component, in hoards from the Levantine littoral and mining districts of the Lower Baetis (Guadalquivir) Valley as late as the 40s B.C.[73]

Denarii and asses, limited to the camps of Roman armies in 200–125 B.C., seeped into and transformed native markets after 125 B.C. so that they circulated alongside and then, by the early imperial age, displaced Iberian coins. In the Baetis Valley, veteran colonies such as Carteia and Corduba (Cordova) and native communities filled with Italian miners and settlers issued bronze denominations as fractions of the denarius from the early second century B.C. By the last quarter of the second century B.C., cities on the Mediterranean shore and Celtiberian towns in the Ebro Valley too commenced striking Roman-style denominations ranging from the as to sextans and with types and legends that betray a mix of Iberian, Punic, and Roman influences.[74] As urban life and commerce quickened, the peoples of Spain adopted Roman coins and monetary habits, although far more gradually than provincials in Sicily or Carthage, but by the time of Augustus they too were full members of the Roman monetary order.

In contrast to Spain, the Roman conquest ended abruptly the native Celtic gold and silver coinages of Cisalpine Gaul (the lands of North Italy between the Rubicon and Alps) and Transalpine Gaul. Celtic peoples dwelled in hill towns and traded in native and foreign coins for two centuries prior to the Roman conquest so that Gauls readily adopted Roman currency in the first century B.C. As early as the mid-third century B.C. leading tribes of central and northern Gaul had minted gold staters (8 g) patterned after Macedonian and Tarantine staters, but the types rapidly deteriorated into jumbles of geometric patterns. Although Gallic princes showered gold staters and later silver coins as gifts binding lord and retainer or accumulated them in treasures to buy allies, early in the first century B.C. many tribes, without imports of coin or fresh metal from mines, failed to maintain their gold currencies.[75]

Bellicose Belgic tribes of northeastern Gaul and their cousins in southeastern Britain used only gold staters, but sophisticated Celtic peoples of central and southern Gaul and Northern Italy adopted, from Greek traders, silver and base metal fractional coinages. Massilia (Marseilles), emporium of Gallic river traffic into the Mediterranean, had, since the fourth century B.C., exported light-weight drachmae (3.75 g) and obols to the Celts of southern Gaul and North Italy. By 250 B.C. Massiliot drachmae and obols filled Gallic marts and hill forts from the Garonne to the slopes of the Swiss Alps.[76] Massiliot coins inspired sundry imitations as far away as the Po Valley where immigrant Gauls struck base obols. The Volcae Tectosages, who held the hinterland of the later Roman colony Narbo Maritus (Narbonne), and their neighbors from the Pyrenees to the Massif Central copied coins of the Massiliot Spanish dependents Rhode and Emporiae. Designs fast degenerated into little more than a cross flanked by crescents and dots so that they are dubbed "monnaies-à-la-croix." Romans considered the Celtic "obols" they encountered in Cisalpine Gaul and Gallia Narbonensis as quinarii (half-denarii), and, based on deposits from Entremont and St. Cyr-sur-mer, Gauls in turn used denarii as doubles of their obols. Hence, the word *obol* in the vernacular Latin of Gaul survived into medieval French as the half of a denier.

In 118 B.C. Rome founded Narbo Martius and annexed as the

province of Gallia Narbonensis two huge blocks of territory that flanked the Rhone Valley controlled by Massilia and her Gallic friends. Denarii and asses entered in force with Roman soldiers, contractors, and merchants, and by 75 B.C. Cicero claimed, "No Gaul ever does business independently of a citizen of Rome; not a denarius (*nummus*) changes hands in Gaul without the transaction being recorded in the books of Roman citizens."[77] Gauls of the Rhone Valley, long acquainted with Greek bronze coins, employed Roman coins carried by Italian merchants into the heartland of Gaul. Aedui, Arverni, Sequani, and Lingones, who dominated central and eastern Gaul beyond the province, issued silver obols and bronze or potin fractions for use in collecting lucrative tolls on transit trade or providing small change to town markets engaged in a brisk business for Roman goods. In the fifty years before Julius Caesar, town life, trade, and use of coins boomed, thereby making possible a rapid Romanization of Gaul. Gallic gold coinages ended along with independence, for Julius Caesar used Gallic gold accumulated over centuries as jewelry, coin, and sacred vessels to strike his first great issue of aurei. In 58–49 B.C., Belgic tribes such as the Ambiani and Treveri were soon without sufficient metal to mint staters so that they debased staters with silver into electrum or "pale gold" (50 percent fine), and other tribes issued silver coins as proxies of gold staters.[78] In 49 B.C. Massilia crossed Caesar by backing Pompey, and Caesar humbled the proud Greek city by stripping her of the means to coin drachmae, thus removing the only competitor to the denarius in southern Gaul.

Hoards, however, suggest limited penetration of Roman coins into Gaul in the generation after the Caesarian conquest (48–16 B.C.). Rome was too distracted to forge a Gallic administration requiring payrolls in denarii, and the legions were without base camps or marched off to the distant battlefields of the civil wars. Tribes in central and northern Gaul freely minted their own silver obols and bronze fractions, including many inspired by Roman designs and some marked as semisses. Hybrid Romano-Celtic fractions quickly passed out of use when the emperor Augustus arrived in 16 B.C. to revise the census of Gaul and to open offensives into Germany. As soon as the legions settled into permanent camps, imperial denarii and asses poured into the Rhineland as the axis of economic life shifted to the east of the Gallic heartland. Crude tribal fractional coins, which could not compare to the elegant money of Augustus, quickly disappeared as Gaul too entered the Roman monetary world.

As Rome faced the Hellenistic East at the beginning of the second century B.C., she encountered a mélange of currencies struck by the great Macedonian monarchs, petty dynasts, leagues, and city-states. The principal trade coins were gold staters and silver tetradrachmae issued by the heirs of Alexander the Great—the Antigonid dynasty based in Macedon and the Seleucid monarchs in Syria. Lesser states, too, issued tetradrachmae, many bearing the portrait of Alexander the Great or Lysimachus. The transfers of specie as booty and reparations from the East following Roman victories over Philip V of Macedon in the Second Macedonian War (200–196 B.C.) and the Seleucid monarch Antiochus III in the Asian War (192–188 B.C.) wrought changes in the currencies of the eastern Mediterranean, but the Hellenic monetary system remained essentially the same.

The impact on the Seleucid monarchy and its coinage was dramatic. From 189 to 176 B.C. Rome exacted indemnities of 22.5 million tetradrachmae (equal to over 100 million denarii), and the Seleucids paid an additional 790,802 tetradrachmae to Rome's ally, Eumenes II of Pergamum. But a much greater blow was the redirection to Rome of the flow of bullion previously imported by the Seleucids from the ports of the North Aegean and the Euxine shores of Thrace. By 171 B.C., Antiochus IV had reduced the weight of his tetradrachma, demoting it to a Syrian stater with only regional significance, and, to overcome his lack of silver, issued a bronze fractional currency based on an obol divided into 8 *chalci*.[79] The downfall of the Seleucids marked the rise of Attalid Pergamum and the island republic of Rhodes. Hellenic cities siding with Antiochus were awarded to Eumenes II or the Rhodians. Eumenes II opened six new mints to effect a major recoinage that established the cistophorus or Attalid tetradrachma (12.65 g, or 75 percent of the Attic standard) as the undisputed stater of western Asia Minor.[80]

Macedon fared better. Philip V was assessed an initial indemnity of 500 talents (750,000 tetradrachmae) and annual payments of

50 talents, but he was able to win a reprieve from reparations in 192 B.C. Macedonian mines and commerce restored the royal treasury by the accession of Perseus in 179 B.C., and the Antigonid tetradrachmae and gold staters recaptured primacy in the Aegean markets.[81] The Third Macedonian War (172–167 B.C.) ended with the abolition of the Macedonian monarchy and, to deny her enemy the means for recovery, Rome closed the Macedonian mines for the next decade. In 157 B.C. the client Macedonian republics resumed minting tetradrachmae to meet their fiscal obligations and tribute owed to Rome (pl. 7.46). With the demise of Macedonian currency, Greek cities revived their own silver staters. Athens, inactive for over a century, resumed striking tetradrachmae. The New Style Athenian coins were struck on wide or "spread" flans, and the central types of Athena's head and her owl were executed in a naturalistic style and ringed by a laurel wreath that alluded to the wreaths Greeks offered L. Aemilius Paullus.[82] Athenian tetradrachmae quickly emerged as the trade coins of the Aegean and eastern Mediterranean. The sacred council of Delphi put its seal of approval upon the change by declaring Athenian tetradrachmae as the medium at the panhellenic shrine: "That all Greeks receive the Attic tetradrachma at four drachmae of silver."[83] Other cities followed with their own wreathed civic tetradrachmae. The wars of the first third of the second century B.C. ended the dominance of the Seleucid and Antigonid coinages and elevated the coinages of Athens and Pergamum, but Hellenic monetary traditions were still in place.

After a lull of twenty years, wars again drew the legions across the Ionian Sea. They seized rich plunder in Macedon and the Peloponnesus (148–146 B.C.) and ransacked cities allied to the insurgents who took arms against Rome upon annexation of the Pergamene kingdom as the province of Asia (133–129 B.C.). The Senate, substituting annexation for informal hegemony, organized the Aegean world into the four Roman provinces—the province of Asia in western Anatolia and those of Epirus, Macedonia, and Achaea in European Greece. Although trade brought denarii to Delos even before 146 B.C., thereafter a flood arrived in consignments for forces in Macedon or in the hands of Italian publicans and financiers rushing into Asia to exploit tax contracts. In Asia, Rome created her first provincial silver coin—the cistophorus, patterned after its Pergamene namesake that had been the principal stater in western Asia Minor for sixty years. Cistophori, tariffed at 3 denarii, were named after their obverse type of a serpent emerging from a Dionysiac basket (*cista mystica*). Since they carried no royal portraits, cistophori were permitted to circulate after 133 B.C. and proconsuls continued striking them without altering the familiar design (pl. 7.49). Loyal Greek cities continued to mint their own fractions, pegged to the cistophorus, so that the Romans created the first of several provincial monetary systems whereby Roman authorities minted a familiar silver stater while cities provided fractional currency.

The exactions of Sulla and his legates in 88–70 B.C. removed so many cistophori for recoining that it is impossible to estimate the original size of the cistophoric coinage.[84] Ephesus and Pergamum together must have issued cistophori in the tens of millions in 133–90 B.C. to fulfill the need for coins to pay taxes. Publicans with contracts for Asian taxes took payments in cistophori, which were then exchanged at the tables of bankers so profits could be remitted to Rome in denarii. Governors, as Cicero complained, drew their salaries and met expenditures in cistophori.[85] The success of the Asian cistophorus encouraged Rome to use tetradrachmae in other provinces. Early in the first century B.C. Roman authorities in Macedon minted tetradrachmae with the portrait of Alexander the Great, and bearing the name of the magistrate along with the ethnic "of the Macedonians" (pl. 7.47).[86] During the First Mithridatic War (89–86 B.C.), L. Licinius Lucullus minted tetradrachmae bearing Athenian types (pl. 7.48), probably to pay local contractors and rowers in the fleet, and Plutarch notes, "Most of the money in the Peloponnesus during the Mithridatic War was coined by him. It remained current for a long time, since the wants of the soldiery during the war gave it rapid circulation."[87] A. Gabinius, governor of Syria in 57/6 B.C., minted tetradrachmae with the portrait and name of the deceased Seleucid king Philip I Philadelphus (93–83 B.C.) to finance an Egyptian expedition (pl. 7.51). Later issues by M. Licinius Crassus (53 B.C.), C. Cassius Longinus (51 B.C.) and

Julius Caesar (47 B.C.) enshrined the coin as Syria's stater, and Cicero even quoted prices of wheat in tetradrachmae at the Roman camp near Laodicea ad Mare during the Civil War.[88]

Since Roman legionaries and then tax farmers drained the Greek world of so much of its specie, they inadvertently promoted the development of bronze currency, which Greeks did not esteem as a medium of exchange. The Athenians, during wartime, had struck bronze coins, but they were redeemed in silver once the emergency had passed. Direct Roman rule dealt a quick death to silver fractional currencies in the late second century B.C. In the Peloponnesus, for example, when the sack of Corinth in 146 B.C. ended the Achaean League and its silver *hemidrachmae,* twenty cities immediately began minting bronze obols and chalci that could be exchanged against a Roman denarius.[89] Even the Athenians adjusted. They minted tetradrachmae for export but no silver fractions for home consumption; they placed their drachma at parity with the denarius which they employed in tandem with bronze obols and chalci. In the last century of the Republic (146–30 B.C.) Roman governors and Greek cities forged the currency arrangements for the Roman East for the next three centuries. Roman authorities minted regional tetradrachmae of traditional type and conveniently tariffed to the denarius, while cities manufactured a range of bronze obols and chalci that were readily convertible into denarii.

The Roman imperial monetary order emerged in the East in the wake of the Third Mithridatic War (74–63 B.C.) and administrative reorganization by Pompey. Only silver coinages useful in provincial taxation or fractional issues of friendly kings and free cities remained in circulation. The Sullan exactions in 88–83 B.C. ended many civic coinages in Roman Greece and Asia Minor. Athens suffered a ruthless sack and thereafter had difficulty in producing her famed tetradrachmae. Sulla seized the previously untouched treasures of Delphi, Olympia, and Epidaurus and coined them into aurei and denarii.[90] In 85 B.C. Sulla demanded from the Asian cities 40 million cistophori in back taxes and perhaps another 2.5 million cistophori paid by the wealthy classes in hospitality to his legionaries in winter quarters. Most cities borrowed money from Roman financiers, defaulted, and fell in debt so that interest on loans swelled to 240 million cistophori (720 million denarii) within a dozen years.[91] Pergamum and Ephesus debased the cistophorus from 95 to 80 percent fine, and the old royal mints at Apamea, Laodicea, and Tralles reopened to aid in a massive recoining of Asian silver money in 85–68 B.C. The fiscal reforms of Lucullus in 70–68 B.C. rescued the Asian cities from ruin. Production of cistophori was suspended with his reprieve from taxes and the cistophorus was restored to 90 percent fine when production was resumed in 58–49 B.C. (pl. 7.50).[92] Farther east, the story was much the same. Sulla extorted 18 million denarii in indemnity from Mithridates VI—the largest sum since the Treaty of Apamea in 188 B.C. The legions of Lucullus and Pompey in 71–63 B.C. looted royal treasuries in eastern Anatolia, Armenia, and Seleucid Syria estimated at over 350 million denarii.[93]

The Roman Civil Wars (49–31 B.C.) simplified currency in the East even further. Pompey, Julius Caesar, the Liberators, and Mark Antony each exacted huge sums of hard cash estimated at several hundred million denarii, and each turned the metal into aurei and denarii. Cassius and Brutus collected in 43–42 B.C. gold stocks sufficient to mint over 7 million aurei needed in donatives alone.[94] Athenian tetradrachmae, Rhodian drachmae, and many lesser silver currencies did not survive the Civil Wars, and even the provincial staters, the Asian cistophorus and the Syrian tetradrachma, nearly vanished. In Asia, at the war's outbreak in 49–48 B.C., Q. Caecilius Metellus Pius Scipio, governor of Syria, marched to Pergamum where he wintered, levied two years of taxes, and coined the last cistophori for a decade. Although Mark Antony issued commemorative pieces in 39–38 B.C. (pl. 10.77), Augustus deserves the credit for restoring the cistophorus by a massive recoinage after the Battle of Actium. Augustus did the same for the tetradrachma of Syria. Since Roman commanders recoined and spent much of the money in the East, provincials east of the Aegean began to employ denarii as equivalents of drachmae. The mix of local and Roman denarii is well seen in a hoard near Halicarnassus comprised of denarii and cistophori, or in the savings of a Cretan mercenary secreted at Hieraptyna that included denarii, cistophori, Athenian tetradrachmae, and Cretan civic staters.[95]

The emergence of Rome as the mistress of the Mediterranean witnessed the triumph of the denarius, first in Italy and then in the overseas provinces. The influx of specie from imperial conquest diversified and monetized the Italian economy, but denarii and asses exported in military costs and trade drew the lands of the western Mediterranean into the Roman economic and monetary orbit so that denarius and Roman systems of reckoning triumphed by 30 B.C. In the eastern Mediterranean world, the denarius penetrated more slowly, for Romans learned to adapt silver staters in Asia Minor and Syria for provincial taxation. Inflation in Italy in the second and early first centuries B.C. undermined the traditional bronze currency of the Republic, while the drain of specie out of the East compelled Greeks to experiment with token bronze currency in several metals. From these diverse experiences, Augustus in 23 B.C. would fashion a new imperial base metal currency of orichalcum and copper denominations whose fixed exchange value against full-bodied coins in gold and silver and convenient size and weight ensured the success of Roman currency for the next 275 years. Every element of the currency of the Roman Empire was born in the age of the Republic's overseas expansion, but it would take the genius of Augustus to weld them into the interlocking imperial, provincial, and civic coinages of the Principate.

# Four

# The Augustan Coinage, 30 B.C.–A.D. 235

Augustus achieved a stunning success when he refashioned the coinages of Rome and her provinces to serve a Mediterranean empire. He restored the purity of the denarius, expanded the production of aurei, created a new token bronze currency, reorganized mints, and resumed large-scale minting at Rome, and, in the process, spread the use of Roman coins and systems of reckoning. The denarius aureus, "golden denarius," stood at the apex of a descending chain of denominations in gold, silver, and bronze that were exchangeable at rates fixed by imperial decree. The keystone of this edifice was the denarius, the "link coin" against which all other coins, including provincial and civic ones, could be reckoned and exchanged. For the first and last time in their history the peoples of the Mediterranean enjoyed, in the denarius, a common measure of value. Augustan coinage owed its success foremost to the economic growth stimulated by the Roman peace, but the coinage itself contributed to this growth by facilitating transactions, both large and small. Success also rested upon the utility of the Augustan denominations and the expansion of the money supply. Rising imperial expenditure and collection of taxes in coin led to the widespread distribution and use of Roman coins in the provinces. Utility, numbers, and availability inspired the most critical element of all, public faith in the coins. Public faith ensured the triumph of aureus, denarius, and eventually even imperial *aes* as the preferred currency in the provinces.

Augustus, who premised his coinage upon the denominations of the Republic, offered the Roman public a currency whose design and engraving could not fail to inspire confidence. Republican coin iconography was subtly reshaped into an elegant miniature art that depicted the emperor and his family at the heart of Roman traditions. In 30 B.C. Augustus moved to assure the utility and supply of aurei and denarii—no mean task as Rome had coined erratically in the prior decade, and Mark Antony had minted innumerable alloyed denarii in his final years—by reinstating the bimetallic standard Julius Caesar had created in 47–46 B.C. Augustus issued virtually pure aurei and denarii struck at the respective standards of 40 and 84 to the Roman pound (pl. 8.52 and 54).[1] The two principal denominations, officially called the golden denarius and silver denarius, were customarily minted with identical designs and inscriptions, and, at times, they were even struck from the same dies. Each denarius was provided with a half, the gold or silver quinarius (pl. 8.53 and 55). Precious metal denominations were exchanged at the rate of 25 denarii to an aureus, a silver to gold ratio of approximately 12:1.[2] Imperial coins, given the convenience of this exchange and their impeccable purity, proved their superior utility in taxation and commerce over other media of exchange, and commanded premiums in the marketplace because the purity of most bullion fell short of that of coins.

The purity expected of aurei is revealed by an incident involving the emperor Galba (68–69). Upon discovering that a gold crown of fifteen pounds offered by the citizens of Tarraco as a contribution to his war effort was, when melted down for minting, three ounces short, Galba ordered them to make up the deficiency because gold so alloyed would have produced aurei only 98.33 percent fine.[3] By the late second century Romans were already referring to aurei by the slang "solidi" (or solid bits) because of their purity. Only aurei of pure gold were considered worthy of gifts by the emperor, now expected on a scale far grander than was ever expected of a Republican conqueror. For example, Augustus, while vacationing on the Bay of Naples, was so impressed by the prayers and sacrifices offered to him by the crew of a passing Alexandrine ship that he gave each member of his circle forty aurei (the equivalent of a pound of pure gold) to spend on Alexandrine goods.[4]

The purity of the denarius, which had fallen as low as 92 percent fine in the latter days of the Republic, was restored to its traditional level of 97.5 to 98 percent fine, and quinarii were only slightly more alloyed (94 to 95 percent). Down to the debasement of A.D. 64, silver, whether obtained from the Spanish mines or from melting old coin and plate, was refined to a consistently high standard.[5] Aurei and denarii also were kept to standard whether they were the products of the senatorial moneyers at Rome, who from 23 B.C. resumed minting coins bearing their names in the Republican fashion, or the imperial mint that accompanied Augustus until he located it at Lugdunum (Lyons) by 15 B.C.[6] Since denarii were so scrupulously maintained to the traditional Republican standard, denarii from the mid-second century B.C. continued in use, constituting well over one-half of the silver money in circulation down to the Neronian reform.

Augustus coined on a grander scale than any Republican *triumphator*. Augustus hints at the great size of his coinage in the reports of his gifts and expenditures found on his monumental inscription, *Res Gestae divi Augusti*. In 30–27 B.C. Augustus converted the spoils from three continents into aurei and denarii to pay off war debts and to fund building programs, ceremonies, and distributions costing at least 750 million denarii. The 120,000 legionaries marching in his triumph each received 120 aurei (= 3,000 denarii) so that donatives were in excess of 360 million denarii (without consideration of the higher bounties given to centurions and officers).[7]

As prices ebbed from the record highs they had reached due to the heavy minting and expenditure in 30–27 B.C., the need for an adequate fractional coinage for a Roman public numbering some 2 million urban residents in the imperial capital and Campanian cities once again became acute. The renewed minting of quinarii after the Battle of Actium had not furnished sufficient substitutes for the worn Republican *aes* still in use.[8] In forging his new fractional coinage, Augustus was inspired by Greek cities in Asia Minor that, due to shortages of silver, had experimented with copper alloys since the late second century B.C.[9] He also owed a debt to Mark Antony, whose legates had devised a set of bronze denominations based upon the sestertius (one-quarter denarius) previously struck in silver (pl. 7.45). Augustus turned these precedents into a new currency anchored on a brass sestertius.

Augustus conducted a dress rehearsal of his reform in 25 B.C. at Pergamum, capital of Asia, which minted two series of Roman-style denominations bearing Latin legends. The portrait of Augustus occupies the obverse; a laurel wreath enclosing either the name AVGVSTVS or C.A., the abbreviation of the Asian assembly (*commune Asiae*) that promoted the imperial cult, is found on the reverses (pl. 11.94–95).[10] Coins were minted from brass and bronze alloys used by Anatolian cities earlier in the first century B.C. Sestertii, along with dupondii and semisses, were struck in brass, but asses, the most numerous denomination, were made from bronze. The coins, although Roman denominations, were intended for use in Asia where they were readily exchanged against imperial aurei and denarii or provincial cistophori.

Shortly after his constitutional settlement of 23 B.C., Augustus introduced his new token currency to Rome (pl. 8.56–59). As in the Asian reform, two metals were used, a brass alloy called orichalcum (20 to 25 percent zinc) for the two higher valued coins—the sestertius (25 g) and dupondius (12.5 g)—and pure copper for two lower denominations—the as (11 g) and its quarter, the quadrans (3 g).[11] These four denominations provided a range of fractions that facilitated even the humblest of transactions. The Republican *aes*, improvised cut fractions, and worn civic pieces were retired and reminted. For the next two decades (23 to 2 B.C.) senatorial moneyers, in keeping with Republican custom, placed their names on the coins. The iconography of the coins reflected a Republican tone—the obverses of sestertii and dupondii show the oak wreath awarded Augustus for valor rather than his portrait, and the letters S.C. (*Senatus consulto*, "by consent of the Senate") encircled by a laurel wreath dominate the reverse. Asses too display the letters S.C. on the reverse.[12] Names of moneyers and the abbreviation S.C. were crowded into the designs to give the new denominations an air of authority to ensure their acceptance. This was particularly true of sestertii and dupondii, newcomers to the denominational system; they did not carry imperial portraits until the reign of Tiberius (14–37). Augustan asses became the prime coins in daily use throughout Italy and in the western provinces as well. In A.D. 8–12, when imperial iconography began to dominate, asses henceforth carried portraits of Augustus or Tiberius. Imperial names and titles ousted names of moneyers, but the letters S.C. were retained, although as a subordinate element in the design, because Romans accepted the letters as a guarantee of the exchange value of *aes* against aurei and denarii.

Brass sestertii and dupondii were deliberately struck in comparatively fewer numbers than asses and quadrantes so their relative scarcity would win public approval. The Augustan sestertius and dupondius were overvalued—the brass sestertius, tariffed at four asses, was only slightly more than double the weight of the as struck in copper—but they were accepted because they could be readily exchanged against higher and lower denominations. The coins themselves inspired trust by their superb workmanship and attractive appearance; sestertii and dupondii had the shiny surface of brass while asses and quadrantes gave off a reddish glow. The coins were lighter and easier to use than their cumbersome bronze predecessors of the Republic. Augustus resisted the temptation to overproduce lucrative fiduciary *aes*. He thus won the critical first round in gaining public faith, and he assured the future utility of token imperial money. As imperial fiscal needs mounted so did public demand for imperial money. Augustus augmented the money supply not only by reintroducing base metal fractions for general circulation, but also by coining aurei to replace denarii for ceremonial gifts and large-scale purchases. Gold, immobilized in plate and votive offerings up until the last fifteen years of the Republic, became again an integral part of the money of the Mediterranean world. The growth of the money supply of the Roman Empire can in part be told as the shift from a silver to a gold currency between the reigns of Augustus and Constantine (306–37).

The number of coins in circulation at any time during the imperial age is beyond counting, but the scale of their numbers can be sensed by the reserves accumulated by Tiberius (14–37) and Antoninus Pius (138–61); each emperor is credited with leaving 675 million denarii in the treasury, an extraordinary sum exceeding by over thirty times the greatest reserves of the Republican treasury.[13] Taxation, imperial expenditure, and trade kept coins in perpetual motion between Rome and the provinces, but the cycle depended upon fresh infusions of coin to meet growing demand as well as to replenish dwindling stocks due to loss, wear, and the export of coins beyond the imperial frontiers. The minting of accumulated reserves and the reminting of earlier coin were insufficient; demand was satisfied by the minting of gold and silver specie obtained by conquest, imports, and mining. The constant, although hardly even, increase in the money supply contributed to mild, long-term rises in prices, but markets were always prey to violent, short-term surfeits or famines, as when Josephus reports that Syrian cities were glutted with the gold and silver captured by Titus's legions at Jerusalem in 70.[14] Moralists of the first century lamented drains of specie in the Far Eastern trade, but long-term expansion of the money supply offset outflows in commerce or diplomacy. The triumph of Roman coins in the provinces during the first and second centuries was largely due to the unprecedented supply of fresh metal available to the imperial government.

War remained a main source of specie. Augustus and Trajan (98–117) built the two greatest dynasties of Rome out of the profits of victory. In 30–27 B.C. Augustus coined spoils taken in Spain, Illyricum, and Egypt into aurei and denarii worth as much as 1 billion denarii at the same time he lavishly endowed shrines, bestowing on Capitoline Jupiter alone 16,000 pounds of gold (equivalent to 640,000 aurei).[15] Ptolemaic treasures (long immobilized in royal coffers and temples), when coined, sparked sharp increases in Italian prices followed by secondary price rises across the empire.[16] Even after the imperial mint in the Flavian age commenced annual striking of "full-bodied" coins, booty remained the readiest source of fresh metal. Trajan netted two major windfalls. In the Second Dacian War (104–5) he seized royal treasures that had been stockpiled over nearly two centuries from the profits of mining and commerce; these were valued at perhaps 1.5 billion denarii, and, in 107, Trajan initiated the most ambitious building program in Rome since Augustus, repaved the empire's highways, and showered his largess on Roman plebeians and provincial cities.[17] The impact of Trajan's new coinage is sensed in a letter penned by Heliodorus, a Greco-Egyptian landowner of Hermopolis, who reports that soon after the Second Dacian War the price of gold bullion in Alexandria had fallen by 25 percent.[18] Trajan's soldiers also seized rich plunder in the Parthian capitals Seleucia and Ctesiphon that provided metal for another vast coinage of aurei and denarii under Hadrian (117–38). This second windfall allowed Hadrian, soon after his accession, to forgive 225 million denarii in tax arrears owed by Roman citizens.[19]

Commerce provided a second source of fresh specie for the Roman mint, but, except for African gold, bullion imports were on a modest scale. In Egypt, Roman prefects succeeded to Ptolemaic contacts that drew gold out of Nubia and the Axumite kings of Ethiopia profited as middlemen in exporting gold from East African mines located far beyond Roman horizons in exchange for wine, cloth, and other manufactured goods.[20] Augustus secured Carthage and the Punic towns on the Syrtic Gulf that were termini of trans-Saharan caravans. The Garamantes, ancestors of the Berbers, had, since the sixth century B.C., engaged in a "silent trade," bartering salt and finished wares in exchange for gold from peoples of the West African savannah. Rome succeeded Carthage as the principal consumer of West African gold, but the Garamantes kept control of the transit trade so that Romans never founded an equivalent to Sidjilmasa, the celebrated medieval base south of the Atlas Mountains that put Arab merchants in direct touch with the goldfields of Ghana.[21] Even less evidence survives about bullion imports on the northern and eastern frontiers. Tacitus assures us that German soil yielded neither gold nor silver—the silver strikes of Goslar and Freiburg lay in the distant tenth and thirteenth centuries.[22] Just beyond the frontier of Asia Minor, mines in Colchis and Armenia exported gold to the Roman world, but this trade seems to have peaked in the early Byzantine age.[23] Strabo also notes routes linking Hellenic cities on the eastern Euxine shores with the caravan centers of Bactria and Sogdiana, but the profits from the rich silver deposits in Central Asia went first to the Arsacid kings of Parthia, and then to the Kushan emperors.[24]

The mining of mineral deposits in the provinces was the other great source of fresh bullion. Archaeological excavations are confirming the picture found in late Roman legal texts that mining was a perpetual cycle of opening and closing many small-scale operations as miners quickly exhausted easily worked surface deposits by "open-cast" methods or panned for fluvial gold.[25] In the first and early second centuries A.D., gold strikes in Spain, Dalmatia, and Dacia, and steady production from silver mines in Spain, the Balkans, and eastern Anatolia dumped fresh bullion on the markets of the Roman Empire. The impact of Roman mining upon currency and prices at least equaled that of the richest late medieval strikes in Central Europe, and it was only dwarfed by the fabulous Spanish American silver production that brought on the price revolution of the sixteenth and seventeenth centuries.

The imperial peace provided optimal conditions for the exploitation of mineral deposits so that the output from mines for the whole of classical antiquity peaked during the two centuries between the reigns of Augustus and Septimius Severus (193–211). Emperors suppressed brigands, provided military escorts for bullion shipments, and appointed procurators to impose efficiency in mines. A revolution in transportation during the imperial peace reduced costs and facilitated distribution of bullion and coin. For example, after Augustus secured the mines of northwestern Spain by 15 B.C., Spanish gold and silver could be shipped across the Bay of Biscay and conveyed by military highways to the mint of Lugdunum (Lyons) where mint workers turned bullion into aurei and denarii which were then shipped via Gallic highways and canals to the armies on the Rhine. The Roman state mobilized manpower on a scale hitherto unparalleled by a mix of inducement and compulsion not unlike that employed in colonial Latin America. Imperial authorities transferred officials and soldiers to the most lucrative mines. Seasoned miners, such as the Dalmatians who signed on to work in the Dacian goldfields, were lured with contracts offering good pay, board, and perhaps a tacit understanding that miners could cart off unreported production.[26] Roman officials and contractors exploited at a profit even relatively small or almost inaccessible deposits (such as Dolaucothi in Wales) by deep mining techniques or "hushing."[27] Roman hydraulic engineering expertise prevented flooding of shafts at deep levels so that miners worked strikes to exhaustion over the course of two or three generations. During their boom years, big mines generated tremendous sums of gold and silver that had an immediate impact on the empire's currency.[28] Three complexes of mines—in Spain, Dalmatia, and Dacia—met the growing demand for Roman coins during the first and second centuries.

In Spain, the silver mines in the southeastern Pyrenees and Lower Ebro Valley, productive since the late Republic, fed imperial mints into the second century A.D. The Sierra Nevada was studded with famed mines of gold, argentiferous lead, copper, and zinc; Strabo in Augustus's day praised Murcian goldfields, perhaps near Bilbilis. Although silver mines near New Carthage had declined since the second century B.C., other Murcian mines must have taken up the slack, for Pliny the Elder reports mines at Baebelo yielded 300 pounds of silver daily or an annual revenue to the state of over 10 million denarii.[29] Pliny the Elder reports only state revenues so that the total production, legal and surreptitious, far exceeded the emperor's equivalent of the later "royal fifth" taken by the Spanish Crown. Once Augustus conquered the Cantabrians in the northwest (25–19 B.C.), Romans swarmed into Gallaecia and Asturias to exploit hundreds of alluvial terraces. Pliny the Elder claims that these gold mines alone netted the treasury annually 20,000 pounds (900,000 aurei), valued at 22.5 million denarii, or as much as 7 percent of all revenues of the Flavian emperors. The heart of the district, the mines of the Rio Duerna, yielded close to half of this income for nearly 150 years (ca. 20 B.C.–A.D. 125).[30] Booms in the northwestern mines spurred discoveries and intensive mining of new veins in districts long worked such as the alluvial gold terraces of southern Lusitania, silver mines of the Rio Tinto, and goldfields near Murcia.[31] Mining of copper and zinc, vital for manufacturing brass sestertii and dupondii, soared in districts near Corduba (Cordova) and Vipasca (Aljustrel, Portugal).[32]

When Augustus subdued the northern and central Balkan lands to secure the Macedonian borders, he opened the mineral wealth of Dalmatia and Upper Moesia. His timing was propitious because deposits of Attic and Thraco-Macedonian silver and of Alpine and Apennine gold were giving out. During the reign of Nero (54–68), a gold rush followed strikes in the Bosnian alluvial fields that made Dalmatian gold proverbial by the Flavian age when annual output climbed to a record 18,000 pounds (810,000 aurei or 20,250,000 denarii in value).[33] Romans expanded the prospecting and mining of silver in Upper Macedon. In the mountains above the Jadar Valley of eastern Bosnia and northwestern Serbia, they hit major silver deposits at Argentica (Srebrenica), the Roman Silverado, and Domavia (near Gradina). Imperial authorities, save for a brief disruption in the mid-third century, mined Dalmatian argentiferous ores for nearly four centuries, and big strikes in the fourth century fed imperial mints at Siscia and Sirmium.[34] As output of Spanish mines ebbed sometime in the second century, Dalmatian production surged ahead.

A third complex of mines that poured gold into the empire's money supply for well over a century was added when Trajan annexed Dacia in 105–6. Although no figures survive for the volume of Dacian gold, hints in literary sources and archaeological finds of shafts, tools, and mining contracts on wax tablets suggest that operations in the second century reached levels comparable to those of the Spanish and Dalmatian gold mines. Dalmatian miners came in force to Alburnus Maior (Rosia Montana in modern Rumania) in the Transylvanian Erzgebirge, and, probably, to mines to the north near Nagy Bánya and Rodna and to southern Transylvanian placer mines.[35] The conquest of Dacia stimulated economic growth south of the Danube, and Romans commenced tapping argentiferous lead ores in Upper Moesia and in eastern Thrace.[36]

Roman coins then owed much of their success to the steady expansion of the supply of specie for well over two centuries. Although, unfortunately, this process can not be quantified, literary sources and archaeology paint an irrefutable picture that stocks of specie in the Roman world grew by great, albeit sporadic, leaps until the close of the second century. The imperial government could depend upon a considerable amount of freshly mined gold and silver (as well as Spanish orichalcum and Cypriote copper) each year, and this supply contributed decisively to the remarkable stability of money and prices down to the reign of Marcus Aurelius (161–80).[37] But even Roman organization and technology had limits. The great mines were usually worked to exhaustion within a century, and small operations were productive for far shorter periods. By the early third century the fabulous gold strikes of the high empire had passed, and so infusions of specie fell even though small mines opened and closed with regularity and imported stocks still arrived down to the fifth century. Imperial expenditures kept mounting, and costs of frontier warfare far exceeded any booty captured. In the 170s, Moorish raiders disrupted mining in Lusitania long enough for rising water levels to flood out some mines, while Germanic invaders in 167–70 interrupted production at Rosia Montana in Dacia and, most likely, at Moesian and Dalmatian mines as well.[38] As the high tide in mining receded, supplies of fresh bullion dipped, perhaps in the Severan age, and then contracted during the chaotic invasions and civil wars of 251–74, pressing emperors already facing fiscal and political crisis to debase the Augustan currency into oblivion.

The imperial mint achieved astonishing success in turning bullion into vast numbers of coins, which imperial fiscal institutions distributed widely, if unevenly, over the Roman world. The output from the imperial mints in the Julio-Claudian age is unknown, and the surviving coins suggest that aurei and denarii were minted annually only after Nero reorganized the mint. Tentative estimates of annual output of denarii under Domitian (81–96) and Marcus Aurelius (161–80) point to figures running into the tens, most likely hundreds, of millions.[39] Likewise, no reliable estimates exist for the production of dupondii and asses, which formed the bulk of *aes* in circulation down to the Severan age. The best statistics for the output of *aes*, which are probably too low, are based on die studies of sestertii issued by Galba and Vespasian during the Civil War of 68–71 and on analysis of the surviving dies of sestertii of 98–147 contained in the Garonne hoard. They suggest an average output of 12 to 15 million sestertii per year, but even in the second century production of *aes* oscillated between periods of little or no mintage and bursts of activity.[40]

Such estimates of output rule out recent opinions, based on casual finds from Roman military and native sites, that *aes* failed to arrive in sufficient numbers to monetize the western and northern provinces. For example, the votive offerings of Roman coins found in the sacred springs of Bath have been advanced to argue that Britain received annually as few as 100,000 sestertii in bronze money even at the height of production in 150.[41] Such implausibly low figures, based on samples hardly representative of the currency, are easily discounted, but they spring from a premise that the state's indifference to economic needs (in distinction to its fiscal needs) inhibited large-scale production as well as widespread distribution and use of coins throughout the Roman West. Brass and copper coins, whatever their numbers, frequently changed hands so that a single coin facilitated many transactions each day since *aes* seldom were put aside as savings until the run-away inflation of the third century. As token money *aes* also seldom fell prey to recoining. The composition of sestertii, dupondii, and asses discovered in a shipwreck of about 160 in the Garonne suggests that most *aes* passed current for at least sixty years and a sizeable proportion stayed in circulation as long as a century. The most recent coins in the hoard, struck during the reign of Antoninus Pius in the decade prior to their loss, are a small part of the hoard—the hoard, perhaps, is a reflection of the coins in circulation.[42] The "restored" *aes* with Julio-Claudian types, which Titus and Domitian minted in 80–82, also confirm the long life of fractional currency, since designs of Flavian "restored" coins were based on prototypes that were still circulating some forty to seventy years after they had been issued (pl. 10.73).[43] Since even very worn pieces had value (although they were often discounted), the Roman state, as in the Republic, obtained maximum use of its token coinage.

Countermarking of *aes* by military commanders has, at times, been cited as evidence that imperial *aes* were in short supply, but the circumstances under which the coins were countermarked and the rarity of the practice are indications to the contrary. Commanders resorted to countermarking worn *aes* only when fresh supplies of small change were in short supply, either because the imperial mint was preparing a coinage for a new emperor or because shipments were interrupted during civil war. Thus, at the accession of Tiberius (14–37), Germanicus counterstamped asses of Augustus and *aes* of Lugdunum with imperial monograms at the camps of Noviomagus (Nijmegen) and Novaesium (Neuss) on the Lower Rhine, while Drusus similarly countermarked sestertii, dupondii, and asses at Carnuntum (near Vienna) in Pannonia (pl. 9.69–70). Countermarks bearing Nero's monogram were similarly applied to *aes* of Caligula and Claudius found at legionary camps in the Upper Rhineland. In camps on the Lower Rhine, counterstamps denoted coins as "good" (*bonus*) or "approved for use" (*probavit*); some sestertii and dupondii were countermarked and retariffed at half their face value, that is as dupondii and asses. In the Civil War of 69, legions countermarked not only to revalidate old coins, but also to declare partisan loyalties.[44] In the East during the First Jewish War (66–70) and the Parthian Wars of Trajan (115–17) and Marcus Aurelius (161–66), provincial and civic bronze coins were countermarked with legionary symbols or numerals because soldiers on campaign ran short of change when they outran the supply lines from their base camps (pl. 9.71).[45]

The recent estimates of total wealth or tax revenues of the Roman Empire are not a reliable guide to the number of coins in use because taxes are only a part of the economy, and, in addition, the figures include taxes collected in grain and other commodities converted into coin based on average prices.[46] More helpful are the measures emperors took to restore the money supply. Tiberius ended the financial panic of 33 when he provided bankers an interest-free loan of 25 million denarii to restore liquidity to the capital's money market without increasing production of new coins.[47] Nero promised that whenever revenues ran low in the state treasury (*aerarium*), he would furnish from the *fiscus* (the emperor's account) 15 million denarii, a sum well within the capacity of the mint's yearly output.[48] Even more telling are the reserves of 675 million denarii that Tiberius and Antoninus Pius each amassed or the donatives in tens of millions aurei or hundreds of millions of denarii which emperors from Augustus to Severus Alexander regularly paid.

The imperial government, which struck coins in unprecedented amounts, achieved an equally remarkable success in the distribution of its money. For reasons of security, the manufacture of imperial money was concentrated initially at two central mints, Rome and Lugdunum, and after 64 Rome alone struck imperial coins. The imperial government was, in normal times, able to provide a steady flow of coins to the provinces for its own needs without a system of branch mints until the reign of Gordian III (238–44). Branch mints in the provinces were used only during civil wars—Vespasian issued aurei and denarii from a mint operating successively at Alexandria, Antioch, and Ephesus in 69–73, and Pescennius Niger (193–94) and Septimius Severus (193–211) improvised coinages at Antioch and Laodicea ad Mare, respectively.[49] The imperial mint primarily met fiscal needs for coin to be disbursed in payrolls, purchases, and imperial gifts rather than for the needs of commerce. Yet, even if only indirectly, the imperial mint fed the hunger of the capital, Italy, and the western provinces for Roman coins as the pace of commercial and urban life quickened. Imperial expenditures put vast numbers of Roman coins into provincial markets, while taxation removed only part of this money back to Rome. Commerce dispersed the rest of the coins over a superb network of roads, canals, and sea lanes linking the Roman world. A cycle of imperial expenditure and commerce kept most Roman coins in perpetual circulation. The effectiveness of vast numbers of Roman coins penetrating provincial markets is undeniable, and is documented by the rising use of Roman aurei, denarii, and *aes* throughout the empire.

The aureus passed unchallenged as the coin of high finance and international trade. The triumph of the denarius was not quite as complete, but in the Julio-Claudian age denarii penetrated every quarter of the Roman Empire so that, with the exception of Egypt, denarii came into general use in all markets of the Roman world by the Flavian age. Mints in Asia Minor and Syria continued to coin Greek-style silver staters with fresh metal from imports and the

Anatolian mines, but even here denarii circulated as equivalents of Attic drachmae and acted as the link coin in exchange and taxation. Hence, Jesus of the Synoptic Gospels designated the denarius as the coin rendered in tax unto Caesar.[50]

The spread of denarii reflected imperial wars of conquest and establishment of secure frontiers. By A.D. 1 denarii circulated unchallenged in the western and Balkan provinces, North Africa, and Greece, because each year great numbers of denarii arrived in military expenditures. In contrast to the Republic, whenever the legions conquered new provinces as in Germany, Britain, Dacia, or Mesopotamia, Roman coins swiftly followed. Augustus made Roman coin the currency of the West for the next 450 years. During his conquest of northwestern Spain and Lusitania (Portugal and central Spain) in 25–15 B.C., Augustus coined Spanish bullion into aurei and denarii at one or two mobile mints. His legate P. Carisius, in Republican fashion, included his name on denarii, quinarii, and *aes* struck at the Lusitanian captial of Emerita (Merida) from 23 B.C. (pl. 8.55).[51] Henceforth, aurei and denarii were the sole "full-bodied" coins circulating in the Iberian peninsula. The pattern was repeated in Gaul where by 16 B.C. Augustus moved the mint to Lugdunum, ceremonial capital of the Gallic provinces and conveniently located between the Spanish mines and the legionary camps on the Rhine. Lugdunum soon emerged as the sole imperial mint of aurei and denarii so that the last Gallic silver obols (equal to half-denarii) expired in a flood of imperial coins. In the reign of Tiberius, Strabo still praised Lugdunum as the city where "the Roman emperors coin their money . . . both the silver and the gold."[52] As Augustus's legions after 16 B.C. mastered trans-Rhenan Germany, the Alpine lands of Rhaetia and Noricum, and the Balkan provinces of Dalmatia, Pannonia, and Moesia, native peoples ceased striking Celtic-style gold and silver coins or imitative denarii.[53] In A.D. 14 the Britons and Dacians alone in Europe escaped subjugation and issued their own gold and silver coins. Belgic kings in southeastern Britain shifted from gold staters to silver and base metal fractions inspired by Roman prototypes.[54] The Dacians curtailed production of native coins as imports of denarii declined in the first century. The Roman conquest of Britian under Claudius and of Dacia by

Trajan doomed both native currencies to rapid extinction.

An even greater testimony to the genius of imperial fiscal and monetary organization was the penetration of imperial *aes* into so much of the Roman world during the first and second centuries. In the late second and first centuries B.C. many cities of Spain, North Africa, and the Greek world had commenced coining their own *aes* as local versions of Roman denominations to be used as fractions of the denarius. This unplanned division of labor proved sensible, because *aes,* although lucrative to mint, were cumbersome and expensive to ship. It was more economical to manufacture fractional bronze coins at civic or provincial mints than to mass produce and ship them from a central mint. Augustus continued this arrangement, and in the East, Greek cities struck most of the bronze coins in daily use for the next three centuries. Augustus sponsored several Roman-style provincial bronze coinages. At the Spanish city of Emerita, his legate P. Carisius minted bronze dupondii and copper asses with iconography closely modeled after their Roman counterparts. In the East, Pergamum, in 25–23 B.C., and Antioch, in about 6–4 B.C., struck *aes* that were Roman in value and iconography (pl. 12.94–97). In the West most cities adopted the Latin inscriptions, Roman types, and imperial denominations on their own initiative. In the reigns of Augustus and Tiberius, Spanish towns minted prolific Roman-style *aes,* often with value marks and sometimes designated as struck "by permission of Caesar." Punic cities in Africa and Numidia did the same, basing their coins on a heavier bronze sestertius (30 g) and including value marks in asses (pl. 9.68).[55] Romanized cities of the southern Gallic province of Narbonensis struck similar *aes* that circulated widely over southern and eastern Gaul. The colony of Nemausus (Nîmes) shortly after 30 B.C. minted heavy bronze dupondii (17 g) and asses (14–11.75 g) carrying on the obverse the heads of Agrippa and Augustus back to back, and on the reverse a crocodile and palm tree in commemoration of the Battle of Actium (pl. 9.66–67).[56] In 10 B.C., Lugdunum, capital of the Three Gauls, commenced striking bronze coins equivalent in weight and tariffing to the four Augustan denominations plus a semis (pl. 9.65).[57] Their numbers, provincial types, and lack of a city name marked the coins for general circulation and they quickly displaced the last Celtic tribal issues in central and eastern Gaul.

It is remarkable how swiftly Roman *aes* were dispersed throughout the Roman world during the Julio-Claudian age. Augustus introduced his orichalcum and copper coins to replace wretched Republican pieces circulating in peninsular Italy and among the frontier armies. Excavations reveal shortages at the military camps in the Rhineland and Upper Danube in the early Augustan age, and soldiers customarily halved uncial asses with the head of Janus when they needed fractions and used local *aes* of Tarraco, Nemausus, and Lugdunum as proxies of Roman ones (pl. 9.65–67).[58] Imperial *aes* ousted tribal currencies in the northern provinces in the Augustan age, and then, within a generation, supplanted municipal bronze coinages of the West. The demise of tribal coinages in the Celtic and Thraco-Illyrian provinces was perhaps inevitable. These silver, potin, and bronze coins were awkward divisions of the denarius and singularly ugly, and the miscellaneous Celtic, Norican, Pannonian, and Thraco-Illyrian coins that have surfaced at sites soon after the Roman conquest were probably curiosities of no monetary value. The preference for Roman *aes* is best seen in Britain during the first decade of the conquest (43–54). Britons, when they ran short of *aes,* manufactured blundered copies of Claudius's asses rather than Celtic-style coins (pl. 9.72).[59]

The triumph of Roman *aes* in the urbanized, Mediterranean provinces of the West was surprising, especially in Iberian and Punic towns with centuries' old traditions of civic coinage. The reigns of Augustus and Tiberius had witnessed an outpouring of Roman-style bronze money at civic mints hugging the Mediterranean shores in Gaul, Spain, Sicily, Africa, and Cyrene that satisfied demand for a generation, but most city mints suspended or reduced operations in the 30s. When this body of local bronze currency needed replenishment by Flavian times, economic growth, a transportation revolution, and increased output of the Roman mint eliminated the need for a second wave of municipal issues in the West, although Spanish towns, such as Corduba, reissued worn coins by countermarking.[60] The mint at Rome, imperial expenditures and trade henceforth ensured that sufficient numbers of *aes* reached provincal economies. In the Flavian age, Tarraco and Lugdunum might have struck sporadic issues of imperial *aes*, but emperors never used these mints as the basis for a network of branch mints in the provinces manufacturing *aes* with dies cut either by local engravers or shipped from Rome.

Within a generation of the death of Augustus, the entire Roman West employed a single fiduciary base metal currency exchangeable against aureus and denarius and manufactured by a single central mint at Rome. As prices rose, production of sestertii leaped ahead of dupondii and asses by the reign of Hadrian (117–38) so that the semis and quadrans dropped out of use by the end of the second century. By the Flavian age, the imperial government so successfully solved the problems of volume and distribution that it was supplying the *aes* as well as "full-bodied" coins to the entire western half of the Roman world. The impact of this achievement was no less far-reaching even if it resulted primarily from the state meeting its own fiscal needs, for it ensured the monetization of the empire's economy and the rapid Romanization of the currency in the West.

Ironically, public faith in imperial coins made possible the policies of debasement that eventually eroded the Augustan currency. When, as frequently happened, imperial expenditure exceeded income and reserves, emperors debased the denarius to cover the budgetary shortfall, but the Augustan tariffing was preserved by adjusting the standards of aureus and base metal fractions. For nearly a century (30 B.C.–A.D. 64) Julio-Claudian emperors maintained the standards set by Augustus, and Tiberius (14–37) even slightly improved the fineness of the denarius as he built his reserve of 675 million denarii.[61] In 64, Nero—under the pressures of debts incurred in a desultory war in Armenia, rebuilding Rome after the Great Fire, and his own depraved extravagance—conducted the first major debasement since the Second Punic War. Nero saddled the exchequer with a fiscal disaster, but the Augustan currency sustained the strain. Official tariffing among coins in all metals was preserved by lowering the standards for all denominations, an action having the added attraction of yielding more coins per pound of metal. The weight standard of the aureus was reduced to 45 to the pound, a decrease of about 11 percent from the 40 to the pound set by Augustus (pl. 8.60). In his eagerness to expand his money supply, Nero resorted to melting down and minting gold votive offerings at Rome, and he even sought out buried treasures such as a gold hoard rumored to have been unearthed in Africa.[62] Nero, cleverly applying lessons learned in manipulating the billon tetradrachmae of Egypt, debased the denarius by more than 20 percent. Its weight was reduced by one-eighth, from 84 to 96 to the pound, and its fineness was lowered from 98 to 93 percent (pl. 8.61). Thus, 1 million old denarii taken in taxes could be reminted into about 1.2 million debased denarii, but the overall profits were greater because Nero demanded taxes in heavy "fresh" coins and worn denarii were either discounted or treated as bullion. Furthermore, many denarii were deliberately struck below standard so that actual debasement probably ranged upward to 25 percent or more.[63] Nero also abandoned, at least temporarily, the Augustan scheme of fractional coinage in two base metals by discontinuing copper asses and quadrantes in favor of ones struck from the brass alloy used for sestertii and dupondii (pl. 8.62–64). Nero raised the weight of the dupondius by 10 percent (from 14.5 to 16 g) and added a semis (one-half as), but his new brass as at 9 g was about 20 percent lighter than its copper predecessor (11 g). The change permitted the manufacture of more asses from less metal, but the new asses failed to win acceptance, and Nero returned to copper asses and quadrantes.[64]

Debasement netted Nero revenues, but it also courted risks. Price increases sparked by the debasement in 64 apparently had little long-term impact, but imperiling confidence in the currency was the first step toward financial disaster. The international reputation of Roman coins was tarnished. Merchants ceased to export aurei and denarii to South India soon after 64, and Tacitus acidly notes how untutored Germans outwitted Romans by insisting upon Republican denarii instead of debased imperial ones.[65] Coins, however, were a minor part of overseas trade, for once they crossed the imperial frontiers, they passed in local marts by intrinsic worth rather than tariffing. It was public trust within rather than outside the empire that was critical to the success of imperial coinage.

Civil war (68–69) assured the triumph of the Neronian standards because none of the imperial contenders could afford the luxury of reform. In 68, Galba, in command of the mineral wealth of Spain, produced his first denarii just below Augustan fineness (96.5 percent). His improvised mint at Tarraco struck aurei and denarii first professing Republican values and appeals to the legions and provinces, but coins with his portrait and titles followed when Galba assumed the purple.[66] Galba, once in Rome, mass produced *aes* and denarii, but now on the baser Neronian standard (93 percent fine). In 69, Otho and Vitellius each adopted the Neronian standard, although Vitellian generals on their march to Italy struck finer denarii (95 percent) either at Lugdunum or from mobile military mints.[67]

In 70, Vespasian reported to the Senate that to prevent the treasury from defaulting he needed 10 billion denarii in cash, a sum nearly fifteen times greater than the largest surplus ever reported in the treasury.[68] Vespasian slashed the standard of the denarius (89 percent fine), and for the next dozen years Flavian emperors exploited provincial mines and devised new taxes. As revenues varied considerably from year to year, many denarii deviated from this new, lower standard, falling to as low as 80 percent fine. In 82, Domitian ordered the second recoinage of the Principate, returning the denarius to its Augustan purity (98.5 percent fine), although he retained the Neronian weight standard of 96 to the pound. By a single stroke, Domitian "cried up" the value of silver money and canceled half of the effects of debasement since 64.[69] His bold attempt at reform was a tribute to Flavian fiscal policy, because the treasury forfeited profits as the mint recoined baser older denarii into finer ones. By mid-85, however, war debts from the Chattic War (83–85) and the expense of campaigns against Sueves and Dacians compelled a return to the Neronian standard (93 percent fine). Domitian laboriously conducted another recoinage, turning his fine denarii into baser ones. For the first time, frontier warfare thwarted reform; it was an ominous preview of the fate of imperial currency during the third century.

Trajan's hauls of gold and silver booty in the Second Dacian War (104–5) put the exchequer in the black so that in 107 Trajan "caused all the money that was badly worn to be melted down."[70]

His was no ordinary recoinage, because, as a symbolic gesture, Trajan struck his own versions of early imperial aurei and Republican denarii that announced "the emperor Caesar Trajan Augustus Germanicus Dacicus father of his country has restored [the coinage]." These so-called restored aurei and denarii carried types of earlier coins, but were struck on Neronian standards to pass at par with current coins (pl. 10.74–75).[71] Aurei were struck in the names of Julius Caesar, Augustus, Tiberius, Claudius, Galba, Vespasian, and Titus, offering a portrait gallery of Trajan's deified predecessors. Trajan selected designs for his denarii from prototypes in circulation. Restored denarii included imperfect copies of quadrigati (remembered as denarii), early denarii complete with the old value mark of 10 asses, and topical denarii of the late second and first centuries B.C. A British hoard from Verulamium (St. Albans) reveals the kinds of denarii circulating during the first decade of Trajan's reign. Worn Republican and Antonian legionary denarii comprised nearly 43 percent of the hoard; most of the rest (51 percent) were imperial denarii of 69–102.[72] The numbers of legionary denarii (pl. 6.42) in the hoard suggest that they might not have been reminted because, given their base metal, they were not threatened by Trajan's recoinage. On the other hand, fine denarii of Julio-Claudian emperors and Domitian (82–85) had already vanished from circulation.

One purpose of Trajan's restored aurei and denarii was to steady public confidence against the shock of a sudden disappearance of so many coins hallowed by familiar types and purity. Since acceptance of coins hinged in large measure upon public faith bred from long usage and familiarity, Trajan offered reassuring replicas of ancestral coins to a Roman public that regarded traditional types as guarantees of value as well as symbols of its heritage that echoed messages conveyed by relief sculpture and paintings adorning public monuments. Romans, even though valuing coins for their utility, must have also appreciated the rich designs, beautiful engraving, and fine manufacture that inspired the confidence so crucial and yet so elusive to measure. This Roman love of diversity surprised foreigners who expected from coin designs little more than denominational value; one rajah of Taprobane (Sri Lanka) was startled to discover that denarii, despite their sundry designs, weighed the same.[73] Trajan, by restoring older designs, acknowledged the danger that debasement and recoinage could undermine this trust and trigger a panic.

Within six months of his first recoinage, however, Trajan again tested Roman trust in their money, for he debased the denarius by some 3 to 4 percent so that denarii (89 to 90 percent fine) stood at par with the basest issues of Vespasian in 70–72. Debasement cut short the minting of restored denarii, and repercussions were felt across the empire; in Syria, mints lowered standards of their staters. Trajan took this unexpected action on the heels of his Dacian triumph to meet mounting expenses. Tariffing of the more debased denarii against aureus and base metal coins was unaffected perhaps because infusions of Dacian gold might have depressed prices of gold and driven up the value of silver.[74] Whatever the forces behind Trajan's debasement, imperial revenues rose and prices leveled off in the next half-century. In 118 Hadrian forgave Roman citizens 225 million denarii in tax arrears, a sum that possibly might imply annual revenues of 100 million denarii from indirect taxes alone.[75] In 148, Antoninus Pius lowered by a further 5 percent the purity of the denarius (83 to 84 percent), in part to defray the costs of his millenarian celebrations. He also could have placed his new coins at par with heavily circulated denarii of Flavian and Trajanic vintage.

At their accession Marcus Aurelius (161–80) and Lucius Verus (161–69) inherited from Antoninus Pius a surplus of 675 million denarii, equal to the record sum accumulated by Tiberius, and the last surplus reported until the mid-fifth century.[76] Imperial currency had changed little in the course of two centuries. Debasement had reduced the silver in the denarius by some 26.5 percent (less than 1 g), but in size, weight, and appearance the denarius was unaltered since the Neronian recoinage. The aureus had suffered an official weight loss of only 11 percent. Of far greater importance, Romans, despite fluctuations in silver standards, handled as equivalent the aurei and denarii minted between 64 and 161 (with due allowance for underweight and particularly pure pieces). Furthermore, base metal fractions in 161 were identical to those of 23 B.C., even though Julio-Claudian pieces had long disappeared. Despite rises in prices, asses still were the most commonly encountered coins in small change and the semis and quadrans were useful fractions.

Within months of their accession, Marcus Aurelius and Lucius Verus exhausted reserves and tax revenues on accessional gifts and a Parthian war. They debased the denarius by 4 percent, lowering its fineness to less than 80 percent—the most serious debasement since the Civil War of 68–69. Denarii of 161–68 were the basest yet in Roman history, and many specimens left the mint below this low standard.[77] Victory over Parthia in 166 brought no respite. Within a year Germans crossed the Danube, plundered the Balkans, and disrupted mining in Dalmatia and Dacia, so that Marcus Aurelius faced the same financial challenge that frontier warfare had posed to Domitian. In 168–70 Marcus Aurelius, with the frontier crisis in hand, restored the denarius to its Antonine standard (83 percent fine), but he abandoned reform when fighting erupted again. Marcus Aurelius, just like Domitian, conducted successive recoinages as he shifted standards to meet the costs of frontier war. His recoinages transformed the character of Roman currency, removing many fine old denarii from circulation. Ensuing inflation prompted a sharp halt in output of *aes*. The semis and quadrans were discontinued; sestertius and middle *aes* were henceforth manufactured in a cheaper bronze alloy with a heavy component of lead. Inexorably the logic of debasement forced the denarius out of its role as the prime coin and eliminated the need for token bronze coins so that the imperial government after 235 split the functions of the Augustan denarius between aurei, minted on ever lighter weight standards, and fiduciary low-grade silver or billon coins.

It is a tribute to Augustus how little the imperial government debased its coinage in the two centuries following his reign. The weight of the denarius was lowered only once, from 84 to 96 to the pound in 64, and its purity was reduced just six times—in 64, 68–70, 85, 107, and 148—so that the pure denarius (98.5 percent fine) was transformed into an alloyed coin 84 to 85 percent fine. Domitian returned the denarius to its pristine purity in 82–85, although he was forced to retreat from this standard, but still the denarius averaged nearly 90 percent fine down to 148. Aureus and base metal fractions suffered even less. Nero officially reduced the weight of the aureus by about 11 percent, although many aurei had long left the mint slightly below standard. Nero abandoned the Augustan scheme of fractional coinage in two base metals in favor of orichalcum denominations struck on a lighter weight standard, but he had to return to the heavy weights and two metals.

Finally, erosion of gold and silver standards down to the reign of Marcus Aurelius had a limited impact on prices and exchange rates, because emperors recoined just enough denarii to cover debts. Many heavier and purer denarii, safely tucked away in strongboxes or circulating in remote districts, eluded the melting pot. Periodic infusions of specie from mines and war often spared the need for a thorough recoinage. Between each change of the standard stretched long periods of stable prices and plentiful currency. Although heavy imperial spending and debasement generated sharp bouts of inflation, each crisis subsided quickly. Government and public adjusted so that prices leveled off and the money supply suffered comparatively few adverse effects. The stability of Augustan currency ensured stable prices and wages that, in turn, contributed in no small measure to the legendary prosperity of the Roman peace.

# Five

# Currencies of the Roman East, 30 B.C.–A.D. 200

"For let none of them have currency or weights or measures of their own; instead let them use ours," so Maecenas urged Augustus, at least in the words of the historian Cassius Dio writing in the Severan age.[1] Cassius Dio's rhetorical plea, however, never influenced imperial policy because the polyglot populations of the Hellenic world had always dealt, and continued to deal, in a bewildering array of coins. City markets and rural fairs were filled with a wide variety of bronze coins carrying the name of the issuing city or a regional league (*koinon* or *commune*) that fostered the imperial cult. Such coins comprised most of the money in daily use, and they came in different sizes and denominations under a variety of standards based on Greek obol, Roman as, or *assarion* (the Greek adaptation of the as). Added to this mix were coins struck by Roman provincial authorities or petty dynasts who held sway at Rome's behest. Silver coins, issued by the same consortium of cities, leagues, friendly kings, and Roman governors, were no less complex. Greek staters were known by such nicknames as "the basket bearing coin," "silver of the Tyrian stamp," or "money of the Ptolemy." The story of this currency has three principal themes: the evolution of the silver currencies in Asia Minor and Syria, the varied bronze coins minted by provincial and civic authorities, and the creation of a fiduciary billon currency in Egypt that provided a model for imperial monetary policy during the later third century.

## *Silver Currencies of Asia Minor and Syria*

Silver currencies in the East were premised upon one of three standards. In the most widely used standard—known as the Attic or, in Syria, as the Tyrian—a silver drachma equaled the denarius so the principal stater, a tetradrachma, was exchanged against 4 Roman denarii. Next in popularity was a drachma at three-quarters of the denarius whereby the tetradrachma was valued at 3 denarii. This lighter standard went under various names—Rhodian or cistophoric in Asia Minor, Antiochene in Syria. In Egypt, a more debased standard prevailed and Claudius in A.D. 41/2 tariffed the drachma at one-quarter of a denarius, so that the tetradrachma was equal to 1 denarius.

Five coins—the cistophorus of Asia, the tetradrachmae of Antioch and Tyre, the tetradrachma of Egypt and, to a lesser extent, the drachma (and later, the didrachma) of Caesarea—acted as links between the denarius and the sundry provincial and civic coins. These were the primary coins taken in taxation and, except in Egypt where all outside coin was forbidden, they could be converted via the denarius into Roman aurei or *aes*. The denarius could, in turn, be converted via regional staters into local bronze and silver fractions. The celebrated silver coins of the Greek homeland disappeared as repeated Roman plundering of Greece and Macedon during the Civil Wars of the late Republic and the exhaustion of the mines at Laurium forced Athens to suspend coining her "New Style" tetradrachmae in the early 30s B.C. Roman officials simplified the silver currency in European Greece by calculating taxes in the Attic drachma and collecting them in denarii, and unwieldy staters such as the Thessalian didrachma (exchanged at 1.5 denarii) were abolished.[2]

In 30 B.C., the cistophorus, although it had been debased and its minting discontinued during the Roman civil wars, was still the most important silver stater in Anatolia. Augustus put the cistophorus at the head of Asia's regional currency when he conducted a major recoinage in tandem with a reform of the taxes of Asia. Mints at Ephesus and Pergamum collaborated in striking at least 15 to 20 million cistophori in the decade from 28 to 18 B.C.[3] Cistophori had traditionally carried a laurel wreath enclosing the central design, but an idealized portrait of Augustus was substituted for the *cista mystica* on the obverse, and the Roman goddess Pax appears on the reverse. Dies for the later Augustan cistophori, most likely cut by imperial engravers, bear impeccable Latin legends and reverse types with personal emblems of Augustus or major monuments in Asia or at Rome (pl. 10.76). Augustus's first issue in 28 B.C. must have been struck from metal obtained by melting base Republican cistophori and civic drachmae, for its fineness was noticeably below that of the cistophori Antony had struck in 39 B.C. (Table 5.1).[4] Antony's cistophori were permitted to circulate, not only because of their high quality, but also because

*Table 5.1*
Cistophori of Asia, 39 B.C.–A.D. 205

| | Weight | Silver Content | | Tariffing |
|---|---|---|---|---|
| Issue | Grams | Fineness | Grams | Denarii |
| M. Antony, 39 B.C. | 11.30 | 91.3 | 10.32 | 3 |
| Augustus, 28 B.C. | 11.30 | 88.5 | 10.00 | 3 |
| Augustus, 27–20 B.C. | 11.75 | 88.7 | 10.42 | 3 |
| Augustus, 19–18 B.C. | 11.60 | 89.0 | 10.32 | 3 |
| Claudius, A.D. 50–51 | 11.00 | 90.5 | 9.96 | 3 |
| Vespasian, 72–73 | 10.25 | 89.3 | 9.15 | 3 |
| Titus/Domitian, 79–84 | 10.35 | 87.0 | 9.00 | 3 |
| Nerva, 98 | 10.00 | 91.0 | 9.10 | 3 |
| Trajan, 98–99 | 10.00 | 92.6 | 9.26 | 3 |
| Hadrian, 112–17 | 10.25 | 80.8 | 8.28 | 3 |
| Hadrian Restrikes, 123: | | | | |
| On Antonian issues | 9.85 | 92.4 | 9.10 | 4 |
| On Augustan issues | 10.40 | 92.5 | 9.62 | 4 |
| On unidentified issues | 10.00 | 92.6 | 9.26 | 4 |
| Sept. Severus, 198–205 | 9.10 | 73.4 | 6.68 | 4 |

*Source:* Walker, *MRSC* I, pp. 26–38 and 122–23, and II, pp. 61–70 and 106–7 (reattributing issues from Arabia to Asia), and III, pp. 72–73.

they bore the portrait of the emperor's sister Octavia. The large numbers and improved fineness of the later Augustan cistophori testify to the return of prosperity and an infusion of fresh silver received in trade and from mines in Thrace and Anatolia. Cistophori, given their iconography, likely entered circulation as distributions at festivals of the imperial cult held at the great centers of Asia and Bithynia. Cistophori served the province's needs for the next 150 years, and demands for new silver coin were met by minting more cistophori rather than importing denarii, which apparently did not penetrate Asia Minor in any numbers until the second century. Claudius struck his own sizeable issue, and, in the early Flavian age, worn pieces were revalidated by countermarks (pl. 10.77).[5]

Throughout Anatolia and the Eastern Aegean, cities and leagues continued to coin their own fractional silver coins on the Attic standard and employed cistophori as tridrachmae (pl. 10.78). The free Carian cities of Tabae, Mylasa, and Stratonicea struck didrachmae and drachmae for local consumption.[6] The Lycian League, in the rugged pine-clad southwestern corner of Asia Minor, coined Attic drachmae at par with the denarius in 30–20 B.C., and again, after formal annexation, in A.D. 43 and 95–99 (pl. 10.79). Lycian drachmae, which passed as thirds of the cistophorus, gained popularity far afield, and they were still being set aside in hoards two decades after the debasement by Caracalla.[7] The seven members of Crete's league adopted the cistophoric standard in the Julio-Claudian age, but later switched to the Attic standard when they were united with Cyrene into a single province (pl. 10.80–81).[8] The cistophorus was even popular east of the Taurus mountains, circulating in cities on the Cilician littoral and in the remote mountainous regions of Cappadocia and Pontus. Tarsus coined both tetradrachmae and tridrachmae on the Attic standard, and the lesser Cilician cities of Aegeae, Mopsus, and Seleucia joined in striking the same denominations in the Hadrianic and Antonine ages (pl. 10.82–83).[9] The free city Amisus in 131–38 struck Attic standard tridrachmae (along with didrachmae and drachmae) in a massive recoinage of at least 6 million drachmae that provided the Euxine regions with fine silver money for over a generation (pl.

10.84).[10] The league of Cyprus minted tetradrachmae and didrachmae at Salamis after 76/7, but their light weight (12.5 g) and purity confined their use to the island.[11]

In eastern Anatolia local Attic drachmae were complements rather than rivals to the cistophorus. The client kings, Archelaus of Cappadocia (36 B.C.–A.D. 17) and Polemo II of Pontus (36–64), struck drachmae from silver mined near Mt. Argaeus and in districts southwest of Trapezus.[12] Upon the annexation of Cappadocia, Roman authorities continued striking drachmae and hemidrachmae; the first drachmae bear Latin legends, but their weight, design, and, with Nero, Greek inscriptions marked them for regional use. Claudius introduced the didrachma that became the principal Caesarean denomination in the 90s (pl. 11.85). The mix of silver coins current in Anatolian towns can be seen from the assorted fractions issued by Caesarea in 55–60, which included didrachma, 1.5 drachma, drachma, three-quarter drachma, and hemidrachma. This array of denominations, minted on the Attic standard, provided convenient fractions for both the Attic tetradrachma and the cistophorus. The three standard Attic fractions—didrachma, drachma, and hemidrachma—were also equal, respectively, to two-thirds, one-third, and one-sixth of the cistophorus, and the unusual Attic fractions—1.5 drachma and three-quarter drachma—were the half and quarter of the cistophorus (pl. 11.86).[13]

When Hadrian visited Asia Minor in 123, he ordered the "renewal" (*renovatio*) of Antonian and Augustan cistophori. A dozen leading cities withdrew old cistophori and overstruck them, often with dies cut by local engravers, and most cities used the opportunity to mint reverse types celebrating patron divinities.[14] But of greater significance, Hadrian revalued the cistophorus from 3 denarii to 4 denarii as a delayed move to keep pace with Trajan's debasement of the denarius in 107 (see Table 5.1). Hadrian's tours and his patronage of Hellenic shrines and cities as well as relief to victims of earthquakes poured into Asia Minor unprecedented numbers of denarii, which henceforth formed a significant proportion of the money supply. At its old tariffing of 3 denarii, the cistophorus courted the melting pot, but at the revised rate of 4 denarii it dropped to a slightly overvalued regional coin. Revaluation also netted a windfall profit, covered costs of manufacture, and gave old coins a new lease on life. Hadrian, in effect, turned the cistophorus into an Attic weight tetradrachma. The shift of standard proved convenient because cistophori circulated widely over Asia Minor, and some (along with Amisan and Lycian drachmae) were exported to the silver-hungry Levant.[15] They had become the stater of Bithynia, since Nicomedia participated in the Hadrianic recoinage. After Hadrian revalued the cistophorus from 3 to 4 denarii, Caesarea, Amisus and the Cilician cities began minting tridrachmae, presumably because the old cistophori had popularized a stater equal to 3 denarii (pl. 10.83–84).

The second widely used coin in Asia Minor, the Caesarean drachma tariffed at 1 denarius, often has been considered a coin primarily struck to pay the eastern legions. Caesarea, which commanded the highways across the Taurus into Syria and Armenia, issued didrachmae and drachmae during major Parthian Wars, in 54–65, 112–17, and 163–66 (pl. 11.87). It is, however, more likely that Caesarean drachmae were paid to local contractors supplying the army, rather than as military payrolls. Hoards suggest that Cappadocian drachmae seldom found their way south of the Taurus to Syria and Mesopotamia, and Caesarea struck little or no coinage during the expeditions of Severus Alexander (229–33) or Gordian III (242–44).

Most Anatolian mints struck limited numbers of silver coins during the second half of the second century, in large part because more and more denarii streamed into the peninsula—the Parthian War of Trajan and Hadrian's tours of the Hellenic world glutted many cities of Asia Minor and the Levant with denarii. Philhellene emperors and Roman senators of eastern origin patronized Greek cities, thereby dumping even more denarii into eastern markets. Lycia provides a telling comment about the end of many eastern silver currencies. In 130 the benefactor Opramoas offered 5,000 denarii to the Lycian League to cover the cost of manufacturing a new issue of drachmae, but instead the league opted to distribute the denarii among leading citizens.[16] The Lycians probably decided, as did many other cities and leagues in the second century, that striking their own silver coins was unprofitable with so many denarii on hand.

In Syria, Augustus inherited a less complicated set of silver currencies. The two tetradrachmae in widespread use were those of Tyre (a Levantine version of the Attic stater tariffed at 4 denarii) and the baser coins of Antioch (tariffed at 3 denarii). Silver bullion was imported to Syria from the Aegean world, and as a significant proportion of this specie might have been diverted to the silver-consuming Parthian Empire, many Syrian cities lacked metal to maintain their silver coinages. The Nabataean sheiks east of the Jordan and Arab kings of Oshroene in Upper Mesopotamia minted debased drachmae that passed as fractions of the tetradrachmae of Roman Syria. Trajan in 111–14 and Marcus Aurelius in 166 improved, respectively, the silver coinages of Arabia (pl. 11.93) and Mesopotamia by recoining soon after annexation.[17]

Down to 57/8 Tyre struck her handsome tetradrachma—minted to a consistently high fineness (over 96 percent) and of good weight (14 g). It had been prized as the trade coin of the Levant since the late second century B.C. Aramaic and Greek speakers viewed the city emblems, the obverse portrait of Melqart and the striding eagle on the reverse, as guarantees of "good silver of the Tyrian stamp" (pl. 11.92). Aniconic Jews accepted Tyrian tetradrachmae in payment of temple dues and caravan merchants of Palmyra, Bostra, and Petra popularized the coin from Aela on the Gulf of Aqaba to Charax on the Persian Gulf.[18]

The lighter, more debased tetradrachma of Antioch prevailed in northern Syria. In 30–13 B.C. Antioch resumed minting tetradrachmae, tariffed at 3 denarii, bearing the posthumous portrait of the Seleucid king, Philip Philadelphus (the coin is hereafter referred to as "pseudo-Seleucid"; pl. 7.51). They were accepted in the collection of taxes and used by Roman governors to pay administrative costs and contractors. From Antioch the coins passed eastward into the lands between the Upper Euphrates and Upper Tigris, where they appear in merchant's hoards as late as A.D. 215.[19] Antioch discontinued the imitative Seleucid tetradrachmae by 13 B.C., and in 5 B.C. issued a new series with the portrait of Augustus on the obverse and the city's traditional reverse type of the seated Zeus (pl. 11.88). Later in the same year this series was abandoned in favor of a tetradrachma tariffed at 4 denarii, and, on the reverse, the city's Tyche displaced the seated Zeus (pl. 11.89). The change might have been taken in tandem with the introduction of Roman-style provincial *aes* to impose a single currency in Syria (pl. 12.96–97).[20] The new Augustan tetradrachma failed because the Romans blundered by placing it in competition to two popular staters, the pseudo-Seleucid (which it was intended to replace) and the Tyrian tetradrachma. Although the Tyrian and the new Antiochene tetradrachmae were each tariffed at 4 denarii, outside of northern Syria the Antiochene coin was rejected as overvalued (by nearly 13 percent). The exchange against the pseudo-Seleucid tetradrachma was even less favorable. Four pseudo-Seleucid tetradrachmae, valued at 12 denarii, contained about 19 percent more silver than three of the new pieces, also valued at 12 denarii. Tiberius reduced the fineness (and thereby the silver content), reestablished the tariffing at 3 denarii, and restored Zeus as the reverse type. Claudius improved its fineness, and in 51–54 he struck didrachmae (Table 5.2).

The costs of Nero's war in Armenia (54–66) drove Roman authorities to debase Syrian tetradrachmae to a single standard, thereby netting profits and simplifying tax collection. In 56–57 Antioch debased her tetradrachma and minted large numbers of low-grade didrachmae and drachmae in a great recoinage of north Syrian currency. Tyre halted production of her famed civic-style tetradrachmae forever in 57/8, but Antioch resumed operations in 59/60, providing a uniform silver currency for all of Syria. This new Neronian tetradrachma, sporting on its reverse the striding eagle of Tyre, was tariffed at 4 denarii and overvalued by 25 percent against the denarius (pl. 11.90). The purity and weight standard were again lowered in 65 in response to the denarius's debasement (see Table 5.2). The costs of the Jewish War (66–70) and Roman Civil War (69) resulted in two further debasements. Under Vespasian, mints at Antioch, Laodicea ad Mare, Tyre, and perhaps Seleucia Pieriae, recoined most of Syria's silver currency over the course of the next fifteen years.[21] Domitian and Nerva by stages restored the fineness and weight of the tetradrachma virtually to its earlier Tyrian standard.

Trajan in 98–100 reorganized Syria's currency, adjusting the

*Table 5.2*
Tetradrachmae of Antioch, Syria, 34 B.C.–A.D. 179

| Issue | Weight Grams | Silver Content Fineness | Silver Content Grams | Tariffing Denarii |
|---|---|---|---|---|
| M. Antony, 34–33 B.C. | 15.05 | 81 | 12.19 | 4 |
| Augustus, 30–13 B.C. | 14.20 | 73 | 10.37 | 3 |
| Augustus, 5 B.C. | 14.00 | 73 | 10.22 | 3 |
| Augustus, 5 B.C.–A.D. 12 | 14.75 | 78.5 | 11.58 | 4 |
| Tiberius, 17–37 A.D. | 14.45 | 66 | 9.54 | 3 |
| Caligula, 37–41 | 14.50 | 68 | 9.86 | 3 |
| Claudius, 41–50 | 13.60 | 82.5 | 11.22 | 3 |
| Nero, 56–57 | 14.50 | 63 | 9.14 | 3 |
| Nero, 59–63 | 14.65 | 80 | 11.72 | 4 |
| Nero, 65–68 | 14.35 | 78 | 11.19 | 4 |
| Galba/Otho, 68–69 | 14.50 | 85 | 12.33 | 4 |
| Vespasian, 70–74 | 14.25 | 81 | 11.54 | 4 |
| Domitian, 81–83; 88–92 | 14.45 | 81.5 | 11.78 | 4 |
| Nerva, 96–98 | 14.80 | 89 | 13.17 | 4 |
| Trajan, 98–100; 107–8 | 14.60 | 85 | 12.41 | 4 |
| Hadrian, 108–11 | 14.10 | 65 | 9.17 | 4 |
| Hadrian, 118–20 | 14.00 | 70 | 9.80 | 4 |
| M. Aurelius, 178–79 | 12.65 | 80 | 10.12 | 4 |

*Source:* Based on Walker, *MRSC* I, pp. 68–69 and 133–38 and II, pp. 91–99.

tetradrachma's fineness slightly downward to put it at parity with the denarius. The elegant engraving and manufacture from neat, round flans was a noticeable improvement over the crude, dumpy coins of Nerva. Antioch and Tyre issued didrachmae and tridrachmae (the latter a revival of the old Antiochene stater) bearing beautiful reverse portraits of Heracles, Zeus, and Hera. A second series of exquisite Tyrian coins cut by an artist from Alexandria followed in 107. Trajan's reform required a comprehensive withdrawal and reminting of old money, but late in 107 Trajan placed this splendid currency in jeopardy when he depreciated the denarius, and, as a consequence, in 107–8 Antioch and Tyre undertook, on short notice, another recoinage (pl. 11.91). Trajan's second wave of Syrian tetradrachmae was designed by Roman engravers and filled demand for the next century.

The regional staters sponsored by Roman authorities provided the provinces of Asia and Syria with an adequate supply of coins on a uniform standard. Augustus restored and augmented the money supply of Asia by striking huge numbers of cistophori. Trajan and Hadrian accomplished much the same when Syrian mints, first in 98–100 and again in 107–20, conducted recoinages that apparently satisfied demand for the next century. Tetradrachmae circulated for well over a century, and lives of coins were often extended by overstriking, as in the case of Hadrianic cistophori, or by countermarking, as in the case of Cypriote and Tarsan tetradrachmae (pl. 10.82). Over the long term the imperial government saved expense by its policy of brief peak production followed by occasional modest issues to replenish or expand the money supply.

It is argued that Roman authorities might have deliberately overvalued local drachmae against the denarius (by 5 to 15 percent prior to the Severan age) to restrict their circulation. The imperial government more likely did not regulate the flow of currency or bullion across provinces except in the case of Egypt. Regional patterns of trade still dictated the flow of silver specie; hence, cistophori and drachmae of Amisus and Lycia surface in second-century hoards deposited in Roman Arabia. The regional patterns of trade (and tax obligations to Rome) rather than imperial regulation dictated the use of eastern silver coins. Imperial policy also ensured sound, silver money for the East. The traditional look of eastern silver coins was essential to their acceptance in markets, because provincials viewed ancestral types as guarantees of their money's worth. Roman authorities seldom altered the types of regional staters, and cities and leagues were free to strike silver coins bearing local appeals. Even when imperial engravers designed provincial silver coinages—such as Augustan cistophori or Trajanic drachmae of Crete, Cyrene, Cappadocia, and Arabia—the designs were local.

### *Bronze Currencies of the Roman East*

A medley of bronze fractional coins, much more varied than the silver staters, comprised most of the money circulating in the markets of the East. For over three centuries, Rome was spared the cost of coining and shipping bulky *aes* to the East, as Augustus continued the division of labor seen in the Hellenistic age when royal and civic mints cooperated in supplying a bronze currency. At the former royal mints of Pergamum and Caesarea Mazaca in Asia Minor, Antioch in Syria, and Alexandria in Egypt, Roman governors struck provincial bronze fractions of traditional silver staters for regional circulation. Cities and leagues (*koinon* or *commune*), however, minted the bulk of bronze coins. Although civic coins often bear the imperial portrait, Hellenic cities and Roman colonies included their "ethnic" or name (in the genitive case for Greek legends and in nominative for Latin ones) to denote coins as their legal tender.

Augustus introduced standardized token bronze coins into the Roman East to facilitate the collection of a welter of customs duties and indirect taxes in Asia, Syria, and Egypt. Pergamum and Ephesus minted, under imperial authority, Asian provincial *aes* in 27–15 B.C. The sestertius, dupondius, and semis were struck from brass (orichalcum), while asses were minted from a bronze alloy with a lead content typical of the Greek world (pl. 12.94–95).[22] All denominations were inscribed in Latin, often imperfect, and carry the bare head of Augustus, styled either as CAISAR or AVGVSTVS on the obverse. Reverses show a laurel wreath enclosing either AVGVSTVS or C.A., the latter being the abbreviation of the *commune Asiae* devoted to the imperial cult. These provincial *aes*, which circulated widely in the eastern Mediterranean, provided convenient fractions both for the Asian cistophorus and Roman denarius.

In Syria Roman-style provincial *aes* in two denominations that approximated the Roman dupondius (14.75 g) and as (9.75 g) were introduced, perhaps by the legate P. Quinctilius Varus (7–4 B.C.).[23] Minted from native bronze alloys, the coins seldom weighed the same as their Roman counterparts (pl. 12.96–97). Although the mint of Antioch produced these coins, they bear neither city ethnic nor mintmark. The types were immobilized for the next two centuries (save, from the reign of Trajan, a shift from Latin to Greek in rendering the imperial name); both denominations bear identical, monotonous designs with the imperial portrait and name on the obverse and, on the reverse, a laurel wreath enclosing the abbreviation S.C., borrowed from imperial *aes* as a guarantee of the money's worth. These provincial *aes* were intended for use in the collection of the many surcharges and custom duties imperial agents levied at Syrian caravan towns. The tariff regulations of Palmyra, laid down by Germanicus (16–17) and reissued by the emperor Hadrian (117–38), required imperial customs agents to collect duties levied on the products of the Far Eastern trade in denarii and Italic asses.[24] Syrian provincial *aes* were ready fractions for Antiochene and Tyrian tetradrachmae. The coins, which were minted down to the reign of Severus Alexander (222–35), were popular due to their uniform weight and Roman appearance. The prominent letters S.C. made the coins instantly distinguishable from the mass of civic bronzes circulating in Levantine bazaars. When Antioch was raised to a Roman colony by Elagabalus (218–22), the city incorporated the letters S.C. as part of the reverse design for her own new civic bronze currency based on the assarion.[25]

The history of bronze currency in the Roman East however, largely consists of the individual stories of some 575 Greek cities and Roman colonies that issued *aes* over the course of 300 years. Augustus ingeniously fashioned a token bronze currency in the East as enduring as his Roman one by turning the task over to the cities. Ambitious Greek aristocrats—moved by patriotism and love of honor (*philotimia*) gained from recognition for public largess—provided their cities with bronze currency with the same spirit that inspired them to assume so many other routine tasks. Although such local initiative produced coinages suited to local tastes and needs, the millions of civic bronze coins of the East added up to a successful currency. Their design, weight, and size were stable, and they were readily converted into silver staters or denarii. Civic coins circulated in the markets at a rate even more rapid than imperial ones—attested by the considerable wear that most surviving specimens suffered. The varied denominations offered a remarkably flexible currency, as cities drew upon a diverse body of coins minted by neighbors to augment their own currency. In a great city such as Tarsus her own bronze coins composed most of those in the market, but a modest city such as Aphrodisias depended upon many coins imported from other cities.[26]

Eastern cities deserve credit for two achievements often overlooked. First, they ensured adequate supplies of bronze currency without any central direction, responding surprisingly well to demand for ever more bronze coins from the mid-second century on. The imperial government, so long relieved from providing bronze currency to the East, later proved unequal to a similar challenge once civic mints suspended operations in the 260s and 270s. During the second century A.D., Greek cities also effected with a minimum of difficulty the transition from a bronze currency based on the obol and chalcus to one based on the assarion, the Hellenized version of the Roman as. Inadvertently cities prepared the way for the creation of a single currency by Diocletian (284–305).

There are no reliable means to calculate the volume of civic *aes* issued in each reign; the best indication of their importance is the total number of civic authorities issuing coins in each reign (Figure 5.1). During the Augustan peace almost 150 Greek cities and Roman colonies minted their own bronze coins, but the pace slackened, then dropped and leveled off in the generation after Augustus. The number of mints in operation attained Augustan levels in the reign of Nero (54–68), and thereafter steadily climbed until it peaked in the reign of Septimius Severus (193–211) when nearly 375 cities and leagues were striking their own money. This high fell by some 15 to 20 percent during the reign of Caracalla (211–17), and later activity oscillated between lesser crests and troughs until the abrupt crash of the 260s.[27]

Conditions varied from city to city, and from region to region. Even in the province of Asia, home to the largest number of minting authorities in the Roman world, the volume of civic coinage differed sharply in each region. Cities issuing coins were concentrated in western regions that had been Hellenized under the Roman peace, notably eastern Mysia, Phrygia, Lydia, and Caria. The five great cities of Anatolia, Ephesus, Smyrna, Pergamum, Nicomedia, and Nicaea—homes to ateliers of engravers by the 160s—manufactured huge stocks of bronze currency that served regional needs. Civic mints were scarcer in the Anatolian heartland of Galatia and Cappadocia—a landscape dominated by villages and tribal groups. Admittedly, counting the number of minting authorities offers only an impression of overall output, but it broadly conforms with other evidence

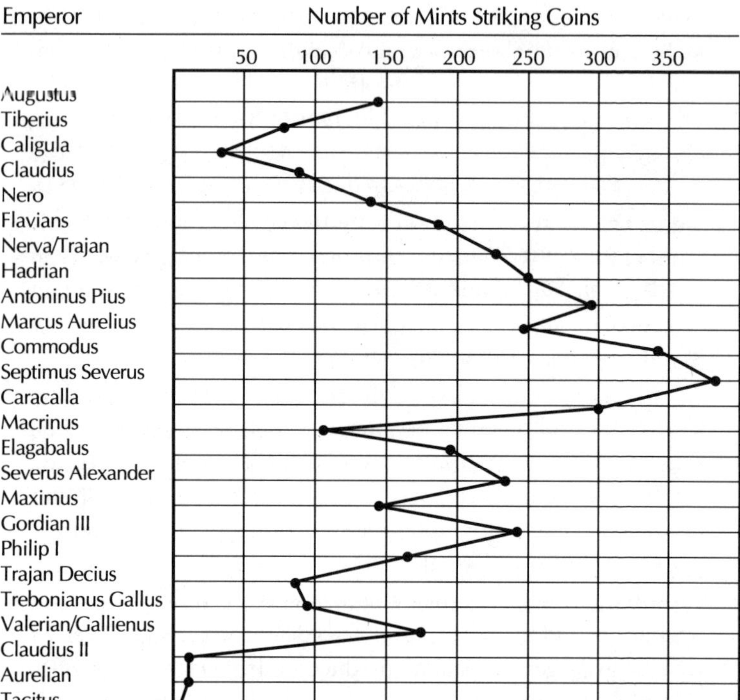


*Figure 5.1* Active Civic Mints, 31 B.C.–A.D. 276.

*Source:* Based on T. B. Jones, "A Numismatic Riddle: The So-called Greek Imperials," *PAPhS* 107 (1963), 310–13 and 334–39. Reprinted by permission of the University of California Press from Harl, *Civic Coins,* p. 107.

suggesting successive surges in the striking of bronze coins during the period 70–235.

The increase in the number of civic mints had a variety of causes. The prosperity of the Roman peace brought a quickening of economic life that fueled demand for more coins. Flavian and Trajanic legates, when they built the strategic highways linking the Bosporus to the Upper Euphrates, prompted cities in Galatia, Lycaonia, and Cappadocia to mint *aes;* the same was true in the Lower Balkans, the southern Levant, and Mesopotamia in the later second and early third centuries.[28] As emperors mounted expeditions against Parthian or Persian foes, Roman forces arriving from Europe dumped denarii on eastern markets, driving up the demand for small change. Visits by emperors, such as those by Hadrian with his large retinue, also stimulated the need for bronze coins. From the Flavian through the Severan ages, cities experienced a boom in public building, and aristocrats sponsored festivals with ever more generous gifts in grain and coin. Large bronze coins, often six- or eight-assaria pieces, were minted for distributions to the crowds on high holidays (pl. 12.100 and pl. 13.101 and 107). Hierapolis, a cult center of Phrygian Apollo, struck a single large issue in 221 just for her Aktia-Pythia celebrations.[29]

Comparison of the relative output by the cities of Smyrna and Stratonicea confirms the main trends of production (Figure 5.2). Smyrna, boasting one-quarter of a million residents, manufactured numerous bronze coins for over three centuries (pl. 12.98–100 and pl. 13.101–103). Output rose steadily in the last decades of the first century and, after a sharp drop, again in the early second century. From the mid-second-century on, it soared to peak in the early Severan age and then dropped to the mid-second century level. In contrast to the general pattern, production skyrocketed in the inflationary post-Severan era (235–60). Stratonicea in western Caria, with less than one-tenth of Smyrna's population, coined intermittently and far more modestly until the late Antonine age when output suddenly leaped to a record high in 198–209 when eight- and six-assaria pieces were commissioned for festivals (pl. 14.107). Thereafter, production plunged. Stratonicea's pattern of minting was repeated at scores of lesser cities which struck the bulk of their coinage in the early Severan age.[30]

As more cities ordered bronze coins, during the great surge in civic minting between the reigns of Marcus Aurelius (161–80) and Gallienus (260–68), engravers organized into ateliers in major cities, minting coins on request or sending dies to more distant customers. By the 160s, four major workshops were mass producing much of the civic bronze currency in western Asia Minor, although a number of smaller operations sprang up to meet the high demand of the early Severan age.[31] Other engravers, such as those who designed the dated *aes* of the cities of Severan Pontus, searched out

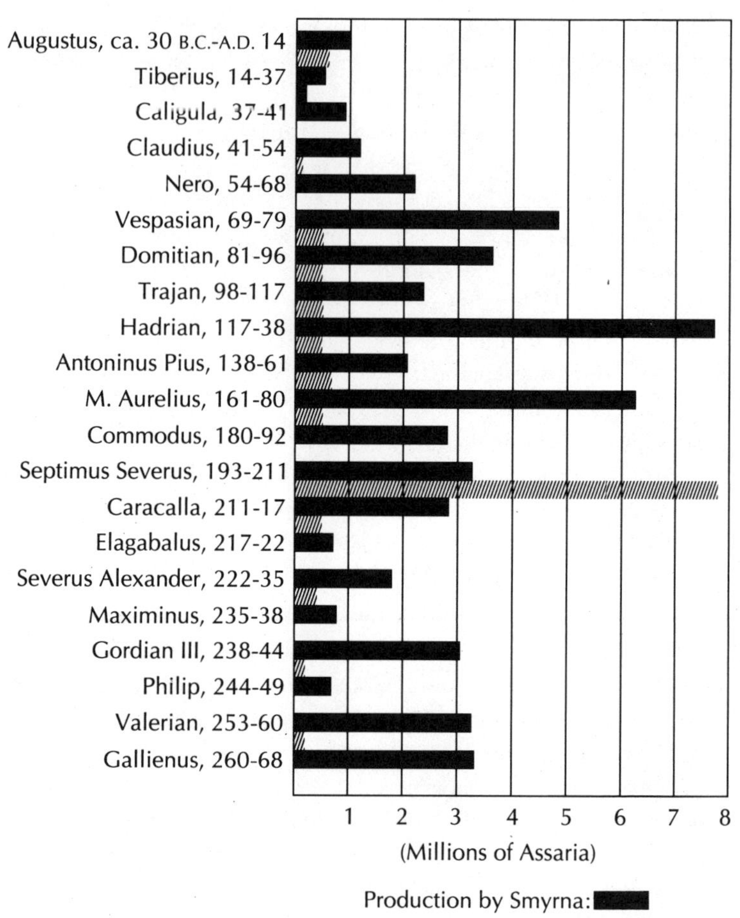


*Figure 5.2* Comparative Production of Coinage—Smyrna, Ionia, and Stratonicea, Caria.

*Source:* Based on D. Klose, *Die Münzprägung von Smyrna in der römischen Kaiserzeit* (Berlin, 1987), pp. 99 and 103–18, and a forthcoming study by K. W. Harl, "The Coinage of Stratonicea in Caria during the Imperial Age."

commissions. Obverse dies, which outlasted the reverse die, frequently were used in combination with many reverse dies to strike coinages for two or more cities. This expedient was adopted because a particular design—a portrait of a member of the imperial family or a personification—was matched to a specific denomination. Thus, engravers at Smyrna used a single obverse die bearing the head of the Roman Senate to mint two-assaria pieces for six different cities in the late 240s and 250s.[32]

Civic *aes,* often struck sporadically and in relatively few numbers, met daily needs because they circulated for a long time within a restricted radius of their place of origin. At times merchants engaged in long-distance trade or Roman soldiers carried a city's coins far from their usual haunts, but this drain had minimal impact upon a region's stock of currency, and exported coins were invariably put to good use. Veterans of Trajan's Parthian War returned to their billets on the Danube with coins of Asian Tabae in their purses, and other veterans of eastern wars in the 240s acquired dupondii and asses of Viminacium, the hub of the middle Danube, which they used at their bases in Pannonia. Peloponnesians serving in Caracalla's expedition of 215–17 spent in the markets of Cilicia, Cyprus, and Syria their native coins which were welcomed to offset shortages brought on by the closure of Antioch's mint by Septimius Severus. Other soldiers and contractors of Caracalla's army brought so many Pontic *aes* to Dura-Europos that the coins still formed the majority of bronze coins in hoards concealed just before the fort fell to Shapur's armies a generation later.[33]

Cities, unlike the imperial government, often revalidated worn *aes* by countermarking, which was more economical than recoining. Cities applied most of the 800 countermarks reported on local *aes*. Approximately 100 of the countermarks are numerical values applied during the inflation of the 260s. The rest date prior to the inflationary spiral (30 B.C.–A.D. 260), but few of these designate a numerical value. Out of the 700 non-numerical countermarks, well over 500 (by a conservative count) denote the emperor, either by his name or portrait (*imago*), or the city, indicated by cult emblems or abbreviations of its ethnic. Six leagues and more than 200 cities (of which nearly two-thirds of the total is located in Anatolia) applied these 500 countmarks for a variety of reasons. Prusias ad Hypium countermarked old coins with the portrait of each new emperor as a gesture of loyalty; Stratonicea stamped eight- and six-assaria pieces with the name of Hecate and the head of Roma for distributions at festivals (pl. 14.107).[34]

By the opening of the second century, cities began replenishing a money supply that was fast wearing out. A large proportion of the bronze currency consisted of dumpy obols and chalci struck in late second and first century B.C. so that moneychangers often demanded fresh coins or discounted worn ones. Vendors and buyers sometimes entered into collusion to buy up bronze coins and set up a private exchange among themselves. In Pergamum, city fathers appealed to the emperor Hadrian to rule against this practice, but most cities reminted their coinage as the best defense against such abuses.[35] During the second century many cities changed their principal denomination from the obol to the assarion. In 30 B.C. few civic bronze denominations, except in colonies, had Roman counterparts (pl. 13.105–6). Whereas the denarius was reckoned only by its quarter, the sestertius, the drachma was divided into two different sets of fractions based on its sixth, the obol, and the obol's eighth, the chalcus ($\frac{1}{48}$ drachma). Since a local drachma was exchanged against the denarius according to its weight and fineness, exchange rates between the denarius and bronze obols or chalci fluctuated widely.

Wherever the Attic drachma was current, a denarius was exchanged for 6 bronze obols. In Thessaly or Asia the drachma was lighter by 25 percent so that 8 obols went to a denarius, giving rise to the common rate of 1 obol to every 2 Roman asses or assaria.[36] Asian cities, when they adopted the assarion, struck multiples of the assarion according to a duodecimal reckoning. Rhodes, down to the reign of Trajan (98–117), minted heavy bronze didrachmae (23–26 g and 36 mm), sporting the radiate head of Helios, which passed as halves of the Asian cistophorus (pl. 13.105). These bronze didrachmae inspired the reckoning of a Rhodian silver drachma at 10 asses so that 3 obols were traded to every 5 assaria.[37] Hence, cities on the southwestern and southern Anatolian littoral such as Aspendus and Side later coined assaria in multiples of five and ten (pl. 18.153–54).

Greek cities retained obol and chalcus both as coins and as units of account and Roman authorities accepted the coins as legal tender. In the early first century, Messenians settled their land taxes in bronze obols and Thessalians paid out obols and chalci for charges levied on the manumission of slaves.[38] Many cities, particularly privileged free cities such as Sparta or the Carian towns Stratonicea and Tabae, long minted obols and chalci with traditional civic designs, introducing multiples such as triobols and diobols. Consequently, a bewildering array of local and Roman bronze denominations passed current in the cities of the East. The currency of Antioch, capital of Syria and third city of the empire, epitomized this diversity. The city issued Roman-style dupondii and asses bearing the prominent S.C. as well as obols and chalci bearing the city ethnic and tutelary divinities. Diobols and obols approximated the size of provincial dupondii and asses, but chalci bore no convenient relationship to the Roman semis or quadrans.[39] In the commercial world painted by the Gospels and Talmudic rabbis, the despised moneychanger alone kept track of the infinite varieties of obol and *issar* (the Aramaic for the as), for the issar might pass at 16, 24, or 30 to the denarius.[40]

By the mid-second century, cities began to adopt the assarion in favor of the obol. Sometimes reform was effected with minimal change to the coins' appearance so that obols and chalci could be revalued in terms of assaria. The island *polis* Chios struck denominations based on the obol and bearing civic emblems without any reference to Rome until the mid-second century.[41] When Chios switched to the assarion, the 3, 2, 1.5, and 1 assaria assumed the sizes and traditional types of their approximate counterparts: the diobol, obol, hexachalcon (three-quarter obol) and hemiobol. Chians went on calling their coins by the old names because the new coins resembled the old money in appearance and buying power. The Chians inscribed the two largest denominations as three- and two-assaria pieces, which were tariffed at par with the earlier diobols and obols. Many other cities effected similar reforms when they recoined large stocks of obsolete or worn obols and chalci—often struck as much as two hundred years earlier—into assaria.[42] They also transformed the size and design of their coins. For over a century, Smyrna minted classic obols, hemiobols, dichalci, and chalci bearing civic types that were direct continuations of her bronze coins since 190 B.C. (pl. 12.98–99). In the Flavian and Trajanic ages, Smyrna introduced the multiples of diobol, triobol, and tetrobol (the respective third, half, and three-quarters of a silver drachma). In the early second century engravers transformed the appearance of Smyrnan coins by adopting the wider, thinner flans of imperial *aes* and adorning larger denominations with imperial portraits. Smyrna applied this new iconography and technology to the assarion and its multiples which were adopted by the reign of Antoninus Pius (138–61).[43] Smyrna was typical of most cities that accommodated the old to new denominations only imperfectly. Although the Asian obol was precisely converted into a two-assaria piece, denominations on either side of the obol were less accurately modified into multiples or fractions of the assarion. If Asian cities had insisted upon precise conversion of each multiple or fraction of obol and chalcus into an equivalent in assaria, their citizens would have been saddled with a conglomeration of unworkable fractions. Instead cities equated old and new denominations with two pragmatic aims in mind: to ensure stable purchasing power, and to provide convenient exchange. Hence, Asian cities commonly minted multiples of six, four, three, and two assaria as handy divisions of the denarius which was widely exchanged at 16 to 18 assaria—the rates decreed at Hadrianic Pergamum (pl. 13.101–103).[44]

Cities adopted a variety of measures to ease the shift from obol to assarion, such as transferring well-known types from old to new denominations and striking new denominations of a size and weight approximating popular older coins. The devices must have worked. At Ephesus in the late second and early third century, commissioners of the markets (*agoranomoi*) cited state-supported bread prices at two and four obols, which Ephesians must have understood as specific denominations of assaria. The word "obol" lived on in Greek slang as the nickname of the prime bronze coin used in daily purchases so that it covered successively the two-assaria piece of the Principate, the Tetrarchic nummus, and the Byzantine follis.[45]

Therefore, for over two centuries the cities of the Roman East produced their own bronze coins, based on either the obol or the assarion, coins that gained public confidence by virtue of their stable appearance, weight, and purchasing power. In a world abounding in local currencies, abuses inevitably arose, but town councils passed ordinances regulating exchange rates and replenished the money supply. Sound bronze currency and fair exchange rates ensured fair pricing in the markets. The longevity of civic bronze coins stands as another tribute to Augustus's statecraft because he mobilized a vast network of sovereign cities to furnish bronze coins, which, for all their diversity, provided a stable, flexible token currency to more than one-half of the residents of the Roman world.

### *The Coinage of Roman Egypt*

In 30 B.C. the prefect of Egypt, the emperor's equestrian deputy, inherited a central mint at Alexandria that struck the currency for the entire province. Augustus extended Ptolemaic monetary regulations into a ban on the import of gold and silver coins so that residents of the Nile Valley used only low-grade silver tetradrachmae and bronze fractions for the next 325 years. Alexandrine coins, often scorned for their shoddy appearance, and imperial monetary regulation have been interpreted as a misdirected experiment in autarky or ruinous exploitation of Egypt. Current scholarly reassessments, however, stress the stimulus of the Roman peace upon the prosperity and rise of population in Egypt. Economic growth owed much to wide use of coins which the Alexandrine mint manufactured in numbers unprecedented in the Ptolemaic age. Tiberius and Claudius pulled off the bold monetary experiment of imposing the first successful fiduciary currency. The Alexandrine tetradrachma and its bronze fractions enjoyed over two centuries of stability and served the needs of the 6 million inhabitants of Egypt who composed 10 percent of the population of the Roman world.

In the Ptolemaic age, Egyptians had grown accustomed to paying taxes and negotiating transactions in grain and heavy copper coins. Gold staters and silver tetradrachmae were reserved for Greek officials and mercenaries because the mint was fed by imported metal—copper was imported from mines of the Sinai and Cyprus, silver from the Aegean world, and gold from Nubia and East Africa. Since Egypt lacked silver, Ptolemy I (305–283 B.C.) lowered the weight of his tetradrachma and his heirs issued bronze coins in lieu of silver fractions. Augustus drastically reduced the supply of specie in Egypt by carrying off royal and sacred treasures accumulated over two centuries and redirecting imported African gold from Alexandria to Rome.

During the first fifty years of Roman rule, Alexandria struck no silver coinage, so that Roman conquerors and Egyptians alike employed the last tetradrachmae of Cleopatra VII (44–30 B.C.), which were nicknamed "silvered Ptolemaic money." At 46 percent fine the Cleopatran tetradrachma contained, on the average, just over one and one-half times the silver in a Roman denarius. Heavy circulation reduced these coins to deplorable condition by 19–20 when Tiberius undertook the first of three reforms that gave to Egypt a new imperial tetradrachma (Table 5.3).[46] The Tiberian tetradrachma, dated by regnal years in the Ptolemaic manner, carried

*Table 5.3*
Standards of Alexandrine Tetradrachmae, Egypt, 73–30 B.C. and A.D. 19–68

| Issue | Weight | Silver Content | | Tariffing |
|---|---|---|---|---|
| | Grams | Fineness | Grams | Denarii |
| Ptolemy XIII, 73–64 B.C. | 13.62 | 91.28 | 12.43 | 3.25 |
| Ptolemy XIII, 60–51 B.C. | 13.52 | 84.86 | 11.47 | 3.00 |
| Cleopatra VII, 44–30 B.C. | 12.66 | 45.72 | 5.79 | 1.50 |
| Tiberius, A.D. 19–20; 31–35 | 13.13 | 30.55 | 4.01 | 1.50 |
| Claudius, 41–48 | 13.04 | 22.94 | 2.99 | 1.00 |
| Nero, 56–57 | 13.19 | 23.15 | 3.05 | 1.00 |
| Nero, 58–67 | 13.22 | 16.54 | 2.19 | 1.00 |

*Source:* Based on Walker, *MRSC*, I, pp. 140–44, and R. A. Hazzard and I. D. Brown, "The Silver Standard of Ptolemaic Coinage," *RN* 6, 26 (1989), 231–39.

distinctive types—the portrait of the emperor on the obverse and on the reverse the portrait of the divine Augustus (pl. 14.108). Egyptians welcomed the new coins as the "silvered money of the Augustus." Alexandria struck the new coins in considerable numbers in 31–35 so that many Cleopatran coins fell prey to recoining, although some better pieces survived as savings in private hands into the 60s.[47] Although he cut the tetradrachma's silver content by nearly 30 percent, Tiberius raised its total weight by 4 percent, maintained its size (25 mm), and held its tariffing at 1.5 denarii. His tetradrachma was manufactured from a silver alloy approaching billon, but it retained the feel and look of its Ptolemaic predecessors. In part, Tiberius slashed fineness because Cleopatran coins had sustained damage that far exceeded, perhaps by several times, modern estimates of a coin's average loss of weight.[48] His debasement also responded to an acute scarcity of silver coins to meet growing fiscal and commercial demands as prosperity returned and more taxes were collected in coin.

Six years later Claudius debased and thereby created the empire's first coin minted in billon (an alloy of bronze mixed with less than 25 percent silver). His tetradrachma was revalued at parity with the denarius to simplify fiscal bookkeeping. The Claudian tetradrachma too retained the Ptolemaic size and weight, but as a billon coin containing but 75 percent of the silver of its Tiberian predecessors this coin doomed the last Cleopatran pieces and Tiberian tetradrachmae to recoinage (pl. 14.109).[49] Tiberius and Claudius, who debased to conserve silver and to net quick profits, created a billon tetradrachma whose official exchange value far exceeded its intrinsic worth and its cost of manufacture. Imperial authorities must have realized how much more lucrative it was to strike overvalued "silver money of the Augustus." At their official rates of exchange against the denarius, Tiberian and Claudian tetradrachmae passed as fiduciary coins overvalued by 27 and 19 percent, respectively.

In 58 Nero ordered a third debasement of the tetradrachma, lowering its silver content by another 28 percent (pl. 14.111). Over the next five years (58–63), the mint of Alexandria recoined the currency of the province on a massive scale. By one estimate as many as 600 million tetradrachma were minted, and over a century later Neronian coins still composed half of the tetradrachmae in circulation.[50] Nero, who applied these lessons in debasement in his recoinage of imperial currency, bestowed on Egypt stable money and prices for the next century. Trajan, Hadrian, and Antoninus Pius struck large numbers of tetradrachmae on the Neronian standard to replenish or increase the money supply.[51] The difference in silver content between Alexandrine tetradrachma and the Roman denarius narrowed as the latter suffered successive debasements. By the accession of Marcus Aurelius, the denarius enjoyed over the tetradrachma an advantage in fineness of only 15 percent. At this tariffing, Marcus Aurelius profitably debased the tetradrachma twice during the Marcomannic War, in 167/8 and 176/7, so that the fineness of his tetradrachma fell by over 28 percent (pl. 14.112). Commodus followed suit so that in 192/3 the tetradrachma contained less than a third of the silver found in the Neronian coin. Marcus Aurelius and Commodus each conducted massive reminting of older coins, possibly on the scale of Nero's recoinage. For the next generation, Alexandria made but modest contributions to the currency in circulation. Severan emperors improved slightly the tetradrachma's fineness. The tetradrachma, coined at its classic weight and size down to A.D. 250, still commanded public trust, because prices after 200 leveled off until the financial crash of the 260s.

Roman authorities also devised bronze fractions for the tetradrachma. Augustus minted two series of bronze denominations on the Ptolemaic standard. In the third century B.C. Ptolemaic kings had substituted bronze coins for the drachma's silver fractions. The silver drachma was divided into several hundred notational units of bronze drachmae so that the obol (1/6 drachma) and chalcus (1/48 drachma) were henceforth minted as large bronze pieces valued in notational copper drachmae at the official rates of exchange. In 30 B.C. the silver drachma was tariffed at 480 copper drachmae so that Augustus struck his first obols and hemiobols marked as pieces of eighty and forty bronze drachmae that passed at par with Ptolemaic obols and hemiobols.[52] Later bronze coins under Augustus and Tiberius carried imperial iconography and, after 3/2 B.C., regnal years, but value marks were discontinued and the weight standard was reduced as the tetradrachma's debasement forced revaluations. By the accession of Claudius (A.D. 41–54), Egyptian bronze currency was in a miserable state, a mix of heavily circulated Ptolemaic, Augustan, and Tiberian coins struck on different weight standards and discounted at the tables of moneychangers.

In 42/3 Claudius created a new fractional currency when he revalued the billon tetradrachma at parity with the denarius. He introduced billon didrachmae and drachmae (pl. 14.110) and a new series of bronze diobols, obols, and hemiobols on a weight standard half that of late Augustan and Tiberian coins, but Claudius soon discontinued the billon fractions. In 64/5 Nero turned the drachma from a bookkeeping unit into a bronze coin subdivided into six obols and forty-eight chalci. The Neronian bronze drachma and its fractions provided subdivisions for the billon tetradrachma that stood in precisely the same relationship as had their silver namesakes to the silver tetradrachma of the Classical age (pl. 14.113–14).[53] The bronze denominations introduced by Nero remained in use for nearly 150 years. Struck on wide, slightly concave flans, bronze drachmae resembled their heavier Ptolemaic predecessors rather than the thicker imperial sestertii. Although scribes had long reckoned in minute fractions of chalci when they drew up tax registers, Egyptians never handled any coin lower than the hemiobol; and, when Marcus Aurelius ceased striking obols and hemiobols, the hemiobol soon fell out of circulation.

In Egypt the coinage endured much more wear than other currencies in the Roman East because the mint of Alexandria replenished or recoined currency at rare intervals. In the reign of Augustus officials already accounted for the loss of weight by charging premiums, dubbed the *prosdiagraphomenon* or "something extra added." In tax receipts from Upper Egypt, fresh tetradrachmae were marked down as "clean" (*hai katharai*), while in other records from Upper Egypt and the Fayyum below-weight tetradrachmae were classified as "dirty" (*rhyparai*) and thus subject to a surcharge of one-sixteenth.[54] In accounts from the reign of Claudius, private individuals reckoned a notational silver drachma at 6.75, 7, or 7.25 obols so that a billon tetradrachma was exchanged against 27, 28, or 29 bronze obols. Officials and bankers employed rates of exchange ranging from 25 to 29 obols to the tetradrachma when they calculated tax obligations.[55] These rates were not official retariffings of the bronze drachma, but rather included premiums of 1 to 5 bronze obols charged whenever billon tetradrachmae fell below full weight. Tax officials also resorted to such rates to exact a penalty for the inconvenience of taking payments in bronze coins rather than tetradrachmae. Tax registers of Karanis reveal that tax collectors in 171–74 employed a tetradrachma of 29 obols when they charged the *symbolikon,* a fee for converting assessments of land taxes reckoned in defunct Ptolemaic money into Roman provincial coins. At Karanis the *symbolikon* was applied automatically to each tax according to a fixed rate. The practice was probably widespread not just in Egypt but throughout the Roman East where many taxes were calculated for centuries in pre-Roman currencies.

Provincials devised sophisticated accounting techniques to cope with the varying currencies and rates of exchange found in many parts of the Roman world. Egyptian papyri reveal what must have been a general practice of accounting in what are called in late medieval Europe "ghost" currencies or money of account. Such money seldom was represented by actual coins. Instead, ghost currencies were a bookkeeping device whereby taxes or prices could be reckoned in consistent accounting units that were then converted into current coins depending on the existing rate of exchange. Officials, bankers, and vendors could reduce to a single set of units tax rates or prices cited in different currencies and according to fluctuating rates of exchange.

As in the rest of the East, the imperial government based its currency and its monetary regulations upon tradition. Since the Roman billon tetradrachma and bronze drachma had the appearance, size, weight, and value of Ptolemaic money, they gained public acceptance as the "money of the Augustus." The success of the billon tetradrachma rested upon four additional measures. First, the tetradrachma was the only legal tender in all obligations, public and private, and it was conveniently exchanged against a set of bronze fractions. Second, the tetradrachma, although it could not be exchanged within Egypt for "full-bodied" gold or silver coins, at least did not circulate in competition with gold or silver coins. There was little risk of an inflationary spiral set off by the dynamics of "Gresham's law" whereby bad money chases out good money. By extending the competence of Ptolemaic monetary regulations, Roman authorities excluded all competitors and upheld the tetradrachma as the premier coin in Egypt. Third, the tetradrachma retained a stable size, weight, and, after the debasement of 58/9, silver content that inspired confidence in its value. Although it lost two-thirds of its silver content by the reforms of Marcus Aurelius and Commodus, the tetradrachma was still of the size and weight of the late Ptolemaic coin and these silver-clad pieces retained their standard, value, and public trust down to the 250s. Confidence was reinforced by a bronze drachma and fractions that remained constant almost as long. Finally, the imperial government strictly regulated production, ensuring adequate supplies of billon currency and stable prices. The imperial government, by judicious regulations, gained public trust so that by A.D. 100 the billon tetradrachma was transformed from an expedient into the venerable ancestral coin. This success was all the more remarkable because it was unprecedented; previous base silver coinages had been despicable expedients.

From their experience with Egyptian coinage emperors learned how to regulate fiduciary currencies. They also learned the potential savings from minting billon coins tariffed far above their intrinsic value. In time, the billon tetradrachma proved its worth even further. Given its overvaluation, the tetradrachma was unaffected by oscillating debasements and reforms afflicting the denarius and it was minted on the Neronian standard until 167/8, and this longevity must have saved the costs of periodic recoinages. Tiberius recoined after reaping the full benefit of fifty years of hard use of the Cleopatran tetradrachmae. Claudius had to remint because he revalued the tetradrachma and his coinage did not last a generation before it too fell victim to a recoinage. On the other hand, Nero, Marcus Aurelius, and Commodus each conducted great recoinages whereby the mint of Alexandria churned out tens of millions of tetradrachmae that circulated for a century.

The impressive achievement of provincial coinage in Egypt profoundly influenced Roman monetary thinking. In the third century, emperors could look to Egypt for a successful case of a billon fiduciary coinage and stable prices. It was as if the emperor had by accident stumbled through an open door into the closed conditions of a laboratory where he could experiment freely in manipulating and debasing coinage. Unfortunately, emperors regarded this laboratory more as a theater, so that regulating Egyptian currency was but a dress rehearsal for a grander performance, the debasement of the Augustan currency. The success of Egyptian billon currency, however, rested upon conditions peculiar to the Nile Valley, and later emperors failed to discern how conditions in the Egyptian laboratory differed from those in the wider world of the Roman Empire.

# Six

# The Great Debasement and Reform, A.D. 193–305

Cassius Dio, writing in the late Severan age, marked the death of Marcus Aurelius (161–80) as the bleak dawn of a troubled era, warning his readers that "our history now descends from a kingdom of gold to one of iron and rust, as did the affairs of the Romans of that day."[1] The Severan emperors (193–235), however, restored much of Rome's splendor, and they paid in coins exchanged according to rates that Augustus had fixed over two centuries earlier. Cassius Dio thus could write that "I here use the name aureus, according to Roman practice, for the gold coin worth twenty-five denarii."[2] Coins retained their values, even though rising costs of war drove emperors to debase the denarius in the half-century after the death of Marcus Aurelius. Severus Alexander (222–35) minted aurei of pure gold, although at 50 to the Roman pound, so that they were 10 percent lighter than Augustan coins. The denarius had fared less well. It contained only 40 percent of the silver content of the Augustan denarius, but it still traded against aureus and *aes* at its traditional rates. Prices were double or triple those of the early second century, but inflation probably rose at a rate proportional to the lowering of the silver content of the denarius so that in 235 the public still had confidence in the worth of its money.

Although the silver content of the denarius had steadily declined since the death of Marcus Aurelius, it was not until 235 that the denarius exhibited the first signs of serious stress from debasement. During the next twenty years emperors funded frontier and civil wars by the time-honored expedient of debasement, quickly reducing the denarius to a miserable billon coinage by 253. Emperors, however, did not net the savings and buying power they might have anticipated based upon their experience with billon currency in Egypt. Instead, debasement destroyed public confidence; panic in turn fueled unprecedented inflationary spirals. Emperors, while engaged in simultaneous wars on the eastern and northern frontiers, blundered into fiscal and economic crises that undermined not just the Roman peace, but the very foundations of classical civilization.

### *Debasement, Inflation, and Collapse, 180–274*

The Parthian and German wars drove Marcus Aurelius to lower the fineness of the denarius (79 to 80 percent), and Commodus (180–92) financed his profligacy with more debasements as he slashed by one-twelfth the average weight of the denarius (3.1 g), which was henceforth minted at 104 to the Roman pound (Table 6.1).[3] Septimius Severus (193–211) and Caracalla (211–17) further alloyed the denarius to pay for their wars and grandiose buildings. Severan increases in military pay suggest that debasement was intended to expand the available denarii by as much as one-third to one-half. Although each debasement drove up wages and prices, the lag in these rises enabled the imperial government to net surplus revenues exceeding the short-term effects of inflation. During war, emperors found it dangerous not to debase. Septimius Severus bluntly advised his sons "to enrich the soldiers and despise the rest," and he implemented his axiom by debasing the denarius and raising salaries.[4] Emperors who improved the purity of the denarius, notably Pertinax in 193, Macrinus in 217, or the senatorial teams of 238, found themselves outbid for the loyalties of the army, and so they

*Table 6.1*
Debasement of the Denarius, 161–241

| Year | Emperor | Weight | Silver Content | |
|---|---|---|---|---|
| | | Grams | Fineness | Grams |
| 148–61 | Antoninus Pius | 3.21 | 83.60 | 2.68 |
| 161–68 | Marcus Aurelius | 3.23 | 79.79 | 2.58 |
| 168–70 | Marcus Aurelius | 3.24 | 82.13 | 2.66 |
| 170–80 | Marcus Aurelius | 3.26 | 79.07 | 2.58 |
| 180–85 | Commodus | 3.07 | 76.18 | 2.34 |
| 186 | Commodus | 2.98 | 74.25 | 2.21 |
| 193 | Pertinax | 3.16 | 87.11 | 2.75 |
| 193 | Didius Julianus | 2.95 | 81.33 | 2.40 |
| 193–94 | Septimius Severus | 3.14 | 78.42 | 2.46 |
| 194–96 | Septimius Severus | 3.07 | 64.58 | 1.98 |
| 196–211 | Septimius Severus | 3.22 | 56.28 | 1.81 |
| 212 | Caracalla | 3.23 | 51.32 | 1.66 |
| 217–18 | Marcinus | 3.15 | 57.85 | 1.82 |
| 219 | Elagabalus | 3.05 | 46.39 | 1.41 |
| 222–28 | Severus Alexander | 3.00 | 43.03 | 1.29 |
| 229–30 | Severus Alexander | 3.24 | 45.11 | 1.46 |
| 231–35 | Severus Alexander | 2.94 | 50.56 | 1.49 |
| 236–38 | Maximinus I | 3.07 | 46.00 | 1.41 |
| 238 | Gordian I & II | 2.77 | 62.80 | 1.74 |
| 238 | Pupienus & Balbinus | 2.80 | 55.00 | 1.54 |
| 241 | Gordian III | 3.03 | 48.11 | 1.46 |

*Source:* Based on Walker, *MRSC* II, pp. 33–45, and III, pp. 1–39.

went down in ignominious defeat. Antonine and Severan emperors eluded the consequences of their debasements and attendant inflation because they inherited a public trust of coins bred from two centuries of stable prices and rates of exchange. Since Severan denarii weighed and looked in their iconography much like those coined since 64, they were accepted at customary rates of exchange against aurei and base metal fractions.[5] The imperial government thus, at least initially, applied the important lesson gained from its manipulation of Egyptian billon currency: maintaining the traditional appearance and reasonable rates of exchange for low-grade silver or billon coins.

In 213, Caracalla recalled and reminted aurei and denarii to pay for huge increases in military salaries and costs of an impending Parthian war. He reduced the fineness of his denarius to 50 percent and lowered the standard of the aureus from 45 to 50 to the Roman pound (pl. 15.115). His measures taxed public patience, but he took a more fateful step in 215 when he introduced the antoninianus (pl. 15.118). The new denomination, bearing a distinctive radiate obverse portrait, circulated as the double of the denarius even though it was only one and one-half times its weight. Since an antoninianus had only 80 percent of the silver content of 2 denarii, widespread hoarding of denarii jeopardized prices and exchange rates. Elagabalus (218–22), grasping the danger of placing the denarius in competiton with its debased double, abandoned the antoninianus, but he retained the debased standards for the aureus and denarius. Severus Alexander restored the tarnished reputation of imperial money by improving the denarius and striking the first substantial numbers of brass sestertii and copper asses in a generation. Production of *aes* had been curtailed during the great recoinages of denarii between 161 and 215. Although late Severan *aes* fall far short of the incomparable beauty of the sestertii of Trajan, Hadrian, and Antoninus Pius; they were well engraved, struck on flans of traditional size and weight, and, as money, the equal of their more elegant ancestors. In the East, civic mints produced tremendous numbers of assaria that held their relative purchasing power as late as 235 (pl. 12.100 and pl. 13.101–5 and 107). In the Roman West grain prices were quoted at 2 to 4 sestertii to the modius, while market commissioners of Ephesus priced loaves of bread by the bronze obol, the equivalent of 2 assaria.[6]

Emperors after 235 debased the silver currency and raised taxes during what they perceived to be a temporary crisis, expecting windfalls of specie from victory, but war had changed from profitable conquest to a grim defense. The Sassanid shahs Ardashir (224–40) and Shapur I (240–70) repeatedly overran and pillaged Mesopotamia, Syria, and Asia Minor, while Saxons, Franks, Alamanni, and Goths surged over northern frontiers. Frontier wars reduced the flow of bullion to the imperial mint, and long-distance trade with the Far East and Africa languished; hence the Axumite kings turned East African gold into their own fractional staters rather than export it to the Roman world. During the 250s and 260s Goths devastated Dacia and Dalmatia and Moors raided Spain, thereby disrupting mining operations. Existing stocks of specie in the Roman world contracted. In 260, Shah Shapur forced the surrender of Valerian and seized hundreds of thousands of antoniniani which his western mints recoined into debased dirhems.[7] German raiders carried off so much gold and silver plate that they changed their taste in coins, preferring aurei over alloyed antoniniani and silver denarii.[8]

Humiliating payments of subsidies to Germanic and Persian foes drained off aurei that seldom returned to the Roman world. In 244 Philip purchased a peace from Shah Shapur to the tune of 500,000 aurei (10,000 pounds of gold), which Sassanid mints recoined into dinars.[9] In the 260s and early 270s the rebel Gallo-Roman emperors paid aurei to Thuringian mercenaries, who carried them back and interred the gold coins in graves in their homeland between the Weser and Vistula.[10] Large sums of money were lost because Roman owners failed to recover their savings in troubled times. Great caches of newly minted antoniniani dispatched as payrolls from Rome were never reclaimed by legionaries who fell fighting on the Lower Danube in the early 250s.[11]

The Civil War of 238 proved a downward step in the history of Roman currency. The senatorial candidates—the Gordiani in Africa and Pupienus and Balbinus at Rome—revived the antoninianus (pl. 15.119), which was struck in massive numbers. Their antoniniani, slightly lighter (4.8 g) and more debased (just under 50 percent fine) than those of Caracalla, contained less than 70 percent of the silver in 2 denarii (Table 6.2). Gordian III (238–44) abandoned the denarius in favor of the antoninianus, and thereby committed the imperial government to a fiduciary currency. As successive debasements between 242 and 253 reduced the antoninianus to a billon coin, Antonine and Severan denarii disappeared into hoards or the melting pot.[12] Each decline in the size and weight of the antoninianus was matched by revisions in its rate of exchange against gold and base metal denominations. In the markets, the population learned to quote prices in terms of notational denarii or

*Table 6.2*
Debasement of the Antoninianus, 215–74

| | | Weight | Silver Content | |
|---|---|---|---|---|
| Year | Emperor | Grams | Fineness | Grams |
| 215 | Caracalla | 5.09 | 52.15 | 2.65 |
| 238 | Balbinus & Pupienus | 4.79 | 49.57 | 2.37 |
| 238 | Gordian III | 4.50 | 48.77 | 2.19 |
| 241 | Gordian III | 4.43 | 44.68 | 1.98 |
| 243 | Gordian III | 4.16 | 41.63 | 1.73 |
| 244 | Philip I | 4.12 | 43.12 | 1.78 |
| 248 | Philip I | 4.12 | 47.07 | 1.94 |
| 250 | Trajan Decius | 3.97 | 41.12 | 1.63 |
| 251 | Trebonianus Gallus | 3.46 | 35.94 | 1.24 |
| 253 | Aemilian | 3.53 | 35.50 | 1.25 |
| 253 | Valerian | 3.10 | 21.86 | 0.68 |
| 255–57 | Valerian | 3.00 | 17.18 | 0.52 |
| 259–60 | Valerian | 3.07 | 19.00 | 0.58 |
| 260–61 | Gallienus | 3.03 | 17.80 | 0.54 |
| 262 | | 2.97 | 15.40 | 0.46 |
| to | Gallienus | 2.75 | 13.05 | 0.36 |
| 266 | | 2.81 | 8.70 | 0.24 |
| 267 | Gallienus | 2.64 | 6.00 | 0.16 |
| 268 | "Postumus"* | 2.69 | 5.60 | 0.15 |
| 268 | Claudius II | 2.95 | 3.16 | 0.09 |
| 269 | Claudius II | 2.60 | 1.71 | 0.04 |
| 270 | Claudius II | 3.39 | 2.85 | 0.10 |
| 270 | Quintillus | 2.50 | 2.62 | 0.07 |
| 270 | Aurelian | 3.15 | 2.64 | 0.08 |
| 274 | Aurelian | 3.88 | 5.00 | 0.19 |

*Revolt of Aureolus in name of Postumus.

*Source:* Based on Walker, *MRSC* III, pp. 36–51, for antoniniani of 215–53. Issues of Valerian in 253–57 from the mint of Rome are based on P. Tyler, *The Persian Wars of the 3rd Century* A.D. *and Roman Imperial Policy* A.D. *253–268* (Wiesbaden, 1975), Appendix 2. Issues of 259–68 from the mint of Mediolanum (Milan) are based on analysis of specimens in Gibraltar hoard by E. Besly and R. Bland, *The Cunetio Treasure: Roman Coinage of the Third Century* A.D. (London, 1983), p. 37. Issues of Claudius II and Quintillus in 268–70 from the mint of Rome are based on L. H. Cope, "The Nadir of the Imperial Antoninianus in the Reign of Claudius II Gothicus, A.D. 268–70," *NC* 7, 9 (1969), 150–53, and C. E. King, "Denarii and Quinarii, A.D. 253–295," in *SNREHS*, pp. 84–85. Issues of 271–93 from the mint of Rome are based on L. H. Cope, "Roman Imperial Silver Alloy Standards: The Evidence," *NC* 7, 7 (1967), 129–30, and King, in *SNREHS*, p. 89.

*denarii communes* (d.c., or "common denarii") which could be converted into antoniniani at the current rate. Since new coins entered circulation in payrolls, the size of military forces determined the structure of a region's currency. The legions concentrated in Illyricum against the Gothic threat were paid mostly in new antoniniani—antoniniani of 238–51 total two-thirds of the silver coins from hoards concealed in military contexts. At the same time, hoards in the Rhineland, a frontier of lesser priority, show the reverse mix of two-thirds denarii and only one-third antoniniani. In the remoter regions, many denarii and purer antoniniani escaped reminting until these coins vanished from hoards shortly after 250.[13]

Trajan Decius (249–51) reduced the antoninianus to a piece of 4 g, 40 percent fine, or roughly the equivalent of the Severan denarius (pl. 15.120). Surviving denarii were restruck as antoniniani so that the antoninianus was likely revalued at 25 to the aureus. This recoinage removed from circulation most silver coins, even debased antoniniani, issued prior to 250. Trajan Decius, however, could not slow the spiraling descent of the antoninianus. Trebonianus Gallus (251–35) slashed the fineness and weight of his coin, which fell to half the silver content of its precursor in 238 and could not even compete with antoniniani of the previous reign. Consequently, coins of Trajan Decius promptly disappeared from circulation. Valerian (253–60) degraded the antoninianus to a billon piece approximating the weight and size, but not the fineness, of a Severan denarius. In just eight years his son Gallienus (260–68) reduced this coin to a miserable specimen with scarcely one-tenth the silver content of the late Severan denarius (pl. 15.121). Yet, even this coin was profitable to debase. Imperial currency hit its nadir in the opening months of the reign of Claudius II Gothicus (268–70) who halved the silver content of the antoninianus (2 percent fine, 2.6 g). The decisive victory over the Goths at Naissus and the recovery of Spain enabled Claudius II to raise the standard (3 percent fine, 3 g)—a trivial improvement but the first in over fifty years.

For two decades, each emperor from Trajan Decius to Claudius II lowered the purity of his antoninianus and thereby condemned the money of his predecessor to the melting pot. Hoards set aside after 251 are comprised almost exclusively of antoniniani of a single standard minted over the span of a few years. The Roman world was treated to the spectacle of imperial mints annually churning out hundreds of millions of silver-clad antoniniani by recycling coins but a few years old. Such rapid recoinages removed older coins from circulation and destroyed public confidence in imperial money by 260. The success of imperial currency had rested on public faith, but the debasements of the 250s and 260s destroyed this faith once new coins ceased to resemble familiar old denominations. Trajan Decius perhaps hoped to avert this loss of faith by striking as "restored coins" commemorative antoniniani in the names of deified emperors (pl. 15.120). Antoniniani from the reign of Trajan Decius were noticeably inferior in manufacture; their shoddy appearance and light feel would have dismayed any who recalled the denominations of less than a generation earlier. Valerian sought to conceal the extent of his debasements by manufacturing antoniniani from bronze cores clad with a silver-enriched coating, and debasements by Gallienus turned the silver surface into a thin wash which, given its poor manufacture, often rubbed off in circulation.[14] Many coins lost their coating as the population grew expert in extracting the silvered veneer, which was sold as bullion, and in disgorging the coins at whatever they could fetch. The abuse plagued billon coins for the next century, generating a spate of legal prohibitions and giving a dark twist to the "sacred money" advertised on the reverse of so many silver-clad antoniniani.

The fate of the aureus paralleled that of the silver coinage.[15] Although Caracalla had lowered the weight of the aureus by one-tenth, he maintained its purity (99.5 percent fine; pl. 15.115). Macrinus (217–18) restored the aureus to its Neronian weight, but Elagabalus and Severus Alexander returned to Caracalla's standard. Severus Alexander reminted many older aurei, thereby popularizing the standard of 50 aurei to the pound, which emperors as late as Diocletian considered appropriate for ceremonial aurei. The aureus, which had been renowned for its consistent purity and weight for 150 years, lost its international reputation and disappeared from the Far Eastern trade soon after Caracalla lowered its weight.

With each debasement of the antoninianus the weight standard of the aureus was lowered to preserve official rates of exchange, but its purity was unchanged because imperial largess required impeccably pure gold coins. Many aurei of Maximinus (235–38) left the mint averaging only 52 or 54 to the pound; Pupienus and Balbinus in 238 minted lighter aurei ranging from 55 to 60 to the pound; and Gordian III fixed his aureus at 65 to the pound, cutting the Severan standard by almost 25 percent. Within the next decade (240–50) the aureus was steadily reduced until it reached the standard of 90 to the Roman pound or one-half the weight of the Neronian coin—a decline of almost 45 percent since 235. The rapidly shrinking aureus of the 230s and 240s resulted in widely fluctuating rates of exchange between aureus and antoniniani that hampered the simplest of transactions. In Upper Egypt, light aurei of Philip (244–49) were trading at perhaps 125 or 175 Alexandrine drachmae, suggesting a local tariffing equivalent to 30 to 45 notational denarii.[16] Trajan Decius might have doubled the notational value of his aureus to 50 denarii so that 25 antoniniani were officially exchanged to the aureus. Romans coped with a baffling array of aurei of different values by calling them after their imperial portrait so that aurei dubbed *philippei* or *valeriani* were quickly recognized and exchanged at separate rates.[17]

Trebonianus Gallus took the next step: he adulterated the aureus by cutting its purity from 99 to 97 percent (pl. 15.116), but he also introduced a heavy aureus, minted at 55 to the pound, which could circulate at par with worn Severan aurei still in use. This heavy aureus, which bears the radiate imperial portrait, must have passed as a double aureus. Later insurgent emperors in Gaul and in the East adopted versions of Gallus's heavy aureus as the standard of their principal gold denomination (although the fineness of these aurei is uncertain).[18] Valerian and Gallienus too minted heavy and light aurei, along with fractional pieces, but they lowered the weight standards so rapidly that their coins still defy classification (pl. 15.117). Their aurei averaged between 93 and 95 percent fine; multiples were usually slightly less pure and fractional pieces dipped as low as 80 percent fine. Claudius II fixed his aureus at 60 to the pound and restored its classic purity (99 percent fine).

The gold currency played a decidedly subordinate role, but emperors needed impressive gold coins as donatives to their soldiers, and hence they issued two or more parallel series of aurei on different standards—a practice that led to the minting of the ceremonial multiples of the solidus in the fourth century. The standards (at 50, 60, or 70 to the Roman pound) did not bear convenient relationships to each other, but aurei were distributed in bags weighing divisions or increments of the pound. Aurei, however, surely circulated as coins, for a Talmudic source, dating from the 260s or early 270s, reports an aureus reckoned at 1,000 denarii.[19] But aurei of such different weight and fineness could not provide an anchor in monetary chaos. Although Severan jurists began recalculating legal fines in aurei, they quickly abandoned the task and, after 235, Romans instead adopted the more pragmatic expression of aurei in terms of so many sestertii or denarii.[20] Throughout the third century, fiscal obligations and prices continued to be cited in denarius, sestertius, or drachma rather than in accounting units based on the aureus.

The demise of the splendid Augustan token base metal currency had far greater consequences, for the widespread use of *aes* stood behind the unprecedented monetization of the Roman economy. In 235 Romans could depend on the purchasing power of their bronze coins, but within fifteen years debasement and inflation ruined the token bronze coins so vital in daily transactions and taxation. The sestertius, dupondius, and as each suffered successive reductions in weight under Maximinus and Gordian III, although each retained the wide flans, types, and reassuring letters S.C. so important in denoting its worth. Philip, however, abandoned the delicate Augustan balance of denominations in orichalcum and copper. Thereafter, bronze denominations were debased with as much as 20 to 25 percent lead and they dropped to about 75 percent of their Severan weight by 260, that is, from a standard of 28 to 38 to the Roman pound. Gallic and British provincials short of fractional *aes* put to use heavily worn pieces of Antonine, Flavian, and even Neronian vintage.[21] As imperial mints flooded markets with debased antoniniani, output of sestertii was expanded at the expense of fractions. Dupondii and asses were in short supply from the 240s so that residents of cities such as Carthage improvised fractions by cutting sestertii into halves.[22]

Many sestertii testify to their hasty mass production. Mint workers cast flans linked together in long bars and they clipped out each flan without trimming its edges. Often sloppy in positioning the dies and hammering, mint workers struck inaccurately or double-struck designs, cracking flans when they employed worn dies. In the reign of Philip they mismatched obverse and reverse dies, producing a bewildering array of "mules." Regulation of weights suffered as officials were satisfied with sestertii that were struck *al marco,* or so many specimens to the pound without scrutiny of each specimen. Sestertii, tariffed at 8 to the antoninianus traded at higher rates in markets by 250. Trajan Decius introduced a double sestertius, sporting the radiate imperial portrait, and revalued upward older heavy *aes* in circulation to double their value (pl. 15.126).

Imperial mints tried to meet demand for *aes* during the most severe inflation of the 260s. Gallienus coined sestertii and asses, including a series in 262 that celebrated the Senate and spirit of Roman people and harkened to the fine money of Augustan days. His Gallo-Roman rival Postumus (260–69) produced superior sestertii for the northwestern provinces (pl. 16.127).[23] Bronze coins, however, ceased to be small change, but instead became a store of wealth. Bronze denominations became so prized that at excavated sites dating from the 250s they were replaced by billon antoniniani as the coins most commonly lost. The composition of hoards changed; henceforth, large numbers of sestertii (or civic *aes* in the East) were set aside as a hedge against inflation. Such hoards of *aes,* which total over one-fifth of those from the third century, include few middle-sized and virtually no fractional pieces.[24] Few Romans willingly parted with their bronze coins down to the reform of Diocletian, thereby ensuring that the sestertius survived as a unit of accounting into the fourth century. Imperial mints after 270 found token bronze coins so costly to produce that they only occasionally coined sestertii and middle-sized *aes* as quaint pieces for donatives.

The disappearance of the token bronze currency removed an essential pillar in the edifice of the Augustan currency. For nearly a century (274–371), emperors reformed imperial currency premised upon billon denominations, but their efforts were doomed to failure as long as they neglected to provide adequate token bronze money. They did not resume minting true bronze coinage until the 370s, but it was still over a century later before Anastasius in 498–512 created the second successful token bronze currency.

### *The Demise of Provincial and Civic Coinages*

Debasement of the imperial currency also spelled the demise of local currencies of the East, but inflation affected at varying rates each of the three major currencies—provincial silver staters, civic bronze coins, and the money of Egypt.

Ever since the Parthian War of Marcus Aurelius (161–66) the fortunes of regional staters had been directly bound to the denarius. Millions of denarii or, after 238, antoniniani arrived with each imperial expedition, disrupting exchange rates and money markets in the East. On each occasion, provincial authorities faced a choice of debasing staters at a rate greater than that of the denarius or suspending the striking of staters whose fineness doomed them to the melting pot. Asian and Syrian mints thus had suspended coining in the face of war debts and debasements of the denarius by Marcus Aurelius and Commodus. The East, by the reign of Septimius Severus, was starved of silver as its silver money was fast wearing out from a century of heavy use. In the tradition of Trajan and Hadrian, Septimius Severus restored silver staters by improving standards and carefully regulating the silver content of local drachmae at 90 percent of that of the denarius. The size of his cistophoric coinage is difficult to judge given its poor survival rate, but it is significant that Ephesus resumed production in 198, after a lull of seventy years. Severan cistophori, debased by over 25 percent, resembled didrachmae rather than tetradrachmae due to their thick fabric, small size, and light weight. Mints in Cappadocia and Syria effected substantial recoinages intended to supply needs for the next two generations (Table 6.3).[25] Caesarea discontinued didrachmae in favor of finer drachmae and tridrachmae that were overvalued against the denarius by 10 percent (pl. 17.137). Tarsus

*Table 6.3*
Debasement of Syrian Tetradrachma, 178–254

| | | Weight | Silver Content | |
|---|---|---|---|---|
| Year | Emperor | Grams | Fineness | Grams |
| 178–79 | Marcus Aurelius | 12.66 | 80.00 | 10.13 |
| 193–94 | Pescennius Niger | 11.56 | 58.00 | 6.70 |
| 202–12 | Septimius Severus: | | | |
| | Antioch | 13.32 | 59.81 | 7.97 |
| | Laodicea ad Mare | 13.49 | 63.03 | 8.50 |
| | Tyre | 14.34 | 62.00 | 8.89 |
| 213–17 | Caracalla | 12.94 | 35.59 | 4.61 |
| 217–18 | Macrinus | 12.94 | 29.23 | 3.78 |
| 218–19 | Elagabalus | 12.64 | 19.40 | 2.45 |
| 220–22 | Elagabalus | 13.10 | 32.21 | 4.22 |
| 238–39 | Gordian III | 12.27 | 35.77 | 4.39 |
| 240 | Gordian III | 12.63 | 24.30 | 3.07 |
| 244–45 | Philip I | 11.71 | 23.63 | 2.77 |
| 246 | Philip I | 11.90 | 27.31 | 3.25 |
| 247–48 | Philip I | 12.08 | 18.78 | 2.27 |
| 249 | Philip I | 11.98 | 16.58 | 1.99 |
| 249–51 | Trajan Decius | 11.99 | 14.99 | 1.80 |
| 251–53 | Trebonianus Gallus | 12.06 | 10.77 | 1.30 |
| 253–54 | Uranius Antoninus | 12.90 | 14.50 | 1.87 |
| 254 | Uranius Antoninus | 8.31 | 93.60 | 7.78 |

*Source:* Based on Walker, *MRSC* II, pp. 91–97, and III, pp. 83–96, and H. R. Baldus, MON*(eta)* URB(is) ANTIOXIA: *Rom und Antiochia als Prägestätten syrischer Tetradrachmen des Philippus Arabs* (Frankfurt/Main, 1969), pp. 40–42.

and Seleucia followed with similar issues in Cilicia. In 202 Antioch, joined by Laodicea ad Mare in 205 and Tyre in 208, undertook a major recoinage of Syrian silver currency that spanned a decade (202–13).[26] These incarnations of the Tyrian tetradrachma compared favorably with those of Trajan or Hadrian. As in Trajan's day, Tyre minted the heaviest and purest coins (62 percent fine and 14.35 g) and Antioch the most debased (60 percent fine and 13.35 g), but the average standard was regulated so that tetradrachmae, at the tariffing of 4 denarii, were overvalued by 7 to 12 percent. Syrians accepted these Severan staters as "fine silver of the Tyrian stamp."

The debasement by Caracalla transformed the currency in the East forever. He had to remint older staters because they posed a challenge to his base denarii, which were flooding eastern markets as Roman forces massed against Parthia. Caracalla also profited by paying contractors supplying his army in debased tetradrachmae. Asian mints could not resume striking cistophori even on a baser standard; most older cistophori were either reminted into denarii or turned into plate. Caesarea resurrected the didrachma (40 percent fine), which passed as an equivalent to the antoninianus. Tarsus struck base didrachmae and tridrachmae, and countermarked and reissued silver coins of Trajan and Hadrian, but the latter coins, given their purity, could not have circulated long.[27] In 214 twenty-five cities in the Syrian cities withdrew and reminted local silver of every description into lighter tetradrachmae containing half the previous silver content (pl. 16.135). Macrinus and Elagabalus cut the standard even further. Within six years (214–19), the mints opened by Caracalla replaced Syrian silver currency so rapidly that Elagabalus closed the auxiliary mints and again centered production at Antioch.[28] Hoards reveal the thoroughness of reminting. In 212, on the eve of the recoinage, imitative Seleucid coins of Augustan date formed the bulk of a merchant's hoard found near Nineveh, but less than a decade later hoards from the Roman Levant contained overwhelmingly base tetradrachmae minted after 213.[29] So drastic a recoinage so soon after the renewal by Septimius Severus undermined public faith. Caracalla's tetradrachmae, although bearing the striding eagle, must not have been accepted as "good silver of the Tyrian stamp," because the expression vanished from common parlance.

The Caesarean didrachma and Syrian tetradrachma of Caracalla circulated for the next twenty years as the sole survivors of once numerous provincial staters. At the accession of Gordian III (238–44), Caesarea and Antioch resumed minting (pl. 17.137). In fineness, Caesarean drachmae and tridrachmae stood at parity with the denarius, whereas Antiochene tetradrachmae were on the Caracallan standard (35 percent fine). With the outbreak of the Persian War (240–44), Caesarea cut standards and soon halted production forever. Antioch coined tetradrachmae for a decade longer because the coins were entrenched in tax collection and were convenient doubles of the antoninianus. Gordian III reorganized the mint into workshops, and annual production henceforth soared in the tens of millions of tetradrachmae. Caesarea and Antioch both have been estimated to have struck for Gordian III staters to the tune of 45 to 50 million denarii in value, but Antioch simultaneously struck five times this value, 235 million denarii, in antoniniani.[30] Within twelve years (240–53), the tetradrachma lost over 70 percent of its silver content, tumbling to the level of an overvalued billon coin only 11 percent fine (see Table 6.3). These later tetradrachmae carry on the reverse, besides the striding eagle, the additional guarantee of the letters S.C.—long familiar from Antioch's *aes*. Philip in 246 (pl. 16.136) and the usurper Uranius Antoninus of Emesa (253–54) each briefly improved the fineness of the tetradrachma, but Shapur ended the series when he sacked the city in 253.

Most eastern cities were without adequate silver or billon currency when the regional staters disappeared from circulation in the generation between the reigns of Caracalla and Trebonianus Gallus. Imperial mints at Cyzicus and Antioch recoined staters into antoniniani to meet the emperor's expenditures. Hoards and casual losses at eastern cities suggest that imperial officials, soldiers, and contractors were the recipients of the new money. Hoards of antoniniani unearthed in Asia Minor and Syria were savings concealed by soldiers on campaign between 240 and 270.[31]

Debasement and inflation after 235 compelled eastern cities to issue more bronze coins, but many, for their own reasons, had been increasing production since late Antonine times. Hoards confirm that the bronze currency of eastern cities at mid-third century contained a high proportion of Antonine and Severan pieces.[32] The great surges in minting assaria during the Antonine and Severan ages thus furnished the East with much of its bronze money during the third century. The noticeable rise in minting authorities and longevity of assaria in circulation suggest that overall numbers of bronze coins in circulation must have peaked by 250, although conditions varied from city to city. Great cities such as Smyrna increased output steadily from 200 to 260, while production at modest cities such as Stratonicea peaked in 190–210, and then fell sharply.

Inflation prompted adjustments from the reign of Septimius Severus. Greek cities in Asia Minor and Syria seldom minted denominations below one assarion, and they began to alloy their bronze coins with as much as 25 to 30 percent lead. As emperors from Gordian III to Trebonianus Gallus debased the antoninianus to a billon coin, cities responded by lowering the weight of their token bronze coins. During the century spanning 161–260, Smyrna reduced the weight of her six-, four-, three-, and one-assaria pieces by 50 to 65 percent, with the most drastic reductions during the last fifteen years of this period.[33] Smyrna's actions were repeated at scores of Greek cities across the East. Civic bronze coins, despite losses in their weight, gained intrinsic value with the swift depreciation of the antoninianus. By the reign of Trajan Decius (249–51), civic *aes* were circulating at double or triple their face value. At the Severan rate of 32 or 36 assaria to a silver-clad antoninianus, five or six six-assaria pieces exceeded by many times the intrinsic value and cost of manufacture of an antoninianus. Furthermore, antoniniani suffered by comparison to civic *aes* that had retained their traditional design and size—crucial in denoting denominational value. The debasement of the antoninianus by Valerian (253–60) compelled eastern cities either to suspend minting or to slash the weight and size of their denominations lest freshly minted *aes* disappear from circulation. Civic mints drastically cut the weight and diameters of all denominations in 255–60; six assaria usually fell to the size of a four- or three-assaria piece. Once local bronze money lost its customary size, feel, and iconography, public trust in exchange rates collapsed, prices soared, and provincials hoarded city coins over wretched imperial money.

Side was typical of how cities reduced weight standards and added higher denominations.[34] In 253, Side slashed the weight of her five-assaria piece by over 40 percent, but concealed the depreciation by increasing the coin's diameter. Side also introduced a double carrying on its obverse the value mark of ten assaria (IA; pl. 18.148). In 255 Side cut the standard of the ten assaria (pl. 18.149) so that it resembled in weight and fabric the earlier five assaria (the latter was almost certainly revalued to ten assaria). Soon after 260 Side replaced the ten with a twelve-assaria piece (pl. 18.150), and then with a fourteen-assaria denomination in 270–74 (pl. 18.151). In retariffing bronze coins at higher values and regulating prices and wages, civic officials provided precedents for measures that Diocletian would adopt to combat inflation in 301. Some cities backed up retariffing by countermarking coins with denominational marks of ten, eight, six, four, and three assaria. In the early 260s, Bithynian cities revalued coins upward by 33 to 200 percent, devising a wide range of new multiples from two to twenty-four assaria (pl. 17.140–44), and similar actions were taken in Asia and Pisidia.[35] By countermarking, cities unwittingly announced that inflation had ruined their bronze currency. Most suspended striking *aes* soon after 260. The destruction wrought by Goths in the Balkans and the Aegean and by Sassanid armies in Syria and eastern Anatolia completed the ruin of civic minting. Only cities on the Pamphylian shore or in the Pisidian highlands remote from the fighting struck coins down to the reign of Tacitus (275–76). Yet, civic *aes* continued to circulate down to Diocletian's reform in 293, and some survived as curiosities in family savings as late as the mid-fourth century.

The currency of Egypt long escaped the scourge of inflation, because the tetradrachma, as a fiduciary coin, was affected only when it approached parity to the denarius as a result of imperial debasement. Three successive debasements between 167/8 and 191/2 lowered the silver content of the tetradrachma to one-third of the Neronian coin (Table 6.4). Each time many coins on the Neronian standard were recoined and thus removed from circulation as competitors to the baser tetradrachmae.[36] Since the population accepted the baser coins, prices and wages seem to have risen only in proportion to each debasement. Septimius Severus restored the fineness of the tetradrachma, but his son Caracalla returned to the standard of Marcus Aurelius. Emperors down to Trajan Decius (249–51) maintained the weight of the tetradrachma at the Neronian standard (12.75 g) so that Egyptians handled staters that, while containing only half the silver, resembled the Neronian coins

*Table 6.4*
Debasement of Alexandrine Tetradrachma

| | | Weight | Silver Content | |
|---|---|---|---|---|
| Year | Emperor | Grams | Fineness | Grams |
| 58–67 | Nero | 13.22 | 16.54 | 2.19 |
| 167–70 | Marcus Aurelius | 12.68 | 12.39 | 1.57 |
| 178–82 | M. Aurelius & Commodus | 11.90 | 7.75 | 0.92 |
| 191–92 | Commodus | 11.90 | 6.20 | 0.74 |
| 193–211 | Septimius Severus | 11.55 | 10.01 | 1.16 |
| 212–17 | Caracalla | 12.62 | 7.00 | 0.88 |
| 218–22 | Elagabalus | 12.28 | unknown | |
| 224–27 | Severus Alexander | 12.75 | 6.84 | 0.87 |
| 235–38 | Maximinus I | 12.41 | 6.00 | 0.74 |
| 238 | Gordian I | 12.90 | 7.50 | 0.96 |
| 238–44 | Gordian III | 12.38 | 6.00 | 0.74 |
| 244–49 | Philip I | 12.20 | 5.00 | 0.61 |
| 249–51 | Trajan Decius | 12.56 | 7.00 | 0.87 |
| 251–53 | Trebonianus Gallus | 10.59 | unknown | |
| 253–60 | Valerian | 10.52 | unknown | |
| 260–61 | Macrianus & Quietus | 10.49 | unknown | |
| 261–68 | Gallienus | 9.97 | 4.00 | 0.40 |
| 268–70 | Claudius II | 9.71 | 2.70 | 0.26 |
| 270–74 | Aurelian | 9.24 | unknown | |
| 274–75 | Aurelian | 7.99 | unknown | |
| 275–76 | Tacitus | 8.05 | unknown | |
| 276–82 | Probus | 7.78 | unknown | |
| 282–84 | Carus & Carinus | 7.77 | unknown | |
| 284–96 | Diocletian | 7.47 | 0.50 | 0.04 |

*Source:* Fineness is based on Walker, *MRSC* I, pp. 149–57, and II, pp. 114–16, and E. R. Caley, "Chemical Composition and Chronology of the Alexandrine Tetradrachma," in *CPANS*, pp. 167–80. Weight standards for tetradrachmae of 192–296 are based on West and Johnson, *Currency*, pp. 172–73.

in size and appearance. Exchange rates and prices were maintained down to the 260s since the tetradrachma was the sole legal tender and was issued in comparatively limited numbers. Septimius Severus also restored the weight of the bronze drachma, which had suffered a reduction in 168/9, and the mint at Alexandria provided suitable bronze fractions for the tetradrachma down to the reign of

Philip (244–49). Trebonianus Gallus (251–53) debased the tetradrachma for the first time in fifty years, significantly reducing its weight (to 10.75 g), size, and probably its fineness. Valerian (253–60) and Gallienus (260–68) followed with further debasements, which within fifteen years reduced the tetradrachma to a dumpy, thick coin possessing one-half its former silver and three-quarters of its former weight (pl. 17.138). The imperial government also committed a fatal blunder by overproducing tens of millions of crudely manufactured base coins. Egyptians panicked by the mid-250s, hoarding earlier coins, hallowed by such nicknames as "ancient" or "Ptolemaic-looking silvered money," over "newfangled money."[37] The mint of Alexandria, just like imperial mints, was swept up into wasteful recycling of tremendous numbers of recent billon coins into more debased ones.

Massive recoinages by Gallienus and Claudius II, which removed so many older coins from circulation, did little to restore confidence. Nor did the occupation of Egypt by forces of the usurpers Macrianus and Quietus (260–61) or Prince Vaballathus (271–72) of Palmyra. Few willingly accepted money of usurpers that would be declared void when the rule of the legitimate Augustus was restored, so that each occupation might have sparked record rises in prices. The strategos Aurelius Ptolemaeus, when bankers in the Oxyrhynchite nome refused tetradrachmae of Macrianus and Quietus, mandated that "all those who own these banks to open them and to accept all coinage except such as is counterfeit and spurious and to exchange it."[38] Inflation eliminated the need for the bronze fractions, which Alexandria had minted only in limited numbers under Gallienus and Aurelian, and in less than twenty years the bronze drachma had shrunk to the dimensions of an undersized Severan diobol. By 274 Egyptians employed a single billon denomination, the tetradrachma.

### *The Reform of Aurelian, 274*

In 274 Aurelian restored some measure of monetary stability, after he defeated the secessionist Palmyrene Empire in the East and the Gallo-Roman Empire in the West and reunited the Roman world.

Aurelian was indebted to his predecessors who had forged a network of imperial mints. The mint of Rome, which had met demands for fresh money since 64, had been strained by the unprecedented scale of the recoining between 238 and 274. *Officinae* at Rome were relocated in the provinces as permanent mints to convert coins taken in tax into antoniniani for military payrolls. Gordian III established the first at Antioch in 240; Valerian and Gallienus added four more mints and decentralized production as barbarian invasions and civil wars disrupted communications.[39] Valerian opened a second eastern mint at Cyzicus on the Bosporus during his first Persian campaign (253–55). In 256/7 the first western mint at Treveri (Trier) went into production with staff Gallienus brought from Rome. When he departed from Gaul in 259, he used Treverian engravers to open a fifth imperial mint at Mediolanum (Milan) to supply the Upper Danube. Soon after, the Gallo-Roman emperor Postumus drew on Treveri for a second mint in the Rhineland at Colonia Agrippina (Cologne). In 262 Gallienus opened Siscia in Illyricum because Goths and rebel emperors interrupted shipments of payrolls from Rome to the legions on the Middle and Lower Danube. The network of imperial mints more than proved their worth; the six in operation in 260 rose to eight in 274, and then to fifteen by 300. Mints conducted recoinages efficiently and safely, because they were located beyond the range of barbarian attacks, except for Antioch which suspended operations several times when Shah Shapur invaded Syria. Officials imposed tight regulations so that mints struck to a uniform standard. Fields and exergues on the reverses of antoniniani carry mintmarks, numerals of *officinae*, control marks denoting the sequence of issues, and value marks so that malefactors could be swiftly detected and punished. Crude aurei and antoniniani of usurpers from temporary mints such as Emesa or Carnuntum fall far short of the well-regulated products from imperial mints. Valerian and Gallienus thus created in the network of imperial mints the means to impose a single uniform currency. Treveri, for example, brought the currency of the northern provinces into line with that of the rest of the empire by recoining surviving denarii and earlier antoniniani in 256–60.[40]

The network of imperial mints eventually proved useful for

*Table 6.5*
Debasement of Gallo-Roman Antoninianus, 260–74

| | | Weight | Silver Content | |
|---|---|---|---|---|
| Year | Emperor | Grams | Fineness | Grams |
| 260 | Postumus | 3.00 | 20.00 | 0.60 |
| 261–67 | Postumus | 3.35 | 15.00 | 0.50 |
| 268–69 | Postumus | 3.00 | 8.00 | 0.24 |
| 268–69 | Laelianus | 3.00 | 4.00 | 0.12 |
| 269 | Marius | 3.00 | 4.00 | 0.12 |
| 269–70 | Victorinus | 3.00 | 2.50 | 0.08 |
| 270–74 | Tetricus I | 2.40 | 1.50 | 0.04 |

*Source:* Based on Besly and Bland, *Cunetio Treasures,* pp. 57–65.

monetary reforms, but in the troubled 260s and early 270s when usurpers seized imperial mints, they could immediately mass produce their own coinage. Macrianus and Quietus (260–61), candidates of the eastern army, issued at Antioch and Cyzicus heavy aurei and antoniniani equaling the best that Gallienus could produce. Antioch later minted antoniniani in the name of Prince Vaballathus of Palmyra (268–72).[41] Postumus owed part of his success in founding a Gallo-Roman empire to his control of the mints of Treveri and Colonia Agrippina, where he struck a superior antoniniani (15 percent fine; pl. 16.129), great numbers of sestertii (pl. 16.127), and heavy aurei bearing exquisite portraits of Postumus as Hercules reborn. Given their relative scarcity, his antoniniani gained a good reputation and circulated uncontested by baser late coins of Valerian or Gallienus (Table 6.5).[42] Hoards concealed in the 260s suggest that Gallo-Roman antoniniani remained in the Gallo-Roman heartland, seldom straying south of the Alps or the Pyrenees where the more debased coins of Gallienus held sway. Civil wars and the loss of Spain in 270 ruined this regional currency, and it sank to levels even more base than the worst issues of Rome under Claudius II (pl. 16.130). Western provincials were already importing superior antoniniani from the central empire several years before Aurelian's reconquest.

In 274, Aurelian had the means to conduct the first major improvement of the currency since Domitian. Even though he evacuated Dacia, the famed gold mines were probably worked out, and any lost Dacian revenues were more than offset by reopening other mines and resuming regular tax collection in the rest of the Roman world. Aurelian reorganized and raised the number of imperial mints to eight, totaling forty *officinae;* returned to imperial currency some of its appearance and reputation; imposed fixed rates of exchange; and so rolled back prices. Personnel of the Gallo-Roman mints at Treveri and Colonia Agrippina were relocated to Lugdunum (Lyons); the mint of Mediolanum was transferred to Ticinum (Pavia); and new mints at Serdica (Sofia) and Tripolis joined sister mints in Illyricum and the East. Within two short years Aurelian demonetized, withdrew, and recoined radiate billon coins on a scale that impressed the historian Zosimus over two centuries later when he recalled how the emperor "gave to the fiscus new silver coin [*neon argyron*]."[43]

The new radiate aurelianianus (pl. 15.122), called after the emperor, was of improved manufacture, weight (3.88 g), and silver content (4.5 to 5 percent fine), and was tariffed at an acceptable rate of 5 *denarii communes,* acknowledging a notational inflation of two and one-half times over the antoninianus of 215. In the exergue aureliani often bear the value mark XXI (or the Greek equivalent KA), indicating a tariffing of 20 sestertii to 1 aurelianianus.[44] Aurelian also minted new billon fractions, probably called by the classic names of denarius and quinarius, and bronze sestertii and asses on a light-weight standard so that they passed at par with worn imperial *aes* in circulation (pl. 15.123 and pl. 16.128). The chain of denominations, premised on traditional denarii and sestertii, was reassuring. Aurelian might have recognized the sunken value of the denarius, accepting the aureus as revalued between 600 and 1,000 d.c. so that 120 to 200 aureliani were exchanged against the aureus.[45] Aurelian, who inherited an improved aureus from Claudius II (99 percent fine), minted many of his aurei to the Severan weight (50 to the pound). Western mints, however, struck aurei at 70 or 72 to the Roman pound, anticipating the standard adopted by Constantine.

Aurelian's reform of imperial currency prompted measures to

improve currency in the eastern provinces. Roman authorities at Alexandria in 274 struck a new tetradrachma on a thick, dumpy flan, which perhaps was tariffed at par with the aurelianianus (pl. 17.139). Another massive recoinage of Egyptian currency ensued, but Aurelian and his successors maintained the standard and returned stable prices and rates of exchange. Even though Aurelian's coin bore little resemblance to earlier tetradrachmae, it earned such acceptance by the population, who considered it the venerable "ancient coin," that Diocletian found it politic to replace it gradually with silver-clad "Italic nummus" in 293–96.[46] In response to Aurelian's reform, Greek cities revalued coins downward by countermarking.[47] Asian cities such as Smyrna countermarked coins of 180–250 at their original value, often stamping the new value mark over countermarks applied in 260–68 (pl. 17.145–47). Sardes sorted out her own coins and those from over two dozen other towns by size and counterstamped all of them with the city ethnic and values of one, two, three, or four assaria. Side halved the value of both heavy and light ten-assaria pieces of 253–68 and neatly countermarked an epsilon for five assaria over the prior value mark iota for ten assaria (pl. 18.152–53). The countermark was also applied to imported coins of equivalent size, such as light-weight ten-assaria coins of Cilician cities, and the heavy three and four assaria struck by Asian towns prior to 253. Hard-pressed cities saved costs by retariffing and countermarking in 274, and so extended the lives of worn civic *aes* down to the great reform of Diocletian.

The success of Aurelian's reform can only be inferred from the stability his denominations enjoyed for the next twenty years, but his recoinage and revaluation generated fourfold price surges detected in Egyptian papyri.[48] His successors preserved the purity of the aureus, although they minted aurei on several distinct standards. In 276 Tacitus doubled the silver content of the aurelianianus to 10 percent fine and revalued it to 2.5 denarii, but only Antioch and Tripolis ever issued the new pieces, which were duly marked as coins of ten sestertii (pl. 16.124). Western mints never implemented the reform; in the East, Probus (276–82) quickly returned the aurelianianus to its original tariffing (pl. 16.125).[49]

The reform of Aurelian was a modest success in comparison to the bolder reform of Diocletian. Hoards down to the reform of Diocletian reveal that aurelianiani failed to penetrate in sufficient numbers to many parts of the Roman world. The northwestern provinces suffered acute shortages after Aurelian relocated the mints in the Rhineland to Lugdunum in southern Gaul.[50] Provincials in Britain and Gaul reused Gallo-Roman antoniniani and struck crude imitative pieces or even counterfeits, the so-called barbarous radiates (pl. 16.131). Britain was starved for coinage until the usurpers Carausius (287–93) and Allectus (293–96) coined at Londinium (London) and Camulodunum (Colchester) aurei and aurelianiani inspired by Gallo-Roman and barbarous prototypes. In the East, Aurelian improved the Alexandrine tetradrachma, but city councils took their own measures when imperial mints failed to provide adequate currency.

## *The Great Reform, 293–305*

Diocletian (284–305) aimed at a far more comprehensive reform of the currency than Aurelian had attempted in 274. Since Diocletian conducted reform by successive measures, he was able to achieve more far-reaching results, effecting nothing less than a complete change of the empire's currency. During his first dozen years, Diocletian improved the gold standard, raising the weight of the aureus from 70 to 60 to the Roman pound (pl. 19.155).[51] He still struck heavy ceremonial aurei (50 to the pound), and he began coining gold medallions that were multiples of the aureus (pl. 19.154). At the same time, Diocletian and his colleague Maximianus (285–305) struck silver-clad aurelianiani on the same standard as the 274 pieces, many carrying the value marks of XXI and KA. When the usurper Carausius founded his own Romano-British Empire, he and his successor Allectus opened mints at Londinium and Camulodunum, relieving the chronic shortage of money in the island province and northwestern Gaul. Carausius minted his own version of aurelianiani (also carrying XXI), along with aurei and rare "denarii" of pure silver that were intended for donatives (pl. 16.132–33).[52] Allectus introduced a half of this denomination—a billon piece carrying on its reverse a galley and letter Q in the exergue (and hence dubbed a "quinarius"; pl. 16.134). His smaller radiate denomination, intended to replace the larger aurelianianus, was nothing more than an official adaptation of the light-weight "barbarous radiate" that long circulated in Britain, Gaul, and Rhineland after the reform of 274.

In 293, Diocletian took three decisive steps. He fixed the standard of the aureus once again at 60 to a pound. He also renewed minting of a pure silver coin, dubbed *argenteus nummus,* at 96 to the pound and tariffed at 25 d.c. so that it was a reincarnation of the Neronian denarius (pl. 19.156). Finally, he introduced a laureate silver-wash piece rated at 5 d.c., the nummus, to replace radiate aurelianiani in circulation (pl. 19.157–58).[53] Diocletian, just as Aurelian, premised his system of denominations upon a bronze denarius communis, the depreciated remnant of the silver denarius (pl. 19.160). Although he introduced the first true silver coins in well over a century, these *argentei,* unlike the denarii of the Principate, played a subsidiary role, for the aureus and the silver-clad nummus were intended as the principal coins.

The gold coin, denarius aureus, henceforth passed officially under the name "solidus" (from the slang for a "solid bit") or its Greek nickname "the golden coin" (*to nomisma khryson*).[54] The terms *solidus* and *nomisma,* by convention, are reserved hereafter for the later Constantinian coin minted at 72 to the pound to avoid confusion. The aureus of Diocletian, just as its lighter weight successor, contained twenty-four *siliquae* or "carats" (Greek *keratia*). The carats served as theoretical weights against which silver denominations were struck according to current gold to silver ratios. The argenteus of 293 was equivalent to a carat of the Tetrarchic aureus; hence, twenty-four were exchanged to each aureus, implying a gold to silver ratio of 1:15. Since the full-bodied coins were close to their intrinsic worth, some later aurei and argentei included on the reverse the numerals 60 and 96 to designate their weight standard. Diocletian put the seal on the shift from a silver to a gold standard and handed down a system of reckoning that was employed into the Middle Ages.

The billon nummus replaced the earlier radiate aurelianianus as the 5-d.c. piece in daily fiscal and commercial transactions. Nummi of Alexandria and Siscia carried the value marks XXI and XX denoting them as coins of 20 sestertii, and Antioch marked some nummi with the numerals of K and V, the equivalent values of 20 sestertii and 5 d.c. (pl. 19.157–58). Diocletian deliberately broke with iconographic canons to give his coinage a new look. The nummus, by its appearance and heavy weight, was readily distingished from its inferior radiate predecessor. Nummi carry on the obverse stylized identical portraits of a Tetrarch who is distinguished only by name, and on the reverse the universal appeal "To the Spirit of the Roman People" (GENIO POPVLI ROMANI). Manufacture also was improved: nummi show neat preparation of flans, careful striking, and a better process of fusing the silver coating onto the bronze core. The nummus, most of all, was a major improvement of the standard. In its average weight (10.75 to 11 g) it was the equal of the as of the high empire. Down to 307, nummi were struck to a consistent standard of 32 to the bronze pound and with a silver surface of at least 4, and possibly 5, percent. The nummus thus enjoyed a decided superiority over the aurelianianus, possessing three times its weight and two and one-half times its silver enrichment.[55]

Since Diocletian planned for the argenteus and nummus to replace all other currencies, his reform required two ambitious measures, the recall of old money and the striking of new coins, notably nummi, in unprecedented numbers. He accomplished both tasks with surprising success. Diocletian demonetized and reminted a heterogeneous mass of clipped, worn, and even counterfeit coins, including the last of the countermarked civic assaria and the dregs of the billon radiates. Britain under rebel emperors clung to the radiate coins until 296 when Caesar Constantius Chlorus recovered the lost province and immediately imposed the new coinage. In Egypt, Alexandria briefly minted both old and new currencies and the abortive revolt of L. Domitius Domitianus (295–96) delayed full implementation of reform.[56]

Many radiate coins of better quality did continue in use after the reform as fractions of the nummus. The nummus was accompanied by two subdivisions, a small copper laureate coin and a radiate piece, also of copper but containing a coating of perhaps 1 to 1.5

*Table 6.6*
Tariffing of Denominations, 293–305

| Denominational Values in *denarii communes* | Official Values 293–99 | Values at Panopolis, Egypt 299–300 | Values in Price Edict 301 | Official Values 301–305 |
|---|---|---|---|---|
| AU Aureus | 600 | 1000/1050 | 1,200 | 2,400 |
| AU Quinarius | 300 | 500/525 | 600 | 1,200 |
| AR Argenteus | 25 | 50 | 50 | 100 |
| Billon Nummus | 5 | 12.5 | 12.5 | 25 |
| Billon Radiate | 2 | 2.5 | 2.5 | 5 |
| AE Laureate | 1 | 1 | 1 | 1 |
| Number of Nummi to the Aureus | 120 | 80/84 | 96 | 96 |

percent silver. The radiate, a ringer for the aurelianianus save for its lack of the value mark XXI, was minted in limited numbers (pl. 19.159). The laureate and radiate fractions were almost certainly tariffed at 1 and 2 d.c., respectively.[57] Diocletian probably sanctioned the use of aureliani ani on par with his new radiates. If the aurelianianus were revalued from 5 d.c. to 2 d.c., a cut of 60 percent in its value might have been justified, because aurelianiani surviving in hoards deposited after 293 commonly lack much or all of their silver coating.[58] Within five years (from 293 to 297) Diocletian and his colleagues had imposed the first uniform coinage throughout the Roman world and had provided sufficient numbers of new coins for its 60 million inhabitants. Official tariffing of the denominations was maintained probably until January 1, 300 (Table 6.6).

Treveri (Trier), the residence of the Western caesar, might have struck the first nummi in 293, but nine other mints were soon opened across the empire in Gaul, Italy, Illyricum, and the East. In 296 Londinium and Alexandria supplied the recovered provinces of Britain and Egypt with the new money, and Carthage swung into action briefly when the Western Augustus Maximianus arrived to wage his Mauretanian War. The last mint opened at Thessalonica two years later. Diocletian modified the system of mints he inherited from Aurelian to suit his reorganization of civil administration into dioceses.[59] Tetrarchic mints struck hundreds of millions of nummi, along with copper fractions and silver argentei, in what must have been by far the largest single coinage prior to the modern age. The volume of this coinage is staggering, for nummi not only displaced older currencies but relieved regions long suffering from chronic shortages of coinage. The Tetrarchs effected not just a recoinage, but one of the most successful replacements of a currency in history.[60]

The achievement of Diocletian is all the more remarkable for its rapid failure. From the start, the nummus encountered a public reluctant to accept it at its stated value. Prices rose as confidence in the nummus sank. Twice the imperial government responded by decreeing higher values for nummus and argenteus without any change in the standard. In January of 300, perhaps on the first of the year, the nummus was officially revalued from 5 to 12.5 d.c., while the argenteus was raised from 25 to 50 d.c.[61] The gold currency, and perhaps the fractions, were not under the same pressure, for at the same time, a pound of gold bullion in Egypt sold at prices of 60,000 to 63,000 d.c. If this gold was of the purity required of coins, the aureus was trading around 1,000 to 1,050 d.c., suggesting that its rate of inflation was half that of the nummus (see Table 6.6). The rate of 20 or 21 argentei to the aureus might, in part, reflect conditions in Egypt where pure silver coins remained scarce throughout the fourth century. The price of gold at Panopolis, however, must have been quoted often through the empire in 300–301, because one Greek stonecutter mistakenly cut 60,000 d.c. rather than 72,000 d.c. as the price in the Elatean copy of the Price Edict.[62]

Less than six years after his grand reform of the currency, market forces compelled Diocletian to decree a new set of values if his coinage were to keep pace with inflation. The nummus had failed to win public trust because it was tariffed at too high a rate. The argenteus too was probably deemed overvalued, for surviving specimens fall well short of the equivalent of a full carat.[63] The radiate and laureate fractions suffered the least. Their official values of 2.5

and 1 d.c. in 300 can be deduced from a register of Karanis recording various taxes paid in coin during the years 296 through 300, including *adaeratio* or commutation of grain taxes into money.[64] The depth of mistrust for the nummus is best seen in the persistence of the imperial government and public in quoting prices by ghost currencies or money of account. During the inflationary spiral of the mid-third century, ghost currencies provided the only secure yardstick for reckoning prices or taxes in a world of widely varying rates of exchange. In Egypt, officials throughout the fourth century assessed taxes in Alexandrine drachmae and talents, which were then exchanged into nummi according to the going rate. The Attic drachma or the denarius communis were similarly employed elsewhere in the empire. The Tetrarchs unwittingly revealed their own nervousness about their fine-looking nummi and argentei because, when they issued the Edict of Maximum Prices in 301, they too quoted prices in d.c. rather than in nummi.

Revaluation achieved little. In 301 the Tetrarchs took more drastic steps, promulgating an edict regulating maximum prices for goods throughout the empire. The Price Edict stipulates a single price of 72,000 d.c. for a pound of gold whether it was composed of refined ingots (*obryzae*), minted coin (*solidi*), or "spun" gold (*aurei neti,* presumably used in the manufacture of ceremonial plate).[65] Since the price applied only to objects produced for imperial fiscal needs, it did not apply to unrefined gold in private use or on the free market. The aureus was thus revalued slightly to a value of 1,200 d.c., but the rates of other denominations, including the argenteus, did not change (see Table 6.6). The Tetrarchs combated ruinous fourfold and eightfold inflation by fixing prices. Lactantius reports that the Price Edict failed miserably and Diocletian was soon compelled to rescind it, because vendors withdrew their goods from the market.[66] Regulation of prices could not substitute for sound currency.

On September 1, 301, the Tetrarchs issued the second Monetary Edict, doubling the value of all denominations above 1 d.c. By a single stroke, Diocletian immediately halved all prices, salaries, and taxes computed in d.c., but he preserved the rates of exchange among the higher denominations (see Table 6.6). The fragmentary copy of this decree, found at Aphrodisias, preserves only the rates of argenteus and nummus, and those assigned to aureus and the fractions, if originally recorded, have not survived. In an Egyptian register from Hermopolis, several payments of taxes in 303–5 still required fractions, and laureate and radiate fractions of 1 and 2.5 d.c. would have best served, but other evidence suggests that the radiate fraction might have passed at 5 d.c.[67] The Monetary Edict neither improved the currency nor slowed the pace of inflation. Officials, moneychangers, and vendors had learned to respond to an imperial revaluation in the third century by marking up their rates in d.c. In practice, coins were worth whatever they could fetch in the marketplace on any given day and not what edicts pronounced. The imperial government willingly participated in undermining the value of its own currency by doubling salaries of many officials after revaluation in 301.

Despite two revaluations and the Price Edict, the nummus was never degraded, and it is astonishing that so handsome a coin failed to win acceptance inasmuch as an entire generation of the Roman world was accustomed to dealing largely in billon radiate coins. On several possible grounds, consumers, vendors, moneychangers, and even officials, however, adamantly rejected the nummus. Since billon coins inevitably possess a greater "exchange" value than the intrinsic value of their metal and the cost of their manufacture, they are overvalued coins. Such coins are extremely profitable to mint, but a public accepts them only under certain conditions. In late medieval Europe, residents of cities and villages alike willingly employed "black money," the low-grade silver deniers. The coins enjoyed faith sanctioned by long usage; they could be exchanged against "full-bodied" silver coins; they faced no competing token bronze currency so that the billon deniers functioned as the sole fiduciary coinage; and they were minted in relatively scarce numbers.

In 284 Diocletian inherited a billon coinage of radiate aureliani, and in Egypt tetradrachmae, which commanded little respect inasmuch as they were the legacy of a century of shameless debasement. Although Diocletian must have sensed the lack of public faith in billon coins, he premised his reform in 293 upon a new silver-clad nummus, assigning only subsidiary roles for traditional pure silver and token copper coins, and he furthermore revalued the billon aurelianianus downward to act as a fraction of his nummus. His approach put pressure on the nummus from three directions. First, the official value of the nummus had to be fixed precisely in relationship to coins in pure gold and silver as well as lower denominations in both billon and copper. This, in turn, required that nummus not be placed in competition with its own fractions, notably the billon radiate pieces. Finally, Diocletian had to regulate the volume of nummi so that overproduction did not drive up prices and undermine the currency's exchange rates. It is doubtful that Diocletian ever grasped these complexities, for he probably just acted in good faith, "crying up" the value of imperial money.

The nummus quickly failed. They were issued in such great numbers that they inevitably sparked a general rise in prices. Since the imperial government was unable to judge the scope of the prodigious task of replacing the entire supply of the empire's money, mints inevitably struck too many nummi; and, just as inevitably, inflation followed. Billon currency had functioned so well in Egypt because the tetradrachma had circulated as the unchallenged premium coin. Likewise, the aurelianianus in 274 was virtually the sole coin in general use, because numbers of aurei and rare token bronze coins were relatively few. In 293, the nummus circulated side by side with gold and silver denominations as well as older billon coins. The public soon grew aware of the disparities between intrinsic and official worth of its coins. The silver in the nummus, given the official rates of exchange, fell far short of that in the argenteus or the aurelianianus. The 24 argentei exchanged to the aureus contained 40 and 76 percent more silver than the equivalent of 120 nummi in 293 and 96 nummi in 301; hence the argenteus was preferred to the nummus. The 480 aureliani with full silver coating were marginally superior (by 2.3 percent) to the 120 nummi exchanged to the aureus in 293, but the difference grew to nearly 78 percent with retariffing in 301. Consequently, the nummus was exchanged in favor of the better coins. As the worth of the nummus sank, it was quoted at ever higher rates of d.c., and revaluations in 300–301 simply worsened the position of the nummus. Aureliani became worth hoarding in large numbers or they were melted down or sweated for their silver content. Hoards suggest that aurelianiani had passed out of circulation before 305 and soon after imperial mints ceased striking pure silver argentei.

If Diocletian never pegged his nummus at its proper value, his successors, who were committed to policies of debasement, met with less success. Despite much public opposition, the imperial government found silver-clad nummi profitable to mint, and the historical experience of the Egyptian tetradrachma suggested that a successful billon currency was possible. Diocletian, however, just as his predecessors, had only read part of the lesson correctly. Billon currency required careful regulation of its quantity and exchange rates. Diocletian can be criticized for setting the pattern of failure repeated many times during the next seventy-five years until Valentinian (364–75) and Valens (364–78) finally scrapped the minting of billon currency. Yet, Diocletian pulled off a major achievement by his recoinage and replacement of the currency of the entire Roman world. He set forth the fundamentals of reform and regulation of billon currency for the next century. Although he failed to select acceptable values for his coins, he never reduced the weight or silver content of the nummus, but rather combated inflation by regulating prices or revaluation.

The demise of the Augustan currency and monetary reforms of Aurelian and Diocletian often have been cited as primary causes for the loss of Roman monetary ways. It is argued that the imperial government countered the effects of inflation by reassessing tax obligations in kind or bullion, while most ranks of Roman society turned from coins to barter. In short, inflationary fiscal demands ruined the monetized economy of the High Roman Empire. Coins, however, suggest the opposite. Emperors debased to augment their supply of coined money and thereby their ability to hire more soldiers and officials to stave off political collapse. Whatever its social and economic consequences, debasement had worked, for Gallienus, Claudius II, and Aurelian financed the restoration of Roman unity with hundreds of millions of silver-clad antoniniani. As inflation mounted sharply after 260, emperors and town councils in the East responded by revaluing upward the notational value of money, often expressed in units of account such as *denarii communes* (d.c.) or Attic drachmae. When these measures failed to stem rising prices, Aurelian in 274, and then Diocletian in 293, took the drastic step of demonetizing the old currency and replacing it with a new set of denominations.

Diocletian's improvements in assessment and collection of taxes have been often taken in tandem with his reform of the currency as a comprehensive policy to protect the imperial government from inflation by putting fiscal needs on a "natural economy" so that taxes were exacted in kind or bullion. Far from moving the Roman Empire off a monetarized economy, Diocletian aimed for the opposite. He boldly combined the silver standard of the Augustan age with lessons on billon coinage drawn from Egyptian provincial currency and the debasements of the third century. Foremost, he hoped to return monetary stability both for fiscal needs and public utility. He aimed correctly, but he failed in details. With his retirement in 305, a new round of civil wars ruined the nummus and monetary stability.

# Seven

# Imperial Regulation and Reform, A.D. 305–498

Diocletian transmitted to his successors a monetary system based upon the silver-clad nummus and an efficient network of mints that facilitated the production of huge quantities of nummi. For the next sixty years (305–67) successors of Diocletian, by reductions in the size and silver content of the nummus, exploited this legacy to finance civil and foreign wars and rising bureaucratic and ceremonial costs. Constantius II (337–61) resumed large-scale production of fine silver coins in 355–56, and Valentinian I (364–75) and Valens (364–78) restored the purity of gold and silver currencies and reintroduced a token bronze coinage. This currency suffered debasement when the barbarian migrations after 395 destroyed the Western Empire and shattered the monetary unity of the Roman world.

## *Regulation and Reform, 305–395*

As civil war engulfed the Roman world from 306 to 324, rival emperors needed ever more men and money. Constantine (306–37), saluted emperor by the Western army, took the lead in debasing the silver-clad nummus in 307. His opponents, Maxentius

(306–12) in Italy and Galerius (305–11) and his rebel Caesar Maximinus Daia (308–13) in the East kept pace. Despite divided control over the mints, the unity of the billon coinage was maintained. At the same time, Constantine suspended the minting of aurei and argentei as prices of gold and silver climbed.[1] When his mint at Treveri resumed striking gold coins by 309, it was on a new standard. The new coin, known as the solidus (4.54 g; pl. 20.161), was struck at 72 to the Roman pound or five-sixths the weight of aurei that Maxentius and Galerius continued to issue in Italy and the East. Constantine is often credited with foresight for devising a gold standard in line with market values, but his solidus was merely a debasement. His victories on the battlefield, followed by reminting of the heavy aurei of his pagan rivals, rather than bullion prices, imposed the solidus on the Roman world.[2]

In the eastern provinces, controlled by Licinius (308–24), as early as 316–18 the aureus was perhaps tariffed at 288 nummi, still rated at 25 d.c. each (indicating a price of 17,280 nummi for a pound of gold refined to imperial standard). Several years later, perhaps in 321, Licinius must have doubled this rate to 576 nummi, when he halved the notational value of the nummus to 12.5 d.c. (pl. 21.179). The lighter solidus used in the West passed at 240 nummi (again a price of 17,280 nummi for a pound of gold) down to the final clash between Constantine and Licinius in 323–24.[3] In addition to reducing their weight, Constantine lowered the purity of gold coins for the first time in over fifty years. Solidi in his closing years average 97.7 percent fine, a fall of nearly 2 percent from the Tetrarchic standard. Civil and foreign wars drove Constantine's heirs to debase further until the solidus averaged less than 95 percent fine by 366. Magnentius (350–53), usurper in Gaul, even lowered the weight of his solidus (3.78 g) by one-sixth to the equivalent of 20 carats in weight.[4]

In 366–67, the fraternal emperors Valentinian I and Valens promulgated laws to crack down upon abuses and payments of taxes in underweight or counterfeit solidi, decreeing that "when solidi are collected into any account, they must be reduced to a firm and solid mass of refined gold (*obryza*)."[5] The count of the sacred largesses (*comes sacrarum largitionum*) enforced a strict exchange of 72 pure solidi to a Roman pound. Parallel laws, which do not survive, imposed the same regulations on silver coins. Ingots cast from solidi or silver coins were stamped either *obryziatum* ("certified pure gold") or *pusulatum* ("certified pure silver"). The bullion was turned into new coins, medallions, or ceremonial plate at "sacred mints," located at imperial palaces (*comitatus*). Henceforth, solidi and silver coins carry in the exergue of their reverses the abbreviations COMOB = COM(itatus) OB(ryziatum) or PS = P(u)S(ulatum). These measures restored solidi to 99.5 percent fine, and argentei were improved to 97.5 to 98 percent fine (pl. 20.162 and 169).[6] The solidus thereafter gained an international reputation for its fineness that was still a marvel to the geographer Cosmas Indicopleustes in the sixth century. The laws of 366–67 did not, as sometimes argued, alter imperial fiscal policy by stipulating that thereafter all taxes were to be collected in solidi or bullion, nor is there any evidence to support the view that sacred mints were under a mandate to remint all full-bodied coins taken each year in taxes. Annual reminting would have been wasteful; other laws reveal that emperors must have periodically recoined inferior coins, but otherwise decreed that solidi of good weight, regardless of age or the effigy they bore, were the equivalent of new coins.[7] Furthermore, the wear on numerous specimens indicates that they had a long circulation life, and the hoards of the fifth and sixth centuries reveal that solidi, once they left the mint, were widely dispersed throughout the empire.[8]

The driving force behind the laws of 366–67, and the surge in the minting of solidi, was change in military recruitment and payment, a change that steadily altered the structure of imperial currency. Emperors from Constantius II to Theodosius I (379–95) needed solidi and argentei of impeccable integrity to pay tribes hired as federates and the barbarians enrolled into elite Roman units who demanded gold coins of honest weight and fineness. The monetary regulations of the 360s also followed at least a decade of special taxes collected either in solidi or gold bullion from the propertied classes (*honestiores*). Socrates, the ecclesiastical historian writing early in the fifth century, grasped the purpose behind the new fiscal demands (even though his details are inaccurate). He reports that Valens levied the first *aurum tirocinium*, the tax requiring the landed classes to commute military service at sixty solidi per citizen, to pay Gothic federates settled in Moesia in 375–76.[9] Valentinian and Valens also effected the formal reclassification of public mints, which struck bronze coins, and sacred (or palatine) mints, which manufactured gold and silver multiples, coins, ingots, and plate. The aim of this reorganization was to improve the production, both quality and quantity, of gold coins and ceremonial objects. The laws issued in 366–67 were some of many measures to meet changes in imperial fiscal obligations.

Silver coins fared far worse than gold during the first half of the fourth century. Diocletian had resurrected the Neronian denarius in the guise of his *nummus argenteus,* but argentei disappeared into the melting pot in 305–7. European mints must have struck considerable numbers, because many argentei survive from hoards unearthed in the frontier provinces of the Middle Danube and northwestern Europe. Papyri reveal a dearth of silver coins in Egypt. Output at the Asian mints is less certain, since a considerable number of argentei might have been drawn out of the Roman East into Iran to be recoined into Sassanid dirhems.[10] All emperors ceased striking fine argentei by 307, in large part because silver was vital in the manufacture of nummi. In the East, Galerius and Maximinus II Daia halted silver coinage altogether. In Italy, Maxentius (306–12) coined argentei and tiny fractions in a quite debased alloy, and the mint at Treveri supplied the West with equally base argentei in the name of Constantine. The circulation of silver currency from 293 to 355 prefigures medieval patterns: silver coins were favored in northwestern Europe and the Balkans but saw limited use in the Mediterranean and eastern regions of the Roman Empire that relied upon the solidus.

Constantine's advent into Rome was commemorated with the usual gold multiples depicting the triumphant emperor greeted by the tutelary gods of the Eternal City, but also by the first silver multiples. During the Civil Wars of 306–24, emperors rewarded supporters at quinquennalian or decennalian festivals with gold coins and well-wrought silver plate, sometimes stamped with dies depicting the imperial effigy. In 324, Constantine revived fine silver coins in a new capacity as ceremonial gifts. He reintroduced the

Tetrarchic argenteus minted at 96 to the Roman pound (pl. 20.168) and representing a carat of the solidus or siliqua (although it is by no means certain the coin passed under the latter name). Constantine also struck a silver multiple at 72 to the pound, called a *miliarense* by numismatic convention, but this name dates only from 384 at the earliest (pl. 20.167). His three sons introduced two larger denominations, a heavy miliarense and a triple miliarensia (pl. 20.165–66).[11] These large silver denominations were not easily exchangeable for argentei or nummi, but were reckoned by the carat and so stood in convenient relationship to the solidus and its ceremonial multiples. Miliarensia thus occupied the lower rungs of an ascending order of ceremonial coins in gold and silver distributed to exalt the emperor's majesty. In their size and weight, miliarensia recalled Hellenic preferences for large silver coins; their iconography marked them as ceremonial pieces to be handed out as donatives to officials and soldiers, or scattered among the urban plebeians on high holidays.[12]

For over fifty years considerable quantities of silver were distributed as plate, ingots, or ceremonial multiples, and large stocks of silver became immobilized as treasure in private hands or Christian churches, but supplies of silver did not abruptly disappear. Mining, resumed in the fourth century after its disruption during the third, poured fresh silver into the money supply. Following the lead of their predecessors in the third century, fourth-century emperors employed silver to produce hundreds of millions of billon nummi. Although the silver coating of each nummus was measured in milligrams, billon coinage consumed tremendous amounts of silver. Relentless debasement of the billon currency fueled alarming rates of inflation and affected the ratio between gold and silver; and, as a result, the minting of full-bodied silver coins, which would quickly end up in melting pots, was discontinued. Over the next two centuries the populace was treated to the continuing spectacle of emperors decreasing the size of the nummus, and then, on occasion, revaluing the depreciated nummus and introducing large-sized multiples that quickly tumbled to the level of the wretched nummi they were intended to replace. The names and tariffing of each reincarnation of the nummus over the next two centuries are so

*Table 7.1*
Classification of Billon and Bronze Coins, 305–498

| Module | Diameter |
|---|---|
| AE1 | 32–26 mm |
| AE2 | 25–21 mm |
| AE3 | 20–17 mm |
| AE4 | less than 17 mm |

obscure that modern numismatists have classified billon and base metal denominations by diameter or module (Table 7.1).

The nummus lost some 35 to 40 percent of its weight and silver content when Constantine's mints at Londinium, Treveri, and Lugdunum, probably in April and November of 307, conducted two separate reductions of its weight (pl. 21.172–73). Constantine's new nummi, struck on a small AE2 module, must have been viewed as a full denominational grade below Diocletian's nummus minted on the larger AE1 module; this, however, was but the start of a decline in the weight and silver content that took place over the next half-century (Table 7.2).[13] The monetary situation grew chaotic during the Wars of Succession in 306–24 (pl. 21.172–77). Constantine rated his smaller nummus at 25 d.c. and his mint at Lugdunum marked some of its first nummi as pieces of 100 sestertii (= 25 d.c.; pl. 21.173). Nicomedia and Cyzicus, controlled by Galerius, followed with nummi on the second Constantinian standard carrying the Latin value mark of 100 sestertii (= 25 d.c.) and Greek numerals designating the standard as 48 to the Roman pound. In 307–9, each of the four competing Augusti—Constantine in the West, Maxentius in Italy, and, in the East, Galerius and his exiled Western colleague Severus II—minted his own nummi, and each fell away at varying speeds from the size, weight, iconography, and credibility of Diocletian's coin. Each debasement of the nummus released more metal for the production of more overvalued nummi, but argentei, billon radiates, and copper laureate denominations disappeared, reducing the empire again to a single billon denomination.[14]

*Table 7.2*
Decline of the Nummus, 305–48 (Tariffed at 25 d.c.)

| Date | Module | Number per Pound | Weight Grams | Silver Content: Fineness | Silver Content: Milligrams |
|---|---|---|---|---|---|
| 305–7 | AE1 | 32 | 10.75 | 4.0 | 430 |
| Apr. 307 | AE2 | 40 | 8.00 | 4.0 | 320 |
| Nov. 307 | AE2 | 48 | 6.70 | 4.0 | 268 |
| 310–13 | AE2 | 72 | 4.50 | 1.5 | 68 |
| 313–18 | AE3 | 96 | 3.36 | 1.4 | 47 |
| 318–24 | AE3 | 108 | 3.00 | 2.0–4.0 | 60–120 |
| 321–24* | AE3 | 132 | 2.40 | 0.1 | 2 |
| 324–30 | AE3 | 108 | 3.05 | 1.9 | 58 |
| 330–35 | AE3 | 132 | 2.48 | 1.0 | 25 |
| 336–37 | AE4 | 196 | 1.61 | 1.3 | 21 |
| 337–41 | AE4 | 196 | 1.64 | 1.1 | 18 |
| 341–48 | AE4 | 196 | 1.65 | 0.4 | 7 |

*Eastern nummi of Licinius, tariffed at 12.5 d.c.

*Source:* Based on *RIC* VI, pp. 93–95, VII, pp. 8–13, and VIII, p. 60.

As prices soared in the worst inflation since the 260s, the public reacted as would be expected. Older nummi with higher silver content were preferred to newer, baser ones, as is reflected in fourth-century hoards that are composed of nummi on a single standard.[15] Constantine and Licinius might have curtailed output in an attempt to curb inflation in 314–18 by closing mints or reducing the number of *officinae*. In Italy, Maxentius preserved better standards and introduced billon fractions of the nummus bearing laureate portraits and perhaps tariffed as pieces of 12.5 d.c. and 5 d.c. In the East the nummus lost its silver content more swiftly. The last Alexandrine nummi of Maximinus II Daia bear on their reverse a prominent *N*, designating nummus, and Licinius included the reassuring denominational mark on his first nummi from Alexandria (313–14).[16] The official tariffing of the nummus stood at 25 d.c., but, in less than fifteen years, the rate of exchange of nummi against gold coins rose by threefold that mandated in the Monetary Edict of 301, from 96 to 288 nummi. In Italy, the solidus officially passed at 240 nummi as late as 323. In Egypt, the aureus in 316–18 was exchanged at a rate equivalent to 288 nummi. The functionary Theophanes, upon returning to Egypt from a tour of Syrian towns at this time, boasted of purchasing aurei for 7,000 d.c. (or 280 nummi), but adds that "he was still buying them when they stood at 30,000 d.c."[17] The aureus was thus exchanged for as many as 1,200 nummi or over four times the official rate.

Licinius, short of silver after he lost Illyricum in 316, ordered a recoinage, perhaps in 321. His new nummi carry the radiate imperial portrait and, on the reverse, a heroic Jupiter Conservator who recalled those on late antoniniani (pl. 21.179). The Licinian nummus, however, inspired little confidence; it was struck on a reduced AE3 flan and possessed 20 percent of the weight and 5 percent of the silver of Diocletian's coin. So patently inferior a coin was unwanted in the East and never circulated in the West.[18] The Licinian nummus carries on its reverse a value mark announcing its retariffing at 12.5 d.c., so that an exchange rate of 576 nummi to the aureus obtained, sixfold that of A.D. 301. Since the calculation of fiscal obligations was in d.c., Licinius, by his revaluation, doubled the intake of coins in taxes, but he probably doubled the number paid out in salaries and contracts, meaning that real prices in the East rose rather than leveled off. Panic ensued as many rushed to convert their nummi into other commodities. Apion, an official in Egypt, urged a colleague, "The divine fortune of our lords has decreed that the Italic coin be reduced to half a nummus. Make haste, therefore, to spend all the Italian coinage that you have, and purchase on my behalf goods of every description at whatever price you find them."[19]

The Licinian nummus was demonetized in 324 when Constantine reunited the Roman Empire. In 325, the Constantinian nummus was 30 percent the weight and contained less than 15 percent of the silver of the nummus in 305, but by 336–37 it was reduced to a miniscule coin just 15 percent of the weight and less than 2 percent of the silver of Diocletian's nummus (pl. 21.176–78). Yet, the imperial government apparently refused to revalue this tiny nummus from its Tetrarchic rate of 25 d.c.[20] Officials, moneychangers, and vendors responded by marking up prices in terms of d.c., thereby setting off inflationary spirals, which by mid-century produced fantastic prices, quoted in ghost currencies, for the most modest of purchases. Prices were quoted in the myriads of d.c., or, in the East, myriads of talents and drachmae. Egyptian papyri, so difficult to date during this period, suggest an inflationary surge in the 330s and 340s, followed by a second wave of runaway inflation after the failure of the reform of 348–52.[21] Casual comments in Talmudic texts and costs reported on Syrian funerary monuments near Carrhae (Harran) reveal a society in the early 340s accustomed to citing prices in the myriads of d.c.[22]

Society, however, adjusted. Nummi were sealed up in leather purses (*folles*) with their value in d.c. marked clearly, or, in Egypt, wrapped up into rolls of papyrus or animal skin marked so many "talents of silvered money of the Augusti in nummi."[23] Purses of sealed coins had always been used for transactions requiring large sums of gold or silver coin; moneychangers had, from time to time, bagged and tagged large groups of assayed bronze coins. From the 330s, however, purses containing swarms of nummi became a necessity for everyday transactions. A public monument at Ghirza in Tripolitania, perhaps on the eve of the reform in 348, was priced in *folles singulares* of 45,600 denarii in nummi.[24] Where insufficient nummi were on hand as in Gaul and Britain, provincials manufactured their own imitative pieces that easily escaped detection among the thousands of nummi in a sealed bag. The imperial government too adjusted. Officials in Egypt as early as the mid-330s were calculating payrolls and expenditures in *folles* composed of hundreds, if not thousands, of nummi.[25] The imperial government had two choices. It could revalue the depreciated nummus, but this achieved nothing because prices raced upward to keep pace with each retariffing. Hence, prices found in papyri of the Tetrarchic period were cited in talents and d.c.; in the 330s and 340s this pricing gave way to myriads of d.c. or talents; by the 360s myriads of talents were cited. A second solution was reform based on large-sized multiples of the nummus that could substitute for the bags of tiny nummi.

Imperial efforts to reform failed miserably. For over a century the most common coins in the marketplace were tiny billon or bronze nummi struck on an AE3 or AE4 module, weighing from 0.6 to 2.5 g, and measuring from 15 to 20 mm. The tariffing of the nummus and its rate of exchange against the solidus between 325 and 445 remain speculative. Based on quotations of exchange rates for the solidus, cited in papyri by myriads of talents or myriads of d.c., a series of rates of exchange can be derived to give an approximation of the number of nummi that were exchanged against the solidus (Table 7.3).[26]

In 325, the billon Constantinian nummus, struck on a flan of an AE3 module, was reckoned at 240 to the solidus (pl. 21.176); its distant descendant in 445 had fallen to a bronze piece on an AE4 module (weighing but 10 percent of Diocletian's coin), and it was exchanged at 7,000 to 7,200 to the solidus (pl. 22.191). It seems that sometime between 330 and 335, when the nummus fell to an AE4 module coin, state and public began reckoning nummi at 1,000 to the solidus. The rising numbers of nummi to the solidus made tax collection difficult and spurred on the reform of 348. The price of the solidus then leaped to fantastic sums of d.c. or talents because of imperial reluctance to revalue the nummus. Emperors most likely revalued either when the rate of exchange to the solidus exceeded 12,000 nummi or when the nummi (whatever their size or official tariffing) weighed more than 25 Roman pounds. Rates of exchange beyond either level were just physically unmanageable.[27] Rates of exchange at the turn of the fourth century point to a solidus reckoned by a factor of several thousands of d.c. and they reflect the failure of reforms from 348 to 379.

In 348 the brothers Constans and Constantius II halted minting miniscule nummi, and, in the first improvement of the currency in over a generation, issued three new billon denominations proclaiming the coming eleventh centenary of Rome as "The Restoration of the Felicity of the Ages" (FEL. TEMP. REPARATIO). The main denomination, struck on a large-sized AE2 flan (5.26 g, 23 mm), carries a prominent value mark A on specimens struck at western mints and it was most likely the *maiorina* later banned by the 354 law (pl. 22.180). Its obverse carries the customary imperial effigy facing right. The intermediate-sized denomination, with the mark N on western issues and minted on a small AE2 flan (4.25 g, 21 mm),

*Table 7.3*
Hypothetical Rates of Exchange for Solidus and Nummus, 324–445

| Date | Rate of Exchange for Solidus: Reported in Ghost Currency (d.c.) | Rate of Exchange for Solidus: Surmised in Actual Coins (nummi) | Source |
|---|---|---|---|
| 323 | 6,000* | 240 | *ILS* 9420 (Italy) |
| 325–30 | 50,000 | 2,000 | *PSI* VII. 825 |
| 325–30 | 52,500* | 2,096 | *SB* XIV. 11591 |
| 325–30 | 54,000* | 2,160 | *SB* XIV. 11592 |
| 330–37 | 150,000* | 6,000 | P. Vindob. G. 25840 |
| 330–37 | 160,000 | 6,400 | *PSI* VIII. 1423 |
| 337–39 | 180,000* | 7,200 | *SPP* XX. 96 |
| 338–41 | 275,000 | 11,000 | *SB* XIV. 11593 |
| 350–55 | 7,300,000 | 1,460 | *PO* 2729 |
| 350–60 | 13,500,000* | 2,700 | *PO* 3401 |
| 360–75 | 20,020,000 | 4,004 | *PO* IX. 1223 |
| 360–75 | 22,500,000* | 4,500 | *P. Oslo* III. 88 |
| 360–75 | 22,500,000* | 4,500 | *PO* 3426 |
| 375–85 | 32,450,000 | 6,490 | *PO* 3429 |
| 395–410 | 38,000,000 | 7,600 | *PO* 3629 |
| 395–410 | 38,500,000 | 7,700 | *PO* 3629 |
| 395–410 | 39,000,000 | 7,800 | *PO* 3628; 3630–33 |
| 395–410 | 40,000,000 | 8,000 | *PO* 3628; 3632 |
| 400–25 | 34,500,000* | 5,750 | *PSI* VIII. 959 |
| 400–25 | 40,500,000* | 6,750 | *PSI* VIII. 960 |
| 400–25 | 45,498,000* | 7,583 | *PSI* VIII. 961 |
| 435–45 | 42,000,000* | 7,000 | *CPR* V. 26 |
| 445 | | 7,000/7,200 | *Novel* XVI. 1 (Rome) |

*Sums divisible by 24; nummus could also be reckoned to the carat of the solidus.

*Source:* Based on R. S. Bagnall and P. Sijesteijn, "Currency in the Fourth Century and the Date of *CPR* V. 26, *ZPE* 24 (1977), 123–24; Bagnall, *Currency and Inflation,* pp. 60–61; and Hendy, *SBME,* pp. 464–65. Excluded as defective readings are *P. London* III. 1529 = Bagnall and Worp, *BASP* 20 (1983), 71–72, no. 4; *P. Lips.* 87; and *P. Rylands* III. 713 (p. 181).

might have been the *centenionalis* of the 354 law (pl. 22.181). Its obverse carries an unusual imperial portrait facing left and holding an orb. The fractional piece (2.42 g) bears no value mark and its reverse carries the Phoenix (pl. 22.182). The intermediate "N" coin (1.5 percent fine), whatever its official tariffing, was the half of the larger "A" coin (3 percent fine). The smallest coin (0.4 percent fine) might have been a revalued version of the old Constantinian nummus.[28] Many Constantinian nummi on AE3 flans were overstruck as the fractional denomination of the new currency, and some better Constantinian pieces continued to pass current, probably at a discount. The new coins were of excellent manufacture, impressive in their iconography, and produced in sufficient numbers to replace the old money. In size and weight, if not in silver content, the two larger denominations recalled nummi of 307–13. In the slang of the marketplace, both coins were collectively distinguished from their small predecessors as *pecuniae maiorinae,* "bigger money."

The fine-looking coins soon ran into the inevitable trouble whenever two billon denominations circulated in competition, because the smaller of the maiorinae, the so-called "N" denomination, was perceived as overvalued. The imperial brothers perhaps tried to avoid this difficulty by encouraging regional preferences for each denomination. At Western mints, Constans struck mostly larger "A" denominations, while in the East, where supplies of silver were scarcer, Constantius II concentrated on smaller "N" denominations. Speculation still ensued and widespread sweating of silver off the surface of maiorinae added to the confusion, since coins without a silver coating passed at a considerable discount. Within a year abuses were out of hand and the emperors mandated capital punishment against metal workers who "are purifying the *maiorina* coins no less criminally than frequently by separating off the silver from the copper."[29]

Civil war ruined this troubled currency almost immediately. The usurper Magnentius (350–53), commanding the Western armies, slew Constans and took over the minting of the AE2 denomination, complete with the A value mark. Constantius II, pressed to mount a reconquest of the West, abolished the two lower denominations in 351 and ruthlessly debased the larger maiorina from a hefty coin of

*Table 7.4*
Debasement of "A" Denomination, 348–61

| Date | Module | Average Weight (Grams) | Number per Pound | Silver Content | |
|---|---|---|---|---|---|
| | | | | Fineness | Milligrams |
| 348–50 | AE2, large | 5.26 | 60 | 3.0 | 158 |
| 350–51 | AE2, large | 5.30 | 60 | 0.8 | 42 |
| 351–52 | AE2, small | 4.34 | 72 | 0.4 | 17 |
| 352–55 | AE3 | 2.48 | 120 | 0.6 | 15 |
| 355–58 | AE3 | 2.26 | 130 | 0.5 | 11 |
| 358–61 | AE3, small | 1.96 | 144 | 0.1 | 2 |

*Source:* Kent, *RIC* VIII, p. 64.

Tetrarchic stature to the size of the tiny Constantinian nummus it had replaced (Table 7.4).[30] As soon as he crushed Magnentius, Constantius II moved to impose monetary order, and in 354 he issued an edict outlawing the maiorinae and centenionales as well as a general prohibition covering old nummi, imitative pieces, counterfeits, and coins of Magnentius.

> But it shall be entirely unlawful for anyone to handle forbidden coins, because it is proper for the price of a thing to be in coins established in public use and not in merchandise. . . . And if ships do by chance come with merchandise to whatever province then it shall be sold with all customary freedom, with the exception of the coins which they call *maiorinae* and *centenionales communes* by the usual custom and others which they know to be forbidden.[31]

The reduced "A" denomination struck on an AE3 module alone remained in circulation. The law, however, brought no monetary relief. Constantius's campaigns against the Germans and Persians compelled more debasements, forcing a revaluation of the dismal descendant of the maiorina to a nummus of several thousand d.c. by 360. A new wave of inflation swept over the empire, resulting in the ludicrously high sums in talents or denarii found in Egyptian papyri. In Britain and Gaul, German invasions in the wake of the defeat of Magnentius disrupted the supply. In 354, Constantius II centered production in the West at Lugdunum and Arelate (Arles) in southern Gaul. He closed Ambianum (Amiens), the auxiliary mint of Magnentius in northeastern Gaul, reopened Treveri, but the mints in southern Gaul could not deliver sufficient coins to the northern provinces when Franks, Saxons, and Alamanni crossed the Rhine and cut off Treveri. The swift contraction of currency in the Roman northwest during the late 350s and 360s was the dress rehearsal for the end of Roman currency in Northern Europe in 406–25. Provincials resorted to using coins of Magnentius or striking imitative pieces (pl. 22.183). Fifteen years of hard campaigning by the caesar Julian (355–60) and then Valentinian I were required to restore order and coinage.[32]

The usurper Magnentius (350–53) unwittingly had charted the road to reform of the base metal currency.[33] After his loss of Italy and Illyricum in 352, Magnentius lowered the weight of his solidus to 20 carats (3.78 g), ceased striking silver coins, and discontinued silver-clad coins in favor of a heavy copper coin (8.3 g) struck on a wide AE1 flan bearing the Christogram flanked by the Alpha and Omega on its reverse (pl. 22.184). This giant maiorina, which circulated as a multiple of earlier billon maiorinae of AE2 module, was apparently tariffed as if it contained silver. Magnentius resorted to a bronze maiorina because he lacked the silver to coat it; in two debasements he also halved its weight (pl. 22.185). Magnentius aimed at recreating the Tetrarchic nummus rather than the Augustan as, but he and the Eastern usurper Procopius (365–66), who, out of necessity, struck maiorinae without a silver wash, unintentionally pointed the way back to a token bronze coinage.

The pagan emperor Julian the Apostate in early 362 cut expenditures, revised taxes, and ordered a recoinage of the tiny billon nummi.[34] The new currency consisted of a large silver-clad maiorina (2 percent fine) struck on the heavy standard (8.13 g) introduced by Magnentius and a fraction struck on an AE3 module flan (2.87 g) whose negligible silver content (0.1 percent fine) and tariffing prevented competition (pl. 22.186–87). Julian guarded against overproducing the new coins by closing nearly half of the seventy-three *officinae* operating at the thirteen mints across the empire. His heavy maiorina was a short-lived success, because his Christian successors Jovian (363–64), Valentinian I, and Valens lowered the silver content when they struck their own versions of the maiorina without the pagan bull reverse so offensive to Antiochenes. Valentinian and Valens, who had restored the purity of the solidus and argenteus, could not maintain the silver content of the maiorina and, in 367, halted its production. In 371, the imperial brothers decreed: "The bronze money which is called *dichoneutum* ('alloyed'), not only shall be henceforth delivered to the *largitiones,* but even shall be entirely withdrawn from use and circulation, and nobody shall be allowed to possess it publicly."[35] Thorough recoining of "alloyed bronze money" removed the last billon coins of imperial Rome in favor of a modest bronze denomination on an AE3 module weighing 2.25 g. The silver reclaimed from melting billon maiorinae went into producing argentei. Valentinian and Valens, in the parlance of medieval England, were "crying up the coins" by restoring sound money and low prices. They declared their sanguine hope, "On account of the reduction that is being brought about in the exchange rate of the solidus, the price of all commodities ought also to decrease."[36] It is impossible to assess imperial claims.

It is a historical irony that rampant inflation in the third century brought forth silver-clad coins to the demise of the Augustan token bronze coins, but, in the fourth century, inflation ruined Tetrarchic silver-clad coins in favor of token bronze coins. War drove emperors to debase the silver-clad nummus; each rise in prices forced debasement, revaluation, and restoration of the nummus until another crisis set off the dreary cycle once more. The process relentlessly destroyed the Tetrarchic billon coinage and forced the emperors out of the ruinous business of billon coinage. By their laws Valentinian and Valens buried an experiment in billon coinage that had lasted 350 years, ever since Tiberius had created the Alexandrine tetradrachma.

The days of the billon coins were probably numbered when emperor Constantius II reduced the weight of the argenteus by 50 percent in 355. By pegging his argenteus to current ratios between gold and silver, Constantius II initiated large-scale minting of argentei, and, as a consequence, argentei struck from 355 to 392, unlike their Tetrarchic forerunners, stayed in circulation (pl.

21.169).[37] In the frontier provinces of Britain, Pannonia, and Dacia, the argenteus is the principal coin of high value found in hoards concealed during the troubled period of 380–420, suggesting that solidi and silver multiples were rarely available. Argentei even circulated in the East. The emperor Julian, when he relieved the famine at Antioch in 362, priced grain in argentei, and twice in the next year during his advance down the Euphrates he paid his soldiers donatives of argentei.[38] Since the light argenteus was probably reckoned as the equivalent of a carat (siliqua), the exchange of ceremonial silver multiples against the solidus were adjusted accordingly. Large silver multiples, struck at 24 and 72 to the Roman pound, were issued intermittently after 348 at Western mints, principally under Magnentius and Valentinian I and Valens, but light miliarensia, struck in some numbers, passed as doubles of the new argenteus, acquiring the name of miliarense before the end of the century (pl. 20.167). The Tetrarchic or heavy argenteus proved an awkward denomination that soon fell out of use.

Constantius II and Julian, who waged expensive wars against Shah Shapur II (309–79), debased the argenteus, but Valentinian I and Valens restored its purity. For a generation, the argenteus might have played a role comparable to that of the Augustan denarius until it was ruined by civil wars. Magnus Maximus (383–88), the tenacious usurper in the West, reduced by one-sixth the weight of argentei at Londinium and the Gallic mints (1.9 g), and by even more after he occupied Aquileia and Rome (1.5 g; pl. 21.170). Theodosius suspended striking silver coinage upon recovering the West, but in 392 he adopted the first standard of Magnus Maximus, minting 168 argentei to the Roman pound (1.9 g). Five years later his sons Honorius (395–421) and Arcadius (395–408) lowered the weight standard by one-sixth to 196 argentei to the Roman pound (1.6 g). As Western mints fell into the hands of usurpers or barbarians, each coined small argentei on local standards. These argentei were no longer equivalents of a carat; many after 450 were halves (1.1 g) of the Constantinian argenteus. British provincials soon after 400 even clipped heavier argentei and reissued them as minor fractions of the solidus.[39]

The modest bronze nummi of Valentinian I and Valens, struck

on an AE3 flan and lacking the infamous silver wash, must have been exchanged by the thousands against the solidus. In 379 the brothers Gratian (367–83) and Valentinian II (375–92) reproduced in bronze the three denominations of the reform in 348. The largest coin, on an AE2 module (5.25 g), looked and weighed the same as an earlier maiorina (pl. 22.188). Since this maiorina passed under the nickname "decargyrus" (a silvered piece of ten), it presumably was tariffed at 10 nummi at some point, and it might be the direct ancestor to the Byzantine *decanummia* of the late fifth century. The principal nummus, at least in the East, was the middle denomination of AE3 module (2.45 g; pl. 22.189). It too resembled its counterpart in the currency of 348 from whence it might have received its name centenionalis in the law of 395. The tiny fraction of AE4 size (1.5 g) might have passed as the single nummus (pl. 22.190), and by the 380s this coin was reckoned by the many thousands to the solidus.[40] These bronze coins, intended as fractions of the argenteus, shared the fate of the silver coinage. Magnus Maximus flooded the markets of the Western provinces and Italy with tiny nummi of AE4 module. In Rome, the pagan senator Symmachus championed the complaints of moneychangers arising from confusion over the exchange rates between solidus and competing nummi in 384–85.[41] In 388–92, mints in the West, by order of Theodosius, ceased striking the AE2 denomination or decargyrus, and sharply curtailed production of the intermediate AE3 denomination. Diminutive nummi minimi ("smallest coins"), struck on the AE4 flan, became by default the common coin of the Western realm. In 395 Honorius outlawed by imperial edict the larger coin in favor of the centenionalis:

> We command only the centenionalis nummus to be handled in public circulation, the making of the larger coin (*maior pecunia*) having been discontinued. Therefore, let no one dare exchange the decargyrus nummus for another, knowing it to be forfeit to the treasury if found in public circulation.[42]

A recoinage of maiorinae ensued, and on the eve of the fifth century Rome and Aquileia mass produced the bronze money of the Western Empire in the form of nummi on AE3 and AE4 modules. The Eastern Empire enjoyed a marginally better bronze currency.

### *The Collapse of Imperial Currency, 395–498*

Theodosius I divided the empire between his sons Honorius (395–423) in the West and Arcadius (395–408) in the East, but despite this dynastic division, mints in the West and the East struck full-bodied and token bronze coins to identical standards throughout the fifth century. It was the collapse of the Western Empire that caused the currency of the two halves of the Roman world to diverge so sharply. As the Germans and Huns assaulted the northern frontiers, the solidus emerged as the prime coin of war and diplomacy. Emperors, anxious to feed palatine mints a steady diet of gold, reimposed the laws passed by Valentinian I and Valens banning export of gold and silver coins and bullion. They simplified the denominations of the gold currency in favor of the solidus, its half (the semis), and its third (the tremissis), introduced by 383 and destined to become the gold coin of the barbarian West (pl. 20.163–64). Emperors dispensed with the ceremonial multiples and reduced the number of types found on the solidus and its fractions for ease of mass production and as a guarantee, especially in the eyes of barbarians, of the coins' purity and weight. During the first half of the fifth century, Rome, Ravenna (seat of the Western Empire after 402), and Constantinople together struck one of the largest gold coinages in Roman history, turning out solidi in the tens of millions. The other palatine mints, Thessalonica, Mediolanum, Arelate, and Treveri coined sporadically.[43]

The circulating specie of the Roman Empire might have begun to contract noticeably after the catastrophic defeat at Adrianople in 378. Theodosius I (379–95) rebuilt the imperial army by recruiting large numbers of German federates who demanded payment in gold. The migrations of the Visigoths in 395–417 opened a new wave of barbarian assaults that interrupted and then terminated Roman mining throughout the European provinces. But of more importance, the barbarian onslaught drained specie out of the Roman world, eroding imperial revenues and currency. Even though the process cannot be measured with any accuracy, it is documented by the numerous hoards of solidi, mixed with medallions and gold and silver plate, secreted between the late fourth and early seventh centuries in the barbarian lands of northern and southeastern Europe. Since Germans and Huns viewed solidi as lesser objects, they were mounted in bracelets or melted to be alloyed with silver and cast into ornaments or tableware. Therefore, emperors saved manufacturing costs by paying tributes in the form of *centenarium,* a leather sack containing 100 pounds of gold that could be made up of solidi, ingots, or plate. Treaties referred to *centenaria* and payment could be made by weighing the sacks without the trouble of counting thousands of solidi.[44]

Barbarian migrations ruined the fiscal institutions that had pumped currency throughout the Roman economy. This loss was far more crucial in the demise of Roman coinage and monetary habits in the Western Empire than the loss of specie taken in plunder and subsidies. Emperors responded by amassing great reserves to meet the unpredictable costs of war and diplomacy. The accumulation of such reserves came to characterize the finances of Byzantine emperors throughout the Middle Ages, and the policy was a return to older, less monetized patterns of expenditure reminiscent of Achaemenid kings of Persia. In 468 the Western emperor Anthemius and his Eastern colleague Leo I launched a joint expedition deploying 100,000 men and over 1,000 vessels against the Vandals of North Africa. Costs of this disastrous venture totaled between 7.5 and 9.5 million solidi, and over one-third was paid in silver coin and bullion weighing 700,000 Roman pounds.[45] Theodosius II (408–50) and Marcian (450–57), despite heavy expenditures, each amassed reserves of 1,000 *centenaria* or the equivalent of 7.2 million solidi. Parsimonious Anastasius (491–518) left the treasury brimming with 3,200 *centenaria,* over 23 million solidi, which Justin I (518–27) increased to a record high of 4,000 *centenaria* (28.8 million solidi).[46]

The crisis of the fifth century pushed the imperial government into discontinuing older systems of reckoning fiscal accounts in favor of the solidus. In northwestern Europe and Spain, reckoning in solidi or tremisses followed soon after the collapse of Roman power and the token bronze currency in 406–10. The transition took much longer in Italy, Africa, and the East, where most daily purchases in markets were transacted in bags of tiny bronze nummi expressed as so many to the carat of the solidus. As late as 435–45, officials assessed taxes of most landowners of the Egyptian village of Skar in the Hermopolite nome in talents and collected in AE4 nummi, but some land taxes, perhaps of the wealthier residents were assessed and collected in solidi. Syrian funerary and public monuments, long priced in talents and d.c., were calculated in solidi by the 480s. By the opening of the sixth century, Egyptian tax registers were regularly kept in solidi and carats.[47]

As emperors and their subjects shifted to a gold standard, the silver and bronze subsidiary coinages deteriorated. Silver coins passed out of general circulation during the mid-fifth century. The striking of ceremonial silver multiples virtually ended by 400. The light miliarense, reduced to the size and weight of a Sassanid dirhem (4.3 g), might have earned its nickname as a coin tariffed at 1,000 to a pound of gold.[48] Argentei were manufactured on thin flans, and their fabric and light weight anticipated the barbarian, imitative, and Western Byzantine denominations of the fifth and sixth centuries, and their even more distant hammered progeny, the pennies and deniers of Carolingian Europe (pl. 21.171). Imperial mints lowered the weight of argenteus and miliarense as the value of silver appreciated, but it is misleading to speak of a silver famine. Silver specie was prone to widespread hoarding in troubled times, and vast amounts of silver were immobilized as the sacramental objects of Christian churches, superb silverware of Roman aristocrats, or caches of plunder secreted by barbarians in northern Europe. Emperors too hoarded silver. The usurper Priscus Attalus (409–10) on short notice recoined the silver plate of Rome into spectacular multiples weighing 24 carats (the equivalent of a solidus). In 468 the Eastern emperor Leo I possessed enough silver in his treasury to manufacture over 100 million argentei at 144 to the Roman pound.

Soon after 400 in the East no denomination in silver or bronze stood between the gold tremissis and the millions of nummi minimi (smallest coins), nicknamed "small change" (*lepta* or *kerma*), that comprised most of the money in daily use. In 395 Honorius outlawed in the Western Empire nummi other than two fractional pieces, a tiny coin on an AE4 module, which almost certainly was the nummus of imperial laws, and its possible double struck on an AE3 flan.[49] Maiorinae of the fourth century vanished from use in the West. In the East, Arcadius delayed implementing his brother's edict, and Eastern mints struck maiorinae (of AE2 size) and maintained heavier standards for the AE3 and AE4 denominations in 395–400. During the next quarter century (400–425), Western and Eastern emperors struck the same bronze currency consisting of paltry AE4 and AE3 denominations that were progressively debased with lead. In 425, Valentinian III (425–55) and Theodosius II (408–50) discontinued and demonetized the AE3 nummus. Nummi minimi alone circulated in the wreckage of the Western Empire thereafter. The Eastern emperors Theodosius II, Leo I (457–74), and Zeno (474–91) each coined limited numbers of maiorinae (5 to 6 g) bearing iconography that recalled their counterparts in the 348 and 379 reforms and perhaps passed as pieces of ten nummi.

Emperors attempted to regulate rates so that the number of tiny nummi exchanged to the solidus did not weigh more than 25 Roman pounds of coined bronze. Honorius and Arcadius so mandated in 396 and, at this rate, their AE4 nummus, struck at 216 to the Roman pound, was officially calculated at 5,400 to the solidus (pl. 22.190). But imperial pronouncements did not determine daily transactions in markets. Within a single year during the reign of Arcadius, the solidus at towns in the Fayyum was perhaps cited at 7,600, 7,700, 7,800, and 8,000 nummi, yielding exchange rates of 35 to 37 pounds of coined bronze per solidus.[50] In 425 Theodosius II and Valentinian III slashed by 25 percent the weight of the AE4 nummus as rising prices bid up exchange rates to unworkable levels (pl. 22.191). At Skar in 435–45, tax officials would have handled close to 32.5 pounds of nummi per solidus. In an edict of 445 Valentinian III ordered that moneychangers of Rome accept the solidus from the mint at the rate of 7,000 nummi and exchange it at their tables at 7,200 nummi. Prices rose unabated in the East. By 498 the solidus was trading at 16,800 nummi at Constantinople when the emperor Anastasius (491–518) at last issued a comprehensive reform rather than resort to expedients of debasement and revaluation of the tiny nummi.

The nummi minimi were extremely cumbersome to use without bronze multiples. Victor, the official who drew up the register of Skar in the Hermopolite nome in 435–45, reports that 327 individuals paid taxes and arrears (nearly 60 percent of the land taxes) in nummi of the AE4 module (1.12 g) that totaled 1,522,080 nummi (or 5,285 pounds by weight), the equivalent of 211.40 solidi. In contrast, two collections in gold netted 152 solidi, reckoned by weight as 135.75 solidi or just under 2 Roman pounds.[51] The imperial government lost revenues due to the ease of counterfeiting nummi. Legal and false nummi were sealed up together in leather bags to pass by the hundreds or the thousands. The last hoards of the Roman Britain and Gaul, concealed between 395 and 410, as well as Italian, North African, and Egyptian hoards deposited during the fifth century consisted of thousands of tiny nummi of AE4 module that included many imitations, counterfeits, and even obsolete nummi of the fourth century (minus their silver coating).[52] This dismal token currency was tolerated (and exploited), because, in the face of barbarian onslaughts, the solidus was the key to survival. It was only at the end of the fifth century when the Roman emperor of the East and the Germanic kings in Italy and Africa were willing and able to reform the bronze currency.

### *New Perspectives on Late Roman Coinage*

The demise of the Tetrarchic currency in the fourth century often has been viewed as a sign of the failure of the Roman monetary economy. It has been argued that emperors exacted more and more taxes either in kind or bullion, thereby reducing their dependence upon coins. This selfish policy, aimed to protect imperial revenues from the scourge of inflation, led to the abandonment of Roman monetary habits and reversion to a "natural economy." Although fiscal oppression and bureaucratic corruption abound in the sources of the Dominate, neither Egyptian tax registers (whose rates were reckoned in traditional ghost currencies and collected in bronze or billon coins), nor legal documents, nor even the coins themselves square with this vision of the late Roman economy. Emperors had always exacted their needs in a mix of kind and coin, and there is no evidence of a policy ordering officials to shun billon or bronze coins for public obligations.

More legislation concerning the regulation or reform of the currency survives for the period of 305–498 than from any other in Roman history. Emperors sponsoring reforms stressed public utility, and their coins second such platitudes. Billon and bronze coins, even though their names and tariffing are obscure, document a remarkable series of reforms. If many emperors shamelessly financed public debt by debasement, others such as Constans and Constantius II, Julian, and Valentinian and Valens offered better money and regulated production. The billon and bronze coins of the fourth century were of good manufacture. Large denominations bear imaginative designs so that their attractive appearance would gain public trust and utility, the professed goals of imperial legislation.

Valentinian and Valens issued their laws in 366–67 to restore sound gold and silver coins; the laws did not mark a departure in monetary thinking that converted solidi and argentei into privileged pieces of bullion rather than coins. There is every reason to believe that coins were still playing their customary role in Roman economic and fiscal life when the barbarians toppled the Western Empire at the opening of the fifth century. If this view is correct, Roman currency, along with monetized economic life and fiscal institutions, did not cease suddenly at some point in the fourth century—such as when Diocletian reformed the coinage and tax assessments, or when Constantine introduced the solidus, or even when Valentinian I and Valens restored gold and silver standards. The failure of imperial coinage in the fifth century is instead part of the larger story of the corruption and failure of the whole edifice of imperial government. But in the wake of imperial demise emerged new medieval currencies, for the pace of decline was hardly uniform throughout the Roman world. Where Roman power or institutions survived, Byzantine emperors and Teutonic kings sponsored new currency reforms and thus wrote the last chapter of the history of Roman coinage.

# Eight

# The Loss of Roman Monetary Ways, A.D. 400–700

During the six centuries between 200 B.C. and A.D. 400, Rome promoted a unified currency and greater use of coins throughout the Mediterranean world. In the following three centuries (A.D. 400 to 700), all parts of the Roman world suffered a steady erosion of their economic and social life and, as a consequence, the loss of Roman monetary ways. What seem to have been two divergent paths in the late fifth and early sixth century—the loss of Roman monetary habits in the West and the survival and reform of Roman currency in Italy, Africa, and the East—were actually two parts of a single process leading to the birth of medieval coinages.

When barbarian migrations shattered the monetary unity of the Roman Empire, three distinct monetary zones emerged during the second half of the fifth century: the former northwestern and Iberian provinces; the western Mediterranean lands of Italy, southern Gaul, and North Africa; and the Roman East firmly under the rule of the emperors in Constantinople. In each region late Roman currency was transformed into a new medieval one. The numbers of coins circulating in each region reflected the degree to which Roman social and economic institutions still functioned. In the Roman

East, emperors between Anastasius (491–518) and Constantine IV (668–85) strove to maintain the currency and the monetized fiscal and economic institutions of Rome. Imperial reforms stabilized prices in the early sixth century during the ephemeral "Indian Summer" of Mediterranean urban life. The last chapter of Roman currency is thus the story of the emerging new orders of the early medieval world: the barbarian West, Italy and North Africa, and the nascent Byzantine Empire.

### *The Barbarian West, 450–700*

The withdrawal of Roman forces from Britain in 410 ended the payrolls that put coins into circulation, and the collapse of the Rhine *limes* in 406–10 cut off supplies of fresh coins from the Gallic mints at Treveri (Trier), Lugdunum (Lyons), and Arelate (Arles). Coins rapidly passed out of use in northern and western regions of the island. Britons in the southeast manufactured barbarous nummi minimi as small change, but such coins ceased to circulate shortly after the Gallic bishop Saint Germanus visited British cities in 430.[1] The minting and use of coins in the island had already disappeared when Anglo-Saxon settlers arrived in force from the mid-fifth century. Nearly two centuries later, in the late seventh century, the English learned the use of coins from their Frankish cousins. Anglo-Saxon royal burials at Sutton Hoo (ca. 630) and Crondale (ca. 640) contain gold tremisses of Merovingian Gaul or equivalent blanks as "gifts" for rowers, but this was a ritual use of coins long common in the Germanic world and is not proof of the resumption of monetary ways.[2] Kinglets in southeastern England, perhaps in ca. 650–80, minted tremisses in imitation of their Merovingian counterparts, but they soon replaced this pale gold coinage with series of dumpy, thick silver pennies which are by convention designated "sceats" (pl. 28.230–31).[3]

The collapse of the Roman frontier on the Rhine and Upper Danube in 406–10 disrupted the manufacture and distribution of imperial coins. In remoter regions of Gaul and Spain, as in Britain, provincials ceased to use coins altogether. Treveri was isolated and ceased to coin, and the prefect of Gaul transferred his seat and primary mint to Arelate by 408. Aetius (433–54), *magister militum* of the West, restored a measure of imperial control to central and eastern Gaul so that provincial authorities might have briefly resumed minting gold and silver coins at Treveri. The Roman commanders Aegidius (456–65) and Syagrius (465–86), who operated independently in northeastern Gaul, perhaps minted solidi and argentei in the names of Valentinian III and Theodosius II (pl. 21.171), and Franks and Visigoths issued many inferior imitative pieces (pl. 27.220–21 and 224).[4] Throughout the Spanish and Gallic provinces, as well as on the frontiers of the Rhine and Upper and Middle Danube, tiny nummi on the AE4 module passed out of circulation by 430, soon after imperial mints in the West ceased striking bronze coins. Thereafter, nummi circulated only in North Africa, southern Spain, Italy, and the Rhone Valley (pl. 27.235).[5]

Although the German invaders—first the Visigoths and the Burgundians, and then the Franks who drove the Visigoths into Spain and subjugated the Burgundians—destroyed direct Roman rule in Gaul and Spain, they neither displaced Roman provincial populations (save on the frontiers) nor swept away the use of coins. Towns in the Rhineland, Gaul, and Spain struck solidi, tremisses, and, at times, small silver fractions (called *argentei minimi* in later Frankish sources), because Roman cities and landlords paid land taxes to their Teutonic masters in coin. Germanic kings also exacted rents and tolls or rewarded retainers in solidi.[6] The survival of a system of taxation, albeit rudimentary, ensured continued circulation of imperial solidi and production of imitative pieces until the late seventh century.

In Gaul, the Visigoths, secure in Toulouse from 412, ruled Aquitaine and minted solidi after Ravennate prototypes of Valentinian III and Severus III (pl. 27.224). The Burgundians, settled as federates in regions of the Jura in 443, occupied the Saône and Rhone valleys by 480 and seized the old imperial mint at Lyons. Burgundian kings in 475–532 struck imitative gold solidi and tremisses, silver fractions, and AE4 nummi (pl. 27.225). In the *lex Burgundionum*, King Gundobald (473–516) imposed a rudimentary monetary unity by outlawing various imitative gold coins as well the coins of the Visigothic king Alaric II (484–507) on the grounds that they were base or underweight.[7] The Burgundians also ruled over the cities of Provence that maintained commercial links with Italy and the Roman East. Marseilles struck solidi (weighing either 20 or 21 carats), silver fractions, and bronze nummi that bear the imperial name and portrait. Frankish kings, who occupied Marseilles and Arles in 537, permitted production of these "pseudo-imperial" light solidi, which were based on Byzantine prototypes, for the next century (pl. 27.226).[8]

The Franks, the most adaptable of Rome's western heirs, encountered many different late Roman and imitative coinages when they conquered Gaul. The tiny argentei—with stylized portraits of Honorius, Valentinian III, and Johannes—might have been minted by the first Franks settling in northern and eastern Gaul who hoarded silver (customarily cut-up plate or "hack silver") rather than gold.[9] Merovingian kings, however, coined solidi either to display their largess in emulation of Roman emperors or to pay for eastern luxuries (pl. 27.227). The prime source of the gold was sundry imitative, Byzantine, and Ostrogothic solidi taken in plunder or tribute: for example, King Theodebert of Austrasia (534–48) acquired 50,000 solidi as the price of his support of the Ostrogothic Witigis, and in 584 Childebert II (575–95) received the same sum from the emperor Maurice Tiberius for an attack against the Lombards in Italy.[10]

Supplies of gold in Gaul were contracting by the late 580s when Frankish kings discontinued the solidus in favor of its third, the tremissis, but the tremissis was steadily debased by being alloyed with silver and the miserable pale gold coinage expired in 670 (pl. 28.228). Frankish kings lost control over the production of tremisses as territorial prelates and secular lords either usurped the right to coin or minted on royal authority. Many tremisses carry the names of moneyers, who perhaps exercised minting as a royal franchise. The individual styles of engraving, the diversity of designs and mintmarks, and the finds at widespread locations confirm that tremisses were struck at many different sites for local circulation.[11] Surviving specimens often are die-linked since they were usually struck in limited numbers for specific payments. Gregory of Tours, for example, reports that the Bishop of Poitiers ordered a gold chalice to be melted down and turned into coin to buy off raiders.[12] This cycle—turning plate into coin and then coin into plate—was repeated many times throughout the barbarian West, and accounts, in part, for the gradual debasement of the tremissis over the course of the sixth and seventh centuries. At the same time, the remnants of the Roman fiscal apparatus disintegrated. Dagobert I (629–39) renounced royal claims to direct taxes, and consequently the minting of tremisses expired in the next generation. When the Merovingian kings suspended minting tremisses in the 670s, they turned to a silver denier (93–94 percent fine), struck on thick flans comparable to Anglo-Saxon and Frisian sceats.

In Spain, imitative Roman coinage followed paths similar to, though less complex than those in Gaul. The Sueves struck crude copies of solidi of Honorius or Valentinian III, along with rare tremisses and silver fractions, down to the Visigothic conquest (ca. 410–580; pl. 27.222–23). Many towns named on coins were located in the mining districts in northwestern Spain where the Sueves still exploited Roman mines. The conquering Visigothic kings, who took over the Suevic mints and mines, initially struck imitative imperial solidi until King Leovigild (568–86) replaced the solidus with a tremissis engraved in a distinct native style and bearing the royal name and portrait (pl. 28.233–34). Visigothic kings, just like their Frankish rulers, debased their tremisses into pale gold by the eve of the Arabic conquest.[13] The Muslim emirs of Cordova briefly struck dinars inspired from late Visigothic tremisses (first with Latin and then with Kufic legends), but by 725 they abandoned the pale gold coins in favor of the silver dirhem of the Umayyad Caliphate (pl. 30.251).

Imitative coinages in Frankish Gaul and Visigothic Spain mask the erosion of the Roman monetary economy rather than prove continuity with the Roman past. Despite minting at many sites scattered across Britain, Frisia, Gaul, and Spain, total coinage numbered only in tens of thousands in 700—trivial in comparison to an annual volume running in hundreds of millions at the three imperial mints of Treveri, Arelate, and Lugdunum in 395. Germanic kings, without the huge budgets of the Roman state, lacked both reasons and means to put coins into circulation. Specie was immobilized in royal and ecclesiastical treasuries or it was drained off to the eastern Mediterranean in payments for luxury goods. Western European monarchs abandoned imitative Roman coinages by 750 in favor of a new silver denier or penny manufactured from "hammered" sheets of metal in the fashion of Sassanid dirhems. Struck in the millions rather than the thousands, deniers and pennies suited the local markets and petty commerce of Dark Age Europe.[14] The monetary future of medieval Europe lay in the denier of Carolingian Gaul (pl. 28.229), the penny of Anglo-Saxon England (pl. 28.232), and the dirhem of the Muslim Spain, but these coinages had traveled far from their Roman antecedents.

### *Vandalic North Africa and Ostrogothic Italy*

In Italy and North Africa, in the towns on the shores of southern Gaul and Dalmatia, and on the islands in the western Mediterranean the fate of Roman coins was quite different from that in Gaul and Spain. Roman civic life and administration survived, although on a reduced scale, so there still was a need for token bronze nummi and silver fractions, and a brisk trade linking Italy and Africa with the Byzantine East, although again on a reduced scale, required gold coins.

The Vandal conquest of North Africa in 427–39 reduced the number of coins imported from Rome and the eastern mints. Since Vandal kings never minted their own solidi, existing stocks and imports apparently proved sufficient not only for royal gifts and purchases of luxuries, but also for commercial transactions even in remote African towns such as those reported in the *Tablettes Albertini*. The failure to mint a gold currency suggests that the Moors disrupted the trade in West African gold and restricted Vandal control and taxation of the Numidian hinterland.[15] The Vandals, however, minted subsidiary silver and bronze coinages bearing imperial-style portraits and reverse types. Even though obverse legends name a Germanic king, the coins by virtue of their Roman appearance passed as divisions of the solidus. From 455 to 477 King Gaiseric struck argentei at 192 to the Roman pound. The coins, called siliquae by numismatic convention, were similar in style and in weight standard to contemporary Suevic and Frankish imitative issues of Valentinian III and Johannes. Wide variations in fineness (from 43 to 71 percent) and the limited number of surviving specimens suggest that Gaiseric minted siliquae from windfalls of plunder.[16] Gunthamund (484–96) and his successors struck in their own names a heavier and finer siliqua (168 to the pound and 99 percent fine) with corresponding halves and quarters (pl. 29.236). On the reverse of each denomination is an appropriate value mark—100, 50, or 25 denarii equivalent, respectively, to 500, 250, or 125 bronze nummi.[17]

Roman nummi of AE4 module circulated throughout the fifth century, and finds at Carthage and smaller African sites reveal that the one nummus was the most common denomination casually lost well into the Byzantine age. Dealing in large numbers of tiny nummi was always cumbersome, but it was especially so in Vandal North Africa which depended on imported *aes* and numerous imitations and counterfeits in circulation. Gaiseric in the late 470s and 480s struck quasi-imperial nummi to replenish declining stocks of *aes*.[18] In ca. 480 the imperial solidus in Vandal North Africa was officially tariffed at 12,000 bronze nummi or approximately 40 percent more than the value mandated at Rome in 445. The rate climbed to between 14,400 and 14,700 nummi by 498.[19] In ca. 487–88 King Gunthamund reformed the dismal bronze currency by issuing a series of multiple denominations including a follis of 42 nummiae (or nummi) and fractions of 21 and 12 nummiae (pl. 28.237and pl. 29.238). The coins carried marks of value, ancient civic and imperial types, and the obverse legend KARTHAGO.

The odd denominations of 42, 21, 12, and eventually 4 nummi were an awkward adaptation of the bronze denominations to a dual system of decimal and duodecimal reckoning. The solidus was reckoned in a decimal scheme as 12,000 bronze nummiae. Silver coins, however, were based on a duodecimal reckoning of 24 siliquae or 2,400 denarii to the solidus so that silver denominations were minted as 1, ½, or ¼ siliqua, representing respectively 1/24, 1/48, and 1/96 of the solidus. Silver pieces were neatly converted into the decimal system of bronze coins; a siliqua of 100 d.c. (1/24 of a solidus) was equivalent to 500 nummi. The bronze coins, however, were not so readily reconciled to the duodecimal reckoning of the siliqua. The Vandals selected the peculiar multiples of 42, 21, 12, and 4 nummiae as approximate fractions of 1/12, 1/21, 1/12, and 1/125 siliqua, respectively, because they rounded off to the nearest whole number quotients resulting from dividing these fractions into a silver siliqua of 500 nummiae. Given the limited number of precise combinations of bronze coins and fluctuating exchange rates, vendors and purchasers must have constantly bargained and rounded off fractions in daily transactions. In the *Tablettes Albertini,* the follis was exchanged at rates of 343 to 350 to the solidus, and prices of olive trees and property were reckoned in large units to avoid dealing in bronze denominations less than the follis.[20] Vendors created further bronze multiples by incising the value marks of 83 nummiae (1/6 siliqua) and 42 nummiae on obsolete Flavian and Antonine sestertii and middle *aes,* respectively (pl. 29.239).[21] Since Vandal denominations did not fit Byzantine reckoning, denominations above the single nummus were recoined soon after Belisarius recaptured Carthage in 533.

In Italy, the celebrated Ostrogothic king, Theodoric (489–526), conquered and restored order to a kingdom embracing Italy, Sicily, Narbonensis, and Dalmatia. Theodoric fell heir to a currency virtually identical to that current in the Roman East. His opponent Odovacer (476–93), the German generalissimo who deposed the last phantom Western emperor Romulus Augustus (475–76), had minted imitative solidi, semisses, and tremisses in the name of Zeno at the Italian mints of Rome, Ravenna, and Milan, and at Arles in southern Gaul. Theodoric centered minting at Rome and closed mints at Milan and Ravenna, but Arles struck quasi-imperial coins for Provence and Salonae minted coins for Dalmatian towns on the eastern shores of the Adriatic. Theodoric and his successors struck large numbers of solidi in the name of the Eastern Roman emperor, but the coins were distinguished from their imperial prototypes by the monogram of the reigning Gothic king on the reverse (pl. 29.240). Since Gothic kings faced substantial military, administrative, and ceremonial costs, older imperial solidi and solidi imported from Constantinople also circulated. Theodoric also provided an appropriate subsidiary coinage in silver based on a theoretical siliqua at 96 to the Roman pound, the Constantinian standard of the early fourth century. Rome and Milan struck a half-siliqua (1.6 g) and quarter-siliqua (0.8 g). The obverses carry the imperial portrait and name, and the royal name or monogram occupy the reverse fields. His grandson Athalaric (526–34) reduced the weights of silver denominations (pl. 29.241). When Belisarius occupied Rome in 537–45, Roman engravers struck, in the name of Justinian, versions of the lighter weight coins but with the Greek value marks of 240 and 120 nummiae (exchanged at 50 and 100 to the solidus, respectively).[22]

In contrast to the rest of the Western Empire, Italian mints produced vast quantities of bronze nummi on an AE4 module during the late fifth century. By 490 the exchange rate for the solidus rose from 7,200 nummi, as laid down in the law of Valentinian III, to 12,000 nummi so that 21 pounds of coined bronze were traded against the solidus. Theodoric, after securing Italy in 491, reintroduced large bronze multiples of the nummus based on a follis of forty nummiae (pl. 29.242). Five *officinae* of the mint at Rome struck forty- and twenty-nummia pieces (at 15 and 7 g, respectively) in a first series; ten- and five-nummia pieces were added in a second series; a third series consisted of only lightweight folles (10 g; pl. 29.243–44).[23] Ostrogothic bronze denominations, far more convenient divisions of the solidus than their Vandal counterparts, inspired the denominational structure of the Anastasian reform at Constantinople. In 490, 300 folles of forty nummiae, with a total weight of just 14 pounds, were exchanged against the solidus. As in Vandal North Africa, the coins bear antique types and, on the reverse, the abbreviation S.C., a detail suggesting that the idea of large bronze coins might have been inspired by the discovery and reuse of *aes* of the Principate.[24]

Eighteen years (536–54) of desultory fighting between the armies of Justinian and the Ostrogoths ruined the cities and currency of Italy. Kings Witigis (536–40), Hildebad (541), Totila (541–52), and Theia (552) concentrated on striking solidi to purchase Frankish and Burgundian allies. Carried north of the Alps in great numbers as subsidies or plunder, late Gothic solidi replaced imperial coins as prototypes for Frankish imitations. Witigis removed his mint from Rome to Ravenna in 537, and, after he surrendered at Ravenna, his successor Hildebad relocated the court and mint to Ticinum (Pavia) in the Po Valley (540–52). The Gothic War ruined the silver and bronze coinages. First Ravenna and then Ticinum sporadically coined silver fractions and light-weight decanummiae and nummiae for regions still under Gothic control. Meanwhile, when Byzantine forces retook Rome in 537, the Eternal City commenced striking bronze currency on the standard of the East. Rome soon suspended minting, for she endured two grueling sieges and ruthless sacks by the Goths in 545–46 and 549–50. Imperial authorities were in no position to furnish Italy with adequate currency for a dozen years, until after the victory at Busta Gallorum in 552.

Finds at Italian sites point to serious shortages of coins of all denominations, and bronze coins in circulation included those from Byzantine metropolitan and auxiliary Italian mints, Gothic pieces, and stray Vandal coins, including unofficially marked obsolete Roman *aes* carried to Italy by Belisarius's veterans from Africa. In 552 Justinian faced the daunting task of restoring the fiscal institutions and currency when he issued his administrative reforms known as the Pragmatic Sanction. Justinian sanctioned as legal tender solidi of former emperors and Gothic foes, provided the coins were of proper weight.[25] Whatever Justinian's plans were for the reconstruction of Italy, they came to naught. In 568 the Lombards invaded the peninsula, shattered Byzantine control, and swept away the vestiges of Roman economic and social life.

Vandal and Ostrogothic coinages were one of the important links with the Roman past after the collapse of the Western Empire. The reforms of Gunthamund in Africa inspired Theodoric to reform Italian currency; both reforms in turn stood behind Anastasius's decision to reform the bronze currency of the Eastern Roman Empire. Subsidiary silver and bronze coinage in Italy and Africa provide an index of the survival not only of Roman monetary habits, but also of fiscal institutions and long-distance trade with the East. Germanic kings, wedded to the Roman past, hesitated to reform without the sanctity of Roman tradition. Solidi almost invariably bear the emperor's name, suggesting that imperial solidi were preferred; silver fractions and nummi in type and fabric were intended to pass as equivalents to imperial originals. Even when they initiated reforms of the bronze money, Germanic kings chose archaizing types that recalled emblems and legends of Carthage or Rome (inspired by Punic *aes,* Roman *aes* of the Principate, Tetrarchic nummi, and Constantinian *contorniates*) thereby conferring an air of legitimacy on the new bronze coins. Justinian easily adapted the imitative currencies to imperial needs, for they were part of the late Roman heritage that enabled him to reincorporate the lost provinces of the West.

The significance of the imitative Roman coinages struck under Vandal and Ostrogothic auspices should not be exaggerated. The size of these coinages remains uncertain, and Vandal silver issues were apparently coined in modest numbers at best. Vandal and Gothic kings countenanced production of solidi, siliquae, and nummi based on imperial prototypes when the stock of circulating money contracted due to wear and loss in the last quarter of the fifth century. The extent of circulation of these coinages is also far from certain. Excavations at Carthage and lesser African towns point to an expansion in the supply of silver and bronze coins from the last quarter of the fifth century until the Arabic conquest. The commercial documents of a sleepy African town, known as the *Tablettes Albertini,* reveal local elites transacting sales in solidi and folles. The picture from Vandal Africa and Ostrogothic Italy is one of continuity in Roman monetary habits in contrast to the northern and Iberian provinces of the Roman West. Imitative coinages, although based on the Roman solidus, were evolving into new systems of reckoning and currency, when the Byzantine conquest abruptly ended these coinages. But the victories of Justinian only retarded rather than reversed the disintegration of the Roman Mediterranean order and its monetary unity.

## *Recovery and Reform in the East, 498–540*

At the close of the fifth century, since the emperors of the East had weathered the military crisis, they could reform the currency and take fiscal measures to restore revenues and promote prosperity. Although emperors between Justinian (527–65) and Maurice

Tiberius (582–602) occasionally minted grandiose golden medallions, the solidus (or *nomisma* in Greek) was the prime high-value gold coin of the nascent Byzantine state. The two palatine mints of Constantinople and Thessalonica monopolized the striking of solidi, which were impeccable in their purity and weight. Argentei, miliarensia, and silver multiples on the Constantininan standard were occasionally used, but most silver coins were recast into plate or were exported to the Sassanid Empire where the shah turned them into dirhems or ornate silver plate destined as gifts for his own barbarian allies in Central Asia and southern Russia.[26] As silver coins vanished from general circulation during the fifth century, tiny bronze nummi (or, in Greek, *nummiae*) served as the sole fractions of the solidus in daily transactions, and they were often exchanged in sealed purses sometimes containing thousands of nummi.

In 498, in the first of two reforms, Anastasius (491–518) recoined nummi minimi of the past century into bronze multiples. John Malalas, the Antiochene chronicler of the sixth century, reports a major recoinage directed by John Caiaphas, the *comes largitionum*: "And he made all the current small change (*kerma*), the *lepta,* into folles, and ordered them to be current throughout the Roman empire thereafter."[27] Anastasius offered a coinage worthy of public trust—it was attractive and functional, and struck on well-manufactured flans in the best traditions of Diocletian. The follis, called in Greek slang an "obol," headed a chain of denominations bearing, on their central reverse, Greek numerals to denote values of forty, twenty, and ten nummiae. Mint and *officina* marks designated responsibility for ease of imperial supervision. The follis (8.5 g) was coined at 36 to the Roman pound—hence its Latin nickname of *terentianus,* a corruption for one-third of an ounce (pl. 23.201). The half-follis of twenty nummiae (4.5 g) was popular because it approximated the size and weight of the AE2 denominations of the late fourth and early fifth centuries.

The better specimens of existing nummi were allowed to circulate as single nummia pieces; hence the underlying coin in the reformed coinage of Anastasius was a nummia (0.56 g) struck at 576 nummiae to the Roman pound—the standard in force since the reign of Leo I (457–74). The chronicler Marcellinus reports approvingly, "By means of the coins called *terentiani* by the Romans and folles by the Greeks, each being marked with its own name, the emperor sold a rate of exchange that was pleasing to the people."[28] Anastasius fixed the rate of exchange at 420 folles (= 16,800 nummiae) to the solidus. In 512 Anastasius doubled the weight of all denominations (pl. 24.202 and 204) and added a *pentanummia* (five-nummiae piece). In effect, this was a return to the weight standard in use in 445, which was based upon a theoretical nummus (1.2 g) minted at 288 to the Roman pound.[29] The solidus was retariffed at 210 folles (= 8,400 nummiae), and light coins of the first reform circulated at one-half their face value so that the follis of 498 passed as a piece of twenty nummiae.

Justinian (527–65) undertook a series of changes in the weight of the follis that are well documented by the coins issued by the mint of Antioch. In 526–29 he reduced the standard of the follis (15 g) from 18 to 22 to the Roman pound but, then, in 529–33 restored the follis (17 g) to 18 to the pound. Two successive debasements in 533 and 537 lowered the follis (13.5 g) to 24 to the pound. In 538/9, as final victory in the West seemed within his grasp, Justinian substantially increased the weight and size of the follis (to 22 g and 42 mm) and lowered the exchange by one-seventh so that a solidus traded against 180 folles (= 7,200 nummiae)—the same rate found in the Novel of 445 (pl. 24.203).[30] Folles, and solidi too, henceforth carry a facing portrait of the emperor holding an orb surmounted by the cross symbolizing his reign over a Christian *oikoumene*. In accordance with regulations for dating official documents, folles struck from year 12 on (= 538/9) bear the regnal year, flanking by the denominational mark, on the reverse, and solidi are marked by indicational year. Justinian by this third and last reform of the bronze money reversed the inflation of nearly a century and created a follis that in size and buying power matched the sestertius of the Principate.

Concessions were made to regional preferences. During the fifth century, the nummus had suffered depreciation at varying rates in each province, thereby spawning different systems of reckoning. The mint of Alexandria, reopened under Justin I, issued a unique denomination, the *duodecanummia* or twelve-nummiae piece (5.25 g), which initially traded at 700 to the solidus, but, as exchange rates changed in 538–39, went at 600 to the solidus (pl. 26.216). Justinian added fractions of six and three nummiae and an ephemeral multiple of possibly thirty-six nummiae (14.5 g; pl. 26.215).[31] In size, fabric, and weight the duodecanummia recalled the Alexandrine tetradrachma, and it appealed to the Egyptians' sense of reckoning in units of four. The duodecanummia was complementary to rather than competitive with the imperial follis so that vendors and buyers probably grouped duodecanummiae in tens or fives so that purses of 120 and 60 nummiae could be exchanged as the equivalent of 3 and 1.5 folles, respectively. Thessalonica resumed operations in the reign of Justinian to supply northern Greece and the Lower Balkans with similar duodecimal fractions of one, two, four, eight, twelve, and sixteen nummiae. Justinian, however, late in his reign reorganized the mint of Thessalonica, which thereafter struck standard half-folles and decanummiae.

The reforms responded primarily to the demands of the state and the needs of the capital Constantinople and its heartland of Thrace, Greece, and Asia Minor. In contrast to the great recoinages of the third and fourth centuries, Anastasius and Justinian lacked the network of imperial mints to impose a single currency. Anastasius failed to reactivate the powerhouse of mints on the Propontis, for Constantinople and Nicomedia alone coined folles; Heraclea never reopened and Cyzicus did not resume production until the reign of Justin I (518–27). Antioch struck only folles on the heavier standard of 512. Even so, Anastasius and Justinian achieved stunning success in minting reformed folles in vast numbers, thereby replacing older coins and relieving chronic shortages. The known obverse dies for folles struck during the first, and more modest, reform of Anastasius could have produced over 10 million coins. Estimates of the actual volume point to perhaps over ten times this number.[32] The relative size of Justinian's vast coinage in 538–42 can be sensed from the fact that nine *officinae* at the metropolitan mints—five at the capital and two each at Cyzicus and Nicomedia—operated each year.[33] Since Justinian never ordered a comprehensive recoinage, many older folles and fractional pieces continued to circulate, at a discount, for many were later overstruck by Heraclius (610–41). Justinian imposed the follis on the reconquered West as first Carthage, in 534–41, and then Rome, in 538–45, each issued its own distinct version of the follis and its fractions (pl. 24.205).[34]

### *The Birth of Byzantine Coinage, 540–717*

Justinian abruptly terminated his restoration of imperial currency soon after 540, for he had financed his early victories by exhausting a reserve of almost 29 million solidi amassed by Anastasius and Justin I. The Second Persian War (540–45), the unexpected resurgence of Gothic arms under Totila, and rebellions in North Africa wiped out imperial reserves. From 540 on, Justinian faced skyrocketing costs for men, ships, and materiel for his expeditionary forces. Twice, in 543–44 and 549–51, the field army in Italy was rebuilt. Plague sweeping over the empire in 541–43 carried off so many victims that Justinian had to recruit numerous barbarian mercenaries who demanded wages in gold. Justinian, facing enormous debts and an impoverished empire, debased the currency and slashed expenditure in the first of a series of cuts that ultimately reduced the late Roman budget to its modest Byzantine scale. Final victory in the West brought no relief, because the successors of Justinian faced new folk migrations of the Lombards into Italy and of the Slavs and Avars into the Balkans as well as two Persian wars (572–91 and 602–28).

Justinian was guilty, as Procopius charges, of alloying the solidus with silver, but it was a modest debasement as the solidus was maintained at a standard of 97 to 98 percent fine throughout much of the sixth and seventh centuries. Miserly Maurice Tiberius (582–602) even issued virtually pure gold solidi (98.5 to 99 percent fine).[35] It is astonishing that the purity of the solidus was maintained during this period of supreme financial emergency, especially since no emperor before Heraclius (610–41) dared to coin gold and silver immobilized in ecclesiastical plate. The ingenious finance minister Peter Barsymes, perhaps in 540–43, devised the clever expedient, the so-called light-weight solidi, by lowering the weight standard of the gold coinage.

Light-weight solidi were a fiscal fiction—a controlled debasement of coins to be used for internal payments rather than as trade coins for the West or as subsidies to barbarians.[36] Solidi had often not been struck to standard and most coins suffered weight loss after they left the mint. The majority of solidi in circulation probably averaged 23 or 23.5 carats by weight. Egyptian tax registers and private accounts from the mid-fifth through the seventh centuries employ a method of reckoning this weight loss by designating solidi short so many carats or fractions of carats, which presumably had to be made up by fractional silver or bronze coins.[37] Shortly after 540 the mint of Constantinople struck a proportion of its solidi below the full standard of 24 carats. Light-weight solidi, carrying types identical to solidi of full weight, are marked as containing 20, 22, or 23 carats so the aim was neither deception nor an official reduction of the standard (pl. 23.192–93). Most likely, officials and contractors were compelled to accept light-weight solidi which imperial authorities decreed as equivalent to full solidi and, in effect, the recipients paid an indirect tax.[38] Heraclius, upon concluding his Persian War (629–31), dispensed with light-weight solidi, but the Arabic onslaught compelled his heirs Constans II (641–68), Constantine IV (668–85), and Justinian II (685–95) to revive them.

After increasing the weight of the follis in 538, Justinian and his successors relentlessly lowered it, and by 551 the follis had lost 25 percent of its weight, falling to the standard of A.D. 512. At the accession of Tiberius II (578–82), the follis had, in less than a generation, declined to one-half the standard of A.D. 538 (Table 8.1).[39] Fractional pieces suffered equally drastic reductions in weight. Justinian attempted to enforce the tariffing of his new, lighter folles at 180 to the solidus, but with so many different folles current, rates in markets fluctuated widely and many coins must have been severely discounted.[40] Prices rose as debasement and inflation during the late sixth and seventh centuries first simplified and then ruined the last successful token bronze currency of imperial Rome. In the last eight years of his reign, Justinian perhaps

*Table 8.1*
Weight and Tariffing of Follis, Mint of Constantinople, 498–717

| Period | Number per Pound | Average Weight (Grams) | Folles to the Solidus |
|---|---|---|---|
| 498–512 | 36 | 8.5 | 420 |
| 512–38 | 18 | 17.5 | 210 |
| 538–42 | 14 | 22.0 | 180 |
| 542–47 | 16 | 20.0 | 180 |
| 548–51 | 18 | 18.0 | 180 |
| 551–65 | 19 | 17.0 | 180 |
| 565–70 | 21 | 15.0 | 240 |
| 570–78 | 25 | 13.0 | 288 |
| 578–615 | 29 | 11.0 | 288 |
| 615–24 | 36 | 9.0 | 352* |
| 624–29 | 54 | 6.0 | 532* |
| 629–31 | 32 | 10.0 | 288 |
| 631–39 | 56 | 5.5 | 576* |
| 639–41 | 72 | 4.5 | 704* |
| 641–75 | 96 | 3.5 | 950* |
| 675–85 | 18 | 18.0 | 210 |
| 685–95 | 72 | 4.5 | 704* |
| 695–717 | 96 | 3.5 | 950* |

*Values surmised based on practice of trading coins by weight at rate of 10 pounds of folles per solidus.

*Source:* Table 8.1 is based on Grierson, *DOC* II. 1, p. 23, and III, p. 70, and C. Morrisson, *Catalogue des Monnuies Byzantines de la Bibliothèque Nationale* (Paris, 1970), II, pp. 611–26.

responded by reducing output of folles, reflected in the steady reduction of *officinae* striking dated folles at the metropolitan mints and Antioch. With Justin II production quickly leaped to the levels of the 540s and nine *officinae* regularly coined dated folles into the early years of Heraclius (610–41).

Soon after 565, as Justin II slashed the weight of the follis (pl. 24.206), heavy Justinianic folles disappeared from circulation. The official rate of exchange in the East leaped from 180 to 240, and then to 288 folles to the solidus. Tiberius II (578–82) and Maurice Tiberius (578–602) stabilized the weight of the follis so that prices might have leveled off. Smaller fractions were discontinued and then dropped out of circulation.[41] Finds of stray coins recovered in excavations of eastern sites document the process. The nummia vanished from circulation in the 550s; pentanummiae and decanummiae, in the 580s. Half-folles were still found as late as the 680s, but they were few in comparison to the wretched Heraclian folles comprising the bulk of the bronze money. In response to inflation, Tiberius II introduced a fraction of thirty nummiae (pl. 26.218) and the Crimean port Cherson marked bronze coins in increments of five nummiae instead of single nummiae so that forty- and twenty-nummiae pieces of Maurice Tiberius carry value marks designating them as eight- and four-pentanummiae pieces (pl. 27.219).

Justinian opened imperial mints in the West, but their production was at best sporadic. Migrations of the Lombards, Slavs, and Avars thwarted efforts to reintegrate the recovered lands into the fiscal and monetary life of the empire. Maurice Tiberius consolidated the distant African and Italian provinces by appointing exarchs at Carthage and Ravenna with supreme military and civil authority, including the right to coin in all three metals. In the reign of Justinian, Carthage struck solidi running into the millions to pay for military operations in 537–40 and 546–48 and the reconstruction of the famed African desert fortifications. Production leaped further under Maurice Tiberius, and local engravers cut dies in a peculiar style and mint workers often avoided hammering out flans to speed up manufacture. Carthaginian solidi were thus struck on smaller flans of distinct fabric, and by the late sixth century they had assumed a small dumpy or "globular" aspect that persisted down to the Arabic conquest (pl. 23.194).[42] Carthaginian solidi, minted from old coin and fresh metal brought by caravan from West Africa, seldom circulated outside the African exarchate. Africa escaped the scourge of inflation, because in 602 the solidus stood at 240 folles and the one-nummia piece was the most commonly lost coin at African towns until the mid-seventh century—long after the denomination had disappeared in the East.

Imperial authorities in Byzantine Spain and Italy, for want of gold, adopted the Western tremissis as the principal gold denomination. Spanish engravers at Cartagena designed imperial tremisses in the style of Visigothic counterparts, but neither silver nor bronze fractions were minted (pl. 23.195).[43] In Italy, the exarchs at Ravenna preserved the denominational structure of the currency, striking the bronze folles along with fractions and three silver denominations marked as pieces of 125, 150, and 500 nummiae (pl. 23.200). The solidus was officially exchanged at 300 folles (= 12,000 nummiae) or the rate that had obtained under Theodoric. In the reign of Justin II (565–78) the solidus was discontinued in favor of the tremissis, characterized by conservative iconography and a ring in high relief enclosing the designs (pl. 23.196). As imperial forces retreated to cities on the Italian shores, the exarch at Ravenna lost control over this provincial currency, and authorities in Rome, Naples, and the Sicilian cities of Catana and Syracuse minted their own currency.[44]

The assassination of Maurice Tiberius in 602 plunged the empire into a series of catastrophic wars that propelled late Roman society across a watershed into the early medieval age. By the late seventh century the Roman Empire of Justinian had been reduced to its Hellenized core of Thrace, Asia Minor, the Aegean littoral and islands, Sicily, and Southern Italy, with distant outposts on the Crimean and Dalmatian shores and in Cyprus. The Lombards had conquered most of the Italian peninsula, extinguishing urban life. Avars and Slavs migrated into the Balkans isolating Thessalonica and the cities of southern Greece and ending vital mining operations. Egypt fell temporarily to the Persians in 617–28 and then permanently to the armies of Islam in 641–42. Constantinople endured three sieges, in 618–26, 670–74, and 717–18. Constantine IV faced the first Arabic siege with revenues a mere one-quarter of those Justinian had commanded. The emperors Heraclius (610–41), Constans II (641–68), and Constantine IV (668–85) heroically battled invaders from every quarter, strove to restore imperial revenues, and thereby forged a new Byzantine state and currency.

Heraclius came to the throne of a Roman Empire on the brink of collapse. Since 602 the Avars had kept Constantinople in a virtual state of siege; meanwhile the armies of Shah Khusrau II conquered Mesopotamia, Syria, and Egypt, and by 615 a Sassanid army was encamped at Chalcedon on the Asian shore of the Bosporus just opposite Constantinople. Heraclius tapped a heretofore inviolate source of specie when he secured from Patriarch Sergius the loan of the church's wealth. The mint of Constantinople from 615 melted down and coined sacred objects. The chronicler Theophanes reports this action in 622, on the eve of Heraclius's Persian expedition: "Having taken the money of the holy churches in the form of a loan, pressed by difficulties, he [Heraclius] seized the *polykandela* of the Great Church as well as other serviceable equipment and coined large numbers of *nomismata* [i.e., solidi] and *miliarisia* [i.e., *hexagrams*]."[45] The mint, fed from stocks of ecclesiastical gold and silver accumulated over the past three centuries, minted extraordinary numbers of solidi, issuing many of 20 carats at the height of the Persian War.

In 615 Heraclius struck massive numbers of the silver coin known as the hexagram, minted at 48 to the Roman pound (6.75 g), and tariffed at 12 to the solidus (pl. 23.197). It thus passed as a 2-carat coin or a double of the Tetrarchic argenteus. According to the *Paschale Chronicle,* "In this year the silver hexagram coin was introduced by law; and during the same year official salaries were paid in it, at half the former rate."[46] The hexagram with its thick flan, dumpy fabric, and heavy weight recalled Greek staters and its design was thoroughly Christian, with the invocation "God help the Romans." The hexagram, like the light-weight solidus, was an emergency coin minted at the capital to ease pressure on gold stocks that were needed to pay barbarian allies and mercenaries. The first hexagrams were tariffed at 24 folles; in 675–85 Constantine IV, reduced, possibly twice, the weight of the hexagram and revalued it at 20 folles.[47] The hexagram was doomed in the long run, because by 660 silver reserves were exhausted and many hexagrams had found their way to the silver-hungry Sassanid Empire or Caliphate to be recoined into lighter, broad-flan dirhems.

Heraclius inherited a stable follis, weighing 11 g and perhaps tariffed at 288 to the solidus. As the military situation deteriorated after 615, Heraclius faced acute shortages of bronze essential for arms and armor and he had little choice but to slash the weight of the follis. Even during the first six years of Heraclius's reign, the weight of many folles deviated widely from the norm, because they were hastily manufactured or overstruck on older coins (pl. 25.207). The follis tumbled to an unprecedented low (6 g) during the desperate fighting of 624–28, but, with victory in hand, Heraclius in 629–31 restored the standard to 10 g, nearly its prewar level (pl. 25.210). In 632–41, as Arabic armies swept over Mesopotamia, Syria, and Egypt, Heraclius halved the follis (5.5 g) and then cut its weight a further 25 percent (pl. 25.211). Constans II struck miserable folles of varying size and weight (between 5 and 3.5 g; pl. 26.212) that could not even match the decanummiae of Justinian (see Table 8.1).[48]

Inflation wiped out real purchasing power and wreaked havoc on exchange rates in the capital and Anatolian heartland. Since neither Heraclius nor Constans II attempted an orderly recoinage, a bewildering array of earlier coins passed current with masses of new folles of sloppy manufacture and widely varying weights and sizes. In their haste, mint workers prepared flans poorly and made maximum use of dies so that many specimens show doublestrikes, flan cracks, or brockage. When the standard was drastically reduced in the 620s, workers at the metropolitan mints overstruck many earlier coins. They crudely trimmed flans of sixth-century folles or they overstruck half-folles and even wide-flan decanummiae. By the mid-seventh century, the bronze currency of the Byzantine heartland was reduced to chaos as folles were exchanged by weight against the solidus.

The Persian War (602–28) also ruined the network of imperial mints, and Heraclius resorted to mobile mints. During his expedition into southeastern Asia Minor, Heraclius operated a mobile mint at Seleucia (615–17; pl. 25.208) and then at Isaura (617–18). The loss of Egypt and much of Asia Minor in 619 forced Heraclius to retreat to Constantinople and to shut down the military mint at Seleucia and the metropolitan mints at Nicomedia and Cyzicus. During the next decade (619–29), the follis deteriorated in workmanship and weight, as Constantinople alone strained to supply coins to what remained of the eastern half of the empire and the field armies. Nicomedia and Cyzicus resumed minting folles in 625–30, when the emperor scored brilliant victories in Armenia and Iran that compelled Shah Khusrau II to raise the siege of the capital. A mint at Constantia on the isle of Cyprus swung into production in 627–29, perhaps with the intention of its transfer to Antioch upon the recovery of Syria (pl. 25.209).

With the disruption of the network of mints, many regions in the East, denied adequate supplies of coins, lost monetary habits.[49] In 629/30, Thessalonica, seat of the Prefecturate of Illyricum, closed its mint and thereafter the cities of Byzantine Greece imported folles from Constantinople. Excavations document a dramatic contraction of the numbers of bronze coins circulating in Thrace, Macedonia, and Greece from the second half of the seventh century. Syria experienced much the same. Sassanid armies compelled the mint of Antioch to close in 608/9, and neither Shah Khusrau II nor Heraclius reopened the mint so that the currency of Mesopotamia, Syria, and Palestine consisted of a diminishing stock of older worn solidi and folles when the Arabic armies arrived in 636.[50]

Heraclius followed his triumph over Persia with bold measures to restore imperial money in 629–31. He ended production of light-weight solidi and returned the follis (10 g) almost to its standard in the late fifth century, thereby aiming for an exchange rate of 240 or 288 folles to the solidus (pl. 25.210). Fractions of thirty, twenty, ten, and five nummiae were again issued in what was intended to be a thorough recoinage. Heraclius extended monetary unity to Egypt by placing on par with the follis the Alexandrine duodecanummia, which henceforth bears double sets of value marks of twelve and forty nummiae (pl. 26.217). The duodecanummia under Sassanid rule in 619–28 had been improved in weight (to 11 g), design, and manufacture.[51]

Heraclius is credited with dismantling the network of imperial mints, but he might have repeated the measures of Justinian to limit production and roll back wartime prices. In the East, he centered minting at Constantinople, closing mints at Thessalonica, Cyzicus, and Nicomedia, and the military mints at Constantia on Cyprus and at Catana on Sicily. The mint at Antioch remained closed. Alexandria in Egypt and the exarchate mints Carthage and Ravenna continued to strike regional currencies. If Heraclius envisioned this reorganization as the first step to a uniform currency, the Arab conquests cut short his plans. Since the closure of these mints (except for Catana) proved permanent, Constantinople alone after 641 struck the currency of an Eastern empire shorn of Syria and Egypt, while provincial issues in Africa, Sicily, and Italy evolved into independent currencies. Heraclius unknowingly announced the birth of new medieval regional coinages in place of a single Roman currency.

As the first caliphs directed a relentless assault against Constantinople, Heraclius and Constans II resumed minting light-weight solidi and hexagrams and shamelessly debased the folles. Constantine IV gained a brief respite when he repelled the Arabic army that besieged his capital in 670–74. In 675, he abandoned light-weight solidi and reintroduced a heavy follis (18 g; pl. 26.213) on the standard used in 512, along with half-follis and decanummiae, and pentanummiae (see Table 8.1). The mass of clipped and worn folles issued since 610 were recoined, but better specimens were permitted to circulate at half their value. Many reformed folles and half-folles bear double denominational marks of K/M and I/K, denoting a revaluation downward by 50 percent. Two hoards from Cyprus consist of half-folles of Constantine IV and older folles countermarked with the monogram K to denote both the emperor's name and a new value of twenty nummiae.[52] The reform of Constantine IV soon failed, with renewed military crisis. Leontius (695–98) and Justinian II (705–11) quartered folles of Constantine IV and overstruck each fragment as a follis, indicating an inflation rate of 400 percent.

By 700, successive debasements and ruinous inflation had undermined the integrity of Roman imperial money. Bronze coins possessed no discernible weight standard. Although *aes* had, since the early days of the Republic, been minted *al marco,* individual specimens fell within an acceptable range of weights and each coin was traded as a denomination subject to the minor fluctuations of exchange rates. Successive debasements after 616, two abortive reforms in 629–31 and 675–85, and sloppy recycling of older coins by overstriking or countermarking destroyed Roman notions of a chain of denominations in various metals exchangeable at fixed rates. The use of glass weights in early Islamic Egypt reveals perhaps just how far notions of currency had diverged from their Roman heritage. Just after the Arabic conquest, Egyptians coped with a bewildering array of crude, illegible, and worn Heraclian folles and duodecanummiae on varying standards and blundered Muslim imitations (struck from the 660s on; pl. 30.248). Merchants devised glass weights for gold dinars and bronze *fuls* (i.e., solidi and folles). Each weight was marked according to a *kharrubah* or carat. Groups of gold or bronze coins were traded based on their total weight rather than exchanged as fixed denominations. When official tariffing of coins ceased to carry meaning in tax collection or trade, the Mediterranean world had lost its Roman monetary ways. The volume of folles minted from 610 to 675 was enormous; they, along with coins of the sixth century, circulated down to 700. Yet, by the year 700 most inhabitants within the borders of the former Justinianic Empire had ceased to employ bronze coins.

In the Byzantine West, Carthage struck globular solidi, along with peculiar silver and bronze fractions (pl. 23.194 and 199). After the Arabs stormed the city in 696, the Byzantines evacuated the mint to Sardinia where they minted distinct gobular solidi and folles for another generation.[53] Arab conquerors of North Africa briefly struck, on Byzantine standards, gold dinars and bronze fuls carrying proclamations of the Muslim faith in Latin, but Kufic dirhems supplanted these imitative pieces from former Byzantine Africa and Spain by 725 (pl. 30.250).

Byzantine Italy and Sicily were spared the worst of the monetary chaos during the seventh century. Shortages of bronze money ensued in Sicily when Heraclius closed the mint at Catana in 629/30, and soon after Constantinople stamped some of its folles with the countermark SICILIA for use in the island (631–43; pl. 29.214). By 654 Constans II opened a mint at Syracuse, and in 663–68 he transferred his court to the city. Despite its comparative prosperity, Byzantine Sicily lacked a source of specie to strike a fractional silver coinage or to maintain its solidus which was steadily alloyed into an electrum piece, the ancestor of the medieval Arabic quarter-dinar and Norman *tari*. Northern and central Italy drifted out of the Byzantine and into the Carolingian monetary orbit. Lombard rulers reminted solidi as tremisses (pl. 30.245–46) at imperial standards of fineness down to the reign of Liutprand (712–44). Byzantine-style coinages lingered on longest in imperial possessions of the far south, the maritime Republics on the Bay of Naples, and in Lombard Benevento. Rome coined base solidi and bronze pieces until Pope Hadrian I (772–95) broke with tradition by coining in his own name silver deniers on the Carolingian standard.[54]

Persian and Arabic rule rapidly transformed currency in Syria and Egypt. Umayyad caliphs struck imitative gold dinars (pl. 30.247) during the first generation of Muslim rule until Abd al-Malik (685–705) introduced an Islamic dinar (4.25 g) struck at the standard of the worn Byzantine solidus (equivalent to 22.5 carats). The monetary future rested in the dirhem, the old Sassanid denomination. In 695 the caliph Abd al-Malik issued a lighter dirhem (2.97 g) with Kufic script in a major recoinage of vast silver reserves captured from Byzantines and Sassanids, and he radically transformed the face of currency in the Near East and North Africa.[55] The dirhem (pl. 30.249), while Sassanid in metrology, carried the iconography of a triumphant Islam. Imitative Byzantine coins, vestiges of a Roman heritage, vanished forever.

Emperors in Constantinople ruled a Byzantine Empire where the denominational structure of Roman currency survived, but by 700 the production and use of coins had drastically fallen. As urban life languished and population declined to its lowest level since the eve of the Iron Age, demand for coins contracted and so did the private patronage so vital for the monetized commercial life of a classical city. Heraclian emperors slashed military, ceremonial, and administrative budgets, permanently reducing the flow of coins to markets. The evacuation and settlement of eastern armies on lands in the themes of Asia Minor in 636–54 ended the full-time professional army of Rome and removed the most powerful stimulus for pumping coins throughout the economy.

The solidus emerged from the great crisis iconographically transformed into the Christian Byzantine nomisma, but its survival was neither planned nor inevitable. Emperors in Constantinople drastically reduced their annual consumption of gold and thereby avoided the need to adopt either a lighter weight standard for the solidus or the tremissis as the principal denomination. They reimposed laws banning the export of gold and secured fresh supplies of gold from mines and trade, so that far fewer *nomismata* were needed by the Isaurian emperors who ruled a state with a smaller population and fewer pretensions. Silver coins were scarce until Leo III (717–41) introduced the *miliaresion,* tariffed at 12 to the nomisma (pl. 23.198). Its light weight (less than one-half that of the hexagram) and epigraphic design were inspired by the Arabic dirhem, and many were overstruck on clipped-down captured dirhems. Bronze money consisted of tiny folles which, to judge from the stray finds at excavated sites in Greece and Asia Minor, were in limited supply until the end of the ninth century. Decline in the numbers and varieties of denominations paralleled the shift from the monetized fiscal and economic institutions of late Rome to those of the medieval Byzantine state. By 700 the process was complete. A series of independent coinages had emerged from Britain to the Euphrates ultimately based on the coinages of the Roman world, but medieval in their conception and use.

# Nine

# Government's Aims and Needs

The Flavian general Q. Petilius Cerealis reminded the Gauls, "no peace without arms, no arms without pay, no pay without taxes," and, he could have added, "no taxes without coins."[1] His words apply to the Roman government's aims and needs for nearly a thousand years. Although coins were struck for fiscal needs, the dynamics of state expenditures and taxation moved coins through markets and ensured their domination over other media of exchange. Classical authors never describe how coins flowed from the mint to markets, but the main currents of this cycle can be inferred from the coins themselves and documentary sources such as Egyptian papyri and imperial laws. What follows is a reconstruction of how the Roman state minted, used, and put into general circulation hundreds of millions of coins by Cerealis's day.

Financial departments, whether responsible to the Republican Senate or the emperor, directed the flow of coins in three major ways: by regulation of the supply, by expenditures to meet the demands of the budget, and by taxation. It is a moot point whether the treasury and mint framed a deliberate "monetary" policy based on predicted needs. The administrative history of these agencies reveals that the Roman state steadily perfected its supervision of standards, minting, and distribution because it needed ever more coins if it were to deliver on Cerealis's claims.

The late Republic acquired a permanent budget of military payrolls and contracts for victualing armies overseas. Augustus added payment of retirement benefits and a relatively predictable cycle of bonuses to urban plebeians, legions, and the Praetorian Guard. Administrative, building, and ceremonial costs also grew over the next four centuries. The budget was often strained by unforeseeable war costs, emergency relief, and shortfalls in taxes. Estimates of various items in the Roman budget are offered as an indication of the order of magnitude of the number of coins that the state might have been called upon to pay each year. The state, however, often manipulated the budget to issue far fewer coins; nonetheless, the figures put into perspective the mint's output, and they suggest how many and what kinds of coins the government employed in expenditures and tax collection, and thereby the figures convey an impression of the amount of money in circulation. Although the nature of fiscal demands varied from province to province, Roman taxation had a uniform impact: it steadily monetized provincial finances and markets. Provincials acquired coins and monetary habits because they had to pay their taxes in coin.

### *Production, Supply, and Distribution*

Inscriptions and legal texts preserve details of the daily routine within the mint and the organization of its technical staff, but fail to describe how the state assured adequate numbers of coins for fiscal and economic needs. Coins were minted in response to fiscal needs or as specie became available, rather than according to any administrative cycle. Imperial laws issued from the fourth through seventh centuries, along with contemporaneous coins with reverses that bear abbreviations of mint, workshop, and series, give the false impression that coins were struck on a regular pattern such as a five-year cycle (*lustrum*). Schemes of regular production in the Dominate are idealized models reconstructed from administrative documents rather than a living reality. Invariably, emergencies or shortages disrupted any cycle of regular minting just as arrears, remissions, and reassessments continually undermined predictable cycles of tax collection.[2] The vast bulk of coins were put into circulation to meet the demands of the budget, but the state also turned to bankers and moneychangers to act as its agents to distribute coins. The fees charged on the service of exchange fluctuated over the centuries. In Hadrianic Pergamum, moneychangers were allowed a profit of one assarion on the denarius in converting imperial silver into local bronze money, or a profit of 6.25 percent, whereas those at Rome in 445 were allowed a profit of less than 3 percent on the exchange of the solidus into bronze nummi.[3] The state could undermine exchange rates whenever it sold masses of new coins or recalled old ones for recoinage. Ensuing hardships, even panic, were endemic to this system of distribution, and they could threaten the agents of distribution with ruin, as in the case of the moneychangers at Rome who petitioned the emperor Valentinian II for relief in 384–85.[4]

The Romans recognized, and reacted to, some reasons behind fluctuations in the money supply and exchange rates even if they did not articulate a monetary policy. The Senate in the Ciceronian age and the emperor Tiberius in A.D. 33 eased demand for coined money without a recoinage by prohibiting export of specie, renegotiating debts, or offering loans when land speculation by the aristocracy triggered shortages of specie at Rome.[5] Republican and imperial governments also learned the effects of turning surfeits of plundered bullion into coin. Suetonius notes how great coinages by Julius Caesar and Augustus drove up Italian prices; the letter to Sarapion of Hermopolis reports similar rises from Trajan's coinage.[6] The imperial government took longer to learn how to cope with the consequences of its policy of debasement, but the edicts on prices and monetary values in 301 capped a long tradition of regulation of the supply and distribution of coins. On a much humbler level, seasonal tax demands influenced the types and numbers of coins in circulation in every region across the empire. When Papnuthis, a landowner and financier of Oxyrhynchus, advised his brother to buy up solidi, he acted on a tip in Alexandria that an impending *aurum tirocinium*, payable by the landed classes in gold, was bound to cause a run on solidi.[7] Papnuthis in the mid-fourth century differed little from most officials or taxpayers who daily took precautions against shortages of coins or speculated on exchange rates.

Measures to improve the administration of the mint and the manufacture of coins reflect growing sophistication in the Roman state's production and distribution of its coins. In the late Republic, Cato the Younger as quaestor of the public treasury (*aerarium*) sought out previous holders of the office and appointed clerks skilled in accounting.[8] From the 180s B.C. consuls probably appointed the three moneyers of the mint, but the abbreviations EX S.C. or S.C. on late Republican denarii suggest that the Senate determined volume and distribution of coins.[9] In 49 B.C. Julius Caesar assumed direct control over the treasury and the mint, appointing his own slaves and freedmen to the important posts, and demoting the senatorial moneyers to titular officeholders.[10] Henceforth the emperor coined the money of the Roman state. Perhaps it was Nero who divided the mint into either three or six workshops (*officinae*) when he concentrated minting at Rome in A.D. 64. This division of labor proved efficient in the production of coins in three metals. By the Flavian age, an imperial procurator supervised the mint's large technical staff of clerks, engravers, and workers, and he answered directly to the procurator of the treasury. The imperial government forged the *officina* into a flexible corps of specialists, comparable to military units, which could manufacture vast numbers of coins on short notice. The number and complexity of *officinae* increased as the state's demand for coins rose. The *officinae* of Rome even minted, on special order, provincial issues such as the Asian cistophori of Augustus, Cypriote and Caesarean coins of Trajan, Alexandrine tetradrachmae of Severus Alexander, and Antiochene tetradrachmae of Philip. Emperors from Valerian to Aurelian detached or cloned the *officinae* at Rome to establish imperial mints in the provinces when civil war and invasion disrupted communications between Rome and the field armies.

The history of imperial mints is merely the best-documented chapter in the story of the growing sophistication of the imperial government as it met its need for coins in payrolls, taxes, and commerce. Although fiscal needs dictated the choice of mints in 274–96 that distributed coins to the West until the mid-fifth century and to the East until Heraclius reorganized the Eastern mints in 629–31, imperial mints were well placed to supply the markets of the Roman world. Thessalonica, for example as seat of the Praetorian Prefect, was the primary or palatine mint of Illyricum from the fourth through seventh centuries. Although several other cities had equal or better claims as economic centers to be the main mint of the Prefecturate, Thessalonica supplied the Greek and Balkan markets adequately with all types of coins. The finds at sites and hoards suggest no shortages until the collapse of the Danubian frontier at the end of the sixth century. Similarly, northeastern Gaul and Britain were well supplied by the mint at Treveri, suffering shortages only when they were cut off from Treveri either by civil war or barbarian invasion.[11] The Roman state created a system of mints not unlike the twelve Federal Reserve Banks of the United States. Although reasons other than economic determined the location of many banks, the network suits the economic life well enough; likewise, late imperial mints suited the economic life of the provinces, for markets and trade were organized in response to the flow of coins from the mints.

Measures improving efficiency of mints in the late empire thus stood in a long tradition of regulation since Republican days rather than marked a break in the state's conception or use of coins. When Diocletian reorganized his network of mints under a count of the sacred largess (*comes sacrarum largitionum*), he premised his reforms upon the lessons of the Roman past. His division of mints into palatine ones (striking gold and silver coins) and public ones (minting billon or base metal coins) was just the latest version of the division of labor pursued ever since Nero divided the mint at Rome into *officinae*. Valentinian and Valens too reenacted old measures to assure the purity of gold and silver standards and to curb abuses in tax collection. The late Roman state differed little from the Republic or Principate in its desire for full-weight gold or silver coins in taxes and fractional denominations for daily transactions. Far more important than the documented refinements in the technical production of coins and the administration of the mint are the inferences drawn from these changes. As the costs of government rose, the Roman state grew more sophisticated in its use of coins, and, far from abandoning coinage for earlier forms of fiscal and economic organization, emperors from Diocletian to Heraclius sought to exploit the coinage to meet mounting bills. It is time to turn to the driving force behind the government's hunger for coins, the budget.

### *Coins and the Roman Budget*

Since Rome's budget was the legacy of conquest, its largest item was military costs. Military pay remained remarkably stable for 150 years. In Polybius's day, a legionary received annual pay of 108 denarii calculated at 3 asses per diem or the cost of a modius of wheat; centurions and cavalry received, respectively, two and three times this rate. Such rates probably dated from the aftermath of the First Punic War; they certainly were in force when Rome revalued the denarius in 213–12 B.C.[12] The payroll of a legion amounted to at least 625,000 denarii; it was undoubtedly higher, because the pay of officers and specialists, although unknown, must have been higher.[13] Revaluation of the denarius in 141 B.C. slightly altered the annual base pay to 112.5 denarii when the daily wage was recalculated at 5 asses, the then probable price of a modius of wheat. This rate stood until Julius Caesar doubled the annual salary to 225 denarii in 46 B.C.[14] Wages, however, were but part of the expense; the annual cost of a legion serving overseas reached 1.5 million denarii early in the second century B.C. The Republic had long assumed the costs of equipping landless volunteers before it was required by the *lex Sempronia militaris* (123 B.C.). Payrolls rose as the size of the legion increased and as higher pay was offered to attract seasoned centurions and specialists. During the second and first centuries B.C., most increases in army costs came from contracts equipping and victualing expeditionary armies and fleets, even though Rome avoided purchases in cash by drawing men, materiel, and foodstuffs from allies. Prices also were kept down by revaluing the denarius in 141 B.C.[15] With the enfranchisement of Italy after the Social War, payrolls of former Italian and Latin legionaries who had figured so prominently in overseas wars since 200 B.C. were henceforth added to the budget.

In the first six years of the Second Punic War (from 218 to

212 B.C.) payrolls of citizen legions rose by at least four times, as well over 300,000 citizens and allies were called to the standards, and total costs more than doubled. The Republic sustained this prodigious military effort through 207 B.C., and then steadily reduced its costs by two-thirds in 200 B.C. In the next generation (200–168 B.C.) fierce fighting in Cisalpine Gaul and Spain and three major expeditions to the East resulted in a sudden increase of 5 to 6 million denarii in annual costs and tremendous outlays in hard cash to equip and feed a consular army, a fleet of 50 to 100 quinqueremes, and 600 to 800 transports (Table 9.1).[16] After 168 B.C., Rome reduced the number of legions overseas and demobilized most of her fleet, and until the outbreak of the Social War (90–88 B.C.), military costs, although impossible to reconstruct, fell substantially. In 167–149 B.C., four to six citizen legions (along with an indeterminable number of Italian allies and men serving in the fleets) were under arms at an annual cost of at least 6 to 9 million denarii. These costs more than doubled during the Celtiberian Wars and Third Punic War in the 140s B.C. and again during the Jugurthine War. The Civil and Mithridatic wars of the 80s and 70s B.C. produced unprecedented levels of expenditure, followed by even greater costs in the Civil Wars of the 40s and 30s B.C. After 80 B.C. the Roman Republic was committed to maintaining forces comparable to those of the later imperial army, ranging between twenty to forty legions at a cost of 22.5 to 60 million denarii per year.

The loss of Asia and Greece during the First Mithridatic War (89–86 B.C.) revealed Rome's dependence on provincial taxes, and L. Cornelius Sulla reorganized provincial taxes so that an annual income of 50 million denarii was available to pay for the twenty-five to thirty legions deployed to defend the provinces; Pompey and Julius Caesar together augmented revenues by a further 45 million denarii by 48 B.C.[17] The budget was far from predictable, and civil wars of the first century B.C. must have thwarted any attempts to estimate annual state needs for new coinage. Furthermore, the Republic did not increase wages in response to rising prices and the need to attract volunteers into the legions. Commanders instead compensated their men with offers of greater triumphal donatives and promises of land grants upon discharge—these forms of remu-

*Table 9.1*
Estimated Military Expenditures, 218–168 B.C.
(in Denarii)

| Year | Legions Payroll | Fleets Payroll | Allies Grain Costs | Total |
|---|---|---|---|---|
| 218 B.C. | 6,000,000 | 11,000,000 | 1,100,000 | 18,100,000 |
| 217 B.C. | 11,000,000 | 11,000,000 | 2,100,000 | 24,000,000 |
| 216 B.C. | 10,000,000 | 11,000,000 | 2,000,000 | |
| | 5,500,000* | | 875,000* | |
| | 15,500,000 | | 2,875,000 | 29,375,000 |
| 215 B.C. | 15,000,000 | 11,000,000 | 3,200,000 | 28,800,000 |
| 214 B.C. | 20,000,000 | 10,750,000 | 3,200,000 | 33,950,000 |
| 213 B.C. | 22,000,000 | 10,750,000 | 2,300,000 | 35,050,000 |
| 212 B.C. | 25,000,000 | 10,750,000 | 2,800,000 | 38,550,000 |
| 211 B.C. | 25,000,000 | 10,750,000 | 3,200,000 | 38,950,000 |
| 210 B.C. | 21,000,000 | 10,750,000 | 2,800,000 | 34,500,000 |
| 209 B.C. | 21,000,000 | 11,500,000 | 2,800,000 | 35,300,000 |
| 208 B.C. | 21,000,000 | 14,000,000 | 2,500,000 | 37,500,000 |
| 207 B.C. | 23,000,000 | 12,000,000 | 2,800,000 | 37,800,000 |
| 206 B.C. | 20,000,000 | 6,000,000 | 2,400,000 | 26,400,000 |
| 205 B.C. | 18,000,000 | 3,875,000 | 1,100,000 | |
| | | 2,750,000** | | |
| | | 6,625,000 | | 25,725,000 |
| 204 B.C. | 19,000,000 | 5,000,000 | 2,400,000 | 26,400,000 |
| 203 B.C. | 20,000,000 | 8,000,000 | 2,500,000 | 30,500,000 |
| 202 B.C. | 16,000,000 | 10,000,000 | 2,100,000 | 28,100,000 |
| 201 B.C. | 14,000,000 | 5,000,000 | 1,900,000 | 20,900,000 |
| 200 B.C. | 5,500,000 | 3,750,000 | 2,100,000 | 11,350,000 |
| 199 B.C. | 4,000,000 | 3,750,000 | 1,700,000 | 9,450,000 |
| 198 B.C. | 5,500,000 | 3,750,000 | 2,100,000 | 11,350,000 |
| 197 B.C. | 4,000,000 | 3,750,000 | 1,900,000 | 9,650,000 |
| 196 B.C. | 6,750,000 | 3,750,000 | 2,400,000 | 12,900,000 |
| 195 B.C. | 6,750,000 | 3,750,000 | 2,500,000 | 13,000,000 |
| 194 B.C. | 5,500,000 | 1,250,000 | 1,900,000 | 9,650,000 |
| 193 B.C. | 5,500,000 | 1,250,000 | 1,900,000 | 9,650,000 |
| 192 B.C. | 6,750,000 | 7,000,000 | 2,400,000 | 16,150,000 |
| 191 B.C. | 8,000,000 | 7,000,000 | 3,000,000 | 18,000,000 |
| 190 B.C. | 8,750,000 | 7,000,000 | 3,100,000 | 18,750,000 |
| 189 B.C. | 8,000,000 | 7,000,000 | 2,800,000 | 17,800,000 |
| 188 B.C. | 8,000,000 | 7,000,000 | 2,800,000 | 17,800,000 |
| 187 B.C. | 5,500,000 | 1,250,000 | 2,100,000 | 8,850,000 |

*Table 9.1* (*Continued*)

| Year | Legions Payroll | Fleets Payroll | Allies Grain Costs | Total |
|---|---|---|---|---|
| 186 B.C. | 6,750,000 | 1,250,000 | 2,200,000 | 10,200,000 |
| 185 B.C. | 5,500,000 | 1,250,000 | 2,000,000 | 8,750,000 |
| 184 B.C. | 5,500,000 | 1,250,000 | 2,000,000 | 8,750,000 |
| 183 B.C. | 5,500,000 | 1,250,000 | 2,000,000 | 8,750,000 |
| 182 B.C. | 6,750,000 | 1,250,000 | 2,400,000 | 10,400,000 |
| 181 B.C. | 5,500,000 | 1,250,000 | 2,100,000 | 9,750,000 |
| 180 B.C. | 5,500,000 | 1,250,000 | 2,000,000 | 9,650,000 |
| 179 B.C. | 5,500,000 | 1,250,000 | 1,900,000 | 9,550,000 |
| 178 B.C. | 4,750,000 | 2,250,000 | 1,500,000 | 8,500,000 |
| 177 B.C. | 4,750,000 | 2,250,000 | 1,500,000 | 8,500,000 |
| 176 B.C. | 6,750,000 | 2,250,000 | 2,000,000 | 11,000,000 |
| 175 B.C. | 4,750,000 | 1,250,000 | 1,500,000 | 7,500,000 |
| 174 B.C. | 4,750,000 | 1,250,000 | 1,500,000 | 7,500,000 |
| 173 B.C. | 4,750,000 | 1,250,000 | 1,500,000 | 7,500,000 |
| 172 B.C. | 4,000,000 | 3,750,000 | 1,300,000 | 9,050,000 |
| 171 B.C. | 7,000,000 | 3,750,000 | 2,100,000 | 12,850,000 |
| 170 B.C. | 7,000,000 | 3,750,000 | 2,100,000 | 12,850,000 |
| 169 B.C. | 5,500,000 | 3,750,000 | 1,800,000 | 11,050,000 |
| 168 B.C. | 7,000,000 | 3,750,000 | 2,300,000 | 13,050,000 |

*After Battle of Cannae.
**After Peace of Phoenice.

*Source:* Based on Brunt, *Italian Manpower,* pp. 418–26 and 501–50, and Hopkins, *Conquerors,* pp. 23–34.

neration spared Rome from taxing citizens since each was paid out of the proceeds of conquest. Veterans received grants of public land (*ager publicus*) appropriated from defeated foes, but the Republic became embroiled in revolutionary politics as it had to alienate public lands to reward veterans in the late second and first centuries B.C. Augustus converted both forms of remuneration into regular payments in coin, and Julius Caesar and Augustus together created the imperial military budget. Each year from A.D. 6 on, the government expended coins reckoned in tens of millions of denarii on four major items: wages (*stipendium*), retirement benefits (*praemia*), bonuses (*donativa*), and purchases for supply and equipment (*coemptio*). These four expenditures remained the lion's share of the budget, affecting fiscal policy, inflation, and reform of the currency into the early Byzantine age. For the era of the Principate, it is possible to calculate the level of costs of the first three items for the army and to suggest a plausible order of magnitude for the fourth. The naval budget, although considerable, is unknown.

Legionaries of Augustus received annually 225 denarii paid in three installments and calculated as a daily wage of 10 asses, which—despite complaints of mutineers to the contrary—was top pay for coveted full-time employment.[18] The legionary's base pay was raised by Domitian (to 300 denarii), Septimius Severus (to 400), and Caracalla (to 600) so that in over 250 years salaries of soldiers rose by two and two-thirds times, an increase that kept purchasing power even with or ahead of rates of inflation prior to A.D. 235.[19] The imperial government, however, faced army costs that mounted at rates faster than inflation once Nero restored the number of legions to their original Augustan number of twenty-eight in 66. Thereafter, legions numbered between twenty-eight and thirty until the Severan age, but emperors increased the size of the garrison at Rome and enrolled more auxiliary units, including well-paid elite millenary and citizen cohorts (Table 9.2).[20]

Total payrolls, although estimated conservatively, are for units at full strength and without deductions against a soldier's pay. Salaries of the Julio-Claudian army, numbering between 300,000 and 330,000 men, totaled annually between 60 to 70 million denarii, and Augustus and Tiberius each netted hefty savings by reducing the army to a force of twenty-five legions after the Varian disaster in A.D. 9. Domitian's pay raise and enrollment of more units produced an army that fluctuated between 360,000 and 400,000 men and cost emperors of the Flavian and Antonine ages between 95 and 105 million denarii yearly. Septimius Severus commanded on paper 450,000 to 475,000 men, probably the Roman army's peak during its entire history.[21] Septimius Severus and Caracalla within twenty years added respectively some 55 and 80 million more denarii to the aggregate Antonine payroll. Therefore, in 215 the imperial government had increased its military payrolls by four times in less than two centuries, but only half of this increase can be put down to inflation. Payrolls of late Roman and early Byzantine armies cannot be calculated with any certainty, because the size of units and differences in pay between officers and the ranks are unknown. Pressures to supply more coins, however, were probably even greater. During the crisis of the third century, legionary base pay tripled, from 600 denarii in 235 to the 1,800 d.c. reported in the files of Panopolis for 299–300. If this higher rate was in force by 284, Diocletian's soldiers in 293 received as their annual salary 360 silver-clad nummi, which revaluation in 300 reduced to 144 nummi. By a conservative estimate, payrolls for a Tetrarchic army of 435,000 men totaled over 5 billion notational d.c., which in 293 was converted into 1 billion nummi and then, after retariffing in 300, into 425 million nummi.[22] Diocletian thus paid out in salaries two to four times the number of coins Severus Alexander had paid for his larger army less than fifty years earlier. Military payrolls between 30 B.C. and A.D. 300 reveal that the imperial government was committed to minting staggering numbers of silver or billon coins.

Between the joint reign of Valentinian I (364–75) and Valens (364–78) and that of Heraclius (610–41), annual wages of 9 solidi were paid to each cavalryman and 5 solidi to each infantryman, but salaries were but a fraction of military costs. Tax officials calculated the annual cost of a soldier at 36 solidi, covering pay, provisions, and equipment, and horses were calculated as an additional 20 to 25 solidi.[23] The men of Roman units, native and Romanized barbarian alike, received most payments in silver-clad or bronze fractions, but federates, such as Alaric and his Visigoths, clamored for gold. Justinian (527–65), who reputedly economized by reducing his field army to 150,000 men, would have faced annual salaries for this force that totaled at least 1 million solidi or 180 million bronze folles (although total costs might have run to 6.6 million solidi).[24] The scale of later payrolls is also glimpsed in the reports that the army and armada sent against the Vandals in 468 cost between 7.25 and 9.5 million solidi. The total cost of this abortive operation was of the same order of magnitude as the price of expeditions Justinian dispatched for the reconquest of North Africa and Italy.[25] Justinian, disbursing payrolls either in millions of solidi or hundreds of millions of bronze folles during his wars of reconquest, dealt in coins on a scale no less grandiose than had Diocletian. Frequent mutinies

*Table 9.2*
Men under Arms and Payrolls in Denarii, 30 B.C.–A.D. 235

| | Men under Arms | | | |
|---|---|---|---|---|
| Year | Rome Garrison | Legions | Auxiliaries | Total |
| 15 B.C. | 13,500 | 147,840 | 167,872 | 329,212 |
| A.D. 9 | 13,500 | 132,000 | 150,508 | 296,008 |
| 39–41 | 15,500 | 142,560 | 162,548 | 320,608 |
| 66–68 | 19,000 | 147,840 | 167,872 | 334,712 |
| 70 | 15,000 | 153,120 | 184,649 | 352,769 |
| 83–86 | 15,000 | 158,400 | 184,649 | 358,049 |
| 86–92 | 15,000 | 153,120 | 184,649 | 352,769 |
| 92–100 | 15,000 | 147,840 | 184,649 | 347,489 |
| 101–102 | 16,000 | 158,400 | 186,729 | 361,129 |
| 132–61 | 16,000 | 153,120 | 186,729 | 355,849 |
| 161–66 | 16,000 | 147,840 | 223,690 | 387,530 |
| 166–70 | 16,000 | 158,400 | 223,690 | 398,090 |
| 195 | 27,000 | 174,240 | 274,936 | 476,176 |
| 215 | 27,000 | 174,240 | 274,936 | 476,176 |
| 230 | 27,000 | 179,520 | 274,936 | 481,456 |

*Source:* Based on pay scales proposed by R. MacMullen, "The Roman Emperors' Army Costs," *Latomus* 43 (1984), 579–80, and M. Speidel, "The Pay of the Auxilia," *JRS* 63 (1973), 41–47 (proposing auxiliary pay at five-sixths of the legionary pay).

in Italy and Africa, however, reveal that Justinian was chronically in arrears, even though top base pay in his army (9 solidi) weighed one-half the gold equivalent paid to legionaries of the Augustan army (225 denarii or 9 aurei).

In stark contrast stand the payrolls of the army of the medieval Byzantine state, which was perhaps 20 to 25 percent the size of the Severan army. In the late seventh century, Heraclian emperors abandoned the professional Roman army because they lacked the coins to meet annual payrolls after territorial losses reduced imperial revenues by 75 percent. Emperors compensated soldiers with land and paid out donatives in installments. In the ninth century, the annual cost of a cavalryman was calculated at 18.5 solidi or slightly more than half that in the Dominate.[26] Heraclian and Isaurian

| Payrolls in Denarii | | | |
|---|---|---|---|
| Rome Garrison | Legions | Auxiliaries | Total |
| 5,750,775 | 42,978,600 | 18,992,700 | 67,722,075 |
| 5,750,775 | 37,248,750 | 17,055,450 | 60,054,975 |
| 6,931,325 | 40,228,650 | 18,411,525 | 65,571,500 |
| 7,176,025 | 42,978,600 | 18,992,700 | 69,147,325 |
| 6,546,025 | 43,208,550 | 21,343,725 | 72,358,300 |
| 8,714,700 | 59,598,000 | 28,834,500 | 97,147,200 |
| 8,714,700 | 57,611,400 | 28,834,500 | 95,160,600 |
| 8,714,700 | 55,624,800 | 28,834,500 | 93,174,000 |
| 9,554,700 | 59,598,000 | 29,115,300 | 98,268,000 |
| 9,554,700 | 57,611,400 | 29,115,300 | 96,281,400 |
| 9,554,700 | 55,624,800 | 34,323,330 | 99,502,830 |
| 9,554,700 | 59,598,000 | 34,323,330 | 103,476,030 |
| 23,435,600 | 87,410,400 | 43,614,800 | 154,460,800 |
| 35,033,400 | 131,115,600 | 65,421,600 | 231,570,600 |
| 35,033,400 | 135,088,800 | 65,421,600 | 235,543,800 |

emperors relieved demand on a shrinking stock of specie, but their reforms propelled the Byzantine world out of the monetized world of Rome into the rural economy of the early Middle Ages.

Payrolls formed just one, albeit the greatest, item in the military budget. Retirement benefits, paid in a lump sum on retirement, each year put millions of denarii into the hands of veterans of the legions and the garrison of Rome. Since benefits were paid in proportion to rank and rates were adjusted with each increase in base pay, reasonable estimates of the annual payments of retirement benefits can be made for the period between 6 and 235 (Table 9.3).[27] The estimates represent the potential costs assuming an orderly rate of discharges and few promotions; admittedly, such conditions seldom obtained. The estimates indicate that the imperial government, on the average, paid out hard cash sums amounting to some 40 to 45 percent of payrolls. Caracalla perhaps greatly

*Table 9.3*
Estimated Military Expenditures, A.D. 6–235
(in millions of Denarii)

| Year | Payroll | Retirement Benefits | Equipment and Supplies | Total |
|---|---|---|---|---|
| 6 | 68 | 29 | 27 | 124 |
| 9 | 60 | 28 | 24 | 112 |
| 39–41 | 66 | 29 | 26 | 121 |
| 68–69 | 69 | 30 | 28 | 127 |
| 70 | 72 | 31 | 29 | 132 |
| 83–86 | 97 | 44 | 39 | 180 |
| 86–92 | 95 | 42 | 38 | 175 |
| 92–100 | 93 | 41 | 41 | 171 |
| 101–32 | 98 | 44 | 39 | 181 |
| 132–61 | 96 | 42 | 38 | 176 |
| 161–66 | 100 | 41 | 40 | 181 |
| 166–70 | 104 | 44 | 42 | 190 |
| 195 | 155 | 70 | 62 | 287 |
| 215 | 232 | 104 | 93 | 429 |
| 230 | 236 | 107 | 95 | 438 |

*Source:* The calculation of retirement payments (computed at two-thirds of base pay over twenty years) are based on M. Corbier, "L'aerarium militare," in *Armées et fiscalité,* pp. 220–31.

increased this amount in 212 if he, by extending citizenship to the entire empire, made auxiliaries eligible for benefits.

Ceremonial distributions, known as donatives to soldiers and *congiaria* to the urban plebeians, were less regular items on the budget, but each occasion put millions of aurei or denarii into circulation. Donatives became the greatest inducement after plunder for joining the legions after 200 B.C. Those serving in tough frontier wars where booty was scarce—Cisalpine Gaul, Spain, or Numidia—gained but a fraction of their wages in donatives, but in the eastern theaters as early as 167 B.C. donatives amounted to as much as 100 denarii, equal to a year's pay.[28] Pompey, Julius Caesar, and Augustus handed out donatives that were thirteen to twenty-six times a soldier's annual pay. Over the years, in terms of buying power, soldiers gained even more. A legionary of 150 B.C. who received a donative of 25 denarii had 52 percent of the cost of his family's annual needs for grain, but his great-grandson with a donative of 3,000 or 6,000 denarii gained twenty-five or fiftyfold this amount. Julius Caesar and Augustus set new standards—they paid their gifts in aurei—and not only to soldiers but to urban plebeians as well, the two groups now numbering from one-fifth to one-quarter of the adult male citizens. Tiberius and Caligula transformed donatives from rewards paid out of booty into regular bonuses, for each at his accession granted donatives of 50 million denarii (by matching 25 million denarii in testamentary gifts of his predecessor). Members of the Praetorians regularly received 10 aurei apiece; those of the Urban Cohorts, half this amount; and legionaries and urban plebeians, 3 aurei each.[29] In 41, Claudius set a new level of largess to the Praetorian Guard, promising 150 aurei per man or fifteen times the previous rate, so that he paid the Guard close to 35 million denarii; gifts to legionaries and urban plebeians added another 49.5 million denarii, totaling nearly 85 million denarii in accessional gifts. In 54, Nero offered similar acccessional donatives, and Vitellius promised to his enlarged Praetorian Guard donatives totaling 88.8 million denarii. The thrifty Flavian emperors reduced the size of the garrison of Rome and imposed strict limits on imperial largess in an attempt to restore imperial solvency.

As imperial revenues again mounted after Trajan's conquests and the exploitation of new mines in the Balkans and Dacia, emperors of the second century augmented and institutionalized ceremonial gift-giving. In the ninety-six years between the reigns of Nerva (96–98) and Commodus (180–92) forty-five separate *congiaria* totaling at least 567,250,000 denarii or 22,690,000 aurei are reported. The Severan emperors in the following forty-three years (193–235) distributed twelve *congiaria* totaling at least 431,250,000 denarii or 17,250,000 aurei. In less than 150 years emperors are known to have distributed to the urban plebeians gifts of nearly 1 billion denarii or 40 million aurei.[30] The legions, which totaled between twenty-eight and thirty in the second century, received donatives at rates comparable to those paid to the urban plebeians so that donatives to the army must have more than matched the sums reported at each *congiaria*. Antonine emperors probably handed out to legionaries donatives that each ranged between 14 and 40 million denarii, and Severan emperors gave to their legions (numbering thirty-three or thirty-four) donatives that totaled on each occasion between 30 and 60 million denarii. The garrison of Rome probably received on each occasion donatives equal to the total amount given to both the urban plebeians and legionaries. The total in ceremonial gifts between the reigns of Nerva and Severus Alexander (96–235) reached perhaps 4 billion denarii or 160 million aurei.

The ceremonial expenditures expected of emperors had long-term consequences for the budget and economic life of the Roman world. Emperors down to the seventh century could seldom amass a great reserve since they constantly were distributing vast numbers of coins as ceremonial gifts. The level of display is well seen in the accessional costs of 161. Marcus Aurelius and Lucius Verus bestowed 30 million denarii to 150,000 urban plebeians, 43.5 million denarii to their twenty-nine legions, and 76.6 million denarii to the Praetorian and Urban cohorts. They spent over 150 million denarii in donatives alone, consuming 22 percent of the 675 million denarii left in the treasury by Antoninus Pius.[31] Entertainment and the initial costs of the Parthian War consumed the rest, so that the treasury was soon desperately short of hard cash; yet, they were merely showering the largess expected of emperors. By the Severan age, the imperial government was already running into difficulties in delivering donatives, and Ammianus Marcellinus reports delays of promised donatives in the fourth century.[32]

Although sestertii commemorate imperial largess during the Principate, most donatives were paid in gold or silver, and, from the reign of Hadrian, aurei were deemed most appropriate—Cassius Dio, Herodian, and SHA all report donatives in aurei. The cycle of frequent donatives paid in gold or silver declined during the third century as the value of imperial money dropped and prices rose. Emperors thereafter paid most donatives in billon antoniniani and reserved handouts of aurei for special occasions such as the celebration of quinquennial vows. On such imperial anniversaries soldiers received donatives of four aurei and one pound of silver, and officers and officials were rewarded with much greater gifts. Nonetheless, emperors after Severus Alexander handed out aurei in numbers that exceeded donatives of the second century. Rates per man were almost unchanged, but the number of recipients at court, in the bureaucracy, and in the army had grown. Diocletian exalted the magnificence of these gifts by handing out, in lieu of coins, gold multiples minted at convenient divisions of the pound rather than as increments of the billon nummus.[33] Emperors from Constantine to Heraclius raised the rate of quinquennial donatives to five solidi, and, in the sixth century, they commuted the silver bullion into solidi.

Inflation after 235 compelled emperors to institute a second type of donative, paid annually in billon coins, distinct from anniversary payments in gold coin and ceremonial plate. Military files at Panopolis in 297–300 reveal that soldiers were paid, in each of the four years, donatives in billon nummi as supplements to salaries.[34] The notion of a donative was transformed from a periodic reward into a regular supplement to maintain purchasing power. Thus, a legionary in 300 was paid an annual donative of 800 silver-clad nummi or 5.5 times more than his base pay of 144 nummi. Such annual donatives were issued in billon coins, either antoniniani or nummi, during the third and fourth centuries, and presumably in bronze folles during the sixth and seventh centuries.

The final item in the military budget was the purchase and the cost of distributing supplies and equipment (*coemptio*). During its overseas wars, the Republic engaged contractors to clothe and equip the armies and exacted foodstuffs from allies to avoid dealing in large numbers of coin. Large-scale payments were settled in gold or silver ingots, and few coins were put into the hands of soldiers. Under the Principate expenditures in coin were limited since the army was able to exact certain needs—grain, oil, wine, leather, and salted meat—on the spot in kind. Legionaries also manufactured items such as bricks or arms and armor, but collections in kind and production at the camps could not fill every need so the treasury had to spend coin for raw materials and for contracts let out to civilian manufacturers. Emperors also preferred to purchase and ship supplies lest charismatic governors rebel if the armies became too self-sufficient.

The cost of arms and armor for a soldier is estimated at 200 to

300 denarii, which was recovered by the state in annual salary deductions of 10 to 15 denarii. The arms of 10,000 recruits inducted each year amounted to 2 to 3 million denarii; the capital investment in arms alone was at least 60 to 90 million denarii.[35] At least 100,000 war horses were in service during the Principate and, at the official price of 125 denarii per mount, were valued at 12.5 million denarii. By the early fourth century, the number of war horses was three or four times this number with a value of between 1.5 and 4 million solidi. The annual cost of feeding and maintaining the animals was four to five times their purchase price.[36]

The average military budget of the Principate during peacetime has been reconstructed based on estimates of the numbers of men under arms and relative levels of pay (see Table 9.3). The figures are offered to indicate orders of magnitude; calculations are based on units at full strength, a regular pattern of retirements, and a steady amount of purchases. Given their range and scale in Egypt during the Principate, army purchases are estimated conservatively at one-third of the annual payrolls.[37] The estimates do not include the donatives. As shown by the reconstruction of the budget, Julio-Claudian emperors faced annual costs ranging between 110 and 130 million denarii for an army of 300,000 to 335,000 men. In the Flavian and Antonine ages, when the ranks swelled to 350,000 to 400,000 men, costs rose by one-third to 175 to 190 million denarii. Septimius Severus and Caracalla together, in keeping with the dynasty's axiom of enriching the soldiers and despising the rest, more than doubled the military budget, even though they commanded an army only slightly larger than that of the Antonines, probably 450,000 to 475,000 men at most.

The numbers of coins required annually are so staggering that it is often doubted whether the Roman government had the means to meet its annual budget in coin. It is noted that the base pay of legionaries was held at a minimum for over five centuries, and soldiers endured deductions against their pay and received many needs in kind to spare the state from dealing in coin. Thrifty emperors, like Tiberius and Vespasian, did not replace lost legions and all emperors tolerated unscrupulous practices—withholding pay, retaining veterans under the standards after their service had expired, and keeping units below strength. All these expedients risked mutinies like the ugly outbreaks in Spain and Macedon during the early second century B.C., or, more dangerous still, defeats. Rome could not have consistently pursued these abuses and conquered her overseas empire. Literary sources report remarkably few mutinies by the imperial armies. It was only in the fifth century, after emperors turned to barbarian mercenaries, and in the sixth century, during Justinian's wars of reconquest, that the imperial army was repeatedly rocked by mutinies over back pay.[38]

It also is argued that because of the many costs and pension payments deducted from their pay, the soldiers had little money to spend. Three Flavian payroll records—two preserved on papyri from Egypt and the other from Masada—seem to bear out this argument, but it is uncertain whether the payroll record for any one of these three soldiers was typical.[39] On the other hand, the state was committed to heavy expenditures in reimbursements, donatives, and retirement payments as well as many incidental costs. Recruits, for example, received travel money (*viaticum*) of three aurei, and soldiers on detached service customarily cited this payment as justification for their extortion of civilians. Veterans upon discharge sold back armor, arms, and mounts. Soldiers marketed commodities that they produced at camp, and they found ready markets for the sale of plunder. Josephus reports how Titus's veterans unloaded so much gold captured at Jerusalem that the price of gold in Levantine cities dropped by nearly one-half.[40] Soldiers had money to spend, even though they received their salary in three (or, after 83, four) installments each year and in spite of the customary deductions. So many coins circulated in army camps that the military moralist Vegetius, writing in the late fourth century, recommended that soldiers be kept short of funds lest they grow idle and unruly. The record of hoards and casual finds at military sites across the empire reveal that soldiers had denarii to save and spare change to lose.[41] Emperors were aware, as Severus Alexander reputedly stated, that "one need not fear a soldier, if he is properly clothed, fully armed, has a stout pair of boots, a full belly, and something in his money-belt."[42] A most telling passage comes from Josephus, who reports that Titus ordered the army on parade to receive pay during the siege of Jerusalem in 70. Josephus captures the drama of payday in the Roman army—the ceremony of so many armies throughout history when large amounts of money changed hands:

> When the soldiers' pay-day arrived, he [i.e., Titus] ordered the officers to parade their troops in full view of the enemy and there count out the money to each man. In accordance with custom the soldiers removed their armour from its protective coverings and advanced in full panoply, the horsemen leading their chargers decked in all their trappings. Every yard of ground before the city shone with silver and gold, a spectacle that filled the Romans with delight, their enemies with terror. . . . In four days the Romans completed the payment of all the legions.[43]

Soldiers, some 450,000 strong, formed the best paid and organized profession in the Roman Empire; and reports of the shipment of coins for payrolls abound. Legions of Marius and Pompey in North Africa received their pay in denarii shipped from Rome by sea.[44] Payrolls and donatives to frontier armies of the Principate came by river transport or by cart and mule train. Military files from Panopolis in Upper Egypt in 300 report receiving a routine shipment by mule cart of 50 pounds of coined silver and perhaps 4,000 nummi (with a total weight of 180 pounds) in payrolls.[45] Writers of the early Byzantine age report as a matter of course the transport by mules, camels, and carts of hundreds of thousands of solidi destined for field armies.[46] Each year the Roman government transported coins numbering millions or tens of millions to armies in the provinces. Even granting the fragmentary condition of Classical sources, the low incidence of reports of mutiny over arrears stands as testimony to the triumph of Roman organization in minting and distributing coins. Roman success is all the more astonishing because it is unmatched until the modern age. In the sixteenth century, the Spanish Crown established the first large professional army since the collapse of Roman power—the army of the Netherlands, numbering between 70,000 and 90,000.[47] The Spanish Crown, despite the flow of silver from the New World, went bankrupt in paying for this force and its soldiers came to institutionalize mutiny over arrears.

The military budget has been estimated as consuming one-half to two-thirds of the state's annual income in the Principate, and the remainder went to civil administration, ostentatious display, and building. The growth of ceremonial and building costs is largely undocumented. The Marcian aqueduct was completed in 143 B.C. at the cost of 4.5 million denarii, but major building projects under Augustus, Claudius, Vespasian, and Trajan cost ten and thirty times this sum.[48] Severan, Tetrarchic, and Constantinian emperors too spent lavishly on monuments, following the advice of Cassius Dio that "such expenditures somehow contribute to the sense of awe among our allies and panic among our enemies."[49]

Augustus paid senatorial and equestrian governors handsome salaries ranging from 10,000 aurei (to the senior proconsuls of Asia and Africa) to 500 aurei to an equestrian military tribune. By the Flavian age civil salaries were determined by rank, and most likely the minimum property qualifications of the upper classes (*ordines*) fixed the pay scales of senior officials. In the mid-second century, some fifty senior consular and praetorian governors drew salaries between 10,000 and 4,000 aurei with the majority receiving between 7,500 and 5,000 aurei. The salaries of senatorial governors, along with the great prefects at Rome and in Egypt, totaled perhaps 400,000 aurei or 10 million denarii.[50] Trajan and Hadrian enrolled many more equestrian procurators paid annual salaries rated at 600, 1,000, 2,000, and, with Marcus Aurelius, 3,000 aurei. If the total number of procurators on the payroll in 150 numbered 3,000 *sexagenarii*, 500 *centenarii*, and 100 *ducenarii*, their combined salaries would have been 1.5 million aurei or 37.5 million denarii. The military tribunes who officered the thirty legions and the prefects commanding nearly 375 auxiliary units received an additional 7.5 million denarii or 300,000 aurei.[51] Therefore, Antoninus Pius could have issued his governors, equestrian procurators, and junior officers annual salaries totaling 50 million denarii (2 million aurei or the equivalent of nearly 45,000 pounds of gold). Total annual expenditures on the administration might have approached the same order of magnitude as total military costs, perhaps growing from 100 million to 250 million denarii between the reigns of Augustus and Septimius Severus.

Overall civil costs and corruption sharply increased with the multiplication of salaried posts, but it is impossible to estimate costs. By the best counts, senior career civil servants rose from 300 to over 35,000 during the century between the reigns of Caracalla (211–17) and Constantine (306–37).[52] The emperors of the Dominate faced a mounting budget in civil administration as daunting as their military expenditures. As the numbers of functionaries at court and administrators in the provinces rose, so did pressures to mint more gold coins, adding another incentive to reduce the weight of the aureus, debase gold coins in the mid-third century and again in the first half of the fourth century, and strike light-weight solidi in the sixth and seventh centuries.

### *Inflation and the Budget*

During the First Punic War (264–241 B.C.), Rome substituted silver coins for the clumsy Italic bronze money to facilitate military expenditures, and the denarius became the primary coin of state expenditures for the next five centuries (241 B.C.–A.D. 238). Most expenditures were met with coins reclaimed in taxation because recalling and reminting of full-bodied coins in circulation was costly; if the state were to profit from a recoinage, taxes had to be exacted in full-weight coins and worn pieces had to be discounted. Although Republican commanders in the field might have occasionally used captured coin for donatives or local purchases, foreign coin obtained as spoils or in tribute was returned to Rome, melted down, and reminted. Therefore, the Roman state seldom met fiscal obligations in any money other than its own.

Egypt stood apart as both an exception and lesson in the use of currency. The billon tetradrachma, tariffed at one denarius from the reign of Claudius, circulated as the sole high-value coin. Although imperial officials computed costs in denarii, payrolls were met in tetradrachmae. Legionaries stationed in Egypt at the time of Augustus received approximately the same amount of silver in their coins, whether they were paid in Roman denarii or Cleopatran tetradrachmae. When Tiberius reduced the fineness of the tetradrachma, Roman soldiers serving in Egypt received coins with about 70 to 75 percent of the silver found in an equal number of denarii. Between the reigns of Nero and Marcus Aurelius, legionaries in Egypt received their pay in coins containing between three-quarters and two-thirds of the silver in current denarii, and debasements in 161–215 reduced the silver to just under 40 percent of imperial coin. The lesson was not lost on imperial officials. Caracalla, who charted the course of debasement for the next 150 years, faced staggering military costs, and it is no surprise that he and his successors debased the silver currency to meet their soaring costs. Antonine and Severan emperors did not set out to create a fiduciary billon currency but rather debased the denarius as an expedient after exhausting reserves and other sources of capital. Nonetheless, successive debasements within a century (161–260) replaced the silver denarius with a billon radiate double, the antoninianus.

Total military costs skyrocketed during the third century, but the rate of increase of each of the four main budgetary items was hardly uniform. Salaries and numbers of men under arms rose as emperors enrolled recruits into expeditions against rivals or foreign foes, but Diocletian (284–305) ended civil war and cashiered many veterans, returning the army to its Severan size of 425,000 to 450,000 men. The base pay of legionaries tripled from 600 to 1,800 denarii between 235 and 284, but inflation reduced the buying power of the denarius and payrolls in real terms diminished in comparison to other military expenses. After 235, high casualties during chaotic civil war and the retention of veterans under the standards reduced total retirement payments. Constantine reaffirmed cash payments, but many veterans were granted land in depopulated frontier zones—a policy that provided the precedent for settling *limitanei* in the fourth century. The most ruinous increases in the budget were the costs of supplies, equipment, and transport as legions crisscrossed the empire to battle each other, repel barbarians, or assault Sassanid Persia. Vast amounts of hard cash were needed, not only for foodstuffs, weapons, and armor, but because emperors pensioned off the unfit and advanced pay to recruits swelling the ranks of expeditionary forces. Levies in kind, requisitioning, and pillage did little to relieve the pressure for coin, because armies on the move had access to a narrow band of towns and lands along highways and little time to collect supplies. Expeditionary armies offered a lucrative market, and vendors could cover high costs of transport and still reap big profits by selling to the commissariat.[53] Campaigning proved ruinously expensive, and logistical costs rose at an unrelenting rate because emperors, save for brief respites under Diocletian and Constantine, were continually on campaign during the third and fourth centuries.

The civil and frontier wars in the fourth century generated new waves of price rises, ruining a dozen reforms of the billon currency. These costs in turn drove emperors to the fateful final steps of abandoning the expensive professional imperial army in favor of barbarians, who by the mid-fourth century already figured prominently in the ranks of crack units and frontier garrisons (*limitanei*). Barbarian federates from the 350s on were granted short-term contracts that relieved the imperial exchequer from annual wages, retirement benefits, donatives, and most equipment costs because mercenaries only received wages and supplies for the duration of a campaign. The lump sums of gold paid to Alaric's Goths or the tribute that Attila extorted from the Eastern emperor Theodosius II were far less onerous than the budget of a professional army, but fiscal savings compromised the defense of empire by ruining the imperial army that had acted as the main agent of monetization.

For the six centuries after 200 B.C., Rome had a constant need for coins, numbering in the tens of millions. Government expenditure was the engine that drove the Roman economy. Rome was able, by the fruits of conquest and the exploitation of mines, to secure fresh supplies of bullion on an unprecedented scale, and the state perfected a system of tax collection that recovered and pumped coins through the economy. Despite the loss of the Western Empire, the budget in the East soared again during the sixth and first half of the seventh century so that the Roman state, even in decline, never relented in its demand for huge numbers of coins. It is time to turn to taxation, the means whereby Roman government, long before Cerealis's day, collected and spent hundreds of millions of coins each year.

### *Coins and Taxes*

The Roman system of taxation too was a legacy of conquest. Rome adapted and extended throughout her empire a plethora of money taxes inherited from the Hellenistic world. Rome imposed capitation or head taxes, collected at fixed rates reckoned in denarii or drachmae; provincials detested the census and head tax as Roman oppression made manifest. To regressive head taxes were added a host of other direct taxes, surcharges, rents, and licensing fees on produce and the legal status of land, on livestock, or on the means of production. Indirect taxes were exacted from citizens and provincials alike, notably tolls levied *ad valorem* on the transit trade within the empire and customs duties on commerce beyond the frontiers.

The annual value of transactions in the Roman world—the gross national product, so to speak—is estimated at between 2 and 6 billion denarii in the Antonine age. Such estimates, however, tell little about the amount collected in taxes or the number of coins required.[54] In 118 Hadrian burned in the forum of Trajan arrears of 225 million denarii owed by Roman citizens, suggesting annual receipts of 90 to 110 million denarii from indirect taxes alone.[55] Although they had access to immense taxable wealth, Roman emperors sought popularity as well as profit. They wrote off arrears, forgave taxes of cities stricken by calamities, extended exemptions to favored groups, and, at their accession, reduced or abolished odious imposts as gestures of good will (although the last were invariably reinstated later). The imperial government favored relatively light taxation to save on administrative costs and so invested responsibility for exacting taxes to decurions who administered the cities. Since the fortunes of imperial taxation depended upon cooperation of the civic elites, emperors who raised taxes after 235 risked rebellion from civic elite classes.

It is argued, based on head taxes reported in Egyptian papyri, that taxation was kept simple so that payments were in whole numbers of denarii, drachmae, or tetradrachmae or, in the time of the Dominate, solidi. Under this scenario, peasants sold produce, purchased silver or gold coins, paid off taxes, and then headed home to their world of barter. There are several problems with this vision of tax collection; foremost, taxpayers did not queue up in an orderly fashion to render unto Caesar his due. Taxes were collected throughout the year, often in installments rather than on a fixed due date; arrears, remissions, and reassessments inevitably impeded and thwarted the process. Tax collectors entered villages armed with intimidating commissions and swordbearers, and their success depended upon the accessibility of taxpayers, the number of hired guards, the vicissitudes of harvests, and the urgency of the demands from above. Collection of taxes at any time in the Roman Empire must have been similar to what Charles "Chinese" Gordon, Victorian soldier of fortune and administrator, described in the Sudan, where Ottoman officials and soldiers collected a complicated set of customary and new taxes in coin and kind. Immediate presence and brute force alone assured payment: "The people unless they are physically coerced by the whip will not pay their taxes. . . . By putting them in prison you would need a huge prison of defaulters . . . so they must be beaten into it."[56]

It was a daunting task to reach 15 million reluctant taxpayers with so few senior imperial officials in the provinces during either the Principate or the Dominate, and then to convey the coins to the proper treasuries. In most of the Roman world, civic officials and liturgists assumed liability for their city's taxes. Leading citizens sometimes advanced their city an interest-free loan on the promise of prompt reimbursement from monies collected. One benefactor on the isle of Tenos endowed a fund to pay the capitation taxes of his fellow citizens; other inscriptions laud generous donors like Opramaos of Rhodiapolis who assumed a year's tax obligation at his own expense.[57] At the Egyptian town of Tebtynis in 100, four liturgists drew lots—two for collecting the poll tax in the town and two for collecting it from citizens resident in the villages. The latter two, who were expected to collect a minimum of 3,300 tetradrachmae from 300 village taxpayers, pledged to pay 275 tetradrachmae per month to guarantee against shortfalls arising from arrears, missed taxpayers, or powerful magnates who refused to pay up.[58] Even after Trajan introduced salaried imperial tax officials to track down rural taxpayers in Egypt, local officials and liturgists still provided the information and advanced money. In the fourth century, this obligation was codified into the collective legal responsibility of the ten leading councilmen who were made liable for deficiencies in their city's taxes. The brothers Dorotheus and Papnuthis, petty officials and landowners of Oxyrhynchus, in 365 borrowed solidi to pay in advance taxes due and then exacted what they could from the peasants as their reimbursement and, perhaps, profit.[59] It is hardly surprising that the emperor and his subjects alike repeatedly censured overly zealous collectors who exacted excessive profits.

Even in the best of times, fiscal agents obtained, at most, four-fifths to five-sixths of assessed taxes. Arrears figure prominently in Egyptian registers of all periods. At the Fayyum town of Philadelphia, delinquent taxpayers annually cost the government approximately 15 to 20 percent of expected revenues (between 625 and 750 tetradrachmae) during the reign of Claudius.[60] Contemporary collection of a land tax in Greece was more efficient since only one-eighth of the tax due from Messene—12,639 out of 99,365 denarii—went unpaid.[61] The powerful could resist the longest; hence the conscientious Julian, while caesar in Gaul in 356, refused to forgive arrears since such generosity benefited the wealthy.[62] Lesser men resisted with passive pragmatism, offering partial payment, as apparently did many taxpayers named on rolls of Antonine Karanis. Once again, Gordon's experience captures the essence of how tax collection in the Roman world was the art of the possible. Even so responsible a Victorian governor as Gordon who tirelessly traveled from Khartoum to remote districts of Equatoria could do no better than Roman proconsuls: "We never get in so much as five-sixths of our revenue: the collectors say to the heads of communities, 'Pay me four-sixths of the sum due, and give as *backsheesh* to me one-sixth; then I will certify that you cannot pay the remaining one-sixth.'"[63] Such methods of collection did not make for the tidy sums reported in Egyptian tax registers of the Fayyum and Delta towns.[64] Many are registers that bankers drew up as summary ledgers for each category of tax collected which were used to check against complaints, for copies of them were forwarded along with the sums of money to the appropriate tax office of nome, *dioketes,* or *Idios Logos.* Others were simplified reports of a community's total tax, converted into neat units of four drachmae, for use by fiscal offices; still others were lists issued to collectors to aid in their identification of taxpayers by residence.

Three great papyrus rolls from the modest Fayyum town of Karanis offer a unique glimpse into the actual collection of coins. The register, spanning the regnal years 12 through 14 of Marcus Aurelius (171–75), is part of a "day book" of an unnamed banker (*trapezites*) and his partner Serap(ion) who meticulously recorded the coins taken in each day by their agents as they collected taxes from the villagers. Over forty different taxes, rents, licenses on manufacturing, commutation of labor services, interest payments on loans and mortgages, and even administrative fees appear on the rolls of Karanis. Only three taxes were assessed in units of 4 drachmae and thus easily collected in tetradrachmae: the capitation tax (*laographia*), an otherwise unattested head tax of 16 drachmae abbreviated as *kh,* and a bath tax paid by L. Longinus Gemellus.[65] The other taxes were reckoned in a ghost currency based on the Ptolemaic standard of the third century B.C. In turning ghost currencies into actual coins, the scribe added a variety of surcharges to each transaction and then a *symbolikon* of either 3 or 1.5 obols for the cost of converting the sum into Roman provincial coin at an exchange rate of 29 bronze obols to the tetradrachma, which itself represented a premium of more than 20 percent (5 obols) over the official rate of exchange of 24 obols to the tetradrachma.[66] Since many payments were made in bronze coins and generated surcharges, it was profitable to collect from every small property studded with its vines, fruit-bearing trees, and pigeon coops all of which were subject to tax. For example, the modest Karanian landowner Athenion, son of Pyrrhus, paid in surcharges and fees on his two principal land taxes, the *apomoira* and *geometria,* an additional 43 and 10.67 percent, respectively.[67] By such fiscal manipulating, lesser taxpayers throughout the Roman world probably endured effective increases of 50 to 100 percent on their land taxes while emperors, at least in Egypt, avoided the odium of raising ancestral tax assessments until the Severan age.

The assessment of land taxes in a complicated money of account and the collection of taxes and arrears in installments over the course of the year resulted in numerous payments in bronze drachmae and obols rather than billon tetradrachmae. Tax agents obtained most money as small sums paid by individual farmers. Many taxes such as the *apomoira* and *geometria,* levied on the seasonal produce of garden lands, dumped numerous bronze fractions on the tables of Karanis's bankers at the harvest's peak between the Egyptian months of Phamenoth and Mesore. The register's entries allow for a day-by-day estimate of the number of bronze coins (reckoned in obols and paid in denominations from 1 obol to 1 drachma) and tetradrachmae taken in tax (Table 9.4). The count of the number of bronze coins is a minimum, because many entries reckoned as drachmae or sums of 4 drachmae might have been paid in bronze coins. The rolls preserve payments of nearly twelve continuous months stretching from Choiak in year 13 to Hathyr in year 14, roughly from December 172 through November 173. Surviving receipts for these months show total collections of 10,224 tetradrachmae and 20,855 bronze obols (a combined value of 10,933 tetradrachmae and 4 obols) so that the fractional bronze coins were, at the most, 6.5 percent of the total value, but were about two-thirds of the number of coins collected.

The tax register of Karanis, a small town numbering perhaps 4,000 souls of whom 650 were assessed on the rolls of 171–75, suggests that an Egyptian in the second century was expected to pay annually 25 to 30 tetradrachmae in direct taxes. If eligible taxpayers in Egypt numbered 1.5 million out of 5 to 6 million residents, the imperial government could anticipate 40 to 50 million tetradrachmae in direct taxes alone.[68] Indirect taxes and tariffs within Egypt, profits of justice, administrative fees, and customs levied on imported luxuries of the Far East would have raised annual revenues at least to 100 to 150 million tetradrachmae. Money taxes of Egypt in the second century, even if one-fifth were in arrears, yielded at least 75 to 115 million tetradrachmae, valued at some 3 million aurei (or nearly 66,700 pounds of gold). The figures suggest that recent estimates of Egyptian revenues in the sixth and seventh centuries as between 1 and 2 million solidi (13,900 to 27,800 Roman pounds of gold) might be too low, but reports by Arab chroniclers that revenues ranged between 12 to 20 million solidi

*Table 9.4*
Coins Collected in Taxes at Karanis, Egypt, A.D. 171–74

| Year and Month | Record of Coins Collected in Taxes | | Collections for 12 Consecutive Months | |
|---|---|---|---|---|
| | Tetradrachmae | AE Obols | Tetradrachmae | AE Obols |
| Year 12 (171–72) | | | | |
| Thoth | lost | lost | | |
| Phaophi[1] | 31+ | — | | |
| Hathyr | 468 | 640 | | |
| Choiak | 376 | 591 | | |
| Tybi[2] | 237+ | 502+ | | |
| Mecheir[2] | 147+ | 112+ | | |
| Phamenoth[2] | 743+ | 894+ | | |
| Pharmouthi[3] | 2,190+ | 3,175+ | | |
| Pachon[4] | 579+ | 1,056 | | |
| Payni[1] | 21+ | 12+ | | |
| Epeiph | lost | lost | | |
| Mesore[5] | 130+ | 148+ | | |
| Epagomenoi | — | — | | |
| Total Year 12 | 4,922+ | 7,130+ | | |
| Year 13 (172–73) | | | | |
| Thoth[6] | 377+ | 653+ | | |
| Phaophi | — | — | | |
| Hathyr | — | — | | |
| Choiak[7] | 553+ | 904+ | 553+ | 904+ |
| Tybi | 386 | 1,344 | 386 | 1,344 |
| Mecheir | 487 | 1,470 | 487 | 1,470 |
| Phamenoth | 874 | 1,140 | 874 | 1,140 |
| Pharmouthi | 867 | 1,812 | 867 | 1,812 |
| Paschon | 751 | 1,026 | 751 | 1,026 |
| Payni | 443 | 832 | 443 | 832 |
| Epeiph | 581 | 1,142 | 581 | 1,142 |
| Mesore | 2,253 | 3,614 | 2,253 | 3,614 |
| Epagomenoi | 213 | 750 | | |
| Total Year 13 | 7,785+ | 14,687+ | | |
| Year 14 (173–74) | | | | |
| Thoth | 1,196 | 2,877 | 1,196 | 2,877 |
| Phaophi | 1,015 | 2,897 | 1,015 | 2,897 |
| Hathyr[8] | 818 | 1,797 | 818 | 1,797 |

*Table 9.4 (Continued)*

| Year and Month | Record of Coins Collected in Taxes: Tetradrachmae | Record of Coins Collected in Taxes: AE Obols | Collections for 12 Consecutive Months: Tetradrachmae | Collections for 12 Consecutive Months: AE Obols |
|---|---|---|---|---|
| Choiak | lost | lost | | |
| Tybi | lost | lost | | |
| Mecheir[4] | 319+ | 347+ | | |
| Phamenoth[2] | 442+ | 874+ | | |
| Pharmouthi[8] | 491+ | 1,073+ | | |
| Pachon[9] | 188+ | 521+ | | |
| Payni[2] | 518+ | 1,265+ | | |
| Epeiph[7] | 310 | 1,088 | | |
| Mesore[2] | 644+ | 883+ | | |
| Epagomenoi[1] | 55+ | 196+ | | |
| Total Year 14 | 5,996+ | 13,818+ | | |
| Recorded Collections, Years 12–14 | 18,703+ | 35,635+ | | |
| Collections for 12 Consecutive Months | | | 10,224 | 20,855 |

[1]Fragmentary month represented by few entries.
[2]Partial total, possibly 50 percent of entries preserved.
[3]Perhaps 75–80 percent of receipts preserved.
[4]Perhaps one-third of entires preserved.
[5]Fragmentary entries of Mesore and Epagomenoi reckoned together.
[6]Fragmentary entries of Thoth, Phaophi, and Hathyr reckoned together.
[7]Largely complete; some missing entries.
[8]Possibly two-thirds of entries preserved.
[9]Fragmentary; perhaps 25 percent of entries preserved.

*Source:* Derived from *P. Mich.* 223–225.

(167,000 to 278,000 pounds of gold) are too high.[69] Roman authorities employed fiscal institutions and currency in Egypt that differed from other provinces only by a matter of degree.

Other Egyptian documents reveal the range and potential profits from indirect taxes, licensing fees, profits of justice, and customs duties under the Principate. A month's receipts of Trajanic Bacchias, the customs barrier on the Nile before Memphis, netted a mixed stew of coins—196 tetradrachmae, 162 bronze drachmae, 180 bronze obols, and 15 bronze half-obols having a value of 279 tetradrachmae and 1.5 bronze obols.[70] Since the provinces (Italy was exempt) were grouped into customs zones, imperial agents at each frontier station daily collected sundry coins in *portoria* or percentage taxes on the value of goods. Most lucrative was the tax at 25 percent *ad valorem* on the transit of luxury goods to or from the Far East, possibly yielding over 6 million denarii annually and often paid in aurei or denarii.[71] Philostratus tells a humorous anecdote about an agent at Zeugma, the customs barrier on the Upper Euphrates, who sensed a profit of perhaps 6.5 aurei when he mistook the six virtues declared by the sage Apollonius of Tyana as names of courtesans destined for Indian courts.[72]

The many different direct and indirect taxes inevitably netted huge sums in local currencies and innumerable low-value fractional bronze coins. Many coins collected in taxes were promptly paid out to meet expenses, such as the salaries of two guards of the customs station at Bacchias.[73] Owners of the record office of Tebtynis perhaps operated at a loss, at least during some months, because surviving receipts seem to indicate that they paid out more for food and writing supplies than was taken in as fees.[74] Bankers and moneychangers acted as traffic directors moving the varied coins taken in taxes along appropriate channels to their proper destination. They were found wherever buying and selling took place, in markets, on quays, or at sanctuaries. Their ranks included humble moneychangers who opened once a week to change small sums of silver denarii into *aes* in Galilean villages as well as great bankers who operated tables of exchange at the bourse at Constantinople. Any city of consequence required daily tables of exchange. Jesus cast the moneychangers out of the temple, but they must have returned on the morrow, for otherwise business in Jerusalem could not have proceeded. Much of the success of taxation (and commerce) rested upon the shoulders of moneychangers who performed several vital fiscal tasks that earned them the right to a premium on exchange or *agio*. They had the knowledge of exchange rates and stocks of coins necessary to convert fractional and local coins taken in taxes into the portable billon, silver, or gold denominations demanded by a government which never invented bills of exchange to avoid conveying coins in taxes or payrolls. The importance of moneychangers is illustrated by the situation at Karanis in 172–73 where small denominations were 6.5 percent of the value, but about two-thirds the number of coins collected in taxes. The 21,566 small coins would have weighed about 280 pounds; but, when converted (into 742 tetradrachmae plus 19 obols at 29 obols to the tetradrachmae) the weight would have been about 40 pounds. In the second century, the Egyptian firm of Deius and Sons at Theadelphia routinely exchanged bronze coins taken in tax into tetradrachmae for shipment to state treasuries.[75] Moneychangers streamlined the transport of coins taken in tax—a task they continued to perform under the Dominate. The register from Skar in the Hermopolite nome in ca. 435 records that 60 percent of the land taxes were collected as 1,522,000 bronze nummi of AE4 module or 5,285 pounds of coined metal, which was exchanged into 211.33 solidi, just under 3 pounds of gold, for ease of shipment.[76]

Banks advanced money to local authorities to meet imperial taxes, and they also had the capital to purchase new coins, especially during a recoinage, and then issue them into markets. The strategos of the Oxyrhynchite nome ordered reluctant banks to accept coins of Macrianus and Quietus (260–61) because otherwise the provincial regime, which recognized the usurpers, could not collect taxes and pay its bills.[77] Moneychangers checked for fakes, imitative coins, and underweight pieces at the start and finish of each shipment of taxes. They discounted worn pieces, certified good money, and pulled from circulation counterfeit, imitative, and foreign coins. By screening out most bad coins before they reached tax offices, moneychangers more than earned their fees. Egyptian banks were regulated by imperial authorities because they ensured that only the billon tetradrachma and its bronze fractions passed current in the Nile Valley. It was critical that moneychangers retain a monopoly on exchange among varied coins used in taxation. The council and assembly of the Carian city of Mylasa in the Severan age affirmed that rights of exchange were held exclusively by those leasing from the city and laid down stiff fines for private individuals caught charging on exchange.[78]

Taxation and government expenditures at every level produced varying patterns of circulation that can be illustrated by charts that reconstruct how fiscal demands moved different currencies through the economies of Egypt, the eastern provinces, the western provinces, and Italy (Figures 9.1–5). In Egypt, the best-documented case, taxes were paid in fiduciary billon or bronze coins struck at Alexandria, which bankers in the villages and Greek-style towns converted into tetradrachmae to be forwarded to nome treasuries or provincial financial departments at Alexandria. Bankers, operating as state lessees, returned to circulation a significant portion of the taxes in payrolls and purchases of the nome administration. Bronze drachmae and obols taken in tax were immediately returned to exchange tables in the marketplaces of villages and towns where vendors and buyers needed small change. The balance of taxes, tetradrachmae duly tested and sealed in bags, arrived at the financial offices of Alexandria where they, with or without a stay in a treasury, suffered one of three fates. Whenever a major recoinage was ordered, the coins were returned to the mint and struck into new money which was sold to moneychangers who put it into circulation. If there was no recoinage, tetradrachmae earmarked to meet imperial tax obligations were exchanged into aurei or denarii either by financial departments, which obtained Roman coin through the sale of surplus grain to cities of the eastern Mediterranean, or by Alexandrine bankers, who thereupon returned the tetradrachmae to circulation in Egypt. The balance of tetradrachmae reentered local markets in payrolls and purchases by the Roman civil administration and army in Egypt.

This pattern of circulation required far more billon tetradrachmae than bronze fractions, because banks returned the latter to circulation quickly. Bronze coins passed through the hands of villagers, moneychangers, and tax officials dozens of times a year, as indicated by the high degree of wear suffered by most surviving specimens. Tetradrachmae, on the other hand, must have lain idle for months in strongboxes of moneychangers, in bags of nome treasuries awaiting shipment, or in leather sacks at Alexandria earmarked for payrolls or recoinage. The dynamics of tax collection and government expenditure dictated that most bronze coins were confined to the territory around the city in which they entered circulation, but tetradrachmae often passed current throughout the province.

Rome applied variations of this Hellenistic taxation found in Egypt to the rest of the empire. In the eastern provinces of Asia, Cappadocia, or Syria, regional silver staters struck by Roman authorities served the same fiscal role as the Alexandrine tetradrachma. In contrast to Egypt, where banks bought coins from a central mint, many eastern cities struck their own bronze money and leased to private firms the right to exchange civic bronze into provincial staters or denarii. Moneychangers in Asia, for example, obtained bronze assaria from the city and silver cistophori from the proconsular mints at Ephesus and Pergamum. Dynamics similar to those operating in Egyptian taxation affected the circulation of these currencies. Civic bronze coins circulated in a discrete radius around their mint, whereas cistophori collected in taxes and remitted to the governor were spent in payrolls, exchanged into denarii for shipment to Rome, or recoined.[79] Cistophori were frequently stockpiled; hence Cicero in 59 B.C. fretted over the fact that his brother Quintius received his expenses in the cistophori that Pompey had deposited at Ephesus years earlier.[80] Collection and distribution of coins in taxation provided the means whereby Roman authorities could swiftly recoin the entire silver currency of a province as in the case of Asian cistophori under Augustus, Egyptian tetradrachmae under Nero, or Syrian tetradrachmae under Trajan. The dynamics of taxation had as much to do with confining eastern silver and billon staters to distinct regions as official tariffing that overvalued these coins vis-à-vis the denarius.

A simpler version of this system operated in the western and North African provinces. From the Flavian age on, moneychangers (*nummularii*) acquired Roman coins from either the imperial mint or Roman bankers (*argentarii*). Military expenditures on the frontiers put into circulation vast numbers of Roman coins which bankers and moneychangers rerouted to city and village markets where denarii and *aes* were swept up into the cycle of meeting tax obligations to Rome. Rapid penetration of Roman imperial money into western markets spelled the demise of civic bronze currencies and

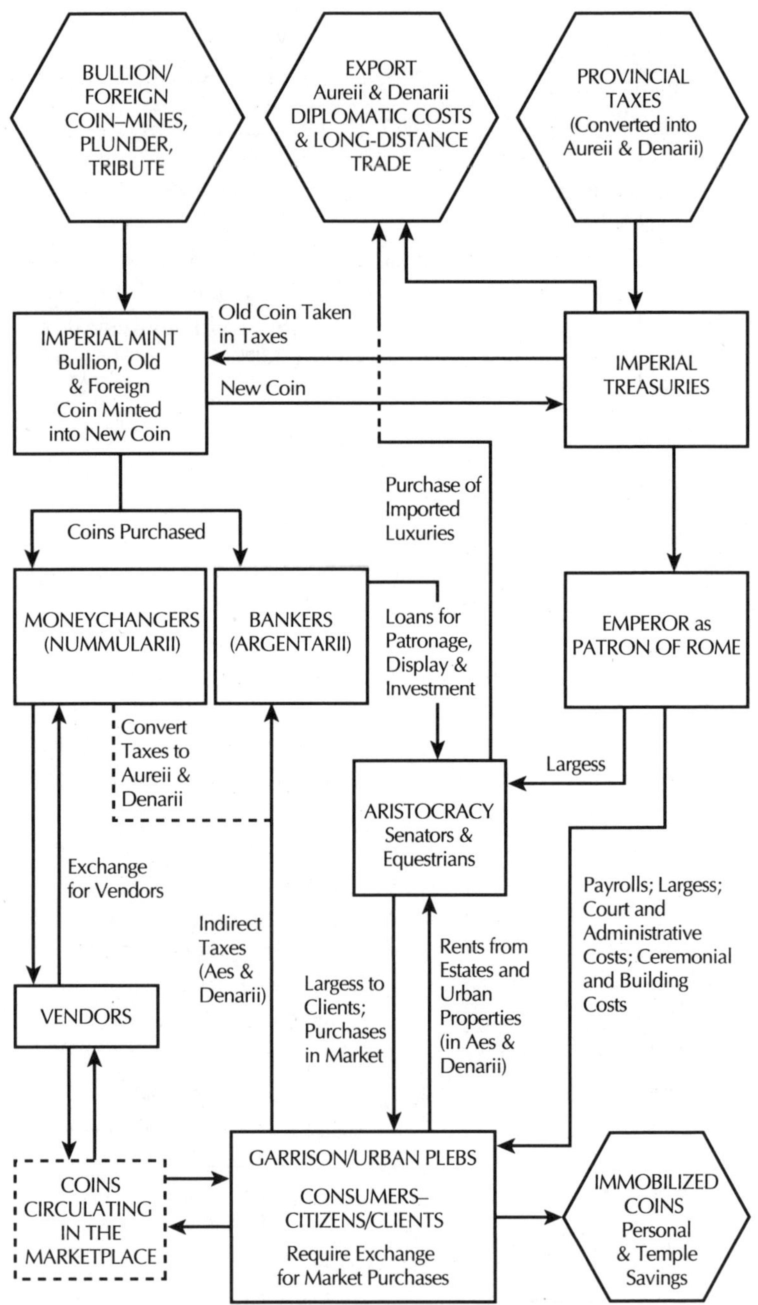


*Figure 9.1* Model for Circulation of Coins in City of Rome A.D. 100.

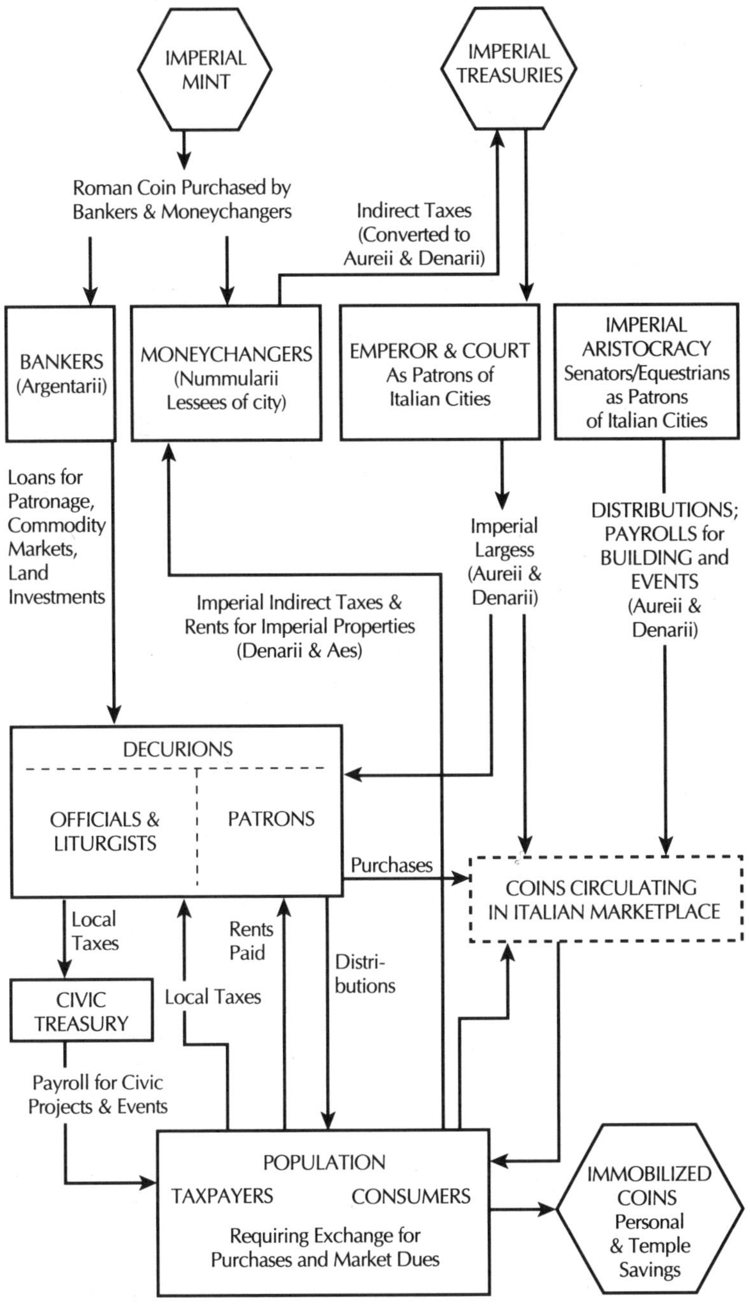


*Figure 9.2* Model for Circulation of Coins in Italy, ca. A.D. 100.

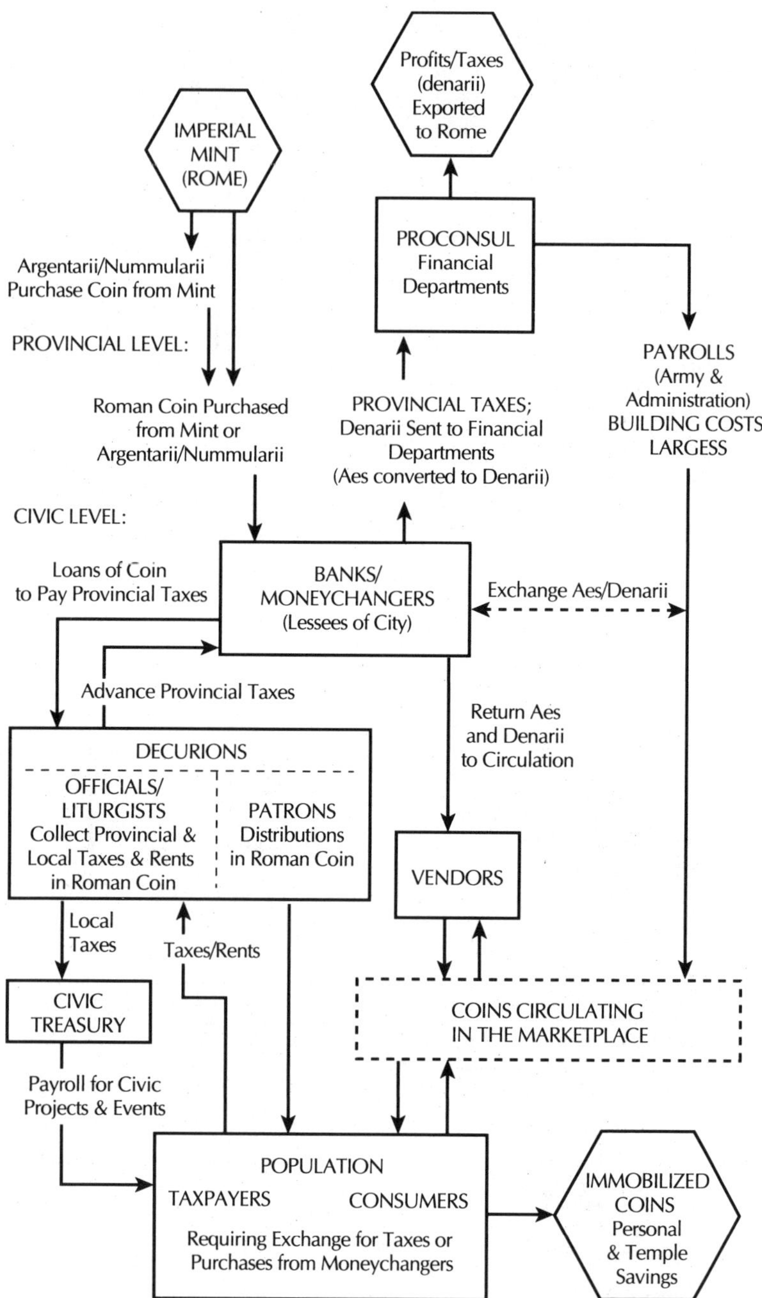


*Figure 9.3* Model for Circulation of Coins in Western Provinces, ca. A.D. 100.

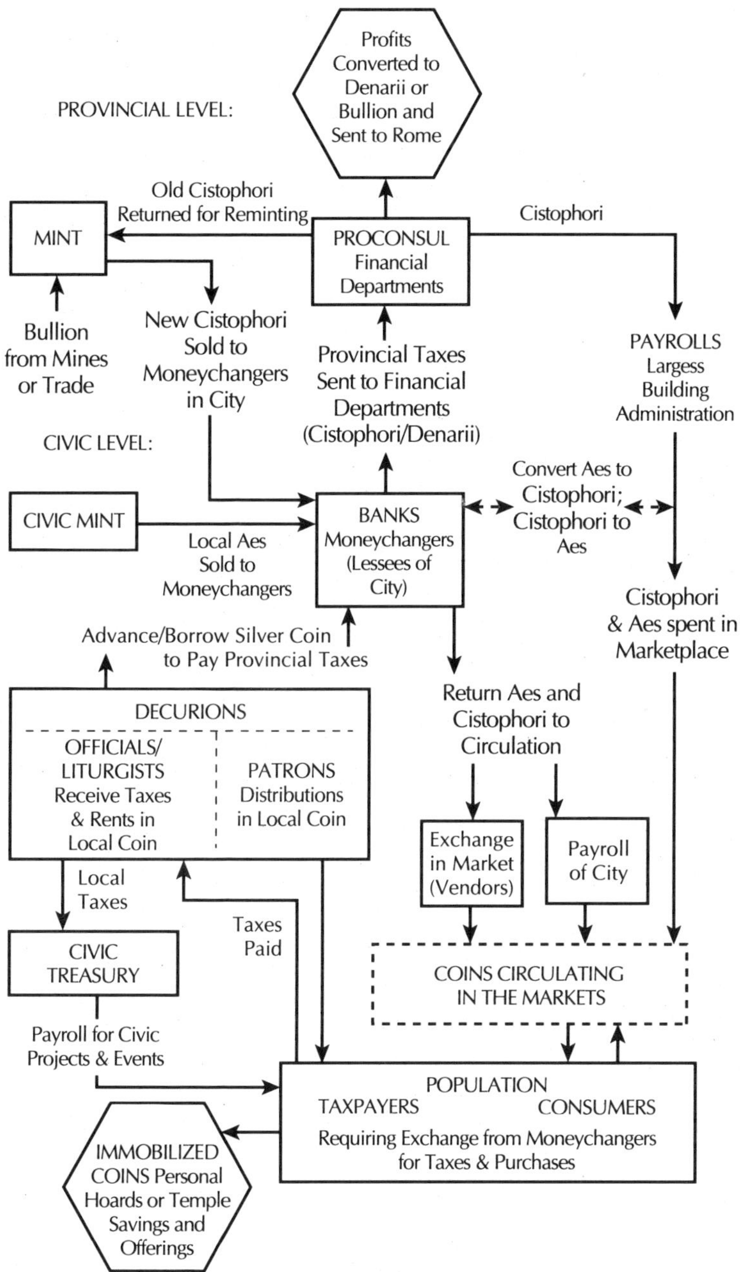


*Figure 9.4* Model for Circulation of Coins in Roman East (e.g., Asia), ca. A.D. 100.

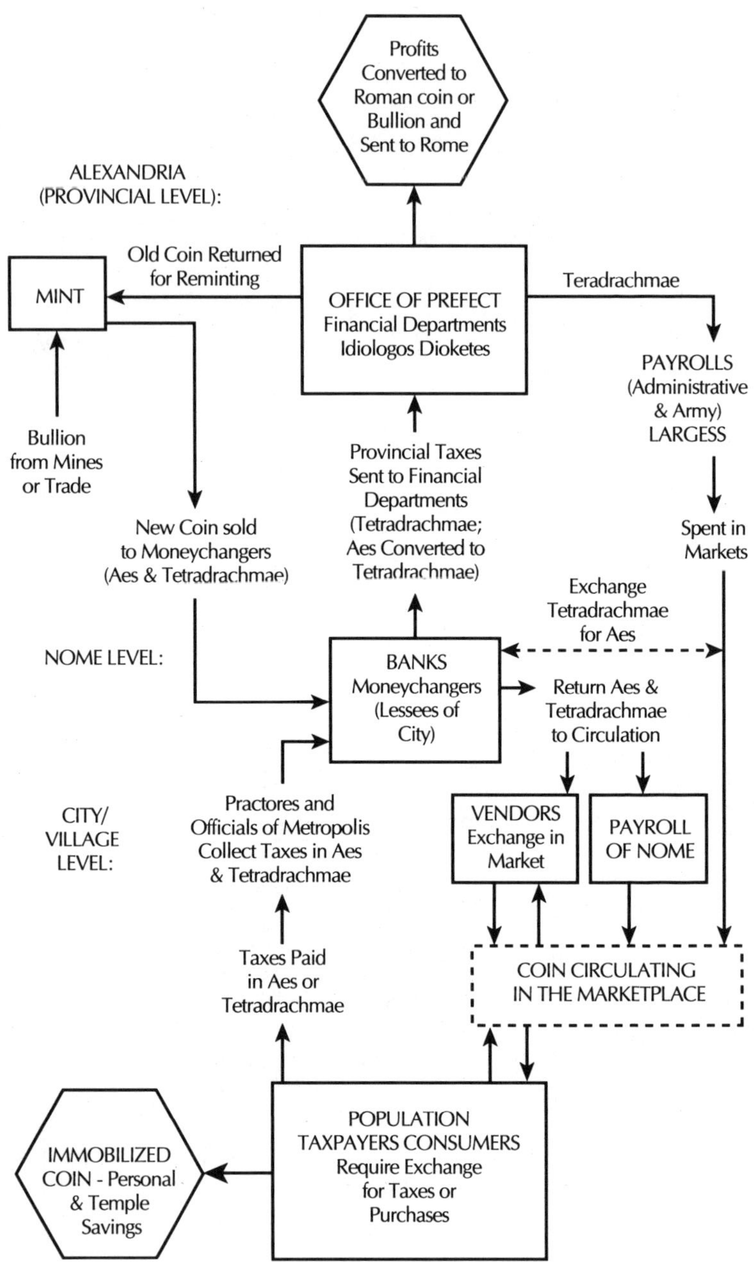


*Figure 9.5* Model for Circulation of Coins in Roman Egypt, ca. A.D. 100.

precluded the need to strike regional silver currencies as in the East. Otherwise, fiscal forces directing the flow of money in the West were the same as those in the East. Roman bronze coins in the western provinces stayed within a relatively restricted area, often where they had originally entered circulation. The *aes* recovered from a sunken ship in the Garonne of A.D. 160 reveal a high velocity of circulation and long use in the provinces, extending over a century for many specimens. Distant provinces such as Britain only suffered shortages in the initial stages of conquest or later in the third century when civil war and invasion disrupted the flow of coins between Rome and the provinces.

The circulation of coins was different at Rome and in Italy, which were glutted by specie obtained from plunder, provincial mines, taxes, and trade. Emperors paid out tremendous sums for buildings at Rome and in distributions to the urban plebs, payrolls, and gifts to Italian municipalities. Since Roman citizens were only subject to indirect taxes, expenditures by the imperial government and gift-giving by the elites primed the Italian economy with coins. The fiscal and monetary conditions in Italy produced a peculiar division of labor between bankers (*argentarii*) and moneychangers (*nummularii*) by the mid-second century B.C.[81] Moneychangers assayed coins and exchanged currencies in the markets of Italian cities. They performed few of the fiscal tasks so lucrative to their counterparts in the provinces, and, consequently, they remained small fry in the social hierarchy of even modest Italian towns. Bankers engaged in deposits and loans and handled transactions that required large sums of denarii or aurei. They advanced hard cash needed by publicans, speculated in commodity markets, and contracted to collect taxes and rents on municipal properties. L. Caecilius Jucundus of Pompeii was representative of bankers in Italian cities—seeking tax-farming contracts and the right to hold auctions, speculating in wine, olive oil, and grain, and advancing credit to decurions purchasing land.[82] His receipts recovered in excavations report that annual profits on investments or loans ranged between 200 and 650 denarii. Bankers like Caecilius Jucundus possessed the hard cash to prime the city government, but they could seldom amass the landed property to enter the decurional order.

The links between fiscal demands and use of coins, it is argued, were snapped by war and inflation from 200 to 400, thereby compelling the Roman government to revert to taxation in kind or bullion. But the imperial government defrayed rising costs by issuing fiduciary currencies so that war and inflation merely simplified regional taxation and imperial money. Diocletian refashioned fiscal institutions to obtain greater tax yields and conducted the greatest recoinage in Roman history to meet his higher tax demands and costs. What is remarkable is how little the use of coins in taxation changed under the Dominate and early Byzantine age. Tax registers preserved on Egyptian papyri also point to the continuity in Roman government's aims and needs. The complicated systems of ghost currencies were devised so taxes could be easily collected in coin during inflationary spirals. Tetrarchic registers reveal that it was worth collecting money taxes from modest landowners who were not unlike their counterparts at Antonine Karanis.[83] Two registers—one of payments at Karanis covering the fiscal years 295/6 through 300/1 and the other from an uncertain town in the Hermopolite nome for the fiscal years of 303/4 and 304/5—span the period when the nummus was tariffed successively at 5, 12.5, and 25 d.c. Obligations were expressed in Alexandrine drachmae or talents, and, despite inflation, even small sums were considered profitable to mark down and collect. Payments at Karanis range from 5 nummi and change to 333 nummi; those at the Hermopolite town from 3 nummi and change to 180 nummi. Ghost units of account offered a means whereby the tax collector could calculate obligations based on the current tariffing of the nummus in a world of widely fluctuating rates of exchange. Tetrarchic registers were thus based on the same accounting principles as those of the Principate and compiled for the same purpose, namely the collection of assorted taxes in billon coins.

Even the process of *adaeratio,* whereby taxes were commuted into either grain or coin, was premised on a monetized market. Officials grew expert in profiting from fluctuations in grain prices and exchange rates between gold and billon coins—well illustrated in payments by landowners at Philadelphia covering the fiscal years 309/10 to 316/7.[84] The imperial government had always exacted many needs in goods. Severan emperors refused to commute taxes in grain and oil into coin whenever they had to feed their traveling retinues, armies, or urban plebeians.[85] Licinius similarly took grain rather than coin from Egyptian taxpayers as supplies during civil war in 314–16. Reports of collections in kind increased not because of a change in monetary policy but because the ruthless efficiency of Tetrarchic officials has left more tax documents of all kinds.[86] Officials often commuted obligations in kind into coin for ease of shipment. For example, the dossier of Aurelius Isidorus, a landowner at Karanis, preserves a list of chaff taxes in 310/11 perhaps commuted into 1,120 nummi, weighing less than 12 pounds, which were far easier to ship and store than 5,250 pounds of chaff.[87] In the fifth and sixth centuries, Byzantine officials followed the same fiscal principles, except that they adopted the solidus and its carats as units of account when reckoning in traditional units of denarius, drachma, and talent by increments of myriads proved too cumbersome.

Since the Roman state's budget generated the means whereby coins were put into circulation, the fiscal and commercial roles of coins were always intertwined. The test of the sophistication of the Roman economy is, given the fiscal means by which money was put into circulation, the extent to which coins were used in daily transactions in markets. It thus is time to consider to what extent Roman coins penetrated markets and transformed the economic life of the Mediterranean world.

# Ten

# Coins in the Cities and Markets of the Roman World

John Chrysostom, bishop and orator of the Theodosian age, declared: "Again, the use of coins welds together our whole life, and is the basis of all our transactions. Whenever anything is to be bought or sold, we do it all through coins."[1] His is a sweeping statement made at the close of the fourth century, a time that many scholars argue the Roman world had already moved away from a monetized economy; hence statements such as John's are set aside as stock archaizing comments of urban mandarins. John, however, spoke to and for his age and his observation should not be dismissed, because Romans of the fourth century were heirs to more than 600 years of coin use. Since fiscal reasons dictated production of coinage, many scholars have doubted John Chrysostom's claim as to the extent to which city and rural economic life in the Roman world was monetized. The importance given to coins in the marketplace depends upon the interpretation of the sophistication of the Roman economy. Two different visions of the Roman economy are currently advanced.

The most commonly advocated vision stresses the overwhelming rural and underdeveloped nature of economic activity in a world thought to be without true market forces. In such a world, coins played but a limited commercial role, and, it is noted, even this role diminished in the fourth century as the imperial government reverted to taxes in kind and bullion.[2] Greco-Roman cities are cast in the role of consumers—or worse, as parasites—exacting rents and taxes from the countryside and giving little in return. The economic life of cities was subordinated to political and religious activities or channeled into purchasing luxuries to exalt the aristocrats of a stratified society. Consequently, decurions are looked upon as a conservative landed elite concerned only with performing political and social dramas on the stage afforded by their city's public places with no interest in developing new methods of commerce, banking, and credit that were so crucial to the capital accumulation and economic transformation of the late medieval and early modern cities of Western Europe.

Based on the premise of a rural, underdeveloped economy, it is deduced that coins were chronically in short supply and that most transactions were conducted by barter.[3] The low yield of coins at excavated rural sites is taken as proof of minimal use of coins by most inhabitants of the Roman Empire. In such interpretations, the fiscal purpose of coins becomes virtually the sole reason for their use, and many large denominations are dismissed as showy expressions of sovereignty rather than true money. The record of excavations at rural sites, however, is far from conclusive proof. Coins are tiny objects easily missed. Furthermore, even fractional bronze coins had considerable buying power and were apt not to be lost except at places where numerous transactions took place—therefore, the low yield of casually lost coins at excavated rural residences is hardly surprising. In cities, such places as markets, ports, temples, and theaters are readily identified and carefully excavated, and the coins recovered at such locales are published in forbidding oversized volumes with lengthy catalogues. Outside the city, locations of weekly village marts and country fairs at crossroads or in fields have largely eluded identification and excavation so that it is not a true test of coin use to compare the coins lost at commercial centers in cities with those recovered from villas and humbler private residences in the countryside.

Furthermore, the literary and documentary sources report the overwhelming preference for quoting prices and settling wages in coin.[4] The notion of widespread barter in rural transactions rests primarily, in the absence of other testimony, on a general probability inferred from a model of an underdeveloped economy.[5] Yet, in Roman Egypt, even though grain had been exchanged as the prime medium since pharaonic times, wages on estates were calculated in obols or drachmae per diem and paid monthly. Although harvesters were hired on terms of remuneration in kind—a percentage of wheat reaped for every *aroura*—they were temporary hands working less than a month so that, in lieu of wages, the ancient method of payment was still convenient.[6] The celebrated relief found at Neumagen in the Mosel Valley shows a Roman banker paying out coins, either in wages or for purchases, to Gallic provincials clad in their native hooded leather jackets and breaches.[7] In putting coins in their rural context, it is best to draw an analogy from practices of early medieval Europe, a world by all accounts far more rural than the Classical Mediterranean. As part of their Roman legacy, Western Europeans still thought in terms of coined money, even when the coins themselves were in short supply. They reckoned the value of transactions in coin even when they settled accounts in kind. Thinking in coins, the hallmark of monetized economic life, must have been even more pronounced in the Roman Empire.

In light of the testimony for ubiquitous use of coins, a second vision of the Roman economy is by far the more plausible. Since taxes imposed by Rome were most often payable in coin, taxation led to rapid dissemination of coins because provincials had to enter the marketplace to trade or sell off produce if they were to acquire sufficient coins to meet their tax obligations. Government aims and needs acted as the engine driving economic growth, creating patterns of coin circulation corresponding well with the remarks by John Chrysostom of how coins welded together the life of the Roman world. In this scheme, cities offered ready markets that made local and regional trade lucrative. The city of Rome stood at the center of economic growth. Her population exploded by twenty times from 50,000 to 1 million between 200 B.C. and A.D. 1, and population in Italy grew by one-half, from 4 to 6 million. As Rome, Ostia, and the Campanian cities swallowed up immigrants, their markets underwent inflation, so that by the Augustan age prices at Rome were three to five times more than those in the provinces. Rome's high prices and insatiable appetite for vendibles attracted merchants from the entire Mediterranean world, and, in turn, specie—acquired by Rome as plunder, indemnities, or tribute—was dispersed to the provinces. Given the high mortality rates in urban centers, Rome replenished her population by attracting immigrants from the Italian countryside. In serving as a safety valve to overpopulation, Rome removed excess laborers from rural Italy, thereby preventing wages from falling to or below subsistence levels. The perpetual flow of immigrants into Rome seeking their fortunes and the retirement from Rome of successful ones carried back to the Italian towns and countryside coins and monetary habits acquired in the imperial capital. The rapid demise of municipal mints in Italy and the concentration of minting at Rome in the second century B.C. marked the emergence of this cycle whereby people and coins were constantly moving between Rome and her Italian hinterland. This circulation of people, goods, and money embraced much of the western Mediterranean, and cities in Africa, Spain, and southern Gaul found minting local coinage superfluous by the reign of Claudius.

The monetization ensuing from the spectacular growth of Rome was repeated at scores of cities in the provinces and around army camps in the frontier lands. A Roman conquest and occupation, like those in Britain or the Rhineland, improved roads and distributed coins in army payrolls and purchases; commerce soon followed inasmuch as soldiers always wanted a host of items to spice up drab military issue and rations. Cities offered markets for the agricultural produce of their hinterlands. Prosperity, from the Flavian through Severan ages, permitted the wave of construction and civic activities in provincial cities that put coins taken in taxes and rents back into local circulation. Although military crisis in the third century disrupted the great building projects and lavish entertainments, Christian cities repeated the process in the fourth and again in the sixth centuries when they remodeled their public space and ceremonies to express their new faith.[8] Thus, circulation of coins in cities inevitably spilled over into the countryside; Greco-Roman cities differed little in their size and markets from medieval towns, which, as we know, were intimately tied to their hinterlands. Weekly markets in Greco-Roman cities engaged at least 5,000 people in coin transactions, and these numbers swelled during festivals.[9] In the world painted in Latin and Greek romances, heroes and heroines, who moved with ease between villages and cities set in Greece, Anatolia, North Africa, and Italy, habitually dealt in coins. It was a literary convention that divine favor restored lost fortunes of men by a chance discovery of a cache of coins.[10] This vision of Roman economic growth is admittedly impressionistic, but it is supported by a wealth of literary and documentary evidence from the Mediterranean heartland of the Roman Empire.

Monetization, however, was hardly an even process, but by mid-first century the markets in the Roman world were by any standard monetized, and the use of coins had even crossed the imperial frontier into adjacent Germany and Dacia. The number of coins available in markets can be inferred from the huge numbers collected in taxes, from estimates of the size of specific coinages, and amounts expended, by both emperor and decurions, on public monuments and entertainment. Such figures support the claim of John Chrysostom that "we do it all through coins."

The impact of Roman rule in promoting the use of coins can be seen in Egypt. After three centuries of Ptolemaic rule, Egyptians rendered one-third of their taxes in coin and the rest in grain; with the advent of Roman rule, the proportion was reversed.[11] In 175, at Karanis 650 taxpayers (out of a population numbering 4,000) needed between 30,000 and 35,000 tetradrachmae to meet their fiscal obligations, and similar amounts were collected from the comparable Fayyum towns of Theadelphia and Tebtynis. At the regional center of Philadelphia some 1,200 taxpayers rendered yearly between 50,000 and 60,000 tetradrachmae.[12] In direct and indirect taxes, licensing fees, and legal fines, an Egyptian taxpayer paid on average 50 tetradrachmae per year. The number of coins passing in private transactions among residents of Egyptian towns can be sensed from the surviving receipts of the record office at Tebtynis. During the course of the regnal year of 45/6, the owners Kronion and Eutychas certified 96 private loans and 133 contracts.

Nearly 4,000 tetradrachmae—often in modest sums of 10 to 30 tetradrachmae—changed hands in the 96 loans, and the 133 contracts that were notarized transferred 4,500 tetradrachmae among private individuals.[13] It is remarkable that, in an incomplete list of what seem routine, small-scale transactions, hard cash equal to about one-fourth of the annual taxes owed by their town changed hands. Kronion and Eutychas, who perhaps operated at a loss, took in at least 680 tetradrachmae in fees, most of which was spent on food and drink, writing materials, and salaries of scribes.[14] Although none of these figures allows for an estimate of the coins circulating in the markets of a Fayyum town, the figures from Karanis and Tebtynis nonetheless point toward the conclusion that markets in Egyptian towns and their hinterlands must have been monetized.

Cases from elsewhere in the Roman world confirm the degree of monetization found in Egypt. From late summer 132 to late autumn 135, Jewish insurgents under Shimon Kochba overstruck silver and bronze coins with Jewish types and Hebrew inscriptions proclaiming the liberation of Israel. Based on specimens whose undertypes are visible, tetradrachmae of Tyre and Antioch were overstruck as *sela;* Bostran drachmae of Trajan and imperial denarii as *zuz;* and city coins of Palestine and Phoenicia as three different bronze fractions.[15] The coins betray themselves as those drawn from circulation and private reserves by Zealots in a restricted area of rural Judaea and the eastern shore of the Dead Sea. The coins were current for just three and one-half years of the rebellion, and a relatively high percentage of the dies used are represented among the surviving specimens because so many owners were killed or enslaved and hence failed to retrieve their savings. The dies point to extraordinary mintages of silver coins: at least 1 million tetradrachmae, 40,000 didrachmae, and 2,280,000 drachmae—a total value of 6,360,000 drachmae in coined silver in three years, an unexpectedly large number of coins circulating in the villages of backwater Judaea. The size of the Judaean population under the control of the insurgents is difficult to estimate; perhaps 150,000 taxpayers were on the rolls in Judaea (excluding Jerusalem) at the outbreak of the revolt. If so, based on the reconstructed output from surviving dies, the coins in circulation were at least 40 silver drachmae per taxpayer. This output of silver currency in 132–35 assumes significance when compared to the reported income of 600 talents (3.6 million drachmae) that King Herod annually levied from Judaea, Idumaea, and Samaria, an area considerably greater in size and wealth than the regions controlled by the insurgents. If Judaea (excluding Jerusalem) yielded as much as one-third of Herod's revenue or 1.2 million drachmae, this figure, when compared to the 6.36 million drachmae struck in 132–35, suggests that the total number of coins in circulation and savings was at least five times greater than the number taken in annual tax collections.[16]

The size of eastern provincial coinages can be sensed from the estimated number of dies employed by Augustus to strike the cistophori of Asia. By C. H. V. Sutherland's conservative count of the number of dies employed, Ephesus and Pergamum produced in 28–18 B.C. at least 20 million cistophori, the equivalent of 60 million denarii.[17] By the year 100 the province of Asia was home to 4 to 4.5 million residents, including at least five cities—Ephesus, Smyrna, Pergamum, Cyzicus, and Miletus—with populations of 100,000 to 200,000 and another two dozen approaching 50,000. If it can be inferred from this figure that 3 million inhabited Asia in 30 B.C., the Augustan coinage of cistophori was minted at an average of at least 30 cistophori (equal to 90 denarii) for each of 750,000 taxpayers. Unfortunately the tax yield of Asia under Augustus is unreported, and the 7 million denarii (equivalent to over 2.3 million cistophori) reputedly paid by the province under Hadrian is suspiciously low.[18]

In the Roman West, the absence of documentary evidence prevents estimates of the volume of coins in circulation, but prodigious cataloguing by archaeologists offers a different way of measuring the number in use. Archaeologists have recovered and published detailed reports of coins casually lost at numerous civilian and military sites in the frontier provinces of Europe. By plotting the collective results on a graph, R. Reece demonstrates the long-term trend in the use of coins in northern Europe under Roman rule from 50 B.C. to A.D. 400, making it evident that Romans minted, used, and lost coins in profusion.[19] In the western provinces the 450 years of Roman rule were an economic continuum that saw a steady absolute and relative rise in the casual loss of coins, and hence the numbers of coins available. The overall trend stands in stark contrast to the low representation of Celtic coins prior to Roman rule and the abrupt decline in the early fifth century with the collapse of imperial power. Roman coins were available in great quantities and they passed in markets at a much faster velocity of circulation than either Celtic or early medieval coins. Reece's analysis and graph, despite its imprecision, confirms the impressions about coin use based on better documented cases in the eastern provinces.

Roman coins circulated for considerable lengths of time prior to the rapid recoinages of the third and fourth centuries. Between 200 B.C. and A.D. 235 the money supply was constantly augmented as bullion from mines and imports flowed to the mint, and even, at times, public and sacred treasures were turned into coin, more than offsetting any diminution suffered from wear or export of specie. Based on rates of wear, Roman coins had a life expectancy of over a century, although gold and silver coins were prone to recoinage with a change of standard. Their long circulation aided denarii and, in the East, Greek-style staters to penetrate markets in sufficient numbers for everyday use. Silver denarii and staters during the Republic and Principate and gold solidi during the Dominate and Byzantine age sustained far more wear than would be expected if they were employed just for fiscal purposes.[20] Denarii of the late Republic and Mark Antony comprised between 55 and 65 percent of hoards buried in the Flavian age. As late as 250, denarii, including many specimens from as early as Nero's reign, make up the majority of coins in hoards such as the great cache of denarii and antoniniani concealed in Thrace at Reka-Devnia, near Macrianopolis.[21] In Egypt, billon tetradrachmae issued by Nero are one-half or more of the coins in hoards concealed as late as 200, and they were still present in hoards as late as 250.[22]

Bronze coins had potentially longer lives because, despite heavy wear, they did not disappear into the melting pots with each recoinage. Heavily worn specimens often were retariffed (usually so designated by countermarks) or halved to provide fractions. Republican uncial asses, circulating fifty years after their production

*Table 10.1*
Bronze Coins in the Garonne Hoard, ca. A.D. 160

| Emperor/Years | Specimens | Percentage |
|---|---|---|
| Claudius, 41–54 | 2 | 0.05 |
| Nero, 54–68 | 2 | 0.05 |
| Galba, 68–69 | 28 | 0.70 |
| Vespasian, 69–79 | 139 | 3.48 |
| Titus, 79–81 | 107 | 2.68 |
| Domitian, 81–96 | 345 | 8.63 |
| Nerva, 96–98 | 182 | 4.55 |
| Trajan, 98–117 | 1,103 | 27.59 |
| Hadrian, 117–138 | 1,655 | 41.41 |
| Antoninus Pius, 138–61 | 434 | 10.86 |
| Total | 3,997 | 100.00 |

*Source:* Based on Étienne and Rachet, *Trésor de Garonne,* pp. 333–34 and 421–22.

had been discontinued, gave rise to calling asses "ships" (*naves*), after their reverse type of the prow—an idiom remembered in the late imperial age. In Greek slang the name "obol" was applied to the obol's successors such as the two-assaria piece of the Antonine and Severan ages and the Byzantine follis.[23] The sestertii, dupondii, and asses recovered from the shipwreck in the Garonne River in southern Gaul give a good index of the long usage of bronze money. In the Garonne hoard, about one-half the bronze coins were less than forty years old, i.e., money issued during the then-current generation; one-third were between forty and sixty years old, or money of the immediately prior generation; and about one-sixth were between sixty and one hundred years old, or money of two or three generations earlier (Table 10.1).[24]

The stray finds and hoards from Dura-Europos reveal how civic bronze coins in the East saw long usage. The first wave of Roman-style *aes,* which probably arrived with the soldiers of Trajan in 116–17, consisted of late Julio-Claudian and Flavian pieces of Antioch. With a permanent Roman garrison by 180, the town acquired bronze coins from civic mints in eastern Asia Minor, Cyprus, and the Greek homeland. Many of these coins were carried in the purses of Peloponnesians serving in Caracalla's famed phalanx in 214–17.[25] In the 240s Dura turned to more immediate sources for fresh supplies of bronze money, when the new colonies in Mesopotamia—Carrhae, Edessa, Nisibis, and Singara—stepped up production. In six hoards concealed just before Shah Shapur sacked the city in 256, 3,449 bronze coins have been identified as to reign; 1,897 coins (55 percent) are Severan pieces, many from Pontic mints striking in 209–12, that is, money that was over a generation old. The rest consisted of Mesopotamian coins, with an admixture of Antiochene pieces, issued in the early 240s, so that they were fifteen to twenty years old.[26] A hoard of 162 Tarsan bronze coins concealed perhaps in 253 shows a similar structure. One-half of the coins were of Severan date, and another 42 percent were issued under Gordian III (238–44).[27] The episodic minting of civic coins is not, as is sometimes claimed, proof of insufficient quantities of bronze money in circulation, since a single major coinage could supply needs of a region for two or three generations.

Given the diversity of coins in circulation, the role of moneychangers was vital in supplying markets with the proper numbers and types of coins. Moneychangers set daily exchange rates, discounted worn coins, and withdrew damaged, counterfeit, and imitative pieces. In the East, they recycled old money by countermarking or withdrawing it for reminting. In the third and fourth centuries, moneychangers acquired the new task of identifying and retiring obsolete coins with each recoinage. Exchange rates such as 17 to 18 assaria to a denarius at Hadrianic Pergamum or 24 bronze obols to an Alexandrine tetradrachma were official ones employed by moneychangers, vendors, and buyers as the starting point from which they negotiated the value of their coins depending on conditions. Coins passed current in Roman markets in much the same fashion as that found in the Ottoman Empire in 1900: "Each village in the Ottoman Empire before 1914 had its own reckoning of 'good' and 'bad' money. In Istanbul, the *mejidie* is 20 piastres, except 19 when buying postage stamps. At Smyrna, it is 25 when buying coffee, 29 for opium, even 47 in Jerusalem and 54 in the Hejaz."[28] The same description, with appropriate change of names, applies as well to the markets of the Roman Empire. Exchange rates were in a constant state of flux responding to the seasonal use of coins, hoarding in times of crisis, surfeits and shortages that arose from the inherent dangers of transporting specie, preferences for coins of a certain type or denomination, and indolence in accepting newfangled or unfamiliar coins. Imperial laws never abolished the daily forces affecting exchange rates in markets—either in the East where so many different coins passed current, or in the northern frontiers where old coins stayed in circulation so long that they were often countermarked or halved for fractions. Under the Principate, token bronze coins, due to their utility and public trust, were easily exchanged into full-bodied silver coins by paying a surcharge that ranged between 2 and 5.5 percent. Talmudic scholars in their parables took it for granted that a traveler could carry his money as Tyrian tetradrachmae (*sela*) and easily turn it into drachmae (*zuz*) or bronze fractions at minimal cost immediately upon arrival at his destination.[29] The inflationary spirals of the third and fourth century did not alter attitudes toward coins, for coins had always been bought and sold at variable rates; what was so troubling was the frequency of change and the range within which rates seesawed with each debasement or reform. Such fluctuations were all the more dismaying in comparison to the stable currency enjoyed over the prior two centuries when rates moved within narrow margins.

Cities employed the coins of an empire that formed a community of cities encircling the Mediterranean Sea, which Romans audaciously called "Our Sea" (*mare nostrum*). "We live around a sea like frogs around a pond" was how Socrates, so Plato tells us, described to his friends the Hellenic cities of the Aegean in the late fifth century B.C.[30] Plato's image was just as apt for the cities of the Roman Empire except that the pond had become the Mediterranean Sea. If imperial expenditures and the demands of Rome were the heart of the Roman economy, the cities of Italy and the provinces acted as the arteries carrying coins through vessels and capillaries to villages and countryside for use in weekly marts and seasonal country fairs.

Civic revenues and budgets are virtually unknown. Cicero reported that the modest Asian city of Tralles netted annual revenues of 225,000 denarii.[31] Receipts of the Pompeian banker L. Caecilius

Jucundus reveal a diverse range of profits from surcharges and indirect taxes, leases on rental properties, tolls, and legal fees, but tell us little about the number of coins in circulation. The dimensions of civic expenditure can best be judged by the public activities and values that inspired decurions. To a man, they were political and social conservatives, obtaining their incomes from rents and public service rather than risky commercial ventures. Decurions, steeped in the polished language and aesthetics of the Classics, fostered loyalty to Rome and promoted the cults of their cities. They were motivated by love of country and love of honor, especially personal honor gained from public recognition by social peers and fellow citizens. The private ambition and wealth of decurions was channeled into public service so that much of the urban civilization of the Principate rested upon voluntary gift-giving by its ruling classes on a scale yet to be equaled. Public responsibilities were taken on as a liturgy, the notion that richer citizens were obliged to assume the costs of an assigned public task, and liturgists often spent far above minimum amounts required as demonstrations of patriotism. It was, as M. I. Finley once noted, as if wealthy taxpayers of the United States voluntarily paid to the IRS many times their assessed taxes as a mark of patriotism.[32] Magistrates and councilors paid (*summa honoraria*) for the privilege of holding an office that brought social distinction. At times, additional amounts were assessed to defray the costs of a specific project. In the second century, Bithynian cities charged each newly appointed member of the town council between 1,000 and 2,000 denarii, which represented 4 to 8 percent of the minimum net worth of 25,000 denarii required of decurions. Their spending in their quest for recognition became a prime means of putting coins into local circulation. As prosperity rose, they endowed permanent funds to defray costs of offices and priesthoods, of oil furnished at gymnasiums, of entertainment and distributions at festivals, and for charitable payments to children of needy citizens.[33] By 200 a not inconsiderable proportion of real properties around cities, either as public lands or endowments, was paying annual returns in coin to fund civic life.

Decurions protected and expanded the money supply of their cities in other significant ways. In the wake of disasters, they petitioned emperors for financial relief lest their city be emptied of money in taxes and rebuilding costs. After a catastrophic earthquake struck Asia in 17, Tiberius forgave taxes of the twelve damaged cities for five years, and he granted 2.5 million denarii (or 100,000 aurei) in direct aid to Sardes. Christian emperors fell heir to this policy, and so Antioch received 324,000 solidi (nearly double the coined gold that Sardes had obtained) and tax remissions for three years after the Syrian metropolis was ravaged by earthquakes and fires in 526–27.[34] Decurions maintained reserves of grain and oil in case of shortages, and, in times of scarcity, fixed ceilings on grain prices and imported grain that was sold to citizens below market prices. Decurions continually returned coins to circulation by two activities often cited as epitomizing the parasitic nature of classical cities: public buildings and public festivals. Decurions in Italy, Africa, and Asia Minor have left inscriptions proudly reporting the amounts of money they spent on such endeavors. Such inscriptions were never intended as a full accounting of their disbursements, but rather stressed donations bringing the greatest prestige—gifts for impressive buildings, spectacular festivals, or distributions to fellow aristocrats. Grants in money or grain to the populace were less worthy and presumably mentioned less frequently. The records of civic costs is thus a selective one coming from the most prosperous regions of the Roman world.

Major donors could affect the money supply of a region by scattering hundreds of thousands of denarii in building projects among favored cities. A laudable contribution ranged between 25,000 and 150,000 denarii—the equivalent of one to six times the minimum property required of a decurion. A sense of the scale of such expenditures can be obtained from the costs of select building projects at cities in Italy, Africa, and Asia Minor.[35] Aqueducts, due to the technical skills and materials required, were extremely expensive, often costing more than 1 million denarii (forty times a decurion's property). Herodes Atticus, the celebrated Athenian philanthropist, contributed 4 million denarii, matched by another 3 million from the emperor Hadrian himself, to pay off the scandalously overpriced aqueduct of Alexandria Troas whose residents numbered perhaps 15,000. Tiberius Claudius Erymaeus spent

2 million denarii (eighty times his property qualification), the largest single gift reported in any inscription, on the aqueduct of Aspendus, a city of perhaps 30,000 on the southern littoral of Anatolia. The impact of such gift-giving on the money supply is seen in Lycia, the southwestern corner of Asia Minor, which was organized into a league of some forty cities whose population totaled 200,000. After the province was devastated by an earthquake in 140/1, the leading men poured money into restoring civic life over the next decade. Opramoas of Rhodiapolis reports in a remarkable inscription decorating the walls of his funerary monument that he had spent several hundred thousand denarii on buildings at six different cities just before the earthquake struck. In the wake of the earthquake, he boasts of three successive grants in 141–48, totaling at least 352,000 denarii, for rebuilding thirty-one cities. At his death soon after 152, Opramoas had donated to nearly every Lycian town hard cash running into millions of denarii. Opramoas was not alone; other benefactors spent enough coins in wages and contracts to monetize the markets of every Lycian town.[36]

The scale of civic building during the Principate was unprecedented, as ambitious decurions remodeled, expanded, or added to the public places and sanctuaries. Buildings regarded as essential to public life such as aqueducts, theaters, and baths drained substantial wealth from decurional families. Dio Chrysostom, Greek orator of the Flavian age, lamented the gift-giving by his grandfather to his native Prusa, which had bankrupted the family and saddled him with a debt of 100,000 denarii (the equivalent of the property requirement for equestrian rank).[37] Maecenas, according to Cassius Dio, warned Augustus that cities must be restrained from excessive buildings and games.[38] Dio Chrysostom reports how the crowds in the assembly cheered his exhortations that Prusa should rival the greatest cities of Asia in her fair buildings, but legal and financial disputes, even when funding was assured, stalled many projects.[39] Money was often wasted in settlements with landlords to gain prime sites. Opramoas might have welcomed the earthquake of 140/1 as divine favor permitting him to rebuild Lycian cities without the usual legal headaches and costs.

Incompetence and corruption left the centers of many cities

cluttered with half-finished buildings inasmuch as donors gleefully promised new monuments bearing their names but were loath to repair existing ones. Pliny the Younger, Trajan's legate and financial trouble-shooter in Bithynia-Pontus, reports how Nicaea raised 2.5 million denarii from private subscription to pay off an overpriced complex of theater, basilica, and stoa.[40] Yet, even if many building projects took years to complete and ruined decurional families, they monetized city markets. Between the mid-second century B.C. and the mid-second century A.D. Roman decurions, exempt from direct taxation, channeled the profits of empire into public buildings that made Italian civic life the envy of the Mediterranean world. Each year tens of thousands of the Italian poor employed on building projects received wages in denarii. The emperor Vespasian was credited with destroying the blueprint of a device to elevate columns lest it put the Roman poor out of work.[41] The magnitude of money and labor poured into Italian construction is glimpsed in the stupendous projects undertaken by Claudius. In the course of eleven years ( A.D. 42–53), he mobilized 30,000 men to drain the Fucine Lake. At a minimum wage of 10 asses per diem, this labor force cost annually 6.75 million denarii and its subsistence between 1.25 and 1.75 million denarii. Claudius also completed the great aqueduct that bears his name at a total cost of 87.5 million denarii, which Pliny the Elder regarded the most expensive known to him, for it was nearly twenty-two times the cost of the Marcian aqueduct completed two centuries earlier.[42]

At festivals, the prizes paid to victors, distributions to spectators, and payment for entertainment were vehicles spreading coins into local economies. Poorer citizens clamored for festivals, preferring their distributions of coins and grain to the seasonal toil and high risk of injury on building projects. Emperors favored buildings over games and festivals that attracted crowds and courted social unrest. Hence, Antoninus Pius supported Vedius Antoninus, the Roman senator who offered Ephesus buildings when the populace voiced its desire for distributions and games, as follows: "I myself have granted him [Vedius Antoninus] whatever he asked, and I received his request because he has not chosen the usual way of men in public life, who expend their patriotic zeal on shows and distributions and on funding competitions in order to achieve an immediate reputation, but a means whereby he hopes that he will make the city more distinguished in the future."[43] Civic centers and sanctuaries, however, were empty theaters devoid of meaning without the dramas of festivals and games. Decurions expended on festivals, games, and distributions amounts that in total probably outstripped sums spent on buildings. By one estimate, expenditures by cities on animal and gladiatorial combats averaged at least 22.5 million denarii per year. At Italian and North African cities in the second century, a typical show of combats lasting three to four days cost a decurion between 25,000 and 50,000 denarii, equal to one to two times his minimum property requirement or to laudable contributions toward public buildings. At a modest city in the Greek East, a gymnasiarch, who provided games and oil to the gymnasium as a liturgy, incurred at least 20,000 denarii in annual expense.[44]

Panhellenic, dynastic, and local games attracted competitors and spectators, and their coins, from afar. The winners of Greek-style musical, dramatic, and athletic contests received purses of prize money, often in sums of 20, 40, or 80 aurei (originally equivalents of one-half, one, and two pounds of gold).[45] Money purses for victors became an iconographic convention on civic bronze coins, mosaics, and relief sculpture across the empire and stand as testimony to the importance of festivals in a city's economic life. Since decurions granted cash handouts (*sportula*) according to social rank, decurions, Augustales, and members of guilds in the cities of Italy, North Africa, and Narbonese Gaul received substantial sums of 2, 3, or 5 denarii, and, at times, even 1 to 4 aurei. Humbler citizens received a sole denarius, but this lesser gift could buy 2 modii of wheat (half the monthly needs of an adult male).[46] Eastern benefactors too favored their peers—priests and their wives and members of the council, *gerousia,* aristocratic youth clubs, and the assembly. Citizens and visitors usually received 1 or 2 denarii at festivals.[47] Mendora, patroness of Sillyum, recognized in two grants of money the hierarchy typical at Greek cities. Citizens received 2 denarii at the first distribution and 9 denarii at the second; councilors and other civic worthies were given nine to ten times these amounts (18 to 20 denarii on the first occasion and 77 to 85 on the subsequent one); and, peasants and freedmen received 3 denarii at the second distribution.[48] Even among the poor citizens there were the favored. In many cities in Italy, Africa, and Anatolia they numbered between 500 and 1,000 adult males who qualified for free public grain and whose children most likely received the subsistence payments from the alimentary endowments.[49]

Distributions influenced the denominational structure of city coinage during the second and third century. The leading families of the Greek city of Stratonicea offered their populace sums of 2, 3, 5, or 10 denarii per man, and so struck commemorative bronze multiples of four, six, or twelve assaria for the distributions at festivals. Stratonicea struck between eight and ten successive issues of six-assaria denominations in 198–209 that bear the names of leading aristocrats who put these coins into circulations at festivals to Zeus of Panamara or Hecate of Lagina. One of ten eponymous magistrates named on Severan coins, Tiberius Claudius Aristeas Menander, reports that he and his wife Aelia Glycinna administered the cult of Hecate at Lagina and "they instituted a festival for the entire city and they carefully gave to each of the citizens assembled in the theater two denarii apiece, summoning them by deme by means of placards."[50] Claudius Aristeas perhaps minted in his name between 60,000 and 120,000 six-assaria pieces (equivalent to 20,000 or 40,000 denarii). If each of the 5,000 citizens of Stratonicea were to receive six bronze coins as his grant, Claudius Aristeas would have put into circulation by his single distribution 25 to 50 percent of the coins bearing his name. The nine other eponymous magistrates struck for similar distributions at high holidays bronze coins with a total value of approximately 375,000 denarii.[51] Stratonicea was but one of several hundred Greek cities striking bronze currency for a schedule of festivals, and quite often these large bronze denominations were reissued at later festivals with appropriate countermarks. Stratonicea recalled six-assaria denominations twice, in 209–12 and in 214–15, when large numbers were countermarked with two different stamps bearing the name of Hecate and head of Roma or with the portrait of Caracalla (pl. 14.107).

Most of the Stratonicean citizens who received two denarii from Claudius Aristeas lived in rural demes; some donors specify that their grants included peasants (*paroikoi*) who dwelled outside the city walls. When he was summoned to the city to settle a legal dispute, the rural protagonist the Hunter, in the *Euboean Oration* of Dio Chrysostom, could offer as proof of citizenship his father's participation in a money distribution at a festival: "We are citizens too of the city, as I used to hear my father say. And once he too came here just when a grant of money was being made, as it happened, and got some too along with the rest [of the citizens]."[52] Such distributions merited far less mention on funerary monuments than other gifts, but they must have been common if the populace at Ephesus and Prusa could cry out that donors give money rather than more buildings.

Festivals also offered occasions for markets and fairs. C. Julius Demosthenes, who endowed a festival at Oenoanda in the time of Hadrian, scheduled events during the three weeks in July just before harvest and included one day reserved for the market, two for sacrifices, three without any events, and the last four for hired entertainment or civic contests. Visitors had plenty of time to shop and vendors to sell their wares most opportunely because business was exempt from all taxes and dues "on any purchases, sales, sacrificed, imported, introduced, or exported during all days of the festival."[53] The atmosphere was the mix of carnival and commerce of medieval fairs that allowed country people to sell their produce and buy essentials and luxuries. Pliny the Younger notes how boisterous rural residents filled theaters, markets, and quays of Italian towns during festivals.[54]

Given the frequent political activities and festivals in Greco-Roman cities and given the long periods of inactivity and underemployment on the countryside, peasants traveled regularly to and from civic centers. They acquired coins by selling produce, laboring on building projects, and receiving cash handouts at festivals. Denarii and bronze coins passed between city and countryside in a seasonal cycle analogous to that of the "black coin," the billon pennies and deniers of Western Europe in the thirteenth and fourteenth centuries. For example, during Michaelmas, English peasants entered towns to sell their grain and purchase goods, carrying the balance of coins back to their villages which then experienced a sudden influx of coins. Slowly the coins were drained out of the village as peasants spent them on goods at country fairs, loaned them to fellow peasants, and used them to buy land, provide dowries, or pay rents and taxes. At the next high holiday, the process was repeated, and so coins circulated in the countryside according to a seasonal cycle of expansion and contraction of the money supply.[55]

The cycle of festivals and civic building also drew coins into the city from the surrounding territory. In the eastern provinces, excavations demonstrate that in any city market a mix of coins from neighboring cities passed current. They arrived in the purses of visitors, merchants, pilgrims, and laborers drawn by the festivals, fairs, and construction. The dedications and archaeological remains at the two shrines of Panamara and Lagina reveal that the aristocrats of Stratonicea remodeled and vastly extended the sanctuaries, improved accommodations for pilgrims, and widened gift-giving at festivals to include visitors who were drawn from ever greater distances. The munificence of the Stratonicean elites was repeated in hundreds of cities across the Roman world from the Flavian through Severan ages.

It is by no means certain how much monetary crisis and inflation after 235 disrupted the civic cycles of taxation and expenditure that kept coins in circulation. In the cities of the Roman East, the number of festivals and games recorded on local coins and inscriptions peaked in the six decades between the reigns of Septimius Severus (193–211) and Gallienus (253–68). The fate of civic endowments made during the Principate is unknown, but, if most investments were in land, cities could have collected rents and interest in the new billon coins of the late third or fourth centuries rather than in denarii. With the return of peace under the Tetrarchs, decurions again donated time and money for festivals, and rebuilt city centers and sanctuaries. The unbroken record of munificence at the shrines of Panamara and Lagina into the fourth century has led Peter Brown to conclude that "the third century, as we know it, does not appear to have happened at Stratonikeia."[56]

The means whereby coins passed between cities and their countrysides were disrupted in the second half of the third century, but there is little to suggest that cities during the fourth and fifth centuries renounced the use of coined money in favor of other media of exchange. Cities acquired new patrons, either the emperor himself or imperial officials and soldiers, who, as they were exempt from taxation, poured their money into new forms of display such as races in the hippodrome or opulent villas that were decorated with costly African-inspired mosaics. In Christian cities, bishops sponsored buildings and festivals in the service of the new faith, and Palestine experienced boom years in construction and the pilgrimage trade between the early fourth and early seventh centuries. The seasonal cycle of coins between city and countryside survived in its essentials. The loss of monetary ways came to the markets of the Roman West during the fifth century with the collapse of the municipal institutions and regional trade, and to the cities of the Mediterranean heartland during the crisis of the late sixth and seventh centuries.

# Eleven

# Coins, Prices, and Wages

Inhabitants of the Roman world came to regard their gold, silver, and base metal coins not only as objects with intrinsic worth but also as stable units of purchasing power. Common denominations, such as denarius and sestertius, tetra-drachma and obol, or solidus and follis, were, with due allowance for seasonal and regional fluctuations, expected to buy goods and services at customary prices. The task of officials, whether market wardens in Antonine Ephesus or imperial bureaucrats implementing the Edict on Maximum Prices, was to uphold fair pricing of goods and services in terms of trusted coins. Associating stable prices and wages with familiar coins endured in medieval Europe under the notion of the "just price." The success of Roman coins contributed in no small measure to the long periods of price and wage stability. Repeated use of the same denominations for the purchase of familiar units of goods bred public faith not so much in the abstract notion of Roman currency (personified as SACRA MONETA on antoniniani and nummi) but rather in specific denominations such as the denarius, and it was this faith that enabled emperors to manipulate the currency during the third and fourth centuries.

During the second century B.C. Roman denarii and asses penetrated greater Italy, ousting local competitors from the markets and thereby simplifying daily transactions. At the same time, the price structure of the Republic was transformed. Since specie was concentrated in Rome, the higher prices and wages found in the imperial capital acted as a magnet for trade from the Mediterranean world during the next five centuries. The rest of Italy south of the Po Valley too experienced sharp price increases. The pace of inflation in 200–30 B.C., however, is not readily documented; classical authors when moralizing only commented on prices paid for luxuries or during periods of exceptional hardship.

There are, however, a few signposts that can be used to calculate differences, or similarities, in the cost of living, both chronologically and geographically, and, therefore, the value of coins. These include the base pay of a legionary, which is known for most periods; the cost of wheat, for which prices at many dates and many locations have come down to us; and scattered reports of prices of other commodities and payment for employment other than military. Calculations based on such data are fraught with pitfalls—the data are incomplete, at times prices are "official" rather than market prices, and they are not always comparable. Wheat and (to a lesser extent) barley were staples of the Mediterranean diet. The adult male Roman citizen required a monthly minimum of 4 modii of wheat or 48 modii annually, representing perhaps two-thirds of his caloric intake with oil, vegetables, and protein accounting for the other one-third. A modius of wheat baked into sixteen to twenty-two loaves of bread weighing one pound each, and an adult male consumed on average two pounds of bread daily.[1] The annual minimum requirement for a family of four was perhaps 120 modii (or approximately 800 kg) of wheat.[2] The modius of barley, which was customarily priced at one-half that of wheat, was considered to have only one-half the nutritional value of wheat so it was most often used as feedgrain for livestock.[3] Surviving grain prices from the Republic are prices fixed by the Roman state and reflect long-term trends of what was considered a just price for the urban plebeians to pay rather than what grain actually might have fetched on the open market.

The state prices assume meaning when compared to wages of the legionary, although grain was issued directly and the price deducted from his salary. In 200–150 B.C. the legionary received 3 asses per diem or an annual wage of 108 denarii. He earned enough in a month (90 asses without accounting for deductions) to purchase about twenty-two modii of wheat at 4 asses per modius or five and one-half times his monthly minimum grain requirement or, to put it another way, it took him about five days to earn a month's supply of his daily bread.[4] When the denarius was retariffed in 141 B.C. at 16 asses (the new asses, at two-thirds of an ounce each, were approximately equal in weight to 10 uncial asses, each of a full ounce), the pay of a legionary was recalculated at 5 asses per diem, or an annual wage of 112.5 denarii. The apparent increase in salary was more than offset by price increases in the markets. In 123 B.C. the tribune Gaius Sempronius Gracchus proposed that the state subsidize a price of 6.33 asses per modius of wheat for the urban plebeians. At this low price, a legionary, who received 150 asses per month, again would have needed about five days to earn his monthly supply of grain. The Gracchan price would have restored the buying power of a legionary, at least for grain, but it provoked such a storm of protest from conservative optimates that it was likely rescinded.[5] Military pay consequently failed to keep pace with rises of even official prices of wheat at Rome. At the price in 73 B.C. of 12 asses per modius, it took the legionary almost ten days to earn the 48 asses needed to purchase his monthly bread. The Caesarian pay increase in 46 B.C. doubled the salary of a legionary to 10 asses per day, and, if the 73 B.C. price of 12 asses per modius still obtained, a legionary would again earn his monthly bread in five days—giving him the buying power advocated by Gaius Sempronius Gracchus. An Augustan legionary, who received 300 asses per month, would, with wheat at a price of 16 asses, need about seven days to meet his monthly needs.

Grain prices, and the prices of other commodities as well, were subject to the unpredictable forces of supply and demand. In 203 B.C. the price of 4 asses per modius of wheat charged in the city of Rome perhaps reflected the arrival of supplies from Spain, but in 211–10 B.C. Hannibal's devastation of Latium had sent prices soaring to five to six times this level. Gluts produced falling prices as in

196 B.C., when *aediles* sold off 1 million modii of wheat in war surplus at a rock-bottom price of 2 asses per modius.[6] Regional prices are even harder to document, but Polybius considered prices in the Po Valley the lowest in Italy. A modius of wheat there in 150 B.C. sold for 1 as and daily subsistence could be purchased for one-half as, so that average prices were considerably lower than state prices at Rome in 203 B.C.[7] Even in the less fertile regions of Lusitania, Polybius reports prices for 1 modius of wheat at just under 2 asses and of barley at 1.5 asses—respectively, one-half and three-quarters of official prices at Rome; however, during the first half of the second century B.C., Rome still paid considerably less than major Hellenistic cities for imported foodstuffs.[8] At the port of Delos, with perhaps the highest costs of living in the Aegean, wheat and barley sold in the market at the equivalent of 15 to 16 and 5 to 6 asses per modius, respectively.[9] Delos, and other cities in the Aegean and Euxine sought out cheaper wheat which was sold to citizens at controlled prices comparable to those at Rome.[10] But Ptolemaic subjects in Egypt too paid higher prices for wheat, 4.5 to 6.33 asses per modius in 210–160 B.C., and then 10 to 13 asses in 130–90 B.C. Since Egyptians were compelled to use fiduciary bronze coins, they endured frequent jumps in prices quoted at ever greater numbers of accounting units of copper drachmae per silver drachma.[11]

There is far less evidence for prices of the other essential foodstuffs of oil and wine, and virtually none for meat, fruit, and vegetables. Legionaries consumed each year perhaps 48 sextarii of oil, and 365 sextarii of wine. A peasant family of four might have required each year 120 modii of wheat, 120 sextarii of oil, and 720 sextarii of wine (often mixed with vinegar as *posca*).[12] Since prices varied so widely due to quality, estimates are only the most approximate for oil and wine. In 175–150 B.C. ordinary oil and wine at Rome might have been sold on average at two-thirds and one-sixth asses per sextarius, respectively, so that a family's mininum annual expenditure on the three most essential staples would be about 68 denarii (480 asses for wheat, 80 asses for oil, and 120 asses for wine) or over 60 percent of a soldier's base pay.[13]

Price levels at Rome continued to mount after 150 B.C. and, at some point in the early first century B.C., surpassed those at the great cities in the Greek East. In 75–73 B.C. Cicero reveals customary Sicilian wheat prices as 25 percent below official and at least 50 percent below market prices at Rome (an indication that actual prices at Rome were at least 50 percent greater than the official price).[14] The daily wage of the legionary doubled to 10 asses in 46 B.C., but even unskilled laborers at Rome earned more, at least 12 asses per diem by Cicero's day.[15] The salary of a legionary, however, probably was premised on the lower prices current in Italy or the western provinces so his daily wage would usually cover the cost of one modius of wheat outside of Rome. As a consequence of the rise in prices, bronze denominations lost their buying power in markets throughout Italy by 80 B.C., and the denarius became a common, if not the principal, coin exchanged in daily transactions.

The imperial peace stretching from the reign of Augustus to the death of Commodus ushered in two centuries of widespread prosperity and comparatively stable prices and wages. This stability, in large part, rested on the public's high confidence in the denarius and aureus and the convenience with which they could be exchanged against base metal fractions or local currencies, the general availability of all types of coins due to the dynamics of imperial fiscal demands, and repeated efforts by imperial and civic officials to provide fair pricing in markets to offset shortages and famines. These conditions did not change significantly until the inflationary spirals of the 240s and 250s. Salaries of legionaries, who received relatively good pay for highly coveted full-time employment, are one indication of long-term stability. The salaries suggest that prices might have risen by less than two times from 46 B.C. to A.D. 195, but then increased 50 percent in the following two decades. Although in A.D. 14 mutinous legionaries complained that 10 asses per day were insufficient, many owed their indebtedness to their own inability to budget expenditures between pay days.[16] During the course of 240 years, army salaries were raised only once, by Domitian, and this single pay increase (along with periodic donatives, which at times were not inconsiderable) probably enabled soldiers to keep pace with inflation until the Severan age.

In the Flavian era, a flat amount of 2.5 asses per diem was

deducted for rations from a legionary's pay. Latin authors of the first century too confirm an impression of stability and comparatively high pay for a legionary, because they cited nostalgically 2 asses as sufficient for daily food wants.[17] The price probably applied to Italian towns rather than Rome, for it yields a low annual cost of 45 to 50 denarii for minimum dietary needs. At the same time, Pompeiian laborers earned daily wages ranging from 5 to 16 asses.[18] A century later skilled Dacian miners commanded daily wages of 6 to 10 asses, approximately one-half to three-quarters of what a legionary earned, but they were also granted room and board—which effectively raised their pay by 2 to 3 asses so that, at the upper level, it approached the pay of a legionary.[19] The relatively low level of wages reflected the high purchasing power enjoyed by the silver denarius, the brass sestertius and dupondius, and the copper as in markets across the empire.

Prices are better documented than wages during the imperial peace, but they exhibit wide fluctuations even for staples such as grain and oil. Rome stood at the center of the highest prices and was ringed by a succession of concentric circles of progressively lower prices covering Italy and the western Mediterranean. Latin satirists and novelists delighted in complaining of the ruinous cost of living in the imperial capital. Great provincial cities such as Alexandria, Antioch, Carthage, and Ephesus too stood at the center of their own rings of descending prices, but, even setting aside the matter of great cities, prices varied from region to region. Prices of staples (except wine) in soil-poor Palestine were customarily 50 percent more than those of Roman Egypt or Parthian Babylonia; one rabbi notes that craftsmen were persuaded to migrate from Alexandria to the Galilee on condition that their salaries were doubled.[20] Literary sources comment on occasions when catastrophes such as famine or war disrupted markets. Cities experienced frequent shortages rather than famines, and although the wealthy at times were reluctant to disgorge stores of grain to poor citizens, noble benefactors often stepped forward to assume the costs of importing and selling foodstuffs at just prices. More often war disrupted prices and bled cities of their coins. During the siege of the Syrian city of Laodicea in 43 B.C., the price of wheat tripled to 3 tetradrachmae (or 12 denarii) per modius, sixteen times official prices at Rome.[21] In the Galilee during the Jewish War, Josephus reports profiteering by the notorious John of Gischala, who contrived to sell two sextarii of olive oil for a denarius, or ten times his purchase price.[22]

The imperial peace of the first and second centuries brought improvements in transportation and communications, reducing many risks associated with commerce. The changes made prices throughout the empire more uniform, although differences, because of the costs of transport, still prevailed. The average market prices for wheat during the first century in Egypt, which produced a surplus of grain, were as little as 25 percent of those in Rome (Table 11.1).[23] The effective cost of wheat to the plebeians in Rome at times probably fell below the fixed price due to the large quantities distributed to the urban plebeians and imperial efforts to impose ceilings on prices.[24] Prices of 16 asses (1 denarius) reported in Africa and Asia Minor were current in cities such as Carthage and Ephesus, but lower prices prevailed in the countryside. The index suggests that a Julio-Claudian legionary, stationed as he was outside of Italy, would earn enough in four or five days to pay for his monthly supply of grain. Members of the Praetorian Guard, who

*Table 11.1*
Average Wheat Prices for Select Regions, A.D. 1–100

| Region | Average/Range of Price per Modius (In Asses) | Average Price Indexed against Price at Rome |
|---|---|---|
| Rome | 32 | 1.00 |
| Italy | 16 | 0.50 |
| Africa | 12.5 (9 to 16) | 0.39 |
| Asia Minor | 12 (8 to 16) | 0.38 |
| Palestine | 11 (10 to 12) | 0.34 |
| Egypt | 8 (7 to 9) | 0.25 |

*Source:* Based on Duncan-Jones, *Economy,* pp. 50–51 and 145–57; Sperber, *Roman Palestine,* pp. 101–3; and Lendon, *Klio* 72 (1990), 109–34.

were based in the city of Rome, received 2 denarii per diem, enough to buy one modius of wheat at the market rate at Rome.[25]

Shortages were common in the early spring when prices in towns could rise by as much as six to tenfold.[26] Even in plentiful times, prices varied. In just over a month in 45/6, which was a time of plenty, owners of a record office at Tebtynis bought their wheat in bulk at prices ranging from just over 1 to 2 tetradrachmae per artaba, equivalent to 4 to 7 asses per modius.[27] Since prices were subject to seasonal conditions, cities took measures to guard against price-gouging and fluctuations. Cyzicus decreed:

> Therefore the council and people have decreed that all the chief magistrates and dignitaries shall support the market commissioners in seeing to it that the same prices prevail for all merchandise in the entire market and that not a single one of the products sold in any way turns out to be sold at more than the existing price. Anyone injuring the common prosperity, or corrupting the markets of saleables in any way, shall be accursed as a public enemy of the city and shall be punished by the chief magistrates.[28]

This was the same logic that inspired the empire-wide regulations of the Price Edict in 301.

Many citizens were favored with some sort of subsidized pricing of their daily bread. In times of scarcity, officials imposed ceilings of 1 or 2 denarii per modius or benefactors absorbed the difference between famine prices and a just price calculated as the mean of the typical low and high on the open market. In 124/5 or 127/8, Sparta sold, and absorbed 70 percent of the cost, of imported Egyptian wheat that it had purchased at the price of 2 denarii per modius (perhaps an indication that a just price in Sparta would have been about 10 asses).[29] A benefactor at the Asian city Sebastopolis assumed total costs of 8,000 denarii by selling wheat at 1 denarius per modius, one-half his purchase price, and, in addition, distributing 1 denarius to each citizen. At the African town of Thuburnica, a generous benefactor expended 100,000 denarii, equivalent to a Roman equestrian's property qualification, for 10,000 modii imported at the ruinous price of 10 denarii per modius.[30] Citizens who received cash handouts of 1 or 2 denarii at festivals had enough to purchase 50 to 100 percent of the monthly requirement of wheat for an adult male.

Most Romans enjoyed this stability in daily purchases of bread during the 250 years from the Augustan through Severan ages. They employed primarily middle-sized base metal denominations that were fractions of a thick brass or bronze prime denomination, whether the brass Roman sestertius, the bronze civic six-assaria piece, or the Alexandrine drachma. The prime denomination of uncial weight (25 g), whatever its tariffing, inspired confidence, proved a handy multiple of considerable value, and was conveniently exchanged against silver coins. At Rome or Pompeii in ca. 50, wheat bread weighing one or one and one-half pounds sold on average for 2 asses, so that a Roman paid out either a shiny brass dupondius (12.5 g) or two reddish copper asses (11 g each). In smaller Italian towns bread went for one-half this price.[31] Contemporaries at Ephesus in Asia Minor expended for the same loaf either 1 or 2 obols—a dumpy bronze denomination of comparable weight (10 to 12 g) and little changed in design since the mid-second century B.C. A century later, even though the notational price had doubled, an Ephesian still paid one or two civic bronze coins, tariffed as four-assaria pieces (13.5 g), which approximated the weight of the obol but were struck on a wide flan similar to those of imperial asses.[32] Prices of bread in Palestine of the mid-second century were comparable to those at Ephesus, either 1 or 2 Syrian *issars,* the Roman-style asses struck at Antioch.[33] Residents of Egyptian towns and villages in the Fayyum paid substantially less for their bread in ca. 50. One loaf of wheat bread cost a single obol (5.5 to 6.5 g). Since an Alexandrine obol was one-half the weight and size of either a Roman as or Asian obol, the coins used by Egyptians to pay for their daily bread weighed only 25 percent of those used by their contemporaries in Rome or Ephesus. This low price of wheat bread in Egypt had only doubled at the end of the second century.[34] Pricing of bread suggests that wages were well in excess of bare subsistence levels, and consequently coins, silver and bronze, must have circulated in great numbers. If daily wheat bread sold at 1 as per loaf in Italy during the first century, legionaries and farm laborers earned daily ten to sixteen times this amount. In

Palestine, hired hands for gathering the harvest or vintage received similar wages.[35] Egyptian laborers hired by estates for agricultural tasks in ca. A.D. 75–125 received only three to seven times the going price of bread (daily wages of 3 to 7 obols), but they were customarily provided with their food and drink. Wage levels increased to 8 to 16 obols sometime after 125.[36]

Fewer records have come down to us for the prices of other staples such as oil and wine, although surviving prices from Italy and Egypt confirm the impression of the high value of token bronze coins. At Pompeii, for example, the day's table wine cost 1 as per sextarius, double or quadruple for superior ones, while the price at Rome started at 5 asses and ranged to perhaps 30 asses or more.[37] Although production of wine increased dramatically during the imperial peace, prices varied widely due to vintage and the cost of transportation. Prices of olive oil distributed in gymnasiums of Greek cities rather than for consumption exhibit variations by fourfold. Wherever soil and climate did not permit cultivation of olive groves, benefactors in Asian cities during the second century paid wholesale 96 denarii per amphora (or 2 denarii per sextarius); elsewhere those with ready access to oil paid 27 to 36 denarii per amphora (9 to 12 asses per sextarius).[38]

In Italy in about 75–125, a family of four would have spent annually 200 denarii on recommended needs of wheat, oil, and wine, an average of 2 to 2.5 asses per diem for each family member.[39] In Africa, such a family might have paid half this amount, as did many others in the European and Anatolian provinces.[40] In Egypt, the scribes operating the record office at Tebtynis in 46/7 bought daily food and drink out of modest fees of 1 to 7 obols charged for writing documents. They presumably drank domestic wine obtained wholesale at 14 to 36 obols per *ceramion* (or 1 to 2.5 obols per sextarius).[41] Common fish sold by weight, eggs, beer, dried fruits, vegetables, oil for dinner, and condiments each were purchased for modest sums of 1 to 3 obols.[42] In short, in about A.D. 50 a petty bureaucrat in a Fayyum town of 4,500 souls ate well at a price of 1 to 2 bronze drachmae each day or what he earned by writing three or four routine documents. A humbler family of four at Tebtynis could buy its annual wheat, beer, and olive oil for

125 tetradrachmae or, if wishing the snob appeal of wine, 150 tetradrachmae.[43]

Few prices and wages survive to document how they were undermined by the great debasements of the third century. The only meaningful records survive from the Egyptian Fayyum during the period of 190–260, and, based on the price of wheat, they might suggest that the fiduciary billon tetradrachma and bronze drachma held their value remarkably well in the Nile Valley.[44] In response to Nero's debasement, the average price of wheat, in terms of tetradrachmae, rose from 25 to 40 percent, but in terms of the silver content of the coins, it remained constant for over a century (ca. 45–160). The debasement of the tetradrachma by Commodus in 190/1 triggered a doubling of prices over those of the first half of the second century, and prices remained at that general level into the mid-third century, although they might have fallen again when Septimius Severus and Caracalla improved the standard by 50 percent. Wine prices suffered corresponding increases. In 247–64 table wine produced on a Fayyum estate of Appianus, citizen and councilor of Alexandria, was marketed at Theadelphia and its surrounding villages at 3 to 4 tetradrachmae per ceramion—as much as three times the 14 to 36 obols paid by the owers of Tebtynis's record office in ca. 45–47.[45] Wages for agricultural laborers too kept pace with inflation, at least on the estate of Appianus, because they were hired at daily rates of 11 to 32 obols, double the rates of the mid-second century.[46] Price stability and faith in fiduciary coins collapsed in Egypt in 255–75. But what was more telling for the fate of the coinage was the increase in the number of fractional coins (billon tetradrachmae or bronze drachmae) needed to make simple purchases, and, as a consequence, Egyptians saw the obol sink in value and fall out of circulation.

In 293, Diocletian reformed the currency and premised it on a silver-clad nummus expected to function as a silver denarius, but he also officially recognized inflation of 200 percent due to the reduction of the denarius's silver content by over two-thirds in the past sixty years. Legionaries and elite cavalrymen of Diocletian received top annual pay reckoned at the notational value of 1,800 d.c., triple the Severan base pay. In its purchases, the imperial government also recognized a threefold rise in prices. At Dura-Europos on the Upper Euphrates in ca. 240, boots were priced at 22 denarii and Dalmatic cloaks (depending on quality and cut) at 17.5 to 60 denarii. In the Price Edict, items of comparable military issue were quoted at 75 and 50 to 200 notational denarii, respectively.[47] Although Diocletian intended that the billon nummus act as the proxy of a silver denarius, his nummus resembled in size and weight the as of the Principate. As prices rose sharply, he strove to maintain the worth of his nummus by retariffing its notational value from 5 d.c. to 12.5 d.c. in 299–301, and then to 25 d.c. in 301. Romans, however, associated the buying power of coins with appearance, and the nummus, whatever its official tariffing, felt and looked like a dupondius or as of the Principate. This resemblance was unfortunately all too often accentuated by illicit extracting of the silver wash from the nummus's surface. Given the nummus's weight, size, and low silver content, Romans in 293 would have instinctively reckoned 8 to 16 nummi as the price of a modius of wheat.

Nearly all prices and wages surviving from the Tetrarchic period are official ones that were below those in the market, but the prices at least reveal what Diocletian planned and why his nummus failed. A legionary in 293 received an annual salary of 360 nummi (tariffed at 5 d.c. each), and most likely he was supposed to purchase with his daily wage of 1 nummus 1 modius of wheat, customarily measured as a heaping "portion of the camp" (*modius castrensis*), which averaged 50 percent more than the standard Roman modius.[48] If such pricing were in effect, his minimum needs, calculated as 32 *modii castrenses* of wheat, would have cost 32 nummi or a low 9 percent of his base pay—a purchasing power comparable to the best times under the Principate. This official price probably lasted but briefly in the marketplace, because the prologue of the Price Edict laments that within less than eight years prices had raced to fourfold or eightfold what Diocletian had intended. The same legionary in early 301 received an annual wage of only 144 nummi (retariffed at 12.5 d.c.). At the official rate of 8 nummi per *modius castrensis* in the Price Edict, he would have expended 256 nummi, over 1.75 times his entire base pay, to purchase annual needs of wheat. Diocletian tried to offset ruinous price increases by issuing wheat rations of 20 *modii castrenses* (just under two-thirds of a soldier's annual needs, which, at state prices, represented a value of 160 nummi), a cash supplement of another 48 nummi for grain purchases (which could purchase six *modii castrenses* of wheat according to the Price Edict), and four donatives each year amounting to 800 nummi.[49] Total remuneration came to 992 nummi in cash or 1,152 nummi if the value of the wheat rations is included, but a daily wage of either 2.75 or 3.2 nummi calculated from these sums fell far short, by at least 60 percent, of the official price of 8 nummi per modius of wheat in the Price Edict. Without yet more supplements in cash or kind, Tetrarchic soldiers could not buy minimum needs of wheat; the erosion of purchasing power was considerable.

Diocletian designed his currency reform to provide his legionaries with silver-clad nummi issued as salary in the same numbers and with the same buying power of denarii of the first century. By early 301, when fourfold and eightfold price rises ruined this scheme, Diocletian promulgated his Edict of Maximum Prices, but this measure swiftly failed as vendors withdrew goods from markets.[50] Thereupon, he rescinded the edict and doubled tariffing of denominations above the denarius communis. In effect, he halved prices so that such staple grains as wheat and millet (at a price of 100 d.c.) were officially halved from 8 to 4 nummi, and barley and rye (at 60 d.c.) from 4 nummi and change to 2 nummi and change per *modius castrensis*. The daily wages mandated in the Price Edict were too low even if markets followed official pricing of basic commodities. A farm laborer was allowed a maximum daily wage of 2 nummi (25 d.c.) so that he earned daily only 25 percent of the price of a modius of wheat, whereas his forefathers in 100 earned two to four times this amount. Craftsmen such as shipwrights and masons fared marginally better with salaries of 4 to 12 nummi. A family of four that purchased its subsistence needs of grain, oil, and wine at official maximum prices expended approximately 1,250 nummi each year, so that an annual subsistence wage of 720 nummi would have defrayed only 60 percent of total costs.[51]

Market prices of wheat in Egypt during the early fourth century suggest how the Roman public reacted to Diocletian's nummus and price schemes. Withdrawal of the Price Edict and retariffing the currency in 301 generated a wave of inflation, but by 305 the public might have begun to accept the nummus, for one modius of wheat sold for 2 nummi in the market of Oxyrhynchus in the Fayyum. Egyptian prices, normally at the most only one-half those elsewhere in the Roman world, suggest that one modius of wheat sold at between 4 and 10 nummi in other markets. The climb in Egyptian wheat prices after 305 mirrored the steady decline of the weight and silver content of the nummus.[52] The price of 2 nummi for a modius of wheat in 305 doubled to 4 nummi by 312, rose by 4.5 times to 18 nummi in 314, and then more than doubled again to 40 nummi by 327. At the same time, the nummus, although officially rated at 25 d.c., was reduced in weight by over 75 percent, from a middle-sized coin (10.75 g) to a miserable-looking fraction (2.4 g). Romans were reduced to employing ever more nummi of ever diminishing size and weight as their sole coins for small-scale purchases. Theophanes, on the staff of the prefect of Egypt, reports that, while traveling on official business in Syria in ca. 317–23, he paid at Antioch prices of 2 nummi for a loaf of bread, 4 to 8 nummi for a pound of meat, and 6 to 14 nummi for a sextarius of wine.[53]

Any conclusions deduced from military pay and the price of wheat for the period between 325 and 650 are highly speculative, so it is best to review what is known. During this period, salaries were 9 solidi per annum for a cavalryman and 5 for an infantryman (56 and 31 percent, respectively, of the gold equivalent of the annual salary of an Augustan legionary).[54] Grain prices were quoted in the quantity—modii or, in Egypt, artabai—that could be bought for a solidus; in other words, what survive for the most part are wholesale prices. The price of 30 modii of wheat per solidus was common in state purchases and taxation during the fourth century and one of 40 modii per solidi in the late fifth and sixth centuries. Prices at Oxyrhynchus early in the reign of Justinian (527–65) ranged from 10 to 14 artabai (or approximately 45 to 63 modii) per solidus, and those quoted at Aphrodito at a slightly later date (ca. 555–80) are similar.[55] Therefore, at the most expensive end of the range (30 modii per solidus), the annual wheat of 48 modii would cost about 1.6 solidi, 18 percent of the annual salary of a cavalryman who would need between five and six days to earn his monthly bread. At the least expensive end of the range (63 modii per solidus), it would cost three-quarters of a solidus, meaning that it would take a cavalryman three days to cover his cost of wheat for a month. An infantryman would have taken ten and five days, respectively, to earn his monthly bread. Such figures are not inconsistent with costs of the Republic or Principate. Regional and seasonal variations cannot be documented, but famine prices of 10 modii (or, in Egypt, 5 artabae) per solidus were universally regarded as catastrophic. Prices in urban markets must have fluctuated violently far more often because far fewer benefactors regulated prices or imported grain during shortages, as decurions abandoned the public service of their forefathers.

It is seldom possible to express wages or prices in terms of billon denominations of the fourth century or bronze nummi minimi of the fifth century, although they were the coins most often spent in daily purchases. Two sets of prices, however, cast light on the buying power of silver argentei and bronze nummi minimi. In the spring of 363, the emperor Julian cited wheat prices at Antioch in accordance with local market practices by numbers of cab (*metra*) per argenteus. Antiochenes, among the most pampered of the empire's inhabitants, expected to pay for one modius of wheat between one-quarter to one-half of an argenteus (almost certainly in the form of billon maiorinae whose tariffing is as yet unknown) and, in hard times, three-quarters of an argenteus. The massing of forces for Julian's Persian war drove up the subsidized price of wheat by 50 percent, from 15 to 10 cab (approximately 3.75 to 2.5 modii) per argenteus. These prices yield a range expressed in wholesale terms of between 90 and 60 modii per solidus, although during the acute scarcity of early spring, the price could be as high as 30 modii per solidus.[56] Julian subsidized low prices for the Antiochenes by importing 100,000 modii of wheat from eastern Syria, 22,500 modii from imperial estates, and unspecified amounts from Egypt. In 445, the Western emperor Valentinian III mandated that taxpayers in Mauretania and Numidia must commute wheat rations due military forces at the rate of 40 modii per solidus. At the then rate of exchange of 7,200 nummi (1.15 g each) per solidus, one modius of wheat in Roman Africa was officially reckoned at 180 nummi minimi or the same as the daily wage of a cavalryman.[57]

The regional structure of prices documented in the sixth century exhibits significant changes as the empire's financial center shifted back to the eastern shores of the Mediterranean during the fifth century. Constantinople displaced Rome as the center of the empire's concentric circles of decreasing wages and prices. As taxes and trade rerouted specie to Constantinople, regions sustaining the new imperial capital also prospered, and consequently prices rose at satellite cities on the Bosporus or Aegean shores of Anatolia. Antioch and Alexandria, populous cities and seats of powerful eastern patriarchs, acquired new patrons and sources of money. Prices mounted in Syria and Palestine during the boom years from the late fourth to sixth centuries as the money supply rose due to the profits from the pilgrimage trade and the largess that pious emperors poured into endowing holy cities. Simultaneously, the money supply of Italy contracted as Rome lost population and imperial patronage. By the time of Alaric's sack in 410, residents of Rome numbered between 500,000 and 600,000, half the inhabitants of Augustan Rome. Rome, despite an ephemeral recovery under Ostrogothic rule, lost her position as the center of the Mediterranean economy.

In the sixth century, stable prices and wages returned in the East with the reintroduction of a heavy token bronze coinage. It was based on a follis that was far larger than any fractional denomination struck in over a century. In diameter and buying power, the folles of 498–512 were comparable to the middle-sized *aes* of the Principate, although their weight (8.5 g) was but two-thirds that of dupondii or asses. The heavier folles, struck between 512 and 565 (ranging in weight from 17 to 22 g) were comparable to Roman sestertii or Egyptian bronze drachmae of the Principate; in 565–615 they fell again to the level of brass dupondii (11 to 15 g). The minting of folles by Ostrogothic and Vandal kings suggests a similar stability in Italy and Africa even though documentation is lacking.

A guide to prices and wages during the sixth century can be constructed by recalculating daily military salaries and the range of wheat prices per modius reported in Egypt in terms of folles at known rates of exchange. Whatever the size and official tariffing of the follis, an elite cavalryman serving in Egypt during the sixth century would have purchased his monthly needs of wheat with the wages of three to four days; infantry with wages of five to six days. Soldiers serving elsewhere paid higher prices. At the most commonly cited official price of 40 modii per solidi, a modius of wheat cost 10 folles in 498–512; 4 to 5 folles in 512–65; and 6 to 8 folles after 578.[58] At these prices, horse soldiers bought their monthly wheat from the wages of six days; infantry from wages of eight days. Yet, even this purchasing power compared favorably to that of legionaries of the middle Republic and Principate, and it was far above that of Tetrarchic soldiers.

Residents of Fayyum towns might have paid average market prices as low as 7 folles per modius of wheat in A.D. 500; 3 folles in 540, and 5 folles in 580 (although transactions were reckoned by artabai and paid in bronze duodecanummiae). Egyptian grain prices were by far the lowest in the Roman world, often averaging between one-third and one-half of official prices. Citizens of Constantinople, a capital so often beleaguered after 578, without subsidized grain prices would have paid at least four or five times as much.

Minimum wages in the sixth century, as in the Principate, were above bare subsistence and, what is more important, they apparently kept pace with price rises in staples resulting from the reduction of the weight of the follis after 542. In the early sixth century, ascetics in Egypt and Palestine who hired out as laborers in the fields or on construction earned a going daily rate of 5 folles (weighing between 17.5 and 22 g each). The amount of 5 folles was also considered appropriate as daily alms to the poor.[59] In 540 an adult male could purchase with 1 follis his daily subsistence of bread, oil, and vegetables (equivalent to 25 percent of his wage, as in the Principate); ascetics could survive on a mere half-follis.[60] Within four months, laborers could earn 3 to 3.5 solidi—a considerable sum, the price of a camel or a young slave at the military post of Nessana in the Negev.[61] Cavalrymen stationed in Egypt ate well on a hearty diet of bread, meat, wine, and oil at 3 to 4 folles each day, while residents of Constantinople, Antioch, or Persian Nisibis paid considerably more.[62]

The price of a loaf of daily bread remained quite low relative to minimum daily wages (10 to 15 percent).[63] In 498 it might have cost a light-weight follis, so that after 512 a loaf sold on average for 20 nummiae (a half-follis) and less in times of abundance. In Egypt, a low average cost of 12 nummiae (or three-tenths of a follis) for daily bread might have popularized the use of the duodecanummia. In the 570s the thirty-nummiae piece was perhaps introduced when daily bread might have risen by 50 percent from 20 to 30 nummiae. An Egyptian laborer in 540 could earn in six months 900 folles (each weighing 22 g) or 5 solidi, with which he could purchase six times his own annual grain needs or cover annual costs of wheat, wine, and oil for a family of four.[64] Such purchasing power was threefold what was envisioned in the Price Edict of 301, and it compared favorably to that under the Principate. Sometimes laborers could demand higher wages. In 506, when Anastasius rushed construction on the fortress of Daras, he offered daily wages of 35 folles per man and 70 folles (equal to 1 gold tremissis) for each man with a draft animal. At the exchange rate current in 540, these wages were three and one-half and seven times greater, respectively, than the typical daily wages.[65]

Natural calamities and war could quickly disrupt prices of staples during the late fifth and sixth centuries. Joshua the Stylite reports that in 495 wheat at Edessa, seat of the governor of Mesopotamia, sold at the comparatively high price of 30 modii to the solidus or the equivalent of 14 folles (8 g each) per modius after the Anastasian reform of 498. Famine raged for three years, in 499–501, after swarms of locusts devoured the crops. In the first year of the famine, prices of wheat and barley rose to 105 and 70 folles per modius, jumped in the next year to 130 and 93 folles, and by the third year, 501, fell to 70 and 42 folles per modius, respectively. Requisitions of grain for Roman forces battling the Persians and ambitious building programs in 505 again drove up prices to the levels of 499–500. Prices at Edessa in 499–501 are among the most catastrophic to survive from any period. The emperor Anastasius remitted taxes in 499 and returned to each villager 2 folles—little more than almsgiving—as prices relentlessly mounted. By 500 prices for all foodstuffs soared; meat and eggs were selling at four to five times customary rates.[66]

By 580 the daily wage of 5 folles in 540 had risen to 10 to 15 folles (weighing 11 g) with corresponding increases in the cost of subsistence and almsgiving.[67] It is difficult to document the rate of inflation in the late sixth and seventh centuries, because solidus and folles were traded in markets at rates well beyond those fixed by imperial decree. On the eve of the Persian War of 602–28, prices and wages stood at perhaps double to triple of those in 540. The follis still commanded public trust and considerable buying power, but its weight had been slashed by one-half (from 22 to 11 g). As Heraclius rapidly debased the currency after 616, he destroyed faith in imperial bronze money, and with it, the stable prices and wages of the Justinianic age.

The extent of monetization was reflected by the widespread willingness of the Roman public for well over eight centuries to employ coins in markets. Prices and wages surviving from the periods of 200 B.C. to A.D. 235 and 500–615 reveal that Romans routinely employed huge numbers of hefty token base metal coins. During these periods, middle-sized bronze coins weighing between one-third and one-half of the Roman ounce passed as the coin of common transactions, easily buying a loaf of bread, whereas its heavy multiple weighing an ounce offered the subsistence of a day. Official tariffing did not matter so much as the constant power of the bronze coins in purchasing staples and the ready exchange of token bronze coins into high-value coins such as the silver denarius or gold solidus. Full-bodied and bronze coins together extended by many times the kinds of daily transactions in which Romans could deal in coin, and this was increased further by the ease of extending private credit quoted in the trustworthy coins of the realm. Token bronze coins, in short, were the final ingredient that ensured the triumph of coins in daily usage that made the monetized markets of the Roman world possible.

Between the two periods of relatively stable currency, prices, and wages stretched over 250 years of debasement, abortive reform, and inflation. Prices and wages during the period of 235–498 can be briefly glimpsed in the years 285–325. The Roman public refused to accept a single billon denomination in place of the silver denarius with its token bronze fractions. A billon currency of a single denomination, although profitable to mint, was too cumbersome for daily markets, particularly when their low value necessitated large batches of them to be sealed in leather purses or wrapped in rolls of papyrus or skin to provide multiple denominations. Despite their silver coating, radiate antoniniani or laureate nummi in size and weight never impressed the public. Consequently, they failed miserably in the marketplace; they were exchanged at values far below the tariffing pronounced in imperial edicts. Radiate antoniniani of the third century, Tetrarchic nummi, and diminutive bronze nummi of the fifth century in large part failed as currency because they failed to facilitate exchange in the marketplace. If coins were created as a fiscal instrument and source of state profit, their success depended upon their usefulness in the marketplace. The reasons for the demise of the Tetrarchic nummus applied to all the sundry billon denominations and bronze nummi minimi struck between 235 and 498. Romans perceived Diocletian's nummus as a fraction for purchasing daily bread rather than as the prime high-value coin for bulk purchases or payment of salaries. Hence, it is no surprise that the disappearance of the denarius and its fractional *aes* panicked Romans and set off the scourge of notational inflation of billon nummi reported in Egyptian papyri. This inflation did not spell the end of monetary habits, for Romans had grown far too accustomed to the convenience of coins. When Anastasius and Justinian rebuilt a version of the Augustan currency based on bronze folles and gold solidi, they restored, however briefly, the stable prices and wages of the Roman monetary order.

# Twelve

# Roman Coins beyond the Imperial Frontiers

The Christian geographer Cosmas Indicopleustes writing in the sixth century declared: "There is another mark of the power of the Romans, which God has given them. I mean that it is in their solidus that every nation conducts its commerce, and it is acceptable in every place from one end of the earth to the other. The solidus is admired by all men and all nations, for in no other nation does such a thing exist."[1] Cosmas's praise of the solidus of his day could apply just as well to aurei and denarii of the Principate, which won admiration from the rajah of Taprobane (Sri Lanka) and the historians of Han China. Roman coins traveled beyond imperial frontiers in long-distance trade, diplomatic subsidies, and, from the mid-third century on, as spoils wrested by Teutonic and Sassanid invaders. Flows of coins out of the Roman world are often viewed as irretrievable drains of specie, but the forces drawing specie back into the empire were just as strong. The export of coins, along with other commodities, from the Roman world required that comparably valued goods (including specie) return, otherwise an imbalance would have quickly ruined what Fernand Braudel terms "trade circuits." Braudel's point applies as much to Roman trade in the Indian Ocean for spices and silks, as to

European trade in the Far East since the sixteenth century.[2]

Literary sources and archaeology offer at best ambiguous details, often distorting rather than clarifying the role of coins in overseas trade. Classical authors mentioned export of coin incidentally in moralizing tales, but they offer few clues concerning the dynamics of specie flows across the Eurasian continent.[3] Coins, unlike many other wares, survive in the archaeological record, but dating finds is complicated by preferences for older coins of a familiar type or those of high purity. For example, a Palmyrene merchant on a caravan bound for Charax in 193, when given a choice, selected 300 "old aurei," presumably Antonine pieces struck at 45 to the pound.[4] The great numbers of denarii found as caches of treasure, burial gifts, or votive offerings in South India, Germany, and Scandinavia—lands where coins were treated as bullion—do not necessarily reflect the scale or main directions of trade. In contrast, aurei and denarii that entered the Parthian or Kushan empires—great states with their own currencies—often were reminted or reexported to the West, leaving little trace in the archaeological record.

Rome never struck trade coins—which, by their immobilized design and unchanging standard passed without examination in foreign markets—like the Austrian thalers of Maria Theresa that were minted long after her death by European governments to settle debts in the Near East. But through usage peoples beyond the frontiers learned to trust denarii, aurei, or solidi as universal media of exchange. As noted previously, the rajah of Taprobane, who entertained a freedman captain of Annius Plocamus, "was most impressed with Roman honesty in that amongst the money in his guest's possession, the denarii were all equal in weight, although the different likenesses on them indicated that they had been struck by various emperors."[5]

At the opening of the second century B.C., the gold stater, minted in the names of Macedonian kings and by weight an Attic didrachma (8.5 g), and its silver teradrachma (17.25 g) were the trade coins of the Mediterranean world and Near East. Denarii, reckoned from 26 to 33 to a gold stater, were awkward to trade against an Attic tetradrachma, and denarii leaving Italy prior to 125 B.C. were probably reminted; hence few surface in hoards outside of Italy. Italian merchants did little to popularize denarii in foreign markets, for their major focus was supplying Roman armies overseas. Roman arms imposed the denarius as the premier silver coin of the Mediterranean world, and Hellenic cities adjusted by placing the Attic-weight drachma at par with the denarius. The mounting numbers of Roman coins penetrating far-flung reaches of Europe and Asia after 125 B.C. marked a fundamental shift in trade patterns, and the rise of the importance of Rome in the Mediterranean economy.

### *Roman Coins in Northern Europe, 125 B.C.–A.D. 300*

Denarii first traveled in large quantities to the northern regions beyond Rome's immediate political horizons at the close of the second century B.C. This movement is documented by the number of denarii, over 25,000 to date, and native imitations unearthed in Dacia and Moesia (modern Rumania and Bulgaria).[6] Dacians and their Getic kinsmen dwelling in the Lower Danube Valley had, from the late fourth century B.C., bartered slaves, hides, salted meat and fish, grain, honey, and wax in return for wine, oil, fine wares, textiles, and silver (first Macedonian and then Thasian tetradrachmae) imported over the Balkan river routes from the North Aegean and Adriatic ports.[7] Denarii, arriving from 125 B.C. on, ousted Hellenic competitors by 70 B.C., but as soon as Augustus secured the imperial frontier on the Lower Danube, the export of freshly minted denarii to Dacia—based on the archaeological record—seems to have fallen abruptly until Trajan's conquest in 105–6.[8] The absence of imperial denarii in Rumanian hoards during the first century A.D. might reflect Dacian preference for Republican denarii, or it might be the result of the capture of many imperial denarii (paid in subsidies by Domitian and Nerva) by Trajan's legions when they sacked Sarmizegetusa. In Dacia, where gold was plentiful, imported silver was exchanged against Dacian gold, which could be sold at a profit in Aegean and Asian markets where gold was dear. Such trade is evidenced by tetradrachmae and denarii that have been unearthed in Dacian mining districts, and the gold staters minted from native metal with types modeled after

Roman denarii from 55 B.C. on (pl. 31.252). Roman exploitation of Spanish and Dalmatian gold mines shifted the ratio between the precious metals, and the trade in Dacian gold now yielding lower profits fell off in the first century A.D.[9] Even though many imported silver coins were cast into ingots or ornaments, most specimens, along with Dacian gold staters and imitative tetradrachmae (based on Macedonian and Thasian prototypes) and denarii (pl. 31.253) exhibit wear and so were circulated. Rulers such as King Burebistas (ca. 60–44 B.C.) presumably paid warriors and craftsmen in coin, but the full monetization of Dacia came with the Roman conquest.[10]

Commerce and diplomacy carried denarii far beyond the limits attained by Roman arms in western Spain, Transalpine Gaul, the Alpine regions of Rhaetia and Noricum, and the lands of the Middle Danube. The Celts of Noricum (modern Austria) exploited gold and iron deposits that attracted Italian merchants, who familiarized natives with Roman coins. By 70 B.C. Noricans struck, for local consumption, light-weight silver tetradrachmae (9.6 g) and fractions with native designs at the royal capital Noreia (modern Magdalensberg). Farther east in Pannonia, the Illyro-Celtic Eravisci occupying the regions around present-day Budapest and Lake Balaton in Hungary struck a short-lived series of imitative denarii, possibly in ca. 50–10 B.C.[11] In Noricum and Pannonia, as in Dacia, trade with Rome transformed commercial habits by introducing coins and thereby prepared for rapid assimilation within the Roman monetary world upon conquest.

The campaigns of Augustus opened trade with Scandinavia, the southern shores of the Baltic Sea, and the central European lands between the Rhine and Vistula occupied by the free Germans. Germany and Scandinavia emerged as markets hungry for denarii for the next three centuries.[12] The Romans surveyed the coastal waters from the mouth of the Rhine to the Elbe during the military operations of Drusus in 12–9 B.C. and Germanicus in A.D. 16. Augustus boasted that his fleet penetrated Danish waters in A.D. 5: "My fleet sailed through the Ocean eastwards from the mouth of the Rhine to the territory of the Cimbri, a country which no Roman had visited before either by land or sea, and the Cimbri, Charydes, Semnones, and other German peoples of that region sent ambassadors and sought my friendship and that of the Roman people."[13] Gallo-Roman and Frisian merchants soon after undertook regular voyages to Jutland, the Danish isles, and southern Sweden to sell wine and other Roman goods to markets with sophisticated tastes for imports since Celtic times, and in return they carried amber, slaves, and raw materials to the Rhineland, Gaul, and Britain. In the process, Scandinavians acquired denarii with which they purchased Roman imports.

Overland routes radiated across Central Europe following the river systems.[14] Cities in the Roman Rhineland like Colonia Agrippina (Cologne) profited not only from the new markets offered by the imperial frontier army, but also from commerce with the northern lands. From Castra Vetera (Xanten) and Moguntiacum (Mainz), routes up the Rhine's tributaries Lippe and Main connected Roman Germany via the Fulda Gap to the Upper Elbe, and thence to Scandinavia. The eastern trade axis or "Amber Route" started from Carnuntum, on the Upper Danube downstream from Vindobona (Vienna), and followed the March until it forked into two tracks, each leading to the Baltic. The northerly route descended the Oder Valley, while a northeasterly route ran over Kalisia (the modern Polish town Kalisz) to the middle Vistula, where it merged with routes coming from the Black Sea along the Bug and Dneister river valleys, and followed the Vistula to its mouth in the Danzig Bay. Carnuntum also faced south, offering a direct route over the Alps by imperial highways to Aquileia in Northern Italy. Denarii passed along these routes in both directions. The Hermunduri regularly traveled from their homes in Thuringia to trade at the Rhaetian captial of Augusta Vindelicorum (Augsburg).[15] Marcomanni and Quadi purchased Roman goods at markets held on fixed days on the Pannonian border in the first and second centuries; Goths were permitted the same privileges on the Lower Danube in the fourth century.[16] Germans welcomed Roman traders, and wily king Maroboduus (6 B.C.–A.D. 20), who welded the Suevic tribes of the Marcomanni and Quadi into an effective kingdom in Bohemia, lured Roman traders and sutlers to his capital with promises of privileges and profits. Denarii also came north in the purses of discharged German auxiliaries or as subsidies to princes friendly to

Rome. The Cherusci in northwestern Germany and the Marcomanni and Quadi were the principal beneficiaries of this flow of Roman coins. With regard to the latter, Tacitus summed up imperial policy: "These kings [of the Marcomanni] occasionally receive our armed assistance, more often our financial, and it is equally effective."[17] Tacitus notes how the influx of Roman coins changed native commercial habits:

> The Germans nearest to us value gold and silver for their use in trade, and recognize and prefer certain types of our coins. Those of the interior, truer to the plain old ways, employ barter. They like the old and well known money, denarii with notched edges [*serrati*] or with the type of the two horses [*bigati*]. They likewise prefer silver to gold, not from any special liking, but because a large number of silver coins is more convenient for use among dealers in cheap and common wares.[18]

Tens of thousands of denarii, found in well over 400 hoards and numerous stray finds bear out Tacitus's observation that the Germanic peoples preferred silver money—a taste that endured long into the Middle Ages save for a brief influx of solidi into Scandinavia in the fifth century. Even Germans dwelling far beyond the direct reach of Rome, such as the tribes occupying the Danish peninsula and islands, treated denarii as money to purchase coveted wares from the south rather than bullion for jewelry and plate. Germans desired the purest denarii available, accepting Republican over imperial denarii and then finer Julio-Claudian denarii over later baser ones.[19] As late as 300, denarii were interred among weapons, arms, and clothing dedicated as votive offerings to the god Wotan (Norse Odin) in the eerie peat-bog deposits at Thorsbjerg and Ejsbol in Jutland, and at Nydam and Vimose on the Danish islands of Als and Fyn.[20]

Given the nature of their trade with Rome, the volume of denarii exported to the northern peoples could not have been a major drain of the empire's money supply. As Tacitus noted, and archaeology confirms, the Germans mined no significant deposits of gold and silver, and Baltic amber was the principal precious commodity exported to the Roman world.[21] In the first century, Germanic peoples of western Germany, Jutland, the Danish islands, the Swedish island of Gotland, and along trade routes of eastern Europe minted limited numbers of imitative denarii (pl. 31.254), but for the most part they depended upon Roman coins. Those dwelling in East Prussia even placed sestertii in the mouths of the deceased interred in graves of the second century.[22] The use of Roman coins was widespread and commonplace among Germans living in proximity to Roman frontiers. Archaeology documents the stages whereby the Suevic Marcomanni and Quadi, living in present-day Bohemia and Slovakia, adopted Roman material culture, including the use of denarii and fractional *aes*. Their King Vannius was levying taxes on transit traffic (*vectigalia*) across Suevic lands by the year 50; most likely he collected this most Roman of taxes in Roman coin.[23] Trade and coins so transformed Suevic life that a century later Marcus Aurelius could contemplate the smooth annexation and assimilation of the Sueves. A similar process is suggested by the numerous coins found in Moldavia, which the Carpi probably occupied during the second and early third centuries. The Carpi too became addicted to Roman coins and wares by frequent commerce on the northeastern frontier of the province of Dacia.[24] From the Carpi and the Greek port of Olbia, denarii, along with imperial and civic *aes*, passed farther north into the Dnieper Basin, heartland of the Cherniakhov Culture of the East Slavs.

Therefore, a large body of Roman coins circulated across the northern frontier from the first through early third centuries. This continual movement of money across political boundaries was not an exodus of specie but rather the forging of a network of trade circuits that drew Germanic societies into the monetary and economic orbit of the empire. But regular trade and diplomatic contact with the Germanic world depended upon the Roman peace, and the migrations of the later third and fourth centuries disrupted trade routes and reduced the flow of coins northward. Saxon and Frankish pirates in the late third and early fourth centuries cut off Scandinavia from regular supplies of silver coins. Their raids proved an inadequate substitute for trade, impoverishing many tribes and compelling many Germans to seek fortunes and lands within the Roman Empire. Most Germans reverted to older habits of exchange, treating looted gold coins as treasure, or as models for jewelry rather than as money to buy Roman wares.

*The Eastern Trade and the "Specie Drain"*

The passage of aurei and denarii to lands far east of the imperial frontier has often been viewed as a sign of Rome's decadent craving for luxuries, which created an unfavorable balance of payments and drained specie from the empire. Classical authors complained of Roman coins flowing eastward in exchange for wares originating in China (raw silk), India (spices, aromatics, and gems), and Arabia (spices and aromatics). What they overlooked was the fact that much of the price paid in Rome covered costs incurred or profits earned within the empire. These goods traveled over varied routes before they reached the markets of Rome. Raw silk left China by one of two principal routes. The first was the famous "Silk Road," whereby Sogdian caravans skirted the wastes of the Tarim Basin and arrived at the cities of Bactria and Sogdiana—Bactra (Balkh), Maracanda (Samarkand), or Antiochia Margiane (Merv)—in Central Asia. A second route passed overland via Burma to ports at the mouths of the Ganges and on to Cholan ports on the Coromandel coast in southeast India. These centers of commerce were destinations for Roman traders seeking silk and other goods from the Far East.

There were two sets of routes available to Roman merchants traveling east. The first was the series of caravan trails crossing the Roman and Parthian empires. Caravans departed from the Greek cities Phasis and Trapazeus on the southeastern shores of the Black Sea, headed toward the Caspian Sea or across the Armenian plateau, passed through the cities of northern Mesopotamia, Media, and Bactria, and arrived at the cities of Sogdiana. Another well-traveled route crossed the Euphrates at Zeugma, a Roman customs station, and entered Parthian domains bound for the Hellenized cities Seleucia and Ctesiphon in Babylonia, Ecbatana (Hamadan) in Iran, and Susa, or Aramaean Charax, entrepot of maritime traffic in the Persian Gulf. A third caravan route, farther south, crossed the northern rim of the Arabian desert, avoiding Parthian domains, and linked the Aramaean cities of Petra (in modern Jordan) and Bostra and Palmyra (in modern Syria) to Charax at the head of the Persian Gulf. From Charax, there were two choices—traveling by sea to ports at the mouths of the Indus River, or overland via Hecatompylos (Damghan) to Antiochia Margiane (Merv) on the edge of the Parthian eastern frontier. The second set of routes started from the Egyptian ports of Myos Hormos and Berenice on the Red Sea for African and Arabian ports on the Gulf of Aden, and then either across the Arabian Sea with the aid of monsoon winds to cities on the western shores of India or south along the East African coast to Rhapta (a trading post on the coast of modern Tanzania near Dar es-Salaam).

In the time of Augustus, diverse currencies, based on Attic-weight denominations introduced by the Macedonian conquerors, circulated in the area that was the source of the goods sought by Roman merchants—it encompassed the lands bounded on the north and west by the southern slopes of the Caucasus Mountains and the Euphrates River and enclosed by an eastern frontier sweeping in a great arc from Transoxiana across the Hindu Kush to include northwestern India and the middle Gangetic plain. When the Seleucid and Mauryan empires fragmented by the early second century B.C., their royal currencies dissolved into a medley of silver drachmae and bronze or copper fractions.[25] This economic world included the Sabaean Kingdom (modern Yemen and known to the Romans as Arabia Felix) on the Red Sea, which minted tetradrachmae copied after Athenian prototypes and then the ubiquitous tetradrachmae of Alexander the Great. Indian kingdoms south of the Vindya Mountains and Narbada River (which separate the Indo-Gangetic plain of northern India from the rest of the peninsula) employed "punchmarked" silver coins, the *karshapana* (1.7 g), along with potin and bronze fractions rather than Hellenic-style coins. Therefore, Roman traders and their money entered markets that (save for southern India) had a long tradition of dealing in coin. Since few of the eastern currencies matched the fineness of imperial money, aurei and denarii were prized and often used to settle accounts in international trade.

None of the imperial governments on the Eurasian continent—

Rome, Parthia, the Kushans, or Han China—forbade trade in specie or luxury goods; but Chinese chronicles report that Parthian kings discouraged direct trade between Rome and China. In 166, during Marcus Aurelius's Parthian War, Roman merchants are reported to have arrived at the Han court by sea to open direct trade for Chinese silks. Representing themselves as envoys of the emperor, they claimed "their kings always desired to send embassies to China, but the An-hsi [i.e., Parthians] wished to carry on trade with them in Chinese silks, and it was for this reason that they were cut off from communication."[26] But, for the most part, the Arsacid kings of Parthia and later the Sassanid shahs of Persia taxed (and the duties were quite lucrative) rather than blocked the brisk transit trade for eastern luxuries. Merchants who avoided routes through Parthian domains did so to escape the delays or disasters that caravans risked whenever Roman and Parthian armies clashed over Armenia. Borders were not barriers to international trade, but, by the use of custom stations, they served as filters whereby governments could secure hard cash and, to some extent, control importation of foreign coin.

Merchants from Rome carried aurei and denarii to purchase luxury goods at the commercial centers in Central Asia and India. Most of the coins were spent for wholesale purchases of silks or spices; but along the way they exchanged Roman wares for local products to be later traded or sold and they paid customs officials, tolls, bribes, and the expense of their daily sustenance. Few Roman coins strayed beyond the limits of commercial centers, and they suffered one of three fates: many were melted and reminted as local currency, as was probably the case of aurei in the Kushan Empire, or turned into private jewelry and plate; some, aurei and denarii in southern India or Tyrian and Antiochene tetradrachmae in Parthian Mesopotamia, circulated as trade coins; and many returned home in payment for goods imported from the Roman world. Moneychangers in the centers of commerce routinely exchanged varied currencies, including popular trade coins and obsolete coins, and incoming Roman coins were directed westward back along the narrow channels of trade or into their government's coffers (and thence to the mint for recoining).

There are no records of wholesale prices Romans paid for eastern luxuries. Pliny the Elder quotes prices in the Roman world for frankincense, myrrh, pepper, cassia, cardamom, malabathrum, and cinnabar ranging from 1 to 16 denarii per pound, although superior-grade spices, nard, and rare perfumes sold at prices between 50 and 100 denarii.[27] In 301 Diocletian's Price Edict set maximum prices for malabathrum, cinnamon, bdellium, parsley, frankincense, marjoram, celandine, and ginger at amounts ranging from 5 to 20 silver-clad nummi per pound; more expensive items—oil of myrrh and Arabian saffron—were priced at 48 and 160 nummi, respectively.[28] Pliny's prices and the official ones in the Price Edict suggest that spices and aromatics, while costly, were not prohibitively so either during the Principate or the Dominate. Comparatively low retail prices suggest that Roman traders bought quality goods at reasonable wholesale prices in the eastern markets. Much of the retail price must have covered costs of transportation, customs fees, tolls, and kickbacks, which, in one case reported by Pliny the Elder, amounted to 688 denarii per camel load of frankincense conveyed by caravan from Sabbatha in Arabia Felix (Yemen) to Petra in modern Jordan.[29] What little is known about silk prices confirms the high purchasing power of imperial coin. The prices paid and those charged by Aramaeans in Central Asia or Levantine Greeks in India for raw silk or silk floss are not known, but they were trading in what was a raw commodity. The big profits came from the meticulous respinning of silk fibers, the weaving of cloth dyed in Tyrian purple (often intertwined with gold and silver threads), and the conversion of the cloth into garments. Phoenician cities producing ceremonial garments, rather than the Aramaean and Sogdian middlemen shipping raw silk west, reaped the lion's share of the profits. The Price Edict fixed one pound of silk dyed purple and spun into fine threads at 125 aurei (nearly 3 pounds of gold), 12.5 times higher than the price of undyed white silk.[30] The scale of profits also can be sensed by comparing the price of finest domestic wool, 16 nummi per pound, to that of ceremonial garments of dyed wool marketed at prices 20 to 250 times higher (ranging from one-quarter aureus to 42 aurei).[31] Such prices put the flow of coin in trade into a new perspective. Roman ships returning from India carried cargoes differing little from those on board Dutch and English vessels coming home from the Far East during the seventeenth or eighteenth centuries. Roman merchants employed gold or silver to buy into eastern markets much as Europeans employed silver mined in the New World to pry open closed Asian markets from the mid-sixteenth to mid-nineteenth centuries.

The greater number of Roman coins leaving the empire in trade entered lands just east of the imperial frontier. The Spartocid kings reigning over Greek cities on the eastern shores of the Cimmerian Bosporus (Crimea) and Tauric (Taman) peninsula minted Greek-style gold staters and bronze fractions (pl. 31.256–57). Bosporan coins circulated as the trade currency from the Lower Don to the western slopes of the Caucasus, and so Roman coins were either exchanged or reminted.[32] In border lands of the Caucasus (known to the Romans as Iberia and Albania) and Armenia, a mix of denarii, Cappadocian and Parthian drachmae, Seleucid and Roman provincial tetradrachmae, and Asian cistophori have surfaced in hoards concealed along trade routes.[33] Farther east, in Mesopotamia and Iran, the Arsacid kings of Parthia, after they lost the Central Asian silver mines soon after 88 B.C., debased their drachma from 90 to 40 percent fine (pl. 31.259). By the reign of Augustus, the Parthian drachma contained two-thirds the silver of the denarius and the Parthian tetradrachma had half the silver content of the pseudo-Seleucid tetradrachma of Antioch (pl. 31.258).[34] Denarii and Antiochene tetradrachmae circulated as the preferred coins on both sides of the boundary that cut the Fertile Crescent into Roman and Parthian halves down to the Severan age.[35] Arsacid kings, habitually short of hard cash, counted on imported Roman coins to sustain their own silver coinage. Parthian coins did not penetrate Roman markets because merchants would have exchanged their money into aurei and denarii at bourses in Charax or Seleucia ad Tigrim rather than face unfavorable rates for the Parthian drachma in Antioch and Tyre. Tariffing of silver coins and the dynamics of trade in the Fertile Crescent probably resulted in many aurei and denarii streaming back into the Roman Empire.

Aurei and denarii that escaped reminting by Parthian kings or were not returned to Rome passed farther east to cities of Central

Asia and northern India. Early in the first century, Kushan emperors united the Tocharian nomads who had swept away the Greek political order in Bactria, and welded together an empire embracing Central Asia, eastern Iran, Afghanistan, Pakistan, and northwestern India. They controlled the crossroads of Eurasia, rich gold deposits in the Punjab and Kashmir, and alluvial gold fields in the Gangetic Valley. Vima Kadphises (ca. 78–126) introduced a gold stater (pl. 32.265)—almost equal in weight (7.9 g) and purity to the Augustan aureus—and a chain of fractions based on a bronze drachma (17 g; pl. 32.266).[36] Iranian-speaking Sogdians in Transoxiana, the lands between the Oxus (Amu Darya) and Jaxertes (Syr Darya), struck as silver trade coins Attic-weight tetradrachmae copied after Seleucid and Bactrian originals that circulated widely until ousted by Sassanid dirhems in the late fourth century (pl. 32.267).[37] The fate of Roman coins in Kushan domains is unclear because, with the exception of the excavations at Taxila, few efforts have been made to publish finds. British travelers of the nineteenth century, however, reported that Indo-Greek and Roman coins were sold as old gold or silver in the bazaars of Pakistan and northwestern India.[38] Stylistic and iconographic features of the copper coins of Kujula Kadphises (ca. 45–64) and staters of Kanishka I (ca. 128–51) point to familiarity with aurei and denarii that must have been gained in trade. Aurei could circulate at par with Kushan staters, as suggested by the three aurei found in a hoard unearthed near Jalalabad in Afghanistan, but aurei and denarii were likely reminted into Kushan gold staters and Sogdian tetradrachmae, respectively.[39] The same probably was true for Roman coins arriving by sea at the ports of Barbaricum and Pattala at the mouths of the Indus, which acknowledged Indo-Parthian kings of Taxila in the early first century and Kushan emperors from the late first to mid-third centuries. If Kushan emperors reminted imported coin as policy, many Roman merchants would have avoided coin in favor of other commodities. Pausanias apparently refers to such transactions at Kushan ports: "The sailors on ships that go to India say that the Indians will give produce in exchange for a Greek cargo, but coins are meaningless to them, even though they have an enormous amount of gold and bronze ones."[40]

It is unlikely that Roman gold and silver reached Han China in any significiant quantity, even though Pliny the Elder asserts that the Chinese (known to him as Seres) were the ultimate beneficiaries of the specie drain. Aurei and denarii (or any other Roman wares) have not been recovered from any of the thousands of Han graves in China or burials of Central Asia. Commerce between the two great empires of Rome and China was in the hands of middlemen, even though Han armies imposed Chinese overlordship upon nomads straddling the Tarim Basin. The Han court presumably saw aurei and denarii, for the chronicle of *Hou-han-shu*, written in the fifth century, preserves what purports to be a description of the Roman Empire (Ta-t'sin) based on envoys received from An-tun (Marcus Aurelius) in 166.

> The country contains much gold, silver, and rare precious stones. . . . They make coins of gold and silver. Ten units of silver are worth one of gold. They traffic by sea with An-shi [Parthia] and T'ien-chu [India], the profit of which trade is tenfold. . . . They are honest in their transactions, and there are no double prices. Cereals are always cheap. The budget is based on a well-filled treasury. When embassies of neighboring countries come to their frontier, they are driven by post to the capital, and, upon arrival, are presented with golden money.[41]

Roman coins and wares were novelties to Chinese of the late second century; in large part, aurei and denarii were also prized by (and useful to) Parthians, Sogdians, Kushans, Arabians, and Indians.

Pliny the Elder, writing under Vespasian, gave a false air of precision to stock Stoic complaints that luxury bred indolence by asserting that 13.75 million denarii (550,000 aurei or nearly 12,225 pounds of gold)—a figure possibly inferred from imperial customs receipts—were sent to India each year to buy gems and spices. He also claimed that total payments to Arabia Felix, India, and China topped 25 million denarii (1 million aurei or nearly 22,225 pounds of gold).[42] Over 1,350 aurei and 6,000 denarii dating from the Augustan to the Severan ages have been published from finds in central and southern India—the lands that figure prominently in *Periplus*, a manual composed by an Alexandrine Greek merchant in about A.D. 40. The *Periplus* and Roman geographers paint a picture of commerce in the Erythraean Sea quite different from impressions gained from complaints in Pliny, Dio Chrysostom, and Tacitus. On the eve of the first century B.C., Greek sailors from Egypt learned how to use the monsoons to navigate the Arabian Sea. The Greek geographer Strabo, visiting Egypt in ca. 25–19 B.C., noted that the number of ships bound for India from the port of Myos Hormos had risen by sixfold, from 20 each year to 120.[43] The imperial aristocracy at Rome offered a market for eastern luxuries that turned voyages of discovery into regular commerce with India. Private fortunes were to be made, and imperial officials augmented considerably customs receipts. The capital investment and organization required for Roman trade in the Erythraean Sea could have only been sustained if it were a profitable venture—a trade circuit benefiting all participants. Otherwise, it is difficult to explain why it lasted over 250 years and, then, was revived in the fourth century.

Roman merchantmen docked at a number of ports on the Red Sea and Gulf of Aden en route to India. They sailed to Muza, the Himyarite capital on the coast of Arabia Felix (North Yemen), to purchase frankincense and myrrh. The rapid growth of Roman trade on the Erythraean Sea drew the Arabian ports of present Yemen into the Roman economic orbit. Himyarite sheiks discouraged the export of their hard-earned specie, reminting denarii into fractional denominations based on a half of the denarius (pl. 32.262–63).[44] The Himyarite trading stations on Pemba Island and at Rhapta on the coast of Azania (modern Tanzania) funneled more denarii spent on the East African coast back to the royal mint at Muza. Himyarite prosperity depended on commerce with Rome; once the Erythraean trade waned in the early third century, the reserves amassed in trade proved insufficient to sustain a currency.

Roman merchants spent heavily in Indian ports dotting the western shores from Barygaza (Broach) to Muziris (Cranganore). In the first century, native vendors and moneychangers eagerly accepted aurei and denarii over aged Greco-Bactrian drachmae (struck 175 to 150 years earlier), base Greek-style and Mauryan punch-marked karshapanas, and square copper, potin, and lead fractions. Hoards and stray finds of denarii, totaling over 6,000 specimens, are almost exclusively Julio-Claudian issues, with the overwhelming majority being Augustan pieces with Gaius and Lucius Caesars on the reverse (pl. 8.54) or Tiberian ones with a seated goddess. Virtually all denarii have been found in Indian states south of Kristna River—Mysore, Kerala, Madras, and the southern districts of Andhra and Madhya Pradesh—due to the efforts of the British Colonial Service. The native punch-marked coins were so base and variable in weight that denarii of Augustus and Tiberius became the preferred medium in regional trade between 5 B.C. and A.D. 70. Julio-Claudian aurei, most of the same Augustan and Tiberian designs, circulated along with the denarii, but soon after the Neronian recoinage in 64–68 only aurei struck at 45 to the Roman pound were imported as late as 215.[45]

Romans flocked to the port of Barygaza (modern Broach at the mouth of the Narbada River and on the Gulf of Cambay opposite the Saurashtra peninsula), just beyond Kushan domains, to buy Chinese silks, Indian cottons, ivory, gems, and spices. In the last quarter of the first century, Satavahana rulers who dominated Barygaza and her hinterland covering western Madhya Pradesh and northern Bombay perhaps reminted Greco-Bactrian drachmae and denarii into punch-marked karshapanas because few finds of Roman coins have been reported in this region.[46] Few Roman goods and coins reached Paithana (modern Paithan), seat of the Andhran Empire in the Telagu country of the northern Deccan, whose rulers struck bronze and lead fractions for local consumption. From Barygaza, Roman vessels made for ports on the Malabar coast in the Tamil-speaking lands of the far south where gold and silver were in high demand.

Romans purchased spices (pepper and malabathrum) and gems (beryls, diamonds, and sapphires) at Muziris (Cranganore) and Nelkynda (Kuttanadu), the principal ports of the Chera and Pandya kingdoms, respectively. They obtained Chinese silks at Cholan ports, such as Korkai and Kaveripatanam, on the Coromandel coast. By the reign of Claudius (41–54), Romans also opened direct trade with Taprobane (Sri Lanka), but few Roman coins dated prior to the fourth century have surfaced on the isle.[47] The numerous aurei and denarii unearthed in the Chera and Pandya kingdoms reflect the volume of Roman commerce. Many specimens suffered wear, apparently from heavy use in native markets; others were pierced or bent for mounting in jewelry. Tamil monarchs saved as treasure rather than reminted the fine gold and silver coins brought by Yavanas ("Ionians" or Greek-speaking westerners). Their subjects trusted denarii of Augustus as pure silver. When denarii of this type were unavailable in the late first century, Tamils accepted only aurei, red coral, and fine wares in exchange for pepper and gems.[48] Southern Indians, although conducting most trade with foreigners by barter, learned to use aurei and denarii as trade coins.

The total of aurei and denarii from published Indian finds falls far short of those found in Dacia or Germany. Some Indians struck imitations of denarii based on Augustan prototypes in the later first century and of aurei from the second through early fourth centuries, and others cut deep slashes across the imperial portrait on aurei, virtually halving the coins so the damage would discourage merchants from accepting them for export back to the Roman West or eastward toward the Chinese world. Most denarii found in a large hoard from Pudukota were defaced by chiseling out the imperial visage and counterstamping with punch marks, perhaps so that the coins were acceptable for use among followers of aniconic Hinayana Buddhism dwelling in the Krishna Valley during the first century (pl. 31.255).[49]

The impact of Roman coins upon the economic life of central and southern India was uneven. Indians, just like the Germans, manufactured copies of Roman coins for decorative arts as much as for money. They too depended upon imported specie, and their striking of imitative pieces and the measures taken to prevent the export of aurei suggest that imported coins were insufficient for local needs. Kingdoms south of the Narbada River outside the Kushan or later Gupta empires failed to amass from trade bullion sufficient to maintain a native currency in gold or silver. They minted base silver fractions and token copper and lead coins betraying no influence of Roman weight standards or types. The currency of kingdoms in central and southern India rested upon the demand of Roman markets for their luxuries, and as commerce between India and the Mediterranean world contracted and fell off, these kingdoms first reduced and then, in the seventh century, suspended minting coins for nearly four centuries.

*Decline and Revival of Long-Distance Trade, 235–650*

The might and prosperity of imperial Rome fostered trade across the Eurasian continent during the Principate, but conditions rapidly changed after 235. The military crisis that compelled emperors to debase the currency, and so to fuel inflation, forever altered commerce and the use of Roman coins beyond the imperial frontiers. The emergence of the Sassanids, who overthrew the Parthians and subjected the Kushans, profoundly affected trade and currency east of the Euphrates. Roman and Sassanid armies clashed over the Fertile Crescent and Armenia throughout the third and fourth centuries, and they renewed the struggle with greater ferocity in the sixth and early seventh centuries. Campaigns of the shahs Ardashir (224–40) and Shapur I (240–70) disrupted the network of Aramaean communities so vital to trade in the Fertile Crescent. The armies of Shapur ravaged Roman cities in Mesopotamia, Syria, and eastern Asia Minor, and twice, in 253 and again in 260, sacked Antioch. Roman armies in turn invaded and sacked Ctesiphon so that by the time of Julian's campaign in 363, Sassanid Babylonia was a borderland bristling with fortifications rather than dotted with cosmopolitan commercial centers. The sacks of Bostra and Palmyra in the Roman Civil Wars of 270–73 and raids by nomadic Nobades and Blemmyes against caravans passing between Coptos and the Red Sea ports impaired trade in the Persian Gulf and Erythraean Sea.

Once the shahs Ardashir and Shapur I brought their Kushan foes to heel, the rich gold and silver deposits in Central Asia henceforth fed Sassanid mints. Ardashir resurrected the Augustan aureus and denarius in Iranian guise as gold dinars (8.1 g) and fine silver dirhems (4 g and 93 percent fine) with Zoroastrian iconography and Pahlavian legends (pl. 32.260).[50] The dirhems (pl. 32.261), by weight a drachma, approached in size (25–30 mm) a trade coin, a tetradrachma, because they were struck on wide, thin flans cut from sheets of rolled metal—a manufacturing technique transmitted to the medieval world. As Roman emperors rapidly debased the aureus and denarius, the Sassanid heavy dinar and dirhem circulated as the prime trade coins from the Fertile Crescent to Central Asia, supplanting Sogdian tetradrachmae and Kushano-Sassanid coins by 375. The Chonites, Hun allies of Shapur II, and the Hephthalites or "White Huns" (who overran Sassanid frontiers in Transoxiana during the fifth century) popularized dirhems on the steppes of Turkestan. Sogdian merchants carried Sassanid and Hephthalite imitative dirhems to Turks in the Tarim Basin and Chinese of the western provinces, where dirhems were interred in graves by the mid-fifth century.[51]

Constantine's solidus reestablished the reputation of imperial money in international trade. Shah Barham IV (388–99) discontinued the Sassanid heavy dinar in favor of a lighter one struck on the same standard as the solidus (4.5 g). Procopius later claimed that "while the Persian king is accustomed to make silver coinage as he likes, still it is not considered right for him or any other sovereign in the whole barbarian world to imprint his own likeness on a gold stater [i.e., solidus]."[52] The solidus facilitated the revival of eastern commerce between the fourth and seventh centuries as Aramaic, Levantine Greek, and Sogdian merchants adjusted to new conditions and resumed trade along familiar patterns.

After the suspension of commerce between India and the Mediterranean world during the third century, Roman merchantmen returned to their old haunts on the Gulf of Aden and the western shores of India in the early fourth century, but they found that the Axumite emperors of northwestern Ethiopia had gained control of the ports on the Somalian and Yemenite coasts. Axumite emperors minted their own tiny gold coins from East African metal that circulated on both sides of the Horn of Africa as fractions of solidi imported from the fourth through sixth centuries (pl. 32.264).[53] In the fourth century, Roman traders also returned to the Indian ports to purchase spices, gems, cottons, and raw silk. Cosmas Indicopleustes, who traveled to India during the early sixth century, remarked on the wide acceptance of the solidus; Roman merchants must have circumvented imperial edicts banning the export of specie as readily as their counterparts in the sixteenth and seventeenth centuries ignored similar regulations of the Spanish Crown.[54] Solidi have surfaced at Taprobane (Sri Lanka), where Romans bought pepper and pearls; many Constantinian nummi of AE3 module, maiorinae of 348–52, and nummi minimi of the fifth century were also imported and imitated. In southern India, a large hoard of solidi deposited in ca. 525 was unearthed at Pudankavu, Travancore, in the heart of the Pandya Kingdom which Roman merchants had long frequented for gems and spices.[55] The Gupta emperors in northern India, like their Kushan predecessors, probably reminted solidi received in trade.

Justinian (527–65) and his successors sought alliances with Axumite emperors and Turkomens of Central Asia to assure access to silk should war with Persia disrupt caravans across Iran or traffic in the Arabian Sea. In 551/2, Nestorian monks brought to Constantinople the knowledge of sericulture from Gupta India, but the demand for silk in Constantinople outstripped home-grown supplies so that Roman merchants continued to import silk from Arabian, Indian, and Sogdian middlemen.[56] Hence solidi and barbarous imitations passed along caravan routes linking the Tarim Basin to western China during the late sixth and seventh centuries.[57] The cultivation of silk worms in the eastern Mediterranean increased Byzantine profits from the sale of silk vestments to the Germanic West, and this trade steadily emptied Western Europe of its gold specie to the benefit of the New Rome during the seventh and eighth centuries.

The most serious drain of specie from the Roman Empire came from tribute, subsidies, and diplomatic payments rendered to barbarian invaders and Sassanid shahs. The emperors Valentinian I and Valens banned the export of gold and silver to curtail the flow of specie to Northern Europe. Since many Germans purchased foodstuffs, wines, and fancy Roman wares, any drain of specie probably did not become serious until the collapse of the Roman West after 395. Alaric and his Visigoths extorted gold from the courts at Constantinople and Ravenna, disrupted mining in the Balkans during their migration to Italy, and, in 410, pried a ransom from Rome of 5,000 pounds in gold (360,000 solidi) and 30,000 pounds in silver; the Vandals hauled off more rich spoils in their sack of Rome in

455.[58] Plunder was immobilized in royal coffers as ancestral treasures and consequently lost as circulating money for centuries. The Eastern emperor Theodosius II paid Attila and his Huns the first substantial annual tributes in imperial history. The total tribute payments imposed by three humiliating treaties between 422 and 450 were at least 1,335,600 solidi and, in addition, numerous captives were ransomed at rates of 8 to 12 solidi per head.[59] Marcian (451–57) ended payments to Attila, but he settled the Ostrogoths as federate allies in Pannonia in 454, offering a yearly subsidy of 300 pounds of gold (21,600 solidi). King Theodoric and his Ostrogoths received at least 2,304,000 solidi before they departed for Italy in 489.[60] Lombards and Avars posed the principal threats to Byzantine Italy and the Balkans between the reigns of Justin II (565–78) and Constans II (641–68). The Lombards extorted large payments from Phocas and Heraclius, for each negotiated armistice at rates of 12,000 to 36,000 solidi.[61] The Avars, dominating the steppes stretching from the Middle Danube to the Lower Volga and northern slopes of the Caucasus, proved such useful allies and dangerous foes that they received at least 2.8 million solidi in imperial subsidies between 574 and 623.[62]

The Eastern emperors purchased political survival at onerous rates, but it is difficult to judge how much subsidies, ransoms, and plunder seized by barbarians reduced the money supply of the Eastern Roman Empire. Theodosius II and Marcian, despite large payments, each amassed a reserve of 100,000 pounds of gold (7.2 million solidi), and emperors withheld payments of subsidies at the first opportunity. Germanic raiders, without a commissariat, spent solidi on necessities at high prices in provincial markets. Although they acquired Roman gold, East Germans, Scandinavians, Huns, and Avars failed to pick up Roman monetary habits. The large hoards of solidi secreted in Scandinavia, Eastern Europe, and the Balkans from the fifth to seventh centuries represent only a fraction of these windfalls that failed to monetize the economic life of barbarians dwelling north of the Roman Empire.[63] Barbarian rulers preferred ostentatious objects such as cords worked with gold, couches, silk garments, well-wrought plate, gems, and spices which they either purchased with solidi or demanded as gifts valued in so many solidi. East Germanic and Scandinavian craftsmen mounted solidi and gold medallions in jewelry, used them as models for decorative arts, or melted them to alloy with silver and cast as plate. Germanic invaders settling in the western provinces and Hun or Avar khans who took up residence on the Danube near modern Budapest spent much of their gold with Roman merchants who flocked to buy captives and booty and offer expensive wares. In short, the flow of specie in subsidies and plunder out of the eastern Roman world was offset by an even greater return of gold to Constantinople that emptied Western and Central Europe of most of its gold by 700. The money supply of the Roman world did contract, but the shrinkage was felt most acutely in the former provinces of northwestern Europe, the Iberian peninsula, and finally Italy, rather than in the Eastern Roman Empire which had paid off the invaders. The flow of solidi across imperial frontiers, and back, from 400 to 700, concentrated gold in the eastern Mediterranean until the opening of the thirteenth century, and thereby reversed the decision of 200–30 B.C. that had put Rome and Italy at the center of the economy of the Mediterranean world.

Rome suffered her most humiliating losses of gold to Sassanid Persia, but emperors attempted to avoid the odium of rendering annual tribute to the shah by offering bulk payments. In 244 Philip I negotiated a disgraceful peace with Shah Shapur I to the tune of 500,000 aurei, probably Severan pieces minted at 50 to the pound or the equivalent of 10,000 pounds of gold.[64] The emperors Anastasius and Justinian each opted to buy out of ruinous Persian Wars. In 505–13, Anastasius paid under treaty to Shah Kavad I seven installments and the ransom of the cities of Amida and Edessa to the tune of 6,500 pounds of gold (468,000 solidi) or two-thirds of the sum that Philip I had promised to Shapur I in 244.[65] Justinian, in order to free his armies to reconquer the western provinces, negotiated the most costly treaties in Roman history. Shah Khusrau I obtained nearly 1.6 million solidi (22,150 pounds of gold) over the course of thirty years (532–62), which he used, not to strike a major gold currency, but to meet his own diplomatic and military costs in trans-Caucasia and southern Russia.[66] Imperial diplomatic costs during the sixth century should be put in perspective, because the total was but a fraction, 9 percent and 7 percent respectively, of the great reserves of 320,000 and 400,000 pounds of gold amassed by Anastasius and Justin I. Diplomacy cost far less than war. Since Iran was a silver-consuming region, its gold to silver ratios could well have been higher than the rates of 1:14.4 to 1:18 that prevailed in the Roman world during the fifth and sixth centuries, so that many solidi entering the Sassanid Empire could be exported back to the Roman world at a profit.

Roman coins regained their international primacy in the fourth century with the recovery of long-distance commerce. The reputation of the solidus depended foremost upon the return of fiscal and monetary stability and on the wealth and social needs of the Roman elite who backed ventures and provided so much of the market demand. Success rested too on the solidus itself. Procopius reports that the Frankish king Theodebert, upon capturing Marseilles in 537, dared to strike solidi in his own name, but his solidi failed to gain acceptance in markets because it was not considered proper for any barbarian sovereign "to imprint his own likeness on a gold stater, and that, too, though he has gold in his kingdom, for they are unable to tender the coin to those with whom they transact business, even though the parties concerned in the transaction happen to be barbarians."[67] For the next six centuries Byzantines and barbarians refused to accept any gold coin in trade that was not a legitimate solidus or "besant."

It was, however, a conditional revival, perhaps even survival, of long-distance trade that reflected the contraction of Roman prosperity. The most grievous blows dealt to Roman coinage were not specie drains but rather internal monetary crises during the third and fourth centuries that eroded Roman money and monetary ways. As humiliating as tribute payments were for the Romans, still the Germanic kings, nomadic khans, and Sassanid shahs spent their windfalls of solidi. Long-distance commerce in 300–650 ensured, however tenuously, that Roman notions of coined money survived in the barbarian West, and so contributed to the revival of trade and spread of coinage beyond the limits of the Roman Empire between the ninth and thirteenth centuries.

## *The Return of Coins to the Empire*

The export of aurei and denarii to the Far East reflected the vigor of Roman commerce and great purchasing power of imperial money rather than a drain of specie. In lands where few or no native coins were minted such as Germanic Europe, the Caucasus, or southern and central India, Roman coins circulated as trade coins in regional and international commerce. Elsewhere, as in the Parthian and Küshan empires and the Himyarite Kingdom of Arabia, Roman coins were exchanged against or reminted into local currency. Two flows of gold bullion ran opposite to the export of specie. First, Rome fell heir to the trans-Saharan trade that had fed gold to Carthage. Although the Romans facilitated desert travel by introducing the camel, the Garamantes, ancestors of the Berbers, controlled the caravans across the Sahara that conveyed gold from mine fields in West Africa to the Romano-Punic towns on the Tunisian and Libyan coasts. East African gold entered the Roman Empire each year, either by caravans passing down the Nile Valley from the mines of Meroe (northern Sudan) or on board Roman merchantmen calling at ports on the Somalian and Kenyan coasts.[68]

Even more important was the return flow of aurei, denarii, and, in the Fertile Crescent, Syrian tetradrachmae into the Roman world due to war and commerce. Trajan seized vast stocks of denarii in Dacia, and legions captured many coins and treasures whenever they sacked Parthian cities in Babylonia. Punitive expeditions against restless northern barbarians must have repeatedly carried gold and silver back to the Roman world. Far greater numbers of coins returned in commerce. This movement of specie in trade is difficult to document, but Roman coins, given their unmatched purity and numbers, were surely the preferred trade coins of the Eurasian continent for over 250 years. If many aurei and denarii ended up in melting pots or were reminted into exotic foreign coins, virtually none of their eastern competitors, mostly issued for local or regional use, has surfaced at Roman sites. Imperial customs officials did not need to impose strict currency regulations at the frontiers, because exchange rates in Roman markets put foreign coins at a disadvantage. Foreign merchants, whenever possible, obtained aurei and denarii from moneychangers in cities such as Charax, Seleucia ad Tigrim, Antiochia Margiane, or Barygaza, before venturing west. Cosmas Indicopleustes, writing of an incident in the early sixth century, conveys the respect accorded Roman coins. When a rajah of Taprobane challenged a Roman envoy and a Sassanid envoy to prove the superior wealth and power of his master, the Roman easily won the contest by producing a golden solidus, while his Persian opponent could offer only a silver dirhem.[69] The great sovereigns of the East as much as German tribesmen paid homage to Roman coins by imitation, adoption of Roman weight standards, and adaptation of imperial iconography. Roman coins enabled merchants to buy into distant Asian markets, thereby priming economic growth at home and abroad, further monetizing fiscal and commercial life in the Roman world, and exporting Roman monetary habits and coins. The imperial government too profited from this international trade, levying customs duties of 25 percent on the value of imported eastern luxuries and tolls payable in imperial money. The aurei and denarii, carried by merchants in search of profit or granted as rewards to dutiful allies, marked the triumph, not the demise, of Roman imperial currency.

# Appendix

# Weights and Measures in the Roman World

### *Weights*

The Roman pound (*libra*) is reckoned at 322.5 grams divided into 12 ounces (*uncia*). An *uncia* is reckoned as 26.875 grams.

### *Measures of Capacity*

Romans measured dry capacity (grain) by the modius (8.62 liters or approximately 1 peck; by weight nearly 6.67 kilograms or 14.67 pounds) and wet capacity (oil and wine) by the amphora (26.2 liters or nearly 7 gallons). In markets, oil and wine were customarily cited by the sextarius (0.546 liters or just under 1 pint) and dry foodstuffs by the sextarius (0.539 liters).

| DRY MEASURES | LIQUID MEASURES |
|---|---|
| 1 modius = 16 sextarii | 1 culleus = 20 amphorae |
| 1 sextarius = 16 cyathi | 1 amphora = 48 sextarii |
| | 1 sextarius = 16 cyathi |

In the Price Edict (A.D. 301), many foodstuffs are priced in terms of the modius castrensis, equivalent to 1.5 modii.

Greeks measured dry capacity (grain) by the medimnos (52.5 liters or nearly 6 pecks; by weight 25 kilograms or 55 pounds) and wet capacity (wine or oil) by the metretes (nearly 39 liters or 10.2 gallons). In markets, oil and wine were usually cited in the kotyle (0.27 liters) and dry foodstuffs in the choenix (1.087 liters).

DRY MEASURES

1 medimnos = 48 choenikes = 192 kotylai
1 choenix = 4 kotylai = 24 kyathoi
1 kotyle = 6 kyathoi

LIQUID MEASURES

1 metretes = 12 choes = 144 kotylai = 864 kyathoi
1 chous = 12 kotylai = 72 kyathoi
1 kotyle = 6 kyathoi

The Attic medimnos was reckoned as equivalent to 6 Roman modii and 1 kotyle was reckoned as equal to one-half sextarius. For liquid measures, the Attic metretes equaled 1.5 Roman amphora and 1 kotyle was reckoned as one-half sextarius.

In Egypt, grain was measured by the artaba (38.78 liters or 4.4 pecks; by weight nearly 30 kilograms or 66 pounds). The Roman army reckoned 10 artabai of grain as equivalent to 45 modii of grain. Wine and oil were reckoned by ceramion. The ceramion monochoron is reckoned as 7.2 liters; it was subdivided into 36 kotylai (0.2 liters each). Multiple jars such as ceramion dichoron (14.4 liters) are commonly cited.

In Syria, grain was reckoned by the *sea* or, more often, by its sixth the cab (2.16 liters or nearly 0.25 peck; by weight nearly 1.67 kilograms or 3.67 pounds). The cab was divided into 24 log or xestae (0.546 liters). Four cab were customarily reckoned to the Roman modius.

The *metron* was the indefinite term "measure" used to translate an unfamiliar unit of measurement. Cicero (*Ad Fam.* 12. 13. 4) and the emperor Julian (*Misop*. 369A), who reckoned by the Roman modius, employed *metron* to translate the cab of Syria. Josephus (*Ant. Jud*. 16. 2. 2) and Eusebius (*HE* 9. 8), natives of the Levant who measured by the cab, employed it to translate the Roman modius.

# PLATES

*PLATE 1*

*Monetization of Roman Italy, 500–200 B.C.*

1. Neapolis, Campania, didrachma, ca. 350–300 B.C., 7.36 g, American Numismatic Society = *SNGANS* 401
2. Taras (Tarentum), Calabria, didrachma, ca. 272–238 B.C., 6.39 g, American Numismatic Society = *SNGANS* 1160
3. Roman Republic, didrachma (heavy denarius), Rome mint, ca. 310–300 B.C., 7.26 g, Crawford, *RRC* I, p. 133, no. 13/1, American Numismatic Society
4. Roman Republic, didrachma (heavy denarius), Rome mint, ca. 269–264 B.C., 7.41 g, Crawford, *RRC* I, p. 134, no. 15/1a, American Numismatic Society
5. Roman Republic, didrachma (heavy denarius), Rome mint, ca. 269–264 B.C., 7.24 g, Crawford, *RRC* I, p. 137, no. 20/1, American Numismatic Society
6. Roman Republic, didrachma (heavy denarius), Rome mint, ca. 264–241 B.C., 6.47 g, Crawford, *RRC* I, p. 138, no. 22/1, American Numismatic Society
7. Roman Republic, didrachma (heavy denarius), Rome mint, ca. 264–241 B.C., 6.38 g, Crawford, *RRC* I, p. 141, no. 25/1, American Numismatic Society
8. Roman Republic, didrachma (heavy denarius), Rome mint, ca. 264–241 B.C., 6.68 g, Crawford, *RRC* I, p. 142, no. 26/1, American Numismatic Society

9. Roman Republic, drachma (quinarius), Rome mint, ca. 264–241 B.C., 3.26 g, Crawford, *RRC* I, p. 142, no. 26/2, American Numismatic Society

10. Roman Republic, didrachma (heavy denarius), Rome mint, ca. 261–241 B.C., 6.66 g, Crawford, *RRC* I, p. 143, no. 27/1, American Numismatic Society

*PLATE 2*

*Monetization of Roman Italy, 500–200 B.C.*

11. Roman Republic, quadrigatus, Rome mint, 218–214 B.C., 6.48 g, Crawford, *RRC* I, p. 143, no. 29/3, American Numismatic Society

12. Roman Republic, aureus, Rome mint, 217–216 B.C., 6.87 g, Crawford, *RRC* I, p. 145, no. 29/1, American Numismatic Society

13. Roman Republic, aureus of 60 asses, Rome mint, 212–209 B.C., 3.35 g, Crawford, *RRC* I, p. 154, no. 44/2, American Numismatic Society

14. Roman Republic, aureus of 30 asses, Rome mint, 212–209 B.C., 2.23 g, Crawford, *RRC* I, p. 154, no. 44/3, American Numismatic Society

15. Roman Republic, aureus of 20 asses, Rome mint, 212–209 B.C., 1.12 g, Crawford, *RRC* I, p. 154, no. 44/4, American Numismatic Society

16. Roman Republic, denarius, Rome mint, 213–212 B.C., 3.78 g, Crawford, *RRC* I, p. 155, no. 44/5, American Numismatic Society

17. Roman Republic, quinarius, Rome mint, 213–212 B.C., 2.26 g, Crawford, *RRC* I, p. 155, no. 44/6, American Numismatic Society

18. Roman Republic, sestertius, Rome mint, 213–212 B.C., 1.05 g, Crawford, *RRC* I, p. 155, no. 44/7, American Numismatic Society

19. Roman Republic, victoriatus, Rome mint, 213–212 B.C., 3.16 g, Crawford, *RRC* I, p. 154, no. 53/1, American Numismatic Society

20. Populonia, Etruria, gold fraction of 25 asses, 215–212 B.C., 1.39 g, American Numismatic Society = *SNGANS* 5

21. Populonia, Etruria, didrachma of 20 asses, 215–212 B.C., 7.96 g, American Numismatic Society = *SNGANS* 80

22. Populonia, Etruria, drachma of 10 asses, 215–212 B.C., 3.95 g, American Numismatic Society = *SNGANS* 26

*PLATE 3*
*Monetization of Roman Italy, 500–200 B.C.*

23. Roman Republic, libral as, Rome mint, ca. 300–270 B.C., 336.95 g, Crawford, *RRC* I, p. 123, no. 14/1, American Numismatic Society

*PLATE 4*
*Monetization of Roman Italy, 500–200 B.C.*

24. Roman Republic, reduced libral as, Rome mint, 241–217 B.C., 252.59 g, Crawford, *RRC* I, p. 147, no. 35/1, American Numismatic Society

*PLATE 5*
*Monetization of Roman Italy, 500–200 B.C.*

25. Roman Republic, quadranal as, Luceria mint, 214–212 B.C., 81.81 g, Crawford, *RRC* I, p. 153, no. 43/1, American Numismatic Society

26. Roman Republic, sextanal as, Rome mint, 211–210 B.C., 49.75 g, Crawford, *RRC* I, p. 158, no. 56/2, American Numismatic Society

27. Roman Republic, quadranal semis, Luceria mint, 214–212 B.C., 26.01 g, Crawford, *RRC* I, p. 153, no. 43/3a, American Numismatic Society

28. Roman Republic, quadranal triens Luceria mint, 214–212 B.C., 10.63 g, Crawford, *RRC* I, p. 154, no. 43/4, American Numismatic Society

29. Roman Republic, sextanal semis, Rome mint, 211–210 B.C., 17.06 g, Crawford, *RRC* I, p. 158, no. 56/3, American Numismatic Society

30. Roman Republic, uncial as, Rome mint, ca. 165 B.C., 27.03 g, Crawford, *RRC* I, p. 397, no. 184/19, American Numismatic Society

31. Roman Republic, semuncial as, Rome mint, 91–90 B.C., 12.22 g, Crawford, *RRC* I, p. 388, no. 337/5, American Numismatic Society

*PLATE 6*

*The Denarius and Overseas Expansion, 200–30 B.C.*

32. Roman Republic, aureus, L. Cornelius Sulla, Rome mint, 81–79 B.C., Crawford, *RRC* I, p. 397, no. 381/a, and II, pl. XLVIII

33. Roman Republic, aureus minted by Caesarian prefect A. Hirtius, Rome mint, 46 B.C., 8.13 g, Crawford, *RRC* I, p. 478, no. 466/1, American Numismatic Society

34. Roman Republic, aureus, Octavian and divus Julius Caesar, Rome mint, 43 B.C., 8.1 g, Crawford, *RRC* I, p. 500, no. 490/2, American Numismatic Society

35. Roman Republic, aureus, M. Junius Brutus, eastern mint, 44–42 B.C., Crawford, *RRC* I, p. 517, no. 507/1b, and II, pl. LXI

36. Roman Republic, denarius, Rome mint, ca. 167–160 B.C., 3.72 g, Crawford, *RRC* I, p. 246, no. 200/1, American Numismatic Society

37. Roman Republic, denarius with value mark XVI, Rome

mint, 141 B.C., 3.64 g, Crawford, *RRC* I, p. 260, no. 224/1, American Numismatic Society

38. Roman Republic, quinarius, Rome mint, 98 B.C., 1.83 g, Crawford, *RRC* I, p. 331, no. 332/19, American Numismatic Society

39. Italian insurgents, denarius minted by C. Papius, 90–88 B.C., 3.53 g, Sydenham, *Coinage of Roman Republic*, p. 94, no. 641, American Numismatic Society

40. Roman Republic, serrate denarius, Rome mint, 79 B.C., 3.63 g, Crawford, *RRC* I, p. 397, no. 382/1b, American Numismatic Society

41. Roman Republic, denarius, Julius Caesar, Rome mint, 44 B.C., 3.69 g, Crawford, *RRC* I, p. 488, no. 480/3, American Numismatic Society

42. Roman Republic, legionary denarius, Mark Antony, eastern mint, 32–31 B.C., 3.72 g, Crawford, *RRC* I, p. 546, no. 544/8, American Numismatic Society

43. Roman Republic, dupondius issued by Caesarian prefect C. Clovius, uncertain Italian mint, 45 B.C., 16.01 g, Crawford, *RRC* I, p. 486, no. 476/1a, American Numismatic Society

44. Roman Republic, dupondius, Octavian and divus Julius Caesar, uncertain Italian mint, ca. 38–35 B.C., 20.6 g, Crawford, *RRC* I, p. 535, no. 535/1, American Numismatic Society

*PLATE 7*

*The Denarius and Overseas Expansion, 200–30 B.C.*

45. Roman Republic, sestertius, issued by Antonian legate L. Sempronius Atratinus, Corinth, 38–37 B.C., 20.62 g, Amandry, *RSN* 65 (1986), 81, no. 8, pl. II. 8

46. Macedonia, Republic A, tetradrachma, Amphipolis mint,

158–150 B.C., 16.87 g, H. Gaebler, *Die antiken Münzen Nordgriechenlands* (Berlin, 1906), III, p. 57, no. 176, American Numismatic Society

47. Macedonia, Roman province, tetradrachma, in name of quaestor Aesillas, Amphipolis mint, ca. 95–60 B.C., 16.6 g, Gaebler, *Antiken Münzen Nordgriechenlands* III, p. 70, no. 217, American Numismatic Society

48. Imitative Athenian tetradrachma, issued by L. Licinius Lucullus, 87–84 B.C., 14.25 g, Thompson, *New Style Coinage of Athens*, p. 427, no. 1301a = American Numismatic Society

49. Asia, Roman province, cistophorus, Pergamum mint, 95–67 B.C., 12.30 g, American Numismatic Society

50. Cilicia, Roman province, cistophorus, issued by M. Tullius Cicero, Laodicea ad Lycum mint, 51–50 B.C., 11.38 g, American Numismatic Society

51. Syria, Roman province, pseudo-Seleucid tetradrachma in name of Philip I Philadelphus (93–83 B.C.), Antioch mint, 45/4 B.C., 15.18 g, American Numismatic Society

*PLATE 8*
*The Augustan Coinage, 30 B.C.–A.D. 235*

52. Augustus (31 B.C.–A.D. 14), aureus, Rome mint, ca. 19–18 B.C., 7.93 g, *RIC* $I^2$ , p. 83, no. 521 = *BMCRE* I, p. 100, no. 680, American Numismatic Society

53. Augustus (31 B.C.–A.D. 14), gold quinarius, Spanish mint, ca. 18–16 B.C., 3.94 G, *RIC* $I^2$, p. 49, no. 121 = *BMCRE* I, p. 73, no. 424, American Numismatic Society

54. Augustus (31 B.C.–A.D. 14), denarius, Lugdunum mint, 6 B.C.–A.D.4, 3.78 g, *RIC* $I^2$, p. 49, no. 207 = *BMCRE* I, p. 73, no. 533, American Numismatic Society

55. Augustus (31 B.C.–A.D. 14), silver quinarius, Emerita

mint, issued by P. Carisius, 25–23 B.C., 1.63 g, *RIC* I$^2$, p. 41, no. 1a = *BMCRE* I, p. 54, no. 293, American Numismatic Society

56. Augustus (31 B.C.–A.D. 14), orichalcum sestertius, Rome mint, issued by moneyer C. Gallius Lupercus, ca. 22–21 B.C., 22.88 g, *RIC* I$^2$, p. 70, no. 377 = *BMCRE* I, p. 34, no. 171, American Numismatic Society

57. Augustus (31 B.C.–A.D. 14), orichalcum dupondius, Rome mint, issued by moneyer C. Cassius Celer, ca. 23–22 B.C., 9.38 g, *RIC* I$^2$, p. 70, no. 376 = *BMCRE* I, no. 166, American Numismatic Society

58. Augustus (31 B.C.–A.D. 14), copper as, Rome mint, issued by moneyer Cn. Piso Cn. f., ca. 23–22 B.C., 11.65 g, *RIC* I$^2$, p. 72, no. 395 = *BMCRE* I, p. 29, no. 137, American Numismatic Society

59. Augustus (31 B.C.–A.D. 14), copper quadrans, Rome mint, issued by moneyers Regulus, Pulcher, and Taurus, ca. 8 B.C., 3.19 g, *RIC* I$^2$, p. 75, no. 424, American Numismatic Society

60. Nero (54–68), aureus, Rome mint, A.D. 65–66, 7.29 g, *RIC* I$^2$, p. 153, no. 59 = *BMCRE* I, p. 211, p. 87, American Numismatic Society

61. Nero (54–68), denarius, Rome mint, A.D. 64–65, 3.3 g, *RIC* I$^2$, p. 153, no. 55 = *BMCRE* I, p. 211, no. 83, American Numismatic Society

62. Nero (54–68), orichalcum as, Rome mint, A.D. 64, 8.71 g, *RIC* I$^2$, p. 163, no. 214, American Numismatic Society

63. Nero (54–68), orichalcum semis, Rome mint, A.D. 64, 4.84 g, *RIC* I$^2$, p. 164, no. 233, American Numismatic Society

64. Nero (54–68), copper quadrans, Rome mint, A.D. 62–66, 2.09 g, *RIC* I², p. 158, no. 93 = *BMCRE* I, p. 256, no. 286, American Numismatic Society

*PLATE 9*

*The Augustan Coinage, 30 B.C.–A.D. 235*

65. Lugdunum, Gallia Lugdunensis, sestertius, Augustus, ca. A.D. 9–14, 25.28 g, *RIC* I², p. 57, no. 231a = *BMCRE* I, p. 94, no. 565, American Numismatic Society

66. Nemausus, Narbonensis, as, Augustus and Agrippa, ca. 20–11 B.C., 12.95 g, *RIC* I², p. 51, no. 158, American Numismatic Society

67. Nemausus, Narbonensis, halved as, Augustus and Agrippa, ca. 20–11 B.C., 5.97 g, *RIC* I², p. 51, no. 158, American Numismatic Society

68. Utica, Africa, as, Tiberius (14–37), minted by proconsul C. Vibius Marsus, A.D. 26/7–29/30, 16.35 g, L. Müller, *Numismatique de l'ancienne Afrique* (Copenhagen, 1862), II, p. 160, no. 356, American Numismatic Society

69. Countermarked as, Augustus, on obverse IMP AVG and on reverse TIB AV, Upper Rhineland, A.D. 12–23, 8.85 g, *RIC* I², p. 71, no. 389 = *BMCRE* I, p. 31, no. 153var., American Numismatic Society

70. Countermarked as of Lugdunum, Augustus, on reverse TIB, Lower Rhineland, A.D. 14–16, 9.30 g, cf. *BMCRE* I, p. 93, no. 559, American Numismatic Society

71. Countermarked worn as of Antioch, on obverse FVLM, XII (= legion XII Fulminata), A.D. 115–17, Howgego, *GIC*, p. 255, no.736

72. Imitative as of Claudius, Britain, ca. A.D. 43–54, based on prototype of *RIC* I², p. 127, no. 95, 10.79 g, American Numismatic Society

*PLATE 10*
*The Augustan Coinage and Currencies of the Roman East, 30 B.C.–A.D. 200*

73. Restored sestertius of divus Augustus, issued by Nerva (96–98), Rome mint, 22.56 g, *RIC* II, p. 233, no. 136 = *BMCRE* III, p. 233, no. 149, American Numismatic Society

74. Restored aureus of divus Augustus, issued by Trajan, Rome mint, A.D. 107, *RIC* II, p. 312, no. 828, pl. II. 166

75. Restored Republican denarius of moneyer Marcellinus, issued by Trajan, Rome mint, A.D. 107, *RIC* II, p. 310, no. 809 = *BMCRE* III, p. 136, no. 659, American Numismatic Society

76. Asia, Roman province, cistophorus, Augustus, Ephesus mint, 25 B.C., 12.01 g, *RIC* I$^2$, p. 80, no. 477 = *BMCRE* I, p. 122, no. 691, American Numismatic Society

77. Asia, Roman province, cistophorus, Mark Antony, Ephesus mint, 39–38 B.C., countermarked by Vespasian in A.D. 69–71, 9.16 g, Howgego, *GIC*, p. 293, no. 840 = American Numismatic Society

78. Nicopolis, Epirus, silver quinarius, Antoninus Pius (138–61), 1.81 g, M. K. Oikonomides, *He Nomismatokia tes Nikopoleos* (Athens, 1975), p. 92, no. 12a = American Numismatic Society

79. Lycia, Roman province, drachma, Domitian (81–96), 2.81 g, American Numismatic Society

80. Crete, Roman province, drachma, Caligula and divus Augustus (37–41), 2.66 g, American Numismatic Society

81. Cyrene, Roman province, hemidrachma, Trajan (98–117), 1.91g, Sydenham, *Coinage of Caesarea,* p. 62, no. 178, American Numismatic Society

82. Tarsus, Cilicia, tetradrachma, Trajan, countermarked in A.D. 180–92, 12.28 g, Howgego, p. 294, *GIC,* no. 842 = American Numismatic Society

83. Tarsus, Cilicia, tridrachma, Hadrian (117–38), 9.65 g, *SNGLevante* I. 996

84. Amisus, Pontus, tridrachma, Hadrian, A.D. 135/5, 7.86 g, American Numismatic Society

*PLATE 11*

*Currencies of the Roman East, 30 B.C.–A.D. 200*

85. Caesarea, Cappadocia, didrachma, Nero (54–68), 7.12 g, *RIC* I², p. 185, no. 607, American Numismatic Society

86. Caesarea, Cappadocia, half-cistophorus or 1.5 Attic drachma tariffed at 24 asses, Nero, A.D. 54–56, *RIC* I², p. 186, no. 614, pl. 22. 614

87. Caesarea, Cappadocia, didrachma, Lucius Verus (161–69), 6.68 g, Sydenham, *Coinage of Caesarea,* p. 90, no. 354, American Numismatic Society

88. Syria, Roman province, tetradrachma, Augustus, ca. 5 B.C., Antioch mint, Wruck, *Die syrische Provinzialprägung,* pp. 178–79, no. 1, pl. I.1

89. Syria, Roman province, tetradrachma, Augustus, Antioch mint, A.D. 5/6, 15.19 g, American Numismatic Society

90. Syria, Roman province, tetradrachma, Nero, Antioch mint, A.D. 60/1, 15.51 , Wruck, *Die syrische Provinzialprägung,* pp. 182–83, no. 38, American Numismatic Society

91. Syria, Roman province, tetradrachma, Trajan, Antioch mint, A.D. 110–11, 14.03 g, Wruck, *Die syrische Provinzialprägung,* pp. 194–95, no. 158, American Numismatic Society

92. Tyre, Phoenicia, tetradrachma, A.D. 44/5, 14.35 g, American Numismatic Society

93. Bostra, Arabia, drachma, Trajan, A.D. 114–16, 3.31 g, American Numismatic Society

*PLATE 12*

*Currencies of the Roman East, 30 B.C.–A.D. 200*

94. Asia, Roman province, sestertius, Augustus, Pergamum mint, 25–23 B.C., 24.27 g, *BMCRE* I, p. 116, no. 721, American Numismatic Society

95. Asia, Roman province, as, Augustus, Pergamum mint, 25–23 B.C., 11.93 g, *RIC* I$^2$, p. 84, no. 529, American Numismatic Society

96. Syria, Roman province, dupondius, Augustus, Antioch mint, ca. 5 B.C.–A.D. 14, 18.36 g, *RIC* I$^2$, p. 84, no. 528, American Numismatic Society

97. Syria, Roman province, as, Augustus, Antioch mint, ca. 5 B.C.–A.D. 14, 9.01 g, *RIC* I$^2$, p. 84, no. 529, American Numismatic Society

98. Smyrna, Ionia, bronze obol, Nero and Poppaea, A.D. 62–65, Klose, *Smyrna,* p. 231, no. 11, pl. 25 V5/R8

99. Smyrna, Ionia, bronze hemiobol, Augustus and Tiberius, A.D. 4–14, Klose, *Smyrna,* p. 210, no. 12, pl. 18 V3/R11

100. Smyrna, Ionia, bronze medallion of 18 assaria, Caracalla, minted by Aurelius Charidemus, A.D. 211–14, 53.87 g, Klose, *Smyrna,* p. 286, no. 12, American Numismatic Society

*PLATE 13*

*Currencies of the Roman East, 30 B.C–A.D. 200*

101. Smyrna, Ionia, 6 assaria, Septimius Severus, minted by

Claudius Aristophanes, A.D. 193–95, 17.22 g, *SNGvAulock* 2216 = Klose, *Smyrna,* p. 268, no. 6

102. Smyrna, Ionia, 4 assaria, Caracalla, minted by Claudius Rufinus, A.D. 198–202, 12.06 g, Klose, *Smyrna,* p. 285, no.7, American Numismatic Society

103. Smyrna, Ionia, 3 assaria, Geta, A.D. 198–202, 8.60 g, Klose, *Smyrna,* p. 294, no. 17, American Numismatic Society

104. Antiochia, Pisidia, sestertius, Caracalla, A.D. 198–205, 25.64 g, American Numismatic Society

105. Rhodes, bronze didrachma, ca. 40 B.C.–A.D. 96, 25.86 g, American Numismatic Society

106. Cyprus, Roman province, sestertius, Trajan, A.D. 114–15, 25.13 g, American Numismatic Society

*PLATE 14*
*Currencies of the Roman East, 30 B.C.–A.D. 200*

107. Stratonicea, Caria, 6 assaria, Caracalla and Geta, minted by Epitychanon, ca. A.D. 208–9, with countermarks to Hecate and Rome in A.D. 209–11 and *damnatio memoriae* of Geta in 212, 19.47 g, *SNGvAulock* 2686

108. Alexandria, Egypt, tetradrachma, Tiberius, A.D. 20/1, 13.67 g, Milne, *Alexandrian Coins,* p. 2, no. 38, American Numismatic Society

109. Alexandria, Egypt, tetradrachma, Claudius, A.D. 44/5, 13.56 g, Milne, *Alexandrian Coins,* p. 6, no. 203, American Numismatic Society

110. Alexandria, Egypt, drachma, Claudius, A.D. 42/3, 2.6 g, American Numismatic Society

111. Alexandria, Egypt, tetradrachma, Nero, A.D. 67/8, 13.16 g, Milne, *Alexandrian Coins,* p. 8, no. 292, American Numismatic Society

112. Alexandria, Egypt, tetradrachma, Marcus Aurelius, A.D. 169/70, 12.01 g, Milne, *Alexandrian Coins,* p. 63, no. 2603, American Numismatic Society

113. Alexandria, Egypt, bronze drachma, Antoninus Pius, A.D. 138/9, Milne, *Alexandrian Coins*, p. 40, no. 1608, 24.29 g, American Numismatic Society

114. Alexandria, Egypt, bronze hemidrachma, Antoninus Pius, A.D. 138/9, 8.46 g, G. Dattari, *Monete imperiale greche* (Cairo, 1901), no. 2799, American Numismatic Society

*PLATE 15*

*The Great Debasement and Reform, A.D. 193–305*

115. Caracalla (198–217), aureus, Rome mint, A.D. 217, 6.38 g, *RIC* IV. 1, p. 257, no. 296 = *BMCRE* V. 1, p. 463, no. 186, American Numismatic Society

116. Trebonianus Gallus (251–53), light aureus, Rome mint, 3.98 g, *RIC* IV. 3, p. 161, no. 22, American Numismatic Society

117. Gallineus (253–60), heavy aureus, Rome mint, 6.24 g, *RIC* V.1, p. 135, no. 52var., American Numismatic Society

118. Caracalla (198–217), antoninianus, Rome mint, A.D. 215, 4.94 g, *RIC* IV. 1, p. 239, no. 259 = *BMCRE* V. 1, p. 459, no. 152, American Numismatic Society

119. Pupienus (238), antoninianus, Rome mint, 5.15 g, *RIC* IV. 2, p. 174, no. 11b = *BMCRE* VI, p. 258, no. 92, American Numismatic Society

120. Divus Augustus, antoninianus minted by Trajan Decius (249–51), Rome mint, 4.28 g, *RIC* IV. 3, p. 130, no. 78, American Numismatic Society

121. Gallienus (253–68), antoninianus, Rome mint, A.D. 260–68, 2.99 g, *RIC* V. 1, p. 144, no. 157var., American Numismatic Society

122. Aurelian (270–75), aurelianianus with value mark XX, Ticinum mint, 3.82 g, *RIC* V. 1, p. 281, no. 154, American Numismatic Society

123. Aurelian (270–75), denarius communis, Rome mint, 3.51 g, *RIC* V. 1, p. 273, no. 74, American Numismatic Society

124. Tacitus (275–76), aurelianianus with value mark XI, Antioch mint, *RIC* V. 1, p. 347, no. 211 = J.-P. Callu, *NAC* 8 (1979), 245, pl. I. 10

125. Probus (276–82), aurelianianus with value mark KA, Serdica mint, 3.91 g, *RIC* V. 2, p. 109, no. 839, American Numismatic Society

126. Trajan Decius (249–51), double sestertius, 33.39 g, Rome mint, *RIC* IV. 3, p. 135, no. 115, American Numismatic Society

*PLATE 16*
*The Great Debasement and Reform,* A.D. *193–305*

127. Gallo-Roman Empire, Postumus (260–69), sestertius, Colonia Agrippina mint, 16.27 g, *RIC* V. 2, p. 348, no. 123, American Numismatic Society

128. Aurelian and Severina (270–75), sestertius, Rome mint, 13.56 g, *RIC* V. 1, p. 313, no. 1, American Numismatic Society

129. Gallo-Roman Empire, Postumus (260–69), antoninianus, Colonia Agrippina mint, A.D. 261, 3.43 g, *RIC* V. 2, p. 348, no. 76, American Numismatic Society

130. Gallo-Roman Empire, Tetricus I (270–74), antoninianus, Colonia Agrippina mint, 2.17 g, *RIC* V. 2, p. 343, no. 56, American Numismatic Society

131. Barbarous radiate, imitative antoninianus based on prototype of Tetricus I (270–74), 1.41 g, American Numismatic Society

132. Romano-British Empire, Carausius (287–93), silver denarius, Londinium mint, 2.99 g, *RIC* V. 2, p. 514, no. 595var., American Numismatic Society

133. Romano-British Empire, Carausius (287–93), antoninianus with value mark XXI, Londinium mint, 4.3 g, *RIC* V. 2., p. 471, no. 98var., American Numismatic Society

134. Romano-British Empire, Allectus (293–96), billon "Q" denomination, Camulodunum mint, 2.48 g, *RIC* V. 2, p. 569, no. 125, American Numismatic Society

135. Syria, Roman province, tetradrachma, Caracalla (198–217), Antioch mint, A.D. 214–17, 12.90 g, Bellinger, *Syrian Tetradrachms,*p. 24, no. 18, American Numismatic Society

136. Syria, Roman province, tetradrachma with mintmark MON(eta) VRB(is), Philip II (247–49), Antioch mint, A.D. 246, 10.17 g, American Numismatic Society

*PLATE 17*
*The Great Debasement and Reform,* A.D. *193–305*

137. Caesarea, Cappadocia, tridrachma, Gordian III (238–44), A.D. 239/40, 9.12 g, Sydenham, *Coinage of Caesarea,* p. 129, no. 599, American Numismatic Society

138. Alexandria, Egypt, tetradrachma, Gallienus (260–68), A.D. 264/5, 12.15 g, Milne, *Alexandrian Coins,* p. 98, no. 4098, American Numismatic Society

139. Alexandria, Egypt, tetradrachma, Severina, A.D. 274/5, 6.69 g, Milne, *Alexandrian Coins,* p. 107, no. 4470, American Numismatic Society

140. Countermarked aes, A.D. 255–60, 12 assaria of Gordian III (238–44) revalued at 24 assaria, Prusias, Bithynia, 33.98 g, Howgego, *GIC*, p. 293, no. 837 = American Numismatic Society

141. Countermarked aes, A.D. 255–60, heavy 4 assaria of Maximus (235–38) revalued at 12 assaria, Prusias, Bithynia, 15.28 g, Howgego, *GIC*, p. 292, no. 836

142. Countermarked aes, A.D. 255–260, 4 assaria of Severus Alexander (222–35) revalued at 8 assaria, Heraclea, Bithynia, 12.36 g, Howgego, *GIC*, p. 288. no. 824, American Numismatic Society

143. Countermarked aes, A.D. 255–60, 3 assaria of Gordian III (238–44) revalued at 6 assaria, Tium, Bithynia, 6.92 g, Howgego, *GIC*, p. 281, no. 809, American Numismatic Society

144. Countermarked aes, A.D. 255–60, 2 assaria of Caracalla (212–17) revalued at 4 assaria, Heraclea, Bithynia, 5.41 g, Howgego, *GIC*, p. 275, no. 789

145. Countermarked aes, A.D. 274, 6 assaria of Severus Alexander (222–35) revalued at 4 assaria, Aspendus, Pamphylia, 15.98 g, Howgego, *GIC*, p. 277, no. 796

146. Countermarked aes, A.D. 274, 6 assaria of Caracalla (212–17) revalued at 3 assaria, Ephesus, Ionia, 21.05 g, Howgego, *GIC*, p. 271, no. 776

147. Countermarked aes, A.D. 274, light 3 assaria of Salonina, ca. A.D. 258–60, revalued at 2 assaria, Tabae, Caria, Howgego, *GIC*, p. 267, no. 765i

*PLATE 18*
*The Great Debasement and Reform, A.D. 193–305*

148. Side, Pamphylia, heavy 10 assaria with value mark I, Gallienus, A.D. 253–55, 23.16 g, *SNGvAulock* 8546 = American Numismatic Society

149. Side, Pamphylia, light 10 assaria with value mark I, Gallienus, A.D. 255–60, 17.78 g, *SNGvAulock* 4848

150. Side, Pamphylia, 12 assaria with value mark IB, Gallienus, A.D. 260–68, 15.46 g, *SNGvAulock* 4845

151. Side, Pamphylia, 14 assaria with value mark **IΔ**, Aurelian, A.D. 270–74, 15.46 g, *SNGvAulock* 4864

152. Side, Pamphylia, light 10 assaria of Gallienus, ca. A.D. 255–60, countermarked at new value of 5 assaria in A.D. 274, 13.75 g, Howgego, *GIC*, p. 280, no. 805, American Numismatic Society

153. Side, Pamphylia, heavy 5 assaria of Maximus (235–38) countermarked at new value of 5 assaria in A.D. 274, 19.17 g, Howgego, *GIC,* p. 280, no. 805, American Numismatic Society

*PLATE 19*

*The Great Debasement and Reform, A.D. 193–305*

154. Diocletian (284–305) and Maximianus (285–305), 10 aurei multiple, Treveri mint, A.D. 293/4, 54.45 g, *RIC* VI, p.163, no. 2 = American Numismatic Society

155. Diocletian (284–305), aureus, marked as struck at 60 to Roman pound, Antioch mint, ca. A.D. 296–97, 5.39 g, *RIC* VI, p. 614, no. 13, American Numismatic Society

156. Diocletian (284–93), argenteus, marked as struck at 96 to Roman pound, Aquileia mint, ca. A.D. 300, 3.12 g, *RIC* VI, p. 312, no. 16a, American Numismatic Society

157. Constantius I (305–6), nummus with value mark XXI, Alexandria mint, ca. A.D. 298–99, 10.45 g, *RIC* VI, p. 665, no. 31a, American Numismatic Society

158. Diocletian (284–305), nummus with value mark K/V, Antioch mint, ca. A.D. 298–99, 9.98 g, *RIC* VI, p. 620, no. 54a, American Numismatic Society

159. Diocletian (284–305), radiate fraction, Rome mint, ca.

A.D. 297–98, 3.31 g, *RIC* VI, p. 359, no. 77a, American Numismatic Society

160. Maximinus II Daia (309–13), laureate fraction, Siscia mint, A.D. 305–6, 1.6 g, *RIC* VI, p. 475, no. 171b

*PLATE 20*
*Imperial Regulation and Reform,* A.D. *305–498*

161. Constantine I (306–37), solidus, Rome mint, A.D. 325, 4.45 g, *RIC* VII, p. 327, no. 273, American Numismatic Society

162. Valens (364–78), solidus with certification OB, Treveri mint, A.D. 367–75, 4.44 g, *RIC* IX, p. 16, no. 16c, American Numismatic Society

163. Arcadius (395–408), semis, Constantinople mint, A.D. 383–88, 2.21 g, cf. *RIC* IX, p. 231, no. 71a, American Numismatic Society

164. Theodosius I (379–95), tremis, Constantinople mint, A.D. 383–88, 1.47 g, *RIC* IX, p. 232, no. 75b, American Numismatic Society

165. Constans (337–50), triple miliarensia, Siscia mint, A.D. 337–40, 13.24 g, *RIC* VIII, p. 352, no. 45, American Numismatic Society

166. Valentinian I (364–75), heavy miliarense, Treveri mint, A.D. 367–75, 4.82 g, *RIC* IX, p. 18, no. 23b, American Numismatic Society

167. Constantius II (337–61), light miliarense, Treveri mint, A.D. 336–37, 4.30 g, *RIC* VII, p. 222, no. 583, American Numismatic Society

168. Constantius II (337–61), argenteus, Thessalonica mint, A.D. 340–50, 3.01 g, *RIC* VIII, p. 410, no. 93, American Numismatic Society

*PLATE 21*
*Imperial Regulation and Reform,* A.D. *305–498*

169. Valentinian I (364–75), argenteus with certification PS, Treveri mint, A.D. 367–75, 2.11 g, *RIC* IX, p. 19, no. 276, American Numismatic Society

170. Magnus Maximus (383–88), argenteus, Aquileia mint, A.D. 387–88, 1.66 g, *RIC* IX, p. 105, no. 54a, American Numismatic Society

171. Theodosius II (408–50), argenteus, Treveri mint, ca. A.D. 450–65, minted either by Aetius (435–54) or Aegidius (456–65), J. Lafaurie, "Les dernères émissions de Trèves au V siècle," in *Mélanges de numismatique offerts à Pierre Bastien,* ed. H. Huvelin, M. Christol, and G. Gautier (Wetteren, 1987), p. 320, type IA, no. 2, pl. 25. 2.

172. Constantine I (306–37), nummus (AE2 module), Lugdunum mint, A.D. 307, 8.5 g, *RIC* VI, p. 239, no. 231, American Numismatic Society

173. Constantine I (306–37), nummus (AE2 module) with value mark CIHS, Lugdunum mint, A.D. 308–9, 7.07 g, *RIC* VI, p. 264, no. 295, American Numismatic Society

174. Constantine I (306–37), nummus (AE2 module), Londinium mint, ca. A.D. 310–12, 5 g, *RIC* VI, p. 135, no. 153, American Numismatic Society

175. Constantine I (306–37), nummus (AE3 module), Treveri mint, A.D. 316, 3.6 g, *RIC* VII, p. 173, no. 105, American Numismatic Society

176. Constantine I (306–37), nummus (AE3 module), Treveri mint, A.D. 322, 3.39 g, *RIC* VII, p. 194, no. 341, American Numismatic Society

177. Constantius II (337–61), nummus (AE4 module), Treveri mint, A.D. 335–37, 1.6 g, *RIC* VII, p. 223, no. 592, American Numismatic Society

178. Constans (337–50), nummus (AE4 module), Arelate mint, A.D. 347–48, 1.69 g, *RIC* VIII, p. 208, no. 81, American Numismatic Society

179. Licinius II (308–24), nummus (AE3 module), with value mark for 12.5 d.c., Cyzicus mint, A.D. 321–24, 2.67 g, *RIC* VII, p. 646, no. 18, American Numismatic Society

*PLATE 22*

*Imperial Regulation and Reform, A.D. 305–498*

180. Constantius II (337–61), maiorina (large AE2 module), Arelate mint, A.D. 348–50, 5.04 g, *RIC* VIII, p. 211, no. 120, American Numismatic Society

181. Constantius II (337–61), centenionalis (small AE2 module), Alexandria mint, A.D. 348–50, 4.41 g, *RIC* VIII, p. 542, no. 54, American Numismatic Society

182. Constans (337–50), AE3 billon fraction, Lugdunum mint, A.D. 348–50, 2.46 g, *RIC* VIII, p. 183, no. 96, American Numismatic Society

183. Imitative maiorina (AE2 module) based on prototype of Constantius II, Gaul, ca. A.D. 350–55, 2.36 g, American Numismatic Society

184. Decentius (351–53), large maiorina (AE1 module), Treveri mint, A.D. 352, 9.06 g, *RIC* VIII, p. 164., no. 319, American Numismatic Society

185. Magnentius (350–53), maiorina (AE2 module), Ambianum mint, A.D. 352, 4.16 g, *RIC* VIII, p. 122, no. 14, American Numismatic Society

186. Julian II (360–63), maiorina (AE1 module), Lugdunum mint, A.D. 362–63, 8.58 g, *RIC* VIII, p. 195, no. 236, American Numismatic Society

187. Jovian (363–64), AE3 billon fraction, Sirmium mint, 3.24

g, *RIC* VIII, p. 394, no. 118, 3.24 g, American Numismatic Society

188. Theodosius I (379–95), AE2 denomination, Antioch mint, A.D. 378–83, 5.28 g, *RIC* IX, p. 283, no. 20d, American Numismatic Society

189. Gratian (367–83), AE3 denomination, Rome mint, A.D. 378–83, 2.72 g, *RIC* IX, p. 126, no. 46a, American Numismatic Society

190. Valentinian II (375–92), nummus minimus (AE4 module), Nicomedia mint, A.D. 388–92, 1.3 g, *RIC* IX, p. 261, no. 45a, American Numismatic Society

191. Theodosius II (408–50), nummus minimus (AE4 module), Cyzicus mint, ca. A.D. 425–35, 1.08 g, *RIC* X, p. 275, no. 451, American Numismatic Society

*PLATE 23*
*The Loss of Roman Monetary Ways,* A.D. *400–700*

192. Phocas (602–10), solidus, Constantinople mint, 4.44 g, *DOC* II. 1, p. 150, no. 10e = Wroth, *BMC* I, p. 162, no. 6, American Numismatic Society

193. Phocas (602–10), light-weight solidus of 20 carats marked on reverse OBXX, Constantinople mint, 3.23 g, cf. Adelson, *Light Weight Solidi,* p. 159, American Numismatic Society

194. Heraclius (610–41), globular solidus, Carthage mint, A.D. 626/7, 4.46 g, cf. DOC II. 1, p. 345, no. 217 = Wroth, *BMC* I, p. 237, no. 337, American Numismatic Society

195. Justinian I (527–65), tremissis, Cartagena mint, 1.49 g, ca. A.D. 550–65, *DOC* I, p. 193, no. 376, American Numismatic Society

196. Heraclius (610–41), tremissis, Ravenna mint, 1.36 g,

*DOC* II. 1, p. 368, no. 275 = Wroth, *BMC* I, pp. 245–46, no. 474, American Numismatic Society

197. Heraclius (610–41), hexagram, Constantinople mint, 6.51 g, *DOC* II. 1., p. 271, no. 62 = Wroth, *BMC* I, p. 195, no. 99, American Numismatic Society

198. Leo III (717–41), miliaresion, Constantinople mint, 2.08 g, *DOC* III. 1, p. 252, no. 22b, American Numismatic Society

199. Justinian I (527–65), silver half-siliqua, Carthage mint, 1.02 g, *DOC* I, p. 160, no. 281 = Wroth, *BMC* I, p. 62, no. 339, American Numismatic Society

200. Justinian I (527–65), silver half-siliqua, Ravenna mint, 1.45 g, *DOC* I, p. 182, no. 338, American Numismatic Society

201. Anastasius I (491–512), follis (40 nummiae), Constantinople mint, A.D. 498–512, 15.07 g, *DOC* I, p. 12, no. 16a = Wroth, *BMC* I, p. 6, no. 41, American Numismatic Society

*PLATE 24*
*The Loss of Roman Monetary Ways, A.D. 400–700*

202. Anastasius I (491–512), follis (40 nummiae), Constantinople mint, A.D. 512–18, 16.96 g, *DOC* I, p. 20, no. 23f = Wroth, *BMC* I, p. 4, no. 24, American Numismatic Society

203. Justinian I (527–65), follis (40 nummiae), Constantinople mint, A.D. 538/9, 22.81 g, *DOC* I, p. 84, no. 37c = Wroth, *BMC* I, p. 31, no. 42, American Numismatic Society

204. Anastasius I (491–518), half-follis (20 nummiae), Constantinople mint, A.D. 512–18, 8.85 g, *DOC* I, p. 23, no. 24b = Wroth, *BMC* I, p. 5, no. 30, American Numismatic Society

205. Justinian I (527–65), half-follis (20 nummiae), Rome mint, A.D. 538–44, 5.89 g, *DOC* I, p. 176, no. 325, American Numismatic Society

206. Justin II (565–78), follis (40 nummiae), Cyzicus mint, A.D. 573/4, 13.82 g, *DOC* I, p. 235, no. 121a, American Numismatic Society

*PLATE 25*

*The Loss of Roman Monetary Ways, A.D. 400–700*

207. Heraclius (610–41), follis, Constantinople mint, A.D. 615/6, overstruck on follis of Maurice Tiberius minted at Antioch in A.D. 586/7, 12.42 g, *DOC* II. 1, pp. 284–85, no. 81, American Numismatic Society

208. Heraclius (610–41), follis, Seleucia mint, A.D. 616/7, 10.56 g, *DOC* II. 1, p. 339, no. 18b, American Numismatic Society

209. Heraclius (610–41), follis, Cypriote mint, A.D. 626/7, 4.42 g, *DOC* II. 1, pp. 331–32, no. 184, American Numismatic Society

210. Heraclius (610–41), follis, Constantinople mint, A.D. 629/30, 11.35, g, *DOC* I. 1, p. 296, no. 105c = Wroth, *BMC* I, p. 203, no. 149, American Numismatic Society

211. Heraclius (610–41), follis, Constantinople mint, A.D. 633/4, 4.42 g, *DOC* I, p. 298, no.100var., American Numismatic Society

212. Constans II (641–68), follis, Constantinople mint, A.D. 654/5, 2.59 g, *DOC* II. 2, p. 451, no. 72c, American Numismatic Society

*PLATE 26*

*The Loss of Roman Monetary Ways, A.D. 400–700*

213. Constantine IV (668–85), follis, Constantinople mint, A.D.

675–83, 18.80 g, *DOC* I. 2, p. 537, no. 28c, American Numismatic Society

214. Countermarked follis of Anastasius by Heraclius for use in Sicily, A.D. 631–41, 16.12 g, *DOC* I. 1, p. 198, no. 23, American Numismatic Society

215. Justinian I (527–65), 36 nummiae denomination with value mark **ΛΓ**, Alexandria mint, 12.81 g, *DOC* I. 1, p. 157, no. 273 = Wroth, *BMC* I, p. 62, no. 339, American Numismatic Society

216. Justinian I (527–65), duodecanummia, Alexandria mint, 5.43 g, *DOC* I, p. 157, no. 274 = Wroth, *BMC* I, p. 62, no. 342, American Numismatic Society

217. Heraclius (610–41), duodecanummia with dual value marks IB and M, Alexandria mint, A.D. 629–31, 7.13 g, cf. Wroth, *BMC* I, p. 226, nos. 297–301, American Numismatic Society

218. Tiberius II (578–82), 30 nummiae denomination, Constantinople mint, 12.81 g, *DOC* I. 1, p. 273, no. 15d = Wroth, *BMC* I, p. 110, no. 40, American Numismatic Society

*PLATE 27*
*The Loss of Roman Monetary Ways,* A.D. *400–700*

219. Maurice Tiberius (582–602), 8 pentanummiae denomination (40 nummiae), Cherson mint, 12.51 g, *DOC* I. pp. 373–74, no. 299, American Numismatic Society

220. Franks, Eastern Gaul, ca. A.D. 450–500, solidus based on prototype of Honorius (395–423) struck at Mediolanum, 4.38 g, American Numismatic Society

221. Franks, Eastern Gaul, ca. A.D. 450–500, argenteus based on Rprototype of Honorius (395–423), 0.78 g, J. Lafaurie, "Les dernères émissions de Trèves au V siècle," in

*Mélanges de numismatique offerts à Pierre Bastien,* ed. H. Huvelin, M. Christol, and G. Gautier (Wetteren, 1987), p. 317, no. 4, pl. 23. 4

222. Sueves, Spain, ca. A.D. 425–75, solidus based on prototype of Honorius (395–423), 3.71 g, American Numismatic Society

223. Sueves, Spain, ca. A.D. 450–500, tremissis based on prototype of Valentinian III (425–55), 1.42 g, W. Reinhart, *MBNG* 55 (1937), 185, no. 42, pl. XXXIII. 1 = American Numismatic Society

224. Visigoths, Gaul, ca. A.D. 425–500, solidus, based on prototype of Valentinian III (425–55), 4.42 g, W. Reinhart, *DJBN* 2 (1939), 55, no. 20, = American Numismatic Society

225. Burgundians, Gaul, ca. A.D. 500–525, solidus based on prototype of Anastasius I (498–518), Lyons mint, 4.44 g, cf. A. de Belfort, *Description général des monnaies mérovingiennes* (Paris, 1892) II, p. 173, no. 2241, American Numismatic Society

226. Pseudo-imperial solidus based on prototype of Maurice Tiberius (582–602), Arles mint, 3.79 g, American Numismatic Society

227. Clothaire II (613–29), King of Franks, solidus, Marseilles mint, 3.49 g, cf. M. Prou, *Les monnaies mérovingiennes (Catalogue des monnaies de la Bibliothèque Nationale)* (Paris, 1892), pp. 303–5, nos. 1380–88, American Numismatic Society

*PLATE 28*

*The Loss of Roman Monetary Ways, A.D. 400–700*

228. Franks, Gaul, ca. A.D. 600–700, electrum tremissis issued by moneyer Madelinus, 1.24 g, Belfort, *Description général* II, p. 73, no. 1760, American Numismatic Society

229. Pepin I (751–68), King of the Franks, silver denier, Antrain mint, 1.29 g, K. F. Morrisson and H. Grunthal, *Carolingian Coinage* (New York, 1967), p. 78, no. 26, American Numismatic Society

230. Anglo-Saxons, Britain, thrysma (tremissis), ca. A.D. 650–75, 1.27 g, J. J. North, *English Hammered Coinage* (London, 1994), I, p. 56, no. 29, American Numismatic Society

231. Anglo-Saxons, Britain, silver sceatta (penny), ca. A.D. 675–710, 1.23, J. J. North, *English Hammered Coinage* I, p. 66, no. 126, American Numismatic Society

232. Offa, King of Mercia (757–96), silver penny, Ealred moneyer, 1.16 g, J. J. North, *English Hammered Coinage* I, p. 87, no. 293, American Numismatic Society

233. Visigoths, Spain, solidus based on prototype of Justinian (527–65), Seville mint, 4.39 g, X. Barral y Altet, *La circulation des monnaies suèves et visigotiques* (Munich, 1976), pl. V. 3, American Numismatic Society

234. Leovigild, King of Visigoths (568–86), tremissis, 1.49 g, Tomasini, *Barbaric Tremissis,* p. 18, no. 19, American Numismatic Society

235. Seville (Ispali), Visigothic Spain, AE4 nummus, ca. A.D. 600–705, 1.08 g, Crusafont, *Problems of Medieval Coinage* III, pp. 60–61, no. 5, American Numismatic Society

236. Gunthamund (484–96), King of the Vandals, siliqua, Carthage mint, 2.14 g, Wroth, *BMC* II, p. 3, no. 1, American Numismatic Society

237. Vandals, North Africa, follis (42 nummi), Carthage mint, ca. A.D. 487–96, 11.05 g, Wroth, *BMC* II, p. 3, no. 13, American Numismatic Society

*PLATE 29*
*The Loss of Roman Monetary Ways, A.D. 400–700*

238. Vandals, North Africa, half-follis (21 nummi), Carthage

mint, ca. A.D. 487–96, 8.69 g, Wroth, *BMC* II, p. 3, no. 14, American Numismatic Society

239. Vandals, North Africa, as of Titus (79–81) incised as follis (XLII = 42 nummi), ca. A.D. 500–33, 9.94 g, American Numismatic Society

240. Theodoric (487–526), King of Ostrogoths, solidus struck in name of Justin I (518–27), Ravenna mint, 4.44 g, Wroth, *BMC*, II, p. 48, no. 12, American Numismatic Society

241. Athalaric (526–34), King of Ostrogoths, half-siliqua in name of Justin I, Rome mint, 1.41 g, Wroth, *BMC* II, p. 63, no. 27, American Numismatic Society

242. Ostrogoths, Italy, follis, Rome mint, ca. A.D. 491–522, 14.32 g, Wroth, *BMC* II, p. 104, no. 25, pl. XIV. 2

243. Ostrogoths, Italy, follis, Rome mint, ca. A.D. 522–34, 10.02 g, Wroth, *BMC* II, p. 102, no. 6, American Numismatic Society

244. Theodahad (534–36), King of Ostrogoths, follis, Rome mint, 9.09 g, Wroth, *BMC* II, p. 75, no. 19, American Numismatic Society

*PLATE 30*

*The Loss of Roman Monetary Ways, A.D. 400–700*

245. Lombards, Italy, ca. A.D. 584–615, tremissis based on prototype of Maurice Tiberius (582–602), 1.46 g, cf. Grierson and Blackburn, *European Medieval Coinage,* pl. 15. 301–4, American Numismatic Society

246. Lombards, Italy, ca. A.D. 615–50, tremissis based on prototype of Maurice Tiberius (582–602), 1.35 g, cf. Grierson and Blackburn, *European Medieval Coinage,* pl. 15. 304–6, American Numismatic Society

247. Umayyad Caliphate, gold dinar, ca. A.D. 640–92, based

on solidus of Heraclius (610–41), 4.4 g, American Numismatic Society

248. Umayyad Caliphate, bronze fuls (follis) based on prototype of Constans II (641–68), 3.62 g, American Numismatic Society

249. Abd al-Malik (685–705), Umayyad caliph, silver dirhem, Damascus mint, A.H. 85 = A.D. 704/5, 2.97 g, American Numismatic Society

250. Umayyad Caliphate, gold dinar, Carthage mint, ca. A.D. 698–710, 4.27 g, American Numismatic Society

251. Umayyad Caliphate, gold dinar, al-Andalus (Spanish mint), A.H. 98 = A.D. 717/8, 4.12 g, American Numismatic Society

*PLATE 31*
*Roman Coins beyond the Imperial Frontiers*

252. Imitative aureus, Dacia, Koson, ca. 50–30 B.C., based on prototype of denarius struck by M. Junius Brutus, 8.5 g, cf. Crawford, *CRR* I, p. 445, no. 433/1, American Numismatic Society

253. Imitative denarius, Dacia, ca. 75–50 B.C., based on prototype struck by moneyer M. Lucilius Rufus, 3.53 g, cf. Crawford, *RRC* I, 375, no. 324/1, American Numismatic Society

254. Imitative denarius, Central or Northern Europe, ca. A.D. 1–75, based on prototype of Augustus, 3.04 g, *RIC* $1^2$, p. 35, no. 207 = *BMCRE* I, p. 90, no. 533, American Numismatic Society

255. Augustus (31 B.C.–A.D. 14), denarius, Lugdunum mint, imperial portrait defaced, Akkenpalle Hoard, Turner, *Roman Coins from India,* p. 140, pl. VII. 730

256. Cotys II (124–32/3), King of the Bosporus, with portrait

of Hadrian (117–38) on reverse, aureus, A.D. 123, 7.85 g, Frolova, *Coinage of Bosporus* I, pp. 133–34, American Numismatic Society

257. Cotys II (124–32/3), King of the Bosporus, sestertius, A.D. 125, 12.42 g, Frolova, *Coinage of Bosporus* I, pp. 139–40, American Numismatic Society

258. Gotarzes II (41–51), King of Parthia, tetradrachma, Seleucia ad Tigrim mint, 11.13 g, American Numismatic Society

259. Orodes I (57–37 B.C.), King of Parthia, drachma, Rhagae mint, 4.04 g, American Numismatic Society

*PLATE 32*
*Roman Coins beyond the Imperial Frontiers*

260. Khusrau II (590–628), Sassanid Shah of Persia, dinar, uncertain Iranian mint, A.D. 613/4, 4.61 g, Göbl, *Sasanian Numismatics,* III/4, no. 217, American Numismatic Society

261. Shapur I (240–70), Sassanid Shah of Persia, dirhem, uncertain Iranian mint, Göbl, *Sasanian Numismatics,* III/1, American Numismatic Society

262. Himyarite Yemen (Arabia Felix), silver didrachma based on obverse of a denarius of Augustus, ca. A.D. 1–50, 5.42 g, *SNGANS* 1486 = American Numismatic Society

263. Himyarite Yemen (Arabia Felix), silver drachma based on prototype of denarius of Augustus, ca. A.D. 1–50, 2.71 g, *SNGANS* 1492 = American Numismatic Society

264. Ousanas (ca. 300–25), Emperor of Axum, gold fraction, 1.64 g, American Numismatic Society

265. Vima Kadphises (ca. 78–126), Kushan emperor, gold stater, Lahore mint, 7.95 g, American Numismatic Society

266. Kanishka I (ca. 128–51), Kushan emperor, bronze drach-

ma, Lahore mint, 15.85 g, American Numismatic Society

267. Sogdiana, silver tetradrachma based on prototype of Euthydemus I (230–190 B.C.), Bactra mint, ca. A.D. 1–200, 9.44 g, American Numismatic Society

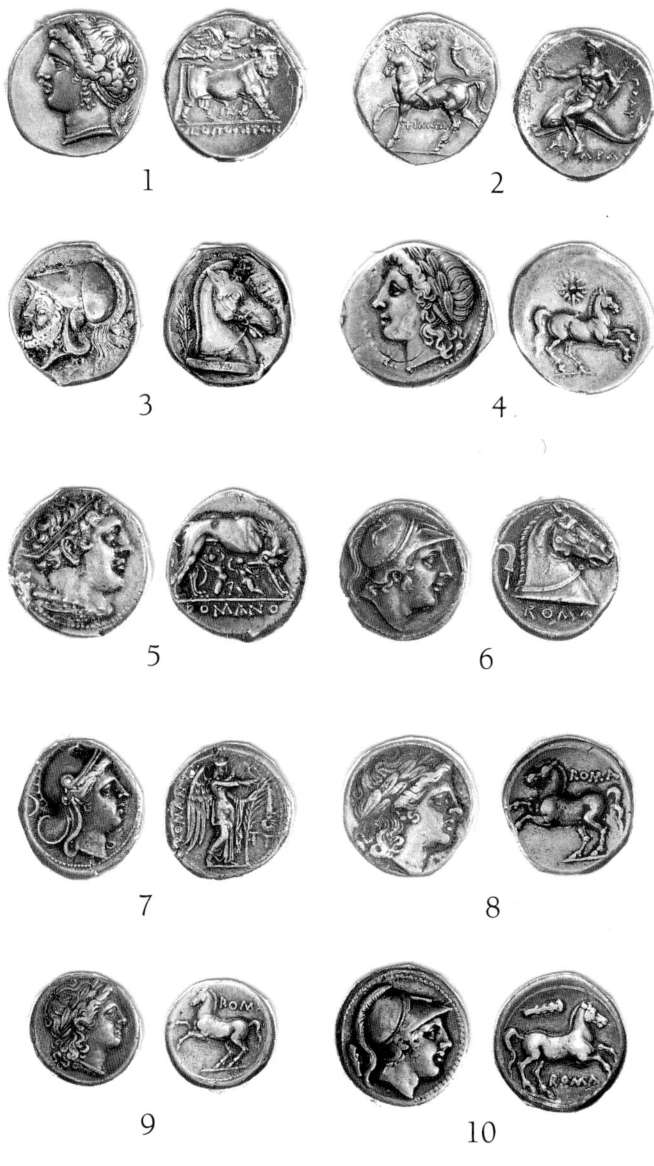


1 2 3 4 5 6 7 8 9 10

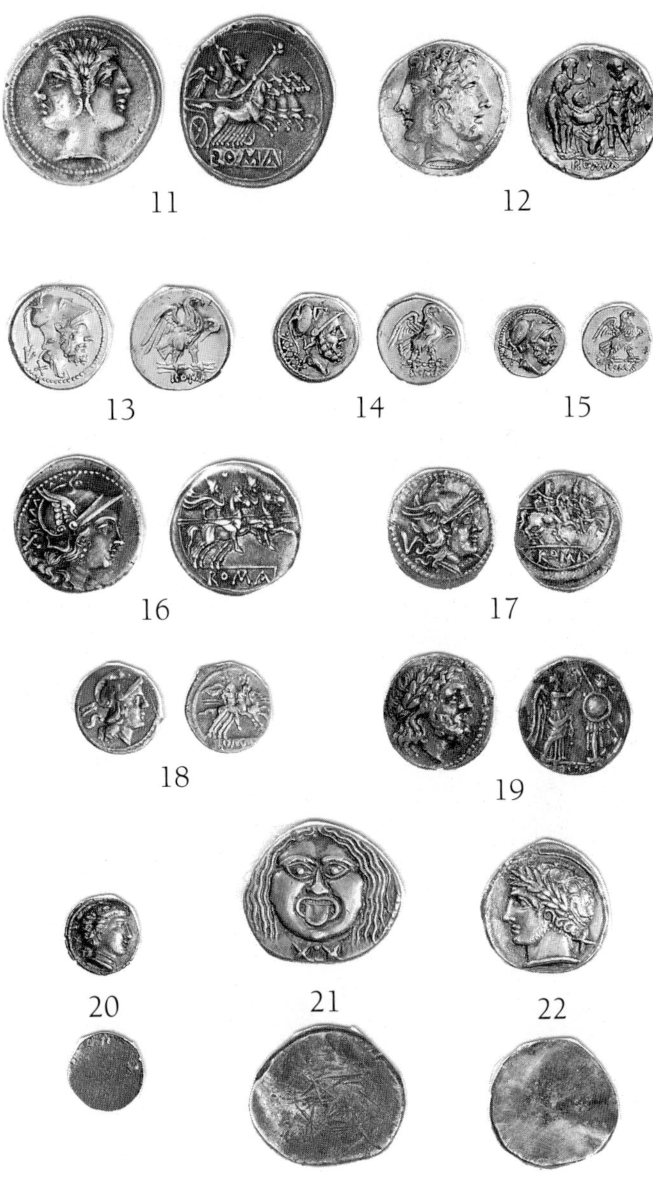


11 12 13 14 15 16 17 18 19 20 21 22

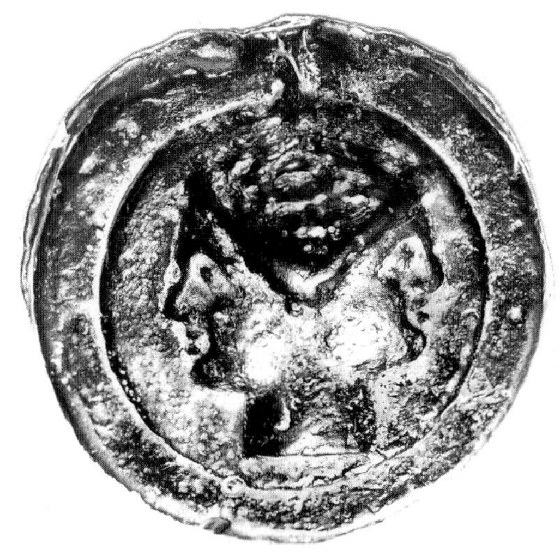

23

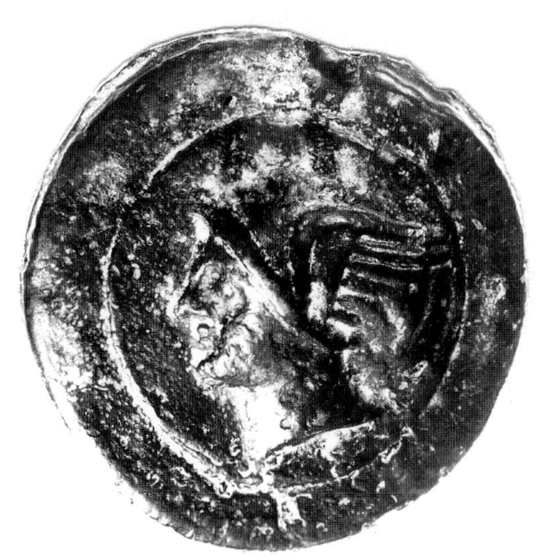

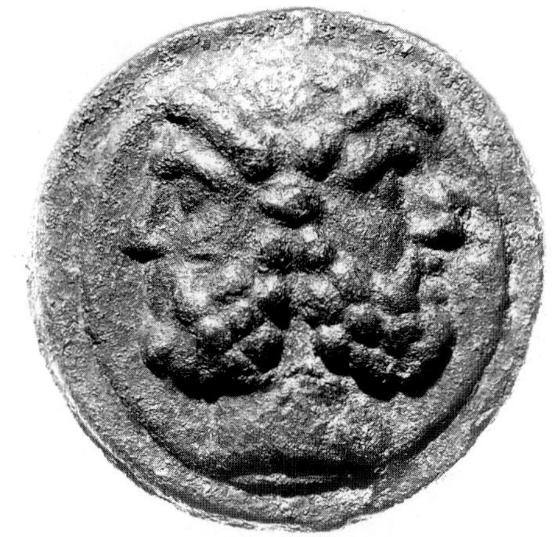

24

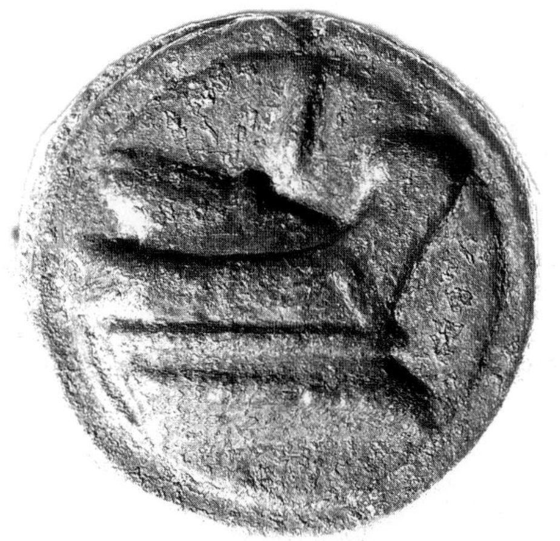

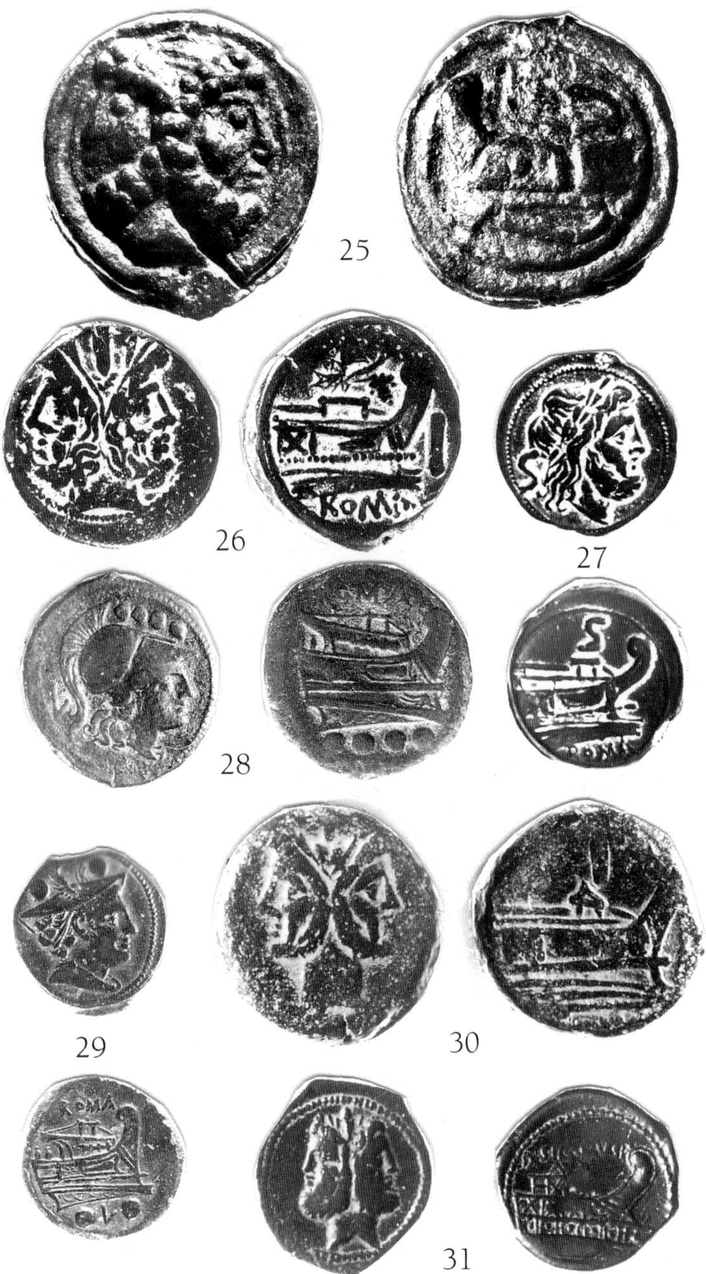
25
26
27
28
29
30
31

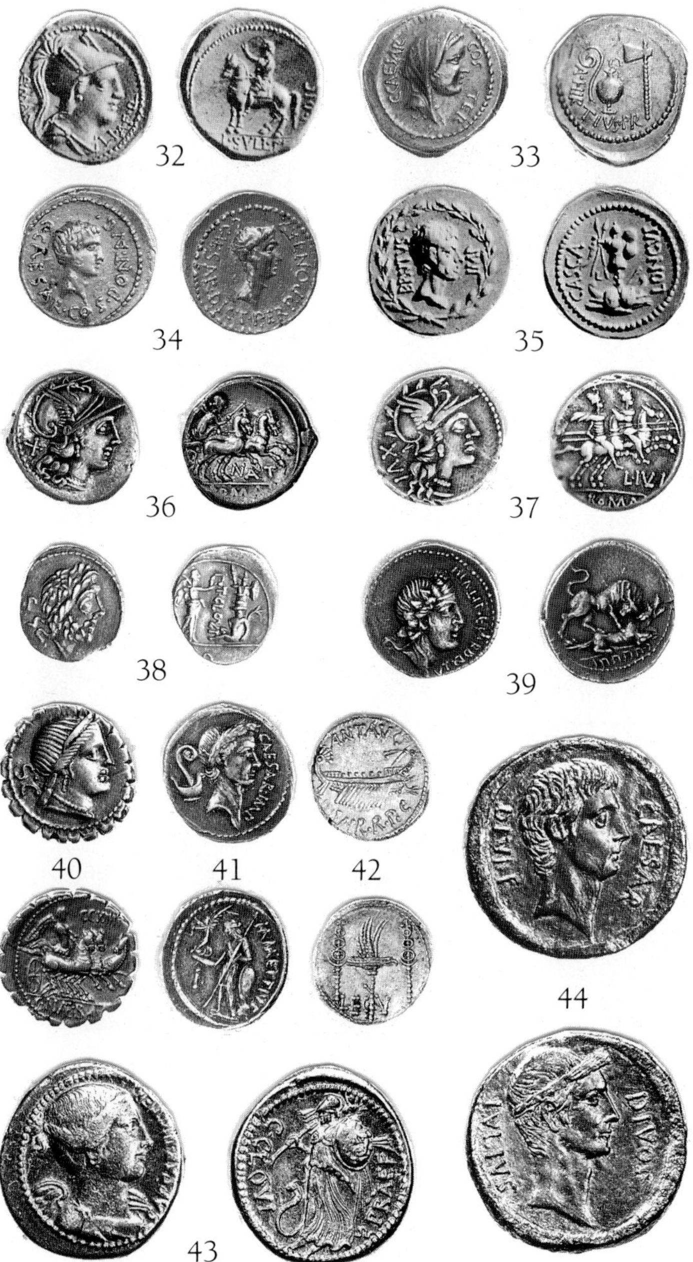
32
33
34
35
36
37
38
39
40
41
42
43
44

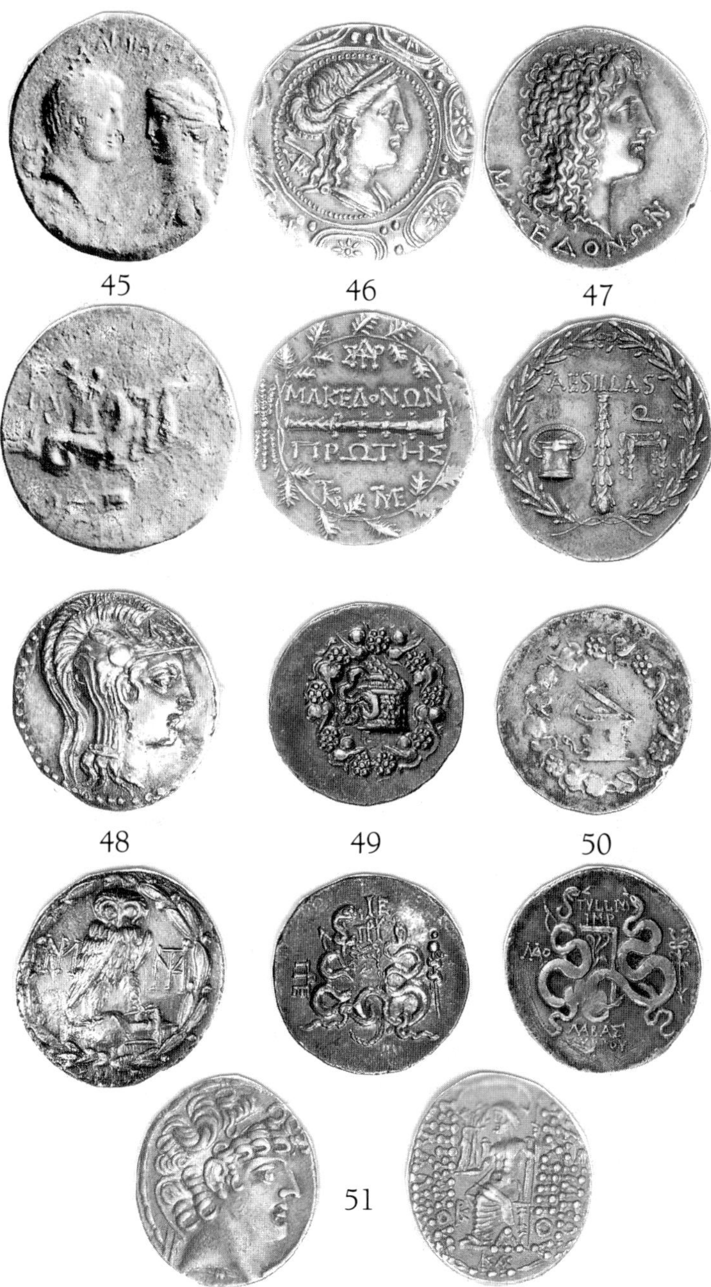


45 46 47

48 49 50

51

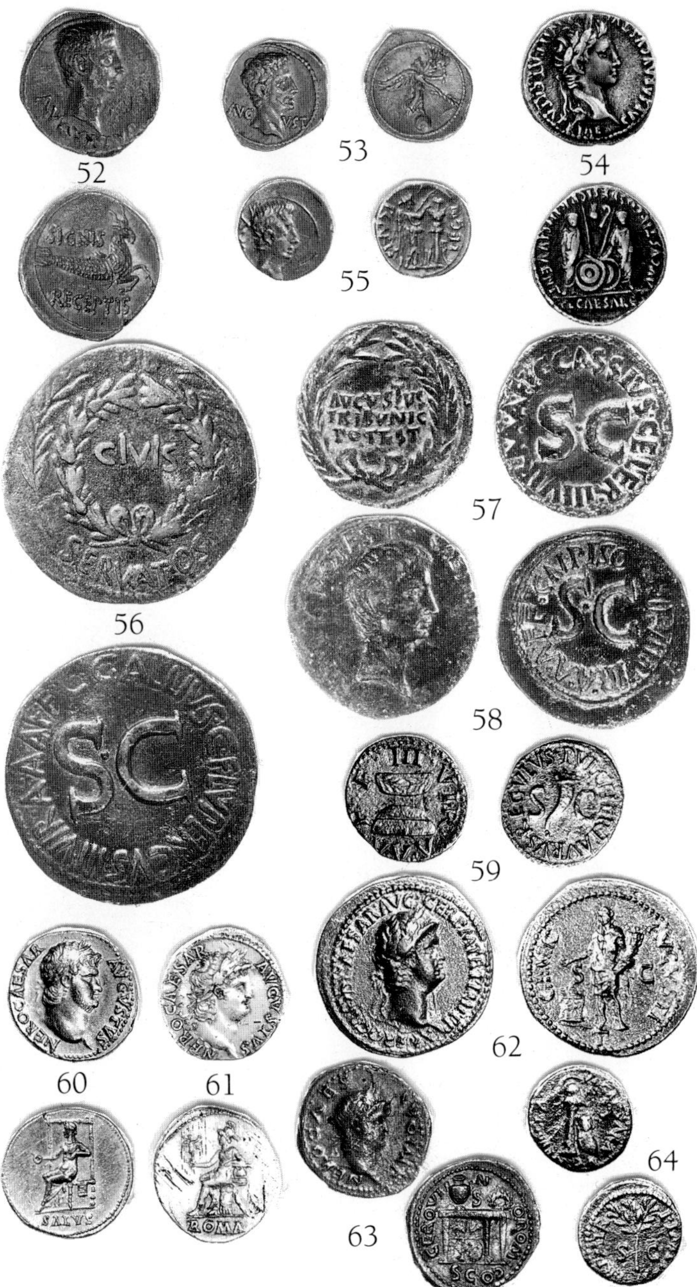
52
53
54
SIGNIS
RECEPTIS
55
CIVIS
SERVATOS
56
AVGVSTVS
TRIBVNIC
POTEST
57
58
59
60
61
62
SALVS
ROMA
63
64

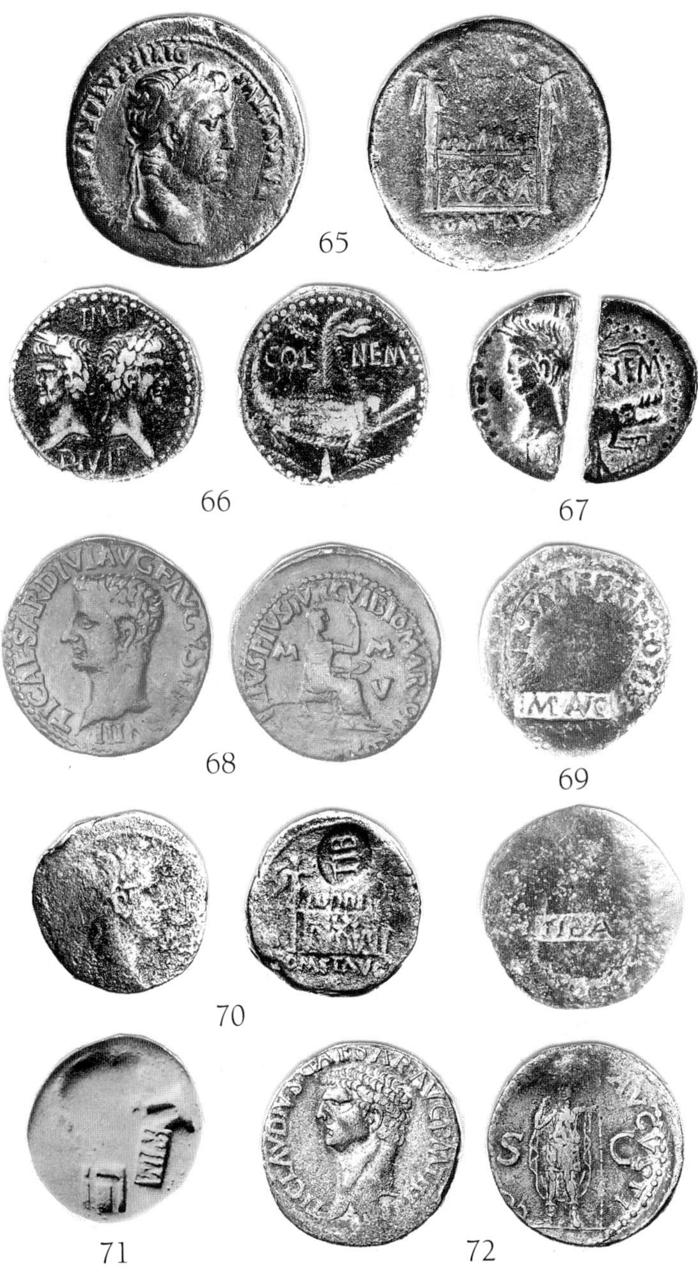
65
COL NEM
66
67
68
69
TIB
70
71
72

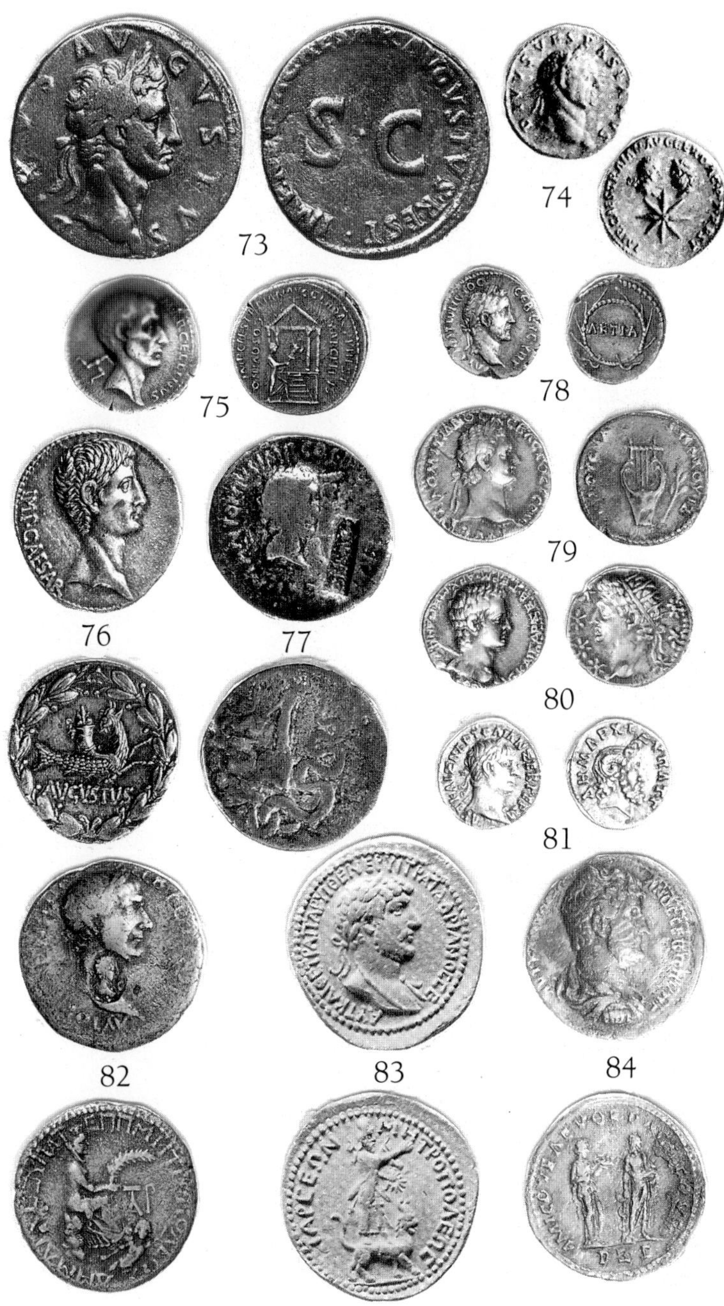
73
74
75
78
76
77
79
80
81
82
83
84

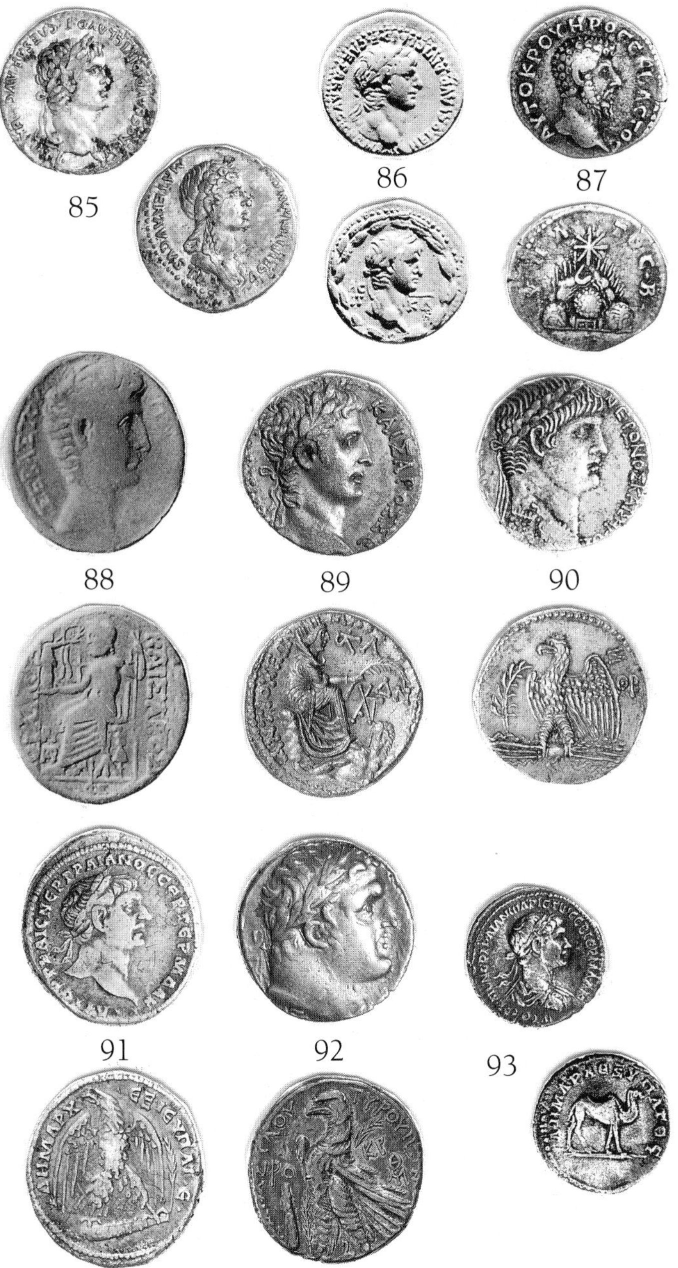

85 86 87

88 89 90

91 92 93

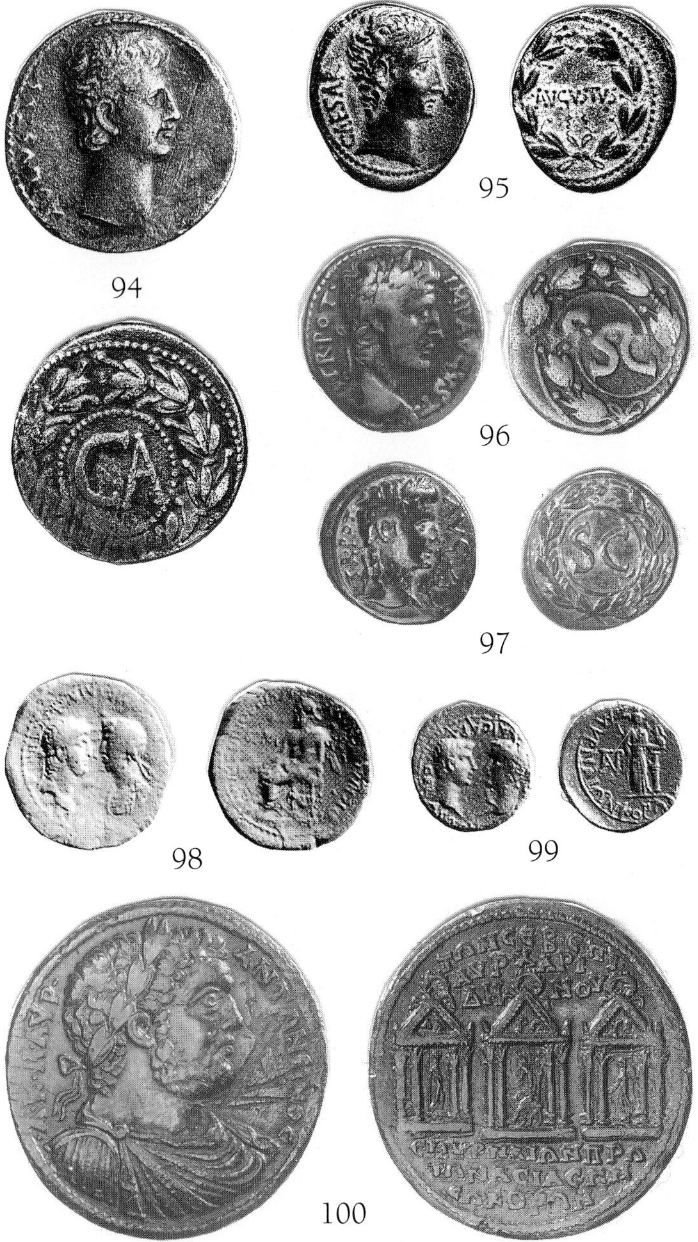
94
95
CAESAR
AVGVSTVS
CA
96
SC
97
SC
98
99
100

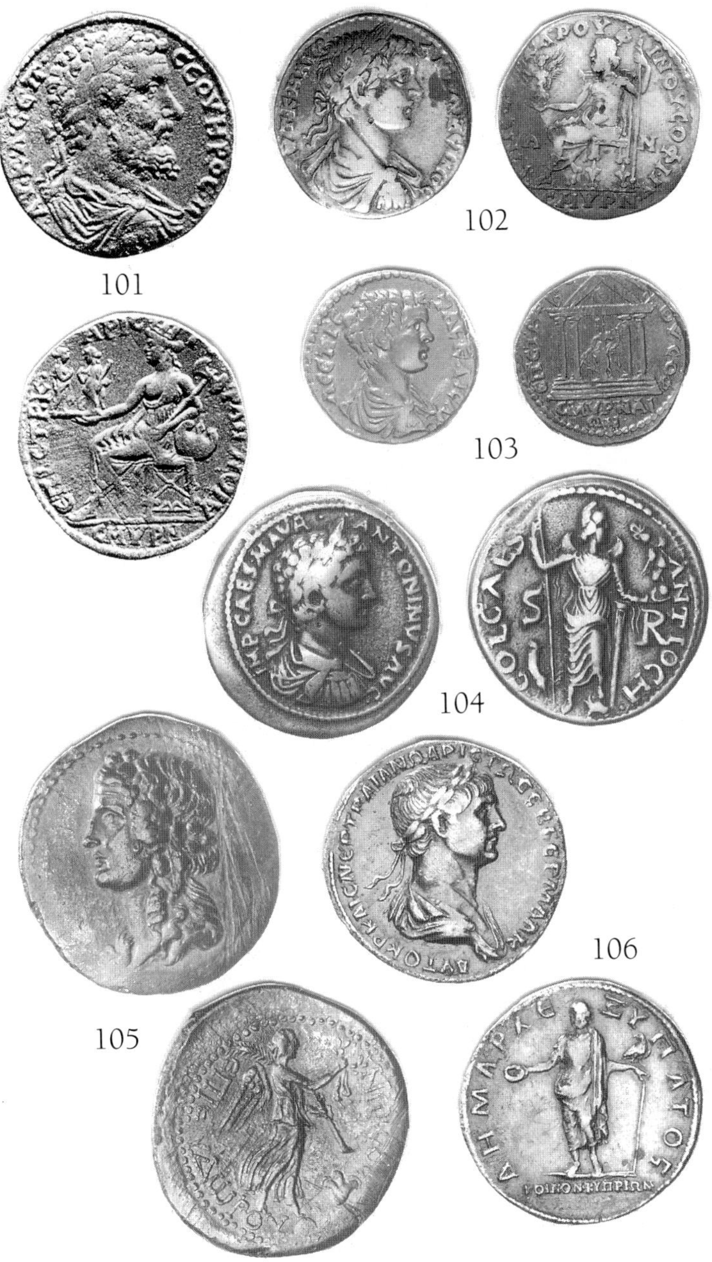
101
102
103
104
105
106

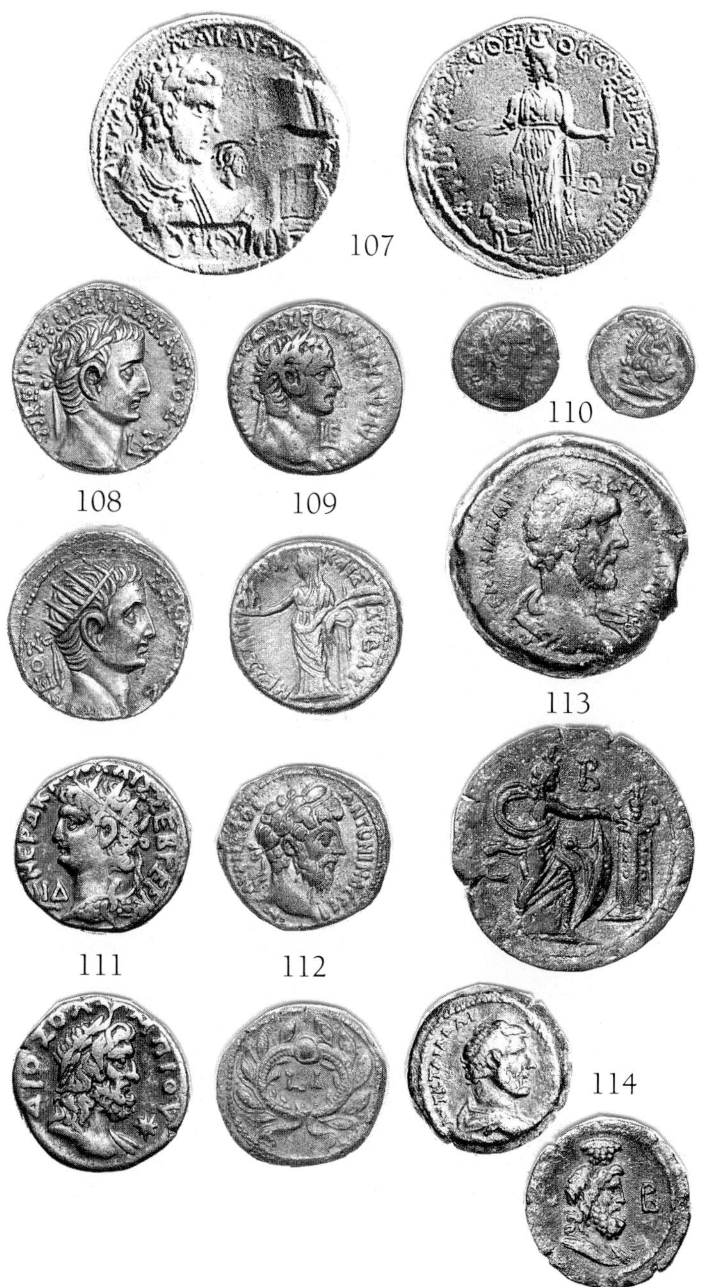
107
108
109
110
111
112
113
114

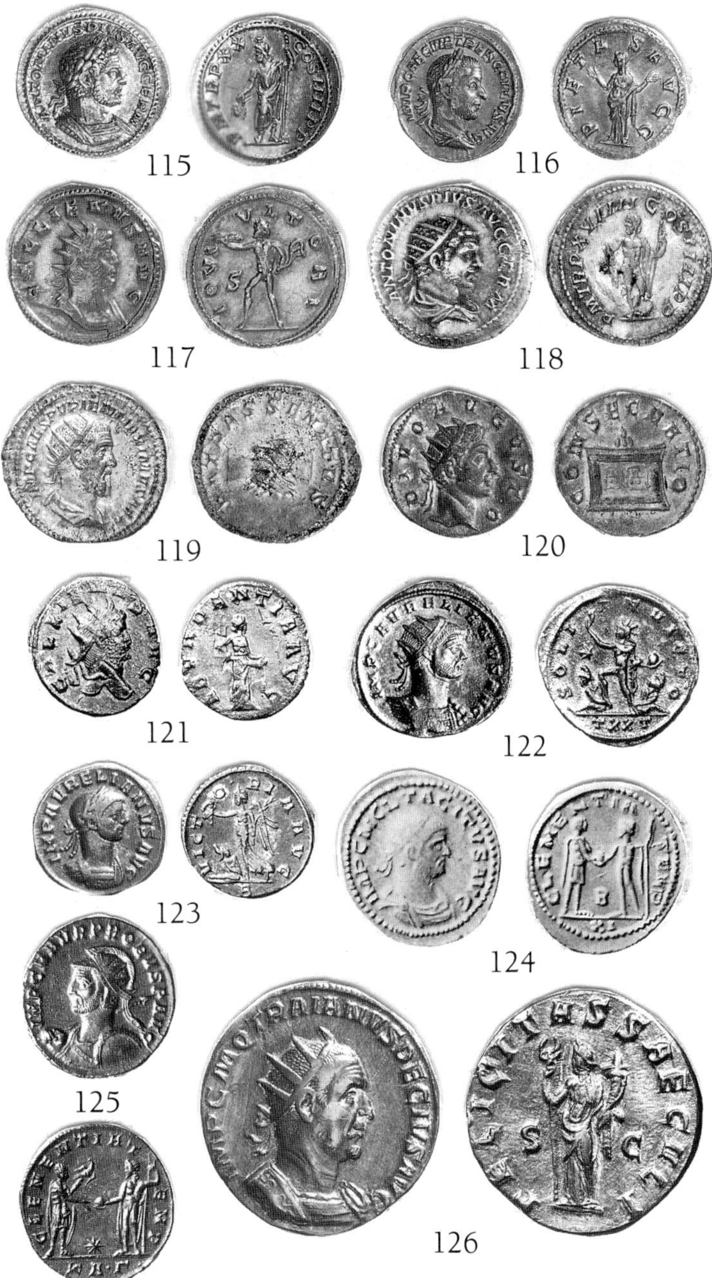
115
116
117
118
119
120
121
122
123
124
125
126

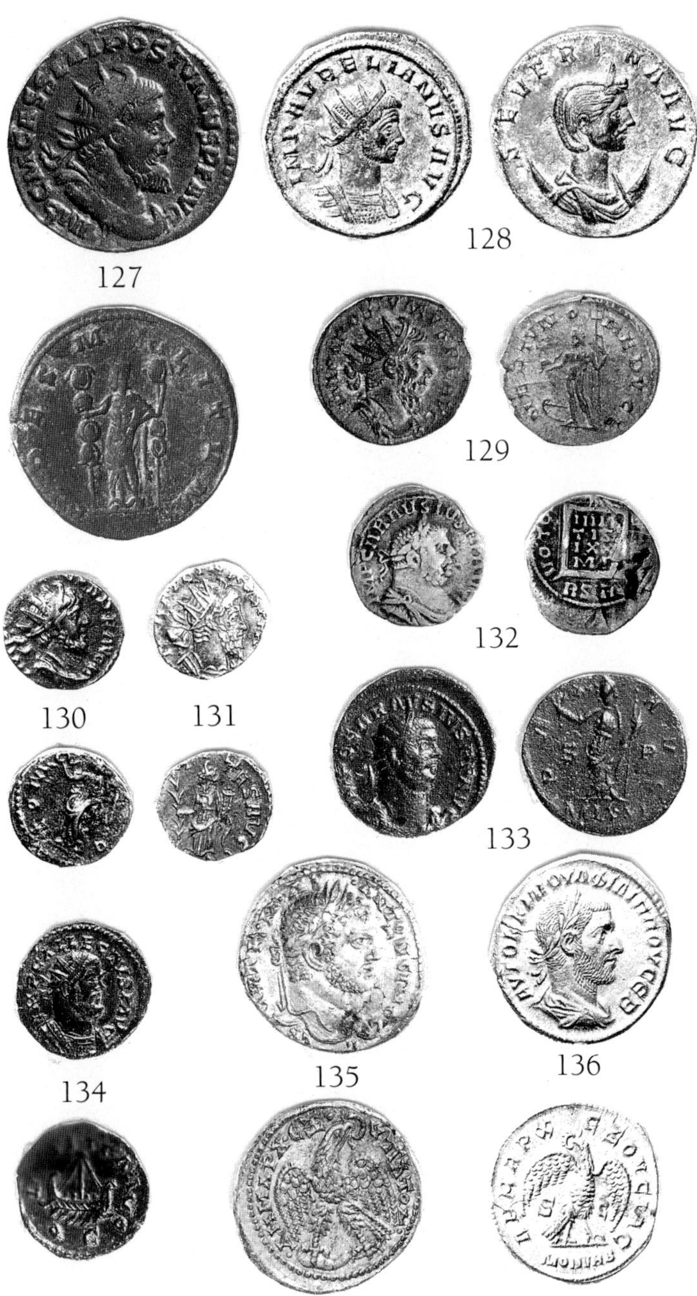

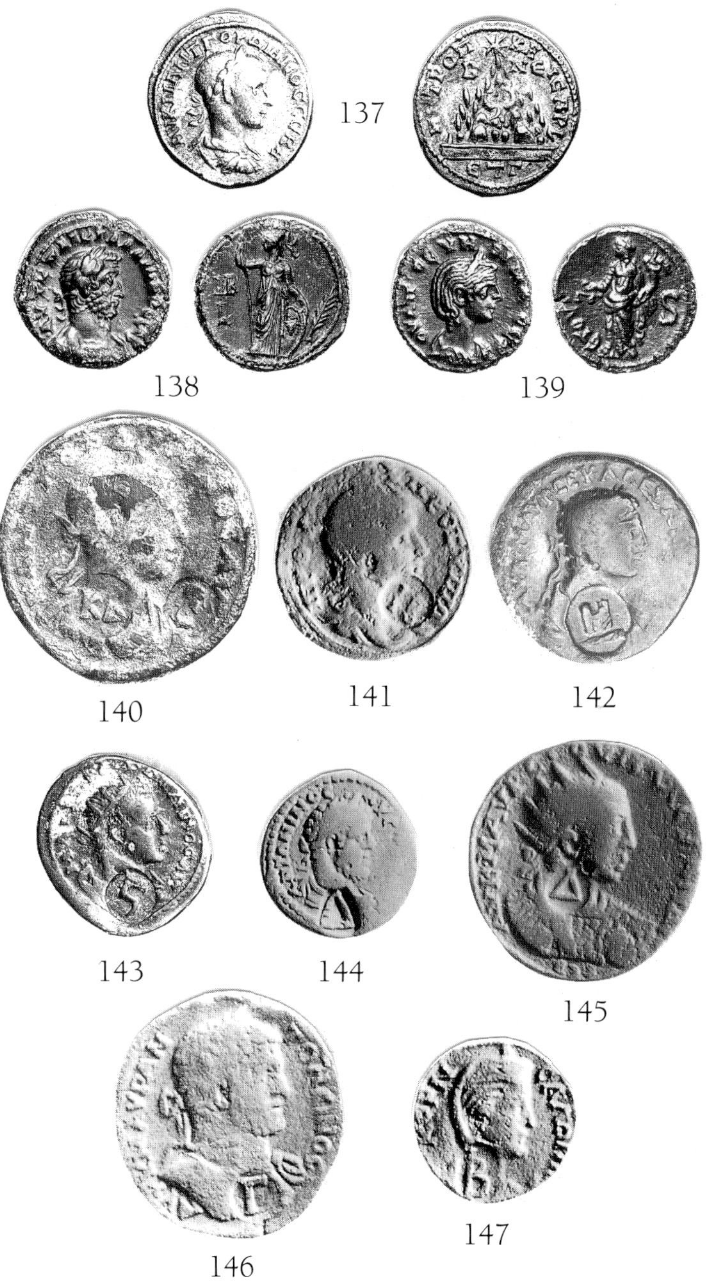
137
138
139
140
141
142
143
144
145
146
147

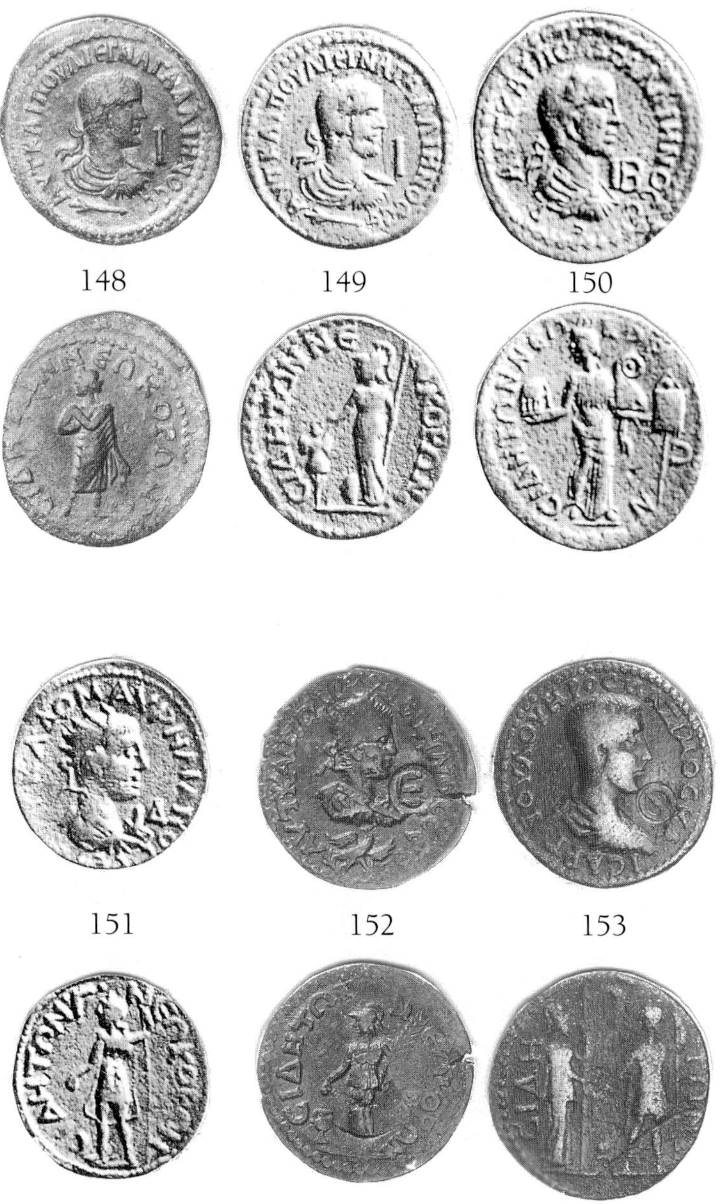

148 149 150

151 152 153

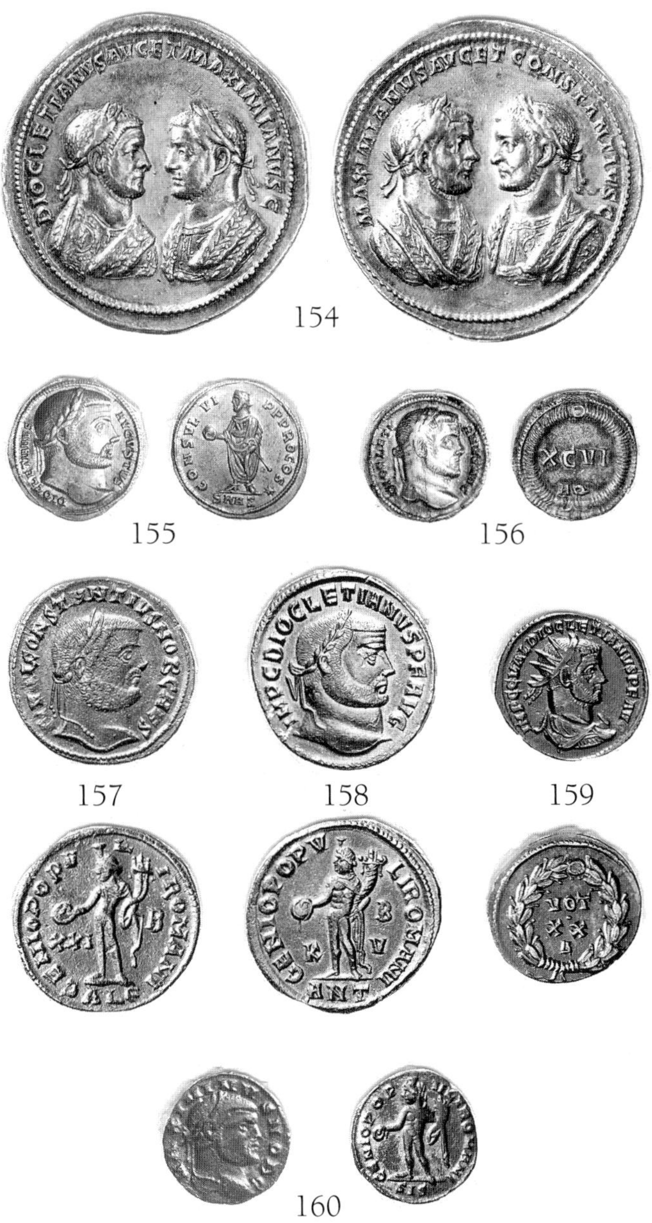


154

155

156

157

158

159

160

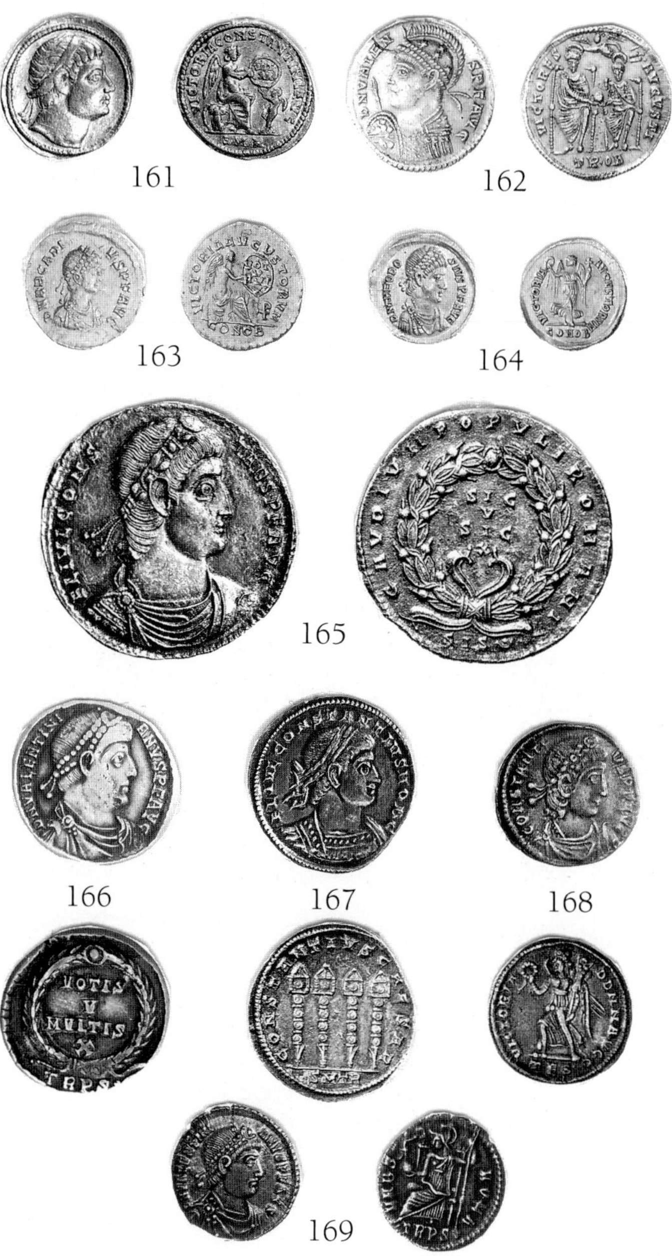

161 162 163 164 165 166 167 168 169

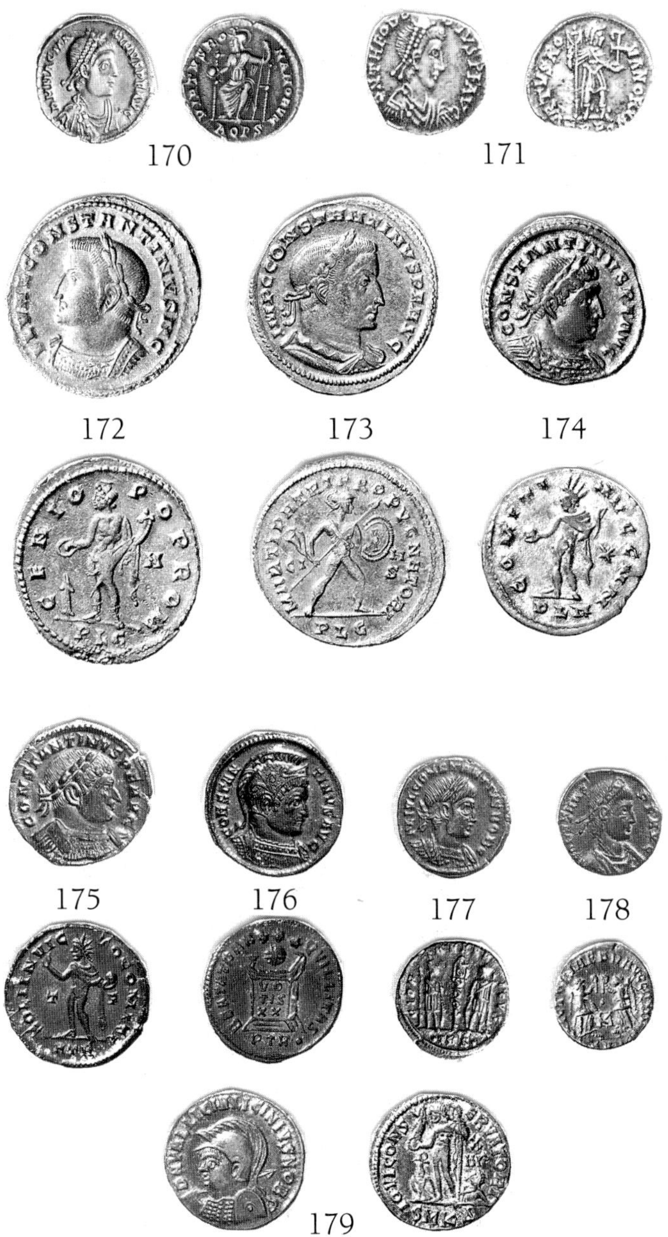

170 171

172 173 174

175 176 177 178

179

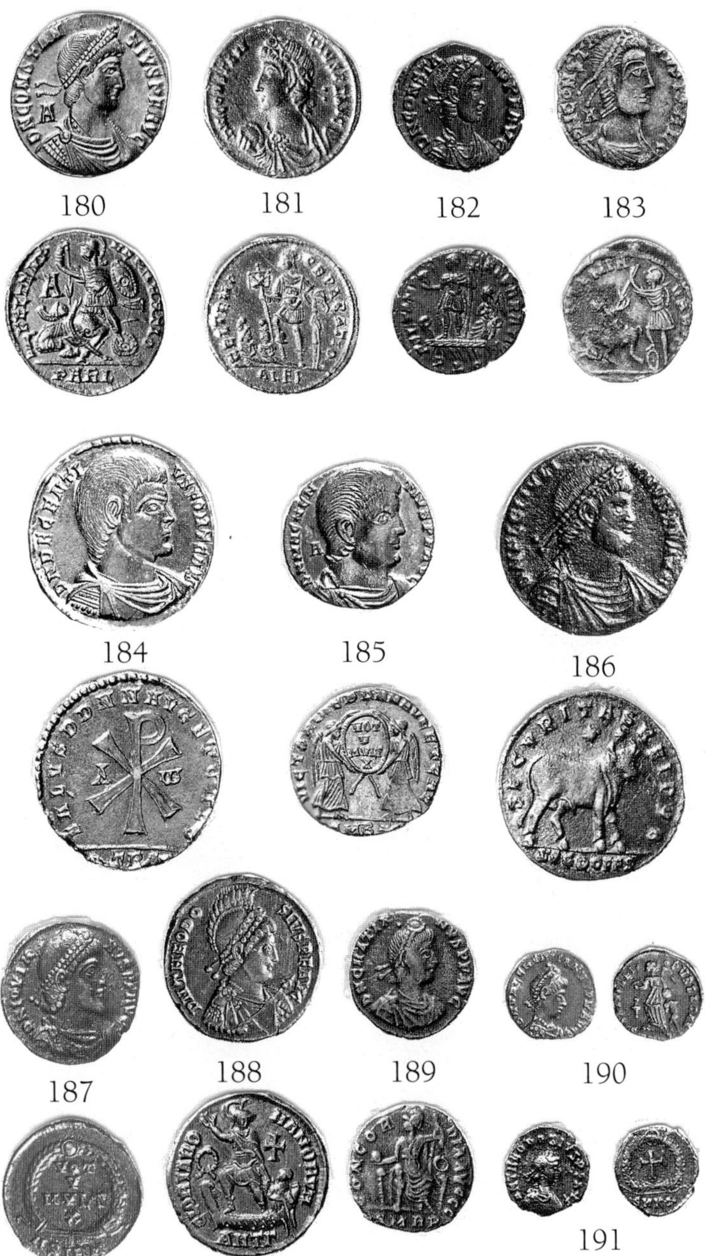

180 181 182 183

184 185 186

187 188 189 190

191

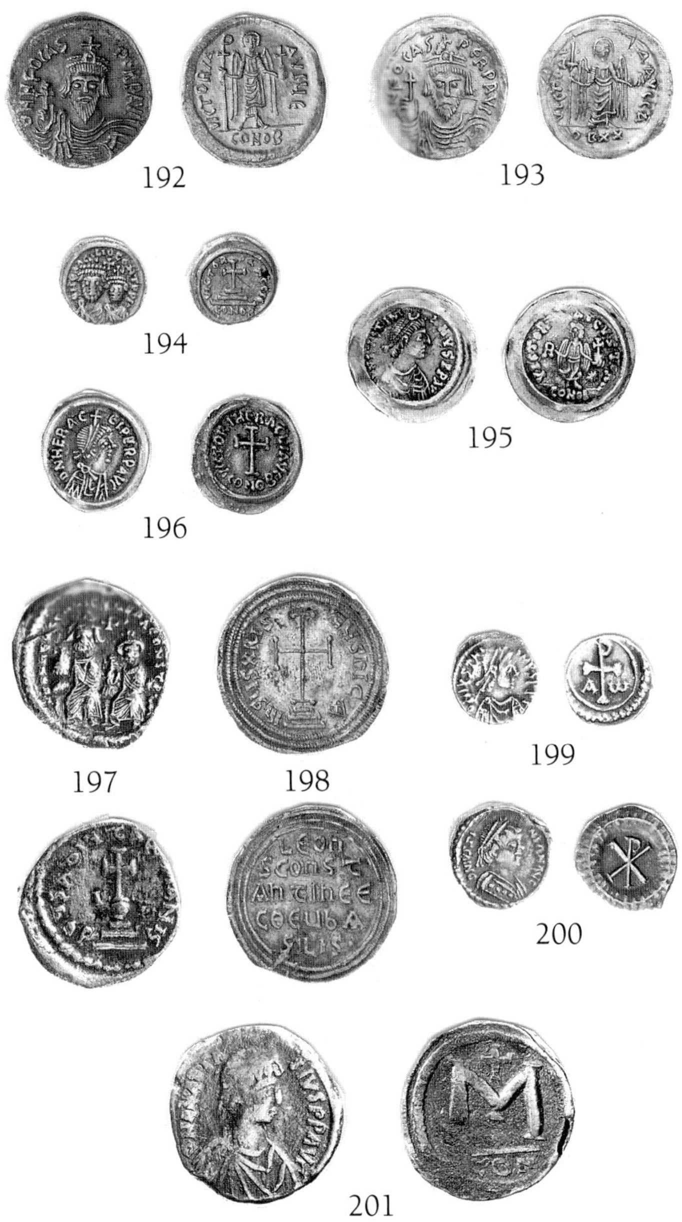
192
193
194
195
196
197
198
199
200
201

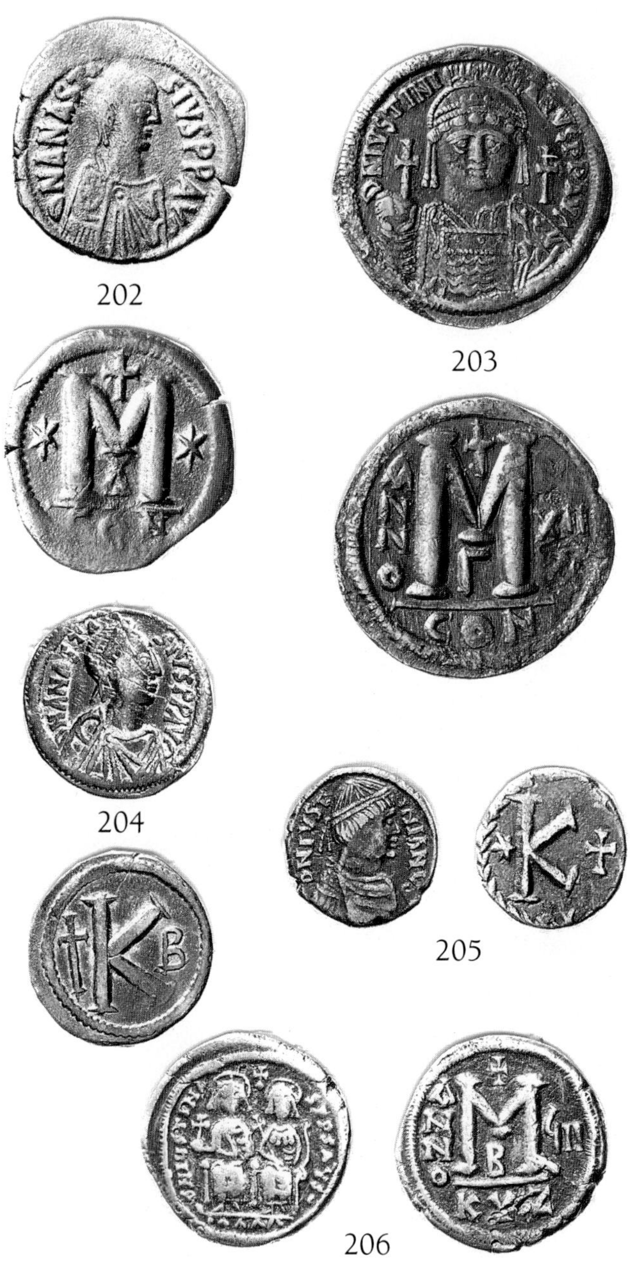

202 203 204 205 206

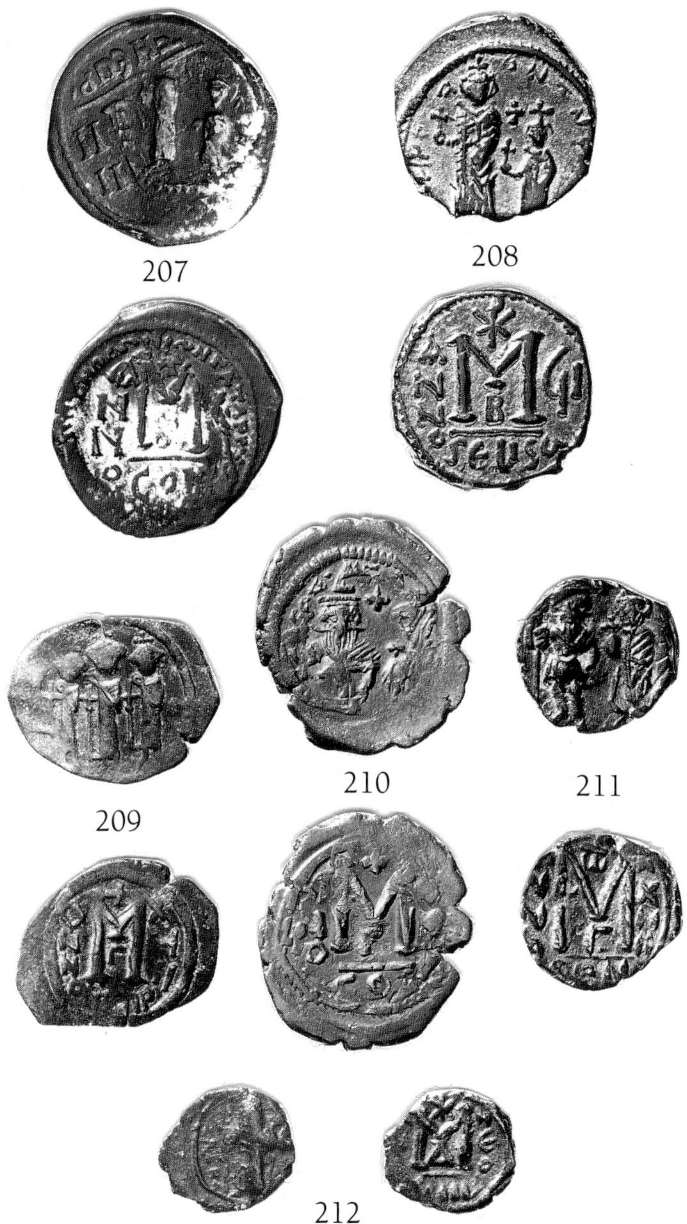

207 208

209 210 211

212

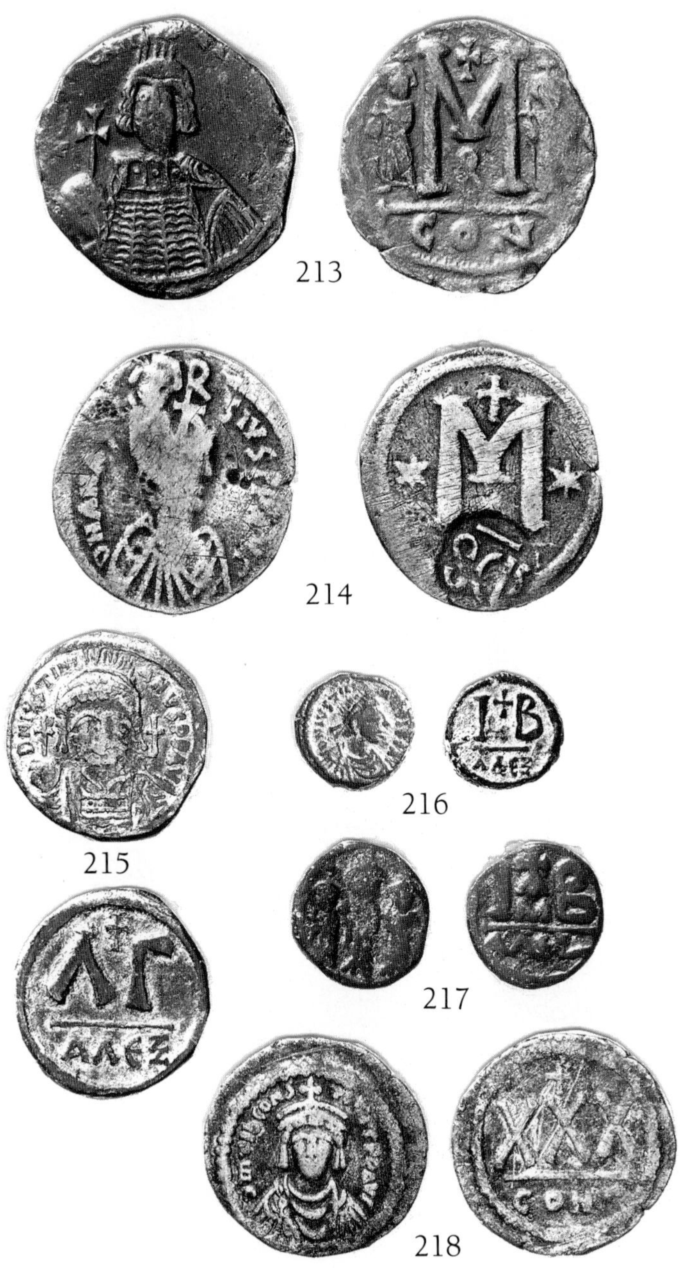

213

214

215

216

217

218

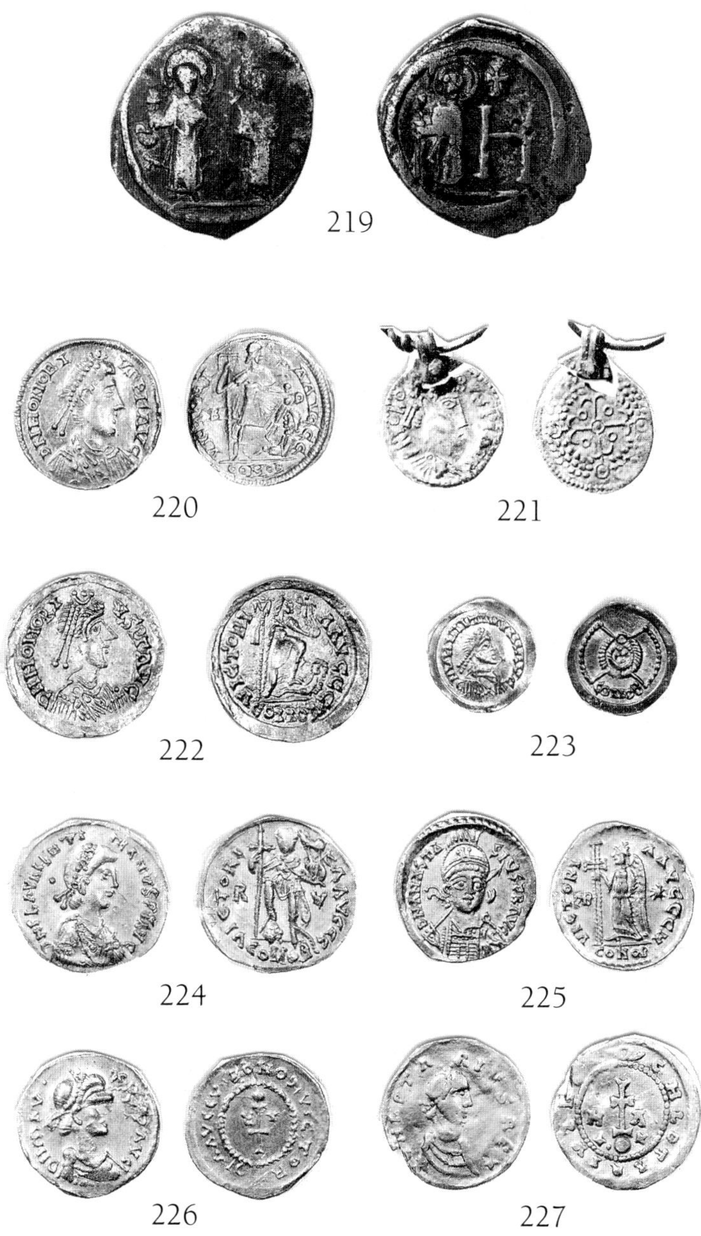

219

220

221

222

223

224

225

226

227

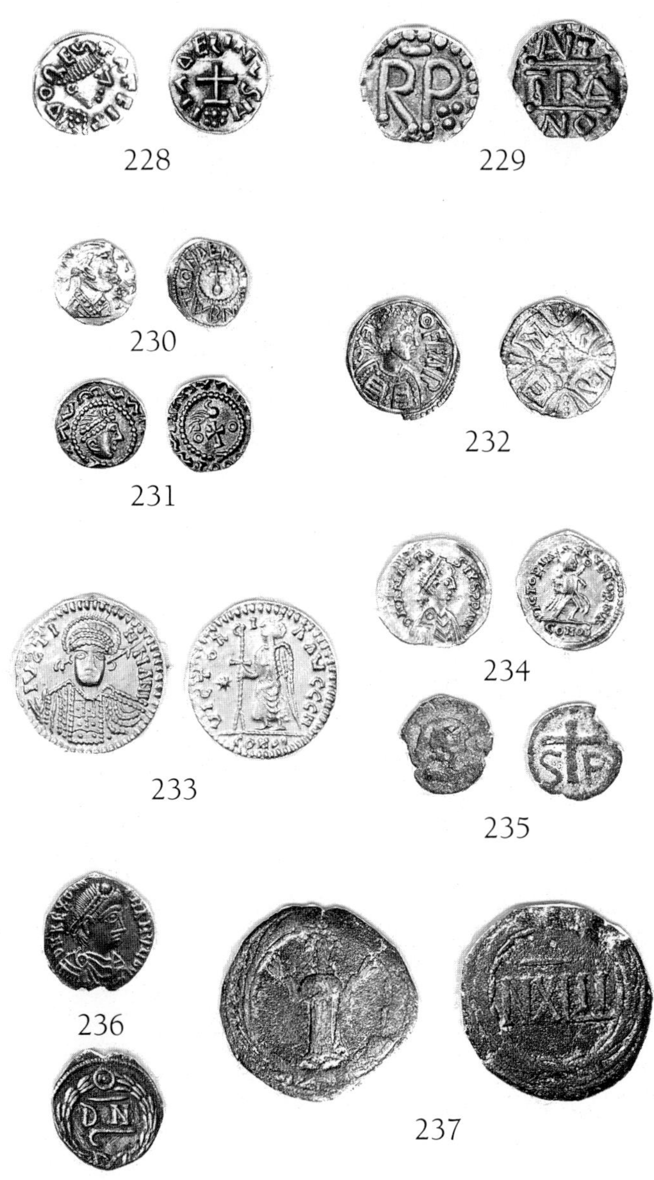
228
229
230
232
231
234
233
235
236
237

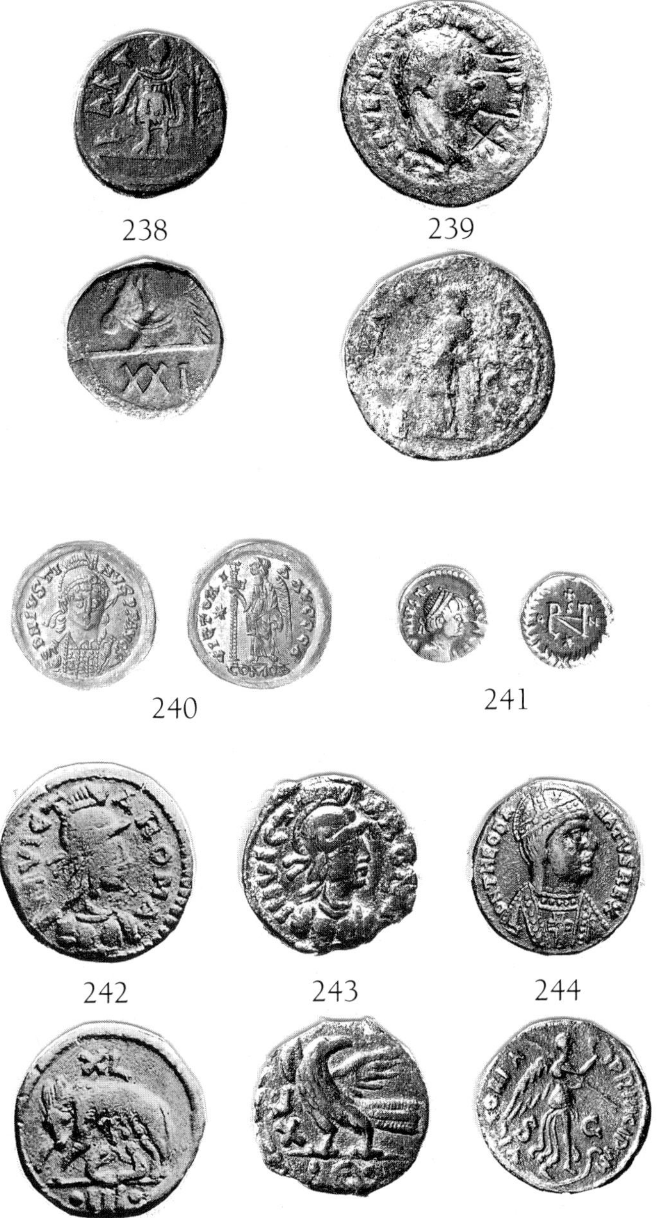
238 239

240 241

242 243 244

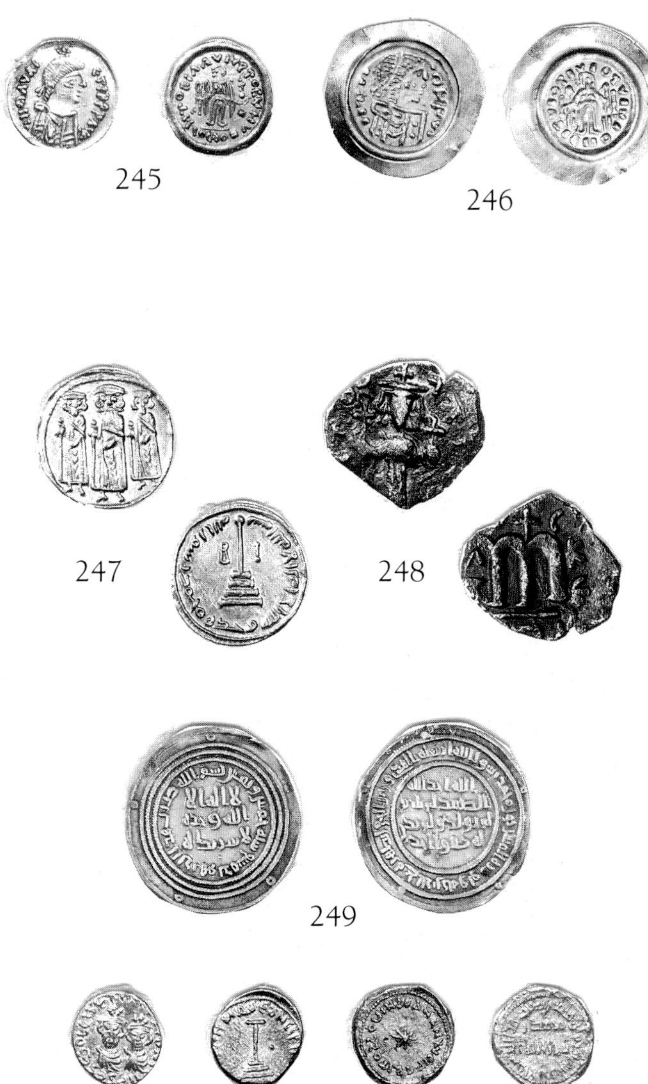
245
246
247
248
249
250
251

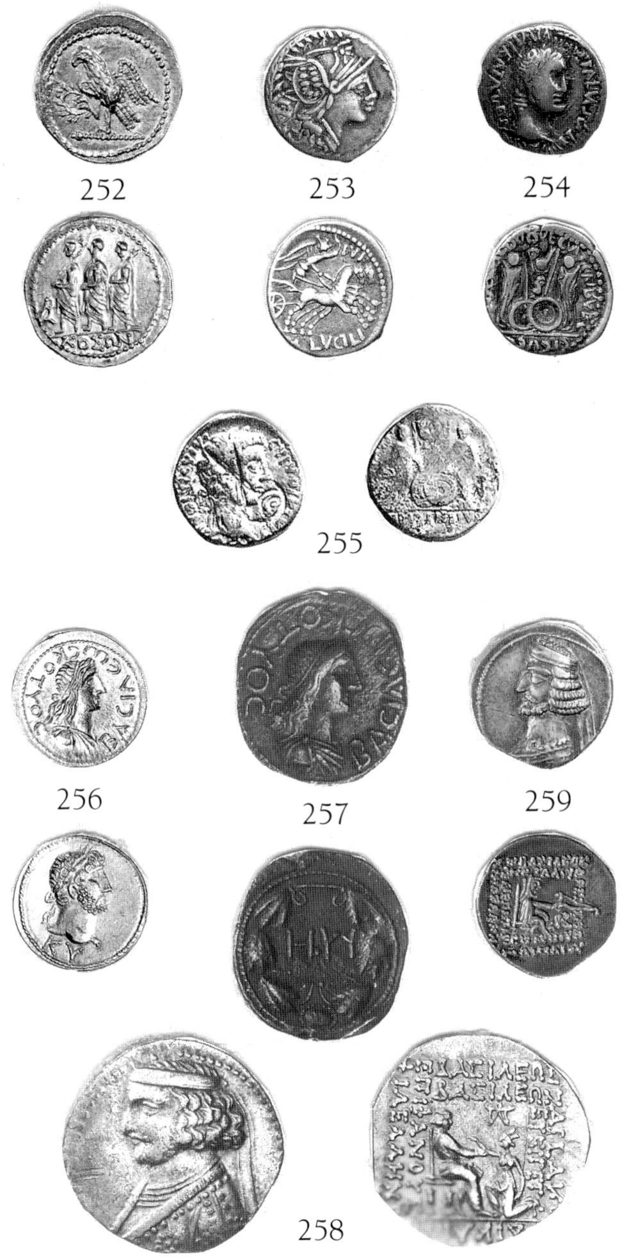
252
253
254
255
256
257
259
258

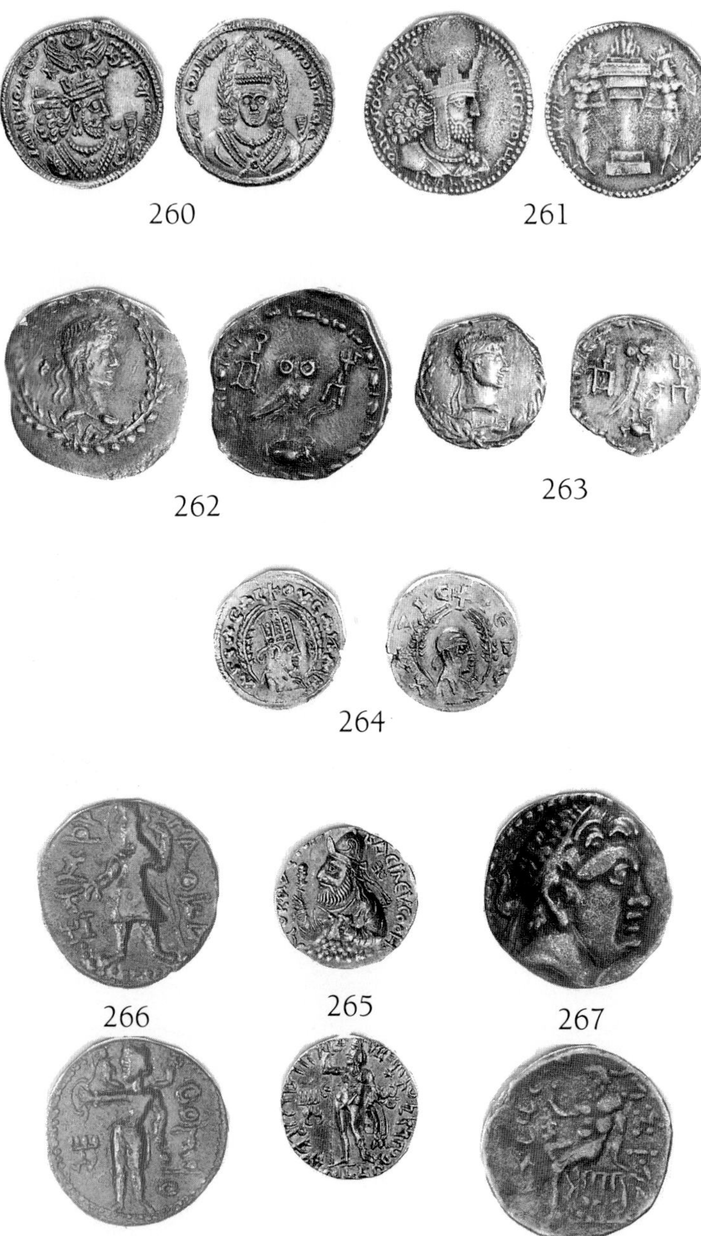
260 261

262 263

264

266 265 267

# Abbreviations

The following list covers abbreviations of numismatic and secondary works not generally familiar. This work has employed the standard abbreviations of classical authors, papyrological and epigraphic collections, reference works, and journals throughout.

*ANRW* — *Aufstieg und Niedergang der römischen Welt* (Berlin, 1972–).

*BMC* — *Catalogue of Greek Coins in the British Museum*, vols. 1–29 (London, 1873–1974).

*BMCRE* — H. Mattingly et al., *Catalogue of Coins of the Roman Empire in the British Museum*, vols. 1–6 (London, 1923–62).

*BMCRR* — H. A. Grueber, *Catalogue of Coins of the Roman Republic in the British Museum*, vols. 1–3 (London, 1910).

*CPANS* — *Centennial Publications of the American Numismatic Society*, ed. H. Ingholt (New York, 1958).

Crawford, *CMRR* — M. H. Crawford, *Coinage and Money under the*

| | |
|---|---|
| | *Roman Republic: Italy and the Mediterranean Economy* (Berkeley, 1985). |
| Crawford, *RRC* | M. H. Crawford, *The Roman Republican Coinage,* vols. 1–2 (Cambridge, 1974). |
| Crawford, *RRCH* | M. H. Crawford, *Roman Republican Coin Hoards,* Royal Numismatic Society, Special Publication 4 (London, 1969). |
| *CRWLR* | *The Coinage of the Roman World in the Late Republic,* ed. A. M. Burnett and M. H. Crawford, BAR Int. Ser. no. 236 (Oxford, 1987). |
| *DOC* | A. R. Bellinger et al., *Catalogue of the Byzantine Coins in the Dumbarton Oaks Collection and in the Whittemore Collection,* vols. 1–3 (Washington, D.C., 1969–73). |
| *ENMPG* | *Essays in Numismatic Method Presented to Philip Grierson,* ed. C. N. L. Brooke, B. H. I. H. Stewart, J. G. Pollard, and T. R. Volk (Cambridge, Mass., 1983). |
| *ERCHM* | *Essays in Roman Coinage Presented to Harold Mattingly,* ed. R. A. G. Carson and C. V. Sutherland (Oxford, 1956). |
| *ESAR* | *An Economic Survey of Ancient Rome,* vols. 1–5, ed. T. Frank (Baltimore, 1935–40). |
| Giard, *CBN* | *Catalogue des monnaies de l'empire romaine, Paris, Bibliothèque nationale,* vols. 1–2 (Paris, 1976–88). |
| Grant, *FITA* | M. Grant, *From Imperium to Auctoritas: An Historical Study of Aes Coinage in the Roman Empire 49 B.C.–A.D. 14* (Cambridge, 1946). |
| Hahn, *MIB* | W. R. O. Hahn, *Moneta Imperii Byzantini,* vols. 1–3 (Vienna, 1973–81). |

| | |
|---|---|
| Hendy, *SBME* | M. F. Hendy, *Studies in the Byzantine Monetary Economy, c. 300–1453* (Cambridge, 1985). |
| Howgego, *GIC* | C. J. Howgego, *Greek Imperial Countermarks: Studies in the Provincial Coinages of the Roman Empire*, Royal Numismatic Society, Special Publication 15 (London, 1985). |
| *IGCH* | *An Inventory of Greek Coin Hoards*, ed. M. A. Thompson, O. Mørkholm, and C. M. Kraay (New York, 1973). |
| Jones, *LRE* | A. H. M. Jones. *The Later Roman Empire, 284–602: Social, Economic and Administrative Survey*, vols. 1–2 (Oxford, 1964). |
| *PNIC* | *Proceedings of the Numismatic International Convention, Jerusalem, 27–31 December 1963*, ed. A. Kindler and C. H. V. Sutherland (Jerusalem, 1964). |
| *RIC* | H. Mattingly et al., *The Roman Imperial Coinage*, vols. 1–9 (London, 1983–91). |
| *RIC* I$^2$ | C. H. V. Sutherland, *The Roman Imperial Coinage*, vol. I, rev. edition (London, 1984). |
| *SEBGC* | *Studies in Early Byzantine Gold Coinage*, ed. W. R. O. Hahn and W. E. Metcalf, American Numismatic Society, Numismatics Studies 17 (New York, 1988). |
| *SNGANS* | *Sylloge Nummorum Graecorum, The Collection of the American Numismatic Society* (New York, 1969–94). |
| *SNGvAulock* | *Sylloge Nummorum Graecorum Deutschland. Sammlung von Aulock* (Berlin, 1957–68). |
| *SNREHS* | *Scripta Nummaria Romana: Essays Presented to Humphrey Sutherland*, ed. R. A. G. Carson and C. M. Kraay (London, 1978). |

| | |
|---|---|
| Thomsen, *ERC* | R. Thomsen, *Early Roman Coinage,* vols. 1–3 (Copenhagen, 1957–61). |
| Walker, *MRSC* | D. R. Walker, *The Metrology of Roman Silver Coinage,* 3 parts, British Archaeological Reports, supplementary series 5, 23, and 60 (Oxford, 1976–78). |
| Wroth, *BMC* I | W. Wroth, *Imperial Byzantine Coins in the British Museum* (London, 1908). |
| Wroth, *BMC* II | W. Wroth, *Western and Provincial Byzantine Coins of the Vandals, Ostrogoths and Lombards and the Empires of Thessalonica, Nicaea and Trebizond in the British Museum* (London, 1911). |

# Notes

*Chapter 1: Coins, the Money of the Roman Economy*

1. See S. Bolin, *State and Currency in the Roman Empire to 300 A.D.* (Uppsala, 1958), pp. 3–46 and 51–130; but see reviews by T. V. Buttrey, Jr., *AJA* 65 (1961), 84, and P. Grierson, *JRS* 50 (1960), 267–68.
2. M. I. Finley, *The Ancient Economy* (Berkeley, 1973), p. 166, but see critique by T. Martin, *Sovereignty and Coinage in Classical Greece* (Princeton, 1985), pp. 166–85. For nature of Roman financial crises, see M. H. Crawford, "Money and Exchange in the Roman World," *JRS* 60 (1970), 40, n. 6; M. W. Frederiksen, "Caesar, Cicero, and the Problem of Debt," *JRS* 56 (1966), 128–41; and C. Rodewald, *Money in the Age of Tiberius* (Totowa, N.J., 1976), pp. 1–17 and 70–72.
3. S. Mrozek, "*Abundantia Pecuniae,*" *Historia* 25 (1976), 122–23; and "*Inopia rei nummariae* et l'usure dans l'historie romaine," in *Rythmes de la production monétaire, de l'antiquité à nos jours,* Actes du colloque international organisé à Paris du 10 au 12 janvier 1986, ed. G. Depeyrot et al. (Louvain-la-Neuve, 1987), pp. 323–33.
4. See review of opinions in C. Morrisson, J.-N. Barrandon, and C. Brenot, "Composition and Technology of Ancient and Medieval Coinages: A Reassessment of Analytical Results," *ANSMN* 32 (1987), 181–209.
5. See P. Spufford, *Money and Its Use in Medieval Europe* (Cambridge, 1988), pp. 382–86, and cf. F. Millar, "The World of the Golden Ass," *JRS* 71 (1981), 63–75, and R. MacMullen, "Roman Market Days," *Phoenix* 24 (1970), 333–41.

6. See critiques by Crawford, *JRS* 60 (1970), 40–48, and Hendy, *SBME,* pp. 257–329 and 613–57, and contrast views of E. Lo Cascio, "State and Coinage in the Late Republic and Early Empire," *JRS* 71 (1981), 76–86, and M. G. Fulford, "Coin and Circulation and Mint Activity in the Later Roman Empire," *Archaeological Journal* 135 (1978), 59–69.
7. See R. Reece, "The Use of Roman Coinage," *Oxford Journal of Archaeology* 3 (1984), 198–200, and Fig. 1.
8. Str. 4. 2. 3 (191) and Athenaeus, *Deipnosophistae* 4. 152D (Posidonius, frag. 67) are applied to models proposed by K. Polanyi et al., *Trade and Market in Early Empires* (Glencoe, Ill., 1957).
9. K. Greene, *The Archaeology of the Roman Economy* (Berkeley, 1986), pp. 40–41, critiquing gift exchange proposed by L. Hedeager, "A Quantitative Analysis of Roman Imports to Europe North of the Limes (0–400 A.D.)," in *New Directions in Scandinavian Archaeology,* ed. K. Kristiansen and C. Palaudan-Muller (Lyngby, 1977), pp. 191–216.
10. See R. Duncan-Jones, "Weight-loss as an Index of Coin-wear in the Currency of the Roman Empire," in *Rythmes,* p. 249, Table XIV and *Money and Government in the Roman Empire* (Cambridge, 1994), pp. 180–212.
11. See F. C. Lane and R. C. Mueller, *Money and Banking in Medieval and Renaissance Venice* (Baltimore, 1985), I, pp. 24–28. The rate of loss for a medieval silver coin in active circulation is 0.2 percent according to P. Grierson, "Numismatics," *Medieval Studies,* ed. J. A. Powell (Syracuse, 1976), p. 125. For comparable estimates, see J. Craig, *The Mint: A History of the London Mint from A.D. 287 to 1948* (Cambridge, 1953), pp. xvi, 26–27, and 60 (10 percent loss in fifty years), and N. J. Mayhew, "Numismatic Evidence and Falling Prices in the Fourteenth Century," *EcHR* 2, 27 (1974), 1–15 (10–20 percent loss including exports of silver). Far less likely are the higher annual rates argued by P. Spufford, *Monetary Problems and Politics in the Burgundian Netherlands, 1453–1496* (Leiden, 1970), p. 11 (1 percent per year), or C. C. Patterson, "Silver Stocks and Losses in Ancient and Medieval Times," *EcHR* 2, 25 (1976), 207–8 and 220 (2 percent in Roman world and 1 percent in medieval Europe and the Caliphate).
12. See Lane and Mueller, *Money and Banking,* pp. 24–44. Analysis of silver currency is based on W. R. Walker, "The Silver Content of Roman Republican Coinage," in *Metallurgy in Numismatics* I, ed. D. M. Metcalf and W. A. Oddy (London, 1980), pp. 55–72, and *The Metrology of Roman Silver Coinage,* 3 parts, BAR Int. Ser. 5, 22, and 40 (Oxford, 1976–79).
13. G. F. Hill, "Ancient Methods of Coining," *NC* 5, 2 (1922), 1–22; see surviving ancient dies in in C. C. Vermeule, *Ancient Dies and Coining*

*Methods* (London, 1954), and "Minting Greek and Roman Coins," *Archaeology* 10, 2 (1957), 100–107.

14. See P. Kinns, "The Amphictyonic Coinage Reconsidered," *NC* 143 (1983), 1–22 (40,000 coins per obverse die). and Crawford, *RRC* II, pp. 694–97 (30,000 coins per obverse die). For comparable output at medieval mints, see J. D. Brand, "The Shrewsbury Mint, 1249–50," in *Essays Dedicated to the Memory of Albert Baldwin,* ed. R. A. G. Carson (London, 1971), pp. 129–50; M. Mate, "Coin Dies under Edward I and II," *NC* 7, 9 (1969), 207–18; and A. Stahl, *The Venetian Tornessello: A Medieval Colonial Coinage* (New York, 1985), pp. 50–51. I regard as too low estimates of 11,500 to 20,000 coins per obverse die proposed by D. G. Sellwood, "Some Experiments in Greek Minting Techniques," *NC* 3, 7 (1963), 217–31; and T. V. Buttrey, Jr., "The Denarii of P. Crepusius and Roman Republican Mint Organization," *ANSMN* 21 (1976), 67–108; and H. B. Mattingly, "The Management of the Roman Republican Mint," *AIIN* 29 (1982), 27–28.
15. See G. F. Carter, "A Simplified Method for Calculating the Original Number of Dies from Die Link Statistics," *ANSMN* 28 (1983), 195–206.
16. See J. P. C. Kent, "Interpreting Coin Hoards," in *Coins and the Archaeologist,* ed. P. Casey and R. Reece, BAR Int. Ser. 4 (Oxford, 1979), pp. 188–89.
17. Jos., *BJ* 6. 6. 1 (317).
18. See T. R. Volk, "Mint Output and Coin Hoards," in *Rythmes,* pp. 156–60.
19. See M. H. Crawford, "Coin Hoards and the Pattern of Violence in the Late Republic," *PBSR* 37 (1969), 79.
20. Artemidorus, *Oneirokritikon* 2. 59; cf. Phil., *VA* 6. 39; Tac., *Ann.* 16. 1; and Suet. *Nero* 31. 4.
21. Plut., *Pomp.* 11. 3–4; cf. Jos., *BJ* 7. 122.
22. App., *BC* 4. 73 and 81–82.
23. *P. Rylands* II. 125.
24. Crawford, *RRC* I, pp. 47–74, and II, 633–40, and 694–707, but see critique by Volk, *Rythmes,* pp. 156–59.
25. The statistics are based on I. Carradice, *Coinage and Finances in the Reign of Domitian* A.D. *81–96*, BAR Int. Ser. 178 (Oxford, 1973), p. 91.
26. See Duncan-Jones, *Money and Government,* pp. 82–179, whose reconstructed mintages of imperial aurei and denarii are vitiated by failure to account for distorted record offered by hoards.
27. See Volk, *Rythmes*, pp. 142–55, criticizing stray finds as proof that military pay was in bronze coins as argued by C. H. V. Sutherland, "The Intelligibility of Roman Coin Types," *JRS* 49 (1959), 53, and K. Kraft,

"Bemerkungen zur keltischen Neusaufnahme der Fundmünzen," *JNG* 7 (1976), 39–40.

28. See J. Casey, *Roman Coinage in Britain* (Aylesbury, 1980), p. 31, Figs. 5–6.
29. B. W. Frier and A. J. Parker, "Roman Coins from the River Liri," *NC* 7, 10 (1970), 89–109; W. E. Metcalf, "Roman Coins from the River Liri II," *NC* 7, 14 (1974), 42–53; and T. V. Buttrey, Jr., *Cosa: The Coins* (Rome, 1980), pp. 31–35.
30. Fulford, *Archaeological Journal* 135 (1978), 67–114.
31. See C. Morrisson, "Coin Finds in Vandal and Byzantine Carthage: A Provisional Assessment," in *A Circus and a Byzantine Cemetery at Carthage,* ed. J. H. Humphrey (Ann Arbor, Mich., 1989) I, pp. 423–36; and W. E. Metcalf, "A Heraclian Hoard from Syria," *ANSMN* 20 (1975), 109–38, and "Three Seventh-Century Byzantine Gold Hoards," *ANSMN* 25 (1980), 87–108.

*Chapter 2: Monetization of Roman Italy, 500–200* B.C.

1. Plin., *NH* 33. 42–44, and Crawford, *RRC* I, no. 5/1.
2. Coins of Vetulonia and Populonia date to the Second Punic War; see I. Vecchi, "The Coinage of the *Rasna*: A Study in Etruscan Numismatics," *SNR* 67 (1988), 43–52, and P. Visonà, "Foreign Currency in Etruria *circa* 400–200 B.C.," in *Ancient Coins of the Greco-Roman World: The Nickle Numismatic Papers,* ed. W. Heckel and R. Sullivan (Waterloo, Ont., 1984), pp. 221–40.
3. See C. M. Kraay, *Archaic and Classical Greek Coins* (Berkeley, 1976), pp. 161–79 and 206–24, and N. K. Rutter, *The Campanian Coinages, 475–380* B.C. (Edinburgh, 1979), pp. 3–16, 21–22, 32–34, and 99.
4. See Kraay, *Greek Coins,* p. 185, and N. H. Gale, W. Genter, and G. A. Wagner, "Mineralogical and Geographic Silver Sources of Archaic Greek Coinage," in *Metallurgy in Numismatics,* ed. D. M. Metcalf and W. A. Oddy, (London, 1980), I, pp. 48–49.
5. See C. H. V. Sutherland, "Overstrikes and Hoards: The Movement of Greek Coinage down to 400 B.C.," *NC* 6, 2 (1942), 1–18. For circulation of Corinthian coins after 400 B.C., see R. J. A. Talbert, "Corinthian Silver Coinage and the Sicilian Economy, c. 390-c. 290 B.C.," *NC* 7, 11 (1971), 53–66.
6. See Martin, *Sovereignty*, pp. 196–214, and cf. C. Starr, *Athenian Coinage, 480–449* B.C. (Oxford, 1970), pp. 6–7 and 75–86.
7. See C. Boehringer, "Zu Finanzpolitik und Münzprägung des Dionysios von Syrakus," in *Greek Numismatics and Archaeology: Essays in Honor of Margaret Thompson,* ed. O. Mørkholm and N. Waggoner (Wetteren, 1979), pp. 9–33. For comparable Carthaginian currency, see G. K. Jenkins and R. B. Lewis, *Carthaginian Gold and Electrum Coins,* Royal

Numismatic Society, Special Pub. 2 (London, 1963), pp. 11–12, and G. K. Jenkins, "Coins of Punic Sicily," *RSN* 56 (1977), 4–66.

8. See Kraay, *Greek Coins*, pp. 189–96, and A. M. Burnett, "Naples and South Italy, Coinage and Prosperity, ca. 300 B.C.," in *La monetazione di Neapolis nella Campania antica = Atti del VII convegno del centro internazionali di studi numismatici, Napoli 20–24 aprile 1980* (Naples, 1986), pp. 25–28.
9. See Thomsen, *ERC* I, pp. 55–89 and 191–97; and A. M. Burnett, "The Coinages of Rome and Magna Graecia in the Late Fourth and Third Centuries B.C.," *SNR* 56 (1977), 93–94. For the corpus of *aes grave*, see E. J. Haeberlin, *Aes Grave: Das Schwergeld Roms und Mittelitaliens* (Frankfurt/Main, 1910), II, pl. 70–78, 82–92, and 96.
10. See Crawford, *RRC* I, pp. 29–31; Thomsen, *ERC* I, pp. 191–209; and Haeberlin, *Aes Grave,* I, pp. 57–280, and II, pl. 62–96.
11. See *RRCH,* nos. 13–21, 23–28, 30–31, and 38–50.
12. The chronology of the first three issues of the didrachma is based on A. M. Burnett, "The Coinages of Rome and Magna Graecia in the Late Fourth and Third Centuries B.C.," *SNR* 56 (1977), 116, and "The Second Issue of Roman Didrachms," *NAC* 9 (1980), 169–74. See Table 2.1.
13. Liv. 9. 37. 10. The first didrachmae, minted at 44 or 45 to the Roman pound, give a silver to bronze ratio of 1:120; see Burnett, *SNR* 56 (1977), 95, n. 5. Early didrachmae were probably tariffed at 10 asses and termed denarii as Pliny, *NH* 33. 43 states. The later nicknames *quadrigatus* and *bigatus* designated denarii derived from their reverse types; see Plin., *HN* 33. 46, and Festus 347M; cf. Thomsen, *ERC* I, p. 35.
14. See A. M. Burnett, "The First Roman Silver Coins," *NAC* 7 (1978), 125–54; cf. Frank, *ESAR* I, pp. 47–48, for prices and fines in the Twelve Tables cited in asses.
15. Liv. 10. 46. 5 and 14, for totals of 2,533,000 and 380,000 *aeris gravis* or 2,913,000 asses in 293 B.C., and contrast Liv. 10. 46 for 1,830 pounds of silver taken in Samnium. See Liv. 10. 37. 5, for fines of 500,000 asses imposed on Volsinii, Perusia, and Arretium, and Liv. 10. 46. 12, for 100,000 asses assessed against the Faliscans. In 295 B.C. ransoming of captives netted 539,400 asses (Liv. 10. 31. 3).
16. Liv., *Periocha* 15 ("tunc primum populus R. argenteo ut coepit"); cf. Zon. 8. 7 and Dio. Hal. 10. 17. The coins were heavy denarii (didrachmae) of the second and third series, see A. M. Burnett, "The Second Issue of Roman Didrachms," *NAC* 9 (1980), 169–74, and *SNR* 56 (1977), 106–14; and Thomsen, *ERC* I, p. 34, superseding Crawford, *RRC* I, pp. 38–42.
17. Crawford, *RRC* I, pp. 44–45. The weight standard of heavy denarii (didrachmae) was lowered slightly from 7.3 in 310 B.C. to 7.1 g by 268

B.C. so the new denarii could circulate at par with worn older Italiot coins issued on a reduced standard during the Pyrrhic War (Tarantine coins classified as Evans Groups VI and VII); see Burnett, *SNR* 56 (1977), 106–14. Didrachmae of the first ROMANO series and Tarantine coins of Evans Group V are deposited in hoards of the Lucanian War (303–302 B.C.). Didrachmae of the second and third ROMANO series are hoarded with coins of Tarantine Group VI or VII (ca. 270–250 B.C.), dating either to the Pyrrhic War or early stages of the First Punic War. Those of the fourth ROMANO series and of the three ROMA series are found with Tarantine Group IX (ca. 250–240 B.C.) and late Neapolitan coins in hoards of the later First Punic War. The hoards suggest that the ROMA series were minted during rather than after the First Punic War as argued by Crawford, *RRC* I, pp. 40–46, and Burnett *SNR* 56 (1977), 114–16.

18. Calculations are based on A. M. Burnett, "The Beginnings of Roman Coinage," *AIIA* 36 (1989), 44–45, and Jenkins and Lewis, *Carthaginian Gold and Electrum Coins,* pp. 35–42.
19. The rate of pay is surmised from Plin., *HN* 18. 17, recording the price of one as per modius of wheat offered in 250 B.C. at the triumph of L. Caecilius Metellus (cos. 251).
20. See Polyb. 1. 20. 9–10 and 13–14. Most of the coins were minted in 300–270 B.C.; see A. M. Burnett, "Naples and South Italy, Coinage and Prosperity, ca. 300 B.C.," *Atti del VII convegno del centro internazionale di studi numismatici, Napoli 20–24 aprile 1980* (Naples, 1986), pp. 28–38; A. Johnston, *The Coinage of Metapontum,* Part 3 (New York, 1990), pp. 57–63; and R. Williams, *The Silver Coinage of Velia,* Royal Numismatic Society, Special Pub. 25 (London, 1992), pp. 93–133.
21. Polyb. 1. 19. 15, and cf. 1. 24. 10–13.
22. See *CIL* I. 2. 25 = A. Degrassi, *Inscriptiones Italiae* XIII. I. 77. The numbers are corrupt but the total was between 2 million and 3 million asses in value. The aurei were gold Attic tridrachmae (12.5 g and valued at 22 shekels or 40 Attic drachmae each); most silver coins were shekels (7.6 g, equivalent to an Attic didrachma); see Jenkins and Lewis, *Carthaginian Gold and Electrum Coins,* pp. 13 and 27–38. The 3,600 gold staters = 144,000 Attic drachmae = 24 talents = 92,160 Roman denarii (i.e., 24 × 80 × 48) or 921,600 asses. Deducting this sum from the total of 2 million to 3 million asses, yields a remainder in silver coins valued between 1,078,400 and 2,078,400 asses (equivalent to 107,840 and 207,840 Roman denarii or between 2,246.67 and 4,330 Roman pounds of silver).
23. See Crawford, *CMRR,* pp. 43–51, and Buttrey, *Cosa,* pp. 25–27; many series are undated or unassigned to mints. Burnett, *SNR* 56 (1977), 93–95, notes bronze series bearing ROMA were issued in tandem with

the ROMA series of heavy denarii (didrachmae). These bronze series must date to 264–241 B.C., and weight standards were progressively reduced by 12 to 17.5 percent. The as fell to a light libral standard (282 to 266 g) or 2 ounces below a full Roman pound; see Crawford, *RRC* I, pp. 44–45 and nos. 25/4–9 (Janus/Mercury series), 26/5–8 (Apollo/Apollo series), and 27/5–10 (Roma/Roma series).

24. Polyb. 1. 63. 1–2 and 1. 88. 12; the silver was assayed and melted down as in 199 B.C.; cf. Liv. 32. 1. 1–12. The loan of 242 B.C. was paid off from booty taken at Aegetes Islands; see Polyb. 1. 61. 6–8.
25. See P. Le Gentilhomme, "Le quadrigati nummi et le dieu Janus," *RN* 4, 37 (1934), 1–36; and cf. Thomsen, *ERC* II, pp. 259–60, and Crawford, *RRC* I, pp. 44–45 and 103–19. The first series (incuse legend) was the largest, but the dies defy counting. The 16,896,000 quadrigati potentially coined from Carthaginian silver would have required 425 obverse dies and 1,275 to 1,700 reverse dies.
26. The portrait of Janus on quadrigati must allude to the closing of the temple doors in 241 B.C.; see Liv. 1. 19. 3 and Varro, *LL* 5. 165, and discussion by W. Harris, *War and Imperialism in Republican Rome 327–70 B.C.* (Oxford, 1979), pp. 190–91, and H. W. Ritter, *Zur römischen Münzprägung in 3 Jh. v. Chr.* (Marburg, 1983). The prow on asses alludes to the naval victories; see Plin., *NH* 33. 44, and Thomsen, *ERC* III, pp. 147–49. Dating the first quadrigati to ca. 225 B.C. is argued by E. A. Sydenham, *The Coinage of the Roman Republic* (London, 1952), pp. xx–xxi, and Crawford, *RRC* I, pp. 103–5, and II, p. 715, on two untenable iconographic grounds. The reverse type of the quadrigatus is interpreted as honoring a victory over Gauls in 225 or 223 B.C. and the prow on the as a copy from coins of Antigonus Doson in 227 B.C.
27. Walker, in *Metallurgy in Numismatics,* I, pp. 56–57; the first issues with incuse legend are 96.7 to 97.3 percent fine and on a weight standard of 48 to the Roman pound. See Crawford, *RRCH*, nos. 35–37 and 59–60 (Italian hoards) and 32 (Cagliari), and L. Villaronga, "The Tangier Hoard," *NC* 149 (1989), 149–52 (quadrigati hoarded by a Punic mercenary as equivalents of Neapolitan, Velian, and Tarentine didrachmae).
28. See Crawford, *RRC* I, nos. 28–29, and Walker, *Metallurgy in Numismatics,* I, pp. 56–57, for reduction from 6.4 g (97 percent fine) to 6 g (91 percent fine).
29. See Crawford, *RRC* II, p. 691 and I, nos. 28/1–2 and 29/1–2, and Plin., *NH* 33. 4; the coins were most likely called *denarii aurei* rather than staters and they were tariffed at a gold to silver ratio between 1:8 and 1:12.
30. See E. G. R. Robinson, "Carthaginian and Other South Italian Coinages of the Second Punic War," *NC* 7, 4 (1964), 37–64.
31. Festus, 87L and cf. 468L, and Plin., *NH* 33. 44 (mistakenly dating the

action to the First Punic War). The as suffered four successive weight reductions in 218–213 B.C., falling from a light libral (268 g), to semilibral (133 g), *triental* (83 g), *quadranal* (69 g), and finally *sextanal* (40.5 g) standard. See Crawford, *RRC* I, pp. 11–12, and *CMRR*, pp. 59–61, and Thomsen, *ERC* II, pp. 229–31.

32. See Crawford, *RRC* I, nos. 41/1–11, and *CMRR*, pp. 39–40; many fractions of libral and semilibral standards were probably retariffed at higher values.
33. T. V. Buttrey, Jr., "The Morgantina Excavations and the Date of the Roman Denarius," in *Atti del Congresso internazionale di Numismatica 1961* (Rome, 1965), pp. 261–67 = *Morgantina Studies: The Coins* (Princeton, 1989), pp. 215–19, and cf. pp. 220–26. The date of 214–211 B.C. is fixed by a find of uncirculated specimens of the first quinarii and sestertii at Morgantina sacked by the Romans in 214 and 211 B.C. Quadrigati are also last named in ransoms and payrolls in 216–215 B.C., see Liv. 23. 17, 54. 2, and 52. 3.
34. See Plin., *NH* 33. 46, and C. Seltman, "Argenteum Oscense and Bigati," *NC* 6, 4 (1944), 79, for *bigatus* as army slang denoting "two-horsed" rather than a two-horsed chariot (*biga*). The term denoted denarii in triumphal reports of 197–191 B.C.; see Thomsen, *ERC* I, pp. 42–43 and 184–85, and cf. Liv. 33. 23. 7 and 37. 11; 34. 10. 4 and 46. 2; 36. 21. 11 and 40. 12. Soldiers coined the term to distinguish the new lighter denarii from heavier denarii or quadrigati; see Liv. 22. 52. 2 and 4, and 59. 18.
35. See Crawford, *CMRR*, pp. 56–57 and 107–12, and *RRCH*, nos. 86, 93, and 103; cf. Thomsen, *ERC* II, pp. 332–37.
36. Cato, *De Agr.* 15 and cf. 145. See Thomsen, *ERC* II, pp. 320–91, and C. A. Hersh, "A Quinarius Hoard from Southern Italy," *NC* 7, 12 (1972), 75–88, and "Notes on the Chronology and Interpretation of the Roman Republican Coinage," *NC* 7, 17 (1977), 19–36.
37. Crawford, *RRC* I, nos. 56/1–8.
38. Calculations are based on dies in Crawford, *RRC* II, p. 691. The production of 1,800,000 heavy aurei (1/48 pound) in 218–214 B.C. consumed 26,666.67 Roman pounds of gold whereas 1,800,000 light aurei (1/96 pound) consumed 18,750 pounds. See Frank, *ESAR* I, pp. 89–91, estimating from reports by Livy and Polybius that at least 14,000 pounds of gold were collected in 211–209 B.C.
39. Polyb. 15. 18; Liv. 30. 37. 5; and Plin., *NH* 33. 51, for an indemnity of 20,000 talents payable in fifty years in annual installments of 200 talents or 1,152,000 denarii (struck at 1/72 Roman pound).
40. Polyb. 9. 10. 11, and, Crawford *RRC* I, pp. 299–315. See Frank, *ESAR* I, pp. 80–81, for windfalls in 211–205 B.C. Spoils from New Carthage (Polyb. 2. 10. 19; 600 talents), the Metaurus (Polyb. 2. 11. 3; 300

talents), and Taras (Plut., *Fab.* 22; 3,000 talents) were valued at 3,900 talents or the equivalent of 22,464,000 denarii (struck at 1/72 Roman pound). Silver windfalls from Capua (Liv. 26. 14. 8; 31,200 pounds) and New Carthage (Liv. 26. 47. 7; 14,342 pounds) totaled 45,542 pounds or 3,279,024 denarii (struck at 1/72 Roman pound).

41. See Vecchi, *RSN* 67 (1988), 53–57; Populonia and Vetulonia minted four gold denominations (marked 10, 12.5, 25, and 50 asses) and five silver denominations (marked 1, 2.5, 5, 10, and 20 asses) that parallel a denarius struck at 72 to the Roman pound in 215–213 B.C. Vulci, Volsinii, Populonia, and Vetulonia had coined earlier series based on a silver denomination (11.3 g), marked as 5, or its fractional gold equivalent (1.13 g), that was perhaps deemed a double of the quadrigatus, but their tariffing and fineness are uncertain.
42. See Crawford, *CMRR,* pp. 108–10, and A. S. Walker, "Some Hoards from Sicily and a Carthaginian Issue of the Second Punic War," in *Festschrift für Leo Mildenberg,* ed. A. Houghton, S. Hurter, P. E. Mottahedeh, and J. A. Scott (Wetteren, 1984), pp. 269–88. See R. R. Holloway, "Numismatic Notes from Morgantina: Half-coins of Hiero II in the Monetary System of Roman Sicily," *ANSMN* 9 (1960), 65–73.
43. See Crawford, *RRCH*, nos. 33, 75, 91, 104, and *IGCH* 2330 and 2337–39.
44. See L. Villaronga, "La monnaie d'argent en Éspagne de l'arrivée des Romains jusqu'à la moitié du II siècle," in *Rythmes,* pp. 99–117, for drachmae of Emporiae minted from an estimated 378 obverse dies, but the issues probably date from 200–180 B.C.; see R. Knapp, "The Purpose of Iberian Denarii," *NC* 7, 17 (1977), 2–18.

*Chapter 3: The Denarius and Overseas Expansion, 200–30 B.C.*

1. See Walker, *Metallurgy in Numismatics,* I, pp. 58–61, for a standard above 96 percent fine in 212–170 B.C.; nearly 98 percent fine in 169–91 B.C. Temporary debasements in Social (90–88 B.C.) and Civil wars were never more than 3 percent below a standard of 98 percent fine. See Harris, *War and Imperialism,* pp. 68–74, and Frank, *ESAR* I, pp. 126–45 and 228–31, who rule out arguments that the Roman state was perpetually short of specie and coin as proposed by Crawford, *RRC* II, pp. 633–95.
2. Liv. 38. 40. 15. See H. Zehnacker, "Monnaies de compte et prix à Rome au IIe siècle avant notre ère," in *Les dévaluations à Rome* (Paris, 1980), II, pp. 40–47, for donatives of 42, 84, and 124 denarii in 187 B.C. which were probably based on a standard of 84 denarii to the Roman pound so that the sums represent 0.5, 1, and 1.5 pounds of silver.
3. Plin., *NH* 33. 44; see Thomsen, *ERC* II, pp. 181–92.
4. Plin., *NH* 33. 45; but see Thomsen, *ERC* III, pp. 15–72 and Crawford,

*RRC* I, pp. 42–46 and II, pp. 595–97 and 615–17. Many specimens of uncial asses weigh 18 g due to heavy wear.

5. See Liv. 32. 1. 1–2 (199 B.C.), for melting down and assaying the Carthaginian indemnity. For use of bullion bars (*lateres*) of gold and silver, see Plin., *NH* 33. 55–56, (49 B.C.); and cf. *RRCH*, no. 357, for a hoard of 80,000 denarii and bars of gold. For comparable use of certified bars in medieval and Renaissance bulk payments, see Spufford, *Money*, pp. 209–14.
6. The silver content of the victoriatus was half that of the denarius; see Walker, *Metallurgy in Numismatics,* I, pp. 58–61, and Cato, *De Agr*. 15. 1, for a tariffing of five asses in 180 B.C. See C. A. Hersh, "A Quinarius Hoard from South Italy," *NC* 7, 12 (1972), 75–88, and *NC* 7, 17 (1977), 28–29, for discontinuing quinarii and sestertii soon after 200 B.C., redating quinarii in Crawford, *RRC* I, no. 133/3, to the Second Punic War, and rejecting those in no. 156/2 as bogus.
7. Crawford, *RRC* I, pp. 71–75, and II, pp. 635–37, and *CMRR*, p. 57, n. 10, who posits a gap in minting denarii during the period 168–157 B.C. Crawford argues that the Roman state suffered chronic shortages of silver specie. This argument is based on two untenable grounds. First, output is reconstructed based on dies preserved in hoards, but this record distorts rather than mirrors production; see Volk, *Rythmes,* pp. 158–89, and the comparable case in E. Besly, *English Civil War Coin Hoards* (London, 1987), pp. 53–68. The poor survival of specimens results from the low incidence of hoards during a period of comparative peace and later reminting. The fifty-nine hoards of the Second Punic War (218–201 B.C.) are over three times more numerous than those dated to 200–150 B.C. (eighteen hoards), a period over twice as long; see Crawford, *PBSR* 37 (1969), 76–81. The estimate of dies based on these hoards is untrustworthy; see reviews by T. V. Buttrey Jr., *CW* 20 (1977–78), 151–53, and B. W. Frier, *Phoenix* 30 (1976), 375–82, for criticism of the method and mathematics of estimating dies by Crawford, *RRC* II, pp. 640–94.

   Second, Crawford's sequence of issues and dating of denarii and *aes* need revision in light of Hersh, *NC* 7, 17 (1977), 19–23. See also A. M. Burnett, "The Authority to Coin in the Late Republic and Early Empire," *NC* 7, 17 (1977), 43, and Mattingly, *AIIN* 29 (1982), 12–16. Denarii depicting Luna in *biga* were minted from the Macedonian spoils seized in 168–167 B.C., notably Crawford, *RRC* I, nos. 156, 159, 162–63, 166, 168, and 172. See Burnett, *NC* 7, 15 (1977), 43, for redating Crawford, no. 162/1 (ca. 179–170 B.C.) to 163 B.C. See Hersh, *NC* 7, 17 (1977), 19–23, for reattribution of many denarii from the Second Punic War to ca. 200–190 B.C. based on Sydenham's relative chronology for the development of Roma's portraits (helmet A, B, C, and E) as successive types; hence the following must be reattributed: Crawford, *RRC* I, nos. 53/2, 57/2, 58/2, 80/1, 88/2, and 89/2 (denarii), 57/1, 58/1, and 89/1 (victoriati). Consequently, denarii attributed by Crawford to 200–168 B.C. must be redated later to the period 168–150 B.C., thereby eliminating the so-called hiatus in minting.

8. The silver sums shown in Table 3.1 are converted at rate of 1 Attic talent = 80 Roman pounds (Polyb. 1. 16. 9). The *Oscense argentum* is reckoned 1 to the denarius and the Attalid cistophorus at 3 denarii; see Knapp, *NC* 7, 17 (1977), 11–18, and K. W. Harl, "Livy and the Date of the Introduction of the Cistophoric Tetradrachma," *CA* 10 (1991), 290–94. The annual income of the Spanish mines as 1,500 talents (25,000 drachmae per day) after 177 B.C. is based on Str. 3. 14. 8 = Polyb. 34. 9. See Harris, *War and Imperialism,* p. 69, n. 2, arguing that the sum represents state profits rather than total output, and *contra* E. Badian, *Publicans and Sinners* (Ithaca, N.Y., 1972), pp. 33–34. The annual profits of 500 talents from Spanish mines prior to 177 B.C. is offered as a conservative estimate. There is no reason to believe that mining profits were included by Livy among spoils carried in triumphs; see J. S. Richardson, "The Spanish Mines and the Development of Provincial Taxation in the Second Century B.C.," *JRS* 66 (1976), 140–41, and *contra* Frank, *ESAR* I, pp. 138 and 154–55.
9. See Badian, *Publicans and Sinners,* pp. 29–31, and P. A. Brunt, *Italian Manpower, 225 B.C.–A.D. 14* (Oxford, 1971), pp. 419–20 and 671–76.
10. See Liv. 31. 13. 5–9, for the *trientabulum* offering the use of public land at a nominal rent of one as per *iugum* to raise hard cash for the war against Philip V in 200 B.C. This was the third repayment of a loan in 210 B.C.; the first two repayments in 204 and 202 B.C. were made out of the spoils of Spain (Liv. 26. 36 and 29. 16. 1–3 and cf. 28. 38. 5).
11. C. Nicolet, *Tributum: Recherches sur la fiscalité directe sous la république romaine* (Bonn, 1976), pp. 19–33.
12. See Liv. 39. 7. 5; the *tributum* was presumably levied in 192–189 B.C. The text does not support the view that the profits from the Asian booty were applied to reimburse the landed classes for 22.5 successive earlier *tributa*—this view assumes an impossibly high number of unpaid levies at 1 percent since 210 B.C. (or at 2 percent since 198 B.C.); *contra* Frank, *ESAR* I, pp. 124–25 and 137–38, and Crawford, *RRC* II, p. 635.
13. Crawford, *RRC* I, nos. 197–200 and 202–8; dating to ca. 168–160 B.C. is based on Burnett, *NC* 7, 17 (1977), 43–44.
14. Plin., *NH* 33. 56 ("tributum pendere desiit"), and cf. Cicero, *De Off.* 2. 76, and Plut., *Aemil.* 38.
15. Since donatives were generous enough to ensure a high turnout of soldiers at triumphs, the sums shown in Table 3.2 are calculated after

accounting for losses from attrition; see K. Hopkins, *Conquerors and Slaves* (Cambridge, 1978), pp. 38–39.

16. See Plut., *Pomp.* 45, and Liv. 45. 34. 5–6 (167 B.C.).
17. Crawford, *RRCH*, no. 255 (200+ denarii, 108 tetradrachmae, 13 drachmae, and 250 triobols). See M. Thompson, *The New Style Silver Coinage of Athens* (New York, 1958), p. 504, and D. M. Lewis, "The Chronology of the Athenian New Style Coinage," *NC* 7, 2 (1962), 281–82.
18. Liv. 39. 44. 5 and Dio. Hal. 3. 67. 5.
19. Front., *Aq.* I. 7, and T. R. Wiseman, "Roman Republican Road Building," *PBSR* n.s. 38 (1970), 122–51.
20. See Plin., *NH* 33. 16. 55; conversion of gold bullion at a ratio of 1:10. The *lateres* of gold and silver in 49 B.C. have been conservatively reckoned at one Roman pound each, because their total value was comparable to or greater than the reserve reported in 157 B.C.; see Harris, *War and Imperialism,* p. 70.
21. Liv. 45. 18. 5, Diod. Sic. 31. 8. 6, and Cassid. 616M, for the Macedonian mines. Macedonian silver after 157 B.C. was coined by Republic A rather than exported to Rome; see C. Boehringer, "Hellenistischer Münzschatz aus Trapezunt, 1970," *RSN* 54 (1975), 62, and Mattingly, *AIIN* 29 (1982), 37–38; *contra* Crawford, *RRC* I, pp. 74 and 235, and *CMRR*, pp. 128–32. For Spanish mines, see Richardson, *JRS* 66 (1976), 143–44, and O. Davies, *Roman Mines in Europe* (Oxford, 1935), pp. 107–10.
22. Plin., *NH* 33. 45, and Crawford, *RRC* II, pp. 636–38. The measure was never implemented because denarii were struck to standard and plated coins once considered the products of a Drusan debasement are contemporary forgeries; see Walker, *Metallurgy in Numismatics,* I, pp. 61–68, and M. C. Crawford, "Plated Coins, False Coins," *NC* 7, 8 (1968), 55–59.
23. See Burnett, *NC* 7, 17 (1977), 39–41.
24. See A. M. Burnett, "The Currency of Italy from Hannibalic War to the Reign of Augustus," *AIIA* 29 (1982), 128–35, and Reece, *Oxford Journal of Archaeology* 3 (1984), 201–2, for analysis of finds at Minturnae, Cosa, and Liri. See Volk, in *Rythmes,* pp. 156–66, for comparison of Roman *aes* to token bronze currency of early modern France and Sweden. Volk's point rules out the contention that Rome alienated gold and silver to purchase bronze as its prime coin metal in 170–157 B.C., as argued by Crawford, *RRC* I, pp. 49–53 and 74–75, and II, pp. 634–35, and *CMRR,* pp. 94–96, 116–17, and 143–44.
25. Plin., *NH* 33. 45, and Crawford, *RRC* I, nos. 225–28, and discussion in T. V. Buttrey, Jr., "On the Retariffing of the Denarius," *ANSMN* 7 (1957), 57–65.
26. Plin., *NH* 33. 46; see Crawford *RRC* II, pp. 678–79, and Walker,

*Metallurgy in Numismatics,* I, p. 61. For the need for fractions, see halved denarii in Crawford, *RRCH*, no. 151 and discussion in Lo Cascio, *JRS* 71 (1981), 83–84, and Rodwell, *Money in the Age of Tiberius,* pp. 91, nn. 130–31, p. 105, nn. 267–68, and pp. 146–47, Table I. Quinarii were hoarded in Northern Italy (as the Roman successor to Massiliot and Celtic drachmae), but they were intended for general rather than regional circulation, *pace* Crawford, *RRC* I, p. 81, and *CMRR,* pp. 181–83.

27. Plin., *NH* 33. 44, and Festus 516; see Crawford, *RRC* I, no. 338, and Lo Cascio, *JRS* 71 (1981), 83.
28. Crawford, *RRC* I, no. 548.
29. See Cic., *In Vat.* 12, and *Pro Flacc.* 67, for ban on exports of specie in 63 B.C.; cf. Zon. 8. 19. 2 and Diod. Sic. 5. 27, for ban on export of gold to Celts in 230 B.C.
30. See J. G. Milne, "The *Philippeus* Coin at Rome," *JRS* 30 (1940), 11–15. M. Fulvius Nobilior permitted the Aetolians to pay one-third of their indemnity in Macedonian gold staters rather than silver; see Liv. 38. 9. 9, and Polyb. 21. 30. 1–3 (189 B.C.). The exchange was probably 1 Attic gold stater (8.5 g) to 10 silver didrachmae on the Corcyrean standard (10.3 g), for a gold to silver ratio of 1:12 that favored Rome rather than the typical 1:10 (Liv. 38. 11. 8–9, and Polyb. 21. 32. 8–9); see R. S. de Laix, "The Silver Coinage of the Aetolian League," *CSCA* 6 (1973), 37–75.
31. Crawford, *RRC* I, no. 547, and see overstrikes in T. V. Buttrey, Jr., "The Unique As of Cn. Piso Frugi, An Unrecognized Semuncial Dupondius," *Studia Oliveriania* 11 (1963), 7–14, and C. A. Hersh, "Additional Roman Republican Overstrikes," *ANSMN* 32 (1987), 92, no. 10a.
32. Crawford, *RRC* I, nos. 337 and 340, whose die estimate suggests outputs of at least 24 and 34.5 million, respectively. See A. Campara, *La monetazione degli inserti italici durante la Guerre Sociale (91–87 a.C.)* (Soliera, 1987), whose die count suggests a mintage of at least 5.25 million denarii by the Italian insurgents—a low estimate since many denarii were later reminted.
33. See Walker, *Metallurgy in Numismatics,* I, pp. 61–64, issues at Rome fell to 94.5 percent in 89–87 B.C.; Italians minted in 90–88 B.C. at 96.6 percent, but later denarii were baser.
34. App., *Mithr.* 84. The sum is equivalent to 7,560,000 denarii (at the gold to silver ratio of 1:10) or the annual costs of five legions.
35. Cic., *De Off.* 3. 80.
36. Plin., *NH* 33. 46 ("ars denarios probare"), and see M. H. Crawford, "The Edict of M. Marius Gratidianus," *PCPS* n.s. 14 (1968), 1–4.
37. See Crawford, *RRC* I, nos. 354 (EX S.C.) and 355 (D.S.S.). Simultaneous use of uncial and semuncial asses implied variable rates of

exchange and discounting prior to 86 B.C.; see Crawford, *RRC* I, pp. 77–78, and II, 596–97.

38. See Cic., *Pro Front.* 1; Vell. Pat. 2. 23. 2; and Sall., *Cat.* 32. 2; and discussion in C. M. Bulst, "*Cinnanum Tempus;* A Reassessment of the *Dominatio Cinnae,*" *Historia* 13 (1964), 331–34. See E. Badian, "The Testament of Ptolemy Alexander," *RhM* 110 (1967), 178–92; Walker, *Metallurgy in Numismatics,* I, pp. 61–62; and Crawford, *RRC* I, nos. 351–53.
39. See Crawford, *RRC* I, nos. 350–54 and 356–64, with die count of nos. 357 and 361 based on Hersh, *NC* 7, 17 (1977), 30–33. The die numerals on Crepusius's coins are taken as sequential and continuous; see C. A. Hersh, "Sequence Marks on Denarii of Publius Crepusius," *NC* 6, 12 (1952), 52–66, T. V. Buttrey, Jr., "The Denarii of P. Crepusius and Roman Republican Mint Organization, *ANSMN* 21 (1976), 67–108, and H. Zehnacker, "L'évaluation des masses des émissions à l'époque republicaine," *Dévaluations* (1978), I pp. 31–54.
40. See Plut., *Sulla,* 22–23 and 2, and *Luc.* 4, and cf. App., *Mithr.* 55–56, for alternate reports of 2,000 and 3,000 talents. See T. R. Martin, "Sulla *Imperator Iterum,* the Samnites, and Roman Coin Propaganda," *SNR* 68 (1989), 19–44, for redating aurei (Crawford, *RRC* I, no. 367) to 86–82 B.C. See Crawford, *NC* 7, 4 (1964), 141–55, arguing for a mobile mint in Italy in 83–82 B.C. because aurei fail to surface in eastern hoards, but Romans would not have concealed their savings in the East but rather *sub signa* so that the absence of aurei in eastern hoards is not proof of Italian minting.
41. Crawford, *RRC* I, no. 402, minted at 38 to the Roman pound and perhaps were tariffed at 25 denarii. For the date of 81 B.C. rather than 71 or 61 B.C., see E. Badian, "The Date of Pompey's First Triumph," *Hermes* 83 (1955), 107–18, and "Servilius and Pompey's First Triumph," *Hermes* 89 (1961), 254–56.
42. Cic., *Phil.* 12. 20.
43. See Plut., *Pomp.* 45 (61 B.C.); Suet., *Iul.* 38; and App., *BC* 3. 44 (46 B.C.). The Augustan donative is inferred from Dio 51. 21. 5–7; see Hopkins, *Conquerors,* pp. 38–39.
44. Suet., *Iul.* 54. 2–3.
45. Val. Max. 7. 6. 4, and Plin., *NH* 33. 16; cf. Diod. Sic. 38–39, frag. 14.
46. Plin,. *NH* 33. 26.
47. Walker, *Metallurgy in Numismatics,* I, pp. 65–67.
48. Plut., *Luc.* 13 (74 B.C.); App., *Mithr.* 420 (67 B.C.); cf. *Pomp.* 25.
49. Plut., *Pomp.* 45, and Suet., *Iul.* 25, and cf. Eutrop. 6. 17, but the total probably includes the value of grain taxes of Sicily, Sardinia, and Africa; see Frank, *ESAR* I, pp. 323–24.
50. Cic., *Ver.* 2.3. 163 and 5. 52, reports purchases of 3,000,000 modii at 3

HS and then 800,000 *modii* at 3.5 HS, or 2,250,000 and 700,000 denarii, respectively. At the Gracchan price of 6.33 asses per *modius,* the state would have reaped 1,180,000 denarii or only 40 percent of the initial outlay. See Cic., *Ad Quint. fr.* 2. 6 (5), for an outlay of 10 million denarii for grain purchases in 56 B.C.

51. See Walker, *Metallurgy in Numismatics,* I, p. 67; Crawford, *CMRR,* pp. 246–47, and F. Bertrandy, "Remarques sur l'origine romaine de monnayage en bronze et en argent de Juba Ier, roi de Numidie," *Bulletin Archéologique du Comité des Travaux Historiques* B.12–14 (1976–78), 9–22.
52. See A. Wallace-Hadrill, "Image and Authority in the Coinage of Augustus," *JRS* 76 (1986), 74–83.
53. App., *BC* 2 102, and Vell. 2. 56. 3. Donatives are reported as either 5,000 (App., *BC* 2. 102, and Dio 43. 21) or 6,000 denarii per man (Suet., *Iul.* 38). Ten legions would have received, at 5,000 denarii each, donatives totaling 300 million denarii or 12 million aurei.
54. Vell. 2. 60. 4; Cic., *Phil.* 2. 93, 5. 11, 8. 26, and 12. 12; and Plut., *Cic.* 43. 6, and *Ant.* 15 (private estate).
55. See Crawford, *RRCH*, nos. 358, and cf. nos. 557–58 (157–133 B.C.) and 362 and 372 (ca. 75–74 B.C.).
56. See Crawford, *RRC* I, no. 476, and E. R. Caley, *Orichalcum and Related Ancient Alloys* (New York, 1964), pp. 3–31. The ore was probably mined near Mediolanum (Milan); see. Grant, *FITA*, pp. 7–11.
57. Crawford, *RRC* I, no. 535.
58. See P. Amandry, "Le monnayage de Bibulus et Capito," *RSN* 65 (1986), 73–85 and 66 (1987), 102–34. P. Amandry, "Le monnayage émis en Orient, sous l'autorité d'Antoine par L. Calpurnius Bibulus, L. Sempronius Atratinus et M. Oppius Capito: Un essai d'estimation quantitative," in *Rythmes,* p. 224, estimates production of at least 3 million coins.
59. App., *BC* 4. 31 (cf. Frank, *ESAR* I, pp. 340–42), indicates that assets in excess of 200 million denarii were seized. Die counts suggest at least 21.7 million denarii and 5.6 million aurei (= 140 million denarii) were struck; see Crawford, *RRC* II, pp. 662–65 and 668–689.
60. Cic., *Ad Att.* 16. 8, and App., *BC* 3. 40 and 44.
61. App. *BC* 4. 74 and 5. 5, and cf. Frank *ESAR* I, pp. 340–42.
62. Dio 46. 25. 3, or Plut., *Brut.* 40, and see Crawford, *RRC* II, p. 741 and I, nos. 498–500 (Cassius) and 501–8 (Brutus). See Crawford, *RCC* I, no. 511, and D. R. Evans, "The Sicilian Coinage of Sextius Pompeius," *ANSMN* 32 (1987), 97–158.
63. See Crawford, *RRC* I, nos. 536–38, 540, 544, and II, pp. 668–71 and 690, and Walker, *Metallurgy in Numismatics,* I, pp. 67–68. See Plin.,

*NH* 33. 13, with corrections to text by Crawford, *PCPh* n.s. 14 (1968), 1–2, for Antony's debasement.

64. See Crawford, *RRC* I, nos. 516–17, 520–22, 527–28, and C. H. V. Sutherland, *RIC* I², pp. 59–60, nos. 250–63 (ca. 32–29 B.C.), and "Octavian's Coinage from c. 32 to 27 B.C.," *NAC* 5 (1976), 129–58.
65. See L. Villaronga, "Troballa esporàdica de bronze romans republicans," *Gaceta Numismatica* 74–75 (1984), 113–17, and R. C. Knapp, "Spain," in *CRWLR*, p. 19, n. 4.
66. *ID* 1421 Ab. 1. 3. For Athenian coins in accounts, see L. Robert, "Monnaies dans les inscriptions grecques," *RN* 6, 4 (1962), 12–13; and J. R. Melville-Jones, "Greek Coin Names in -phoros," *BISC* 21 (1974), 55–71.
67. See M. H. Crawford, "Republican Denarii in Romania: The Suppression of Piracy and the Slave-Trade," *JRS* 67 (1977), 117–20, but he stresses the slave trade to exclusion of other commodities. For denarii in Macedon, see I. Touratsoglou, "Macedonia," in *CRWLR*, pp. 57–58.
68. See Burnett, *RSN* 62 (1983), 5–26, and Walker, in *Festschrift für Leo Mildenberg*, pp. 275–81, for import of quadrigati, denarii, and victoriati. Aurei (Crawford, *RRC* I, nos. 42 and 67–82) attributed to a mint in Sicily were struck at Rome; see Hersh, *NC* 7, 17 (1977), 22–23 and 28.
69. See M. H. Crawford, "Sicily," in *CRWLR*, pp. 49–51, and *CMRR*, pp. 114–15 and 344–45.
70. See Jenkins and Lewis, *Carthaginian Gold and Electrum Coins*, pp. 51–53. For overstrikes of Punic coins, see Hersh, *ANSMN* 32 (1987), 86–88, and Crawford, *RRC* I, pp. 31–32.
71. See J. Alexandropoulos, "La circulation monétaire en Afrique Proconsulaire de 146 avant J.-C. à la fin du règne de Tibère," *REA* 84 (1982), 96–103, and A. M. Burnett, "Africa," in *CRWLR*, pp. 178–79. For denarii minted in Africa, see Crawford, *RRC* I, nos. 459–62 (Metellus and Cato) and 458 (Julius Caesar).
72. See Knapp, *NC* 7, 17 (1977), 8–17, and R. C. Knapp, in "Spain," in *CRWLR*, pp. 21–22, for date and identity of the *Oscense argentum* named in Roman triumphs of 196–180 B.C. Weight standards follow those of denarii; see M. H. Crawford, "The Financial Organization of Republican Spain," *NC* 7, 11 (1969), 81–82.
73. See Knapp, *NC* 7, 17 (1977), 4–7, and H. J. Hildebrandt, "Zur Chronologie keltiberischer Münzfunde in Spanien," in *Keltische Numismatik und Archeologie*, ed. G. Grasmann, W. Janssen, and N. Brandt, BAR Int. Ser. 200 (Oxford, 1984), pp. 151–63. Mixed hoards show progressively fewer native silver coins from 89 to 46 B.C.; see A. M. de Guadan, *Numismatica ibérica e ibero-romana* (Madrid, 1969), pp. 178–210.

74. See L. Villaronga, *Los tesoros de Azaila y la circulación monetaria en el valle del Ebro* (Barcelona, 1977), pp. 18–21 and 34–44. Latin towns minted primarily asses and semisses; see R. C. Knapp, "The Coinage of Corduba, *Colonia Patricia*," *AIIN* 29 (1989), 185–89 and 194.
75. See D. E. M. Nash, *Coinage in the Celtic World* (London, 1987), pp. 118–24, and J.-B. Colbert de Beaulieu, "Umlauf und Chronologie der gallokeltischen Münzen," *JNG* 16 (1966), 45–62.
76. See J.-N Barrandon and C. Brenot, "Le monnayage de Marseille," *MEFRA* 90 (1978), 637–65. For the imitative drachmae, see D. F. Allen, "Monnaies-à-la-croix," *NC* 7, 9 (1969), 33–78, and P. P. Ripolles-Alegie and L. Villaronga, "La chronologie des monnaies à la croix de poids lourd d'après les trésors d'Éspagne," *Acta Numismatica* 11 (1981), 30–39.
77. Cic., *Pro Font.* 5. 11, and cf. Caes, *BG* 7. 3. 1 and 55. 5. Few hoards survive prior to Caesar's conquest; see Crawford, *CMRR,* pp. 166–70 and 317–18, and *RRCH,* nos. 110 and 560.
78. S. Scheers, "Coinage and Currency of the Belgic Tribes during the Gallic War," *BNJ* 41 (1972), 1–6, for debasement, and Colbert de Beaulieu, *JNG* 16 (1966), 58–62, for abrupt end of Gallic gold coinage. Exclusive use of Celtic coins by natives is revealed by the pattern of finds from Alesia in 53 B.C.; see J. B. Colbert de Beaulieu, "Numismatique celtique d'Alésie," *RBN* 101 (1955), 88–93, and Crawford, *RRCH,* no. 343.
79. See Harl, *CA* 10 (1991), 280–82 and 295–97. For Seleucid currency, see C. Boehringer, *Zur Chronologie mittelhellenischen Münzenserien 220–160 v. Chr.* (Berlin, 1972), pp. 63–64, and O. Mørkholm, *Studies in the Coinage of Antiochus IV* (Copenhagen, 1963), pp. 7–22.
80. See Harl, *CA* 10 (1991), 267–97, for the introduction of cistophorus in the late 190s B.C. rather than in ca. 180–166 B.C. as argued by F. S. Kleiner and S. W. Noe, *The Early Cistophoric Coinage* (New York, 1977), pp. 10–15; G. Le Rider, "La politique monétaire du royaume de Pergame après 188," *Journal des Savants* (1989), 169–72; and R. Bauslaugh, "Cistophoric Countermarks and the Monetary Policy of Eumenes II," *NC* 150 (1990), 22–23.
81. Liv. 33. 30. 7, Polyb. 18. 44, and see P. R. Franke, "Zur Finanzpolitik des makedonischen Köings Perseus wahrend des Krieges mit Rom 171–168 n. Chr.," *JNG* 8 (1957), 31–50.
82. See O. Mørkholm, "Chronology and Meaning of the Wreathed Coinages of the Early 2nd Century B.C.," *NAC* 9 (1988), 145–46, and Harl, *CA* 10 (1991), 278–79, noting that the wreathed design did not denote Roman direction or regional monetary unions as argued by A. Giovannini, *Rome et la circulation monétaire, en Grèce au IIe siècle avant Jésus Christ* (Basel, 1978) pp. 16–21 and 81–100, and Boehringer, *Zur*

*Chronologie,* pp. 14–19 and 31–91. The "low" chronology of ca. 167–165 B.C. for the inception of New Style Athenian coinage is accepted throughout; see Lewis, *NC* 7, 2 (1962), 275–300, and E. Badian, "Rome, Mithridates, and Athens," *AJAH* 1 (1976), 105–28. Hoards vitiate the "high" chronology of 197 B.C. advocated by M. Thompson, *New Style Silver Coinage of Athens,* pp. 473–74 and 622–31, and "Athens Again," *NC* 7, 2 (1962), 301–33. The overstrike of an Athenian tetradrachma on a Macedonian tetradrachma in the name of the quaestor Aesillas offers no chronological assistance, because Macedonian coins carry *types immoblisés* during ca. 95–60 B.C.; see A. M. Burnett, *Coin Hoards* 7 (1985), 54–67.

83. *FD* III. 2. 139 = $SIG^3$ 729.2–3, and cf. 10–13 (ca. 160 or 120 B.C.). See Robert, *RN* 6, 4 (1962), 18–24, and Boehringer, *Zur Chronologie,* pp. 33–36, for the drachma *stephanophoros* designating Athenian coins.
84. K. Rigsby, "The Era of the Province of Asia," *Phoenix* 33 (1979), 39–47, notes that the first Ephesian cistophori date to 134/3 B.C. See F. S. Kleiner, "Hoard Evidence and the Late Cistophori of Pergamum," *ANSMN* 23 (1978), 77–106, and "The Dated Cistophori of Ephesus," *ANSMN* 18 (1972), 17–32. But his absolute chronology needs revision in light of the facts that most hoards were concealed during the First Mithridatic War and many specimens were recoined by Sulla; see *IGCH* 1359, 1456, 1458–62, and F. S. Kleiner, "The Girseun Hoard," *ANSMN* 19 (1974), 3–26.
85. Cic., *Ad Quint. fr.*. 1. 3. 7, and see J. Andreau, *La vie financière dans le monde romain* (Rome, 1987), pp. 509–10.
86. See R. S. Fischer, "Two Notes on the Aesillas Tetradrachms: Mint Attribution and a Die Control System," *ANSMN* 30 (1988), 69–88, for an inception from 90 to 88 B.C.
87. Plut., *Luc.* 2. 1–2, and see Thompson, *New Style Silver Coinage of Athens,* pp. 425–39.
88. See A. R. Bellinger, "The Early Coinage of Roman Syria," in *Studies in Economic and Social History to Allan Chester Johnson,* ed. P. R. Coleman-Norton, F. C. Bourne, and J. V. A. Fine (Princeton, 1951), pp. 58–67.
89. See Crawford, *RRCH*, no. 158, and M. Thompson, *The Agrinion Hoard* (New York, 1968); Athenian tetradrachmae should be redated to ca. 157–36 B.C.
90. Plut., *Sulla* 12 and 19; Diod. Sic. 38–39, frag. 7; and Paus. 9. 7. 4.
91. See Plut., *Sulla* 25. 2, and App., *Mithr.* 62–63.
92. See Walker, *MRSC* I, pp. 26–36, and P. Kinns, "Asia Minor," in *CRWLR*, pp. 109–11.
93. See Plut., *Luc.* 29 and 37 (Lucullus); Plin., *NH* 37. 16; Plut., *Pomp.* 45; and App., *Mithr.* 116 (Pompey).

94. App., *BC* 4. 100, and see T. R. S. Broughton, "Asia Minor," *ESAR* IV, pp. 585–90.
95. See B. Overbeck, "Ein Schatzfund der späten Republik von Halikarnassos," *SNR* 56 (1978), 164–73 (ca. 48 B.C.), and *IGCH* 352 = *RRCH*, no. 374 (42 B.C.), with addition of *IGCH* 318.

*Chapter 4: The Augustan Coinage, 30 B.C.–A.D. 235*

1. For fineness, see C. Morrisson, C. Brenot, J.-P. Callu, J. Poirier, and R. Halleux, *L'or monnayé* (Paris, 1985), I, p. 82, and Walker, *MRSC* I, pp. 18 and 108–9, and cf. Lane and Mueller, *Money and Banking*, I, pp. 174–79 and 493–530, for mint charges in manufacture of full-bodied coins. For weight standards, see C. H. V. Sutherland, "Some Observations of the Coinage of Augustus," *NAC* 7 (1978), 164, and *RIC* I², p. 4. Aurei of 12 B.C.–A.D. 37 were struck at 41 to the Roman pound; those from A.D. 60–64 at 42 to the Roman pound, but in markets 40 aurei or 1,000 denarii were long reckoned as equal to 1 Roman pound of gold; see Hendy, *SBME*, p. 462, and J.-P. Callu, "Les prix dans deux romans mineurs d'époque impériale: Histoire d'Apollonius roi de Tyr—Vie d'Ésope," *Dévaluations* (1978), I, pp. 197–205.
2. Dio 55. 12. The exchange rate is confirmed by *congiaria* and *sportula*; see S. Mrozek, "Les espèces monétaires dans les inscriptions latines du Haut-Empire," *Dévaluations* (1978), I, p. 84, and R. P. Duncan-Jones, *The Economy of the Roman Empire: Quantitative Studies*, 2nd ed. (Cambridge, 1974), p. 105, no. 290, and p. 188, nos. 818–26.
3. Suet., *Galba* 12. 1, and cf. Plut., *Galba* 20. 2. The usual range is 98.5 to 99.5 percent fine; see L. H. Cope, "The Complete Analysis of a Gold Aureus by Chemical and Mass Spectrometric Analysis Techiques," in *Methods in Chemical and Metallurgical Investigation of Ancient Coinage*, ed. E. T. Hall and D. M. Metcalf (London, 1972), pp. 307–13, and Morrisson, *L'or monnayé*, I, pp. 82–83. In markets, coins were weighed and assayed only when noticeably underweight or suspected as counterfeits; see Plin., *NH* 33. 42–43, and J. E. Lendon, "The Face on the Coins and Inflation in Roman Egypt," *Klio* 72 (1990), 113–14.
4. Suet., *Aug.* 98. 2–3.
5. Walker, *MRSC* I, pp. 22–25.
6. See C. H. V. Sutherland, *RIC* I², pp. 24–39, and "Octavian's Gold and Silver Coinage from c. 32 to 27 B.C.," *NAC* 5 (1976), 129–58; but his attributions of aurei and denarii of 32–16 B.C. to mints outside of Rome based the subjective criteria of style and iconography must be rejected. Rome coined aurei and denarii bearing CAESAR DIVI F and IMP CAESAR in 32–29 B.C. (*BMCRE* I, pp. 97–105, nos. 596–643) and then aurei, denarii, and quinarii celebrating Augustan victories after 29 B.C. (*RIC* I², p. 85, nos. 544–47, and p. 84, nos. 536–43). The mean

fineness of denarii is 96 to 97 percent and of quinarii 92 to 93 percent; see Walker, *MRSC* I, pp. 4–7 and 13. In 23–12 B.C., the college of moneyers at Rome resumed striking aurei and denarii carrying their names (*RIC* I$^2$, pp. 62–74, nos. 278–322, 337–44, 350–69, and 397–414); see Wallace-Hadrill, *JRS* 76 (1986), 77–79 and 85–86. In 11 B.C. Rome ceased minting coins in precious metals.

In Spain, Emerita initially struck aurei and denarii from Iberian bullion during the Cantabrian War (25–19 B.C.); then possibly two mobile military mints operated in the later stages of the war; see Sutherland, *NAC* 7 (1978), 163–64 and 172–73, and Walker, *MRSC* I, pp. 8–10 and 23. When Augustus shifted his military efforts to the Rhineland in 16 B.C., the prime imperial mint was opened at Lugdunum, which coined aurei and denarii down to the Neronian reform in A.D. 64. See C. H. V. Sutherland, *The Emperor and the Coinage* (London, 1978), pp. 46–47; W. E. Metcalf, "Rome and Lugdunum Again," *AJN* 1 (1989), 51–52; and Walker, *MRSC* I, pp. 11–12 and 23–24. For dies of aurei and denarii found in France (presumably plundered from the mint), see Vermeule, *Ancient Dies,* pp. 24–28, nos. 24–37 and 42–46; J. Lafaurie, "Coins monétaires de Tibère trouvés à Auxerre," *BSFN* 24 (1970), 544–47; and R. A. G. Carson, "Roman Coinage and Metal Production," *NAC* 10 (1981), 311. See Walker, *MRSC* I, pp. 5–7 and 12; metrology vitiates attributions of denarii to the Peloponnesus and Samos in 21–20 B.C. (*RIC* I$^2$, pp. 34–35 and 79, nos. 472–75) and aurei and denarii to Pergamum in 19–18 B.C. (*RIC* I$^2$, p. 79, nos. 472–75, and pp. 82–83, nos. 511–26). All were struck at Rome, and the engraving and iconography most likely indicate that Asian cistophori of Sutherland Group VII (*RIC* I$^2$, p. 82, nos. 505–10) were products of the Roman mint; see C. H. V. Sutherland, "Augustan Aurei and Denarii Attributable to the Mint of Pergamum," *RN* 6, 15 (1973), 129–51.

7. *RGdA* 15–21; donative rates are based on P. A. Brunt, "The Army and the Land in the Roman Revolution," *JRS* 52 (1962), 78–81.
8. *RIC* I$^2$, p. 85, no. 547. See Sutherland, *NAC* 5 (1976), 156, and Rodewald, *Money in the Age of Tiberius,* pp. 82–83, n. 47, for Rome as the mint.
9. See A. M. Burnett, P. T. Craddock, and K. Preston, "New Light on the Origins of Orichalcum," in *Actes du 9ème congrès international de numismatique, Berne 1979,* ed. T. Hackens and R. Weiller (Louvain-la-Neuve, 1982), pp. 263–68, for orichalcum with 20 to 25 percent zinc.
10. See *RIC* I, p. 80, nos. 483–88 (CAISAR/AVGVSTVS series) and pp. 81–82, nos. 495–504 (C.A. series). Metrology and iconography locate the mint at Pergamum; see Burnett, *NC* 7, 17 (1977), 45–46, and Wallace-Hadrill, *JRS* 76 (1986), 79–84.

11. See Wallace-Hadrill, *JRS* 76 (1986), 79–83, conclusively dating the reform to 23 B.C. because sestertii bear the legend TRIBVNICA POTESTAS (*RIC* I, pp. 22–27, nos. 41–42). Hence, local issues with such types in Spain were inspired by imperial issues rather than minted prior to the reform as argued by Grant, *FITA*, pp. 119–23, and Sutherland, *RIC* I², p. 25, who date analogous Spanish *aes* from Emerita to 25–23 B.C. (cf. *RIC* I², p. 42, nos. 22–25).
12. See Wallace-Hadrill, *JRS* 76 (1986), 82–87, reviving the argument of Grant, *FITA*, pp. 91–98, and Mattingly, *BMCRE* I, pp. xciv–xcvii, that the coins must honor the grant of tribunician power in 23 B.C. The series terminated by 2 B.C.; see Burnett, *NC* 7, 17 (1977), 48–50. A date of inception in 19 B.C. based on a rigid reconstruction of the *cursus honorum* of the moneyers is implausible, *contra* K. Kraft, "Zur Datierung der Münzmeisterprägung unter Augustus," *NZ* 46–47 (1951–52), 28–35; A. Bay, "The Letters S.C. on Augustan *Aes* Coinage," *JRS* 62 (1972), 111–22; Giard, *CBN* I, pp. 41–43; and Sutherland, *RIC* I², pp. 61–78.
13. Suet., *Calig.* 37. 2–3; Dio 73. 8. 8; and Eutrop. 8. 8.
14. Jos., *BJ* 6. 5. 1.
15. *RGdA* 16–21, and Suet., *Aug* 30, and see Frank, *ESAR* V, p. 14; reported sums in 30–28 B.C. total 630 million denarii.
16. See Suet., *Aug.* 41. 2, and Flor. 2. 33; cf. Oros., *Ad Pag.* 9. 19, and Dio. 51. 17. 6–8 and 21. 5, and see Rodewald, *Money in the Age of Tiberius*, p. 81, n. 36.
17. Dio 68. 15. 3 = John Lyd., *De Mag.* 2. 28; calculations are based on figures emended by Frank, *ESAR* V, pp. 65–66; denarii are reckoned at 90 percent fine.
18. *P. Heid.* 40 = *P. Bad.* 37 = J. Schwartz, *Les archives de Sarapion et de ses fils* (Cairo, 1961), no. 90 (from the archive of Sarapion, ca. 107–13). See L. C. West and A. C. Johnson, *Currency in Roman and Byzantine Egypt* (Princeton, 1944), pp. 90–93, and *contra* objections raised by Walker, *MRSC* II, pp. 117–18, n. 3. The price is for an unspecified amount of gold of unstated purity that had fallen from 15 to 11 drachmae or by 26.67 percent. One pound of gold is priced at 3,962 drachmae (= 990.5 denarii) in A.D. 97 (*BGU* 1065) and then 3,800 drachmae (950 denarii) in 127 (*P. Oxy.* 496), but the gold's purity is not specified so that the figures do not offer a means to calculate the value of the aureus.
19. Dio 69. 8.
20. See M. G. Raschke, "New Studies in Roman Commerce in the East," *ANRW* 2, 9, 2 (Berlin, 1978), 858–69, n. 899, and 930–34, n. 1141a.
21. S. Gsell, *L'histoire ancienne de l'Afrique du Nord* (Paris, 1921–29), IV,

p. 140, and E. W. Bovill, *The Golden Trade of the Moors,* 2nd ed. (Oxford, 1968), pp. 12–41.

22. Tac., *Germ.* 5, and see Spufford, *Money*, pp. 74–85.
23. Str. 14. 5. 28, and see S. Vryonis, "The Question of Byzantine Mines," *Speculum* 37 (1962), 5–8.
24. See R. J. Forbes, *Studies in Ancient Technology* (Leiden, 1964) VIII, p. 212, and Raschke, *ANRW* 2, 9, 2 (1978), 745–46, n. 435, for trade routes to Bactria.
25. See J. C. Edmondson, "Mining in the Later Roman Empire and Beyond: Continuity or Disruption?" *JRS* 79 (1989), 96–97. The reopening of small mines after 300 reproduced the mining pattern of the Principate. See Richardson, *JRS* 66 (1976), 144–50, for comparable operations in Republican Spain.
26. See Richardson, *JRS* 66 (1976), 142–43. For wages and inducements to lure miners to Dacia, see S. Mrozek, "Die Goldbergwerke im römischen Dazien," *ANRW* 2, 6 (Berlin, 1977), pp. 99–104. For transfers of skilled staff, see Edmondson, *JRS* 79 (1989), 96, nn. 99–100, and P. R. Lewis and G. D. B. Jones, "The Dolaucothi Gold Mines, I: The Surface Evidence," *Antiquaries Journal* 49 (1969), 244–72.
27. See Davies, *Roman Mines,* pp. 154–55, and R. Jones, "The Roman Mines at Rio Tinto," *JRS* 70 (1980), 162.
28. See C. Domergue, "À propos de Pline, *Naturalis Historia* 33. 70–78, et pour illustrer sa description des mines d'or romaine d'Éspagne," *Archivo Español de Arqueologia* 47 (1974), 499–548, for "hushing" and *ruina montium.*
29. See Davies, *Roman Mines,* pp. 96–99. See Plin., *NH* 33. 6. 97, and Edmondson, *JRS* 79 (1989), 89–91, for mines of Baebelo; at 300 pounds per day for 360 days. Its annual production of 108,000 pounds is equivalent to 10,368,000 denarii of A.D. 64 or 1,650 Attic talents—a sum comparable to the 1,500 talents from mines near New Carthage in 150 B.C.
30. Plin., *NH* 33. 6. 97, and see C. Domergue and G. Hérail, *Mines d'or romaines d'Éspagne: le district de la Valduerna (Léon): Étude géomorphologique et archéologique* (Toulouse, 1978), p. 278, and Edmondson, *JRS* 79 (1979), 89–90.
31. See Lewis and Jones, *JRS* 60 (1970), 169–85, and Jones and Bird, *JRS* 62 (1972), 59–74, estimating 3,000 kilograms annually or 9,302 Roman pounds—the equivalent of 418,505 aurei or 10,465,116 denarii. See Edmondson, *JRS* 79 (1979), 90–91, for gold mines of Vipasca (Aljustrel).
32. Plin., *NH* 34. 1–2, and see D. W. MacDowall, *The Western Coinages of Nero* (New York, 1979), pp. 24–26.
33. Plin., *NH* 33. 4. 67 (50 pounds per day); cf. Stat., *Silvae* 1. 2. 153, 3. 3.

90, and Mart., 10. 78. 5. See S. Dušanić, "Aspects of Roman Mining in Noricum, Pannonia, Dalmatia, and Moesia Superior," *ANRW* 2, 6 (Berlin, 1977), 61–78, and Davies, *Roman Mines,* pp. 182–97.

34. Davies, *Roman Mines*, pp. 196–97 and 211–28, and Edmondson, *JRS* 79 (1989), 93, but the richest silver veins such as Novo Brdo escaped Roman notice; see D. Kovacevic, "Dans la Serbie et la Bosnie médiévales: Les mines d'or et d'argent," *Annales E.S.C.* 15 (1964), 248–58.
35. See Davies, *Roman Mines,* pp. 198–206. The presence of a procurator of mines at Ampelum (Zlatua) indicates major operations; see S. Mrozek, "Aspects sociaux et administratifs des mines d'or romaines de Dacie," *Apulum* 7 (1968), 307–26.
36. See Dušanić, *ANRW* 2, 6 (1977), 62–78, for silver deposits at Mt. Kosmaj south of Singidunum and in the Mlava and Pek valleys south of Viminacium. See Davies, *Roman Mines,* p. 217, for Thracian mines near Ruplje and Glogovica. See A. Mócsy, *Pannonia and Upper Moesia* (London, 1974), pp. 132–33, for mines in Pannonia and Moesia.
37. Plin., *NH* 34. 1–2, and cf. Jos., *Ant.* 16. 5. 5, and Galen 9. 214.
38. For disruptions of Spanish mining, see SHA, *Vita M.A.* 21. 1, and J. C. Edmondson, *Two Industries in Roman Lusitania: Mining and Garum Production,* BAR Int. Ser. 362 (Oxford, 1987), pp. 223–41. For disruption of Dacian and Balkan mining, see *CIL* III, pp. 921–60, and A. Birley, *Marcus Aurelius* (New Haven, 1987), p. 151.
39. See Carradice, *Coinage of Domitian,* pp. 83–96.
40. For output in 68–71, see C. M. Kraay, *The Aes Coinage of Galba* (New York, 1956), pp. 50–62, and "The Bronze Coinage of Vespasian: Classification and Attribution," in *SNREHS*, pp. 47–57. Estimates for 98–147 are based on R. Étienne and M. Rachet, *Le trésor de Garonne: Essai sur la circulation monétaire en Aquitaine à la fin de règne d'Antonin le Pieux (159–161)* (Bordeaux, 1984). For inadequate sample of Julio-Claudian dies, see Burnett, *NC* 7, 17 (1977), 55, and R. Reece, "Coin Finds and Coin Production," in *Rythmes,* pp. 335–40.
41. See D. R. Walker, "The Roman Coins," in *The Temple of Sulis Minerva at Bath* II. *The Finds,* ed. B. Cunliffe (Oxford, 1988), based on 12,595 coins, but the method and conclusions are vitiated by critique by C. L. Clay, *NC* 149 (1988), 209–24.
42. See tables in Étienne and Rachet, *Trésor de Garonne,* pp. 421–26.
43. H. Mattingly, "The Restored Coinage of Titus, Domitian and Nerva," *NC* 4, 20 (1920), 187–201; see *RIC* II, pp. 141–48, nos. 184–249 and pp. 211–13, nos. 453–61. Nerva in 98 restored types of divus Augustus and Agrippa; see *RIC* II, pp. 232–33, nos. 127–37.
44. See H. Chantraine, *Die antiken Fundmünzen von Neuss. Gesamtkatalog der Ausgrabungen, 1955–1978* (Berlin, 1982), pp. 33–38, for finds at Neuss. See C. M. Kraay, "The Behavior of Julio-Claudian Counter-

marks," *ERCHM*, pp. 119–22; C. M. Kraay, *Die Münzfunde von Vindonissa bis Traian* (Basel, 1962), pp. 45–51; and T. V. Buttrey, Jr., "Observations on the Behavior of Tiberian Countermarks," *ANSMN* 18 (1970), 58–59, for Rhenish countermarks. See D. W. MacDowall, "An Early Imperial Countermark from Pannonia," *NC* 7, 6 (1966), 124–33, for countermarks at Carnuntum retariffing sestertii as dupondii and dupondii as asses. For partisan loyalties declared in A.D. 68–69, see A. M. de Guadan, "Sobre una contremarca inédita de la Legio VI en un Sextercio de Claudio," *Numisma* 8, 32 (1958), 13–17, and D. W. MacDowall, "Two Roman Countermarks of A.D. 68," *NC* 6, 20 (1960), 103–9 and pl. VII. 1–9.

45. See Howgego, *GIC*, nos. 726–39, and G. G. Brunk, "A Hoard from Syria Countermarked by Roman Legions," *ANSMN* 25 (1980), 63–85, for countermarks of 66–70. For countermarking in Syria or Palestine in 115–117, see Howgego, *GIC*, no. 738. For countermarking of *aes* of Caesarea and Tyana in camps on Upper Euphrates in 160s, see ibid., nos. 740–41.
46. See Suet., *Calig.* 37. 2–3 (A.D. 37), and Dio 73. 8. 8 and Eutr. 8. 8 (A.D. 161). See K. Hopkins, "Taxes and Trade in the Roman Empire (c. 200 B.C.–A.D. 400)," *JRS* 70 (1980), 116–19, for tax revenues, and R. W. Goldsmith, "An Estimate of the Size and Structure of the National Product of the Early Empire," *Review of Income and Wealth* 30 (1984), 263–88.
47. Tac., *Ann.* 6. 17, and Suet., *Tib.* 48, and see Andreau, *La vie financière,* pp. 656–58, and Rodewald, *Money in the Age of Tiberius,* pp. 1–17.
48. Tac., *Ann.* 15. 18.
49. See W. E. Metcalf, "The Flavians in the East," *Actes du 9ème congrès international de numismatique, Berne, 1979*, ed. T. Hackens and R. Weiler (Louvain-la-Neuve, 1982), pp. 332–35. Alexandria minted aurei in A.D. 69; Antioch (cf. Tac., *Ann.* 2. 82) struck aurei and denarii in 69–72; Ephesus struck denarii in 69–74. Antioch (and possibly Caesarea and Alexandria) minted aurei, denarii, and *aes* for Pescennius Niger (193–94) and Laodicea ad Mare minted aurei and denarii for Septimius Severus in 198–202; see *BMCRE* V, pp. clxi–clxvii, and R. F. Bland, A. M. Burnett, and S. Bendall, "The Mints of Pescennius Niger in Light of Some New Aurei," *NC* 147 (1987), 65–83. Clodius Albinus minted at Lugdunum in 195–97; see *BMCRE* V, pp. cii–cvi. Aurei and denarii of Macrinus attributed to Antioch were coined at Rome, see C. L. Clay, "The Roman Coinage of Macrinus and Diadumenian," *NZ* 73 (1972), 21–40.
50. See Mark 12:17; Math. 22:21, and Luke 20:24.
51. See Rodewald, *Money in the Age of Tiberius,* pp. 29–45.
52. Str. 4. 3. 2.

53. See M. Torbágyi, "Die Münzprägung der Eravisher," *Acta Archaeologica Academicae Scientiarum Hungaricae* 36 (1984), 161–96, and H.-J. Kellner, *Die Münzfunde von Marching und die keltischen Fundmünzen aus Südbayern* (Stuttgart, 1990), pp. 26–39.
54. M. R. Cowell, W. A. Oddy, and A. M. Burnett, "Celtic Coinage in Britain and Recent Analyses," *BNJ* 57 (1987), 1–23.
55. See K. W. Harl, *Civic Coins and Civic Politics in the Roman East,* A.D. *180–275* (Berkeley, 1987), p. 134, n. 46, and Wallace-Hadrill, *JRS* 76 (1986), 73 and 79–80.
56. *RIC* I$^2$, pp. 51–52, nos. 154–61. See C. M. Kraay, "The Chronology of the Coinage of Colonia Nemausus," *NC* 6, 12 (1958), 75–86, and C. M. Wells, *The German Policy of Augustus* (Oxford, 1972), pp. 272–77, for the date of inception in ca. 20 B.C. rather than 30 B.C. For iconography, see Grant, *FITA*, pp. 55–57 and 69–70.
57. *RIC* I$^2$, pp. 57–58, nos. 227–48; cf. p. 25, and Sutherland, *NAC* 7 (1978), 165. The series dates from 10 B.C. after dedication of the altar (Suet., *Claud.* 2); see Kraay, *NC* 6, 12 (1958), 75–87, and Wells, *German Policy,* pp. 272–77.
58. See Wells, *German Policy,* pp. 268–69, and Rodewald, *Money in the Age of Tiberius*, pp. 67–68, 136, nn. 554–55, and p. 150, Table IV.
59. See B. Overbeck, "Celtic Chronology in South Germany," in *CRWLR,* pp. 1–12, who redates late Vindelican, Norican, and Pannonian coinages before the Roman conquest. Finds at Magdalensberg (Noreia) reveal Roman *aes* crowding out native coins after 15 B.C.; see Kellner, *Münzfunde von Marching,* pp. 26–39, and H. Bannert and G. Piccottini, *Die Fundmünzen von Magdalensberg* (Klagenfurt, 1972), pp. 20–34. For Britons imitating Roman coins, see C. H. V. Sutherland, *Romano-British Imitations of Bronze Coins of Claudius I* (New York, 1935), and G. C. Boon, "Counterfeiting in Roman Britain," *Scientific American* 231, 6 (1974), 120–29.
60. See Hopkins, *JRS* 70 (1980), 101–5, and *contra* M. Grant, "Decline and Fall of City-coinages in Spain," *NC* 6, 9 (1949), 93–106, suggesting political reasons for suppressing civic coinages.
61. See Walker, *MRSC* I, pp. 11–25, and III, pp. 110–14.
62. Plin., *NH* 33. 3, and Tac., *Ann.* 15. 45, and see discussion in C. H. V. Sutherland, *Roman History and Coinage, 44* B.C.–A.D. *69* (Oxford, 1987), pp. 95–100, nos. 39–40.
63. See Suet., *Nero* 44. 2, for demanding "fresh" coins (*nummum asperum*); see Sutherland, *Roman History and Coinage,* pp. 101–3, no. 40. For lowering the fineness, see Walker, *MRSC* I, pp. 16–17 (denarii), and Cope, *Chemical and Metallurgical Investigation,* pp. 307–13 (aurei). See V. C. E. Challis, "The Debasement of the Coinage, 1542–1551," *EcHR* 2, 20 (1967), 441–66, and Craig, *The Mint*, pp. 109–12, for compara-

ble scheme by Henry VIII reminting £1,250,000 in 1544–51 at an official rate less by 16 percent but at an actual rate of 24 percent.

64. See MacDowall, *Western Coinages,* pp. 144–45; the dupondius was increased from 14.5 to 16 g, but in 67–68 returned to 14 g.
65. Tac., *Germ.* 5. 5; and see Bolin, *State and Currency,* pp. 88–103 and 336–57.
66. See *RIC* I², pp. 205–17, nos. 1–132 and 515–21. Aurei and denarii without imperial portraits were struck by Galba in Spain during mid-68; see P.-H. Martin, *Die anonymen Münzen des Jahres 68 nach Christos* (Mainz, 1979), pp. 36–40 and 67–86, and cf. Walker, *MRSC* II, pp. 83–87 and 104–5. The *aes* of Galba (*RIC* I², pp. 239–40, nos. 133–41) must be reattributed from Lugdunum to Rome; see MacDowall, *Western Coinages,* pp. 145–47, and Kraay, *Aes Coinage of Galba,* pp. 55–60.
67. See Walker, *MRSC* I, pp. 85–88.
68. Tac., *Hist* 1. 20, and Suet., *Vesp.* 16. 3.
69. Walker, *MRSC* I, pp. 88–95.
70. Dio 68. 15. 3, undated, but the epitomator Xiphilinius timed the event to just after Trajan's return to Rome and the reconstruction of roads in 107. See Walker, *MRSC* II, pp. 3–12, for fineness of denarii in 98–107.
71. See H. Mattingly, "The Restored Coins of Trajan," *NC* 5, 6 (1926), 265–78, and *RIC* II, pp. 305–10, nos. 766–814: IMP CAES TRAIAN AVG GER DAC P P REST.
72. See C. M. Kraay, "A Hoard of Denarii from Verulamium, 1958," *NC* 6, 20 (1960), 272–73.
73. Plin., *NH* 6. 24. 83–88.
74. The volume of Trajanic and Hadrianic coinages cannot be estimated because hoards preserve insufficient number of specimens and obverse dies and many coins suffered recoining in the Antonine and Severan ages; see P. V. Hill, *The Arrangement of the Undated Coinage of Rome, 98–148* A.D. (London, 1970), pp. 29–39. There is thus insufficient evidence to minimize the impact of Dacian gold on the money supply because of limited mintage of aurei as argued by J. Guey, "De 'l'or des Daces' (1924) au livre de Sture Bolin (1958): Guerre et or. Or et monnaie," in *Mélanges d'archéologie, d'épigraphie et d'histoire offerts à Jérôme Carcopino* (Paris, 1966), pp. 444–75, and Walker, *MRSC* II, pp. 117–18, n. 3.
75. Dio 69. 8. 1, and SHA, *Vita Hadr.* 7. 6, and cf. *RIC* II, p. 466, no. 590–95 (sestertii); see R. MacMullen, "Tax Pressure in the Roman Empire," *Latomus* 46 (1987), 740–41.
76. See Walker, *MRSC* II, pp. 25–33.
77. Walker, *MRSC* II, pp. 36–38. Orichalcum denominations were alloyed

with 5 percent tin under Domitian; from the Severan age on, denominations were minted from bronze with increasing amounts of lead; see R. Turcan, *Le trésor de Guelma: Étude historique et monétaire* (Paris, 1968), pp. 50–57, and L. H. Cope, "The Metallurgical Development of Imperial Coinage in the First Five Centuries A.D.," Ph.D., Liverpool University 1974, pp. 142–72.

*Chapter 5: Currencies of the Roman East, 30 B.C.–A.D. 200*

1. Dio 52. 30 and cf. *IGRR* III. 864.
2. See Davies, *Roman Mines*, pp. 250–51, and Thompson, *New Style Silver Coinage of Athens*, pp. 392–434, with chronological revisions by Lewis, *NC* 7, 2 (1962), 275–300, for end of Athenian silver coinage. For abolition of Thessalian staters, see *IG* V. 1. 1432–33, and B. Keil, "Zur Victoriatusrechnung auf griechischen Inschriften," *ZfN* 32 (1920), 47–71.
3. Dio Chry., *Or.* 31. 66, and Dio 54. 7. 5. See C. H. V. Sutherland, N. Olcay, and K. E. Merrington, *The Cistophori of Augustus* (London, 1970), pp. 85–120, with the mint of the second issue as uncertain, and pp. 105–9. The estimate of an original minimum of 500, based on a single hoard, is too low; at least an excess of 600 dies was employed. Coins of groups III–VII exhibit the style and techniques of Rome, but they were minted from baser metal than comparable denarii; see Walker, *MRSC* I, pp. 12 and 24. It is thus inferred that the dies were engraved at Rome and shipped to Asia rather than at an imperial mint that was opened at Pergamum as argued by Sutherland, *RN* 6, 15 (1973), 129–51.
4. See *BMCRR* II, pp. 502–3, nos. 133–37, for cistophori of Mark Antony. See Sutherland, *Cistophori of Augustus*, pp. 112–13, and W. E. Metcalf, *The Cistophori of Hadrian* (New York, 1980), pp. 130–35, nos. B1–B15, for temples of Roma and *divi*.
5. See Howgego, *GIC*, nos. 839–40, and M. Thiron, "Cistophores contremarqués sous Vespasien," *SMB* 13 (1963), 1–8, and 14 (1964), 148–49.
6. See Walker, *MRSC* II, pp. 69–70 and 117, correcting their misattribution as tridrachmae of Caesarea in E. A. Sydenham, *The Coinage of Caesarea in Cappadocia* (New York, 1978), nos. 186–88.
7. See Walker, *MRSC* I, pp. 56–57, and Harl, *Civic Coins*, p. 133, n. 43.
8. See L. Robert, "Villes et monnaies de Lycie," *Hellenica* 10 (1955), 208–10, and Walker, *MRSC* I, pp. 54–56, and II, pp. 70–71; cf. H. A. Troxell; *The Coinage of the Lycian League* (New York, 1962), pp. 111–84.
9. See J. N. Svoronos, *Numismatique de la Crète antique* (Mâcon, 1890), pp. 113–19, and Walker, *MRSC* I, pp. 50–51 and 79, n. 34, and II,

pp. 60–65, for coinage of Crete. For coinage of Cyrene, see Walker, *MRSC* II, pp. 112–13. For Cilician silver coinages, see J.-P. Callu, *La politique monétaire des empereurs romains de 238 à 311* (Paris, 1969), pp. 154–55, and Walker, *MRSC* I, pp. 56 and 91, and II, pp. 86–91. Civic minting and imperial patronage are documented at Mopsus and Aegeae; see H. von Aulock, "Die Münzprägung der kilikischen Stadt Mopsos," *AA* 78 (1963), cols. 231–78, and H. Bloesch, "Caracalla in Aigeai," in *Congresso internazionale di numismatica, Roma 1961* II. *Atti* (Rome, 1965), pp. 7–23.

10. See Walker, *MRSC* II, pp. 66–70, and J. H. Nordbø, "The Imperial Silver Coinage of Amisus, 131/2–137/8 A.D.," in *Studies in Ancient History and Numismatics Presented to Rudi Thomsen,* ed. A. Damsgaard-Marsden (Arahus, 1981), pp. 166–78.
11. See Walker, *MRSC* I, pp. 130–32, and D. A. Parks, "The Roman Coinage of Cyprus," M.A. Thesis, University of Missouri-Columbia, 1991, pp. 68–74.
12. See Str. 12. 39; Arr., *Peripl.* 16; and Broughton, *ESAR* IV, pp. 620–21, for Pontic silver mines (Argyria). Chaldian silver mines were again exploited from the thirteenth through sixteenth centuries; see A. A. M. Bryer, "The Question of Byzantine Mines in the Pontos," *Anatolian Studies* 32 (1982), 138–41.
13. See Sydenham, *Coinage of Caesarea,* pp. 38–40, nos. 73–79, and Walker, *MRSC* I, pp. 38–39.
14. See Metcalf, *Cistophori of Hadrian,* pp. 110–20, and "Hadrian, Iovis Olympius," *Mn* 4, 27 (1974), 59–67.
15. See Walker, *MRSC* II, pp. 62–64, but the conclusions will be modified due the process of surface enrichment. See K. Butcher and M. Ponting, "Production of Roman Provincial Silver Coinage, A.D. 69–117: Interim Report," unpublished paper, Cambridge, April 1994, pp. 3–15. Many tetradrachmae or tridrachmae of Trajan found in Arabian hoards, attributed to Caesarea or Arabia, are most likely cistophori, because they bear cistophoric types or the Anatolian goddess Artemis Pergaea, and they were struck on flans and of the fineness and weight identical to other Trajanic cistophori; see Walker, *MRSC* II, pp. 67–71 and 109–11, and cf. W. E. Metcalf, "The Tell Kalak Hoard and Trajan's Arabian Mint," *ANSMN* 20 (1975), 91–94 (who suggests an Arabian mint). See, however, Harl, *CA* 10 (1991), 286–97, for comparable export of silver coins of western Anatolia to the Seleucid Empire in the third and second centuries B.C.
16. See *TAM* II. 3. 905 = *IGRR* III. 739, cap. 18, and Harl, *Civic Coins,* pp. 29 and 69, n. 144.
17. See Walker, *MRSC* I, pp. 106–10, and II, pp. 108–11 and 117; and G. F. Hill, "The Mints of Roman Arabia and Mesopotamia," *JRS* 6

(1916), 149–69. For Trajan's Arabian coinage, see Metcalf, *ANSMN* 20 (1975), 90–108, and Y. Meshorer, *Nabataean Coins* (Jerusalem, 1975), pp. 28–77. For Talmudic references to an Arabian *dinar* (or drachma), see D. Sperber, *Roman Palestine 200–400* A.D.*: Money and Prices* (Ramat-Gan, 1974), p. 230, n. 6.

18. See F. M. Heichelheim, "Roman Syria," *ESAR* IV, pp. 213 and 217–20, and Sperber, *Roman Palestine,* pp. 50–53.
19. G. F. Hill, "A Hoard of Coins from Nineveh," *NC* 5, 11 (1931), 160–70, and cf. hoard 16 in A. R. Bellinger, *The Excavations at Dura-Europos: Final Report VI: The Coins* (New Haven, 1949), pp. 207–9.
20. See Walker, *MRSC* I, pp. 67–69 and pp. 74–76, and for date of reform to 5/4 B.C., see C. J. Howgego, "Coinage and Military Finance: The Imperial Bronze Coinage of the Augustan East," *NC* 142 (1982), 7–13.
21. See C. M. Kraay, "Notes on the Early Imperial Tetradrachms of Syria," 6, 7 (1965), 58–63, and Walker, *MRSC* I, pp. 68–69 and 135–38, and III, pp. 114–17. Estimates of dies from hoards are untrustworthy in light of Flavian and Trajanic recoinages.
22. Sutherland, *RIC* I$^2$, p. 80, nos. 483–86 (Ephesus, AVGVSTVS series), and pp. 81–82, nos. 495–504 (Pergamum, C.A. series). For use of orichalcum, see Burnett, Craddock, and Preston, in *Actes du 9ème congrès international de numismatique*, p. 266.
23. See G. F. Carter, "Chemical Composition of Copper-based Roman Coins VIII: Bronze Coins Minted in Antioch," *INJ* 6–7 (1982–83), 22–38, and D. B. Waage, *Antioch-on-the-Orontes: Greek, Roman, Byzantine and Crusader's Coins* (Princeton, 1952), pp. viii–xi; the coins were minted of bronze to pass as equivalents of imperial dupondius and as. See Harl, *Civic Coins,* p. 128, n. 2, and C. H. V. Sutherland, "The Symbolism of Early *Aes* Coinages of Augustus," *RN* 6, 7 (1965), 94–105, for S.C. as honorific. Similar engraving and sharing of obverse dies with civic issues point to a single mint, organized into *officinae;* see Metcalf, *ANSMN* 22 (1977), 67–77.
24. *IGRR* III. 1056 col. IV.a, and cf. col. II. 7; see J. T. Matthews, "The Tax-Law of Palmyra: Evidence for the Economic History of a City of the Roman East," *JRS* 74 (1984), 157–80.
25. See K. Butcher, "The Colonial Coinage of Antioch-on-the Orontes (A.D. 218–53)," *NC* 148 (1988), 63–76. For patterns of circulation, see Waage, *Antioch,* pp. 29–69, and Bellinger, *Dura,* pp. 73–81.
26. See D. J. MacDonald, *Coins from Aphrodisias,* BAR Supp. Ser. 9 (Oxford, 1976), pp. 40–50. Finds suggest that Tarsus provided 90 percent of her needs whereas Aphrodisias provided only 50 percent. At Sardes, 80 percent of the bronze coins were civic. Among the civic coins, 52 percent were minted by Sardes, 22.5 percent by neighboring Lydian cities, and 11 percent by Ionian towns; see A. Johnston, "The Greek

Coins," in *Greek, Roman, and Islamic Coins from Sardis* (1981), pp. 5–6, and T. V. Buttrey, Jr., "The Roman Coins," in ibid., pp. 92–93, and cf. H. W. Bell, *Sardis IX: The Coins, Part I: 1910–1914* (Leiden, 1916), pp. 12–37.

27. For regional patterns of minting, see in W. Leschhorn, "Le monnayage impérial d'Asie Mineure et la statistique," *PACT: Statistics and Numismatics Statistiques et Numismatique* 5 (Paris, 1981), ed. C. Carcassone and T. Hackens, pp. 260–66. See objections in A. Johnston, "Greek Imperial Statistics: A Commentary," *RN* 6, 26 (1984), 240–57, and the reply by W. Leschhorn, "Die kaiserzeitlichen Münzen Kleinasiens: Möglichkeiten und Schwerigkeiten ihrer statistischen Erfassung," *RN* 6, 27 (1985), 203–16.
28. See Harl, *Civic Coins,* pp. 13–14, and 129, n. 2, and pp. 22–23 and 134, n. 46, and E. Gren, *Kleinasien und der Ostbalkan in der wirtschaftlichen Entwicklung der römischen Kaiserzeit* (Uppsala, 1941), pp. 30–59.
29. For festivals as stimulus for civic coinage, see cases in A. Johnston, "Hierapolis Revisited," *NC* 144 (1984), 52–80; P. Weiss, "Ein agonistisches Bema und die isopythischen Spiele von Side," *Chiron* 11 (1981), 315–46; "Ein Altar für Gordian III, die Älteren Gordiane und die Severer aus Aigeai (Kilikien)," *Chiron* 12 (1982), 191–205; and R. Ziegler, "Münzen Kilikiens als Zeugnis kaiserlischer Getriebespenden," *JNG* 27 (1977), 29–63.
30. See S. Grunauer-von Hoerschelmann, "The Severan Emissions of the Peloponnesus," *INJ* 6–7 (1982–83), 36–46, and T. B. Jones, "A Numismatic Riddle: The So-called Greek Imperials," *PAPhS* 107 1963), 310, for patterns of minting in Greece, to be compared to the production in Ionia and Caria shown in Fig. 5.2.
31. See K. Kraft, *Das System der kaiserzeitlichen Münzprägung in Kleinasien* (Berlin, 1972), pp. 16–21 and 90–92. For workshops in Syria, see K. Butcher, "Two Related Coinages in the Third Century A.D.," *INJ* 9 (1986–87), 73–84, and *NC* 148 (1988), 65–76.
32. See Kraft, *Das System,* pp. 28–29, pl. 10.76a–76h.
33. For Peloponnesian *aes,* see Harl, *Civic Coins,* pp. 18 and 135, nn. 52–54. For Pontic *aes,* see Bellinger, *Dura,* pp. 185–89, with reservations by Howgego, *GIC,* pp. 27–28.
34. See Howgego, *GIC,* who lists 837 countermarks, along with 26 supplementary ones, for a total of 863 countermarks. For purpose of countermarking, see M. J. Price, "Countermarks at Prusias ad Hypium," *NC* 7, 7 (1967), 37–42.
35. *OGIS* 484, and cf. *OGIS* 515 (Mylasa, ca. 210).
36. See D. Klose, "As und Assarion—zu den Nominalsystem der lokalen Bronzemünzen im Osten des römischen Reiches," *JNG* 36 (1986),

104–5, and *Die Münzprägung der Smyrna in der römischen Kaiserzeit* (Berlin, 1987), pp. 112–15, and *contra* Howgego, *GIC*, pp. 54–60.

37. R. Ashton, "Rhodian Coinage in the Early Imperial Period (*CH* 3. 82)," in *Recent Turkish Coin Hoards and Numismatic Studies*, ed. C. J. Lightfoot, British Institute of Archaeology Monographs 12 (Oxford, 1991), pp. 71–90. See *IGRR* IV, 915 (Cibyra, A.D. 74), in which a worn Rhodian drachma is discounted at 10 assaria (five-eighths of a denarius) rather than at the expected 12 assaria (three-quarters of a denarius), for an exchange rate of of 1 obol = 1.67 assaria or 3 obols = 5 assaria. This type of reckoning must have prompted the coining of assaria denominations on a decimal system; see Callu, *La politique monétaire*, pp. 59–63 and 93–102, and Howgego, *GIC*, pp. 61–62.

38. For reckoning of taxes at Messene, see A. Wilhelm, "Urkunden aus Messene," *JÖAI* 17 (1914), 51–54. For units of account at Athens, see *IG* II$^2$. 2276 (A.D. 110–50) and S. Millar, "A Roman Monument in the Athenian Agora," *Hesperia* 41 (1972), 50–92. See also *IG* II$^2$. 1368.80 and 82) and J. Notopolos, "Studies in the Chronology of Athens under the Empire," *Hesperia* 18 (1949), 29 and 51. Discussion by Howgego, *GIC*, pp. 54–56, misses the point of reckoning by ghost currencies.

39. See G. MacDonald, "The Pseudo-Autonomous Coins of Antioch," *NC* 4, 4 (1904), 124. For survival of the obol at Antioch and other northern Syrian cities, see forthcoming work by K. Butcher and R. Ziegler, communicated by them to me at "Kolloquium: Die kaiserzeitliche Münzprägung Kleinasiens," Munich, Staatlichen Münzsammlung, April 27–30, 1994. Civic *aes* at Antioch during the Neronian and Flavian ages (2.25 to 2.75 g) are marked "chalci." In the Severan age, Seleucia Pieriae, Rhossus, and Cyrrhus still marked multiple denominations in obols. At an official Tyrian exchange of 1 denarius to 6 bronze obols, the obol would have been reckoned at 2.67 assaria (rather than 2 assaria) so that 3 obols equaled 8 assaria.

40. See Sperber, *Roman Palestine*, pp. 101–5, and *contra* C. J. Howgego, "The Relationship of the Issar to the Denar in Rabbinic Literature," *INJ* 8 (1984–85), 59–64.

41. J. Mavrogordato, "The Chronology of the Coinage of Chios," *NC* 4, 18 (1918), 3–6, with chronological revisions by Klose, *Smyrna*, pp. 114–15.

42. For the example of Athens, see J. H. Kroll, "The Eleusis Hoard of Athenian Imperial Coins and Some Deposits from the Athenian Agora," *Hesperia* 42 (1973), 312–33, and Howgego, *GIC*, pp. 55–58.

43. See Klose, *Smryna*, pp. 103–8 and Tables 13–14.

44. See *OGIS* 484, and A. S. Walker, "16 or 18 Assaria, Drachmai, and Denarii in Mid-Second Century A.D. Athens," *INJ* 6–7 (1982–83), 142–47. There was no single rate of 16 assaria as argued by J. Melville-

Jones, "Denarii, Asses and Assaria in the Eastern Roman Empire," *BICS* 18 (1971), 95–101, and Howgego, *GIC*, pp. 54–56.

45. *Die Inschriften von Ephesos* III, nos. 910, 923–24, 929, 934, and 938, and VII, no. 3010, and Broughton, *ESAR* IV, pp. 879–80. See discussion in Callu, in *Dévaluations* (1980), II, pp. 199–206.
46. Tariffing of Ptolemaic tetradrachmae of 73–64 B.C. and 60–51 B.C. is surmised from its relationship to denarii in 78–62 B.C. (96 percent fine or 3.67 g of silver) and in 61–49 B.C. (97 percent or 3.73 g of silver). See Table 5.3.
47. See C. E. King and D. R. Walker, "The Earliest Tiberian Tetradrachms and Roman Monetary Policy towards Egypt," *ZPE* 21 (1976), 265–69, and Walker, *MRSC* I, pp. 152–54. See West and Johnson, *Currency*, pp. 65–73, and E. Christiansen, "On Denarii and Other Coin-Terms in Papyri," *ZPE* 54 (1984), 292–96; the term "Ptolemaic silver" (denoting imperial tetradrachmae) fell out of use soon after the Neronian reform.
48. See Duncan-Jones, *Rythmes*, p. 249, Table XIV. At an annual loss of weight through wear of 0.05598 percent, Cleopatran tetradrachmae (5.67 g), after fifty to sixty-four years of circulation would have lost 2.95 to 3.76 percent of their original weight in silver. In A.D. 19/20 the coins would have still contained 5.5 to 5.46 g of silver against 4.01 g of silver in the Tiberian coins. Cleopatran tetradrachmae probably contained silver equivalent to that of the Tiberian coins so that they had suffered an average annual rate of loss of 0.5 to 0.7 percent—a rate plausible in light of their heavy wear. For medieval analogies, see Grierson, in *Medieval Studies*, p. 25; Craig, *The Mint*, p. xvi; and Lane and Mueller, *Money and Banking* I, pp. 24–28.
49. See Walker, *MRSC* I, pp. 145 and 155–56.
50. See Walker, *MRSC* I, pp. 155–57, and E. Christiansen, *The Roman Coins of Alexandria: Quantitative Studies* (Aarhus, 1988), I, pp. 28–110. The latter's figures for coinage in circulation is of the proper order of magnitude even though his method for estimating dies is questionable.
51. See Christiansen, *Roman Coins of Alexandria*, I, pp. 237–58 and 295–301. For stability of prices, see Lendon, *Klio* 72 (1990), 110–11.
52. See West and Johnson, *Currency*, pp. 12–17 and 176–77, but the chronology of Milne's series 4 and 5 must be revised in light of A. Gara, "Egitto," in *CRWLR*, pp. 156–57 and 162, n. 26. The denominations, although precise identities are uncertain, are based on Ptolemaic bronze drachmae.
53. See West and Johnson, *Currency*, pp. 15–16 and 176–77, and Christiansen, *Roman Coins of Alexandria*, II, pp. 79–89 and 96–98, for improved weights of diobol (8.85 g), obol (4.8 g), and *hemiobol* (2.65 g). Worn late Augustan and Tiberian coins were perhaps retariffed at half their original value.

54. See West and Johnson, *Currency,* pp. 8–12, and Hendy, *SBME,* pp. 356–60, with the rate of difference representing one-sixteenth and noting that bronze obols were called *rhyparoi*. Surcharges date from at least 11/10 B.C.; see collection of documents in A. Gara, *Prosdiagraphomena e circolazione monetaria* (Milan, 1976), pp. 21–49, but the thesis of Egyptian denominations as direct equivalents of Roman ones is untenable; see King and Walker, *ZPE* 21 (1976), 265–66, and review by E. Christiansen, *JRS* 69 (1979), 204–6. For accounting units, see H. C. Youtie, "A Problem in Greco-Roman Bookkeeping," *ZPE* 15 (1974), 117–41.
55. See J. Day and C. W. Keyes, *Tax Documents from Theadelphia* (New York, 1956), pp. 276–307, and J. C. Shelton, *A Tax List from Karanis (P. Cair, Mich. 359)* (Bonn, 1977), II, pp. 7–18.

*Chapter 6: The Great Debasement and Reform,* A.D. *193–305*

1. Dio 72. 36. 4.
2. Dio. 55. 12. 3–5.
3. See Walker, *MRSC* II, pp. 33–45, and III, pp. 1–39.
4. Dio 77. 15. 2.
5. See T. V. Buttrey, Jr., "Dio, Zonares, and the Value of the Denarius," *JRS* 51 (1961), 40–45. Retariffing of the aureus at 50 denarii is premised upon an implausible identification of a fine of 10,000 HS reported by Gaius (*Comm.* 4. 46) as equivalent to one of 50 aurei reported by Ulpian (*Dig.* 2. 4. 24); see G. Mickwitz, *Geld und Wirtschaft in römischen Reich des vierten Jahrhunderts n. Chr.* (Helsinki, 1932), p. 37, and T. Pekáry, "Studien zur römischen Währungs- und Finanzgeschichte von 161 bis 235 n. Chr.," *Historia* 8 (1959), 481.
6. See Duncan-Jones, *Economy,* pp. 380–81.
7. See A. A. Gordus, "Neutron Activation Analysis of Coins and Coinstreaks," in *Methods of Chemical and Metallurgical Investigation of Ancient Coinage,* ed. E. T. Hall and D. M. Metcalf (London, 1972), pp. 131–38, and "Non-Destructive Analysis of Parthian, Sassanian, and Umayyad Silver Coins," in *Near Eastern Numismatics, Iconography, Epigraphy, and History: Studies in Honor of George C. Miles,* ed. D. K. Kouymjian (Beirut, 1974), pp. 141–62.
8. See Bolin, *State and Currency,* pp. 336–57, based on the finds in S. Bolin, *Fynden av romerska mynt i det fria Germanien* (Lund, 1926).
9. *RGdS* line 9 = A. Marciq, "Classica et Orientalia V: Res gestae divi Saporis," *Syria* 35 (1958), 309. Aurei were presumably those struck on a Severan standard of 50 to the Roman pound; see C. D. Gordon, "Subsidies in Imperial Defense," *Phoenix* 3 (1949), 63–64.
10. See J. F. Drinkwater, *The Gallic Empire: Separatism and Continuity in the*

*North-Western Provinces of the Roman Empire,* A.D. *260–274, Historia* Einzelschriften Heft 52 (Stuttgart, 1987), p. 205.

11. See J. Fitz, *Der Geldumlauf der römischen Provinzen im Donaugebiet Mitte des 3. Jahrhunderts* (Budapest, 1984), pp. 294–96 and 317–36; most hoards were concealed in 251–53.
12. See Walker, *MRSC* III, pp. 36–51.
13. See Fitz, *Geldumlauf,* pp. 317–20; M. Christol, "Effort de guerre et atelier monétaire de la périphérie au IIIe siècle ap. J.-C.: L'atelier de Cologne sous Valérien et Gallien," in *Armées et fiscalité dans le monde antique, Paris 14–16 octobre 1976* (Paris, 1977), pp. 253–55; and Callu, *La politique monétaire,* pp. 204–21. Hoards from Illyricum in 238–49 are comprised of 66 percent new baser issues and 34 percent older purer coins in contrast to those in the Rhineland in 238–51 comprised of 32 percent new coins and 68 percent older coins. See Bellinger, *Dura,* pp. 175–77, 181, and 187, for hoards concealed in 255/6 as comparable to those from Illyricum.
14. See Cope, *NC* 7, 17 (1977), 217–18, and King, in *SNREHS,* pp. 84–85, for process of coating antoniniani with silver as opposed to the superior fusing of silver to cores of nummi. For laws against sweating and clipping, see P. Grierson, "The Roman Laws of Counterfeiting," in *ERCHM,* pp. 240–61.
15. Fineness and weight standards for aurei are based on analyses by Morrisson, *L'or monnayé,* I, pp. 82–84, and Callu, *La politique monétaire,* pp. 430–31. The low survival rate of aurei of 193–285 points to successive reminting, but there is no evidence that aurei were demonetized and so circulated as bullion, as is argued by C. Oman, "The Decline and Fall of the Denarius in the Third Century A.D.," *NC* 4, 16 (1916), 57–60; Mickwitz, *Geld und Wirtschaft,* pp. 35–36, 65–66, and 77–81; and Callu, *La politique monétaire,* pp. 418–28.
16. See *CIG* 5008 (244) and 5010 (248) reporting annual expenses of a high priest, which editors take as equivalent sums (although this is not certain). The first sum is restored as 2,500 or 3,500 drachmae; see West and Johnson, *Currency,* pp. 94–95 and no. 4, and contrast Bolin, *State and Currency,* pp. 278–81, and Callu, *La politique monétaire,* p. 445, n. 1. An aureus of 125 or 175 drachmae gives 31.25 to 43.75 tetradrachmae (= denarii), but the exchange rate between tetradrachma and antoninianus is unknown.
17. See K. Menadier, "Die Münzen und das Münzwesen bei den Scriptores Hitoraie Augustae," *ZfN* 31 (1914), 6–9. For *aurei antoniniani,* see SHA, *Vita Aurel.* 9. 7 and 12. 1, and *Vita Prob.* 4. 5. For *aurei philippei,* see SHA, *Vita Claud.* 14. 3, and *Vita Firm.* 15. 8. For *aurei valeriani,* see SHA, *Vita Claud.* 17. 7.

18. See Morrisson, *L'or monnayé,* I, pp. 82–84. For Gallic aurei, see B. Schulte, *Die Goldprägung der gallischen Kaiser von Postumus bis Tetricus* (Frankfurt/Main, 1983), pp. 17–23. For eastern usurpers, see H. R. Baldus, *Uranius Antoninus: Münzprägung und Geschichte* (Bonn, 1971), pp. 88–95, and Callu, *La politique monétaire,* p. 434.
19. See Sperber, *Roman Palestine,* pp. 44–45 and 302, text M, quoted from R. Johanan.
20. *CIL* XIII. 3167 (Thorigny, A.D. 220), for salary of 25,000 HS *in auro*. See Duncan-Jones, *Economy,* pp. 251–54, and Callu, *La politique monétaire,* pp. 417–19.
21. For alloying with lead, see E. R. Caley, *Orichalcum and Related Ancient Alloys* (New York, 1964), pp. 71–75; Turcan, *Trésor de Guelma,* pp. 57–61; and P. Bastien, *Le monnayage bronze de Postume* (Wetteren, 1967), p. 36, Tables 2–3. For shortages of *aes*, see cases discussed by Turcan, *Trésor de Guelma,* pp. 127–29; T. V. Buttrey, Jr., "A Hoard of Sestertii from Bordeaux and the Problem of Bronze Circulation in the Third Century A.D.," *ANSMN* 18 (1972), 33–55; and R. Reece, "Coinage and Currency in the Third Century" in *The Roman West in the Third Century,* ed. A. King and M. Henig, BAR Int. Ser. 109 (Oxford, 1981), I, pp. 82–83.
22. W. E. Metcalf, "The Coins—1982," in *A Circus and a Byzantine Cemetary at Carthage* ed. J. H. Humphrey (Ann Arbor, Mich., 1989), I, pp. 339 and 342, no. 70.
23. See *RIC* V, 1, p. 36, nos. 1–3; D. Younge, "The So-called Interregnum Coinage," *NC* 139 (1979), 47–50; and Bastien, *Monnayage bronze de Postume,* pp. 31–38.
24. See Callu, *La politique monétaire,* pp. 111–30, and Turcan, *Trésor de Guelma,* pp. 127–29.
25. Severan cistophori (9.06 g) at 73.3 percent fine (6.65 g of silver) were a cut in weight by 29 percent and in fineness by 25 percent from the Hadrianic restrikes; see W. E. Metcalf, "The Severan Cistophori," *RIN* 100 (1988), 155–56, and Walker, *MRSC* III, pp. 72–73. For Cappadocian and Arabian issues, see Walker, *MRSC* III, pp. 74–82, and K. Butcher, "Two Notes on Syrian Silver of the Third Century A.D.," *NC* 149 (1989), 109–72.
26. See A. R. Bellinger, *The Syrian Tetradrachms of Caracalla and Macrinus* (New York, 1940), pp. 21–22, and R. G. McClee, "The Severan Tetradrachmae of Laodicea," *ANSMN* 29 (1984), 46–50.
27. See Ziegler, *JNG* 27 (1977), 35, nos. 1–2, and Walker, *MRSC* III, pp. 81–82. See Howgego, *GIC,* nos. 842–45, for countermarking of Tarsan and Cypriote silver coins.
28. See Bellinger, *Syrian Tetradrachms,* pp. 9–14, and Walker, *MRSC* III,

pp. 99–100, identifying twenty-six mints under Caracalla and nineteen under Macrinus. For a mint at Salamis on Cyprus, see Parks, "Roman Coins of Cyprus," pp. 98–101.

29. See G. F. Hill, "A Hoard of Coins from Nineveh," *NC* 5, 11 (1951), 160–70, and contrast hoards of ca. 220 published by P. Rosenthal-Heginbottom, "The Mampsis Hoard—A Preliminary Report" *INJ* 4 (1980), 39–54, and C. van Hoof, "Zur syrischen Tetradrachmenprägung der römischen Kaiserzeit: Ein neuer Schatzfund," *JNG* 36 (1986), 107–26. Finds at Dura-Europos mirror this pattern; compare Bellinger, *Dura,* pp. 202–3, hoard 5 (ca. 190) to pp. 182–84, hoard 19 (ca. 225).
30. Production is calculated from estimated dies in R. Bland, "The Last Coinage of Caesarea in Cappadocia," in *Ermanno A. Arslan Studia Dicata,* ed. R. Martini and N. Vismara (Milan, 1991), pp. 266–68.
31. See A. Spijkerman, "A Hoard of Syrian Tetradrachms and Eastern Antoniniani from Capharaum," *Studium Biblici Franciscani* 9 (1958–59), 282–327; 1,134 out of 1,272 antoniniani (over 89 percent) are from Cyzicus, when classified according to R. A. G. Carson, "The Hamâ Hoard and the Eastern Mints of Valerian and Gallienus," *Berytus* 17 (1967), 123–42. For comparable hoards, see K. J. J. Elks, "The Eastern Mints of Valerian and Gallienus: The Evidence of Two New Hoards from Western Turkey," *NC* 7, 15 (1975), 91–109, and H. D. Gallway, "A Hoard of Third-Century Antoniniani from Southern Spain," *NC* 7, 2 (1962), 335–408.
32. See A. M. Woodward, "A Hoard of Imperial Coins from Tarsus," *NC* 5, 5 (1925), 301–35, and Bellinger, *Dura,* pp. 185–87, for typical hoards of 253–55.
33. See Klose, *Smyrna,* pp. 108–9 and Tables 15–16, and Callu, *La politique monétaire,* pp. 57–110. See Waage, *Antioch,* pp. x–xi, for Antiochene *aes* in 218–53.
34. See *SNGvAulock* 4837–39 (Valerian, marked IA) and 8540 (Gallienus, marked ϵ), for issues of 253–55. Later ten-assaria pieces, although on a reduced weight standard, were struck on wide diameters (28–31 mm) to distinguish them from heavy five-assaria pieces struck prior to 253; see *SNGvAulock* 4835–36 (Valerian), 4840–44, and 4847–52 (Gallienus), and 4853–63 and 8547–50 (Salonina). For twelve and fourteen assaria, see *SNGvAulock* 4845–46 and 4854.
35. See Howgego, *GIC,* pp. 67–68, and Klose, *Smyrna,* pp. 110–11 and Table 20. The following cities revalued bronze denominations of one to six assaria from one-third to double the original value in ca. 255–70: Heraclea (Howgego, *GIC*, nos. 828–29, 810–11, 789, 771), Nicaea (nos. 833, 821, 807, and 788), Nicomedia (nos. 833, 821, 807, and

788), Prusias (nos. 837, 836, 822–23), Tium (nos. 824, 827–28, 789, and 771), Smyrna (nos. 830–31, 791, 760), a mint in Troas or Mysia (nos. 828–29, 810–11, 790), a Lydian mint (nos. 816i-17i, 775), uncertain Asian mint (nos. 816ii, 815i, 774) and Selge (nos. 832, 797, 779, 768).

36. The standard of tetradrachmae struck at Rome in 224–27 was identical to that of Alexandrine pieces; see A. M. Burnett and P. T. Craddock, "Rome and Alexandria: The Minting of Egyptian Tetradrachmas under Severus Alexander," *ANSMN* 28 (1983), 116–18.
37. See Christiansen, *ZPE* 54 (1984), 296, and Callu, *La politique monétaire,* pp. 186–97, for terms of *palaios* or *ptolemaikos* in papyri dated 266–96 in contrast to coins dubbed *neos* in 255 or *kainos* in the 260s.
38. *P. Oxy.* 1411 = West and Johnson, *Currency,* p. 183, no. 5 (November 24, 260). See Callu, *La politique monétaire,* pp. 186–88, and Lendon, *Klio* 72 (1990), 112–19, reading *to theion ton Sebaston nomisma* as tetradrachmae rejected on political grounds rather than as imported antoniniani.
39. See R. A. G. Carson, "Mints in the Mid-Third Century," in *SNREHS*, pp. 63–74, and E. Besly and R. Bland, *The Cunetio Treasure: Roman Coinage of the Third Century* A.D. (London, 1983), pp. 43–60, for identification of mints. See K. J. J. Elks, "Reattribution of the Milan Coins of Trajan Decius to the Roman Mint," *NC* 2, 12 (1972), 111–15, reassigning to Rome aurei and antoniniani assigned to Sirmium, Viminacium, or Mediolanum on grounds of style and provenance. For the identification of eastern mints, see Carson, *Berytus* 17 (1967), 132–42; Elks, *NC* 7, 15 (1975), 91–109; and Harl, *Civic Coins,* pp. 172–72, n. 71, and pp. 111–12.
40. See Christol, in *Armées et fiscalité,* pp. 253–55.
41. See P. Tyler, *The Persian Wars of the 3rd Century* A.D. *and Roman Imperial Policy* A.D. *253–208* (Weisbaden, 1975), p. 19, for antoniniani of 15 percent fine and hence comparable to those struck at Rome in 258–62. See Callu, *La politique monétaire*, p. 434, for heavy aurei (4.94 g) struck at 65 to the Roman pound. Antoniniani of Vaballathus are of comparable weight to imperial coins of 268–74, but no analysis of their silver content is yet available; see *RIC* V. 2, pp. 584–85, nos. 1–8 and nos. 1–2, and H. Mattingly, "The Palmyrene Princes and the Mints of Antioch and Alexandria," *NC* 5, 18 (1936), 89–114.
42. For chronology and identification of mints of this period, see Drinkwater, *Gallic Empire,* pp. 133–40 and 155–56. For circulation patterns, see J. F. Drinkwater, "Coin Hoards and the Chronology of the Gallic Empire," *Britannia* 5 (1974), 295–302; cf. *Gallic Empire,* pp. 189–214, and I. Pereira, J.-P. Bost, and J. Hiernard, *Les fouilles de Conimbriga* III

*Les monnaies* (Paris, 1974), pp. 236–37, for the composition of Spanish currency.

43. Zos. 1. 61. 3, but the account is otherwise muddled; see Callu, *La politique monétaire,* pp. 323–29, and R. A. G. Carson, "The Reform of Aurelian," *RN* 6, 7 (1965), 232–35. See King, in *SNREHS,* pp. 86–89, noting absence of prereform radiates in hoards of 274–93. For opening mints at Lugdunum, Ticinum, Tripolis, and Siscia, see *RIC* V. 1, pp. 21–25, and P. Bastien, *L'atelier de Lyon de la réouverture par Aurélien à la mort de Carin* (Wetteren, 1976), pp. 38–39.
44. See King, in *SNREHS,* pp. 88–89, and cf. J.-P. Callu C. Brenot, and J.-N. Barrandon, "Analyses de séries atypiques (Aurélien, Tacite, Carus, Licinius)," *NAC* 8 (1979), 241–54, suggesting an ideal weight of 4 g and 5 percent silver. The aurelianianus was thus minted at 80 to the Roman pound with 201.5 mg of silver. See K. W. Harl, "Marks of Value on Tetrarchic Nummi and Diocletian's Monetary Policy," *Phoenix* 39 (1985), 268, for XXI as 20 sestertii = 1 nummus. The denotation of a value of 20 asses is implausible, *contra* M. H. Crawford, "Finance, Coinage, and Money from the Severans to Constantine," *ANRW* 2, 2 (Berlin, 1975), pp. 575–76, and W. Weiser, "Die Münzreform des Aurelians," *ZPE* 53 (1983), 279–95.
45. See Morrisson, *L'or monnayé,* I, pp. 83–84; the aureus was improved from 94 to 99 percent fine. See Sperber, *Dévaluations* (1978), I, p. 182, and Callu, *La politique monétaire,* p. 367, n. 2, and p. 402, n. 1., for a Talmudic report of an aureus of 1,000 denarii in the 260s or 270s. The Tetrarchic rate of 600 d.c. to an aureus (struck at 60 to the pound) might imply a possible rate of 720 d.c. to an aureus struck at 50 to the pound in 274.
46. See Callu, *La politique monétaire,* p. 193, for *palaion nomisma* juxtaposed to *noummion Italikon.* Tetradrachmae of 274–96 weigh 7.75 to 8 g; Tetrarchic specimens have been analyzed at 0.5 percent fine, but modern analyses are lacking. If the tetradrachma was tariffed at par with the aurelianianus, the ideal standard might have been 8 g and 2 percent fine (or 160 mg of silver). A thorough recoinage is suggested by hoards concealed after 274 containing exclusively tetradrachmae of 274–96; see Christiansen, *Coin Hoards* 7 (1985), 81–85.
47. For revaluing in Asia Minor, see Klose, *Smyrna,* pp. 110–12, and cf. Howgego, *GIC,* nos. 559–61 and 802–5. For cities on Euxine shore, see Howgego, *GIC,* p. 76 and no. 626, and Callu, *La politique monétaire,* pp. 60–61.
48. See Lendon, *Klio* 72 (1990), 111–12 and 121–23.
49. See Morrisson, *ANSMN* 32 (1987), 198, and Callu, *NAC* 8 (1979), 241–54. The reform is suggested by the following sequence of antoniniani carrying the reverse CLEMENTIA TEMP. at Antioch.

Sequence of Aurelianiani, Antioch, 276
CLEMENTIA TEMP. Series

| Emperor | Value Mark | No. of Officinae | Fineness (%) | Tariffing (in d.c.) |
|---|---|---|---|---|
| Tacitus | XXI | 7 | 5 | 5 |
| Tacitus | XI | 8 | 10 | 2.5 |
| Probus | XXI or KA | 8 | 5 | 5 |
| Probus | XXI or KA | 9 | 5 | 5 |

There is no discernible relationship between Tacitus's revalued aurelianiani with so-called donative denarii of Carus and the Romano-British emperors. See Bastien, *Lyon*, pp. 274–85 and 289, and cf. *RIC* V. 2, p. 134, no. 5 (Lugdunum, with mark X ET I), and p. 146, nos. 99–100 (Siscia, with marks X.I or X.I.I), for coins of Carus. See N. Shiel, *The Episode of Carausius and Allectus,* BAR Br. Ser. 40 (Oxford, 1972), pp. 185–88, for British issues.

50. See C. E. King, "The Circulation of Coins in the Western Provinces, A.D. 260–295," in *The Roman West in the Third Century: Contributions from Archaeology and History,* ed. A. King and M. Henig, BAR Int. Ser. 109 (Oxford, 1981), pp. 92–97. Hoards of Britain, northern Gaul, and the Rhineland are 60 to 80 percent imitative radiates and Gallo-Roman antoniniani in contrast to hoards of central and southern Gaul, comprised mostly official aurelianiani.
51. See *RIC* V. 2, p. 207, and VI, pp. 93–94, and Morrisson, *L'or monnayé* I, p. 85; aurei were struck at 99 percent fine.
52. See Shiel, *Carausius,* pp. 57–66 and 187–88. See A. M. Burnett, "The Coinage of Allectus," *BNJ* 54 (1984), 27–28, for quinarii (possibly tariffed at 1 or 2 d.c.) as equivalent to pre-274 radiate antoniniani.
53. For the name of the denomination nummus rather than follis, see Crawford, *ANRW* 2, 2 (1975), 580, n. 80. For an initial tariffing at 5 d.c., see Harl, *Phoenix* 39 (1985), 263–70, and Hendy, *SBME,* pp. 452–62; *contra* a value of 10 d.c. proposed by K. T. Erim, J. M. Reynolds, and M. H. Crawford, "Diocletian's Currency Reform: A New Inscription," *JRS* 61 (1971), 175–76, and Crawford, *ANRW* 2, 2 (1975), 580–81. For inception of the reform, see P. Bruun, "The Successive Monetary Reforms of Diolcetian," *ANSMN* 24 (1979), 129–48.
54. The term *solidus* is applied to the gold coin in the Price Edict; see M. H. Crawford, "The Aezani Copy of the Prices Edict," *ZPE* 34 (1979), 176 and 197. See *RIC* VII, pp. 678–79, for gold coins of Licinius, minted at Antioch (ca. 317–19) at 60 to the Roman pound, marked I S(olidus)

INT(eger). The slang dated from the Severan era; see Apul., *Meta*. 9. 18 and 10. 9, and *CIL* VI. 29,700.

55. See King, in *SNREHS*, pp. 88–89; the aurelianianus averages 3.88 g (1/84 pound) and, at 4.5 percent fine, 175 mg of silver. See L. H. Cope, "The Argentiferous Bronze Alloy of the Large Tetrarchic Folles of A.D. 294–307," *NC* 7, 8 (1968), 115–49, for the nummus at 4 percent fine or 430 mg of silver.
56. See W. E. Metcalf, "From Greek to Latin Currency in Third Century Egypt," in *Mélanges de numismatique offerts à Pierre Bastien*, pp. 157–68. The last tetradrachmae of Diocletian, dated year 12 (295/6), were struck just prior to the rebellion of L. Domitius Domitianus (295–96) so that tetradrachmae and nummi briefly circulated together; hence the nummus was dubbed "Italic nummus" (*noummion Italikon*). See J. Schwartz, *Domitius Domitianus* (Brussels, 1974), pp. 141–44.
57. See Harl, *Phoenix* 39 (1985), 263–65, and Hendy, *SBME*, pp. 458–62. The Price Edict is premised on units of one, two, and five d.c., which probably reflect original tariffing in 293; cf. Bolin, *State and Currency*, pp. 300–302.
58. See *P. Ryland* IV. 604; *PSI* 969; and *P Oslo* III. 88, for comparable panic when Licinius halved his nummus to 12.5 d.c. See Hendy, *SBME*, pp. 463–65, and Crawford, *ANRW* 2, 2 (1975), p. 589, n. 105. See E. Haley, "The Roman Bronze Coinage in Britain and Monetary History from A.D. 293 to 350," *AJN* 1 (1989), 89–95, for radiates in hoards from Britain and Egypt as late as 307.
59. See M. F. Hendy, "Mint and Fiscal Administration under Diocletian, His Colleagues, and His Successors," *JRS* 62 (1972), 75–82, and *SBME*, pp. 378–80.
60. See J. Ermatinger, "The Circulation Pattern of Diocletian's Nummus," *AJN* 2 (1990), 107–17, and cf. a modern example in A. J. Dowling, "Calculating Britain's Requirement for Decimal Coins," *BNJ* 41 (1972), 168–75.
61. See Harl, *Phoenix* 39 (1985), 265–67, and Hendy, *SBME*, pp. 459–60.
62. *P. Beat. Pan*. 2. 215–17 (Feburary 16, 300), an official letter authorizing a price of 60,000 d.c. per Roman pound, but later agreeing to 63,000 d.c.; *contra* R. S. Bagnall, *Currency and Inflation in Fourth Century Egypt*, BASP, Supp. 5 (Atlanta, 1985), p. 60, who distinguishes these prices as official and market. The value of the aureus thus rose by either 66.67 or 75 percent in 293–300. For error on stone of Elatea, see M. Crawford and J. M. Reynolds, "The Aezani Copy of the Price Edict," *ZPE* 34 (1979), 176.
63. See Hendy, *SBME*, pp. 449–51; specimens average 3 to 3.2 g, 7.5 to 13.3 percent below the theoretical 3.46 g.
64. *P. Merton* 88.

65. *Edictum de Pretiis Maximis,* XXVIII. 9 (*CIL* III, pp. 802ff. = *ILS* 642); an increase of 14.3 to 20 percent over the rate in 300. The price of 6,000 d.c. for pure silver (*pusula*) is for bullion rather than argentei that were struck considerably below standard, *contra* Hendy, *SBME,* pp. 430–31. For corrections to the text from the copy found at Aezani, see R. and F. Naumann, *Der Rundbau in Aezani mit dem Preisedikt des Diokletians und das Gebaüde mit dem Edikt in Stratonikeia* (*Ist. Mitt.* Beiheft 10, 1973), p. 57 and pl. 14, and Crawford and Reynolds, *ZPE* 34 (1979), 179.
66. *Edictum de Pretiis Maximis, praef.* 14, and cf. with general complaint in *praef.* 6. See Lact., *De Mort. Pers.* 7. 7.
67. *P. Lips.* 84. For the nummus revalued at 25 d.c., see text in Erim, Reynolds, and Crawford, *JRS* 61 (1971), 193, frag. b., with restoration argued in Harl, *Phoenix* 39 (1985), 284–85, and cf. *P. Oxy.* XLIII. 3121. 10, for value of 25 Attic drachmae = 25 d.c.

*Chapter 7: Imperial Regulation and Reform,* A.D. *305–498*

1. Sutherland, *RIC* VI, pp. 41–42. See Bagnall, *Currency and Inflation,* pp. 27–35, and Hendy, *SBME,* pp. 465–67 and 481. The aureus, tariffed at 2,400 d.c. in 301, was struck from a pound of refined gold (99.5 percent fine) valued at 144,000 d.c., twice that in the Price Edict. See *P. Oxy.* XLIII. 3121, for the town council purchasing gold to manufacture a crown for Licinius II in 314–16. This gold (*aurum coronarium*) had to be of imperial standard (99.5 percent fine); its price of 432,000 d.c. per pound reflects the tariffing of the aureus at 7,200 d.c. (= 288 nummi) or the solidus at 6,000 d.c. (= 240 nummi). See A. K. Bowman, "The Crown-tax in Roman Egypt," *BASP* 4 (1967), 59–74, and cf. *P. Oxy.* 1413.

   Other gold prices in papyri cannot be used to document price trends or tariffing because the fineness of the bullion is not specified, notably *P. Oxy.* 2106 and *P. Rylands* IV. 616, in ca. 310–13, citing prices of 100,000 d.c and 110,000 d.c. per pound, respectively. Special levies from landowners in 309–24 netted gold and silver that was not refined to imperial standard so that these prices too do not reflect tariffing of coins; see R. S. Bagnall, "Bullion Purchases and Landholding in the Fourth Century," *Chronique d'Égypte* 52 (1977), 322–36, and R. S. Bagnall and K. A. Worp, "A Receipt for Gold Bullion," *Chronique d'Égypte* 52 (1977), 319–21, correcting readings of J. R. Rea, "*P.S.I.* 310 and Imperial Bullion Purchases," *Chronique d'Égypte* 49 (1974), 165–66.
2. See P. Bastien, *Le monnyage de Magnence (350–353)*, 2nd ed. (Wetteren, 1983), pp. 74–77, and Kent, *RIC* VIII, pp. 74–77, reducing the solidus from 4.54 g to 3.78 g.

3. See Harl, *Phoenix* 39 (1985), 269–70, and Sutherland, *RIC* VI, p. 104; the rate of the aureus is based on a nummus tariffed at 25 d.c., and cf. *P. Oxy*. XLIII. 3121 (316–18). For the solidus of 6,000 d.c., see *ILS* 9420 (Feltre, Italy).
4. Morrisson, *L'or monnayé,* I, p. 84. Constantine and Licinius each minted at 98 percent fine, a reduction by 1 percent; see Morrisson, *ANSMN* 37 (1987), 188–95. Constantine reminted Licinian solidi due to their pagan symbols (Euseb., *Vita Const*. 3. 54) as well as melted and coined gold cult statues (Soz., *HE* 2. 5).
5. *CTh* 12. 6. 12 (366, Pharr translation), and cf. *CTh* 12. 6. 13 (367). See J. P. C. Kent, "Gold Coinage in the Late Roman Empire," in *ERCHM,* pp. 191–93, and Hendy, *SBME,* pp. 387–88.
6. See M. Amandry, et al., "L'affinage des métaux au Bas-Empire," *NAC* 11 (1982), 283–84. The standard was maintained at least to 395; see R. Reece, "Some Analyses of Late Roman Silver Coins," *NC* 7, 3 (1963), 240–41. For stamped gold ingots of 379–83, see R. A. G. Carson, "Roman Coinage Metal and Coin Production," *NAC* 10 (1981), 307–8 and pl. II. 1–4, and Hendy, *SBME,* pl. 3. 9–10.
7. Valentinian III, *Novel*. 16. 1, and *CJ* 11. 11. 1–3.
8. See W. E. Metcalf, "The Minting of Gold Coinage in the Fifth and Sixth Centuries and the Gold Coinage of Illyricum and Dalmatia," in *SEBGC,* pp. 67–69. Hoards alone vitiate a cycle of perpetual reminting of solidi surmised by Kent, in *ERCHM,* pp. 197–98, and Jones, *LRE,* pp. 439–41 and 444–45.
9. Soc., *HE* 4. 34, and Amm. Marcel. 19. 11. 70. The *aurum tirocinium* was introduced during the mid-350s; see C. E. King, "The *Sacrae Largitiones*: Revenues, Expenditures, and the Production of Coin," in *Imperial Revenue, Expenditure and Monetary Policy in the Fourth Century,* ed. C. E. King, BAR Inter. Ser. 76 (Oxford, 1980), pp. 147–50.
10. See A. Jeločnik, *The Sisak Hoard of Argentei of the Early Tetrarchy, Situla* 3 (Ljubljana, 1961), pp. 42–43 and 66–69. For scarcity of silver coins and bullion (*asemos*) in Egypt, see West and Johnson, *Currency,* pp. 112–13.
11. See H. L. Adelson, "A Note on the Miliarense from Constantine to Heraclius," *ANSMN* 7 (1957), 128–31.
12. *CTh* 15. 9. 1 (384), and see Hendy, *SBME,* pp. 193–94 and 468–69.
13. For the fineness of the coinage shown in Table 7.2, see J.-P. Callu and J.-N. Barrandon, "L'inflazioni nel IV secolo (295–361): Il contriobuto delle analisi," in *Società romana e imperio tardoantico, istituzionie, ceti, economie,* ed. A. Giardina (Rome, 1986), pp. 590–91; J.-N. Barrandon and C. Brenot, "Analyse de monnaies de bronze (318–340) par activation neutronique à l'aide d'une source isotopique de Californium 252," in *Dévaluations* (1978), I, pp. 123–44; and J. N. Barrandon, J.-P. Callu,

and C. Brenot, "The Analysis of Constantinian Coins (A.D. 313–40) by Non-destructive Californium 252 Activation Analysis," *Archaeometry* 19 (1977), 173–86.

14. For tariffing of nummus at 25 d.c., see Harl, *Phoenix* 39 (1985), 269–70, and Hendy, *SBME,* pp. 462–63. There is no evidence for successive retariffing in 301–24 from 20 to 100 d.c. as argued by J.-P. Callu, "Denier et Nummus (300–354)," in *Dévaluations* (1978), I, pp. 108–9. For disappearence of argentei and radiates, see E. Haley, "The Roman Bronze Coinage in Britain and Monetary History from A.D. 293 to 350," *AJN* 1 (1989), 94–98.
15. See P. Bruun, "Site Finds and Hoarding Behaviour," in *SNREHS,* pp. 114–23, and "Quantitative Analysis of Hoarding in Periods of Coin Deterioration," *PACT* 5 (1981), pp. 355–56.
16. See C. E. King, "Fractional Coins at Rome, Ostia and Trier, A.D. 310–313," *NAC* 20 (1991), 227–38. Fractions of Maxentius and Constantine are described as half and quarter nummi, but a tariffing as a fifth at 5 d.c. was more probable than a quarter at 6.25 d.c.
17. *P. Rylands* IV. 623, p. 107, dated 317–24, and see A. H. M. Jones, J. R. Martindale, and J. Morris, *Prosopography of the Later Roman Empire* (Oxford, 1971), I, p. 907. If paid in Licinius's debased nummi tariffed at 12.5 d.c., exchange rates ranged from 560 to 2,400 nummi to the solidus.
18. See Bruun, *RIC* VII, p. 12, and Hendy, *SBME,* pp. 463–65, for the years 321–24. The date of 317 proposed by Crawford, *ANRW* 2, 2 (1975), 597, is based on the absence of money payments in *P. Princ.* 1 = *SB* V. 7521 after 316/7, but the taxpayers were profiting from *adaeratio;* see R. S. Bagnall and K. A. Worp, "The Fourth-Century Tax Roll in the Princeton Collection," *Archiv* 30 (1984), 56–58.
19. *P. Rylands* IV. 607. The letter, dated 317–24; is from the archive of Theophanes; see Hendy, *SBME,* p. 464, and Bagnall, *Currency and Inflation,* pp. 12–15. See *PSI* 965 and *P. Oslo* III. 88, reporting revaluation from 25 to 12.5 d.c. The reform failed to stablize prices; see Lendon, *Klio* 72 (1990), 122–24.
20. See Bagnall, *Currency and Inflation,* pp. 33–34 and 44. Tariffing of the nummus is undocumented in 324–48, because papyri quote prices in accounting units. Several schemes of retariffing are conjectured by Callu, in *Dévaluations* (1978), I, pp. 108–9 and 113, and "Rôle de distribution des espèces de bronze de 348 à 392," in *Imperial Revenues,* pp. 44–48 and 68. But Callu's schemes rest on two false premises. First, it is argued that the nummus was revalued upward to 100 d.c when it was debased to a coin of AE4 module in 330 and so occasioned a recoinage as evidenced by the pattern of discrete hoarding discussed by Haley, *AJN* 1 (1989), 105. But recoinage and hoarding patterns were

inevitable whether the nummus was at its old or new tariffing, and only a single retariffing in 321–24 is documented for the period 307–24. Second, it is argued the nummus of AE4 module in 330–48 is identified as the *centenionalis communis* ("common hundreder") named in laws of 354 (*CTh* 9. 23. 1) and 395 (*CTh* 9. 23. 2) and denoting tariffing of 100 d.c.; see Callu and Barrandon, in *Società romana*, 790–91, n. 67. But the *centenionalis* in the 354 law must be one of two AE2 denominations introduced in 348; the centenionalis in 395 is a AE3 rather than AE4 denomination. See Chastagnol, in *Dévaluations* (1980), II, p. 121, and Hendy, *SBME*, p. 291, n. 193.

21. See Chastagnol, in *Dévaluations* (1980), II, pp. 215–32, and Bagnall, *Currency and Inflation*, pp. 37–48, but note reservations by Lendon, *Klio* 72 (1990), 125–26.
22. See Sperber, *Roman Palestine*, pp. 164–66, for Talmudic sources, and pp. 167–68, and Callu, *Dévaluations* (1978), I, p. 116, for Syrian tombs.
23. See Hendy, *SBME*, pp. 338–44, for sealed purses of coins called either *balantion* or *follis*, but there was no single value assigned to a purse as argued by A. H. M. Jones, "The Origin and Early History of the Follis," *JRS* 49 (1959), 34–38. See Apul., *Meta* 4. 9 (*aureos folles*), for sealed bags of aurei in Severan North Africa. For use of papyrus for rolling up billon nummi, see *P. Oxy.* 2571 (A.D. 338) and 3189. For use of animal skin for same purpose, see *P. Oxy*. 1917 (early sixth century); N. Lewis, "Notationes legentis 51," *BASP* 14 (1977), 154–55; and West and Johnson, *Currency*, pp. 136–37.
24. *CIL* VIII. 22,660 ("in nummo X follis singulares quadragatina quinque milia sescentos"). J.-P. Callu, "Follis Singularis (à propos d'une inscription de Ghirza, Tripolitana)," *MEFR* 71 (1959), 321–37, deduces that the *follis singularis* (a sealed bag of nummi) proves a nummus of 100 d.c., but this undated inscription preserves no such tariffing.
25. See P. Bastien, "Imitations of Roman Bronze Coins, A.D. 318–363," *ANSMN* 30 (1985), 148–61. For use of sealed bags (*folles*) in official payments, see P. Cario Inv. 10,570 = K. A. Worp and R. S. Bagnall, "Five Papyri on Fourth Century Coins and Prices," *BASP* 20 (1983), 11–12.
26. Since coins were fiduciary, their tariffing cannot be deduced from bullion ratios as argued by Hahn, *MIB* I, pp. 24–27, and 65, and II, pp. 15–17. See Table 7.3.
27. Rates of exchange are based on analogy to documented rates in fifth and sixth century, but a tax receipt of ca. 400 reports 1 *noummion* reckoned at 4 Alexandrine talents (= 6,000 d.c.); see J.-P. Callu, "Monnaies de compte et monnaies réelles: L'ostracon 54 de Douch," *ZPE* 79 (1989), 73–74. The Register at Skar (ca. 435–45) reckons 28,000

talents to the solidus (*CPR* V. 26. 604–5) and records taxes paid in *ta kermata*, nummi of AE4 module (lines 453, 705–6, 710–10, 869, and 998). If the nummus at Skar were tariffed at 6,000 d.c, then 7,000 nummi would have been exchanged against the solidus—the same rate reported at Rome in 445. See R. S. Bagnall and P. Sijesteijn, "Currency in the Fourth Century and the Date of *CPR* V. 26," *ZPE* 24 (1977), 111–24. The register is redated from 388–90 to 430–45 due to reckoning by gold carats and Christian nomenclature; see R. S. Bagnall, "Conversion and Onomastics," *ZPE* 69 (1987), 243–58.

28. Kent, *RIC* VIII, pp. 61–64, and H. L. Cope, "The Metallurgical Analysis of Roman Imperial Silver and *Aes* Coinage," in *Methods of Chemical and Metallurgical Investigation of Ancient Coinage,* ed. E. T. Hall and D. M. Metcalf (London, 1972), pp. 34–47. Composition of hoards and an end to imitating AE4 nummi prove a recoinage of the AE4 nummi; see Haley, *AJN* 1 (1989), 106–8, and R. J. Brickstock, *Copies of Fel. Temp. Reparatio in Britain*, BAR Br. Ser. no. 176 (Oxford, 1987), pp. 4–26.
29. *CTh* 9. 21. 6 (349).
30. See Kent, *RIC* VIII, p. 64.
31. *CTh* 9. 23. 1; the edict was issued in 354 but perhaps reissued in 356; see Hendy, *SBME,* pp. 470–71. There are two explanations as to the identity of the coins named in *CTh* 9. 23. 1 ("quas more solito maiorinas vel centenionales communes appellant vel ceteras quas vetitas esse cognoscunt"). Hendy, *SBME,* pp. 290–94, takes *vel* as disjunctive, thereby arguing that the passage denotes maiorina and centenionalis as two names for the same coin, the large "A" denomination in Hendy's opinion. But context rules out this reading as forced so that *vel* is conjunctive, linking two separate items and so denoting two different coins; see Chastagnol, *Dévaluations* (1980), II, p. 121.
32. See Brickstock, *Copies,* pp. 28–30, and Bastien, *Magnence,* pp. 113–49 and 288–310. For Gallic hoards reflecting Germanic attacks, see G. Depeyrot, *La numéraire gaulois du IV siècle,* BAR Int. Ser. 127 (Oxford, 1983), pp. 163–78 and 214–16, and Callu, in *Imperial Revenue,* pp. 41–44 and 64–69.
33. Kent, *RIC* VIII, pp. 63–64, and Bastien, *Magnence,* pp. 69–70; the absolute chronology of Kent, *RIC* VIII, pp. 241–42, is to be preferred to that of Bastien.
34. Amm. Marcel. 22. 4. 9–10. See Kent, *RIC* VIII, pp. 46–48 and 63–66, and Amandry, *NAC* 11 (1982), 286–89. The *maiores nummi* named in a government purchase of African wheat (*CIL* III. 17,896) is emended as *maiorinae* by A. Chastagnol, "Un nouveau document sur le majorina?" *BSFN* 30 (1975), 854–57.
35. *CTh* 11. 21. 1, and Hendy, *SBME*, pp. 472–73; *aes dichoneutum* ("alloyed bronze") is translated as billon coins. The term *bicharacta* ("twice

fused") is synonymous; see Erim, *JRS* 61 (1971), 171, and Crawford, *ANRW* 2, 2 (1975), 581, n. 80.

36. *CJ* 11. 11. 2 (371), and see Hendy, *SBME*, p. 473.
37. See Kent, *RIC* VIII, pp. 57–58, and Hendy, *SBME*, p. 468. Argentei, tariffed at 24 to the solidus, were premised on a ratio of gold to silver of 1:12, but see *P. Oslo* III. 162 (ca. 355–75) and *CJ* 13. 2. 1 (397), for a ratio of 1:14.4.
38. Jul., *Misop*, 369D, citing prices in *argyria*, and cf. *P. Oxy*. 2729 (*argyra*) and J. M. Carrié, "Papyrologica Numismatica," *Aegyptus* 64 (1984), 203–27. For donatives in argentei, see Zos. 3. 13. 3 (*argyra nomismata*) and Amm. Marcel. 24. 3. 3. (*nummi argentei*) with discussion by P. Bastien, *Monnaie et Donativa au Bas-Empire* (Wetteren, 1988), pp. 41–42.
39. See Pearce, *RIC* IX, p. xxviii, and P. Grierson and M. Mays, *Catalogue of Late Roman Coins in the Dumbarton Oaks Collection and in the Whittemore Collection* (Washington, D.C., 1992), pp. 37–39. Argentei of 364–95 and of 395–408 were clipped down to 1.2 g and to 0.8 g, respectively, as halves and thirds of the Constantinian argenteus; see C. E. King, "Late Roman Silver Hoards in Britain and the Problem of Clipped Siliquae," *BNJ* 51 (1981), 1–31.
40. *CTh* IX. 32. 2, and see Grierson and Mays, *Late Roman Coins*, pp. 42–43, and Hendy, *SBME*, pp. 473–75 and 490–93.
41. Symmachus, *Relatio* 29, and see Hendy, *SBME*, pp. 250–51.
42. *CTh* 9. 23. 2, and see Grierson and Mays, *Late Roman Coins*, pp. 43–46.
43. See J. M. Fagerlie, *Late Roman and Byzantine Solidi found in Sweden and Denmark* (New York, 1967), pp. 6–7, and Metcalf, in *SEBGC*, pp. 68 and 76–77.
44. Malchus 18. 2 = R. C. Blockley, *The Fragmentary Classicising Historians of the Later Roman Empire* (Liverpool, 1983), II, pp. 430–31, reports that Goths measured out centenaria. See G. Dagron and C. Morrisson, "Le *kentènarion* dans les sources byzantines," *RN* 6, 17 (1975), 145–62, and J.-P. Callu, "Le centenarium et l'enrichissement monétaire au Bas-Empire," *Ktema* 3 (1978), 301–16.
45. See Priscus, frag. 53. 1 = Blockley, *Classicising Historians*, II, pp. 363–63, and Proc., *Bell.* 3. 6. 2, for a sum of 1,300 centenaria in gold (= 9,360,000 solidi). See Candidus, frag. 2 = Blockley, *Classicising Historians*, II, pp. 470–71, for payment by Leo I of 640 centenaria of gold (= 4,608,000 solidi) and 7,000 centenaria of silver with Anthemius paying the balance of the costs; see John Lydus, *De Mag.* 3. 43, for variant of 630 centenaria of gold. At a gold to silver ratio of 1:14.4 to 1:18, 7,000 the centenaria of silver is reckoned between 2.8 and 3.5 million solidi. The total of Candidus is between 7.4 and 8.1 million solidi; that of John Lydus between 7.3 and 8 million solidi.

46. John Lydus, *De Mag.* 3. 43, and Proc., *HA.* 29. 7–8; the sums are equal to 23,040,000 and 28,800,000 solidi, respectively.
47. See Bagnall, *Currency and Inflation,* p. 10, and West and Johnson, *Currency,* p. 129.
48. See Adelson, *ANSMN* 7 (1957), 125–29.
49. See J. P. C. Kent, "The Coinage of Arcadius (395–408)," *NC* 51 (1991), 56–57, and Grierson and Mays, *Late Roman Coins,* pp. 44–47 and 123–25.
50. *CTh* 11. 31. 2 (396); *CTh* 21. 3 (424); and Valentinian III, *Novel.* 16. 1 (445), stipulate 25 Roman pounds of coined bronze to the solidus; after the 498–512 reforms, 20 Roman pounds of coined bronze equaled a solidus (*CJ* 10. 78. 1–3). For weights of nummi minimi, see J. D. MacIssac, "The Weight of the Late 4th and Early 5th Century Nummus (AE4)," *ANSMN* 18 (1972), 62–64, and H. L. Adelson and G. L. Kustas, *A Bronze Hoard of the Period of Zeno* (New York), pp. 38–39. For alloying of nummi minimi with lead, see *RIC* X, pp. 21–22.
51. *CPR* V. 26. 604–5; 1 solidus is reckoned at 28,000 talents (= 42,000,000 d.c.). Taxes in nummi (*kerma*) totaled 5,9191,000 talents (8,878,500,000 d.c.), a sum Victor reckoned as 211 full-weight solidi (= 5,908,000 talents) plus 11,000 talents (just under two-fifths solidus). See *CPR* V. 26. 1009–12, for payments in gold totaling 152 solidi that, by weight, were short 390.25 carats, the equivalent of 135.75 solidi of full weight. The actual weight of the solidi was thus 1.9 rather than 2.1 pounds.
52. See Grierson and Mays, *Late Roman Coins,* pp. 22–23. The pattern is well documented by African hoards; see R. Turcan, "Trésors monétaires trouvés à Tipasa: La circulation du bronze en Afrique romaine et vandale aux Ve et VIe siècle ap. J.-C.," *Libyca* 9 (1961), 201–57, and *Trésors monétaires de Tipasa et d'Announa* (Lyons, 1984), but hoard Tipasa 2 dates from 395–400 rather than 423–30.

*Chapter 8: The Loss of Roman Monetary Ways,* A.D. *400–700*

1. See J. P. C. Kent, "From Roman Britain to Anglo-Saxon England," in *Studies in Anglo-Saxon Coinage Presented to Sir Frank Stenton,* ed. R. H. M. Dolley (London, 1961), pp. 1–22.
2. See P. Grierson, "La function sociale de la monnaie en Angleterre aux VIIe et VIIIe siècles," *Moneta e Scambi nell'alto medievo* 8 (1960), 341–62, and cf. R. E. M. Wheeler, *Rome beyond the Imperial Frontiers* (London, 1954), pp. 23–26.
3. See P. Grierson and M. Blackburn, *Medieval European Coins with a Catalogue of the Coins in the Fitzwilliam Museum, Cambridge, I: The Early Middle Ages (5th–10th centuries)* (Cambridge, 1988), I, pp. 14–16 and 159–64. Silver sceats, initially minted as proxies for tremisses (*thrym-*

*sas*), were debased from 98 to 20 percent fine, see D. M. Metcalf, "Chemical Analyses of English Sceattas," *BNJ* 48 (1978), 12–19.

4. See J. Lafaurie, "Les dernières émissions impériales d'argent à Trèves au 5e siècle," in *Mélanges de numismatique offerts à Pierre Bastien,* pp. 297–323, but heavy argentei date earlier to ca. 425, see Grierson and Mays, *Late Roman Coins,* pp. 150–51. The identity of Frankish and Roman authorities is tentative; see C. E. King, "Fifth Century Silver Issues in Gaul," in *Studia Numismatica Labacensia,* ed. P. Kos and Z. Demo (Ljubljana, 1988), pp. 197–212, and "Roman, Local and Barbarian Coinages in Fifth Century Gaul," in *Fifth-Century Gaul: A Crisis of Identity,* ed. J. Drinkwater and H. Elton (Cambridge, 1992), pp. 185–87. For Visigothic imitations of ca. 425–50, see G. Depeyrot, "Les solidi gaulois de Valentinien III," *RSN* 65 (1986), 111–31.
5. See J. Lafaurie, "Monnaies de bronze marseillaise au VIe siècle," *BSFN* 28 (1973), 480–82. Cities in southern and central Spain minted *aes* based on Byzantine prototypes in 554–624; see M. Crusafont i Sahater, "The Copper Coinage of Visigoths in Spain," in *Problems of Medieval Coinage in the Iberian Area,* ed. M. G. Marques and D. M. Metcalf (Santarem, 1988), III, pp. 35–70.
6. See P. Le Gentilhomme, "Le monnayage et la circulation monétaire dans les royaumes barbares en Occident Ve-VIIIe siècles," *RN* 5, 7 (1943), 46–112; and 5, 8 (1948), 13–59, but his generalizations must be modified in light of recent hoards. See notably J. Lafaurie, "Les routes commerciales indiquées par les trésors de trouvailles monétaires mérovinginens," *Moneta e scambi nell'alto medioevo* 8 (1960), 231–78, and D. M. Metcalf, "For What Purposes Were Suevic and Visigothic Tremisses Used?" in *Problems of Medieval Coinage in the Iberian Area,* III, pp. 15–34.
7. Grierson and Blackburn, *Medieval European Coinage,* I, pp. 44–46 and 75–76.
8. See P. Grierson, "The *Patrimonium in illis partibus* and the Pseudo-Imperial Coinage of Frankish Gaul," *RSN* 105 (1959), 95–111, and cf. Grierson and Blackburn, *Medieval European Coinage,* I, pp. 111–16, but there is no support for papal officials supervising this coinage. For issues minted by Frankish kings, see E. Felder, "Zur Münzprägung der merowingischen Könige in Marseille," in *Mélanges de numismatique offerts à Pierre Bastien,* pp. 223–25.
9. See K. J. Gilles, *Die Trierer Münzprägung im frühen Mittelalter* (Coblenz, 1982), pp. 11–18, and King, "Fifth Century Silver Issues in Gaul," pp. 199–206.
10. Gregory of Tours, *Hist. Franc.* 4. 42, and Fredegarius 4. 69 (*Scrip. rer. Merov.* II. 155), and see J. Lafaurie and C. Morrisson, "La pénetration

des monnaies byzantines en Gaule mérovingienne et visigotique de VIe à VIII siécle," *RN* 6, 29 (1987), 38–98.

11. See J. P. C. Kent, "Gold Standards of Merovingian Gaul, A.D. 580–700," in *Methods of Chemical and Metallurgical Investigations of Ancient Coinage*, ed. E. T. Hall and D. M. Metcalf (London, 1972), pp. 72–73, and A. M. Stahl, *The Merovingian Coinage of the Region of Metz* (Louvain-la-Neuve, 1982), pp. 58–69.
12. Gregory of Tours, *Hist. Franc.* 7. 26, and see P. Grierson, "Commerce in the Dark Ages: A Critique of the Evidence," *TRHS* 5, 9 (1959), 132–35.
13. See P. Grierson, "Visigothic Metrology," *NC* 6, 13 (1953), 74–87, and G. C. Miles, *The Coinage of the Visigoths in Spain: Leovigild to Achila II* (New York, 1952), pp. 154–64. Leovigild minted his tremissis (1.6 g) at 75 percent fine; average fineness fluctuated between 58.3 and 66.7 percent in the seventh century. For Arab imitations, see M. Balaguer, "Early Islamic Transitional Gold Issues of North Africa and Spain," *ANSMN* 24 (1978), 225–41.
14. See D. M. Metcalf, "The Prosperity of North-western Europe in the Eighth and Ninth Centuries," *EcHR* 2, 20 (1967), 344–57, who estimates at least 6.7 million deniers struck by Pepin the Short (752–68) and a like number of pennies by Offa (757–96).
15. See Grierson and Blackburn, *Medieval European Coinage* I, pp. 17–18, and C. Morrisson, "La circulation de la monnaie d'or en Afrique à époque vandal: Bilan des trouvailles locales," in *Mélanges de numismatique offerts à Pierre Bastien*, pp. 325–44.
16. See C. Morrisson and J. H. Schwartz, "Vandal Silver Coinage in the Name of Honorius," *ANSMN* 27 (1982), 149–80.
17. See Hendy, *SBME*, pp. 478–80, reckoning a silver *siliqua* at 1 carat or 500 denarii so that the solidus was 2,400 d.c. or 12,000 nummi, yielding a rate of 1 d.c. = 5 nummi.
18. See Morrisson, in *Circus and Byzantine Cemetery*, pp. 424–36.
19. See P. Grierson, "The *Tablettes Albertini* and the Value of the Solidus in the Fifth and Sixth Centuries A.D.," *JRS* 49 (1959), 77–80.
20. C. Courtois et al., *Tablettes Albertini: Actes privés de l'époque vandal (fin du Ve siècle)* (Paris, 1952), pp. 202–5.
21. C. Morrisson, "The Re-use of Obsolete Coins: The Case of Roman Imperial Bronzes Revived in the Fifth Century," in *ENMPG*, pp. 95–111, and Hendy, *SBME*, pp. 483–84. Specimens found in Italy were carried there by Justinian's soldiers (along with Vandalic four nummi) and were not of Italian origin as argued by Grierson and Blackburn, *Medieval European Coinage*, I, pp. 29–31, and C. P. A. Barcaly, "Countermarked As of Vespasian from South Italy," *NC* 146 (1986), 226–30. The denominations eighty-three and forty-two nummi are not consis-

tent with an Ostrogothic bronze currency based on a follis of forty nummi.

22. See J. P. C. Kent, "The Coinage of Theodoric in the Names of Anastasius and Justin I," in *Mints, Dies and Currency,* pp. 71–74, and "The Italian Silver Coinage of Justinian I and His Successors," *Studia Paulo Naster oblata,* ed. S. Scheers (Louvain, 1982), pp. 275–82.
23. Cassiod., *Variae* 1. 10, and see Hendy, *SBME,* p. 485, dating the gloss to 507–11.
24. See Hendy, *SBME,* pp. 486–87, and Grierson and Blackburn, *Medieval European Coinage,* I, pp. 30–31.
25. *Constitutio Pragmatica* (App. VII), 1. 20; see Hendy, *SBME,* pp. 366 and 485.
26. See R. N. Frye, "Byzantine and Sasanian Trade Relations with Northeastern Russia," *DOP* 26 (1972), 265–69.
27. John Malalas, *Chronographia* XVI (Bonn ed., p. 400), and D. M. Metcalf, *The Origins of the Anastasian Coinage Reform* (Amsterdam, 1969), pp. 82–90. For the exchange of 480 folles to the solidus, see *P. Mich.* II. 607 (sixth century); and see discussion by J.-M. Carrié, "Monnaie d'or et monnaie de bronze dans l'Égypte protobyzantine," *Dévaluations* (1980), II, p. 258, and West and Johnson, *Currency,* p. 135. Many AE4 nummi circulated into the reign of Justinian; see H. L. Adelson and G. L. Kustas, "A Sixth Century Hoard of Minimi from the Western Peloponnese," *ANSMN* 11 (1964), 188–93.
28. Marcellinus Comes, *Chronicon* a. 498; *MGH* AA XI, p. 95; see Hendy, *SBME*, p. 476.
29. See Anon., *Chronicle* = *Scriptores Syri* III. 4, p. 115, s.a. 824 (= 512/3), and Hendy, *SBME*, pp. 476–77.
30. Proc., *HA* 25. 11–12, and, for date of reform, see R. Scott, "Justinian's Coinage and Easter Reforms and the Date of the Secret History," *Byzantine and Modern Greek Studies* 11 (1987), 215–21. Papyri of Justinianic date reckon 1 nummus at 7,200 myriads of d.c. for an exchange rate of 1 solidus = 180 folles = 7,200 nummiae; see *P. Oxy*. 1917–1918, and West and Johnson, *Currency,* pp. 162–63. The same rate is attested later; see *P. Cario Masp*. 367,309 (undated) and *P. Cario Masp*. 267,168 (569).
31. See Bellinger, *DOC* I, pp. 156–57, no. 273; the denomination marked ΛΓ, based on its weight and size, is best interpreted as a coin of thirty-six nummiae introduced to provide a convenient multiple to the duodecanummia with revaluation in 538/9. The value mark might denote three *litai,* but its precise meaning is obscure; see West and Johnson, *Currency,* pp. 130–31. The alternate view that it represents a value mark denoting a piece of thirty-three nummiae results in an otherwise

inexplicable denomination; see L. Schindler and G. Kalmann, "Byzantinische Münzstudien, II. Das 33 Nummistrück Justinians I," *NZ* 72 (1947), 109–12, followed by Hahn, *MIB* I, p. 65, and Hendy, *SBME,* pp. 497–98.

32. See Metcalf, *Origins,* pp. 74–81, estimating between 28 and 112 million small folles in 498.
33. See Hahn, *MIB* I, 59–60, Prägetabelle VI–VIII; five *officinae* regularly operated at Constantinople from 538 to 553; two each at Cyzicus and Nicomedia.
34. See Morrisson, in *Circus and Byzantine Cemetery,* p. 427, ruling out a second mint at Constantine in Numidia. For local minting in Italy and Sicily during the Gothic War, see Hahn, *MIB* I, pp. 73–75 and 90–91.
35. See Morrisson, *L'or monnayé,* I, pp. 202–8, and C. Morrisson, "Carthage: The *Moneta Auri* under Justinian I and Justin II, 537–578," in *SEBGC,* p. 11, n. 28.
36. See H. L. Adelson, *Light Weight Solidi and Byzantine Trade during the Sixth and Seventh Centuries* (New York, 1957), p. 49, but see review by J. P. C. Kent, *NC* 5, 19 (1959), 238–39, for central minting at Constantinople. Light-weight solidi bear the facing portrait introduced in 538/9; see Proc., *HA* 22. 38 and 25. 12, for possible dating of first issues to 547–55 when Peter Barsymes was praetorian prefect for the second time.
37. For "carat minus" reckoning, see West and Johnson, *Currency,* p. 177; Carrié, in *Dévaluations* (1980), II, p. 268; and J. Durliat, "Philologie et numismatique: A propos de quelques prix protobyzantines," in *Rythmes,* pp. 349–50. See Metcalf, *ANSMN* 25 (1980), 107–8, for how exclusive use of worn solidi gave rise to new lighter weight standards in Syria.
38. See M. Hendy, "Light Weight Solidi, Tetartera and the Book of the Prefect," *BZ* 65 (1975), 57–90, ruling out light-weight solidi as trade coins or subsidies to barbarians as argued by Adelson, *Light Weight Solidi,* pp. 16–20 and 104–37, and J. Smedley, "Seventh Century Byzantine Coins in Southern Russia and the Problem of Light Weight Solidi," in *SEBGC,* pp. 123–30. The savings of this expedient for internal payments is readily demonstrated by the fact that for every pound of gold minted into 72 solidi of 23, 22, or 20 carats, the excess bullion was equivalent to 3, 6, or 12 full-weight solidi, respectively. If, for example, 28,000 pounds of gold taken in tax (equal to 25 percent of Justinian's annual revenues) were minted into solidi of 22 carats at the rate of 72 coins per pound, the excess gold would have totaled 168,000 full-weight solidi.
39. See Hendy, *SBME,* pp. 496–99.
40. Malalas, *Chronographia,* XVIII (Bonn ed., p. 486). Papyri report what

appear to be daily fluctuations of exchange rates. For rates of 15.25, 15.5, and 16 folles per carat (or 366, 372, and 384 folles to the solidus) in the 570s, see *P. Cairo Masp.* 26,714, and Carrié, in *Dévaluations* (1980), II, pp. 251–58. The rate of 372 folles = 1 solidus was reported in 579; see *PSI* 8,963 = J. Keenan, *BASP* 9 (1972), 16–18. See *P. Oxy* XVI. 1921 (ca. 560–70), and West and Johnson, *Currency,* pp. 130–31, for 15.5 folles per carat (or 372 folles to the solidus), if 125 *lita* = 1 carat.

Two late Justinianic papyri reported unprecedentedly low exchange rates of 125 to 130 folles per solidus (if the nummus was tariffed at 10,000 d.c.). See *P. Oxy.* XVI. 1911 (557), reckoning 1 solidus at 5,169 myriads of d.c. for an exchange of 5,1569 nummiae = 129 folles, 9 nummiae = 1 solidus. See *P. Oxy.* XVIII. 2195 (562), reckoning 1 solidus at 5,000 myriads of d.c., for an exchange of 5,000 nummiae = 125 folles = 1 solidus. If the nummus had been tariffed at 5,000 d.c. in these documents, the reconstructed exchange rates of 258 and 250 folles are more plausible.

41. See P. Grierson, "The President's Address—Weight and Coinage," *NC* 7, 4 (1960), i–xvii. An official exchange of 240 folles = 1 solidus is inferred from value marks on issues from Carthage under Maurice Tiberius; see Grierson, *DOC* II. 1, pp. 20–21. An undated papyrus of the later sixth century (*SPP* 20. 218) reckons 12 folles to the carat or 288 folles to the 1 solidus; see Carrié, in *Dévaluations* (1980), II, pp. 251–58. The rate rose to 25 folles to the carat or 600 folles to the solidus in 602; see *P. Grenf.* 2. 87 (602), and West and Johnson, *Currency,* p. 135.
42. See Morrisson, in *SEBGC,* pp. 49–60, revising chronology of Hahn, *MIB* I, pp. 51–52, and Bellinger, *DOC* I, pp. 158–62. For volume of Carthage mint, see C. Morrisson, "Estimation du volume de solidi de Tibère et Maurice à Carthage," *PACT* 5 (1981), 267–84, and in *SEBGC,* p. 61.
43. See Hahn and Metcalf, in *SEBGC,* p. 14, and Hahn, *MIB* I, p. 52. Imperial issues in Spain reflected Visigothic standards and denominations; see W. H. Tomasini, *The Barbaric Tremissis in Spain and Southern France: Anastasius to Leovigild* (New York, 1964), pp. 129–31.
44. See Hendy, *SBME,* pp. 624–26, and Hahn and Metcalf, in *SEBGC,* pp. 8–9. See D. M. Metcalf, "North Italian Coinage Carried across the Alps: The Ostrogothic and Carolingian Evidence Compared," *RIN* 90 (1988), 449–51, for export of solidi north of Alps.
45. Theoph., *Chron.,* I, pp. 302–3 (de Boor ed.), under the year 622. See Hendy, *SBME,* pp. 494–95, ruling out the date 615 argued by K. Eriksson, "Revising a Date in the Chronicon Paschale," *JÖB* 17 (1968),

17–28, and "The Cross on Steps and the Silver Hexagram," *JÖB* 17 (1968), 149–64.

46. *Chronicon Paschale,* p. 706 (Bonn ed.), and see P. A. Yannopoulos, *L'hexagramme, un monnayage byzantin en argent du VII siècle* (Louvain, 1978), pp. 6–9 and 86–108.
47. See Hendy, *SBME,* pp. 494–95, for XXIV and XX in the exergue as marking successive tariffings of 24 and 20 folles to the hexagram rather than regnal years proposed by Yannopoulos, *L'hexagramme,* pp. 86–99.
48. G. C. Bates, "Constans II or Heraclonas: An Analysis of the Constantinopolitan Folles of Constans II," *ANSMN* 17 (1971), 141–61.
49. See P. Charanis, "The Significance of Coins as Evidence for the History of Athens and Corinth in the Seventh and Eighth Centuries," *Historia* 4 (1955), 163–72, and cf. D. M. Metcalf, *Coinage in South-eastern Europe, 820–1396,* Royal Numismatic Society Special Publication 11 (London, 1979), pp. 18–24. For comparable situation in Asia Minor, see C. Foss, "The Persians in Asia Minor and the End of Antiquity," *EHR* 90 (1975), 721–47.
50. See W. E. Metcalf, "A Heraclian Hoard from Syria," *ANSMN* 20 (1975), 133–34, for *aes,* and Hahn and Metcalf, in *SEBGC,* p. 10, n. 23, for solidi in Syria.
51. J. R. Phillips, "The Byzantine Bronze Coins of Alexandria in the Seventh Century," *NC* 7, 2 (1982), 225–41; duodecanummiae carry value marks of IB and M to designate parity with the imperial follis. See also W. Hahn, "Alexandrian 3-Nummi and 1-Nummus Types under Heraclius," *NC* 7, 18 (1978), 181–83. During Persian rule in 618, the exchange was improved to 1 solidus = 640 duodecanummiae = 7,680 nummiae (the equivalent of 192 folles); see *P. Oxy.* XVI. 1904.
52. See P. Grierson, "The Monetary Reforms of Anastasius and their Economic Consequences," in *PINC,* pp. 286–87, and *Byzantine Coins* (Berkeley, 1982), pp. 121–22, and cf. *DOC* II. 1, p. 55. The countermark is attributed to Constantia on Cyprus, but examples have been found at Carthage, suggesting that countermarking was widespread; see Morrisson, in *Circus and Byzantine Cemetery,* p. 427, and Hahn, *MIB,* pp. 159–60. A revaluation of 400 percent is suggested by countermarking a follis of Constans II (4.34 g) with X (= 10 nummiae) as a fraction of the reform follis (17 g); see P. A. Yannopoulos, "La réforme de bronze sous Constantin IV à lumière d'un follis contremarqué de Constant II," *RBN* 133 (1987), 721–47.
53. See W. A. Oddy, "The Debasement of Provincial Byzantine Gold Coinage from the Seventh to Ninth Centuries," in *SEBGC,* pp. 135–42, for base standards in Byzantine Sicily, Africa, and Sardinia.

54. See P. Grierson, "The Monetary Reforms of 'Abd al-Malik, their Metrological Basis and their Financial Repercussions," *JESHO* 3 (1960), 241–64, and Metcalf, *ANSMN* 25 (1980), 96–99, for recoinage of imitative dinars and dirhems.
55. See E. Bernareggi, *Moneta langobardorum,* trans. P. Visonà (Lugano, 1989), pp. 40–44, 85–88, and 120–35, and Grierson and Blackburn, *Medieval European Coinage,* I, pp. 62–73. For fineness of Lombard gold coins, see W. A. Oddy, "Analyses of Lombardic Tremisses by Specific Gravity Method," *NC* 7, 12 (1972), 193–215. Initial silver issues were based on prototypes of Justin II and Maurice Tiberius. See P. Grierson, "The Silver Coinage of the Lombards," *Archivo Storico Lombardo* 8, 6 (1956), 130–47.

*Chapter 9: Government's Aims and Needs*

1. Tac., *Hist.* 4. 74, and cf. Dio 52. 28. 1–2.
2. See R. MacMullen, *Latomus* 46 (1987), 737–41, and *Corruption and Decline in the Later Roman Empire* (New Haven, 1988), pp. 129–39. Predictable production of coinage dictated by regular tax cycles is inherently implausible as argued by W. Hahn, *Emission und Lustrum in der byzantinischen Münzprägung des 6. Jahrhunderts* (Vienna, 1971).
3. *OGIS* 484.8–13; see A. D. Macro, "Imperial Provisions for Pergamum," *GRBS* 17 (1976), 174–76, and Valentinian III, *Novel.* 16. 1 (445).
4. Symmachus, *Relatio* 29.
5. See Rodewald, *Money in the Age of Tiberius,* pp. 14–17, and Mrozek, *Historia* 34 (1988), 310–11.
6. See Suet., *Iul.* 54. 2–3, and *Aug.* 41. 2; *P. Heid.* 40 = Schwartz, *Archives de Serapion,* no. 90.
7. *P. Oxy.* 3401; see Bagnall, *Currency and Inflation,* p. 60, for the date of 350–60. See *PSI* VII. 825 = Naldini 44 (ca. 326), for Didymus advising his brother Severus to purchase solidi at 50,000 d.c. and silver bullion (*asemos*) at 300,000 d.c. per pound. See *P. Oxy.* 1223 (ca. 360–75), with discussion by Bagnall, *Currency and Inflation,* pp. 61–62, and A. C. Johnson and L. C. West, *Byzantine Egypt: Economic Studies* (Princeton, 1949), p. 159. Hermias notes to his brother Horion "the solidus (*holokottinos*) is now 2,020 myriads, for it has come down" (lines 31–33).
8. Plut., *Cato* 16; see Hopkins, *JRS* 70 (1980), 111.
9. See Burnett, *NC* 7, 17 (1977), 43–44, and Wallace-Hadrill, *JRS* 76 (1986), 70–77.
10. Suet., *Iul.* 76. 2–3, and see R. J. A. Talbert, *The Senate of Imperial Rome* (Princeton, 1984), pp. 379–83.
11. See Metcalf, in *SEBGC,* pp. 66–67, and Fulford, *Archaeological Journal* 135 (1978), 67–114.

12. Polyb. 6. 39. 12. See Crawford, *RRC* II, pp. 622–25, for two Attic obols (3.33 asses) per diem as Polybius's equivalent of the state minimum wage of 3 asses per diem for 360 days; cf. Plaut., *Most.* 357, and Plut., *TG* 13.
13. See Crawford, *RRC* II, pp. 696–97, but see Badian, *Publicans and Sinners,* pp. 26–47, for contracts to supply legions overseas doubling or tripling the cost of payrolls in 218–167 B.C. The legion is reckoned at 4,140 infantry, 60 centurions, and 300 cavalry (total payroll 619,320 denarii); see Brunt, *Italian Manpower,* p. 67.
14. See Plin., *NH* 33. 45, for revaluation. See Suet., *Iul.* 26. 3, and cf. Tac., *Ann.* 1. 17. 6, for increase to 225 denarii annually in 46 B.C.
15. See Hopkins, *Conquerors,* pp. 38–39, and Frank, *ESAR* I, pp. 97–108, 190–98, and 402–8, for grain prices. See C. Nicolet, "Armée et fiscalité: Pour un bilan de la conquête romaine," in *Dévalutions* (1980), II, pp. 39–42, for Italian allied governments raising their own *tributa* to pay their forces overseas.
16. J. H. Thiel, *Studies on the History of Roman Sea-Power in Republican Times* (Amsterdam, 1946), pp. 210–15, 258–76, and 377–78, notes that fleets averaged between 68 and 77 quinqueremes, but transports must have numbered between 500 and 800. See Polyb. 1. 52. 6, for 800 transports required to ship four legions and their supplies to Sicily in 248 B.C. and Plut., *Pomp.* 11. 2, for 800 transports to convey six legions, siegecraft, and materiel to Africa in 82 B.C.
17. See Plut., *Pomp.* 45; Pompey's fleet of 120 warships and 24 legions in 67 B.C. is priced at 36 million denarii. See Brunt, *Italian Manpower,* pp. 456–57. See Suet., *Iul.* 25, and Eutrop. 6. 17; Caesar's six legions in 58 B.C. cost 9 million denarii.
18. Suet., *Iul.* 26. 3, and Tac., *Ann.* 1. 17. 6; see MacMullen, *Latomus* 43 (1984), 579–80. Praetorians received two denarii per diem; see P. A. Brunt, "Pay and Superannuation in the Roman Imperial Army," *PBSR* 18 (1950), 55, and R. Develin, "The Army Pay Raises under Severus and Caracalla, and the Question of the *Annona Militaris,*" *Latomus* 30 (1971), 691.
19. For Domitian's pay raise, see Suet., *Dom.* 7; and Dio 67. 3. 5; and C. M. Kraay, "Two New Sestertii of Domitian," *ANSMN* 9 (1960), 109–16. For Severan pay raises, see Brunt, *PBSR* 18 (1950), 58–59, and Develin, *Latomus* 30 (1971), 687–96.
20. For the size of the garrison of Rome, see H. Freis, *Die Cohortes Urbanae,* Epigraphische Studien 2 (Cologne, 1967). The cost of the household cavalry (*exploratores*), 1,000 men strong and raised by Trajan, is reckoned at double the payroll of a Praetorian cohort. The number of auxiliary units shown in Table 9.2 is based on P. A. Hodder, *Studies in the Auxilia of the Roman Army,* BAR Int. Ser. 70 (Oxford, 1980),

pp. 214–40 (correcting previous undercounting of Julio-Claudian units). Citizen cohorts were presumably paid higher wages, but their pay has been computed at the same rate as other auxiliary cohorts; pay and numbers of *numeri* in service after Hadrian are unknown.

21. See R. MacMullen, "How Big Was the Roman Imperial Army?" *Klio* 62 (1980), 451–60, and Hendy, *SBME*, pp. 176–77, for Diocletian's army at 435,000 men based on John Lydus (*De Mensibus* 1. 27). This size is preferred to estimates based on Agathias (*Hist.* 5. 13) who cites 645,000 men as the size of the army before Justinian.
22. See Hendy, *SBME,* pp. 176–77. *P. Beat. Pan.* 2. 2–16 (A.D. 299–300) reports a base pay of 1,800 d.c. for legionaries and elite cavalry (*alares*) and 1,200 d.c. for auxiliaries. R. P. Duncan-Jones, "Pay and Numbers in Diocletian's Army," *Chiron* 8 (1978), 551, suggests that officers received five times base pay.
23. See King, in *Imperial Revenues,* pp. 147–50, and Jones, *LRE*, pp. 432 and 625–26. For 20 solidi as commutation rate, see *CTh* 7. 13. 14 (A.D. 397), 18 (409), 20 (410); for 25 solidi, see *CTh* 7. 8. 2 (367), 7. 1 (375), and 13 (397); for 30 solidi, see Valentinian III, *Novel.* 6. 4 (444).
24. See Hendy, *SBME,* pp. 168–69, based on Agathias, *Hist.* 2. 4., and cf. Jones, *LRE*, pp. 684–86, interpreting the figure as the field army (and so excluding *limitanei*).
25. See Hendy, *SBME,* pp. 221–23; the sums, paid in bronze folles on the standard of 512, would have totaled between 1.5 and 2 billion folles. See K. Hannestad, "Les forces militaires d'après la guerre gothique de Procope," *C & M* 21 (1961), 136–83, for the expedition against Africa in 533–34, and the field armies sent to Italy in 536–39, 544–48, and 549–51.
26. See Theoph., *Chron.* p. 486, and Hendy, *SBME,* pp. 181–87 and 645–50. Nicephorus I (802–11) fixed the minimum cost of a *stratiotes* (cavalryman) at 18.5 solidi. For size of the Byzantine army in 650–950, see J. F. Haldon, "Kudama ibn Dj'afar and the Garrison of Constantinople," *Byzantion* 48 (1978), 78–90, and W. T. Treadgold, "Notes on the Numbers and Organization of the Ninth-Century Byzantine Army," *GRBS* 21 (1980), 269–88.
27. In Table 9.3, the rates are adjusted to account for pay raises and higher salaries of officers as argued by R. MacMullen, "The Roman Emperors' Army Costs," *Latomus* 43 (1984). It is assumed that auxiliaries did not receive pensions, but see reservations by Hopkins, *JRS* 70 (1980), 124–25.
28. See Hopkins, *Conquerors,* pp. 38–39, and cf. Brunt, *Italian Manpower,* pp. 393–94.
29. See D. van Berchem, *Les distributions de blé et argent à la plèbe romaine* (Paris, 1939), pp. 145–68. Dio 59. 1–2 notes that Caligula personally

gave a *congiaria* of 12.5 million denarii so that each of the 150,000 urban plebeians received 75 denarii—the common rate of second century.

30. Calculations of *congiaria* (reckoned for 150,000 plebeians or for the same number eligible for the *annona*) are based on van Berchem, *Distributions*, pp. 141–61, and Corbier, *Dévaluations* (1978), I, p. 281. Number and rates of donatives are based on van Berchem, *Distributions*, pp. 152–54, and see SHA, *Vita Had*. 5. 7–8.
31. SHA, *Vita Marc. Aur*. 27, reports 200 denarii to each urban plebeian. See Dio 74. 8. 4, for 200 denarii per legionary and 320 denarii per Praetorian. Each guardsman of the Urban Cohorts is surmised to have received 160 denarii.
32. Dio 46. 46. 7. See SHA, *Vita Sept. Sev*. 7. 6, for soldiers claiming that donatives of 10,000 denarii were promised. For delays in payment during the Dominate, see Hendy, *SBME*, pp. 187–89.
33. See van Berchem, *Distributions*, pp. 152–54 and 159–61, and cf. Hendy, *SBME*, pp. 481–82.
34. *P. Beat. Pan*. 2. 197–203, and cf. *P. Oxy*. 1047. See Duncan-Jones, *Chiron* 8 (1978), 544–45.
35. See L. Wierschowski, *Heer und Wirtschaft: Das römische Heer der Prinzipatszeit als Wirtschaftsfaktor* (Bonn, 1984), pp. 199–201, estimating 200 to 300 denarii as the cost of arms per man. See Brunt, *PBSR* 18 (1950), 60–61, and R. O. Fink, *Roman Military Records on Papyri* (Ann Arbor, Mich., 1971), nos. 68–72, for deductions and pay stoppages.
36. See Wierschowksi, *Heer und Wirtschaft*, pp. 219–24; see R. Davies, *Service in the Roman Army* (New York, 1989), pp. 158–62, for purchase prices of 125 denarii for each mount at Dura-Europos in 246–51. Prices of 5 to 10 solidi per horse in the Dominate are comparable to those at Dura; see Jones, *LRE*, pp. 625–26. A horse consumed annually 140 modii of barley, perhaps 70 denarii (Polyb. 5. 39, and cf. *P. Oxy*. 2046), but grain was a fraction of maintenence; see P. Southern, *The Roman Cavalry* (London, 1992), pp. 210–11.
37. See Carrié, in *Armées et fiscalité*, pp. 384–87.
38. See J. Harmand, *L'armée et le soldat à Rome* (Paris, 1957), pp. 410–16. Back pay was just one objection; see Liv. 32. 3. 2 (mutiny in Macedonia, 199 B.C.); 39. 38. 4; 40. 35. 6–11; and 36. 10 (mutinies in Spain, 184 and 180 B.C.); also Plut., *Luc*. 14 (Lucullus's soldiers in Asia Minor in 70–69 B.C.); and Tac., *Ann*. 1. 17–18 (Tiberius's legionaries). For mutinies in Byzantine armies, see J. Teall, "Barbarians in Justinian's Armies," *Speculum* 40 (1965), 294–322, and W. Kaegi, *Byzantine Military Unrest, 451–843* (Amsterdam, 1981), pp. 41–63.
39. See Fink, *Roman Military Records*, nos. 67–69. High deductions from the payroll of the cavalryman at Masada in A.D. 72 or 74 probably

recovered costs of shipping barley; see H. Cotton, "The Date of the Fall of Masada," *ZPE* 78 (1988), 157–62, and H. Cotton and I. Geiger, *Masada* II: *Final Report on the Masada Excavations* Part 3: *The Papyri* (Jerusalem, 1989), pp. 52–53, no. 722 (A.D. 72 or 74). Such deductions were inapplicable on frontiers where horses could graze or grain was readily available. For grain rations bought at market prices that were reimbursed, see *PSI* 683 (199).

40. Jos., *BJ* 6. 6. 1.
41. See Davies, *Service,* pp. 18–23. Funds of men were kept with *signifer,* see Suet., *Dom.* 7. 3 (Moguntiacum, A.D. 88–89) and Veget., *Epit. rei mil.* 2. 20. For officers and centurions amassing savings, see Caes., *BC* 1. 39, and Suet., *Caes.* 68.
42. SHA, *Sev. Alex.* 52, and cf. *Edictum de Pretiis Maximis,* praef. 4–6.
43. Jos., *BJ* 5. 9. 1–2 (349–56), Penguin translation, p. 316.
44. Sall., *BJ* 27. 5 and 36. 1, and Plut., *Pomp.* 11. 2; see Dio 32. 49–50, and Suet., *Iul.* 19, for Senate controlling funds of governors overseas. See Liv. 40. 51. 8 (180 B.C.), for centurions in Spain remitting to the treasury in Rome money not distributed in payrolls in 180 B.C. Republican denarii found in Sardinia arrived as payrolls of soldiers; see J. R. Rowland, "Numismatics and the Military History of Sardinia," *Limes: Akten XI internationalen Limeskongress (Budapest, 1976),* (Budapest, 1977), pp. 87–112.
45. *P. Beat. Pan.* 2. 303–4, and cf. transport by mules in Cic., *Verr.* 2. 3. 183. See A. S. Robertson, "Evidence for the Transport of Roman Coins in the Mediterranean to Britain," in *Roman Frontier Studies, 1989: Proceedings of the XVth International Congress of Roman Frontier Studies,* ed. V. A. Maxwell and M. J. Dobson (Exeter, 1991), pp. 114–16.
46. See Hendy, *SBME,* pp. 272–75.
47. See G. Parker, *The Army in Flanders and the Spanish Road, 1567–1559* (Cambridge, 1972), pp. 139–57. Roman soldiers demanded pay raises or donatives during the Civil Wars of 69–70 (Tac., *Hist.* 4. 16–19, and Dio 73. 11–12) and 193–95 (Herod. 2. 6., and cf. SHA, *Vita Sev.* 5. 2).
48. Front., *Aq.* 1. 7, for Marcian aqueduct, and contrast Plin., *NH* 36. 122, and *ILS* 218. Claudius completed the aqueduct bearing his name at a cost of 87.5 million denarii or twenty-two times the cost of the Marcian aqueduct.
49. Dio 52. 30. 1.
50. Salaries are estimated based on range 10,000 aurei for the proconsul of Asia or Africa (Dio 78. 22. 5) and 500 aurei for a military tribune (*CIL* XIII. 3161, Thorigny, ca. 220), See Suet., *Claud.* 10, for an annual stipend of 5,000 aurei as the worth of an impoverished senator. Senatorial governors thus received between 4,000 (minimum property requirement of equestrian) and 10,000 aurei (minimum property of

senator); equestrian officials received salaries between 1,000 (minimum property of decurion) and 4,000 aurei (minimum property of equestrian). Equestrian military tribunes were paid less than senior centurions; see B. Dobson, "Legionary Centurion or Equestrian Officer? A Comparison of Pay and Prospects," *Ancient Society* 3 (1972), 193–201.

51. See R. MacMullen, "Roman Bureaucrats in the Provinces," *HSCP* 68 (1964), 305–16. The annual salaries of senior officials include fifty senatorial governors (300,000 to 375,000 aurei), proconsuls of Asia and Africa (20,000 aurei), the Prefect of the City (10,000 aurei), Prefects of the Annona, Vigiles, Praetorian Guard, and Egypt (20,000 aurei). For equestrian officials in service, see H.-P. Pflaum, *Les procurators équestres sous le Haut-Empire* (Paris, 1952), p. 150, and "Les salaries des magistrats et functionnaires du Haut-Empire," in *Dévaluations* (1978), I, pp. 211–15.
52. MacMullen, *HSCP* 68 (1964), 314–15, and Jones, *LRE*, pp. 366–410.
53. See MacMullen, *Latomus* 43 (1984), 576–77, and *Roman Government's Response to Crisis, 235–337 A.D.* (New Haven, 1975), pp. 149 and 281, n. 88. Requisitions and recruitment on the march are best seen in the Civil Wars of 69 and 193–95 (Tac., *Hist* 3. 63–67, and Dio 75. 8. 4). For cities impressed to manufacture arms, see Tac., *Hist*. 2. 82, and M. C. Bishop, "The Military *Fabrica* and the Production of Arms in the Early Principate," in *The Production and Distribution of Roman Military Equipment,* ed. M. C. Bishop, BAR Int. Ser. 275 (Oxford, 1987) pp. 16–17.
54. See R. W. Goldsmith, "An Estimate of the Size and Structure of the National Product of the Early Roman Empire," *Review of Income and Wealth* 30 (1984), 273–74, for GNP valued at 4.5 to 5 billion denarii or 46.9 to 52.5 million pounds of coined silver on the Neronian standard. See Hopkins, *JRS* 70 (1980), 118–19, for coined money equivalent to 1.75 to 2.5 billion denarii or 18.2 to 26 million pounds of coined silver (but provincial silver and billon coinages are omitted).
55. *ILS* 309 = *CIL* VI. 967; Dio 69. 8. 1; and SHA, *Vita Had.* 7. 6. See depictions of coin and relief work in *RIC* II, p. 590, no. 3, and M. Torelli, *Typology and Structure of Roman Historical Reliefs* (Ann Arbor, Mich., 1982), pp. 108–9. Arrears owed by Roman citizens are calculated as one-sixth of indirect taxes of the fifteen-year cycle 103–18; see MacMullen, *Latomus* 46 (1987), 743. But if the remission extended only to A.D. 106 when Trajan burned arrears in the forum, annual revenue was 110 million denarii; see *Chron. Pasch.* MGH AA 9. 223, and Plin., *Paneg.* 29. 4 and 40. 3–4.
56. See C. Trench, *The Road to Khartoum: Life of General Charles Gordon* (New York, 1988), p. 142. See *P. Tebtynis* 391 for tax liturgists paying

for swordbearers in the second century, and *P. Oxy*. 3339–3400, 3402, 3408–9, 3416, and 3419, for hiring armed collectors in 360s and 370s.

57. See J. Robert and L. Robert, *Amyzon* (Paris, 1983), pp. 217–26, no. 28 = *SEG* (1983), 33, and L. Migette, "Note sur l'emploi de *prodaneizein*," *Phoenix* 34 (1980), 219–26, for practice of *prodaneismos* or *proeisphora* whereby citizens advancing money for taxes were reimbursed from taxes. For endowments to pay head taxes, see *IG* XII. 5. 724 (Andros) and XII. 5. 946 = B. Laum, *Stiftungen in der griechischen und römischen Antike* (Leipzig, 1914), I, no. 60 (Tenos). For benefactors paying annual taxes, see *ILS* 6960 = *CIL* II. 3664, *TAM* II. 291 (Xanthus, gift of 30,000 denarii), *IG* IV. 181 (halving of capitation tax, Lampsacus), and *IG* IV. 259 (Assus).
58. *P. Tebtynis* 391 = Johnson, *ESAR* II, p. 536, no. 327, and see Day and Keyes, *Tax Documents from Theadelphia*, pp. 308–16.
59. *P. Oxy*. 3401, 3424, and cf. 3394–95, for outstanding loans of Papnuthis to pay taxes in advance. See *P. Oxy*. 2861, for a certain Apollonius of the second century urging Dioscurides to speed up collections because of loans due to bankers (*trapezitai*).
60. See A. E. Hanson, "The Poll Tax in Philadelphia," *Proceedings of XIVth International Congress of Papyrology* (London, 1975), p. 149, comparing *P. Princ*. 8 to *P. Mich*. 10. 594 (A.D. 51), showing arrears of 2,500 to 3,000 drachmae and 636 delinquient taxpayers for obligations in A.D. 46/7. See parallel case in D. H. Samuel, "Taxation at Socnopaiou Nesos in the Early Third Century," *BASP* 14 (1977), 186–207.
61. *IG* V. 1. 1432–33, and see Wilhelm, *JOAI* 17 (1914), 48–49.
62. Amm. Marcel. 16. 5. 15, and cf. 18. 14. 1–2.
63. Trench, *Road to Khartoum*, p. 142.
64. See W. L. Westerman and C. W. Keyes, *Tax Lists and Transport Receipts from Theadelphia* (New York, 1932), pp. 37–40.
65. See S. L. Wallace, *Taxation in Egypt from Augustus to Diocletiän* (Princeton, 1938), pp. 124–25 and 413–18, and C. W. Keyes, "Syntaximon and Laographia in the Arsinote Nome," *AJP* 62 (1961), 263–69, for the unnamed head tax of 44 drachmae as the *laographia*. The *kh* tax was paid at the rate of 16 drachmae per man, with a remainder (*loipon*) of 20 obols (12 obols for priests) levied upon full payment; see H. C. Youtie, *CW* 30 (1936–37), 200–202 = *Scriptiunculae* (Amsterdam, 1973), II, pp. 852–53. The bath tax (*balaneion*) was paid in worn drachmae (*rhyparai*) at a fixed rate rather than as one-third of gross receipts; see Wallace, *Taxation*, pp. 155–59.
66. See Youtie, *ZPE* 15 (1974), 117–41.
67. *P. Mich*. 224. 1833–36, Pharmouthi 4, year 12. The *apomoira*, assessed in ghost units as 2 drachmae, 3 obols, was raised by surcharges and

conversion fees to 4 drachmae and 17 obols. The *geometria,* assessed at 6 drachmae, 1 obol, and 4 chalci, was raised to 1 tetradrachma and 22 obols (which in coin was just under 8 drachmae).

68. *P. Mich.* 223–25, and see analysis by A. E. Boak, "The Populations of Roman and Byzantine Karanis," *Historia* 4 (1955), 158–60. The 644 names entered under the head tax represent 575 taxpayers (deducting for duplications due to mutilated entries and multiple nomenclature of Egyptians). There are over 72 cleruchs or Roman citizens recorded.

69. See R. S. Bagnall and B. W. Frier, *The Demography of Roman Egypt* (Cambridge, 1994), pp. 53–57. See Hopkins, *JHS* 70 (1980), 116–17, estimating 144 million tetradrachmae in direct annual taxes based on Jos., *BJ* 2. 386, and *Ant.* 19. 352. If money taxes ranged between 100 to 150 million tetradrachmae, they were valued at 4 to 6 million aurei or 90,000 to 135,000 pounds of gold. For Egyptian revenues in the Byzantine era, see estimates by R. S. Bagnall, "Agricultural Productivity and Taxation in the Later Roman Empire," *TAPA* 115 (1985), 304–5, and Hendy, *SBME,* pp. 168–71. For reports in Arab chronicles, see Johnson and West, *Byzantine Egypt*, pp. 263–65 and 287–88, and M. el-Abbadi, "Historians and the Papyri on the Finances of Egypt at the Arab Conquest," in *Proceedings of XIVth International Congress of Papyrology* (Chico, Calif., 1981), pp. 509–16.

70. *P. Wisc.* II. 80 = *SB* 7365 = Johnson, *ESAR* II, pp. 595–601. Incomplete entries for six months from Socnopaiou Nesos in the Antonine or Severan age total 327 tetradrachmae, 55 bronze drachmae, and 181 obols which converts to 383 tetradrachmae, 3 drachmae, and 1 obol (*P. Lond.* III. 1169).

71. See Plin., *HN* 12. 84 and 6. 101, and S. E. Sidebotham, *Roman Economic Policy in the Erythraean Thalassa, 30 B.C.–A.D. 217* (Leiden, 1986), pp. 106–10. Pliny's annual drain of 25 million denarii might represent the value of goods exported. See Raschke, *ANRW* 9, 2 (Berlin, 1978), pp. 632–34, dismissing the authenticity of Pliny's figures.

72. Phil., *VA* 1. 20; at Coptos (*OGIS* 764); twenty-seven denarii were charged on each *hetaira*. See Sidebotham, *Roman Economic Policy,* pp. 102–5, and L. Casson, "P. Vindob G. 40822 and the Shipping of Goods from India," *BASP* 23 (1986), 73–79.

73. *P. Mich.* 127, and see discussion by A. E. R. Boak, *Papyri from Tebtunis* I, *Michigan Papyri,* vol. II (Ann Arbor, Mich., 1933), pp. 92–101.

74. See R. Bogaert, *Banquiers dans les cités grecques* (Leiden, 1968), pp. 403–8, and Westermann and Keyes, *Tax Lists*, pp. 40–45. See F. Oertel, *Die Liturgie: Studien zur ptolemaischen und kaiserlichen Verwaltung Äegyptens* (Leipzig, 1917), pp. 247–48, for liturgists serving as moneychangers.

75. See *CPR* V. 26, and Bagnall and Sijpesteijn, *ZPE* 24 (1977), 111–24. The document is redated from 388–90 to ca. 435–45; see Bagnall, *Currency and Inflation,* p. 10.
76. *P. Oxy*. 1411 = West and Johnson, *Currency,* p. 183, no. 5.
77. *OGIS* 515 (Mylasa, ca. 210), and cf. punishments at Hadrianic Pergamum in *OGIS* 484 = *IGRR* IV. 352.
78. See *OGIS* 484 (Pergamum, A.D. 130) and 515 (Mylasa, ca. A.D. 202). For Hellenistic regulations, see *SIG*[3] 218 (Olbia, ca. 350 B.C.), *SIG*[3] 525 (Gortyn, ca. 250 B.C.), *IG* VII. 2426. 16–17 (Thebes, ca. 230 B.C.), and *OGIS* 339 (Sestos, ca. 130 B.C.).
79. Cic., *Ad Quint. fr.*. 1. 3. 7, and *Ad Att*. 2. 6. 2 and 2. 16. 4, for *permutatio* or exchange of his profits as governor from cistophori into denarii. See Andrieu, *La vie financière,* pp. 509–10.
80. Cic., *Att*. 2. 6. 2, and cf. 2. 16. 4 and *De Domo* 52.
81. See Andrieu, *La vie financière,* pp. 359–444, 503–21, and 644–56.
82. See J. Andrieu, *Les affairs de M. Jucundus* (Rome, 1974), pp. 223–71 and 312–38.
83. *P. Merton* 88 (Karanis) and *P. Lips*. 84, corrected by U. Wilcken, *Archiv* 4 (1908), 481–82 (Hermopolite nome). For continuity in head taxes, see L. Neesen, *Untersuchungen zu den direkten Staatsgaben der römischen Kaiserzeit* (Bonn, 1980), pp. 125–34, and A. Déléage, *La capitation de Bas-Empire* (Nancy, 1945), pp. 146–47. For continuity in landholding patterns, see R. S. Bagnall, *Egypt in Late Antiquity* (Princeton, 1993), pp. 68–78 and 110–21.
84. Kase, *P. Princ.* 1 = *SB* 7621, reedited by Bagnall and Worp, *Archiv* 30 (1984), 33–82. The few collections in nummi in 316–17 might reflect inflation resulting from Licinius's halving of the nummus to 12.5 d.c. (although many payments in coin are more likely missing for these years).
85. *AE* (1978), 109 (215/6), and see Corbier, *Dévaluations* (1978), I, pp. 292–93.
86. See R. MacMullen, "Some Egyptian Tax Statistics," *Aegyptus* (1964), 98–102.
87. *P. Cairo Isid.* 17; the twenty-four legible payments total 1,125 nummi (weighing 11.7 pounds), the commutation of over 35 *sargane* of chaff (150 Roman pounds).

*Chapter 10: Coins in Cities and Markets of the Roman World*

1. John Chrys., *In Princep. Actorum* 4. 3. = Migne, *PG* 51. 99, translation from S. J. B. Barnish, "The Wealth of Julius Argentarius: Late Antique Banking and the Mediterranean Economy," *Byzantion* 55 (1985), 37.
2. See Max Weber, *The Agrarian Sociology of Ancient Civilizations* (London, 1976), and M. I. Finley, *The Ancient Economy* (London, 1973). See also

C. R. Whittaker, "Trade and the Aristocracy in the Roman Empire," *Opus* 4 (1985), 49–75, and collected articles of A. H. M. Jones, *The Roman Economy,* ed. P. A. Brunt (Oxford, 1974).

3. See Finley, *Ancient Economy,* pp. 165–66, and cf. Crawford, *JRS* 60 (1970), 40–43, citing as evidence stock complaints or incidents when aristocrats ran short of hard cash in buying up a glut of confiscated property from 62 B.C. to A.D. 33. See critique by Mrozek, *Historia* 25 (1976), 122–23, and discussion of financial crises by Frederiksen, *JRS* 56 (1966), 128–61, and Rodewald, *Money in the Age of Tiberius,* pp. 1–17 and 138–39.
4. See Millar, *JRS* 71 (1981), 72–73, and see prices complied from literature, papyri, and inscriptions in Johnson, *ESAR* II, pp. 302–21 (Egypt), and Heichelheim, *ESAR* IV, pp. 182–88 (Levant).
5. See E. Patlagean, *Pauvreté économique et pauvreté sociale à Byzance, 4e à 7e siècles* (Paris, 1977), pp. 353–543, and cf. Hendy, *SBME*, pp. 640–69. See S. J. B. Barnish, "Pigs, Plebeians and *Potentes*: Rome's Economic Hinterland, c. 350–600 A.D.," *PBSR* 55 (1987), 179–85, for use of coins in rural Italy in same period. See Y. Hirschfeld, *The Judaean Desert Monasteries in the Byzantine Period* (New Haven, 1992), pp. 102–11, for monetizing impact of monasteries.
6. See Schwartz, *Archives de Serapion,* pp. 77–79, nos. 49–51, and pp. 111–23. For prevalence of wages in coin during the third century, see D. Rathbone, *Economic Rationalism and Rural Society in Third-Century* A.D. Egypt (Cambridge, 1991), pp. 148–74 and 265–330.
7. See P. Veyne, "Les cadeaux de colons à leur proprietère," *RA* (1981), 245–52, and J. Drinkwater, "Money Rents and Food Renderers in Gallic Funerary Reliefs," in *The Roman West in the Third Century,* BAR Supp. Reports no. 109 (Oxford, 1981), pp. 223–31 and pl. 15. VIII–IX. Twelve out of fifteen reliefs depict tenants making courtesy gifts rather than paying rents in kind; see Whittaker, *Opus* 4 (1985), 74, n. 61, and cf. Mart. 8. 44. 4 and 10. 72. 1–2.
8. See M. Avi-Yonah, "The Economics of Byzantine Palestine," *IEJ* 8 (1958), 39–51, and D. Claude, *Die byzantinische Stadt im sechtsen Jahrhundert* (Munich, 1969), pp. 15–106.
9. R. MacMullen, "Market Days in the Roman Empire," *Phoenix* 24 (1970), 333–41, and L. de Ligt and P. W. de Neeve, "Ancient Periodic Markets: Festivals and Fairs," *Athenaeum* 66 (1988), 391–416. See Braudel, *Wheels of Commerce,* pp. 42–43, for weekly town markets engaging 6,000 to 7,000 people in the eighteenth century.
10. See Artemidorus, *Oneirokrition* 2. 69 (dreams of divine favor promising coin hoards), and Phil., *VA* 6. 39 (sage aids suppliant with hoard of coins). For soldiers searching out caches of coins, see Plut., *Pomp.* 11. 3–4, and App., *BC* 4. 73, 81–82.

11. See Samuel, *BASP* 21 (1984), 187–206.
12. See Bagnall and Frier, *Demography of Roman Egypt*, pp. 53–57 and 171–78.
13. See *P. Mich.* 123. Loans include *daneion, paratheke, paramone;* see A. E. R. Boak, *Papyri from Tebtunis* 1, *Michigan Papyri*, vol. II (Ann Arbor, Mich., 1933), pp. 88–89, and R. Taubenschlag, *The Law of Greco-Roman Egypt* (Warsaw, 1955), pp. 113–18, 285–93, 349–52, and 499–501.
14. See Boak, *Papyri from Tebtunis*, II. 1, pp. 92–103, but Boak's sums must be recalculated at 6 obols to the drachmae (rather than 7 obols); see Youtie, *ZPE* 15 (1974), 117–41.
15. L. Mildenberg, *Coinage of Bar Kokhba War* (Frankfurt/Main, 1984), pp. 22–29, and "A Bar Kokhba Didrachma," *INJ* 8 (1984–85), 33–36, pl. 24. 4–5.
16. Calculations based on dies reported in Mildenberg, *Bar Kokhba War,* pp. 57–60. If the Zealots controlled 750,000 inhabitants, adult male taxpayers totaled 150,000; see Dio 69. 13. 3, SHA, *Vita Had.* 14, and Euseb., *HE* 4. 6. 1–2, and discussion by S. Applebaum, *Prologemena to the Study of the Second Jewish War (A.D. 132–135)*, BAR Suppl. Series 7 (Oxford, 1976). For population and revenues under Herod, see Jos., *Ant.* 17. 11. 4–5, 318–19; 18. 1. 1–2; 19. 8. 2. 352; and *BJ* 1. 18. 5, and 2. 6. 3 and 95–96.
17. See Sutherland, *Cistophori of Augustus*, pp. 105–9, but his estimates of 500 obverse and 2,000 reverse dies are too low, because many new dies have since been noted.
18. See Phil., *VS* 2. 1, and cf. Cic., *De Imp. Pomp.* 14; see discussion by Hopkins, *JRS* 70 (1980), 116. For population figures, see Broughton, *ESAR* IV, p. 815.
19. See Reece, *Oxford Journal of Archaeology* 3 (1984), 197–210.
20. See Hahn, in *SEBGC*, pp. 67–69, for circulation of solidi. *CTh* 9. 22 (343) and Justinian, *Edictum* 11 (559), outlawed the 12.5 percent premium on solidi, but reckoning solidi by carats arose because of the weight loss suffered from wear; see Johnson and West, *Byzantine Egypt*, pp. 140–56, and Hendy, *SBME*, pp. 356–60.
21. Bolin, *State and Currency*, pp. 336–39, and N. A. Mouchmov, *Le trésor numismatique de Réka-Devina* (Sofia, 1934), pp. 5–6.
22. See Christiansen, *CH* 7 (1985), 80–82, and cf. Lendon, *Klio* 72 (1990), 118–19.
23. Macrobius, *Saturnalia* 1. 7. 22; *Origo gentis Romanae* 3.5 refers to heads and tails of Republican asses as *capita aut navia,* "heads and ships." See Callu, *Dévaluations* (1980), II, 199–206, for obol to denote civic two-assaria pieces of the Principate and Byzantine folles.
24. See Étienne and Rachet, *Trésor de Garonne*, pp. 421–26.

25. See Bellinger, *Dura*, pp. 199–203.
26. See ibid., pp. 186–87, and Howgego, *GIC*, pp. 27–28. See J. Simon, "Dura-Europos and the Chronology of Syria in the 250s A.D.," *Chiron* 15 (1985), 111–24, for concealment of hoards in 254–56.
27. See W. Woodward, "A Hoard of Imperial Coins from Tarsus," *NC* 5, 5 (1925), 301–35.
28. P. Grierson, "Review of S. Bolin, *State and Currency in the Roman Empire*," 50 (1960), 267–68.
29. *OGIS* 484. 8–12 authorizes a 5.5 percent charge (*aspouratia*) at exchange of 17 assaria to the denarius; Valentinian III, *Novel.* 14 (445), a 2 percent charge in exchanging 7,200 nummi to the solidus. For moneychangers in Talmudic sources, see M. Goodman, *State and Society in Roman Galilee, A.D. 132–212* (Totowa, N.J., 1983), pp. 56–57. "Fresh" coins (*asper*) could be demanded in taxes, see Suet., *Nero* 44, and cf. usage by Mart., *Epigr.* 4. 28. 5; Persius, *Sat.* 3. 69–70; *IGRR* IV. 494 (Pergamum); and *REG* 6 (1893), 187 (Iasus). Egyptian tax officials distinguished "clean" (*katharai*) from "dirty" (*rhyparai*), i.e., worn, tetradrachmae; see Johnson and West, *Currency*, pp. 30–42. In sixth century, *obryza* designated the discount charged on worn solidi; see Hendy, *SBME*, pp. 356–60, and Johnson and West, *Byzantine Egypt*, pp. 140–45.
30. Plato, *Phaedr.* 109B.
31. Cic., *Pro Flacco* 91; the sum suggests light taxation as argued by Hopkins, *JRS* 70 (1980), 116–20.
32. See Finley, *Ancient Economy*, pp. 150–51.
33. See B. Laum, *Stiftungen in der griechischen und römischen Antike*, 2 vols. (Leipzig, 1914), and Broughton, *ESAR* IV, pp. 797–98. S. Mitchell, "Festivals, Games and Civic Life in Roman Asia Minor," *JRS* 80 (1990), 183–93, and G. M. Rogers, *The Sacred Identity of Ephesos* (London, 1991), pp. 39–79, offer model discussions on civic endowments that yielded annual returns of 6 to 12 percent on investments in land.
34. Tac., *Ann.* 2. 47; Vell. Pat. 2. 126; and Dio 58. 17; cf. *ILS* 156; *Sardes* VII. 1, no. 9; and *IGRR* IV. 1351. For relief to Antioch, see Hendy, *SBME*, p. 201.
35. See Duncan-Jones, *Economy*, p. 91, nos. 27–31 (Africa), and p. 157, nos. 439, 442, 443, 445a, 449 (Italy). For building costs in Asia Minor, see Plin., *Epist.* 10. 33–34 and 37 (Bithynia); *IGRR* III. 804 (Aspendus); Phil., *VS* 2. 1 (Alexandria Troas); A. Balland, *Fouilles de Xanthos* VII (Paris, 1961), no. 67; and *IGRR* III. 739 (Tlos).
36. See *TAM* II. 2. 905 = *IGRR* III. 739, cc. 53, 59, and 63; chronology is based on E. Ritterling, "Zur Zeitsbestimmung einiger Urkunden vom Opramoas Denkmal," *RhM* 73 (1920–24), 35–45. For Opramoas's endowment of Tlos, see *TAM* II. 2. 578–579 = *IGRR* III. 679, and

Balland, *Xanthos* VII, pp. 173–85, no. 66. For gifts over 1,138,000 denarii by an unknown donor to Xanthus, Tlos, Patara, and Myra, see ibid., pp. 185–224, no. 67, and J. J. Coulton, "Opramoas and the Anonymous Benefactor," *JHS* 107 (1987), 171–78. See *IGRR* III. 704–5, for comparable gifts by Jason of Cyaenae to sixteen eastern Lycian cities.

37. See Dio Chrys., *Or.* 46. 3, and *Or.* 45. 5–6.
38. Dio 52. 30.
39. Dio Chrys., *Or.* 40; cf. 45. 8–10 and 47. 19. See also Ael. Arist., *Or.* 23. 24, and Phil., *VA* 8. 7–8. See Mitchell, *JRS* 70 (1990), 183; a Hadrianic endowment of 15,000 denarii for a market at Oenoanda included the costs of buying up and removing old buildings from the site.
40. See Plin., *Epist.* 10. 39, and cf. 33 and 37 (Nicomedia) and 39. 5 (Claudiopolis), and cf. Dio Chrys., *Or.* 40. 14, for Prusa raising funds by selling seats on the council.
41. Suet., *Vesp.* 18, and see P. A. Brunt, "Free Labour and Public Works at Rome," *JRS* 70 (1980), 81–100.
42. Suet., *Claud.* 20; cf. Plin., *NH* 36. 122–24, Dio 60. 11. 5 and 33. 3–5, and *ILS* 218;. See M. K. and R. L. Thorton, *Julio-Claudian Building Programs: A Quantitative Study in Political Management* (Chicago, 1989), pp. 66–73, estimating 3,000 men engaged in the construction. The minimum wage is calculated at 225 denarii per year or 10 asses per diem; subsistence is reckoned at between 2 and 2.5 asses per day (or an annual cost of 45.5 to 57 denarii per man) for an annual total of 1,365,000 to 1,710,000 denarii. See B. Levick, *Government in the Roman Empire* (London, 1985), p. xvii, for a higher estimate of 1,725,000 to 2,075,000 denarii.
43. See *IBM* 491 = *SIB*[3] 850, and cf. Plin., *Ep.* 10. 75, and Mitchell, *JRS* 70 (1990), 190.
44. See Duncan-Jones, *Economy,* pp. 245–46, and cf. nos. 281–89 and 1074a-49, for cost of gladiatorial games. For the cost of gymnasiarchy, see L. Robert, *Études anatoliennes: Recherches sur les inscriptions grecques de l'Asie mineure* (Paris, 1937), pp. 344–45, and A. H. M. Jones, *The Greek City from Alexander to Justinian* (Oxford, 1966), pp. 221–26.
45. See *CIG* 2758, and Broughton, *ESAR* IV, pp. 856–57; sums are expressed in denarii and all but two are readily convertible into whole numbers of aurei.
46. Duncan-Jones, *Economy,* pp. 139–41 and 105–6, nos. 290–320 (Africa), and pp. 188–99, nos. 818–1050 (Italy).
47. See Robert, *Études anatoliennes,* pp. 343–45, no. 41, for 1 denarius per citizen and 3 denarii per councilor. Distributions at Stratonicea distinguished classes; see C. M. Sahin, *Die Inschriften von Stratonikeia* (Bonn, 1981–82), nos. 662 (10 denarii), 192, 309, 311, and 313 (5 denarii),

no. 527 (3 denarii), and 701 (2 denarii). The sum 1 drachma per man (rather than unprecedented 1,000 drachmae) should be restored for Balland, *Xanthos,* VII, no. 67. 22–24.

48. *IGRR* III. 800–801; and cf. 802.
49. *CIL* IX. 1149 (Veleia, Italy), and see Duncan-Jones, *Economy,* pp. 207–9, 300–30, and 333–42, and nos. 1165, 1167, and 1168. For alimenta in the East, see *IGRR* III. 801–2 (Sillyum), LBW 1228 (Balbura), *IGRR* III. 676 (Tlos), and Balland, *Xanthos* VII, no. 67. 23, and pp. 212–14 (with 1,000 *andres sitometroumenoi* as beneficiaries), and Mitchell, *JRS* 70 (1990), 184 (Oenoanda, with *boule* and *sitometroumenoi* as beneficiaries). See *P. Oxy.* 2941–42, and N. Lewis, "The Recipients of the Oxyrhynchus Siteresion," *Chronique d'Égype* 49 (1974), 158–62, for distributions in Egyptian towns.
50. See Sahin, *Stratonikeia,* no. 701.
51. See Harl, *Civic Coins,* pp. 29 and 36; denominations based on comparison to Klose, *Smyrna,* pp. 103–12. The average weight is 22 g, but many specimens were damaged by *damnatio memoriae* so that their diameter has been widened.
52. Dio Chrys., *Or.* 7. 49, LCL translation; see also *IGRR* 69 (Prusa), and 800–801 (Sillyum), for grants to *paroikoi.*
53. See Mitchell, *JRS* 70 (1990), 184–85 and esp. doc. III. 80ff., and V. 100f. See *IGRR* IV (Cyzicus), for exemption from market dues at the panegyris, except for itinerant merchants.
54. Plin., *Epist.* 9. 39.
55. See Spufford, *Money,* pp. 382–85, and Braudel, *Wheels of Commerce,* pp. 57–63.
56. P. R. L. Brown, *The Making of Late Antiquity* (Cambridge, Mass., 1978), p. 51, and see Sahin, *Stratonikeia,* no. 310. For record of gift-giving, see A. Laumonier, *Les cultes indigènes en Carie* (Paris, 1958), pp. 292–323 (Panamara) and 342–406 (Lagina).

*Chapter 11: Coins, Prices, and Wages*

1. Plin., *NH* 18. 89–90; finest meal of winter wheat yielded 16 pounds of bread. Daily consumption was between 2.5 to 3 pounds. See *SB* 4640–49, for 1 pound of bread as daily allotment of laborers in Upper Egypt. Bread rations of 2 to 4 pounds of bread issued either daily to a cavalryman and his groom or issued every second day in the sixth century; see *P. Oxy.* 2046 and 1920, and Jones, *LRE,* pp. 629 and 1261, n. 44. Soldiers in the Spanish army of the sixteenth century were issued two loaves of bread each weighing 1.5 pounds every two days; see Parker, *Army of Flanders,* pp. 162–64.
2. Polyb. 6. 39. 13–15. See L. Foxhall and H. A. Forbes, "Sitometria: The Role of Grain as a Staple Food in Classical Antiquity," *Chiron* 12 (1982),

41–89. Roman soldiers received monthly two-thirds medimnos of wheat (= 4 modii) or 2 sextarii (850 g) of wheat per day. Soldiers in Egypt received 1 artaba (= 4.5 modii) per month. The ration of 4 modii per month is comparable to the recommended rate of 7.5 medimnoi per year or 1 choenix per day in Greek and Macedonian armies; see Hdt. 7. 187. 2, and Xen., Anab. 7. 3, but P. Garnsey, *Famine and Food Supply in the Graeco-Roman World: Responses to Risk and Crisis* (Cambridge, 1988), pp. 91–92, suggests a low annual minimum of 6 medimnoi of wheat (= 36 modii) per Athenian adult of the thetic class. Cato the Elder (*De Agr.* 56–58) recommended monthly rations of 3 modii of wheat for slaves with light duties, 4 to 4.5 modii for unchained slaves, and 4.8 to 6 modii for those in chain gangs.

3. See Duncan-Jones, *Economy,* pp. 50–51.
4. See Liv. 30. 26. 5–6 (203 B.C.) for price of 4 asses per modius. See Plaut., *Most.* 357, and Plut., *TG* 13, for 3 asses per diem as subsistence wage; see Crawford, *CMRR*, p. 14. The cost of subsistence was deducted from army pay; J. Roth, "Logistics of the Roman Army in the Jewish War," Ph.D. Dissertation, Columbia University, 1991, pp. 203–4.
5. Cic., *Pro Sestio* 55, Liv, *Epit.* 68, and Ascon., *Ad Pison.* 4; see P. Garnsey and D. Rathbone, "The Background to the Grain Law of Gaius Gracchus," *JRS* 75 (1985), 21.
6. Liv. 30. 38. 5 and 33. 42. Imported Sicilian wheat in 211–10 B.C. cost 12 drachmae per medimnos (Polyb. 9. 44) or the equivalent of 22.5 asses per modius with the denarius at 1/84 to the Roman pound or 26 asses with the denarius at 1/72 to the pound.
7. Polyb. 2. 15, pricing 1 medimnos (= 6 modii) of wheat at 4 obols (or 6 asses) and of barley at 2 obols (or 3 asses); price of daily keep at inn for one-half as (= one-quarter obol).
8. Polyb. 34. 8. 7–10, pricing 1 medimnos of barley at 1 Attic drachma or 9 asses and 1 medimnos of wheat at 9 Alexandrine obols or 11.5 asses. Imported wine, sold at 1 *metretes* per 1 drachma or 9 asses, suggests a price of 6 asses per Roman amphora. See O. Mørkholm, *Early Hellenistic Coinage from the Accession of Alexander the Great to the Treaty of Apamea (336–186 B.C.)* (Cambridge, 1991), p. 10, for the Alexandrine drachma (3.6 g) as 15 percent lighter than the Attic drachma (4.25 g) so that 9 Alexandrine obols = 7.65 Attic obols or just under 11.5 asses.
9. J. A. O. Larsen, "Roman Greece," *ESAR* IV (1938), pp. 384–86, with reservations by M. Rostovtzeff, *The Social and Economic History of the Hellenistic World,* 2nd ed. (Oxford, 1953), pp. 1488–89, nn. 110–11. In 190–169 B.C., 1 medimnos of wheat sold at 10 to 11 drachmae or 90 to 99 asses (9–10 denarii); 1 medimnos of barley sold at 3 drachmae, 4.5 obols and 4 drachmae or 33.75 to 36 asses (an average of 3.5 denarii).

10. See Larsen, *ESAR* IV, p. 384, and P. Garnsey, T. Gallant, and D. Rathbone, "Thessaly and the Grain Supply of Rome during the Second Century B.C.," *JRS* 74 (1984), 43–44. Wheat donated to Delos by Massinissa in 179 B.C. sold at 3 drachmae to 4 drachmae, 1 obol per medimnos or 4.5 to 6.25 asses per modius. Soon after 188 B.C. Samos purchased wheat at 5 drachmae, 2 obols per medimnos or 8 asses per modius; see *SIG*³ 976 = M. M. Austin, *The Hellenistic World from Alexander to the Roman Conquest* (Cambridge, 1981), pp. 198–201, no. 116. In the late second century B.C., at Priene the price was 4 Attic drachmae per medimnos or 10.67 asses per modius; at Megalopolis 5.5 Corinthian drachmae per medimnos or 7.33 asses per modius.

    During a shortage at Olbia in 225–175 B.C. wheat prices rose to 5 medimnoi per gold stater or 7.2 asses per modius; see *SIG*³ 495 = Austin, *Hellenistic World,* pp. 170–74, no. 97. A benefactor sold 10,000 medimnoi at half this price or 3.6 asses per modius. During a later shortage, the price rose to 1.33 medimnoi per gold stater or 21.6 asses per modius, and a benefactor sold 500 medimnoi at 4.16 medimnoi per stater or 8.64 asses per modius and 2,000 medimnoi at 2.583 medimnoi per stater or nearly 14 asses per modius. See Mørkholm, *Early Hellenistic Coinage,* pp. 66–67, for 24 Attic drachmae per gold stater.

11. See F. M. Heichelheim, *Wirtschaftliche Schwankungen der Zeit von Alexander bis Augustus* (Jena, 1930), pp. 51–52, 67–77, and 118–22, Table VIII, but note revisions and discussion in T. Reekmans, "The Ptolemaic Copper Inflation," *Ptolemaica (Studia Hellenistica)* 7 (1951), 61–119, and "Economic and Social Repercussions of the Ptolemaic Copper Inflation," *Chronique d'Égypte* 48 (1949), 324–42. In markets of 210–160 B.C. 1 artaba of wheat sold at the equivalent of 2 to 3 silver Alexandrine drachmae or 4.25 to 6.33 asses per modius of wheat. In 130–90 B.C. wheat prices are cited as the equivalent of 3 to 4 silver drachmae or 9.75 to 13 asses per modius. The exchange rate is reckoned at 1 Alexandrine tetradrachma (14 g, 98 percent fine) equaling 3.67 denarii (1/84 pound); see R. A. Hazzard and I. D. Brown, "The Silver Standard of the Ptolemaic Coinage," *RN* 6, 26 (1984), 238–39.

12. See Hopkins, *Conquerors,* p. 39, n. 52, and Roth, "Logistics," pp. 206–10. Needs of a family of four are reckoned on the assumption that the adult male consumed 40 percent of the total. Wine rations varied from one-half to 1 sextarius (or 1 to 2 Attic Kotylai) per day. For one-half sextarius, see *SB* 4640–49 (sixth century). For 1 sextarius, see Polyaenus, *Strat.* 8. 16. 2, and cf. *P. Oxy.* 2046 and 1920, for presumably double rations of 2 sextarii of wine per day. Cato the Elder (*De Agr.* 56–58) recommends annual rations of unchained slave and slave on chain gang at 7 and 10 amphorae, respectively, or 1 to 1.33 sextarii per diem.

For oil rations, see *P. Beat. Pan.* 2. 245–49, setting the monthly rate of 4 pounds (= 4 sextarii) of olive oil per soldier or 1 *acetabula* per day (one-eighth sextarii). See *P. Oxy.* 2046 and 1920, for rations of one-eighth or one-tenth sextarii; contrast R. P. Duncan-Jones, *Scale and Structure in the Roman Economy* (Cambridge, 1990), pp. 109–10, arguing for one-eleventh sextarius per diem.

For meat rations, see Roth, "Logistics," pp. 207–8, and Davies, *Service in the Roman Army* pp. 191–96, suggesting one-half pound of pork (or one-quarter pound of beef) issued daily or 80 percent of the meat *annona* granted to the urban plebeians by Aurelian; see *CTh* 14. 4. 10. 3.

13. The price of wine is based on Polyb. 2. 15, who reports that 1 metretes of wine in the Po Valley cost 2 obols (= 3 asses) or 2 asses per Roman amphora. At Rome, the price would have been at least four to five times higher or 8 to 10 asses per amphora so that the sextarius sold at one-sixth as. The price of oil is based on 16 drachmae (= 144 asses) per metretes at Delos or 96 asses per Roman amphora. If prices at Delos were three times those of Rome, the cost per amphora at Rome might have been at 32 asses or two-thirds asses per sextarius. The price of one-half sestertius (= 2.5 asses) per sextarius of oil in rural Italy 180 B.C. is inferred from Cato, *De Agr.* 22. 3, but see reservations in Crawford, *CMRR*, p. 346.
14. Cic., *Ver.* 2. 3. 179 and 188–89, and cf. Frank, *ESAR* I, pp. 402–3. Verres was ordered to buy Sicilian wheat at 12 asses, but he charged the state 14 asses, even though he purchased wheat at prices ranging from 8 to 12 asses. His excessive allowances to his staff of 16 asses per modius of wheat (and 8 asses per modius of barley) possibly reflect high market prices at Rome.

    Prices of oil and wine are difficult to estimate; see Frank, *ESAR* I, pp. 403–5. Choice wines are reported at 8.33 to 33.33 asses per sextarius. See Plin., *HN* 14. 56, for choice Falernian wine at 25 denarii per amphora in 121 B.C. See Diod. Sic. 37. 2 and Plin, *NH* 14. 95, for censors in 89 B.C. fixing a maximum price of 100 denarii per amphora.
15. Cic., *Pro Rosc. Comm.* 28, considered 12 asses per diem for a slave laborer (paid to the owner) a minimum.
16. Tac., *Ann.* 1. 17.
17. Seneca, *Epist.* 2. 18. 7, and Petron., *Satyr.* 16. 14. See S. Mrozek, "Zu den Preisen und Löhnen bei Lukian," *Eos* 59 (1978), 235, no. 15, for comparable price of 1 obol (2 assaria) in the East.
18. *CIL* IV. 4428, 5380, and 8566. See Breglia, *Pompeiana* (1950), 48–53, estimating an average daily wage of 8 asses and food costs of 24 to 28 asses; see Callu, *Dévaluations* (1980), II, p. 209, for slightly higher

daily wages based on *CIL* IV. 4000 and 6877.

19. See Callu, *Dévaluations* (1980), II, p. 209, and Mrozek, *ANRW* 2, 6 (1977), pp. 100–104, for Dacian mining contracts in A.D. 164–65. For subsistence deductions against legionary pay, see Fink, *Roman Military Records,* no. 68 (A.D. 88–90), and Cotton and Geiger, *Masada II,* pp. 46–47, no. 722 (A.D. 72). Twenty denarii (26.6 percent of the pay) or 2.5 asses per diem is deducted, reckoned at 1 as for bread and 1.5 asses for other food; see Roth, "Logistics," pp. 203–4.
20. See Heichelheim, *ESAR* IV, pp. 181–82 and 196–97, and Sperber, *Roman Palestine,* pp. 126–27 and 174–77.
21. Cic., *Ad Fam.* 12. 13. 4; the measure of modius rather than of medimnos is intended because 1 medimnos at 12 denarii produces a price of only 2 denarii per modius. Pompey's army in 67 B.C. paid a comparable price of 11 denarii per modius in Palestine; see Jos., *Ant.* 16. 2. 2., reporting 11 Tyrian drachmae per "measure" (*metron*), by which he intends a modius rather than cab. A price of 11 drachmae per cab gives an unprecedented price of 66 denarii per modius.
22. Jos., *BJ* 2. 21. 2.
23. See Duncan-Jones, *Economy,* pp. 145–57 and nos. 1161–83, for Italian and African prices. Pompeiian graffiti report prices of 12 asses to 1 denarius, 14 asses per modius; see E. Diehl, *Pompeianische Wandinschriften,* 2nd ed. (Berlin, 1930), nos. 391–92.

    For Anatolian prices, see *AE* (1925), no. 162b = *TAPA* 55 (1924), 5–20 = *JRS* 16 (1926), 116; the edict of the legate L. Antistius Rusticus fixes the price of wheat at 1 denarius per modius during a shortage when the usual market price was 8 to 9 asses in 92/3. A price of 8 asses per modius is cited as just in a Severan novel set in Tarsus; see *Historia Apol. Tyr.* cc. 9–10. See *IGRR* IV. 492 (Oenoanda, Lycia), for endowment providing each councilor monthly 4 modii of wheat and 2 denarii, perhaps equivalents that suggest an average price of 8 asses.

    For Palestinian prices, see Sperber, *Roman Palestine,* pp. 102–3, and Heichelheim, *ESAR* IV, p. 187; Talmudic sources considered 1 *sea* of wheat per denarius as a fair price, but 2–4 denarii as high. See Lendon, *Klio* 72 (1990), 131–34, for Egyptian market prices (as opposed to state prices of 8 drachmae per artaba) reported in *P. Mich.* II. 123 and 127; *P. Lond.* 131; *P. Amh.* 133 = *P. Sarap.* 92; *P. Oxy.* 2351; and *P. Bad.* IV. 79.
24. See Tac., *Ann.* 2. 89 and 15. 39, for imperial ceiling of 8 and 14 asses per modius, and cf. Mart. 12. 76, noting that it was unprofitable to sell wheat below 1 denarius per modius. See Plin., *NH* 18. 90, for the flour of 1 modius of the finest wheat priced at 40 asses or 2.5 denarii, but this includes milling and grinding charges.

25. Tac., *Ann.* 1. 17, and cf. Dio 76. 1. 1.
26. Cic., *Ver.* 2. 3. 214, for a rise from 8–12 asses to 5 denarii in Sicilian towns. See Sperber, *Roman Palestine,* pp. 102–3, and Heichelheim, *ESAR* IV, p. 187, for seasonal fluctuations from 1 to 4 denarius per *sea* of wheat, the equivalent of 11 to 43 asses per modius.
27. *P. Mich.* II. 127; see R. Duncan-Jones, "The Price of Wheat in Roman Egypt under the Principate," *Chiron* 6 (1976), 253–54. Prices are 4.4, 5.7, 7.3, and 8 drachmae per artaba from Thoth (September) 7 to after Phaophi (October) 1; they are equivalent to 4, 5, 6.5, and 7 asses per modius.
28. *IGRR* IV. 146 = *SIG*[3] 799 (A.D. 38), translation from N. Lewis, *Roman Principate* (Toronto, 1974), p. 49, no. 18.
29. For Tenos, Cyclades, see *IG* XIII. 5. 947. 79. Barley was bought at 5 denarii per medimnos and sold at 5 assaria (= 3.75 Roman asses) per medimnos. The purchase price was 13.33 asses per modius; the sale price five-eighths of the Roman as per modius. If the price of barley was double that of wheat, the purchase price of wheat would have been 26.67 asses per modius and the sale price 1.67 to 1.25 asses. For Antioch, Pisidia, see *AE* (1925), no. 162b = *TAPA* 55 (1924), 5–20 = *JHS* 16 (1926), 116. For Sebastopolis, Caria, see Robert, *Études anatoliennes,* pp. 342–45, no. 4; wheat was purchased at 4 denarii per *kyprios* or 2 denarii per modius. For Sparta, see *IG* V. 1. 44 = *SEG* XI. 486 = A. W. Woodward, "Excavations at Sparta, 1926," *ABSA* 28 (1925–26), 228. C. Julius Theophrastus during a scarcity in 124/5 or 127/8 imported wheat at 40 denarii per medimnos (or 6.67 denarii per modius) and sold it at 1 denarius per *hemihectus* (or 2 denarii per modius). See P. Cartledge and A. Spawforth, *Hellenistic and Roman Sparta* (London, 1989), pp. 258–59, n. 13.
30. *CIL* VIII. 25,703–4 (Thuburnica, Africa), for 10 denarii per modius (ten to eighteen times the average price). See *Apocalypse* 6, for 8 denarii per modius in Asia (eight to fourteen times the average price), or 1 aureus per modius at Tarsus in a Severan novel *Historia Apol. Tyr.* cc. 9–10 (fifty times the average price).
31. Petron., *Satyr.* 16. 44, for nostalgic price of two loaves of bread (presumably each of 2 pounds) at 1 as; cf. Plin., *NH* 18. 90, for 1.5 to 2 asses per loaf. See *CIL* IV. 5380 (Pompeii), and Duncan-Jones, *Economy*, p. 244, n. 4, for a loaf at 2 asses per day to feed a slave; and cf. *ILS* 7212 (A.D. 117–38), for 2 asses per loaf at Lanuvium.
32. See *Die Inschriften von Ephesos* III, nos. 910, 923–24, 929, 934, and 938, and VII. 1, no. 3010, for official prices of 2 or 4 obols (= 4 or 8 assaria) per loaf (weighing from 0.75 to 1.25 pounds depending on quality).
33. See Heichelheim, *ESAR* IV, p. 184, and Sperber, *Roman Palestine,* p. 103.

34. See *P. Mich.* 123 and 128 for 1 obol per loaf at Tebtynis in A.D. 45/6 and 46/7. The same price is cited in a Severan military requisition; see *SB* 7181 (Oxyrhynchus). For rise of prices in late second century, see Lendon, *Klio* 72 (1990), 107–9, and cf. *O. Brussels* 71 (undated), for a daily bread allowance of 2 obols for a builder. The price of one-half obol per loaf in *P. Oxy.* 736 (A.D. 1) was based on a tetradrachma tariffed at 1.5 denarii.
35. Matt. 20:2, and see Sperber, *Roman Palestine,* pp. 101–2.
36. See *P. Lond.* 131 (Hermopolis, A.D. 78–79); *P. Oxy* 871 (ca. A.D. 100); *P. Fay*. 102 (A.D. 105); *P. Lond.* 1177 (A.D. 113); *PSI* 688; and *Tait O. O.* 89. For wages in later second century, see Johnson, *ESAR* II, pp. 307–9.
37. See Duncan-Jones, *Economy,* pp. 46–47. Columella, *De Re Rust.* 3. 3, notes a break-even price of wine at Rome as 3 denarii per amphora or 5 asses per sextarius. An endowment in A.D. 153 provides wine priced at 61 and 88.5 sestertii (15 to 23 denarii) per amphora or 5 to 8 asses per sextarius; see *ILS* 7213, and Duncan-Jones, *Economy,* pp. 364–65. Customs dues on Spanish wine imply wholesale prices of 2 to 3 denarii per amphora (0.67 to 1 as per sextarius); see T. Frank, "On the Export Tax of Spanish Harbors," *AJP* 57 (1936), 87–90.
38. Prices of olive oil are inferred from five prices of oil issued or sold to citizens for use in the gymnasium. This oil (for cleansing and fuel) was cheaper than grades of olive oil for consumption. At Sebastopolis and Thyatira, where oil had to be imported, 1 denarius per kotyle or the equivalent of 2 denarii per sextarius was charged; see Robert, *Études anatoliennes,* pp. 343–45, no. 4. At Derriopus, olive oil was bought at a high market price of 12 asses per sextarius and sold at an official price of 7 asses per sextarius; see N. Vulić, *CRAI* (1939), 221 = "Bull. Épigr." (1939), no. 161bis. At Stratonicea where olive groves were plentiful, 9 asses per sextarius was common; see Sahin, *Stratonikea,* no. 678, and L. and J. Robert, *La Carie* II, pp. 320–23 (cited at wholesale prices 40 denarii per metretes or 26.67 denarii per amphora). The price of 2.75 denarii (= 44 asses) per sextarius was paid in a shortage at Sparta during Hadrian's visit; see *SEG* XI. 492 = Woodward, *ABSA* 27 (1925–26), 231–32. The price is cited as 30 denarii per *hydria,* equal to 105 denarii per amphora or, reckoning 3.5 hydria = 1 amphora, 35 asses per sextarius.
39. Subsistence for four is calculated by two methods. First, wheat is priced at 120 denarii for 120 modii; 720 sextarii of wine at 45 denarii (at 1 as per sextarius), and 120 sextarii of olive oil at 30 denarii (assuming olive oil at four times the cost of table wine). Total annual costs are 195 denarii. At a religious distribution in the first half of the second century, 1 *mine* of meat (= 15.2 Troy ounces or approximately

1 pound) was priced at 1.5 denarii; see Sahin, *Stratonikeia,* no. 281 = Robert, *Études anatoliennes,* p. 346, with Balland, *Xanthos* VII, p. 189, n. 110, for correction of price. Second, subsistence is reckoned from monthly alimentary rates of legitimate children at Trajanic Tarracina (*CIL* X. 6328 = *ILS* 6278) and Veleia (*CIL* XI. 1147); see Duncan-Jones, *Economy*, pp. 144–45 and 339–50. At Tarracina a boy received 2.5 asses per diem or 60 denarii per year; a girl received only 2 asses per diem or 48 denarii per year. At Veleia, a boy was paid 2 asses per diem or 48 denarii per year; a girl 1.5 asses per diem or 36 denarii per year. For a family of four a daily rate of 2 to 2.5 asses per person yields a total annual expenditure between of 182.5 to 228 denarii.

40. See *CIL* VIII. 1641 = Duncan-Jones, *Economy*, p. 102, no. 248 (Sicca, ca. 175–80), for monthly rates of 40 and 32 asses for boys and girls, respectively, or 1.25 and 1 asses daily.
41. *P. Mich* II. 123 and 127, and see Johnson, *ESAR* II, p. 314. The price on Thoth 4 records 18 obols per ceramion of new wine and 36 obols per ceramion of old wine. The *keramion monochoron* is estimated at 7 liters or approximately 3.5 ceramia = 1 Roman amphora; see Rathone, *Economic Rationalism,* pp. 469–71.
42. *P. Mich* II. 123 and 127, and see Johnson, *ESAR* II, pp. 316–18. Daily ration of beer is reported at 1 to 1.5 obols daily, common fish (braize, perch, thrissa, and clibanita) at 1 to 3 obols, fancy catch (thrissa, latis, and salachii) at 10 to 24 obols, eggs at five for 2 obols or thirty for 10 obols, cabbage and oil for dinner at 1 obol, beets and oil for dinner at 1 obol, cucumbers at 1.5 obol, onions at 1 obol, relishes for dinner at 2 obols, figs at 100 for 1.5 obols, and 3 measures of dates at 8 obols or 10 measures and 8 artabai at 7 tetradrachmae (112 obols).
43. The equivalent Egyptian annual subsistence was 10 artabai of wheat, 240 kotylai of oil, and 720 sextarii of wine. Based on prices in *P. Mich.* II 123 and 128, annual wheat cost 50 tetradrachmae (at 2 tetradrachmae per artaba) and wine 45 tetradrachmae (at 2 obols per sextarius), whereas the cost of daily beer was half that of wine (or 22.5 tetradrachmae per year). Oil is estimated at 60 tetradrachmae at a price of 6 obols per kotyle. Total annual cost is 165 tetradrachmae with wine or 132.5 with beer. The price of oil is based on *P. Oxy* 739, 819, and 1143 (A.D. 1), pricing oil at 2.33 to 4 obols per kotyle (but revaluation of tetradrachma by Claudius requires that prices be recalculated by 50 percent to 3.5 to 6 obols). See *P. Amh.* 126 (ca. A.D. 110–30) and *P. Grenf.* II. 51 and *P. Ross georg.* II. 51, for prices of 5.67, 7, and 8 obols per kotyle in the early second century.
44. Prices based on Lendon, *Klio* 72 (1990), 109–11, and Rathone, *Economic Rationalism,* pp. 464–66.

45. See Rathbone, *Economic Rationalism,* pp. 466–68, and cf. 278–305; domestic table wine is assumed at Tebtynis.
46. See ibid., pp. 156–58; reapers received 9, 12, or 16 drachmae per *aroura* harvested.
47. For prices at Dura-Europas, see *SEG* VII. 423 (boots), 417 and 419–20 (dalmatics). See *Edictum de Pretiis Maximis* 9. 1.1A (boots), and 19. 12–16, and cf. 22. 8 (dalmatics). Citations are taken from S. Lauffer, *Diokletians Preisedikt* (Berlin, 1971).
48. See R. Duncan-Jones, "The Size of the Modius Castrensis," *ZPE* 21 (1976), 53–62.
49. See Duncan-Jones, *Structure and Scale,* pp. 108–9; *annona* reckoned at 600 d.c. and the donatives at 2,500 d.c. each.
50. Lac., *De Mort. Pers.* 7. 6.
51. *Edictum de Pretiis Maximis* c. 1; 80 modii *castrensis* = 120 modii of wheat cost 640 nummi; 120 sextarii of lowest grade oil (at 12 d.c.) cost 115 nummi; 730 sextarii of wine (at 8 d.c.) cost 470 nummi. Pork sausage (at 16 d.c. per pound) cost 576 nummi for annual consumption of 450 pounds; beef sausage (at 10 d.c. per pound) cost 180 nummi for annual consumption of 225 pounds.
52. Prices are collected by Lendon, *Klio* 72 (1990), 133; prices reckoned at the rate of 25 d.c. to the nummus. The price of 100 nummi (2,500 d.c.) per modius (*metron*) of wheat during a famine in Palestine during 312–13 is twenty to twenty-five times greater than the average price in Egypt; see Euseb., *HE* 9. 8.
53. Prices are reckoned by the nummus of 12.5 d.c; if the tariffing of 25 d.c. applied, prices are halved. See *P. Rylands* IV. 630, col. ii, 36 and 50, and 631, col. ii, 112ff., for bread priced at 25 d.c. See ibid IV. 629, 24 and 630, col. 11, 91, and cf. IV. 637, 403, for meat prices at 50, 75, and 100 d.c. See ibid IV. 629, 91, 631, 101, and 636, 267, for wine at 100 and 175 d.c. A comparable price of 4 nummi per sextarius is reported in the Talmud; see Sperber, *Roman Palestine,* p. 104. In 311/2, an imperial gift of oil was priced at 400 nummi (10,000 d.c). per *stamnos* (amphora) or 8.33 nummi per sextarius; see Sahin, *Stratonikeia,* no. 310.
54. See Jones, *LRE*, pp. 623–26. See Amm. Marcel. 28. 1. 18 (372), for purchase of 30 modii per solidus and Valentinian III, *Novel.* 13. 4, for 40 modii per solidus. The official rate in Egypt in the sixth century was 1 solidus per 10 artabai (= 45 modii); see *P. Oxy* 1909 and 1920, and cf. *SEG* VIII. 335. *P. Cairo* 67,320 (A.D. 541) cites 40 modii per solidus and *P. Oxy* 1907 reports 9.5 artabai (= 42.75 modii) per solidus.
55. See Jones, *LRE*, pp. 445–46 and 1185–86, nn. 85–87.
56. Julian, *Misop.* 369A. Julian denotes the argenteus (2.25 g) by *argyrion*

and the unfamiliar Aramaic cab by *metron* so that his prices of 5, 10, and 15 *metra* per *argyrion* were equal to 1.25, 2.25, and 3.75 argentei per modius.

57. Valentinian III, *Novel*. 13. 4; see Justinian, *Edict*. 13. 18 (4 solidi), and *CJ* 1. 27.1. 22–38 (5 solidi).
58. See Johnson and West, *Byzantine Egypt*, pp. 177–78, and Jones, *LRE*, pp. 622–23. The rate of 10 artabai per solidus was used as an approximation; see *P. Oxy*. 1909 and 1920, and cf. *SEG* VIII. 355. The low official price of 8 artabai (= 36 modii) per solidus is excluded; see *P. Masp. Cario* 67,062.
59. See John Moschus, *Pratum Spirituale*, c. 85, col. 2941, and c. 11, col. 2976, for 5 folles as daily alms in Cilicia and Alexandria. See Marc. Diac., *Vita Porphy*. c. 94, set in Gaza in ca. 402, but written in the sixth century, for daily alms of 6 to 10 folles (called obols).
60. For daily subsistence at 1 follis, see F. Nau, "Histoire des solitaires égyptiens," *Revue de l'Orient chrétien* 5 (1900), 256, line 14, for stonecutter in Egypt in ca. 570. Egyptian ascetics in ca. 600 sustained themselves on 1 folles per day, a rate at least half of the current minimum; see Leont. Neapolit., *Vie de St. Jean l'Aumonier*, ed. H. Gelzer, p. 70. John Moschus, *Pratum Spirituale*, c. 42, col. 2896, reports an ascetic abbot surviving for days with daily bread bought at one-half follis (20 *lepta*). *Apophthegmata Patrum* = *PG* 65. 253C reports that the monk Lucius of Enaton, ca. 500–35, labored for 16 *noumia* per day, spending 14 *noumia* on food and giving 2 nummi in alms; see D. J. Chitty, *The Desert A City* (Crestwood, N.Y., 1966), pp. 73–74, and p. 80, n. 111. Such a low wage (paid in a duodecanummia and its third) stressed the ascetic's endurance. *Noumia* is unlikely to be a follis as argued by G. Ostrogorsky, "Löhne und Preise in Byzanz," *BZ* 32 (1932), 293–41. The rate is comparable to Saint Mark who begged 100 nummiae daily, kept 10 nummiae and donated the rest (set in Alexandria in the sixth century); see Nau, *Revue de l'Orient chrétien* 5 (1900), 60, line 15.
61. John Moschus, *Pratum Spirituale*, c. 134, col. 2997, for a monk hired at 5 folles daily for construction on a resevoir in the Sinai directed by Patriarch John II of Jerusalem (516–27), earning for purchase of a New Testament 3 solidi (630 folles) in 126 days; see Grierson, *PINC*, pp. 298–99, and Callu, *Dévaluations* (1960), II, pp. 210–12. Cf. Proc., *HA* 17. 5, and 25. 12, for 3 folles daily wage of prostitutes in Constantinople. See *P. Colt* 89 (ed. Kraemer), pp. 253–60, for a boy slave costing 6 solidi, a girl slave 3 solidi. Camels sold at 4 to 7 solidi; see Grierson, *PINC*, p. 299.
62. At Constantinople, one loaf of bread cost perhaps 1.5 to 4 folles in 545–75; see Patlagean, *Pauvreté*, pp. 185–86 and 405–6, based on

prices quoted by John of Ephesus, *HE* 3. 2. 41 and 3. 14. See *CTh* 14. 20. 1 (413), for fresh fish at 1 solidus for 10, 20, or 30 pounds (depending on quality); in 540 this would be 6 to 18 folles per pound. See Malalas, *Chron.*, p. 439, for a daily allowance of 15 folles for a reputable young woman at Antioch in ca. 540. See John Moschus, *Pratum Spirituale,* c. 187 (pp. 3057–61), for a Sassanid dirhem buying supper (bread, fish, and wine) for two adult males at Nisibis. The cost was 6–7 folles per man; the silver dirhem (4 g) is reckoned at 12 to 14 folles by the exchange rate of 539; see Grierson, *PINC,* pp. 298–99.

63. One artaba of wheat baked into 80 one-pound loaves of bread (*P. Oxy.* 1920) or the equivalent of 18 loaves per modius (Plin., *NH* 18. 89–90). Bread prices in Egypt can be inferred at the usual rates of 10, 12, 15 artabae per solidus. In 498, one loaf cost 17 to 24 nummiae; in 512, 8.5 to 12 nummiae; in 539, 7 to 11 nummiae; in 565, 9.5 to 14.5 nummiae; and in 578, 11.5 to 17 nummiae. Official prices of 30, 40, or 60 modii per solidi yield a price per loaf of 18.5 to 37 nummiae in 498, 9 to 19 nummiae in 512, 8 to 16 nummiae in 539, 10.5 to 21 nummiae in 565, and 13 to 27 nummiae in 578.

64. The annual cost of a family of four is reckoned at 1,025 folles: 120 modii of wheat at 360 folles, 120 sextarii of oil at 300 folles, and 720 sextarii of wine at 365 folles. At the rate of 180 folles to the solidus, 1 modius of wheat is estimated at 3 folles. Low-grade wine is estimated at one-half follis per sextarius; oil at 2.5 folles per sextarius.

    Prices of wine and oil are based on those in military accounts in ca. 550–65; see Carrié, *Dévaluations* (1980), II, pp. 255–63. One sextarius of oil is valued at 5 folles and 1 *angeia* of wine at 6.5 folles (or 1 sextartius of wine per follis); see *P. Masp. Cairo* 67,145, and L. Casson, "Wine Measures and Prices in Byzantine Egypt," *TAPA* 70 (1939), 5–6, for 1 *angeion* reckoned at 7 sextarii.

65. Zach. of Mytilene, *Chron.* 7. 6.

66. Pseudo-Joshua the Stylite, *Chron.* cc. 26, 39, 43, 45–46, and 87, translated by W. Wright, *The Chronicle of Joshua the Stylite* (Cambridge, 1882). See Garnsey, *Famine,* pp. 7–11, and cf. Cassid., *Var.* 10. 27 and 12. 27–28, for contemporary famine prices in Liguria. The price fluctuations were not seasonal as argued by Patlagean, *Pauvreté,* pp. 403–7. Other famine prices at Edessa (Ps.-Josh., *Chron.* cc. 39) such as 25 folles per pound of meat, 7.5 folles per fowl, and 1 follis per egg are four times higher than comparable prices at Aphrodito, Egypt, in ca. 550–75; see Johnson and West, *Byzantine Egypt,* pp. 176–78.

67. See *Apophthegmata Patrum* = *PG* 65. 369, for Nitrine monk Pambo toiling for 2 carats daily (perhaps 20 or 24 folles at 11 g each) in ca. 575–615. See *Vie de St. Jean l'Aumonier* (ed. H. Gelzer), p. 70, for John the Almoner giving daily alms at Alexandria to refugees of the Persian

War (ca. 610–12) of 1 *keration* per man and 2 *keratia* per women (including children), for perhaps 12 and 24 folles, respectively. The monk Vitalis in Alexandria, in ca. 600, earned 1 *keration* (= 12 folles) each day, but he lived on a low rate of 1 follis daily. The ascetic hero John the Almoner fed himself and two others on bread and vegetables bought for 5 folles (1.67 folles per man); see *Vie de St. Jean l'Aumonier* (ed. Festugiere), p. 502. See *Vie de St. Jean l'Aumonier* (ed. H. Gelzer), pp. 76.17–77.13 (composed ca. 650), for recommended daily alms of 10 folles as opposed to a miserly 5 folles.

*Chapter 12: Roman Coins beyond the Imperial Frontiers*

1. Translation adapted from Cosmas Ind., *Christian Topography,* II, c. 148, ed. E. O. Winstedt, p. 81 (translating *nomisma* as Latin solidus), and cf. Hendy, *SBME,* pp. 276–78.
2. See F. Braudel, *Civilization and Capitalism 15th–18th Century:* II, *The Wheels of Commerce,* trans. S. Reynolds (New York, 1979), pp. 138–44.
3. See Raschke, *ANRW* 2, 9, 2 (1978), 625–43.
4. Cantineau, *Inventaire* III, p. 35, no. 28 = *IGRR* III. 1050 = *CIS* II. 3. 1. 2948.
5. Plin., *NH* 5. 85.
6. See I. Glodariu, *Dacian Trade with the Hellenistic World and Rome,* BAR Supp. Ser. 8 (Oxford, 1976), pp. 48–52 and 70–73, analyzing 228 hoards and 210 stray finds. Comparable finds are unavailable for Moesia due to poor publication of hoards in Bulgaria; see Crawford, *JRS* 67 (1977), 117, n. 5.
7. Polyb. 4. 38. 4–5; see Rodewald, *Money in the Age of Tiberius,* pp. 40–41. Slaves were a primary export to Rome rather than the exclusive one as argued by Crawford, *JRS* 67 (1977), 117–24, and *CMRR,* pp. 231–40.
8. Dio 67. 7 and 68, and Dio Chrys. 12. 16–17. See L. Winkler, "Schatzfunde römerischer Silbermünzen in Dakien bis zum Beginn der Dakerkriege," *JNG* 17 (1967), 133–56, and Glodariu, *Dacian Trade,* pp. 50–55. Hoards deposited in the imperial age reflect insecurity rather than volume of trade. Winkler notes twenty-four hoards deposited in the reign of Augustus, three in the period A.D. 14–68, and thirteen in the period A.D. 69–105.
9. See Glodariu, *Dacian Trade,* pp. 35–37. For mix of coins, ingots, and jewelry in hoards, *IGCH* 586, 600, 625, 641, 648, 650, 674, and 685; Crawford, *RRCH,* no. 331 = *IGCH* 662; and Winkler, *JNG* 17 (1977), no. 36A. For Dacian mines, see Davies, *Roman Mines,* pp. 198–206, and Glodariu, *Dacian Trade,* pp. 57–58 and Maps 12–13. Classical sources fail to mention trade in metals, but it is presumed to have followed analogous medieval cases; see, for example, Spufford, *Money,*

pp. 252–55, for trade in precious metals between Venice and Egypt in 1324–1438.

10. See O. Iliescu, "Sur les monnaies d'or à la légende ΚΟΣΩΝ," *NAC* 19 (1990), 185–214, and M. Chitescu, *Numismatic Aspects of the History of the Dacian State: The Roman Republican Coinage in Dacia and Geto-Dacian Coins of Roman Type,* BAR Int. Ser. 112 (Oxford, 1981), pp. 46–61. For bronze coins, see Glodariu, *Dacian Trade,* pp. 26–37 and 88–90, but with reservations by Crawford, *JRS* 67 (1977), 116–20.
11. See Polyb. 34. 10. 10 = Str. 4. 6. 12, for Norican gold strikes. See Bannert and Piccottini, *Fundmünzen von Magdalensberg,* pp. 20–31, and Torbágyi, *Acta Archaeologica Scientarium Hungaricae* 36 (1988), 161–96.
12. See Bolin, *Fynden av romerska mynt,* for corpus of finds, and see discussion by O. Brogan, "Trade between the Roman Empire and the Free Germans," *JRS* 26 (1936), 204–5, and in Raschke, *ANRW* 2, 9, 2 (1978), 667–68.
13. *RGdA* 26. 4, and cf. Vell. 2. 106; Plin, *NH* 2. 167; and Str., 7. 2. 1.
14. See U. L. Hansen, *Römischer Import im Norden: Warenaustauch zwischen römischen Reich und dem freien Germanien während der Kaiserzeit unter besonderer Berücksichtigung Nordeuropas* (Copenhagen, 1987), pp. 125–51 and 219–32, and H. J. Eggers, *Der römische Import in freien Germanien* (Hamburg, 1951), pp. 43–51 and 64–69.
15. Tac., *Germ.* 41, and see J. Künow, *Negotiator et Vectura: Händler und Transport in freien Germanien* (Marburg, 1980), pp. 8–18.
16. Plin., *NH* 27. 43. For the treaty of 173, see Dio 71. 11. 15–16, 18–19; 72. 2 and 15; and L. F. Pitts, "Relations between Rome and the German 'Kings' on the Middle Danube in the First to Fourth Centuries A.D.," *JRS* 79 (1989), 51. For trading rights of Goths, see Them., *Or.* 10. 135C, and cf. E. A. Thompson, *Romans and Barbarians: The Decline of the Western Empire* (Madison, Wisc., 1982), pp. 3–22.
17. Tac., *Germ.* 42–43, and cf. Tac., *Ann.* 11. 16, and Dio 67. 5, for subsidies to the Cherusci. See C. D. Gordon, "Subsidies in Roman Imperial Defence," *Phoenix* 3 (1949), 60–69.
18. Tac., *Germ.* 5. 5; adapted from Modern Library translation. See also Dio 56. 18 and Vell. Pater. 2. 117–18.
19. See Greene, *Archaeology,* pp. 40–41. Denarii arrived as payments in commerce rather than for use as "gift exchange" as argued by Hedeager, *New Directions in Scandinavian Archaeology,* pp. 191–217. For analysis of hoards of denarii, see S. Nielsen, "Roman Denarii and Iron-Age Denmark," in *Coins and Archaeology,* ed. H. Clarke and E. Schia, BAR Int. Ser. 553 (Oxford, 1989), pp. 29–35, and L. Lind, *Roman Denarii found in Sweden,* 2 vols. (Berlin/Stockholm, 1979–81).
20. Wheeler, *Rome beyond the Imperial Frontiers,* pp. 54–60. For analysis of

Danish hoards, see A. Krommann, "Recent Roman Coin Finds from Denmark," in *Proceedings of the 10th International Congress of Numismatics, London, September 1986,* ed. I. Carradice (London, 1989), pp. 263–65 and 268. A comparable Frankish hoard is discussed by P. Bastien and C. Metzger, *Le trésor de Beaurains (dit d'Arras)* (Wetteren, 1977), pp. 206–7.

21. Tac., *Germ.* 5 and 46.
22. Tac., *Germ.* 5. 3–4. For imitative denarii, see Giard, *CBN* I, p. 228, nos. 1667–76, pl. LXII, and discussion by A. Kunisz, "Les imitations des deniers du 1er et du 2e siècle de notre ère hors des frontiers de l'Empire Romaine," in *Proceedings of the International Numismatic Symposium, Budapest,* ed. I. Gedai and K. Bíró-Sey (Budapest, 1980), pp. 24–29, and L. Lind, "Roman Denarii Found in Sweden," in *Studien zu Fundmünzen der Antike* I. *Ergebnisse des FMRD-Colloqiums vom 8–13 Februar 1976 in Franfurt am Main and Bad Homburg V.D.H.*, ed. M. R. Alföldi (Berlin, 1976), pp. 139–41. Sestertii in East Prussian graves arrived as "tag items" rather than a principal export; see Wheeler, *Roman beyond the Imperial Frontiers,* pp. 23–25. Antoniniani and *aes* arrived as plunder after 235; see M. Todd, *The Northern Barbarians, 100 B.C.–A.D. 300* (London, 1987), pp. 35–37 and 63–64, and Harl, *Civic Coins,* pp. 18–19 and 135, nn. 52–53.
23. Tac., *Ann.* 12. 29–30, cf. 2. 63; and Plin., *NH* 4. 80, and see Pitts, *JRS* 79 (1989), 48.
24. See G. Bichir, *The Archaeology of the Carpi* (Oxford, 1976), pp. 119–25, and Raschke, *ANRW* 2, 9, 2 (1978), pp. 626–27 and 737, nn. 373–74.
25. See G. F. Hill, "Ancient Coinage of Southern Arabia," *PBA* 7 (1915), 57–84, and C. Arnold-Biucchi, "Arabian Alexanders," in *Mnemata: Papers in Memory of Nancy M. Waggoner,* ed. W. E. Metcalf (New York, 1991), pp. 95–115.
26. See Ying-shih Yu, *Trade and Expansion in Han China* (Berkeley, 1967), pp. 159–60, and Raschke, *ANRW* 2, 9, 2 (1978), 642–44. For the Roman mission to China, see F. Hirth, *China and the Roman Orient* (Shanghai, 1885), pp. 40–43, translation from *Hou-han-shu,* c. 88. See also ibid. pp. 68–73, from *San-kuo-chih,* c. 30, a chronicle compiled before 429, reporting that Romans employed sea routes to avoid Parthia in 220–64.
27. Plin., *NH* 12. 42. 93 and 59. 129. See Sidebotham, *Roman Economic Policy,* pp. 33–36, noting that Pliny's prices of 1,000 to 1,500 denarii per pound of Arabian cinnamon are probably a copyist's error.
28. *Edictum de Pretiis Maximis,* 32. 34–86. Saffron was priced at 1,000 to 2,000 d.c. (80 to 160 nummi); aromatic oils at 100 to 600 d.c. (8 to 48 nummi), other spices ranged between 60 and 120 d.c. (between 4 and 20 nummi).

29. Plin., *NH* 12. 32. 63–65.
30. See *Edictum de Pretiis Maximis,* 23. 1–2 and 24. 1–1a; prices of silk quoted at 12,000 and 150,000 d.c., respectively. See SHA, *Vita Aurel.* 45. 4–5, for comparable price of one pound of gold for every pound of ceremonial silk garments; see Raschke, *ANRW* 2, 9, 2 (1978), 623–25. See Proc., *HA* 25. 16, for undyed raw silk initially at 8 solidi (one-ninth pound of gold), and then at 15 solidi; see R. Lopez, "The Silk Industry in the Byzantine Empire," *Speculum* 20 (1945), 12–13.
31. See *Edictum de Pretiis Maximis,* 34. 1–12 (dyed wool, from 300 to 50,000 d.c. per pound) and 35. 1–9 (raw wool, 25 to 200 d.c. per pound).
32. See N. A. Frolova, *The Coinage of the Kingdom of the Bosporus* A.D *69–238*, trans. H. B. Wells, BAR Int. Ser. 56 (Oxford, 1979), pp. 14–18, 69–73, and 85–92, and N. A. Frolova, *The Coinage of the Kingdom of the Bosporus* A.D. *242–341/342*, trans. H. B. Wells, BAR Int. Ser. 166 (Oxford, 1983), I, pp. 25–26.
33. *IGCH*, 1774, 1745 (= Crawford, *RRCH*, no. 246), and 1746 (= Crawford, *RRCH*, no. 455), and Crawford, *RRCH*, no. 532, with discussion by Rodewald, *Money in the Age of Tiberius*, pp. 46–47 and 115, nn. 359–360.
34. See E. R. Caley, *Chemical Composition of Parthian Coins* (New York, 1955), pp. 27–40, and Gordus, *Near Eastern Numismatics, Iconography, and History,* pp. 152–54, but improved analysis of coins that accounts for surface enrichment is required.
35. See Hill, *NC* 5, 11 (1931), 160–70, Bellinger, *Dura*, pp. 196–97, and Raschke, *ANRW* 2, 9, 2 (1978), p. 828, nn. 759–80. Tetradrachmae were long preferred in Mesopotamia; see O. Mørkholm, "The Parthian Coinage of Seleucia on the Tigris, ca. 90–55 B.C.," *NC* 7, 20 (1980), 33–47. In Iran, Seleucid, Greco-Bactrian, Parthian, and Characene tetradrachmae were hoarded together as late as 30 B.C.; see *IGCH* 1744, 1784, 1786, 1805–6, and 1814.
36. See D. W. MacDowall, "The Weight Standards of the Gold and Copper Coinages of the Kushana Dynasty from Kadphises to Vasudera," *Journal of the Numismatic Society of India* 22 (1960), 64–67. For Kushan mines, see W. W. Tarn, *The Greeks in Bactria and India,* 2nd ed. (Cambridge, 1951), pp. 103–12, and V. Thakur, "Source of Gold for Early Gold Coins of India," *JNSI* 39 (1977), 87–109. The Kushan era is reckoned to begin in ca. A.D. 78; see A. D. H. Bivar, "The History of Eastern Iran," *CHI* III. 1 (Cambridge, 1983), pp. 192–93 and 197–203. The late date of ca. 210–50 argued by R. Göbl, *System und Chronologie der Münzprägung Kusanreiches* (Vienna, 1984), pp. 57–85, is no longer tenable.

37. See E. V. Ziemal, "The Political History of Transoxiana," *CHI* III. 1, pp. 250–60.
38. P. J. Turner, *Roman Coins from India* (London, 1989), pp. 1–4.
39. See ibid., pp. 13–14, correcting finds reported by Rasckhe, *ANRW* 2, 9, 2 (1978), pp. 672 and 1033–34, nn. 1372–74. For Roman influence in style and iconography, see J. M. Rosenfield, *The Dynastic Arts of the Kushans* (Berkeley, 1967), pp. 1–26, and R. Dar, "The Question of Roman Influence on Gandhara Art: Numismatic Evidence," *RIN* 79 (1977), 61–89.
40. Paus. 3. 12. 4.
41. *Hou-han-shu*, c. 88, in Hirth, *China and Roman Empire*, pp. 40–43; see criticisms of translation by Raschke, *ANRW* 2, 9, 2 (1978), 852–53, nn. 849–50. See Yu, *Trade and Expansion*, pp. 113–17, for alternate route through Burma to cities on the Lower Ganges.
42. See Plin., *NH* 6. 26. 101 and 12. 41. 84, and cf. Dio Chrys. 79. 5–6; Tac., *Ann*. 3. 56; and Dio 57. 15. See critiques by Raschke, *ANRW* 2, 9, 2 (1978), 634–36, 725, n. 311, and 774, n. 552, and Sibebotham, *Roman Economic Policy*, pp. 36–47, and cf. p. 36, n. 73.
43. *Periplus* 57. 19. 2–7, and Str. 2. 98–99; see discussion by L. Casson, trans. and ed., *The Periplus Maris Erythraei* (Princeton, 1989), p. 224, and Tarn, *Greeks in Bactria and India*, pp. 366–70.
44. Plin., *NH* 12. 38–39. 78, and Str., 16. 4. 19. For Himyarite recoining of Augustan denarii, see J. H. Nordbø, "A Hoard of Silver Coins from Arabia Felix," *Meddelelser fra Norsk Numismatisk Forening* 1 (1985), 8–26, and Sibebotham, *Roman Economic Policy*, pp. 18–19.
45. See Turner, *Roman Coins in India*, pp. 1–6, 20–26, and 120–22.
46. *Periplus* 47–51. See Sidebotham, *Roman Economic Policy*, p. 31, and E. J. Rapson, *Catalogue of the Coins of the Andhra Dynasty, the Western Ksatrapas, the Traikutaka Dynasty and the "Bodhi" Dynasty* (London, 1908), pp. xcvii–clii.
47. *Periplus* 54, and cf. Plin., *NH* 6. 24. 85–86. See Sidebotham, *Roman Economic Policy*, pp. 31–33 and 114–15, and P. Thomas, "Roman Trade Centers on the Malabar Coast," *Journal of the Madras Geographical Association* 6 (1931), 230–40.
48. See Wheeler, *Roman beyond Imperial Frontiers*, pp. 142–45. See Sibebotham, *Roman Economic Policy*, pp. 114–15, and Millar, *Spice Trade*, p. 209, for Tamil sources.
49. See Turner, *Roman Coins in India*, pp. 26–34.
50. R. Göbl, *Sasanian Numismatics* (Braunschweig, 1971), pp. 25–33. For fineness, see Gordus, in *Near Eastern Numismatics*, pp. 155–61. Chronology of Sassanid kings follows that of R. N. Frye, "The Political History of Iran under the Sassanids," *CHI* III. 1, p. 178.
51. See Amm. Marcel. 24. 3. 1 and 26. 9. 4, and Zon. 2. 15. See R. Göbl,

*Dokumente zur Geschichte der iranischen Hunnen in Baktrien und Indien* (Wiesbaden, 1967), pp. 44–102 and 112–36, for countermarked Sassanid dirhems and imitative dirhems in Central Asia. For hoards, see Raschke, *ANRW* 2, 9, 2 (1978), pp. 731–32, nn. 344–45 and 349–50.

52. Proc., *Bell.* 7. 33. 5–6; LCL, vol. IV, p. 439.
53. See W. Hahn, "Die Münzprägung des axumitischen Reiches," *Litterae Numismaticae Vindoboneses* 2 (1983), 113–80. Axumite coins were minted from crudely refined gold obtained from the silent trade in East Africa; see Cosmas Ind., *Christian Topography* (McCrindle trans.) II. 139, pp. 52–53, and metrological analysis by S. C. Munroy-Hay, W. A. Oddy, and M. R. Cowell, "The Gold Coinage of Aksum: New Analyses and Their Significance for Chronology," in *Metallurgy in Numismatics,* ed. W. A. Oddy (London, 1988), II, pp. 5–10. For a large hoard of Axumite gold coins and solidi minted between the reigns of Constantine and Theodosius II, see S. C. Munro-Bay, "The al-Madhariba Hoard of Gold Aksumite and Late Roman Coins," *NC* 149 (1989), 83–100.
54. Cosmas Ind., *Christian Topography,* XI, pp. 323–24. See R. S. Lopez, "The Dollar of the Middle Ages," *Journal of Economic History* 11 (1951), 209–34, and cf. Braudel, *Wheels of Commerce,* pp. 209–34. Finds vitiate the case of uniform, effective enforcement of bans on export of specie as argued by Hendy, *SBME,* pp. 257–60.
55. See H. W. Codrington, *Ceylon Coins and Currency, Memoirs of the Colombo Museum,* ed. J. Person, series A, no. 3 (Colombo, 1924), pp. 31–53, and Sidebotham, *Roman Economic Policy,* pp. 34–35.
56. Proc., *Bell.* 8. 17. 2–7, and see Lopez, *Speculum* 20 (1945), 12–13.
57. Men. Prot., frag. 10 = Blockley, *Classicising Historians,* II, pp. 110–27 and 262–63, n. 117. See Raschke, *ANRW* 2, 9, 2 (1978), pp. 730–32, nn. 343–51, for solidi found in Tarim Basin.
58. Zos. 5. 41, and see Grierson, *TRHS* 5, 9 (1959), 131–37.
59. Priscus, frags. 2 and 9.3 = Blockley, *Classicising Historians,* II, pp. 224–27 and 236–41. See O. J. Maenchen-Helfen, *The World of the Huns* (Berkeley, 1973), pp. 108–19, and R. Croke, "Anatolius and Nomus: Envoys to Attila," *Byzantinoslavica* 42 (1981), 159–70.
60. Malchus, frag. 2 = Blockley, *Classicising Historians,* II, pp. 489–511. J. Iluk, "The Export of Gold from the Roman Empire to Barbarian Countries from the 4th to the 6th Century," *Münsterische Beiträge zur antiken Handelsgeschichte* 4, 1 (1985), 87–88, argues that payments were annual tribute in 454–73 (representing 5,700 pounds of gold or 410,400 solidi), but Priscus does not specify annual payments. For subsidies to Theodoric, see Jord., *Get.* 50. 264, and Proc., *Bell.* 7. 34.
61. See Men. Prot., frag. 22 = Blockley, *Classicising Historians,* II, pp. 196–97, for armistice costing 216,000 solidi in 577/8. See Paul the Deacon, *Hist. Longobardorum* 4. 32; Anonymous, *Continuatio Havniensis Pros-*

*peri* = *MGH AA* IX, p. 339, and Fredegar, *Chronicarum Libri IV* IV. 66 = *MGH SRMerov*. II, p. 155, for a peace of 606 at 12,000 solidi. See Anonymous, *Continuatio Havnensis Prosperi* = *MGH AA* IX, p. 339, and Fredegar, *Chronicarum Libri IV* IV. 66 = *MGH SRMerov*. II, p. 155, for peaces in 616/7 and 631/2, costing 36,000 solidi each.

62. See Iluk, *Münsterische Beiträge* 4, 1 (1985), 93, but his total of 6 million solidi (based on the erroneous premise of continuous annual payments) must be revised. In 565–73, Justin II suspended payments (Men. Prot., frag. 8 = Blockley, *Classicising Historians*, II, pp. 92–95) until he he was compelled to resume them in 574 at 80,000 solidi annually (Theoph., *Chron*., pp. 246–47, Bonn ed. Maurice Tiberius raised the subsidy to 100,000 solidi in ca. 582 (Theo. Simoc., *Hist*. 1. 3. 7–13 and 6. 4–6), but he ended payments in 591; see M. Whitby, *The Emperor Maurice and His Historian: Theophylact Simocatta on Persian and Balkan Warfare* (Oxford, 1988), pp. 87–89. Phocas renewed annual tribute at 100,000 solidi in 602–10 (Theoph., *Chron*. p. 291); Heraclius purchased annual peace in 619–21 at presumably 100,000 solidi (Theoph., *Chron*., p. 302) and in 622/3 at 200,000 solidi (Nicephorus the Patriarch, *Hist. Syn*. 17. 181–89). Reported subsidies to the Avars are thus recalculated at 800,000 solidi in 574–83, 700,000 solidi in 584–91, 800,000 solidi in 602–10, 300,000 solidi in 619–21, and 200,000 in 622/3, for a total of 2.8 million solidi.
63. See Fagerlie, *Late Roman and Byzantine Solidi*, pp. 6–7, and Smedley, *SEBGC*, pp. 111–30.
64. See *RGdS*, line 9. See J. Guey, "Autour des 'res gestae divi Saporis': Denier (d'or) et denier (de compte) ancien," *Syria* 39 (1961), 263–74, and T. Pekáry, "Autours des 'res gestae divi Saporis': Le 'tribut' au Perses et les finances de Philippe d'Arabe," *Syria* 39 (1961), 275–83.
65. See John Lyd., *De Mag*. 3. 53, and Zach. of Mytilene, *Chron*., 8. 5, for 500 pounds (36,000 solidi), and Michael Syr., *Chron*. IX. 16, for 550 pounds (39,600 solidi). Amida was redeemed at 1,000 pounds (72,000 solidi) and Edessa ransomed at 2,000 pounds (144,000 solidi) in 502/3; see Joshua the Stylite, *Chron*. c. 61. Subsidies were not owed the shah for his defense of the Caspian Gates under the treaties in 363 (Amm. Marcel. 25. 7. 9–14 and Zos. 3. 31) and 422 (Soc., *HE* 7. 20. 1–7); see R. C. Blockley, "Subsidies and Diplomacy: Rome and Persia in Late Antiquity," *Phoenix* 39 (1985), 69.
66. See Proc., *Bell*. 8. 17. 9–10, and see Blockley, *Phoenix* 39 (1985), 72, n. 3. Justinian paid 792,000 solidi for the Perpetual Peace in 532 (Proc., *Bell*. 1. 22. 3); 144,000 solidi for the Five Year Truce in 545 (Proc., *Bell*. 2. 28. 7–11); 187,200 solidi for the Five Year Truce in 551 (Proc., *Bell*. 8. 15. 1–7), and 210,000 solidi as the first bulk payment under the Fifty Year Peace (Men. Prot., frag. 6. 1 = Blockley, *Classicising Histo-*

*rians*, II, pp. 55–77). Justin II paid 45,000 solidi for the 574 armistice (Theoph. Sim. 3. 16. 3) and 90,000 solidi in 575 under terms of the 562 treaty (Men. Prot., frag. 18. 2 = Blockley, *Classicising Historians*, II, pp. 158–59).

67. Proc., *Bell.* 7. 33. 5–6; LCL, vol. IV, p. 439.
68. Plin., *NH* 36. 25. 30, but see reservations by W. E. Kaegi, Jr., "Byzantium and the Early Trans-Saharan Gold Trade: A Cautionary Note," *Graeco-Arabica* 3 (1984), 95–100. See Str. 3. 114 and 17. 2. 2 (Meroe), and 16. 4. 22 (Berenice).
69. Cosmas Ind., *Christian Topography* XI, pp. 323–24.

# Glossary

**AE1, AE2, AE3,** and **AE4** are the four classifications applied to billon and bronze denominations of A.D. 305–498 based on the coin's module. Denominations designated AE1 are equivalent to Diocletian's nummus (32–26 mm). AE2 (25–21 mm), AE3 (20–17 mm), and AE4 (below 17 mm) are reduced versions or fractions of the principal AE1 denomination.

*Aes* is the collective Latin word for base metal denominations struck in orichalcum, bronze, or copper.

*Alexandrine standard* was, in 150 B.C., 15 percent lighter than the Attic standard. The Ptolemaic silver tetradrachma (14 g) was exchanged at 3.67 denarii; in 30 B.C. it was tariffed at 1.5 denarii. When the Alexandrine tetradrachma was retariffed at 1 denarius in A.D. 42, the Alexandrine talent was reckoned at one-quarter of the Attic talent or 1,500 denarii.

*Antiochene standard* was the Seleucid silver standard of northern Syria employed for Roman provincial tetradrachmae from 30 B.C. to A.D. 57. The Antiochene tetradrachma was tariffed at 3 denarii and the Antiochene talent was reckoned as three-quarters of the Attic talent or 4,500 denarii.

*Antoninianus* is the name used for the double denarius introduced by Caracalla in A.D. 215 (5.09 g, 52 percent fine) and discontinued in 219. The Gordiani reintroduced the antoninianus in 238, and it was debased to 2.5 g and 2.5 percent fine by 270. Aurelian demonetized the denomination in 274.

*Argenteus* was the fine silver denomination (3.3 g) introduced by Diocletian in A.D. 293. The Tetrarchic coin, minted at 96 to the Roman pound and tariffed at 25 *denarii communes* was exchanged at 24 to an aureus (5.38 g) minted at 60 to the pound. The argenteus was retariffed at 50 d.c. by 300, and then at 100 d.c. in 301. Constantine revived the argenteus in 320 as the equivalent of a carat of the solidus. Constantius II reduced its weight to 144 to the Roman pound (2.25 g) in 355.

*As* was the principal cast bronze denomination of the Republic, weighing a full Roman pound (322.5 g) and exchanged at 10 asses to the denarius. During the First Punic War, the as was reduced from a libral standard of 12 ounces to a light libral standard of 10 ounces (280 g). In 217–212 B.C. it was lowered successively to the semilibral (162 g), triental (108 g), quadrantal (81 g), and sextantal (54 g) standards. A fiduciary as on an uncial standard (26 g) was struck after 200 B.C. The worn uncial as (18 g) was retariffed at 16 to the denarius in 141 B.C. Augustus introduced a copper as (11 g) that was a quarter of the orichalcum sestertius and exchanged at 16 to the denarius and 400 to the aureus.

*Assarion* is the Greek adaptation of the Roman as, reckoned at 16 to 18 to the denarius. Greek cities minted denominations in increments of assaria on either decimal or duodecimal systems. The two-assaria piece was equated with the earlier bronze obol.

*Attic standard.* In 150 B.C. the Attic talent was reckoned at 80 Roman pounds of silver (or 6,720 denarii at 84 to the Roman pound). The Attic drachma (4.31 g) was 10 percent heavier than the denarius, and the Attic tetradrachma (17.24 g) was equivalent to 4.5 denarii. The gold Attic stater (8.5 g) was exchanged at 20 to 24 Attic drachmae or 22.5 to 27 denarii. By 125 B.C. the Attic drachma was fixed at parity with the denarius and so an Attic talent henceforth was reckoned as equal to 6,000 denarii.

*Aurelianianus* was the silver-clad radiate denomination (3.88 g, 5 percent fine) introduced by Aurelian and tariffed at 5 *denarii communes* (hence its reverse carries the value mark of XXI or KA, twenty sestertii = 1 aurelianianus). The denomination was briefly retariffed at 2.5 d.c. by Tacitus. It was revalued to 2 d.c. and then demonetized by Diocletian.

*Aureus*. The denarius aureus was a term applied to Roman gold coins of the Republic and Principate. Augustus fixed the weight at 40 to the Roman pound (8.16 g) and tariffed it at 25 denarii or 100 sestertii. In A.D. 64 Nero lowered its weight to 45 to the Roman pound (7.16 g). Diocletian fixed the aureus at 60 to the Roman pound (5.38 g) and tariffed at 600 *denarii communes* (d.c.) (= 24 argentei = 120 nummi). The tariffing was raised to 1,200 d.c. in 300, and 2,400 d.c. in 301.

*Barbarous radiates* were unofficial imitations bearing blundered radiate portraits (i.e., those wearing a crown of solar rays), reverse types, and legends copied after Gallo-Roman and imperial antoniniani. They circulated in the northwestern and Iberian provinces between 260 and 293.

*Bigatus* ("two horsed") is the nickname of the denarius introduced in 213–212 B.C. It was so named after its reverse type of the Dioscuri to distinguish it from the heavier quadrigatus.

*Billon* is any alloy of silver of a fineness of 25 percent or less. The term is applied to late Roman denominations manufactured on bronze flans and coated with a silver wash (for a fineness of 2.5 to 10 percent).

*Brockage* is a misstriking of a coin that results in the mirror image of the obverse die appearing on the reverse of the coin.

*Carat* (Roman *siliqua* and Greek *keration*) was a weight (0.189 g) reckoned as 24 to the solidus (4.54 g). From the reign of Diocletian, gold fractions and silver denominations were minted in terms of siliquae for easy exchange against the solidus. The Tetrarchic and Constantinian silver argenteus (3.3 g) was considered the equivalent of a siliqua by weight.

*Centenionalis* was the small AE2 flan denomination bearing the value mark N (4.25 g, 1.5 percent fine) introduced in A.D. 348 and demonetized in 354. The name was perhaps applied to the AE3 bronze denomination (2.45 g) coined in 379–95.

*Chalcus* was the silver one-eighth of the obol, exchanged at 48 to the drachma. The shift to a bronze drachma and obol led to the striking of multiples of a bronze chalcus in the Greek world during the later second and first centuries B.C.

*Cistophorus* ("basket bearer") was the nickname of the Attalid tetradrachma (12.6 g) called after its obverse type of Dionysus's *cista mystica*. Introduced by 190 B.C., the cistophorus was struck on a weight standard that was 25 percent lighter than the Attic. Rome minted the cistophorus, tariffed at 3 denarii, as the provincial stater of Asia; it was retariffed at 4 denarii in 123.

*Countermark* is a small engraved stamp (with a design or letters) applied to the face of a coin. Countermarks revalidate or revalue currency.

*Decanummia* was introduced as a piece of ten nummiae (2 g) or one-quarter of the follis in 498. Its weight was doubled in 512.

*Decussis* was a cast emergency bronze denomination of ten asses or the equivalent of a silver denarius issued on triental and quadrantal standards in 215–213 B.C.

*Denarius* was the principal Roman silver denomination, denoting a piece of ten libral asses. The earliest Roman silver coin, by weight a Campanian didrachma (7.3 g), was presumably the first denarius. Denarius is used to designate the silver denomination (4.5 g), struck at 72 to the Roman pound that was introduced in 213–212 B.C. By 187 B.C., the denarius (3.83 g) was reduced to 84 to the Roman pound—the standard until Nero lowered it to 96 to the Roman pound (3.36 g) in A.D. 64.

*Denarius communis* (abbreviated d.c.) was the depreciated denarius employed as an accounting unit between 250 and 435. Prices and wages in the Edict of Maximum Prices (301) are quoted in *denarii communes*. The small laureate denomination struck by Aurelian in 274 and Diocletian in 293 was probably tariffed at 1 d.c.

*Didrachma* was a double drachma and frequently the principal stater of Greek cities in the Archaic and Classical ages. Roman silver denominations of 300–241 B.C. were by weight didrachmae on a Campanian standard.

*Die break* is a crack in the die into which a portion of the heated metal of the flan was forced by the striking, thereby producing extraneous raised areas on the coins.

*Die duplicates* are two or more coins that were struck from an identical pair of dies.

*Die link* refers to two or more coins that were struck either from the same obverse or reverse die.

*Dies* are engraved devices used for impressing types and legends on coin's flan. The anvil or obverse die is the lower die for striking; the punch or reverse die is the moveable upper die.

*Dinar* is the Aramaic word (which passed into Pahlavian and Arabic) for denarius that denotes a gold denarius. The term is used for the Sassanid gold dinar (8.1 g) introduced by Ardashir (224–40) and lowered to the weight of the solidus (4.5 g) by Barham IV (388–99).

*Dirhem* is the Aramaic word (which passed into Pahlavian and Arabic) for drachma. The term is used for the Sassanid silver dirhem (4 g) introduced by Ardashir (224–40).

*Doublestruck* refers to coins with a duplicate impression resulting from more than one blow of the hammer to the dies.

*Drachma* was the principal silver denomination of the Greek world. The weight of the Attic drachma (4.31 g) was lowered in 172–

125 B.C. until it stood at parity with the Roman denarius. The Attic drachma was the accounting unit employed in the East during the imperial age. In Egypt, the Roman imperial government issued a token currency based on a bronze drachma (34 mm, 25 g) and its sixth, the obol (19 mm, 5 g).

*Dupondius* was the bronze double of the libral as of the Republic. Augustus introduced a fiduciary orichalcum dupondius as the half of the sestertius (12.5 g). It was exchanged at 8 to the denarius and at 200 to the aureus.

*Electrum* is an alloy of gold and silver, also known as pale gold.

*Ethnic* is the part of the legend on a coin that identifies the issuing authority.

*Exergue* is the lower field beneath the central type on the reverse of the coin. Mintmarks and *officina* marks customarily occupy this field on late imperial coins.

*Fabric* is the overall appearance of the coin based on quality of the metal, shape, weight, diameter, and thickness.

*Fields* refer to the regions above, below, and to the side of the main design of the coin.

*Flan* refers to the piece of metal before receiving its impression from dies; also known as coin blank, disc, or planchet.

*Follis,* in Tetrarchic documents, is a purse of sealed coins often valued at 12,500 *denarii communes;* it is incorrectly used to denote Diocletian's silver-clad nummus. During the inflation of the late fourth and fifth centuries, follis designated a large number of tiny AE4 nummi in sealed purses or rolled up in skin or papyrus. In 498, Anastasius introduced a bronze denomination called a follis (8.5 g) that was tariffed at 40 nummiae and exchanged at 420 to the solidus. When its weight was doubled in 512, the follis was exchanged at 210 to the solidus; in 538/9 its weight was raised again (22 g) and the follis was tariffed at 180 to the solidus.

*Ghost currency* is a bookkeeping device to reckon taxes, prices, and wages in a common monetary unit (which is not issued as a coin) that can be converted into actual coins according to current exchange rates. The *denarius communis,* Attic drachma and talent, and Alexandrine drachma and talent were so employed in the later Roman Empire.

*Hexagram* was the silver denomination introduced by Heraclius in 615. The hexagram, struck at 48 to the Roman pound (6.75 g), was reckoned as 2 carats and exchanged at 12 to the solidus.

*Imitation* is a coin minted officially or privately with the intention to pass as legal tender by copying the types and legends of known coins. Such coins were not intended as counterfeits, but rather to meet specific demand.

*Legend* is the main inscription on the obverse or reverse of a coin.

*Maiorina* was the large AE2 denomination bearing the value mark A (5.25 g, 3 percent fine) introduced in 348 and abolished in 354. The term is also applied to the large silver-clad (8.13 g) denomination introduced by Julian in 362 and demonetized by the laws of 366–67. The term *pecunia maiorina* was common parlance to distinguish large-sized denominations from the AE4 nummi minimi of the late fourth and early fifth centuries.

*Miliarense* originally denoted a silver coin exchanged at 1,000 to a Roman pound of gold. Miliarense is used to designate three silver ceremonial multiples struck by Constantine and his successors. In 320–355, the triple miliarensia (13.44 g), heavy miliarense (5.34 g), and miliarense (4.48 g) were equivalents of 18, 15, and 6 carats, respectively; their values shifted to 12, 10, and 4 carats in 355 after Constantius II lowered the weight of the argenteus.

*Module* refers to the diameter of the coin.

*Nummus* (Greek *nummia*) was Diocletian's silver-clad denomination (10.75 g, 5 percent fine) that replaced the aurelianianus. In A.D. 293, the nummus, tariffed at 5 *denarii communes* was exchanged at 120 to an aureus minted at 60 to the Roman pound (5.38 g). In 300, the tariffing was raised to 12.5 d.c., and then to 25 d.c. in 301. Rapid debasement turned the nummus into a coin of AE2 module (4.5 to 8 g) in 307–13, then of AE3 module in 313–35 (2.5 to 3.4 g), and finally a tiny coin of AE4 module (1.65 g) in 335–48.

*Nummus minimus* was any AE4 module coin (between 0.5 and 1.65 g) that was the depreciated remnant of a large-sized billon or bronze denomination. Nummi minimi (called *kerma* in Greek slang) were the prime coins in circulation from 335 to 498 and customarily exchanged in sealed purses. In 445, a nummus minimus (1.12 g) was exchanged at 7,000 to 7,200 to the solidus; in 498 a nummus minimus (0.54 g) was exchanged at 14,400 to the solidus. This nummus (Greek *nummia*) was the unit for tariffing large denominations in reforms of Ostrogothic Italy, Vandalic North Africa, and the Byzantine Empire.

*Obol* was one-sixth of the silver drachma. In the second century B.C. it was turned into the principal bronze denomination of the Greek world.

*Orichalcum* was the Roman brass alloy, comprised of 75 percent copper, 20 percent zinc, and 5 percent tin. The imperial sestertius, dupondius, and semis were struck in orichalcum.

*Overstrike* refers to a coin that has been struck over an existing coin; often part of the underlying original types and legends are visible.

*Pentanummia* was introduced in 512 as a piece of 5 nummiae (2.3 g) or one-eighth of the follis.

*Ptolemaic standard.* See Alexandrine standard.

*Quadrans* was the bronze quarter of the libral as of the Republic; it was minted on an uncial standard down to the Social War. Augustus reintroduced a copper quadrans (3 g) as the sixteenth of the orichalcum sestertius.

*Quadrigatus* was the silver denomination named after its reverse type introduced after the First Punic War in 241 B.C. The coin, minted at 48 to the Roman pound (6.6 g), was debased in 217–214 B.C. during the Second Punic War and so it was demonetized and replaced by a lighter denarius in 213–212 B.C.

*Quinarius* was the silver half-denarius (2.25 g) introduced in 213–212 B.C., but it dropped out of circulation soon after 200 B.C. In 100–90 B.C. the quinarius was revived with the types of the victoriatus. Augustus instituted the practice of striking a gold quinarius (4 g) as the half of the aureus and a silver quinarius (1.92 g) as the half of the denarius.

*Quincussis* was a cast emergency bronze denomination of five asses or the equivalent of one-half silver denarius issued on triental and quadrantal standards in 215–213 B.C.

*Rhodian standard* was equivalent to the Antiochene and cistophoric standards.

*Semis* was the half of the bronze as of the Republic. In 64–66, Nero introduced an orichalcum semis (8 g) that was the quarter of the orichalcum dupondius and the eighth of the orichalcum sestertius. The gold semis (or semissis) was the half (2.27 g) of the Constantinian solidus.

*Serrate denarii* (*denarii serrati*) were Republican denarii of various issues down to 65 B.C. that were notched with decorative scalloped edges by means of a chisel.

*Sestertius* was the silver quarter of the denarius (1.12 g) first minted in 213–212 B.C., but it dropped out of use soon after 200 B.C. With the retariffing of the denarius at 16 asses in 141 B.C., sestertii (abbreviated HS) replaced the asses as the principal unit of accounting. Augustus introduced an orichalcum sestertius (25 g) to head the token currency.

*Sextans* was the sixth of the libral as of the Republic; it was minted on an uncial standard of 213–212 B.C. down to the Social War (90–88 B.C.).

*Siliqua* is the Latin for carat. The term by convention denotes silver denominations of Vandalic North Africa and Ostrogothic Italy.

*Solidus* (Greek *nomisma khrysion* or *holokottinos*) was a nickname denoting a solid gold bit, first applied to the Severan aureus and officially applied to the Tetrarchic aureus minted at 60 to the pound. The term is reserved by convention for the gold coin introduced by Constantine in 309 and struck at 72 to the Roman pound (4.54 g).

*Stater* was the principal silver trade coin issued by Hellenic cities; the most common denominations were the tetradrachma or didrachma. Macedonian kings popularized an Attic weight didrachma as the gold stater (8.5 g) of the Hellenistic world.

*Stephanophoros* refers to "wreath-bearing" civic tetradrachmae struck on broad flans by Greek cities after the Third Macedonian War (172–167 B.C.). In Delian inventories, the term only denotes the so-called New Style Athenian tetradrachmae.

*Symbolikon* was the fee charged on converting taxes assessed in Ptolemaic ghost units into Roman provincial currency. The charges were either 1.5 or 3 obols at Karanis in 171–75.

*Talent* was the principal unit for measuring weight or large sums of money in the Greek world; 1 talent = 60 minae = 6,000 drachmae. Talents of Attic weight (= 6,000 denarii), cistophoric weight (= 4,500 denarii), and Alexandrine weight (= 1,500 denarii) were used in the East during the imperial age.

*Tetradrachma* was a Greek silver denomination of four drachmae. The Attic weight tetradrachma (17.24 g) was the principal trade coin of the Hellenistic world. The denomination was retained as a provincial stater for Roman provinces in Asia Minor, Syria, and Alexandria. The Attic or Tyrian tetradrachma passed at 4 denarii; the Antiochene or cistophoric at 3 denarii. In A.D. 42, Claudius turned the Alexandrine tetradrachma, initially tariffed at 1.5 denarii, into a billon fiduciary coin that was revalued at 1 denarius.

*Token currency*, also known as fiduciary currency, refers to coins struck from base metals such as billon, bronze, copper, orichalcum, or potin (a lead alloy) and tariffed above their intrinsic value.

*Tremis* (or *tremissis*) was the gold third (1.5 g) of the solidus, introduced by Theodosius I (379–95), and the principal gold denomination of the early medieval West.

*Tressis* was a cast emergency bronze denomination of three asses issued on triental and quadrantal standards in 215–213 B.C.

*Triens* was the third of the libral as of the Republic; it was minted on the uncial standard down to the Social War.

*Type* is the central design of a coin.

*Tyrian standard* was equivalent to the Attic standard.

*Uncia*, the Roman ounce (26.875 g), was struck as one-twelfth of the as down to the end of the second century B.C.; its half was the semuncia.

*Unit of accounting* is a monetary unit, either a coin or ghost currency, employed to reckon fiscal and legal obligations. The as was so employed by the Republic down to 141 B.C., when it was replaced by the sestertius (abbreviated HS). When inflation made traditional units cumbersome, the solidus was introduced as the principal accounting unit from the mid-fifth century on.

*Value marks* are numerals or other designations of the tariffing of a denomination.

*Victoriatus* was the nickname based on the reverse type for the silver denomination (3.75 g, 80 percent fine) introduced in 213–212 B.C. It was half of the quadrigatus and three-quarters of the denarius. Worn victoriati circulated as halves of the denarius during the second century B.C. The word *victoriatus* survived as army slang under the Principate to designate the half of the denarius.

# Select Bibliography


## *General Studies and Catalogues*

### GENERAL STUDIES AND HANDBOOKS

Burnett, A. M. *Coinage in the Roman World.* London, 1987.

Carson, R. A. G. *Coins of the Roman Empire.* London, 1990.

Kent, J. P. C., and photographs by M. and A. Hirmer. *Roman Coins.* New York, 1978.

Mattingly, H. *Roman Coins from the Earliest Times to the Fall of the Western Empire,* 2nd ed. London, 1960.

### CATALOGUES AND CORPORA OF THE ROMAN REPUBLIC

Crawford, M. H. *The Roman Republican Coinage.* Vols. 1–2. Cambridge, 1974.

Grueber, H. A. *Coins of the Roman Republic in the British Museum.* Vols. 1–3. London, 1910.

### CATALOGUES AND CORPORA OF THE ROMAN EMPIRE

Giard, J.-B. *Catalogue des monnaies de l'empire romain, Paris, Bibliothèque Nationale* I. *Auguste.* Paris, 1976.

———. *Catalogue des monnaies de l'empire romain, Paris, Bibliothèque Nationale* II. *de Tibère à Néron.* Paris, 1988.

Grierson, P., and M. Mays. *Catalogue of Late Roman Coins in the Dumbarton Oaks and Whittemore Collection.* Washington D.C., 1992.

Mattingly, H. et al. *Coins of the Roman Empire in the British Museum.* Vols. 1–6. London, 1923–62.

Mattingly, H. et al. *The Roman Imperial Coinage.* Vols. 1–10. London, 1923–94.

Sutherland, C. H. V. *The Roman Imperial Coinage.* Vol. 1, revised. London, 1984.

CIVIC AND PROVINCIAL COINAGES

Burnett, A. M., and M. Amandry. *The Roman Provincial Coinage* I. London/Paris, 1992.

*Catalogue of Greek Coins in the British Museum.* Vols. 1–29. London, 1873–1927.

Dembski, G. *Katalog der antiken Münzen Kunsthistorisches Museum, Wien A. Griechen* I. *Hispanien und die römischen Provinzen Galliens.* Vienna, 1979.

Franke, P. R., W. Leschhorn, and A. U. Stylow. *Sylloge Nummorum Graecorum. Deustchland Sammlung von Aulock Index.* Berlin, 1981.

Imhoof-Blumer, F., ed. *Die antiken Münzen Nord-Griechenlands.* Vols. 1–4. Berlin, 1898–1935.

Milne, J. G. *Catalogue of Alexandrian Coins in the Ashmolean Museum.* Rev. by C. M. Kraay. London, 1971.

*Sylloge Nummorum Graecorum. The Royal Collection of Coins and Medals, Danish Royal National Museum.* Copenhagen, 1942–69.

*Sylloge Nummorum Graecorum Deutschland, Sammlung von Aulock.* Berlin, 1957–68.

Waddington, W. H., E. Babelon, and T. Reinach. *Recueil général des monnaies grecques d'Asie Mineure.* Parts 1–4. Paris, 1904–12; 2nd ed. of part 1. Paris, 1925.

BYZANTIUM AND THE MEDIEVAL WEST

Bellinger, A. R. *Catalogue of the Byzantine Coins in the Dumbarton Oaks Collection and in the Whittemore Collection* I. *Anastasius to Maurice, 491–602.* Washington, D.C., 1966.

Grierson, P. *Catalogue of the Byzantine Coins in the Dumbarton and in the Whittemore Collection* II. *Phocas to Theodosius III, 602–717,* 2 vols.; II.1, *Phocas and Heraclius (602–641);* II.2, *Heraclius Constantine to Theodosius III (641–717).* Washington D.C., 1968.

Grierson, P., and M. Blackburn. *Medieval European Coins with a Catalogue of the Coins in the Fitzwilliam Museum* I. *The Early Middle Ages (5th–10th Centuries).* Cambridge, 1986.

Hahn, W. R. O. *Moneta Imperii Byzantini.* Vols. 1–3. Österreichliche Akademie der Wissenschaften, phil.-hist. Klasse, Denkschriften 109, 119, and 148. Vienna, 1973.

Morrisson, C. *Catalogues des monnaies byzantines de la Bibliothèque Nationale* Vols. 1–2. Paris, 1970.

Wroth, W. *Imperial Byzantine Coins in the British Museum.* Vols. 1–2. London, 1908.

———. *Western and Provincial Byzantine Coins of the Vandals, Ostrogoths and Lombards and of the Empires of Thessalonica, Nicaea and Trebizond in the British Museum.* London, 1911.

*Metrology*

Amandry, M., J.-N. Barrandon, C. Brenot, J.-P. Callu, and J. Poirier. "L'affrinage des métaux monnayés au bas-empire: Les réforms valentiniennes de 364–368." *NAC* 11 (1982), 279–95.

Barrandon, J.-N., and C. Brenot. "Analyse de monnaie de bronze (318–340) par activation neutronique à l'aide d'une source isotopique de Californium 252." In *Les dévaluations à Rome* 1. Rome, 1978, pp. 123–44.

Barrandon, J.-N., J.-P. Callu, and C. Brenot. "The Analysis of Constantinian Coins (A.D. 313–320) by Non-destructive Californium 252 Activation." *Archaeometry* 19 (1977), 173–86.

Burnett, A. M., P. T. Craddock, and K. Preston. "New Light on the Origins of Orichalcum." In *Actes du 9ème congrès international de numismatique, Berne 1979,* ed. T. Hackens and R. Weiller. Louvain-la-Neuve, 1982, pp. 263–69.

Caley, E. R. "Chemical Composition of Alexandria Tetradrachms." In *Centennial Publication of the American Numismatic Society,* ed. H. I. Ingholt. New York, 1958, pp. 167–80.

———. *Chemical Composition of Parthian Coins.* Numismatic Notes and Monographs 129. New York, 1955.

———. *The Composition of Ancient Greek Bronze Coins.* Memoirs of the American Philosophical Society 11. Philadephia, 1939.

———. *Orichalcum and Related Ancient Alloys.* Numismatic Notes and Monographs 151. New York, 1964.

Callu, J.-P., and J. N. Barrandon. "L'inflazione nel IV secolo. 295–361): Il contributo delle analisi." In *Società romana e imperio tardoantico, istituzioni, ceti, economie,* ed. A. Giardina. Rome, 1986, pp. 559–600.

Callu, J.-P., C. Brenot, and J. N. Barrandon. "Analyses de séries atypiques. (Aurélien, Tacite, Carus, Licinius)." *NAC* 8 (1979), 241–54.

Cope, L. H. "The Argentiferous Bronze Alloys of the Large Tetrarchic Folles of A.D. 294–307." *NC* 7, 8 (1968), 115–49.

———. "The Fineness and Sequence of Gallienic Antoniniani, A.D. 259–268." *NC* 7, 17 (1977), 216–19.

———. "The Metallurgical Examination of Debased Folles Issued by Constantine." *Archaeometry* 15, 2 (1973), 721–28.

———. "The Nadir of the Imperial Antoninianus in the Reign of Claudius II Gothicus, A.D. 268–270." *NC* 7, 9 (1969), 145–61.

Craddock, P. T., A. M. Burnett, and K. Preston. "Hellenistic Copper-base Coinage and the Origins of Brass." In *Scientific Studies in Numismatics*, ed. W. A. Oddy. British Museum Occasional Papers 18. London, 1980, pp. 53–64.

King, C. E. "The Alloy Content of the Antoninianus, A.D. 253–268." In *Proceedings of the 10th International Congress, London, 8–12 September*, ed. I. Carradice. London, 1986, pp. 289–92.

Morrisson, C., C. Brenot, J.-P. Callu, J. Poirier, and R. Halleux. *L'or monnayé I. Purification et altérations de Rome à Byzance*. Cahiers Ernst Babelon 2. Paris, 1985.

Walker, D. R. *The Metrology of Roman Silver Coinage*, Parts 1–3. BAR Int. Ser. 5, 22, and 40. Oxford, 1976–78.

———. "The Silver Content of the Roman Republican Coinage." In *Metallurgy in Numismatics*, ed. D. M. Metcalf and W. A. Oddy. Royal Numismatic Society Special Publications 13. London, 1980, 1:55–72.

### *Minting Technology, Die Links, Hoards, and Output*

#### MINTING TECHNOLOGY

Hill, G. F. "Ancient Methods of Coining." *NC* 5, 2 (1922), 1–42.

Malkmus, W. "Addenda to Vermeule's Catalogue of Ancient Coin Dies." *SAN* 12, 4 (1989), 80–85; 18, 1 (1990), 16–22; 18, 2 (1991), 40–49; and 18, 3 (1992), 72–77.

Mayhew, J. N., and P. Spufford, eds. *Later Medieval Mints: Organisation, Administration and Technique*. BAR Int. Ser. 389. Oxford, 1988, pp. 30–88.

Sellwood, D. G. "Some Experiments in Greek Minting Techniques." *NC* 3, 7 (1963), 217–31.

Vermeule, C. C. *Ancient Coin Dies*. London, 1954.

#### STATISTICAL METHODS AND OUTPUT

Carter, G. F. "Comparison of Methods for Calculating the Total Number of Dies from Die-link Statistics." *PACT* 5 (1981), 204–13.

———. "A Simplified Method of Calculating the Original Number of Dies from Die-Link Statistics." *ANSMN* 26 (1983), 195–206.

Kinns, P. "The Amphictyonic Coinage Reconsidered." *NC* 143 (1983), 1–22.

Lyon, C. S. S. "Die Estimation: Some Experiments with Simulated Samples of Coinage." *BNJ* 59 (1989), 1–12.

———. "The Estimation of the Number of Dies Employed in a Coinage." *Numismatic Circular* 73, 9 (1965), 180–81.

Morrisson, C., J.-N. Barrandon, and C. Brenot. "Composition and Technology of Ancient and Medieval Coinages: A Reassessment of Analytical Results." *ANSMN* 32 (1987), 181–209.

Volk, T. R. "Mint Output and Coin Hoards." In *Rythmes de la production monétaire de l'antiquité à nos jours. Actes de colloque international organisé à Paris du 10 au 12 janvier 1986,* ed. G. Depeyrot, T. Hackens, and G. Moucharte. Numismatica Lovaniensia 7. Louvain-la-Neuve, 1987, pp. 141–221.

VOLUME OF ROMAN REPUBLICAN COINAGES

Buttrey, T. V., Jr. "The Denarii of P. Crepusius and Roman Republican Mint Organization." *ANSMN* 21 (1976), 67–108.

Carter, G. F. "Die-link Statistics for Crepusius Denarii and Calculations of the Total Number of Dies." *PACT* 5 (1981), 193–203.

Crawford, M. H. "Control Marks and the Organization of the Roman Republican Mint." *PBSR* 34 (1966), 18–23.

Hersh, C. A. "Sequence Marks on Denarii of Publius Crepusius." *NC* 6, 12 (1952), 52–66.

Mattingly, H. B. "The Management of the Roman Republican Mint." *AIIN* 29 (1982), 9–46.

VOLUME OF IMPERIAL AND BYZANTINE COINAGES

Christiansen, E. *The Roman Coins of Alexandria: Quantitative Studies.* Vols. 1–2. Aarhus, 1988.

Metcalf, D. M. *The Origins of the Anastasian Coinage Reform.* Amsterdam, 1969.

Morrisson, C. "Estimation du volume des émissions de solidi de Tibère et Maurice à Carthage (578–602)." *PACT* 5 (1981), 267–84.

Nordbø, J. H. "The Imperial Silver Coinage of Amisus, 132/1–137/8 A.D." In *Studies in Ancient History and Numismatics Presented to Rudi Thomsen,* ed. A. Damsgaard-Madsen. Aarhus, 1988, pp. 166–78.

Sutherland, C. H. V., N. K. Olcay, and K. E. Merrington. *The Cistophori of Augustus.* Royal Numismatic Society Special Publication 5. London, 1970.

VOLUME OF PARALLEL MEDIEVAL COINAGES

Brand, J. D. "The Shrewsbury Mint, 1249–50." In *Mints, Dies and Currency: Essays Dedicated to the Memory of Albert Baldwin,* ed. R. A. G. Carson. London, 1971, p. 129–50.

Craig, J. *The Mint: A History of the London Mint from A.D. 287 to 1948.* Cambridge, 1953.

Grierson, P. "Mint Output in the Tenth Century." *EcHR* 2, 9 (1957), 462–66.

———. "The Volume of Anglo-Saxon Currency." *EcHR* 2. 20 (1967), 153–60.

Mate, M. "Coin Dies under Edward I and II." *NC* 7, 9 (1969), 207–18.

Metcalf, D. M. "How Large was the Anglo-Saxon Currency." *EcHR* 2, 18 (1965), 475–82.

Stahl, A. *The Venetian Tornessello: A Medieval Colonial Coinage.* Numismatic Notes and Monographs 163. New York, 1985.

HOARDS, CIRCULATION, AND STRUCTURE OF CURRENCY

Bates, G. E. *Byzantine Coins.* Archaeological Exploration of Sardis, Monograph 1. Cambridge, Mass., 1971.

Bellinger, A. R. *The Excavations of Dura-Europos: Final Report VI: The Coins.* New Haven, 1949.

———. *Troy: The Coins.* Supplementary Monograph no. 2. Excavations conducted by the University of Cincinnati, 1932–38. Princeton, 1961.

Breglia, L. "Circolazione monetale ad aspetti di vità economica a Pompei." In *Pompeiana: Raccolta di studi per il secondo centenario degli scavi di Pompei,* ed. A. Maiuri. Naples, 1950, 41–59.

Bruun, P. "Quantitative Analysis of Hoarding in Periods of Coin Deterioration." *PACT* 5 (1981), 355–64.

———. "Site Finds and Hoarding Behaviour." *Scripta Nummaria Romana: Essays Presented to Humphrey Sutherland,* ed. R. A. G. Carson and C. M. Kraay. London, 1978, pp. 114–23.

Buttrey, T. V., Jr. *Cosa: The Coins.* Monographs of the American Academy at Rome 34. Rome, 1980.

———. "A Hoard of Sestertii from Bordeaux and the Problem of Bronze Circulation in the Third Century A.D." *ANSMN* 18 (1972), 33–58.

Buttrey, T. V., Jr., A. Johnston, K. M. MacKenzie, and M. L. Bates. *Greek, Roman, and Islamic Coins from Sardis.* Archaeological Exploration of Sardis Monograph 7. Cambridge, Mass., 1981.

Chantraine, H. *Novaesium* VIII. *Die antike Fundmünzen von Neuss. Gesamtkatalog der Ausgrabungen 1955–1978.* Berlin, 1982.

Christiansen, E. "The Roman Coins of Alexandria: An Inventory of Hoards." *Coin Hoards* 7 (1985), 77–141.

Crawford, M. H. "Coin Hoards and the Pattern of Violence in the Late Republic." *PBSR* 37 (1969), 76–81.

———. *Roman Republican Coin Hoards.* Royal Numismatic Society Special Publications 4. London, 1969.

Duncan-Jones, R. "Weight-loss as an Index of Coin-wear in Currency of the Roman Empire." In *Rythmes de la production monétaire de l'antiquité à nos jours. Actes de colloque international organisé à Paris du 10 au 12 janvier 1986,* ed. G. Depeyrot, T. Hackens, and G. Moucharte. Numismatica Lovaniensia 7. Louvain-la-Neuve, 1987, pp. 235–54.

Étienne, R., and M. Rachet. *Le trésor de Garonne: Essai sur la circulation monétaire en Aquitaine à la fin du règne d'Antonin le Pieux (159–161)*. Bordeaux, 1984.

Fitz, J. *Der Geldumlauf der römischen Provinzen in Donaugebiet Mitte des 3. Jahrhunderts*. Vols. 1–2. Budapest, 1978.

Frier, B. W., and A. J. Parker. "Roman Coins from the River Liri." *NC* 7, 10 (1970), 89–109.

Houghtalin, L. "Roman Coins from the River Liri III." *NC* 145 (1984), 67–81.

Kent, J. P. C. "Interpreting Coin Hoards." In *Coins and the Archaeologist*, ed. P. Casey and R. Reece. Oxford, 1974, pp. 184–200.

Lightfoot, C. J., ed. *Recent Turkish Coin Hoards and Numismatic Studies*. British Institute of Archaeology Monographs 12. Oxford, 1991.

MacDonald, D. J. "Aphrodisias and Currency in the East, A.D. 259–305." *AJA* 78 (1974), 276–84.

Metcalf, W. E. "The Coins—1978." In *Excavations at Carthage Conducted by the University of Michigan*, ed. J. H. Humphrey. Ann Arbor, Mich., 1982, 7:63–168.

———. "The Coins—1982." In *A Circus and a Byzantine Cemetery at Carthage*, ed. J. H. Humphrey. Ann Arbor, Mich., 1988, pp. 337–81.

———. "The Michigan Finds at Carthage, 1975–79: An Analysis." *ANSMN* 32 (1987), 61–84.

———. "Roman Coins from the River Liri II." *NC* 7, 14 (1974), 42–53.

Morrisson, C. "Coin Finds in Vandal and Byzantine Carthage: A Provisional Assessment." In *A Circus and a Byzantine Cemetery at Carthage*, ed. J. H. Humphrey. Ann Arbor, Mich., 1988, pp. 423–36.

Mouchmov, L. A. *Le trésor numismatique de Réka-Devnia. (Macrianopolis)*. Sofia, 1934.

Patterson, C. C. "Silver Stocks and Losses in Ancient and Medieval Times." *EcHR* 2, 25 (1972), 205–35.

Pereira, I., J.-P. Bost, and J. Hiernard, eds. *Fouilles de Conimbriga* III. *Les monnaies*. Paris, 1978.

Thompson, M. A., O. Mørkholm, and C. M. Kraay. *An Inventory of Greek Coin Hoards*. New York, 1973.

Turcan, R. *Le trésor de Guelma: Étude historique et monétaire*. Paris, 1963.

Waage, D. B. *Antioch-on-the-Orontes*. Vol. IV part 2 *Greek, Roman, Byzantine and Crusaders' Coins*. Princeton, 1952.

*Mines, Mining, and Specie Flows*

Bird, D. G. "Pliny and the Gold Mines of the North-west of the Iberian Peninsula." In *Papers in Iberian Archaeology*, ed. T. F. C. Blagg, R. F. J. Jones and S. J. Keay. BAR Int. Ser. 193. Oxford, 1984, pp. 341–63.

———. "The Roman Gold Mines of North-west Spain." *Bonner Jahrbuch* 172 (1972), 36–64.

Bryer, A. A. M. "The Question of Byzantine Mines in the Pontos." *Anatolian Studies* 32 (1982), 133–52.

Davies, O. *Roman Mines in Europe.* Oxford, 1935.

Domergue, C. "A propos de Pline *Naturalis Historia* 33.70–78, et pour illustrer sa déscription des mines d'or romaines d'Éspagne." *Archivo Español de Arqueologia* 47 (1974), 499–548.

Domergue, C. and G. Hérail. *Mines d'or romaines d'Éspagne: Étude géomorphologique et archéologique.* Toulouse, 1978.

Dušanić, S. "Aspects of Roman Mining in Noricum, Pannonia, Dalmatia and Moesia Superior." *ANRW* 2, 6 (Berlin, 1977), 52–94.

Edmondson, J. C. "Mining in the Later Roman Empire and Beyond: Continuity or Disruption?" *JRS* 79 (1989), 84–102.

Forbes, R. J. *Studies in Ancient Technology.* Vols. 1–9. London, 1955–64.

Gale, N. H., W. Genter, and G. A. Wagner. "Mineralogical and Geographic Silver Sources of Archaic Greece." In *Metallurgy in Numismatics,* ed. D. M. Metcalf and W. A. Oddy. London, 1958, I, pp. 3–49.

Healy, F. *Mining and Metallurgy in the Greek and Roman World.* Leiden, 1978.

Jones, R. F. J. "The Roman Mines at Rio Tinto." *JRS* 70 (1980), 146–68.

Jones, R. F. J., and D. G. Bird, "Roman Mines in North-west Spain II: Workings on the Rio Duerna." *JRS* 62 (1972), 59–74.

Jones, R. F. J., and P. R. Lewis. "The Dolaucothi Gold-mines." *Bonner Jahrbuch* 171 (1971), 288–300.

Lewis, P. R., and G. D. B. Jones. "Dolaucothi Gold Mines I: The Surface Evidence." *Ant. Journal* 49 (1970), 244–72.

Lewis, P. R., and G. D. B. Jones. "Roman Gold-Mining in North-west Spain." *JRS* 60 (1970), 169–85.

Mrozek, S. "Die Goldbergwerke im römischen Dazien." *ANRW* 2. 6 (Berlin, 1977), 95–109.

Vryonis, S. "The Question of Byzantine Mines." *Speculum* 37 (1962), 1–17.

## *History of the Currency*

### THE ROMAN REPUBLIC, 500–31 B.C.

Amandry, M. "A propos du monnayage de L. Sempronius Atratinus." *SMB* 33 (1983), 82–85

———. "Le monnayage en bronze de Bibulus et Capito." *RSN* 65 (1986), 73–85; and 66 (1987), 102–34.

Burnett, A. M. "The Beginnings of Roman Coinage." *AIIN* 36 (1989), 33–65.

———. "The Changing Face of Republican Numismatics." *JRS* 77 (1987), 177–83.

———. "The Coinages of Rome and Magna Graecia in the Late Fourth and Third Centuries B.C." *SNR* 56 (1977), 92–121.

———. "The Currency of Italy from the Hannibalic War to Augustus." *AIIA* 29 (1982), 125–38.

———. "The Enna Hoard and the Silver Coinage of the Syracusan Democracy." SNR 62 (1983), 5–26.

———. "The First Roman Silver Coins." NAC 7 (1978), 121–42.

———. "The Iconography of Roman Coin Types in the Third Century B.C." *NC* 146 (1986), 67–75.

———. "The Second Issue of Roman Didrachms." *NAC* 9 (1980), 169–74.

Buttrey, T. V., Jr. "Morgantina and the Denarius." *NAC* 8 (1979), 149–57. Reprinted in *Morgantina Studies: The Coins*. Princeton, 1989, 2:220–26.

———. "The Morgantina Excavations and the Date of the Roman Denarius." In *Atti del congresso internazionale di Numismatica, Roma 1961*. Rome, 1965, pp. 261–67. Reprinted in *Morgantina Studies: The Coins*. Princeton, 1989, 2: 215–19.

———. "On the Retariffing of the Roman Denarius." *ANSMN* 7 (1957), 57–65.

Campana, A. *La monetazione degli insorti italici durante la Guerre Sociale (91–87 a. C.)*. Soliera, 1987.

Crawford, M. H. *Coinage and Money under the Roman Republic: Italy and the Mediterranean Economy*. Berkeley, 1985.

———. *Roman Republican Coin Hoards*. Royal Numismatic Society Special Publications 4. London, 1969.

———. *Roman Republican Coinage*. Vols. 1–2. Cambridge, 1974.

Haeberlin, E. J. *Aes Grave: Das Schwergeld Roms und Mittelitaliens*. Vols. 1–2. Frankfurt/Main, 1910.

Hersh, C. A. "The Agrinion Find and the Problem of the Chronology of the Roman Republican Coinage during the Second Century B.C.." *NC* 7, 6 (1966), 71–93.

———. "Notes on the Chronology and Interpretation of the Roman Republican Coinage: Some Comments on Crawford's *Roman Republican Coinage*." *NC* 7, 17 (1977), 19–36.

———. "A Quinarius Hoard from Southern Italy." *NC* 7, 12 (1972), 75–98.

———. "Some Additional Roman Republican Overstrikes." *ANSMN* 32 (1987), 85–95.

———. "A Study of the Coinage of the Moneyer C. Calpurnius Piso L. f. Frugi." *NC* 7, 16 (1976), 7–63.

Hersh, C. A., and A. Walker. "The Mesagne Hoard." *ANSMN* 29 (1984), 103–34.

Le Gentilhomme, P. "Les quadrigati nummi et le dieu Janus." *RN* 4, 37 (1934), 1–36.

Thomsen, R. *Early Roman Coinage.* Vols. 1–3. Copenhagen, 1957–61.
Vecchi, I. "The Coinage of the *Rasna*: A Study in Etruscan Numismatics. Part I." *SNR* 67 (1988), 43–84.
Zehnacker, H. "Monnaies de compte et prix à Rome au IIe siècle avant notre ère." In *Les dévaluations à Rome* II Paris, 1980, pp. 31–48.

HELLENIC COINAGES, 600–30 B.C.

Boehringer, C. *Zur Chronologie mittelhellenistischer Münzserien 220–160 v. Chr.* Berlin, 1972.
Giovannini, A. *Rome et la circulation monétaire en Grèce au IIe siècle avant Jésus Christ.* Basel, 1978.
Harl, K. W. "Livy and the Date of the Introduction of the Cistophoric Tetradrachma." *CA* 10 (1991), 268–97.
Jenkins, G. K. *Ancient Greek Coins.* rev. ed. London, 1990.
———. "Coins of Punic Sicily." *RSN* 50 (1971), 25–78; 53 (1974), 23–41; 56 (1977), 5–66; and 57 (1978), 5–68.
Jenkins, G. K., and R. B. Lewis. *Carthaginian Gold and Electrum Coins.* Royal Numismatic Society Special Publications 2. London, 1963.
Kleiner, F. S. "The Dated Cistophori of Ephesus." *ANSMN* 18 (1972), 17–32.
———. "Hoard Evidence and the Late Cistophori of Pergamum." *ANSMN* 23 (1978), 77–106.
Kleiner, F. S., and S. W. Noe. *The Early Cistophoric Coinage.* Numismatic Studies 14. New York, 1977.
Kraay, C. M. *Archaic and Classical Greek Coins.* Berkeley, 1976.
Lewis, D. M. "The Chronology of the Athenian New Style Coinage." *NC* 7, 2 (1962), 275–300.
Martin, T. R. *Sovereignty and Coinage in Classical Greece.* Princeton, 1985.
Mørkholm, O. *Early Hellenistic Coinage from the Accession of Alexander the Great to the Peace of Apamea (336–186 B.C.).* Cambridge, 1991.
———. "Some Reflections on the Production and Use of Coinage in Ancient Greece." *Historia* 31 (1982), 290–303.
Rutter, N. K. *Campanian Coinages, 475–380 B.C.* Edinburgh, 1979.
Thompson, M. *The New Style Silver Coinage of Athens.* Vols. 1–2. Numismatic Studies 10. New York, 1958.

IBERIAN, CELTIC, AND GETO-DACIAN COINAGES

Allen, D. F. "Monnaies-à-la-croix." *NC* 7, 9 (1989), 33–78.
———. "New Light on the Serra Riccò Hoard of Cisalpine Coins." *JNG* 21 (1971), 97–108.
Allen, D. F., and D. E. N. Nash. *Coins of the Ancient Celts.* Edinburgh, 1980.
Chitescu, M. *Numismatic Aspects of the History of the Dacian State: The Roman*

*Republican Coinage in Dacia and Geto-Dacian Coins of Roman Type.* BAR Int. Ser. 112, Oxford, 1981.

de Guadan, A. M. *Las monedas de plata di Emporion y Rhode.* Vols. 1–2. Barcelona, 1955–58.

———. *Numismatica ibérica e ibero-romana.* Madrid, 1969.

Göbl, R. *Typologie und Chronologie der keltischen Münzprägung in Noricum.* Vienna, 1978.

Knapp, R. C. "The Date and Purpose of Iberian Denarii." *NC* 7, 17 (1977), 1–18.

Nash, D. E. M. "Plus ça change: Currency in Central Gaul from Julius Caesar to Nero." In *Scripta Nummaria Romana: Essays Presented to Humphrey Sutherland,* ed. R. A. G. Carson and C. M. Kraay. London, 1976, pp. 12–31.

———. *Settlement and Coinage in Central Gaul, c. 200–50 B.C.* Parts 1–2. BAR Supp. Ser. 39. Oxford, 1978.

Scheers, S. *L'histoire monétaire de la Gaule belgique du IIIe au Ier siècle avant J.-C.* Louvain, 1973.

———. *Les monnaies de la Gaule inspirées de celles de la république romaine.* Louvain, 1969.

———. *Traité de numismatique celtique* II. *La Gaule belgique.* Centre de Recherches d'Histoire Ancienne, Série Numismatique 24. Paris, 1977.

Torbágyi, M. "Die Münzprägung der Eravisher." *Acta Archaeologica Academia Scientiarum Hungaricae* 36 (1984), 161–96.

Villaronga, L. *Las monedas de Arse-Saguntum.* Barcelona, 1967.

———. *Las monedas ibèriques de Tàrraco.* Tarragona, 1983.

———. *Numismatica antigua de Hispania.* Barcelona, 1979.

———. *Los tesoros de Azaila y la circulacion monetaria en del valle del Ebro.* Barcelona, 1977.

Winkler, L. "Über dako-getische Münzschätze." *Acta Archaeologica Carpathica* 8 (1966), 83–110.

———. "Zur relativen Chronologie der dako-getischen Münzen." *Acta Archaeologica Carpathica* 10 (1968), 111–15.

THE PRINCIPATE, 31 B.C.–A.D. 235

Bolin, S. *State and Currency in the Roman Empire to 300 A.D.* Stockholm, 1958.

Buttrey, T. V., Jr. "Dio, Zonaras and the Value of the Roman Aureus." *JRS* 51 (1961), 40–45.

———. "Observations on the Behavior of Tiberian Counterstamps." *ANSMN* 16 (1970), 57–68.

Carradice, I. *Coinage and Finances in the Reign of Domitian A.D. 81–96.* BAR Int. Ser. 178, Oxford, 1973.

Giard, J.-B. *Le monnayage de Lyon des origins au règne de Caligula (43 avant J.C.–41 après J.C.* Wetteren, 1983.

Grant, M. *From Imperium to Auctoritas: A Historical Study of Aes Coinage in the Roman Empire 40 B.C.–A.D. 14.* Cambridge, 1949.

———. *The Six Main Aes Coinages of Augustus: Controversial Studies.* Edinburgh, 1953.

Hill, P. V. *The Dating and Arrangement of the Undated Coinage of Rome 98–148 A.D.* London, 1975.

———. *The Coinage of Septimius Severus and His Family of the Mint of Rome, A.D. 193–217.* London, 1964.

Howgego, C. J. "Coinage and Military Finance: The Imperial Bronze Coinage of the Augustan East." *NC* 142 (1982), 1–20.

Kraay, C. M. *The Aes Coinage of Galba.* Numismatic Notes and Monographs 133. New York, 1956.

———. "The Behavior of Early Imperial Countermarks." In *Essays in Roman Coinage Presented to Harold Mattingly,* ed. by R. A. G. Carson and C. H. V. Sutherland. Oxford, 1956, pp. 113–26.

———. "The Bronze Coinage of Vespasian: Classification and Attribution." In *Scripta Nummaria Romana: Essays Presented to Humphrey Sutherland,* ed. R. A. G. Carson and C. M. Kraay. London, 1976, pp. 47–57.

MacDowall, D. W. *The Western Coinages of Nero.* Numismatic Notes and Monographs 161. New York, 1978.

Martin, H.-P. *Die anonymen Münzen des Jahres 68 nach Christus.* Mainz, 1974.

Rodewald, C. *Money in the Age of Tiberius.* Manchester, 1976.

Sutherland, C. H. V. "Augustan Aurei and Denarii Attributable to the Mint of Pergamum." *RN* 6, 15 (1973), 129–51.

———. *Coinage and Roman Imperial Policy 31 B.C.–68 A.D.* London, 1958.

———. *Coins and Currency in Roman Britain.* London, 1937.

———. *The Emperor and the Coinage: Julio-Claudian Studies.* London, 1976.

———. "Octavian's Coinage from c. 32 to 27 B.C." *NAC* 5 (1976), 129–58.

———. "Some Observations on the Coinage of Augustus." *NAC* 7 (1978), 163–78.

Wallace-Hadrill, A. "Image and Authority in the Coinage of Augustus." *JRS* 76 (1986), 62–88.

CIVIC AND PROVINCIAL ISSUES

Alexandropoulos, J. "La circulation monétaire en Afrique Proconsulaire de 146 avant J.-C. à la fin du règne de Tibére." *REA* 84 (1982), 96–103.

Amandry, M. *Le monnayage des duovirs corinthiens* BCH Supp. 15. Paris, 1988.

Ashton, R. "Rhodian Coinage in the Early Imperial Period (*CH* 3 82)." In *Recent Turkish Coin Hoards and Numismatic Studies,* ed. C. J. Lightfoot.

British Institute of Archaeology Monograph 12. Oxford, 1991, pp. 71–98.

Aulock, H. von. *Münzen und Städte Lykaoniens.* Tübingen, 1976.

———. *Münzen und Städte Phrygiens.* Vols. 1–2. Tübingen, 1980–87.

———. *Münzen und Städte Pisidiens.* Vols. 1–2. Tübingen, 1977–79.

———. *Die Münzprägung des Gordian III und Tranquillina in Lykien.* Tübingen, 1974.

Bellinger, A. R. *The Excavations at Dura-Europos: Final Report VI: The Coins.* New Haven, 1949.

———. "Greek Mints under the Roman Empire." In *Essays in Roman Coinage Presented to Harold Mattingly,* ed. R. A. G. Carson and C. H. V. Sutherland. Oxford, 1956, pp. 137–48.

———. *The Syrian Tetradrachms of Caracalla and Macrinus.* Numismatic Studies 3. New York, 1940.

Bland, R. "The Last Coinage of Caesarea in Cappadocia." In *Ermanno A. Arslan Studia Dicata,* ed. R. Martini and N. Vismara. Milan, 1991, I, pp. 213–58.

Burnett, A. M., and P. T. Craddock. "Rome and Alexandria: The Minting of Egyptian Tetradrachms under Severus Alexander." *ANSMN* 28 (1983), 109–18.

Butcher, K. "The Colonial Coinage of Antioch-on-the-Orontes, c. A.D. 218–253." *NC* 148 (1988), 63–76.

Buttrey, T. V., Jr. "The Roman Coinage of Cyrenaica, First Century B.C. to the First Century A.D.." In *Studies in Numismatic Method Presented to Philip Grierson,* ed. C. N. L. Brooke, B. H. I. H. Stewart, J. G. Pollard, and T. R. Volk. Cambridge, 1983, pp. 23–42.

Castelin, K. O. *The Coinage of Rhesaena in Mesopotamia.* Numismatic Notes and Monographs 108. New York, 1946.

Christiansen, E. *The Roman Coins of Alexandria: Quantitative Studies.* Vols. 1–2. Aarhus, 1988.

Grunauer-von Hoerschelmann, S. *Die Münzprägung der Lakedaimoner.* Bonn, 1978.

Harl, K. W. "Caracalla or Elagabalus: The Imperial Imago at the Civic Mint of Magnesia ad Maeandrum." *ANSMN* 26 (1981), 163–84.

———. *Civic Coins and Civic Politics in the Roman East, A.D. 180–275.* Berkeley, 1987.

———. "The Coinage of Neapolis in Samaria, A.D. 244–253." *ANSMN* 29 (1984), 61–98.

Howgego, C. J. *Greek Imperial Countermarks: Studies in the Provincial Coinages of the Roman Empire.* Royal Numismatic Society Special Publications 15. New York 1985.

Johnston, A. "Caracalla or Elagabalus? A Case of Unnecessarily Mistaken Identity." *ANSMN* 27 (1982), 97–148.

———. "Die-sharing in Asia Minor: The View from Sardes." *INJ* 6–7 (1982–83), 59–78.

———. "Hierapolis Revisited." *NC* 144 (1984), 52–80.

———. "New Problems for Old: Konrad Kraft on Die-sharing in Asia Minor." *NC* 7, 14 (1974), 203–7.

———. "The So-called Pseudo-autonomous Greek Imperials." *ANSMN* 30 (1985), 89–112.

Jones, T. B. "A Numismatic Riddle: The So-called Greek Imperials." *PAPS* 107 (1963), 308–47.

King, C. E., and D. R. Walker. "The Earliest Tiberian Tetradrachms and Roman Monetary Policy towards Egypt." *ZPE* 21 (1976), 256–69.

Klose, D. *Die Münzprägung von Smyrna in der römischen Kaiserzeit.* Berlin, 1987.

Knapp, R. C. "The Coinage of Corduba, *Colonia Patricia.*" *AIIN* 29 (1982), 183–202.

Kraay, C. M. "The Chronology of the Coinage of Colonia Nemausus." *NC* 6, 15 (1955), 75–96.

———. "Notes on the Early Imperial Tetradrachms of Syria." *RN* 6, 7 (1965), 58–68.

Kraft, K. *Das System der kaiserzeitlichen Münzprägung in Kleinasien.* Berlin, 1972.

Kroll, J. H. "The Eleusis Hoard of Athenian Imperial Coins and Some Deposits from the Athenian Agora." *Hesperia* 42 (1973), 312–33.

Krzyzanowska, A. *Monnaies coloniales d'Antioche de Pisidie.* Warsaw, 1970.

Levick, B. "The Coinage of Pisidian Antioch in the Third Century A.D." *NC* 7, 6 (1966), 47–59.

MacDonald, D. J. *The Coinage of Aphrodisias.* Royal Numismatic Society Special Publications 23. London, 1993.

MacDonald, G. "The Pseudo-Autonomous Coinage of Antioch." *NC* 4, 4 (1904), 105–35.

Melville-Jones, J. "Denarii, Asses and Assaria in the Early Roman Empire." *Bulletin of the Institute of Classical Studies* 18 (1971), 99–105.

Meshorer, Y. *The Coinage of Aelia Capitolina.* Jerusalem, 1989.

———. *Nabataean Coins.* Jerusalem, 1975.

Metcalf, W. E. *The Cistophori of Hadrian.* Numismatic Studies 15. New York, 1980.

———. "A Corrigendum to the Cistophori of Hadrian." *ANSMN* 26 (1981), 185–86.

———. "A Note on Trajan's Latin *Aes* from Antioch." *ANSMN* 22 (1977), 67–70.

———. "The Severan 'Cistophori.'" *RIN* 90 (1988), 155–66.

———. "The Tell Kalak Hoard and Trajan's Arabian Mint." *ANSMN* 20 (1975), 39–108.

Mildenberg, L. *The Coinage of the Bar Kokhba War.* Frankfurt/Main, 1984.

Schönert-Geiss, E. *Die Münzprägung von Byzantion.* Vols. 1–2. Berlin, 1972.

———. *Die Münzprägung von Perinthos.* Vols. 1–2. Berlin, 1966.

Schultz, S. *Die Münzprägung von Magnesia am Mäander in der römischen Kaiserzeit.* Hildesheim, 1975.

Sutherland, C. H. V., N. Olcay, and E. K. Merrington. *The Cistophori of Augustus.* Royal Numismatic Society Special Publications 5. London, 1970.

Svoronos, J. N. *Numismatique de la Crète antique.* Mâcon, 1890.

Sydenham, E. A. *The Coinage of Caesarea in Cappadocia.* With supplement by A. G. Malloy. New York, 1978.

Touratsoglou, I. *Die Münzstätte von Thessaloniki in der römischen Kaisezeit (32/31 v. Chr. bis 268 n. Chr.).* Berlin, 1988.

Vogt, J. *Die alexandrinischen Münzen.* Vols. 1–2. Stuttgart, 1924.

West, L. C., and A. C. Johnson. *Currency in Roman and Byzantine Egypt.* Princeton, 1944.

Wruck, W. *Die syrische Provinzialprägung von Augustus bis Trajan.* Stuttgart, 1931.

Ziegler, R. *Städtisches Prestige und kaiserliche Politik. Studien zum Festwesen in Ostkilikien im 2 und 3 Jahrhundert n. Chr.* Düsseldorf, 1985.

IMPERIAL DEBASEMENT AND REFORM, A.D. 235–498.

Adelson, H. L. "A Note on the Miliarense from Constantine to Heraclius." *ANSMN* 7 (1957), 125–35.

Adelson, H. L., and G. L. Kustas. *A Bronze Hoard of the Period of Zeno.* Numismatic Notes and Monographs 148. New York 1962.

Alföldi, A. "Die Hauptereignisse der Jahren 253–261 n. Chr. im Orient im Spiegel der Münzprägung." *Berytus* 4 (1937), 41–68.

———. "Die römische Münzprägung und die historischen Ereignisse im Osten zwischen 260 und 270 n. Chr." *Berytus* 5 (1938), 47–91.

Amandry, M., J.-N. Barrandon, C. Brenot, J.-P. Callu, and J. Poirier. "L'affinage des métaux monnayés au bas-empire: Les réformes valentinennes de 364–368." *NAC* 11 (1982), 279–95.

Bagnall, R. *Currency and Inflation in Fourth Century Egypt.* BASP Supp. 5. Atlanta, 1985.

Bagnall, R. S., and P. J. Sijesteijn. "Currency in the Fourth Century and the Date of CPR V. 26." ZPE 24 (1977), 111–24.

Baldus, H. R. *Uranius Antoninus. Münzprägung und Geschichte.* Bonn, 1971.

Bastien, P. "Imitations of Roman Bronze Coins, A.D. 318–363." *ANSMN* 30 (1985), 143–77.

———. *Le monnayage de l'atelier de Lyon de la mort de Constantin à la mort de Julien (337–363).* Wetteren, 1985.

———. *Le monnayage de l'atelier de Lyon de la réforme monétaire de Dioclé-*

*tien à la fermeture temporaire de l'atelier en 316 (294–316)*. Wetteren, 1980.

———. *Le monnayage de l'atelier de Lyon du règne de Jovien à la mort de Jovin (363–413)*. Wetteren, 1987.

———. *Le monnayage de l'atelier de Lyon de la réouverture de l'atelier en 318 à la mort de Constantin (318–337)*. Wetteren, 1982.

———. *Le monnayage de l'atelier de Lyon de la réouverture par Aurélien à la mort de Carin*. Wetteren, 1976.

———. *Le monnayage de bronze de Postume*. Wetteren, 1965.

———. *Le monnayage de Magnence (350–353)*. 2nd ed. Wetteren, 1983.

Bastien, P., and H. Huvelin. "Trésor d'antoniniani en Syrie. La *Victoria Parthica* de Valérien. Les Émissions d'Aurélien à Antioche et Tripolis." *RN* 6, 11 (1969), 231–70.

Bastien, P., and C. Metzger. *Le trésor de Beaurains (dit d'Arras)*. Wetteren, 1977.

Besly, E., and R. Bland. *The Cunetio Treasure: Roman Coinage in the Third Century* A.D. London, 1983.

Bolin, S. *State and Currency in the Roman Empire to 300* A.D. Stockholm, 1958.

Brickstock, R. J. *Copies of the Fel. Temp. Reparatio Coinage in Britain: A Study of Their Chronology and Archaeological Significance including Gazetteers of Hoards and Site Finds*. BAR Int. Ser. 1976. Oxford, 1987.

Bruun, P. M. "The Successive Monetary Reforms of Diocletian." *ANSMN* 24 (1979), 129–48.

Burnett, A. M. "The Coinage of Allectus: Chronology and Interpretation." *BNJ* 54 (1984), 21–40.

Buttrey, T. V., Jr. "A Hoard of Sestertii from Bordeaux and the Problem of Bronze Circulation in the Third Century A.D." *ANSMN* 18 (1972), 33–58.

Callu, J.-P. "Approches numismatiques de l'histoire du IIIe siècle (238 à 311)." *ANRW* 2;2 (Berlin, 1975), 594–613.

———. "Denier et nummus (303–354)." In *Les dévaluations à Rome* I. Rome, 1978, 107–21.

———. "Frappes et trésors d'argent de 324 à 392." In *Imperial Revenue, Expenditure and Monetary Policy in the Fourth Century* A.D., ed. C. E. King. BAR Int. Ser. 76. Oxford, 1980, pp. 175–254.

———. *La politique monétaire des empereurs romains de 238 à 311*. Paris, 1969.

———. "Rôle et distribution des éspèces de bronze de 348 à 392." In *Imperial Revenue, Expenditure and Monetary Policy in the Fourth Century* A.D., ed. C. E. King. BAR Int. Ser. 76. Oxford, 1980, pp. 41–125.

Carrié, J.-M. "Monnaie d'or et monnaie de bronze dans l'Égypte protobyzantine." In *Les dévaluations à Rome* II. Rome, 1980, pp. 253–70.

———. "Papyrologica Numismatica." *Aegyptus* 64 (1984), 203–27.

Carson, R. G. A. "The Hamâ Hoard and the Eastern Mints of Valerian and Gallienus." *Berytus* 17 (1967), 123–42.

———. "Mints in the Mid-Third Century." In *Scripta Nummaria Romana: Essays Presented to Humphrey Sutherland,* ed. R. A. G. Carson and C. M. Kraay. London, 1978, pp. 65–74.

Christol, M. "Effort de guerre et atelier monétaire de la périphérie au III siècle ap. J.C.: L'atelier de Cologne sous Valérien et Gallien." In *Armées et fiscalité dans le monde antique, Paris, 14–16 octobre 1976.* Colloques Nationaux du Centre National de la Recherche Scientifique 936. Paris, 1977, pp. 235–77.

Crawford, M. H. "Finance, Coinage and Money from the Severans to Constantine." *ANRW* 2, 2 (Berlin, 1975), 560–93.

Crawford, M. H., and J. M. Reynolds. "The Aezani Copy of the Prices Edict." *ZPE* 34 (1979), 163–210.

Crawford, M. H., and J. M. Reynolds. "The Publication of the Prices Edict: A New Inscription from Aezani." *JRS* 65 (1975), 160–63.

Drinkwater, J. F. "Coin-hoards and the Chronology of the Gallic Empire." *Britannia* 5 (1974), 293–303.

———. *The Gallic Empire: Separatism and Continuity in the North-Western Provinces of the Roman Empire* A.D. *260–274.* Stuttgart, 1987.

Eddy, S. K. *The Minting of Antoniniani* A.D. *238–249 and the Smyrna Hoard.* Numismatic Notes and Monographs 156. New York, 1967.

Elks, K. J. J. "The Eastern Mints of Valerian and Gallienus: The Evidence of Two New Hoards from Western Turkey." *NC* 7, 15 (1975), 91–109.

Erim, K. T., J. Reynolds, and M. H. Crawford. "Diocletian's Currency Reform: A New Inscription." *JRS* 67 (1977), 171–77.

Gallwey, H. D. "A Hoard of Third-Century Antoniniani from Southern Spain." *NC* 7, 2 (1962), 335–406.

Haley, E. "The Roman Bronze Coinage in Britain and Monetary History from A.D. 293 to 350." *AJN* 1 (1989), 89–116.

Harl, K. W. "The Meaning of Value Marks on Tetrarchic Nummi and Diocletian's Monetary Policy." *Phoenix* 39 (1985), 263–70.

Hendy, M. *Studies in the Byzantine Monetary Economy, c. 300–1453.* Cambridge, 1985.

Hill, P. V. *Barbarous Radiates. Imitations of Third Century Roman Coins.* Numismatic Notes and Monographs 112. New York, 1949.

Kent, J. P. C. "Gold Coinage in the Late Roman Empire." In *Essays in Roman Coinage Presented to Harold Mattingly,* ed. R. A. G. Carson and C. H. V. Sutherland. Oxford, 1956, pp. 190–204.

King, C. E. "Denarii and Quinarii, A.D. 253–295." In *Scripta Nummaria Romana: Essays Presented to Humphrey Sutherland,* ed. R. A. G. Carson and C. M. Kraay. London, 1978, pp. 75–104.

———. "Fifth Century Coinage in the Western Roman Empire: The Usurpations in Spain and Gaul." In *Mélanges de numismatique offerts à Pierre Bastien à l'occasion de son 75e anniversaire,* ed. H. Huvelin, M. Christol, and G. Gautier. Wetteren, 1987, pp. 363–73.

———. "Fifth Century Silver Issues in Gaul." In *Studia Numismatica Labacensia Alexandro Jeločnik oblata,* ed. P. Kos and Z. Demo. *Situla* 26. Ljubjlana, 1988, pp. 197–211.

———. "A Hoard of Clipped Siliquae in the Preston Museum." *NC* 7, 21 (1981), 40–64.

———. ed. *Imperial Revenue, Expenditure and Monetary Policy in the Fourth Century* A.D. BAR Int. Ser. 76. Oxford, 1980.

Lafaurie, J. "La chronologie des empereurs gaulois." *RN* 6, 6 (1964), 91–127.

———. "Les denières émissions impériales à Trèves au 5e siècle." In *Mélanges de numismatique offerts à Pierre Bastien de l'occasion de son 75e anniversaire,* ed. H. Huvelin, M. Christol, and G. Gautier. Wetteren, 1987, pp. 297–323.

———. "Monnaies de Tacite, Carus et Carin, marquées XI, XII, IA." *BSFN* 29 (1974), 666–69.

———. "Réforms monétaires d'Aurélien et de Dioclétien." *RN* 6, 17 (1975), 73–138.

Mattingly, H. "The Coinage of Macrianus II and Quietus." *NC* 6, 14 (1954), 53–61.

———. "The Palmyrene Princes and the Mints of Antioch and Alexandria." *NC* 5, 16 (936), 89–114.

Metcalf, W. E. "The Antioch Hoard of Antoniniani and the Eastern Coinage of Trebonianus Gallus and Volusian." *ANSMN* 22 (1977), 71–94; and 223 (1978), 129–32.

Schulte, B. *Die Goldprägung der gallischen Kaiser von Postumus bis Tetricus.* Frankfurt/Main, 1983.

Shiel, N. *The Episode of Carausius and Allectus.* BAR Br. Ser. 40. Oxford, 1977.

Tyler, P. *The Persian Wars of the 3rd Century* A.D. *and Roman Imperial Monetary Policy* A.D. *253–56. Historia* Einzelschriften 23. Wiesbaden, 1975.

Voetter, O. "Die Münzen der Kaisers Gallienus und seine Familie." *NZ* 32 (1900), 117–47; and 33 (1901), 73–110.

———. "Valerianus Junior und Saloninus." *NZ* 39 (1908), 69–101.

BYZANTIUM AND THE MEDIEVAL WEST, A.D. 400–700

Adelson, H. L. *Light Weight Solidi and Byzantine Trade during the Sixth and Seventh Centuries.* Numismatic Notes and Monographs 138. New York, 1957.

———. "A Note on the Miliarense from Constantine to Heraclius." *ANSMN* 7 (1957), 125–35.

———. "Silver Currency and Values in the Early Byzantine Empire." In *Centennial Publication of the American Numismatic Society*, ed. H. Ingholt. New York, 1958, pp. 1–26.

Barral y Altet, X. *La circulation des monnaies suèves et visigotiques: Contribution à l'histoire économique de royaume visigot. Francia* Supp. 4. Munich, 1976.

Carrié, J.-M. "Monnaie d'or et monnaie de bronze dans l'Égypte proto-byzantine." In *Les dévaluations à Rome* II. 1980, pp. 253–69.

Grierson, P. *Byzantine Coins.* Berkeley, 1982.

———. "Coinage and Money in the Byzantine Empire, 498–c. 1090." *Moneta e scambi nell'alto medioevo* 8 (1980), 411–53.

———. *Dark Age Numismatics.* London, 1970.

———. "The Monetary Reforms of 'Abd al-Malik, their Metrological Basis and their Financial Repercussions." *JESHO* 3 (1960), 241–64.

———. "The Monetary Reforms of Anastasius and their Economic Consequences." In *Proceedings of the International Numismatic Convention, Jerusalem, 27–31 December 1963*, ed. A. Kindler and C. H. V. Sutherland. Jerusalem, 1967, pp. 283–302.

———. "The *Patrimonium in illis partibus* and the Pseudo-Imperial Coinage in Frankish Gaul." *RBN* 105 (1959), 95–111.

———. "The *Tablettes Albertini* and the Value of the Solidus in the Fifth and Sixth Centuries A.D." *JRS* 49 (1959), 73–80.

———. "Visigothic Metrology," *NC* 6, 13 (1953), 74–87.

Grierson, P., and M. Blackburn. *Medieval European Coins with a Catalogue of the Coins in the Fitzwilliam Museum, Cambridge I: The Early Middle Ages (5th–10th Centuries).* Cambridge, 1988.

Hahn, W. *Emission und Lustrum in der byzantinischen Münzprägung des 6. Jahrhunderts.* Österreichliche Akademie der Wissenschaften, phil.-hist. Klasse 108. Vienna, 1971.

Hahn, W., and W. E. Metcalf, eds. *Studies in Early Byzantine Gold Coinage.* Numismatic Studies 17. New York, 1988.

Hendy, M. "Light Weight Solidi, Tetartera, and the Book of the Prefect." *BZ* 65 (1972), 57–80.

———. *Studies in the Byzantine Monetary Economy, c. 300–1453.* Cambridge, 1985.

Kent, J. P. C. "The Coinage of Theodoric in the Names of Anastasius and Justin I." In *Mints, Dies and Currency: Essays Dedicated to the Memory of Albert Baldwin*, ed. R. A. G. Carson. London, 1971, pp. 67–74.

King, C. E. "Fifth Century Silver Issues in Gaul." In *Studia Numismatica Labacensia Alexandro Jeločnik oblata*, ed. P. Kos and Z. Demo. *Situla* 26. Ljubjlana, 1988, pp. 197–212.

———. "Roman, Local and Barbarian Coinages in Fifth Century Gaul." In *Fifth-Century Gaul: A Crisis of Identity*, ed. J. Drinkwater and F. H. Elton. Cambridge, 1992, pp. 184–95.

Lafaurie, J. "Monnaies d'argent mérovingiennes des VIe et VIII siècles." *RN* 6, 11 (1969), 98–219.

Lafaurie, J., and C. Morrisson. "La pénetration des monnaies byzantines en Gaule mérovingienne et visgotique de VIe à VIIIe siècle." *RN* 6, 29 (1987), 38–98.

Le Gentilhomme, P. "Le monnayage et la circulation monétaire dans le royaumes barbares en occident (Ve–VIIIe siècle)." *RN* 5, 7 (1943), 45–112; and 5, 8 (1948), 13–59.

Metcalf, D. M. *The Copper Coinage of Thessalonica under Justinian I.* Vienna, 1976.

———. "North Italian Coinage Carried across the Alps: The Ostrogothic and Carolingian Evidence Compared." *RIN* 90 (1988), 449–56.

———. *The Origins of the Anastasian Coinage Reform.* Amsterdam, 1969.

Metcalf, W. E. "Three Seventh-Century Byzantine Gold Hoards." *ANSMN* 25 (1980), 87–108.

Miles, G. C. *The Coinage of the Visigoths of Spain: Leovigild to Achila II.* Hispanic Numismatic Studies 2. New York, 1952.

Morrisson, C. "La trouvaille d'Aïn Kelba et la circulation des *minimi* en Afrique au début du VIe siècle." In *Mélanges de numismatique, d'archéologie et d'histoire offerts à Jean Lafaurie*, ed. P. Bastien, F. Dumas, H. Huvelin, and C. Morrisson. Paris, 1980, pp. 239–48

Morrisson, C., and J. H. Schwartz. "Vandal Silver Coinage in the Name of Honorius." *ANSMN* 27 (1982), 149–80.

Spufford, P. *Money and Its Use in Medieval Europe.* Cambridge, 1988.

Stahl, A. M. *The Merovingian Coinage of the Region of Metz.* Louvain-la-Neuve, 1982.

Tomasini, W. H. *The Barbaric Tremissis in Spain and Southern France: Anastasius to Leovigild.* Numismatic Notes and Monographs 152. New York, 1964.

Ulrich-Bansa, O. *Moneta Mediolanensis.* Venice, 1949.

Walker, J. A. *Catalogue of the Arab-Byzantine and Post-Reform Umaiyad Coins in the British Museum.* Vols. 1–2. London, 1956.

———. *Catalogue of the Arab-Sasanian Coins in the British Museum.* Vols. 1–2. London, 1941.

Yannopoulos, P. A. *L'hexagramme, un monnayage byzantin en argent du VII siècle.* Louvain, 1978.

*Coins and Fiscal Demands*

MONETARY POLICY AND MINT ORGANIZATION

Alföldi, M. R. "Epigraphische Beiträge zur römischen Münztechnik bis auf Konstantin den Grossen." *RSN* 30 (1958–59), 35–88.

Carson, R. G. A. "System and Product in the Roman Mint." In *Essays in Roman Coinage Presented to Harold Mattingly,* ed. R. A. G. Carson and C. H. V. Sutherland. London, 1956, pp. 229–39.

Fulford, M. "Coin Circulation and Mint Activity in the Late Roman Empire." *Archaeological Journal* 135 (1978), 67–114.

Grierson, P. "The Roman Law of Counterfeiting." In *Essays in Roman Coinage Presented to Harold Mattingly*, ed. R. A. G. Carson and C. H. V. Sutherland. London, 1956, pp. 440–61.

Hendy, M. "Aspects of Coin Production and Fiscal Administration in the Late Roman and Early Byzantine Period." *NC* 7, 12 (1972), 117–39.

———. "Mint and Fiscal Administration under Diocletian, His Colleges, and His Successors, A.D. 305–324." *JRS* 62 (1972), 75–82.

———. "On the Administrative Basis of the Byzantine Coinage, c. 400–c. 900 and the Reform of Heraclius." *University of Birmingham Historical Journal* 12 (1970), 129–54.

Jones, A. H. M. "Inflation under the Roman Empire." *EcHR* 2, 5 (1952–53), 293–318.

King, C. E. "The *Sacrae Largitiones:* Revenues, Expenditure, and the Production of Coin." In *Imperial Revenues, Expenditure and Monetary Policy in the Fourth Century A.D.*, ed. C. E. King. BAR Int. Ser. 76. Oxford, 1980, pp. 141–73.

Lo Cascio, E. "State and Coinage in the Late Republic and Early Empire." *JRS* 71 (1981), 76–86.

———. "Teoria e politica monetaria a Roma tra III e IV d.C." In *Società romana e imperio tardoantico: istituzioni, ceti, economie,* ed. A. Giardina. Rome, 1986, pp. 535–58.

MacDowall, D. W. "The Organization of the Julio-Claudian Mint at Rome." In *Scripta Romana Nummaria: Essays Presented to Humphrey Sutherland,* ed. R. A. G. Carson and C. M. Kraay. London, 1976, pp. 32–46.

Mattingly, H. B. "The Management of the Roman Republican Mint," *AIIN* 29 (1982), 9–46.

Metcalf, D. M. "Organization of the Constantinople Mint for the Follis of the Anastasian Reform." *NC* 7, 1 (1961), 131–43.

Metcalf, W. E. "The Coinage of Otho and Early Mint Organisation." In *Essays in Honour of G. K. Jenkins and R. A. G. Carson,* ed. A. M. Burnett and M. J. Price (London, 1993), pp. 155–60.

———. "Rome and Lugdunum Again. *AJN* 1 (1989), 51–70.

Nicholet, C. "Pline, Paul et la théorie de la monnaie." *Athenaeum* 62 (1984), 105–35.

STATE BUDGET AND EXPENDITURES

Andréadès, A. M. "Le montant du budget de l'empire byzantin." *REG* 34 (1921), 20–56.

*Armées et fiscalité dans le monde antique, Paris 14–16 octobre 1976.* Colloques Nationaux du Centre National de la Recherche Scientfiique 936. Paris, 1977.

Bastien, P. *Monnaie et donativa au Bas-Empire.* Numismatique Romaine 17. Wetteren, 1988.

Berchem, D. van. *Les distributions de blé et argent à la plèbe romaine dans l'empire.* Paris, 1939.

Brunt, P. A. *Italian Manpower, 225 B.C.–A.D. 14,* Oxford, 1971.

———. "Pay and Superannuation in the Roman Army." *PBSR* 18 (1950), 50–71.

Carradice, I. *Coinage and Finances in the Reign of Domitian A.D. 81–96.* BAR Int. Ser. 178. Oxford, 1973.

Carrié, J.-M. "Le rôle économique de l'armée dans l'Égypte romaine." In *Armées et fiscalité dans le monde antique, Paris 14–16 octobre 1976.* Colloques Nationaux du Centre National de la Recherche Scientifique 936. Paris, 1977, pp. 373–94.

Chastagnol, A. "Remarques sur les salaries de rémuneration de IVe siècle." In *Les dévaluations à Rome* II. Rome, 1980, 215–33.

Corbier, M. "Dévaluations et fiscalité." In *Les dévaluations à Rome* I. Rome, 1978, pp. 273–309.

———. "Salaries et salariat sous le Haut-Empire." In *Les dévaluations à Rome* II. Rome, 1980, pp. 61–101.

Crawford, M. H. "The Financial Organization of Republican Spain." *NC* 7, 9 (1969), 79–93.

Delmaire, P. "La caisse de largesses sacrées et l'armée au Bas-Empire." In *Armées et fiscalité dans le monde antique, Paris 14–16 octobre 1976.* Colloques Nationaux du Centre National de la Recherche Scientifique 936. Paris, 1977, pp. 311–30.

*Les dévalulations à Rome: Époque républicaine et impériale.* Vols. 1–2. Rome, 1978–80.

Develin, R. "The Army Pay Rises under Severus and Caracalla, and the Question of the *Annona Militaris.*" *Latomus* 30 (1971), 687–95.

Duncan-Jones, R. P. *Money and Government in the Roman Empire.* Cambridge, 1994.

———. "Pay and Numbers in Diocletian's Army." *Chiron* 6 (1976), 241–62.

———. *Structure and Scale in the Roman Economy.* Cambridge, 1990.

Hendy, M. *Studies in the Byzantine Monetary Economy, c. 300–1453.* Cambridge, 1985.

Hopkins, K. "Taxes and Trade in the Roman Economy, 200 B.C.–A.D. 400." *JRS* 70 (1980), 101–25.

MacMullen, R. "Emperor's Largesse." *Latomus* 21 (1962), 159–66.

———. "How Big Was the Roman Army?" *Klio* 62 (1980), 451–60.

———. "The Roman Emperor's Army Costs." *Latomus* 43 (1984), 571–80.

Nicolet, C. *Tributum: Recherches sur la fiscalité directe du citoyen romain à l'époque republicaine.* Antiquitas 24. Bonn, 1976.

———. "Le stipendium des alliés italiens avant la Guerre Sociale." *PBRS* 46 (1978), 1–11.

Richardson, J. S. "The Spanish Mines and the Development of Provincial Taxation in the Second Century B.C.." *JRS* 66 (1976), 139–52.

Teall, J. L. "The Barbarians in Justinian's Armies." *Speculum* 40 (1965), 294–323.

Wierschowski, L. *Heer und Wirtschaft: Das römische Heer der Prinzipatszeit al Wirtschaftsfaktor.* Bonn, 1984.

TAXATION

Bagnall, R. S., and P. J. Sijpesteijn. "Currency in the Fourth Century and the Date of *CPR* V. 26." *ZPE* 24 (1977), 111–24.

Brunt, P. A. "The Revenues of Rome." *JRS* 71 (1981), 161–72.

Day, J., and C. W. Keyes. *Tax Documents from Theadelphia.* New York, 1956.

Déléagre, A. *La capitation du Bas-Empire.* Nancy, 1945.

Goffart, W. *Caput and Colonate: Towards a History of Late Roman Taxation. Phoenix* Supplement 12. Toronto, 1974.

Karayannopulos, J. *Das Finanzwesen des frühbyzantinischen Staates.* Munich, 1958.

Laet, S. J. de. *Portorium: Étude sur l'organisation douanière chez les Romains surtout à époque du haut-empire.* Bruges, 1949.

MacMullen, R. "Some Tax Statistics from Roman Egypt." *Aegyptus* 42 (1962), 98–102.

Neesen, L. *Untersuchungen zu den direkten Staatsabgaben der römischen Kaiserzeit.* Berlin, 1980.

Samuel, D. H. "Taxation at Socnopaiou Nesos in the Early Third Century." *BSAP* 14 (1977), 161–207.

Sijpesteijn, P. J. *Customs Duties in Greco-Roman Egypt.* Zutphen, 1987.

Skeat, T. C. *Papyri from Panopolis in the Chester Beatty Library, Dublin.* Dublin, 1964.

Wallace, S. L. *Taxation in Egypt from Augustus to Diocletian.* Princeton, 1938.

Westermann, W. L., and C. W. Keyes. *Tax Lists and Transportation Receipts from Theadelphia.* New York, 1932.

Wilhelm, A. "Urkunden aus Messene." *JOAI* 17 (1914), 48–71.

Youtie, H. C. "A Problem of Graeco-Roman Bookkeeping." *ZPE* 15 (1974), 117–41.

———. *Tax Rolls from Karanis* I. Michigan Papyri vol. 4, Part 1. Ann Arbor, Mich., 1936.

Youtie, H. C., and O. M. Pearl. *Tax Rolls from Karanis*. Michigan Papyri vol. 4, Part 2. Ann Arbor, Mich., 1939.

*Coins and Economic Life*

COINS IN MARKETS

Andreau, J. *Les affairs de Monsieur Jucundus*. Collection de l'École française de Rome 19. Rome, 1974.

———. *La vie financière dans le monde romain: Les métiers des manieux d'argent (IV siècle av. J.-C.–III siècle ap. J.-C.)*. Bibliothèque des Écoles françaises d'Athènes et Rome 265. Rome, 1987.

Bagnall, R. S. "Agricultural Productivity and Taxation in the Later Roman Empire." *TAPA* 115 (1985), 289–308.

Balland, A. *Fouilles de Xanthos* VII. *Inscriptions d'époque impériale de Létôon*. Paris, 1981.

Barnish, S. J. B. "The Wealth of Julianus Argentarius: Late Antique Banking and the Mediterranean Economy." *Byzantion* 55 (1985), 5–38.

Bogaert, R. *Banques et banquiers dans les cités grecques*. Leiden, 1968.

———. "Changeurs et banquiers chez les Pères de l'Église." *Ancient Society* 4 (1973), 239–70.

Bowman, A. K. "The Economy of Egypt in the Earlier Fourth Century." In *Imperial Revenue, Expenditure and Monetary Policy in the Fourth Century*, ed. C. E. King. BAR Int. Ser. 76. Oxford, 1980, pp. 23–40.

Carrié, J.-M. "Les distributions alimentaires dans les cités de l'empire romain tardif." *MEFR* 87 (1975), 995–1101.

Coulton, J. J. "Opramoas and the Anonymous Benefactor." *JHS* 107 (1987), 171–78.

Crawford, M. "Money and Exchange in the Roman World." *JRS* 60 (1970), 40–48.

Duncan-Jones, R. P. *The Economy of the Roman Empire: Quantitative Studies*. 2nd ed. Cambridge, 1982.

———. "Mobility and Immobility of Coin in the Roman Empire." *AIIN* 36 (1989), 121–37.

———. *Structure and Scale in the Roman Economy*. Cambridge, 1990.

Fulford, M. G. "Coin Circulation and Mint Activity in the Late Roman Empire: Some Economic Implications." *Archaeological Journal* 135 (1978), 67–114.

Garnsey, P. A., and C. R. Whittaker, eds. *Trade and Famine in Classical Antiquity*. Cambridge Phil. Soc. Supp. Papers 8. Cambridge, 1983.

Goldsmith, R. W. "An Estimate of the Size and Structure of the National Product of the Early Roman Empire." *Review of Income and Wealth* 30 (1984), 263–88.

Greene, K. *The Archaeology of the Roman Economy.* Berkeley, 1986.

Hendy, M. *Studies in the Byzantine Monetary Economy, c. 300–1453.* Cambridge, 1985.

Hopkins, K. "Taxes and Trade in the Roman Empire, 200 B.C.–A.D. 400." *JRS* 70 (1980), 101–25.

Howgego, C. "The Supply and Use of Money in the Roman Empire 200 B.C. to A.D. 300." *JRS* 81 (1991), 76–86.

Jouffroy, H. *La construction publique en Italie et dans l'Afrique romaine.* Strasbourg, 1986.

Klimowsky, E. W. "The Monetary Function of City Coins." In *Proceedings of the International Numismatic Convention, Jerusalem, 27–31 December 1963,* ed. A. Kindler and C. H. V. Sutherland. Jerusalem, 1967, pp. 129–79.

Laum, B. *Stiftungen in der griechischen und römischen Antike.* Vols. 1–2. Leipzig, 1914.

MacMullen, R. "Roman Market Days." *Phoenix* 24 (197), 333–41.

Millar, F. "The World of the Golden Ass." *JRS* 71 (1981), 63–75.

Mitchell, S. "Festivals, Games, and Civic Life in Roman Asia Minor." *JRS* 80 (1990), 183–93.

Patlagean, E. *Pauvreté économique et pauvreté sociale à Byzance, 4ème–7ème siècles.* Paris, 1977.

Pekáry, T. "Les limites de l'économie monétaire à l'époque romaine." In *Les dévaluations à Rome* II. Rome, 1980, pp. 103–30.

Reece, R. "The Use of Roman Coinage." *Oxford Journal of Archaeology* 5 (1984), 197–210.

Whittaker, C. R. "Trade and the Aristocracy of the Roman Empire." *Opus* 4 (1985), 49–75.

Wipszyeka, E. *Les resources et les activités économiques des églises en Égypte du IVe au VIIIe siècles.* Brussels, 1974.

PRICES AND WAGES

Bagnall, R. S. *Currency and Inflation in Fourth Century Egypt.* BASP Supp. 5, 1985.

Callu, J.-P. "Les prix dans deux romans mineurs d'époque impériale: Historie d'Apollonius roi de Tyr—Vie d'Ésope." In *Les dévaluations à Rome* II. Rome, 1980, pp. 187–214.

Carrié, J.-M. "Monnaie d'or et monnaie de bronze dans l'Égypte protobyzantine." In *Les dévaluations à Rome* II. Rome, 1980, pp. 253–69.

Casson, L. "Wine Measures and Prices in Byzantine Egypt." *TAPA* 70 (1939), 1–16.

Coles, R. "Comparative Commodity Prices." In *The Oxyrhynchus Papyri* LIV. London, 1987, Appendix III, pp. 232–40.

Corbier, M. "Dévaluations et évolution des prix (1er–IIIe siècles)." *RN* 6, 27 (1985), 69–106.

Courtois, C., L. Leschi, C. Perrat, and C. Saumage. *Tablettes Albertini: Actes privées de l'époque vandale (fin du Ve siècle)*. Paris, 1952.

Duncan-Jones, R. P. "The Price of Wheat in Roman Egypt under the Principate." *Chiron* 6 (1976), 241–62.

Foxhall, L., and H. A. Forbes. "*Sitometria*: The Role of Grain as a Staple Food in Classical Antiquity." *Chiron* 12 (1982), 41–89.

Frézouls, E. "Prix, salaries et niveaux de vie: Quelques enseignements de l'Edit du Maximum." *Ktema* 3 (1978), 291–300.

Garnsey, P. *Famine and Food Supply in the Graeco-Roman World: Responses to Risk and Crises*. (Cambridge, 1988).

Irmscher, J. "Einiges über Löhne und Preise im justinianischen Reich." In *Les dévaluations à Rome* II. Rome, 1980, pp. 245–52.

Johnson, A. C., and L. C. West. *Byzantine Egypt: Economic Studies*. Princeton, 1949.

Lendon, J. E. "The Face on the Coins and Inflation in Roman Egypt." *Klio* 72 (1990), 100–34.

Mickwitz, G. *Geld und Wirtschaft im römischen Reich des vierten Jahrhunderts n. Chr.* Helsinki, 1932.

Mrozek, S. "Zu den Priesen und Löhnen bei Lukien." *Eos* 59 (1971), 231–39.

Ostrogorsky, G. "Löhne und Preise in Byzanz." *BZ* 32 (1932), 293–333.

Schwartz, J. *Les archives de Sarapion et de ses fils: Une exploitation agricole aux environs d'Hermoupolis Magna (de 90 à 133 p.C.* Cairo, 1961.

———. "La monnaie et l'évolution des prix en Égypte romaine." In *Les dévaluations à Rome* I. Rome, 1978, pp. 169–79.

———. "Recherches sur l'évolution des prix en Égypte romaine." In *Les dévaluations à Rome* II. Rome, 1980, pp. 141–53.

Sperber, D. "Costs of Living in Roman Palestine." *JESHO* 8 (1965), 248–71; 9 (1966), 182–211; 11 (1968), 235–74; and 13 (1970), 1–15.

———. *Roman Palestine 200–400 A.D.: Money and Prices*. Ramat-Gan, 1974.

Straus, J. A. "Le prix des esclaves dans les papyrus d'époque romaine trouvées dans l'Égypte." *ZPE* 11 (1973), 289–95.

Szilágyi, J. "Prices and Wages in the Western Provinces of the Roman Empire." *Acta Antiqua* 11 (1963), 325–89.

Zehnacker, H. "Monnaies de compte et prix à Rome au IIe siècle avant notre ère." In *Les dévaluations à Rome* II. Rome, 1980, pp. 31–48.

*Coins and Long Distance Trade*

COINS AND TRADE IN THE MEDITERRANEAN WORLD

Crawford, M. H. "Rome and the Greek World: Economic Relationships." *EcHR* 2, 30 (1977), 42–52.

Garnsey, P., and C. R. Whittaker, eds. *Trade and Famine in Classical Antiquity.* Cambridge Phil. Soc. Supp. Papers 8. Cambridge, 1983.

Grierson, P. "Commerce in the Dark Ages: A Critique of the Evidence." *TRHS* 5, 9 (1959), 123–40.

Lopez, R. S. "The Dollar of the Middle Ages." *JEH* 11 (1951), 209–34.

Wickham, C. "Review Article: Marx, Sherlock Holmes and Late Roman Commerce." *JRS* 78 (1988), 190–93.

COINS AND TRADE IN NORTHERN EUROPE

Bichar, G. *The Archaeology and History of the Carpi from the Second to the Fourth Century* A.D., trans. N. Hampartumian. BAR Supp. Ser. 16. Oxford, 1976.

Bolin, S. *Fynden av romerska mynt i det fria Germanien.* Lund, 1926.

Brogan, G. "Trade between the Roman Empire and the Free Germans." *JRS* 26 (1936), 195–222.

Chitescu, M. *Numismatic Aspects of the History of the Dacian State: The Roman Republican Coinage in Dacia and Geto-Dacian Coins of Roman Type.* BAR Int. Ser. 112. Oxford, 1981.

Crawford, M. H. "Republican Denarii in Romania: The Suppression of Piracy and the Slave-Trade." *JRS* 67 (1977), 117–24.

Eggers, H. J. *Der römische Import im freien Germanien.* Hamburg, 1951.

Fagerlie, J. M. *Late Roman and Byzantine Solidi Found in Sweden and Denmark.* Numismatic Notes and Monographs 157. New York, 1967.

Glodariu, I. *Dacian Trade with the Hellenistic and Roman World.* BAR Supp. Ser. 8, Oxford, 1976.

Hansen, U. L. *Römischer Import im Norden: Warenaustausch zwischen dem römischen Reich und dem freien Germanien während der Kaiserzeit unter besondere Berücksichtigung Nordeuropas.* Copenhagen, 1987.

Hedeager, L. "A Quantitative Analysis of Roman Imports in Europe North of the Limes (0–400 A.D.)." In *New Directions in Scandinavian Archaeology,* ed. K. Kristiansen and C. Palaudan-Muller. Lyngby, 1977, pp. 191–216.

Iluk, J. "The Export of Gold from the Roman Empire to Barbarian Countries from the 4th to the 6th Centuries." *Münsterische Beiträge zur antiken Handelsgeschichte* 4, 1 (1985), 79–102.

Künow, J. *Negotiator et Vectura: Händler und Transport im freien Germanien.* Marburg, 1980.

Pitts, L. F. "Relations between Romans and the German 'Kings' on the

Middle Danube in the First to Fourth Century A.D." *JRS* 79 (1989), 45–58.
Wheeler, R. E. M. *Rome Beyond the Imperial Frontiers.* London, 1954.
Winkler, J. "Schatzfunde römischer Silbermünzen in Dakien bis zum Beginn der Dakerkriege." *JNG* 17 (1967), 123–56.

COINS AND TRADE IN AFRICA AND THE EAST

Carson, R. A. G. "Late Roman and Early Byzantine Solidi from India." *Numismatic Digest* 4, 2 (1980), 20–23.
Casson, L., ed. and trans. *The Periplus Maris Erythraei.* Princeton, 1989.
Charlesworth, M. P. "Roman Trade with India." In *Studies in Roman Economic and Social History in Honor of Allan Chester Johnson,* ed. P. R. Coleman-Norton, F. C. Bourne, and J. V. A. Fine. Princeton, 1951, pp. 129–42.
Codrington, H. W. *Ceylon Coins and Currency: Memoirs of the Colombo Museum,* ed. J. Person. Series A, no. 3. Colombo, 1924.
Hill, G. F. "A Hoard of Coins from Nineveh." *NC* 5, 11 (1931), 160–70.
———. "Roman Aurei from Pudukota, South India." *NC* 3, 18 (1898), 304–20.
Hirth, F. *China and Rome.* Shanghai, 1885.
MacDowell, D. W. "The Weight Standards of Gold and Copper Coinages of the Kushana Dynasty from Vima Kadphises to Vasudeva." *JNSI* 22 (1960), 63–74.
McDowell, R. H. *Coins from Seleucia on the Tigris.* Ann Arbor, Mich., 1935.
Matthews, J. T. "The Tax-Law of Palmyra: Evidence for the Economic History in a City of the Roman East." *JRS* 74 (1984), 157–80.
Miller, J. I. *The Spice Trade of the Roman Empire 29 B.C. to A.D. 641.* Oxford, 1969.
Mitterwallner, G. von. *Münzen der späten Kusanas, des Hunnen Kirada/Kidara und der frühen Gupta.* Munich, 1983.
Mørkholm, O. "The Parthian Coinage of Seleucia on the Tigris, ca. 90–55 B.C." *NC* 7, 2 (1980), 33–47.
Munro-Hay, S. C. H. "The al-Madhariba Hoard of Gold Aksumite and Late Roman Coins." *NC* 149 (1989), 83–100.
———. *The Munro-Hay Collection of Aksumite Coins.* Naples, 1986.
Munro-Hay, S. C. H., W. A. Oddy, and M. R. Cowell. "The Gold Coinage of Aksum: New Analyses and Their Significance for Chronology." In *Metallurgy in Numismatics,* ed. W. A. Oddy. Royal Numismatic Society Special Publications 19. London, 1988, II, pp. 1–16.
Nodelman, S. A. "A Preliminary History of Characene." *Berytus* 3 (1960), 83–120.
Raschke, M. G. "New Studies in Roman Commerce in the East." *ANRW* 2, 9, 2 (Berlin, 1978), 604–1361.

Sellwood, D. G. "The Parthian Coins of Gotarzes I, Orodes I and Sinatruces." *NC* 7, 2 (1962), 73–89.

Sewell, R. "Roman Coins Found in India." *Journal of the Royal Asiatic Society* 17 (1904), 591–637.

Sidebotham, S. E. *Roman Economic Policy in the Erythraean Thalassa, 30 B.C.–A.D. 217*. Leiden, 1986.

Simonetta, A. M. "Some Remarks on the Arsacid Coinage of the Period 90–57 B.C." *NC* 7, 6 (1966), 15–40.

Simonetta, A. M., and D. G. Sellwood. "Again on the Parthian Coinage from Mithridates II to Orodes II." *NAC* 7 (1978), 95–119.

Still, J. "Roman Coins Found in Ceylon." *Journal of Royal Asiatic Society (Ceylon)* 19 (1907), 161–90.

Turner, P. J. *Roman Coins from India*. Royal Numismatic Society Special Publications 22. London, 1989.

Yarshater, E., ed. *The Cambridge History of Iran* III. 1–2: *The Seleucid, Parthian and Sasanian Periods*. London, 1983.

Ying-shih Yu. *Trade and Expansion in Han China*. Berkeley, 1967.

# Index

ANCIENT SOCIETY AND HISTORY

The series Ancient Society and History offers books, relatively brief in compass, on selected topics in the history of ancient Greece and Rome, broadly conceived, with a special emphasis on comparative and other nontraditional approaches and methods. The series, which includes both works of synthesis and works of original scholarship, is aimed at the widest possible range of specialist and nonspecialist readers.

*Published in the Series:*

Eva Cantarella, *Pandora's Daughters: The Role and Status of Women in Greek and Roman Antiquity*
Alan Watson, *Roman Slave Law*
John E. Stambaugh, *The Ancient Roman City*
Géza Alföldy, *The Social History of Rome*
Giovanni Comotti, *Music in Greek and Roman Culture*
Christian Habicht, *Cicero the Politician*
Mark Golden, *Children and Childhood in Classical Athens*
Thomas Cole, *The Origins of Rhetoric in Ancient Greece*
Maurizio Bettini, *Anthropology and Roman Culture: Kinship, Time, Images of the Soul*
Suzanne Dixon, *The Roman Family*
Stephen L. Dyson, *Community and Society in Roman Italy*
Tim G. Parkin, *Demography and Roman Society*
Alison Burford, *Land and Labor in the Greek World*
Alan Watson, *International Law in Archaic Rome: War and Religion*
Stephen H. Lonsdale, *Dance and Ritual Play in Greek Religion*
J. Donald Hughes, *Pan's Travail: Environmental Problems of the Ancient Greeks and Romans*
C. R. Whittaker, *Frontiers of the Roman Empire: A Social and Economic Study*
Pericles Georges, *Barbarian Asia and the Greek Experience*
Nancy Demand, *Birth, Death, and Motherhood in Classical Greece*
Elaine Fantham, *Roman Literary Culture: From Cicero to Apuleius*
Kenneth W. Harl, *Coinage in the Roman Economy, 300 B.C. to A.D. 700*

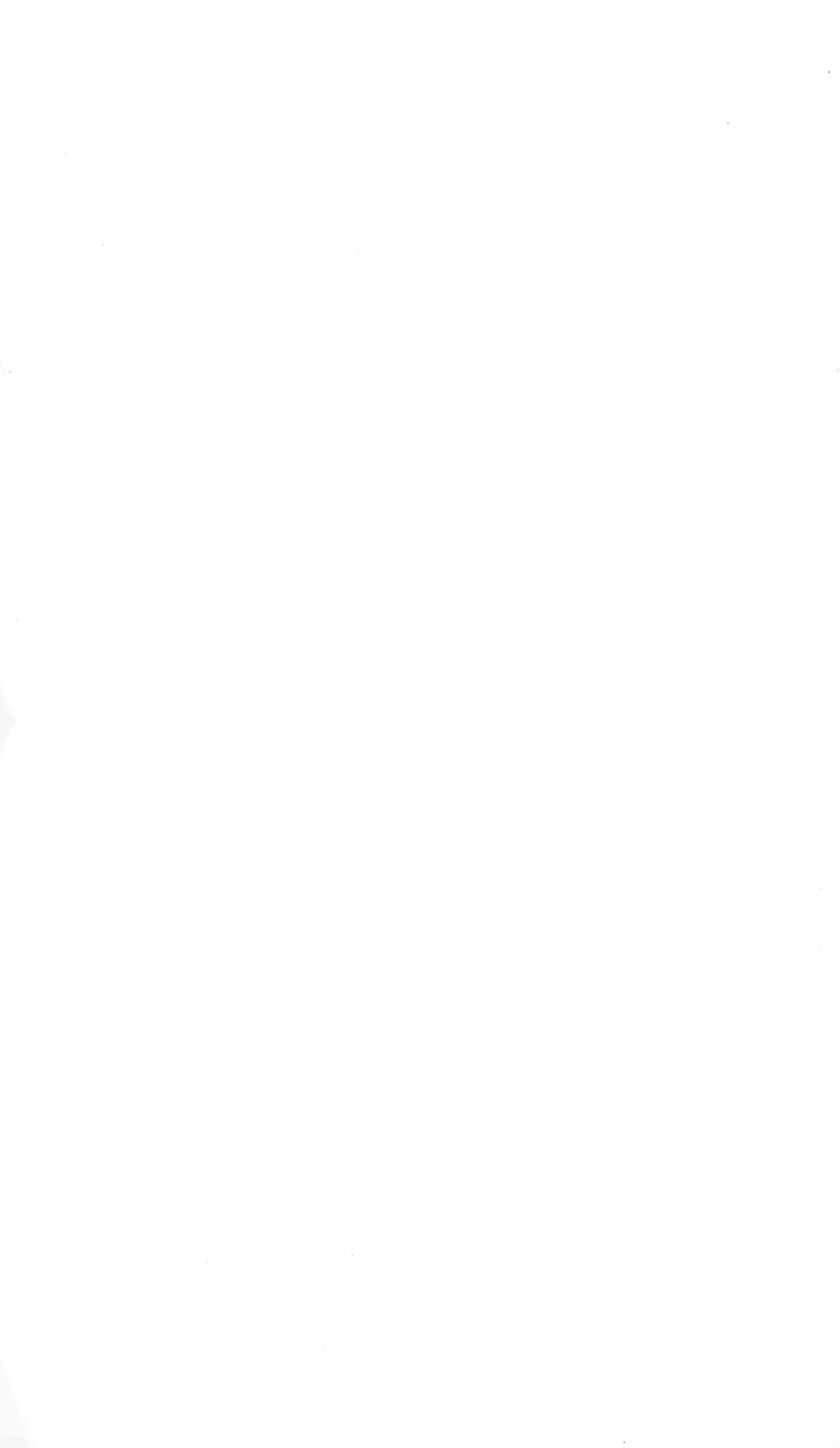